The Woomera Manual on the International Law of Military Space Activities and Operations

The Woomera Manual on the International Law of Military Space Activities and Operations

Edited by
JACK BEARD
AND
DALE STEPHENS
With
DAVID KOPLOW

OXFORD
UNIVERSITY PRESS

Great Clarendon Street, Oxford, OX2 6DP,
United Kingdom

Oxford University Press is a department of the University of Oxford.
It furthers the University's objective of excellence in research, scholarship,
and education by publishing worldwide. Oxford is a registered trade mark of
Oxford University Press in the UK and in certain other countries

© Oxford University Press 2024

The moral rights of the authors have been asserted

All rights reserved. No part of this publication may be reproduced, stored in
a retrieval system, or transmitted, in any form or by any means, without the
prior permission in writing of Oxford University Press, or as expressly permitted
by law, by licence or under terms agreed with the appropriate reprographics
rights organization. Enquiries concerning reproduction outside the scope of the
above should be sent to the Rights Department, Oxford University Press, at the
address above

You must not circulate this work in any other form
and you must impose this same condition on any acquirer

Public sector information reproduced under Open Government Licence v3.0
(http://www.nationalarchives.gov.uk/doc/open-government-licence/open-government-licence.htm)

Published in the United States of America by Oxford University Press
198 Madison Avenue, New York, NY 10016, United States of America

British Library Cataloguing in Publication Data
Data available

Library of Congress Control Number: 2023948493

ISBN 978–0–19–287066–7 (hbk.)
ISBN 978–0–19–287067–4 (pbk.)

DOI: 10.1093/law/9780192870667.001.0001

Printed and bound by
CPI Group (UK) Ltd, Croydon, CR0 4YY

Links to third party websites are provided by Oxford in good faith and
for information only. Oxford disclaims any responsibility for the materials
contained in any third party website referenced in this work.

Foreword

Before 1947, the outback region of South Australia that would become the Woomera Range and village was an unassuming stretch of rugged red earth dotted with salt bush and native daisies. A joint project between the United Kingdom and Australia transformed this area into what would be, by the late 1950s, the second-busiest rocket range in the globe after Cape Canaveral. 'Woomera', the name given to the range and associated township, is the Dharug word for an ingenious Aboriginal spear throwing tool that enabled a spear to be launched with greater speed and force.

Originally established to develop British intercontinental ballistic missiles as a deterrent against possible nuclear war, the focus of the Woomera Range soon turned to the stars. Over the ensuing decades, Australia worked in partnership with the United Kingdom, the European Launcher Development Organisation, and the United States to conduct dozens of space launches and together make a significant contribution to human understanding of outer space. Testing conducted out of Woomera examined a diverse range of problems facing early space exploration: tracking, communications, and re-entry of space vehicles; managing radiation exposure; and measuring the composition of the ionosphere at the edge of space. The first satellite designed and built in Australia, WRESAT, was launched from Woomera in 1967; in the spirit of the international cooperation which is part of the Range's legacy, this occurred with the assistance of a US rocket and ground crew.

Much like its namesake, the *Woomera Manual* is a product of enduring international effort. The creation of the Woomera Range was spurred on by the desire to deter nuclear war. For the *Woomera Manual*, it has been a desire to articulate and clarify the international legal framework for military space activities and, in so doing, to advance the rule of law in space in times of peace, heightened tension, and even armed conflict. Over a span of five years, this basic concept has grown into the work before you today.

The process of creating the *Manual* has involved collaboration with and input from experts from academia and organizations all over the world. The four leading universities in this project are to be congratulated for their tireless efforts in bringing this much needed *Manual* into being. Most importantly, it has involved direct consultation with States—whose views decisively affect the development and correct interpretation of international law—regarding their understanding of the law and of its expression in the *Manual*.

This unique publication provides a clear articulation of the law applicable to the military uses of space, founded on—and shaped by—State practice. In doing so, it makes an impressive contribution to the advancement of the rule of law in space and avoidance of unnecessary conflict. Understanding the law, its application, and where legal thresholds lie should help military forces around the world avoid missteps and miscalculations that could result in escalated tension between States. Further, this *Manual* should act as a catalyst to encourage further discussion and clarification of this important area of the law, as militaries and civilian operators alike, around the globe, continue to reach for the stars.

The Hon Vickie Chapman, LL.B, GDLP.
Former Deputy Premier and Attorney-General of South Australia

Preface

It is our pleasure and honour to present the *Woomera Manual on the International Law of Military Space Activities and Operations*. The *Woomera Manual* is the first comprehensive examination of international law as it applies across the entire spectrum of behaviour: military space operations and activities during peacetime, during times of heightened tension and stress, and during armed conflict.

This *Manual* is a significant and timely undertaking. Human activities in space are growing as never before, with more States and more companies and other non-governmental entities accessing space for a huge and growing array of purposes. There is every reason to anticipate that this surge in diverse space utilization will continue. At the same time, the dangers of arms races and even armed conflict in space are rising too, and attention must be focused on current and potential military activities and operations.

The international legal framework for space is therefore under unprecedented stress. The treaties, customary international law, and related rules for space are vital for peaceful exploration and use of space, but they have received inadequate study and attention. With new opportunities and challenges confronting the international community in this domain, the need for cooperation and a rules-based pursuit of the exploration and use of space has never been greater.

Importantly, the sole focus of the *Woomera Manual* is on summarizing and organizing the *lex lata* (the 'law as it exists'), without any prescriptive agenda. No-one believes that the existing corpus of space law can fully suffice for regulating all future activities. The existing principles and rules are the vital core, but will require supplementation as human activities in space continue—but it is not the task of this *Manual* to speculate or recommend. Where the existing law is unclear, and where authoritative agreed interpretations have not yet emerged, the *Manual* acknowledges that uncertainty.

Fundamental to the *Manual*'s methodology is its central focus on the practice of States. The *Manual* concentrates on the relevant deeds and words of States, and their reactions to the deeds and words of others, to identify and examine existing rules of international law and the contours of its continuing development. This fastidious attention to State practice differentiates this *Manual* from some other works, as it does not rest upon the opinions or interpretations of experts. The *Manual* provides numerous citations, enabling subsequent researchers to identify and scrutinize the State practice underpinning the articulated rules.

In dealing with such a cutting-edge topic, the *Woomera Manual* projects the possible emergence of relevant technologies some years into the future, to anticipate the application of today's rules for tomorrow's circumstances. But it is constrained to relatively proximate developments; it does not speculate about far-distant prospects.

The *Woomera Manual* is the product of a multi-year project by a dedicated and diverse group of experts and researchers from around the world, who contributed insights about a variety of legal and technical specialties. These experts were not asked to endorse the final text of the *Manual*, but they all share the credit for its development.

We are particularly grateful to the Ministry of Foreign Affairs and the Ministry of Defence of the Netherlands for their assistance in organizing and hosting a unique opportunity for State Consultations at The Hague in 2022. During this engagement, we received numerous and valuable comments about an earlier draft of the *Manual* from the representatives of twenty-four States and the International Committee of the Red Cross. These contributions significantly shaped all the Rules and commentary of the *Manual* and helped to make it a unique repository of vital information. States were not asked to endorse the *Manual*, and they did not always agree about points of law or interpretation.

We hope the *Woomera Manual* will provide a useful and compelling resource for military and civilian government personnel, space operators, practitioners, academics, and members of international organizations and non-governmental entities involved in military space activities and operations. With its foundational emphasis on State practice and the rule of law, this *Manual* seeks to advance peaceful cooperation in space and provide a safer and more predictable framework for military space activities and operations.

Jack M Beard
Editor in Chief
*The Woomera Manual on the International
Law of Military Space Activities and Operations*

Woomera Manual Leadership and Experts

Editorial Board

Professor Jack M Beard, Editor in Chief,
University of Nebraska College of Law
Professor Dale Stephens, University of Adelaide
Professor David A Koplow, Georgetown University Law Center

Governance Board

Professor Dale Stephens, Chair, University of Adelaide
Professor Jack M Beard, University of Nebraska College of Law
Mr Duncan Blake, University of New South Wales—Canberra
Associate Professor Aurel Sari, University of Exeter

Core Experts*

Professor Jack M Beard,
University of Nebraska College of Law

Mr Duncan Blake,
University of New South Wales—Canberra

Professor Laurie Blank,
Emory University School of Law

Professor Christopher J Borgen,
St John's University School of Law

Professor Emily Crawford,
University of Sydney

Professor Melissa de Zwart,
University of Adelaide

Dr Heather Harrison Dinniss,
Swedish Defence University

Lt Col Mickael Dupenloup,
French Government

Mr W Renn Gade,
US Department of Defense

Dr Ian Henderson,
Australian Government

Mr Steven Hill,
International Institute for Justice and the Rule of Law

Brigadier-General Rob Holman,
Canadian Armed Forces

---

* All named military and government personnel participated in their personal capacities

Mr Mike Hoversten,
US Air Force

Colonel Matthew T King
US Air Force

Professor David A Koplow,
Georgetown University Law Center

Professor Matthew Stubbs,
University of Adelaide

Professor Kubo Mačák,
University of Exeter

Wing Commander Kieran Tinkler,
UK Royal Air Force

Professor Rob McLaughlin,
University of Wollongong

Lt Col Susan Trepczynski,
US Air Force

Professor Hitoshi Nasu,
US Military Academy

Ms Liis Vihul,
Cyber Law International

Colonel (Res) Noam Neuman,
Ministry of Justice, State of Israel

Dr Jeroen van den Boogaard,
Government of the Netherlands

Professor Michael Schmitt,
US Military Academy

Professor Frans von der Dunk,
University of Nebraska

Professor Dale Stephens,
University of Adelaide

Dr Binxin Zhang,
Sciences Po

Associate Experts*

Dr Stacey Henderson,
Flinders University

Mr Patrick Vermette,
Canadian Government

Dr Cassandra Steer,
Australian National University

Mr Andru Wall,
former US Government

Professor Beth Van Schaak,
Stanford University
(until February 2022)

* All named military and government personnel participated in their personal capacities

Technical Experts

Dr Laura Grego,
Union of Concerned Scientists

Dr Brian Weeden,
Secure World Foundation

Rapporteurs

Ms Joanna Jarose,
University of Adelaide

Mr Jon Natvig,
University of Nebraska

Ex-Officio and Former Board Members

Professor Michael Schmitt,
Senior Executive Advisor,
former member of the Governance Board

Professor Melissa de Zwart,
Inaugural Chair and ex-officio
member of the Governance Board

Professor Rob McLaughlin,
ex-officio member of the Editorial Board

Professor Hitoshi Nasu,
former member of the Governance and
Editorial Boards

---

* All named military and government personnel participated in their personal capacities

Peer Reviewers*

Dr Ntorina Antoni,
Eindhoven University of Technology

Dr Ioana Bratu,
Vrije Universiteit Amsterdam

Professor Rebecca Bresnik,
University of Houston Law Center

Dr Malcolm Davis,
Australian Strategic Policy Institute

Dr Maria Elena De Maestri,
University of Genoa

Lt Col Seth Dilworth,
US Air Force

Commander Nick Minogue,
Legal Adviser and International Civil Servant

Professor Saadia M Pekkanen,
University of Washington

Professor Anél Ferreira-Snyman,
University of South Africa

Major Amy Sfara,
US Air Force

Dr Maria A Pozza,
Gravity Lawyers, New Zealand

Commander Mark Rasmussen,
US Navy

Professor Tim Stephens,
University of Sydney

Lt Col Joshua Wolff,
US Army

Professor Yun Zhao,
University of Hong Kong

Lt Col Timothy Goines,
US Air Force Academy

Dr Andrea Harrington,
McGill University

Legal Research

University of Nebraska College of Law
Professor of Law Library, Stephanie Pearlman

University of Nebraska
Schmid Research Fellowship Program—Students, including Matias Cava, Aaron Graves, Sarah Lauce, Grant Jones, and Max Tierney

University of Adelaide,
Research Unit on Military Law and Ethics—Students

Contents

Table of Cases	xvii
Table of International Agreements and Treaties	xxi
Other International Instruments	xxxi
National Instruments	xxxix
Introduction	1
Overview of the Space Law Regime	15
Note on Legal Connections Between States and a Space Object	25
Note on Outer Space vs Airspace (Delimitation of Outer Space)	26

PART I: MILITARY SPACE ACTIVITIES DURING PEACETIME

Introduction	31

SECTION 1: FREEDOMS AND RESTRICTIONS RELATED TO THE USE OF OUTER SPACE

Rule 1 Freedom of Use, Access, Exploration, and Scientific Investigation and Principles of Cooperation	35
Rule 2 Non-Appropriation of Outer Space and Celestial Bodies	41
Rule 3 Peaceful Purposes in Outer Space	49
Rule 4 Restrictions on Specified Military Establishments and Activities on Celestial Bodies	63
Rule 5 Weapons of Mass Destruction	71
Rule 6 Military Space Activities and Intelligence Collection	82
Rule 7 Jurisdiction	85
Rule 8 Registration of Space Objects	90
Rule 9 Ownership of Space Objects	98

SECTION 2: RESPONSIBILITY AND LIABILITY

Rule 10 Responsibility of States for National Activities in Outer Space	105

Rule 11 Responsibility of International Organizations   118
Rule 12 International Liability for Damage Caused by Space Objects   121

SECTION 3: OTHER OBLIGATIONS

Rule 13 Astronauts and Personnel of a Spacecraft   129
Rule 14 Avoidance of Harmful Contamination   139
Rule 15 Visits to Facilities on the Moon and Other Celestial Bodies 146

PART II: MILITARY SPACE ACTIVITIES DURING TIMES OF TENSION AND CRISIS

Introduction   153

SECTION 1: LEGAL OBLIGATIONS AND PROHIBITIONS OF PARTICULAR RELEVANCE DURING TIMES OF TENSION AND CRISIS

Rule 16 Zones   159
Rule 17 Due Regard   170
Rule 18 Harmful Interference   177
Rule 19 ITU Harmful Radio Interference   185
Rule 20 Non-Intervention Principle   191
Rule 21 Use of Force   201
Rule 22 Threat of Force   222
Rule 23 Armed Attack   226

SECTION 2: RESPONSE ACTIONS

Rule 24 Retorsion   241
Rule 25 Countermeasures   243
Rule 26 Self-Defence   250
Rule 27 Collective Self-Defence   260
Rule 28 Collective Security Measures   263

PART III: MILITARY SPACE OPERATIONS DURING ARMED CONFLICT

Introduction ... 273

SECTION 1: CHARACTERIZATION OF ARMED CONFLICT

Rule 29 International Armed Conflict ... 287

Rule 30 Non-International Armed Conflict ... 294

SECTION 2: CONDUCT IN OR RELATED TO ATTACK

Rule 31 Attack ... 301

Rule 32 Distinction ... 309

Rule 33 Direct Participation in Hostilities ... 312

Rule 34 Military Objectives ... 319

Rule 35 Medical Units and Religious Personnel ... 324

SECTION 3: PRECAUTIONS IN ATTACK

Rule 36 Verification ... 331

Rule 37 Choice of Means and Methods of Attack ... 334

Rule 38 Proportionality in Attack ... 337

Rule 39 Suspension or Cancellation of Attack ... 347

Rule 40 Warnings ... 351

Rule 41 Precautions Against the Effects of Attack ... 357

SECTION 4: MEANS AND METHODS OF WARFARE

Rule 42 Means and Methods of Warfare Generally ... 365

Rule 43 Natural Environment ... 373

Rule 44 Prohibition of Perfidy ... 380

Rule 45 Improper Use of Markings ... 384

SECTION 5: OTHER OBLIGATIONS

Rule 46 Constant Care   391

Rule 47 Belligerent Reprisals   394

Rule 48 Neutrality in Space   399

Index   403

Table of Cases

INTERNATIONAL CENTRE FOR SETTLEMENT OF INVESTMENT DISPUTES

Cargill Inc v United Mexican States (Award) [2009] ICSID Case
   No ARB(AF)/05/02 .... 243n.285
Corn Products International Inc v United Mexican States (Decision on
   Responsibility) [2008] ICSID Case No ARB(AF)/04/01 .... 243n.285

INTERNATIONAL COURT OF JUSTICE

Application of the Convention on the Prevention and Punishment of the Crime
   of Genocide (The Gambia v Myanmar) (Provisional Measures: Order
   of 23 January 2020)... 77n.289
Application of the Convention on the Prevention and Punishment of the Crime
   of Genocide (Bosnia and Herzegovina v Serbia and Montenegro)
   (Counter-claims—Order of 17 December 1997) [1997] ICJ Rep 243 .... 245n.294
Asylum Case (Colombia v Peru) (Judgment) [1950] ICJ 266 .... 20n.72
Case Concerning Application of the Convention on the Prevention and
   Punishment of the Crime of Genocide (Bosnia and Herzegovina v Serbia
   and Montenegro) (Merits) [2007] ICJ Reps 43......................... 112–13n.401
Case Concerning Armed Activities on the Territory of the Congo (Democratic
   Republic of the Congo v Uganda) (Judgment) [2005] ICJ Rep 168
   (Armed Activities in the Congo Judgment) 191n.115, 195n.137, 236n.276
Case Concerning Military and Paramilitary Activities in and against Nicaragua
   (Nicaragua v United States of America) (Merits) [1986]
   ICJ Reps 14 .... 10n.24, 111n.397, 112n.399,
          112–13n.401, 191n.115, 192n.117, 192n.119, 194n.131, 195n.138, 198n.143,
          201n.153, 205, 205n.167, 223n.236, 223n.237, 226n.243, 226n.245, 229–30,
                229n.254, 236n.276, 237n.280, 244n.290, 245n.292, 246n.300, 246n.301,
                   250n.320, 252n.330, 259n.352, 260n.354, 260n.355, 291n.48, 366n.269
Case Concerning Oil Platforms (Islamic Republic of Iran v United States
   of America) (Merits) [2003] ICJ 4 .... 111n.397
Case Concerning Oil Platforms (Islamic Republic of Iran v United States of America)
   (Merits—Judge Simma, separate opinion) [2003] ICJ Reps 161............ 229n.256,
                                                233n.267, 233n.270, 236n.276,
                                         237n.280, 245n.292, 252n.326, 253n.334
Case Concerning The Barcelona Traction, Light and Power Company, Limited
   (Belgium v Spain) (Judgment) [1970] ICJ Repo 3 .... 87n.321
Case Concerning the Right of Passage over Indian Territory (Portugal v India)
   (Judgment: Preliminary Objections) [1957] ICJ Reps 125 .... 11n.26
Corfu Channel Case (United Kingdom v Albania) (Judgment)
   [1949] ICJ Reps 244 .... 244n.290
Fisheries Case (United Kingdom v Norway) (Judgment) [1951] ICJ 116 .... 20n.72
Gabčíkovo-Nagymaros Project (Hungary v Slovakia) (Judgment)
   [1997] ICJ Reps 7 .... 243n.285, 244n.287, 245n.295, 245n.297, 248n.314

xviii TABLE OF CASES

Legality of the Threat or Use of Nuclear Weapons (Advisory Opinion)
    [1996] ICJ Reps 226 .... 14n.41, 74n.273, 77n.288, 77n.291, 78–79, 208n.181,
        216n.214, 222n.232, 223n.237, 251n.323, 273n.3, 275n.8, 309n.89,
        367n.272, 369n.284, 371n.292, 371n.294, 374n.306, 377n.319, 400n.391
North Sea Continental Shelf Cases (Germany v Denmark;
    Germany v Netherlands) (Merits) [1969] ICJ Reps 3 ..... 15n.44, 18n.57, 19n.68, 21n.78
Nottebohm Case (Liechtenstein v Guatemala) (Judgment) [1955] ICJ Reps 1 ...... 87n.320
Reparation for Injuries Suffered in the Service of the United Nations
    (Advisory Opinion) [1949] ICJ Reps 174 .... 15n.44
United States Diplomatic and Consular Staff in Tehran (United States
    of America v Islamic Republic of Iran) [1980] ICJ Reps 3 .... 113n.402, 290–91n.47

INTERNATIONAL CRIMINAL TRIBUNAL
FOR THE FORMER YUGOSLAVIA

Furundžija Case (Trial Judgment) IT-95-17/1-T (10 December 1998) 294n.58
Milošević Case (Decision on motion for judgment of acquittal) IT-02-54
    (16 Jun 2004).. 294n.58
Mucić et al. (Trial Judgment) IT-96-21 (16 November 1998) 294n.58
Prosecutor v Delalić (Trial Judgment) ICTY-04-83-T (15 September 1998) 289n.40
Prosecutor v Galić (Trial Judgement) ICTY-98-29-T
    (5 December 2003)............... 288n.35, 342n.208, 342n.210, 353n.242, 361n.265
Prosecutor v Halilovic (Trial Judgement) ICTY-01-48-T (16 November 2005) 288n.35
Prosecutor v Kupreškić (Judgment) ICTY-95-16-T (14 January 2000) 281n.21,
                                                                    358n.255, 394–95n.360
Prosecutor v Milan Martić (Appeals Judgment) IT-95-11-A
    (8 October 2008)... 394–95n.360
Prosecutor v Pavle Strugar (Trial Judgment) IT-01-42-T (31 January 2005) 319n.137
Prosecutor v Tadić (Decision on the Defence Motion for Interlocutory Appeal
    on Jurisdiction) ICTY-94-1 (2 October 1995) (Tadić decision) 263n.362,
        265n.372, 266n.376, 268n.381, 287n.31, 288n.34, 289n.40, 294n.56, 371n.292

INTERNATIONAL LAW IN DOMESTIC COURTS

Hass and Priebke, In re (Judgment) ILDC 1599-322 (22 July 1997).............. 397n.380

PERMANENT COURT OF ARBITRATION

Guyana v Suriname (Award) [2007] PCA 2004-04 .... 223n.235, 245n.292
In the Matter of the Arctic Sunrise Arbitration (Netherlands v Russia)
    (Award on the Merits) [2015] PCA 2014-02............................. 172n.48
South China Sea Arbitration (Philippines v China) (Award) [2016] PCA 2013-19...... 172n.48

PERMANENT COURT OF INTERNATIONAL JUSTICE

Case Concerning the Factory at Chorzów (Germany v Poland) (Merits)
    PCIJ Series A No 17 .... 116n.407, 120n.426
Case of the S.S. 'Lotus' (France v Turkey) PCIJ Series A No 10.................... 15n.43
Island of Palmas Case (United States of America v Netherlands) (1928)
    II RIAA 829 .... 42n.143, 85n.312
Nationality Decrees Issued in Tunis and Morocco (Advisory Opinion)
    [1923] PCIJ Reps Ser. B No 4, 24....................................... 193n.125
Naulilaa Case (Portugal v Germany) (1949) 2 RIAA 1011 .... 245n.296

SPECIAL COURT FOR SIERRA LEONE (SCSL)

Prosecutor v Taylor (Trial Judgement) SCSL-03-01-T (18 May 2012) 288n.35, 289n.40

UNITED NATIONS WAR CRIMES COMMISSION

Hans Albin Rauter v Netherlands (1949) 14 WCR 120 .... 397n.380
Richard Wilhelm Hermann Bruns and Two Others v Norwegian State
 (1948) 3 WCR 21-22 .... 397n.380

NATIONAL COURTS

Israel

The Public Committee Against Torture in Israel v The Government of Israel
 (2006) HCJ 769/ 02 (Targeted Killings Case) 312n.97, 313n.101,
 314n.113, 315n.120, 315n.122

United Kingdom

Archer Daniels Midland Company and Tate & Lyle Ingredients Americas, Inc v
 United Mexican States (Award) [2007] ICSID Case No ARB(AF)/04/05
 (Archer Daniels case)...................................... 243n.285, 247n.311
In the Matter of the Chagos Marine Protected Area Arbitration
 (Mauritius v United Kingdom) (Award) [2015] PCA 2011-03 .... 172n.47

United States

Fidelity Coal Co. v Diamond, 310 Ill. App. 387 (1941)......................... 88n.326
Principe Compania Naviera, S.A. v Board of Com'rs of Port of New Orleans,
 333 F. Supp. 353 (1971) 88n.326
Union Oil Co. of California v Basalt Rock Co., 30 Cal. App.2d 317 (1939) 88n.326
United States of America v List (The Hostage Case) Case No 7 [1948] reprinted in Trials of
 War Criminals Before the Nuremberg Military Tribunals Under Control
 Council Law No. 10 .... 166–67n.25

Table of International Agreements and Treaties

Agreement Among the Government of Canada, Governments of Member States of the European Space Agency, the Government of Japan, the Government of the Russian Federation, and the Government of the United States of America Concerning Cooperation on the Civil International Space Station (signed 29 January 1998, entered into force 27 March 2001) 41 ILM 1481 .... 15n.46, 100
  Art 2 .... 136n.482
  Art 5 .... 86n.316
  Art 21(2) 100n.371
  Art 22 .... 86n.318, 136n.482
  Art 22(5) 86n.316
Agreement governing the Activities of States on the Moon and Other Celestial Bodies (adopted 5 December 1979, entered into force 11 July 1984) 1363 UNTS 3 ...... 15n.46, 24, 44, 45, 47n.168, 367n.270
  Art 2 .... 24n.100
  Art 3 65
  Art 3(2) 24, 61n.226, 65n.239
  Art 7(1) 140
  Art 11 .... 38–39n.133
  Art 11(1) 44n.153
  Art 11(3) 45n.157
  Art 11(5) 44n.153
  Art 12(3) 134n.475
Agreement on the Rescue of Astronauts, the Return of Astronauts and the Return of Objects Launched into Outer Space' (adopted 19 December 1967, entered into force 3 December 1968) 672 UNTS 119 .... 15n.46, 19–20, 118–19n.421, 129
  Preamble 129–30
  Arts 1–4 131
  Arts 1–5 .... 19n.68
  Art 2 .... 132n.460, 132n.463, 132–33nn.465–66
  Art 3 .... 133, 133n.470, 133–34nn.472–74
  Art 4 .... 134–35, 137n.485

  Art 6 .... 132n.463
  Arts 7–10 .... 20n.73
Air Service Agreement of 27 March 1946 between the United States of America and France (1978) 18 RIAA 417, 443 para 81 .... 244n.287
Antarctic Treaty (signed 1 December 1959, entered into force 23 June 1961) 402 UNTS 71 ... 65–66, 150–51
  Art I 65–66
  Art I.1 .... 66n.242
  Art VII 147n.522
Biological Weapons Convention, BWC see Convention on the Prohibition of the Development, Production and Stockpiling of Bacteriological (Biological) and Toxin Weapons and on their Destruction
Canada–Union of Soviet Socialist Republics: Protocol on Settlement of Canada's Claim for Damages Caused by 'COSMOS 954' (1981) 20 ILM 689
  Art I 123n.441
Charter of the Association of Southeast Asian Nations (adopted 20 November 2007, entered into force 15 December 2008)
  Art 2(e). 200n.151
Charter of the Organization of American States (adopted 30 April 1948, entered into force 13 December 1951, as last amended 10 June 1993) 119 UNTS 48
  Art 3(h) 261n.359
  Art 28 .... 261n.359
Charter of the United Nations (adopted 26 June 1945, entered into force 24 October 1945) 1 UNTS XVI 3–4, 11–12, 15–16, 24n.100, 35–36, 40, 49–50, 52, 54, 55–56, 63–64, 68–69, 110, 111–12, 113–14, 118, 153, 166, 192–94, 207–10, 212–13, 216–17, 219, 226–27, 231, 252, 259, 274–75, 302–3
  Preamble 203n.162

Ch VI 269–70, 388n.349
Ch VII 125, 160–61, 166, 200, 202,
   203nn.161–62, 222–23, 226, 243,
   259, 266, 267n.378, 268–69,
   268nn.381–82, 270–71,
   292n.52, 388n.349
Ch VIII. 266–67, 269–70, 292n.52
Art 2(3) 155
Art 2(4) 110–11, 111n.397, 120,
   153n.2, 201–3, 205n.167,
   205–6n.171, 207–9, 211–12,
   214–15, 216–18, 216n.215,
   220n.230, 223n.237, 236–37
Art 2(5) 266
Art 2(7) 85n.312, 193n.127, 200n.152
Art 5 216–17
Art 11 . . . . 263n.360
Art 12 . . . . 263n.360
Art 24(1) 263n.360
Art 25 . . . . .125n.447, 166n.23,
   264n.364, 266, 270–71
Art 33 . . . . 269n.387
Art 33(1) 155
Art 39 . . . . 263n.361, 265n.370, 268n.381
Art 40 . . . . 263–64, 264n.366,
   265, 268n.381
Art 41 . . . . . 166n.22, 203n.161, 203n.163,
   210–11, 210n.191, 213–14, 228n.251,
   263–64, 265–68, 268n.381
Art 42. . . . . 263–64, 265, 266–68, 268n.381
Art 44 . . . . 203n.162
Art 48 266
Art 49 . . . . .266, 270–71
Art 51 . . . . 12, 68–69, 76–78, 111–12,
   120, 163–64, 202, 202–3n.159,
   208n.181, 216nn.215–216, 217–18,
   226, 227, 233n.269, 236n.277,
   243, 250, 251n.323, 253–55,
   256–57, 259, 260,
   261n.359, 266–67, 301
Art 52(1) 266–67n.377
Art 53 . . . . 264n.365, 267n.378
Art 103 . . . . .111n.398, 125n.447,
   10, 10n.25, 166n.23, 270n.391
Chemical Weapons Convention, CWC
   see Convention on the Prohibition
   of the Development, Production,
   Stockpiling and Use of Chemical
   Weapons and on Their
   Destruction
Chicago Convention *see* International
   Convention on Civil Aviation

Constitution and Convention of the
   International Telecommunication
   Union (adopted 22 December
   1992, entered into force 1 July
   1994) 1825 26 UNTS 3 . . . . 179n.72
Art 1(1)(e) 188n.108
Art 1(2)(b) 188n.108
Art 6(1) 188n.106
Art 6(2) 186n.97
Art 34 . . . . 189n.112
Art 44(2) 375n.311
Art 45 185–86
Art 45(2) 186n.96
Art 45(3) 186n.97
Art 48 . . . . 188n.106
Art 48(1) 188n.106
Art 48(2) 187n.102, 189n.110
Annex, para 1003 . . . . 187n.100
Constitutive Act of the African Union
   (adopted 11 July 2000, entered
   into force 26 May 2001)
   2158 UNTS 3
Art 4(g) 200n.151
Convention on Environmental Impact
   Assessment in a Transboundary
   Context (25 February 1991)
   1989 UNTS 309
Art 2(1) 142–43n.509
Convention on International Liability for
   Damage Caused by Space Objects
   (adopted 29 November 1971,
   entered into force 1 September
   1972) 961 UNTS 187 . . . . .15n.46, 20,
   21–22, 23, 118–19n.421,
   121, 122, 123, 124, 125, 155
Preamble 21n.79
Art I .292nn.49–50
Art I(c) 121n.428
Art II–V 121n.428
Art II 121n.427, 122n.430,
   123n.441, 124, 142n.505
Art III 122n.432, 124
Art III(2)–(3) 122n.433
Art V 122n.433
Art VI(1) 122n.431
Art VI(2) 122n.431
Arts VII–XXXIII 122n.435
Art VII(b) 122n.434
Art IX 123n.436
Art X(1) 123nn.436–37
Art XI(2) 123n.440
Art XII 142n.505

Art XIV 123n.438
Art XIX(2) 123n.439
Convention on Prohibitions or
  Restrictions on the Use of
  Certain Conventional Weapons
  Which May be Deemed to be
  Excessively Injurious or to Have
  Indiscriminate Effects (and
  Protocols) (10 October 1980)
  1342 UNTS 137 .... 61n.227, 366n.268
Art 1(5) 335n.182
Convention on Registration of
  Objects Launched into Outer
  Space (adopted 12 November
  1974, entered into force
  15 September 1976)
  1023 UNTS 15..... 15n.46, 22–24, 90,
                   91, 93–95, 96–97, 99,
                   118–19n.421, 168n.28
Art I(a)................ 22n.88, 95n.352
Art I(b)...................... 92n.341
Arts II–V 22n.88
Art II........... 23, 87–88n.325, 292n.50
Art II(1) 23, 90n.332
Art II(2) 96n.357
Art II(3) 23
Art IV............. 23, 23n.91, 93n.347
Art IV(1) 23n.91, 90n.333,
                       93n.344, 94n.350
Art IV(1)(b)........... 23n.91, 93n.346
Art IV(1)(e)...................... 23
Art IV(2) 93n.345
Art IV(3) 93n.343, 96n.361
Arts VII–XII 23n.96
Convention on Rights and Duties of
  States (adopted 26 December
  1933, entered into force 26
  December 1934) 165 LNTS 19
Art 8 .... 191n.114
Convention on the High Seas (adopted
  29 April 1958, entered into force
  30 September 1962) 450 UNTS 11
Art 12....................... 133n.471
Art 26(3) 172n.45
Convention on the Prevention and
  Punishment of the Crime of
  Genocide (adopted 9 December
  1948, entered into force 12 January
  1951) 78 UNTS 276 .... 77n.289
Art 3(c)..................... 189n.113
Convention on the Prohibition of
  Military or any other Hostile Use
  of Environmental Modification
  Techniques (adopted
  10 December 1976, entered
  into force 5 October 1978)
  1108 UNTS 151......... 14–15, 368–69
Art I 368n.274, 369n.280, 369n.282
Art II................. 367–68, 375–76
Convention on the Prohibition of the
  Development, Production and
  Stockpiling of Bacteriological
  (Biological) and Toxin Weapons
  and on their Destruction (adopted
  10 April 1972, entered into force 26
  March 1975) 26 UNTS 163
Art I 75n.281
Convention on the Prohibition of
  the Development, Production,
  Stockpiling and Use of
  Chemical Weapons and on
  Their Destruction (adopted 3
  September 1992, entered into
  force 29 April 1997) 1974 UNTS 317
Art II........................ 75n.279
Art II (9)..................... 75n.280
ENMOD Convention *see* Convention
  on the Prohibition of Military
  or any other Hostile Use of
  Environmental Modification
  Techniques
Espoo Convention *see* Convention
  on Environmental Impact
  Assessment in a Transboundary
  Context
Geneva Conventions 1949........ 273–74,
                   295–96, 324–25, 395, 396
Common Art 2 .... 14–15, 274n.4,
                      287–89, 289n.43, 293
Common Art 2(1)... 276, 287–88, 289n.39
Common Art 3 .... 276, 281n.21,
                       294–97, 325n.155,
                       394–95n.360
Common Art 3(1)............. 312n.98
Convention (I) for the Amelioration
  of the Condition of the Wounded
  and Sick in Armed Forces in the
  Field of August 12, 1949 (opened
  for signature 12 August 1949,
  entered into force 21 October
  1950) 75 UNTS 31 .... 14n.39
Art 21..................... 325n.156
Arts 24–26................. 310n.93
Art 24................. 310n.94, 328

xxiv   TABLE OF INTERNATIONAL AGREEMENTS AND TREATIES

Art 27 . . . . 326n.158
Art 44 . . . . 386n.343
Art 46 . . . . 395n.364
Art 47 . . . . 395n.361
Convention (II) for the Amelioration of the Condition of Wounded, Sick and Shipwrecked Members of Armed Forces at Sea of August 12, 1949 (opened for signature 12 August 1949, entered into force 21 October 1949) 75 UNTS 85 . . . . . . 14n.39
Art 34 . . . . 325n.156
Art 36 . . . . 310n.93, 328
Art 44 . . . . 386n.343
Convention (III) relative to the Treatment of Prisoners of War of August 12, 1949 (opened for signature 12 August 1949, entered into force 21 October 1950) 75 UNTS 135 . . . . 14n.39
Art 4(2) 316n.128
Art 13 . . . . 395n.362
Art 21 138
Art 118 . . . . 137n.486
Convention (IV) relative to the Protection of Civilian Persons in Time of War of August 12, 1949 (opened for signature 12 August 1949, entered into force 21 October 1950) 75 UNTS 287 . . . . 14n.39
Art 19 . . . . 325n.156
Art 33 . . . . 395n.363
Art 42 . . . . 137n.487
Art 132 . . . . 137n.487
Protocol Additional to the Geneva Conventions of 12 August 1949, and relating to the protection of victims of armed conflicts (Protocol I) (adopted 8 June 1977, entered into force 7 December 1978) 1125 UNTS 3 . . . . . 14n.42, 274n.4, 275, 281, 321–22, 324–25, 365, 371–72, 398
Preamble, para 5 . . . . 275n.11
Pt IV, Sec I, Ch III 378n.323
Art 1(4) 287n.32
Art 8 . . . . 324n.151
Art 8(e) 324n.154
Art 8(f) 324n.152, 326–27n.159
Art 8(g) 324n.152
Art 8(l) 326–27n.159
Arts 9–15 . . . . 325n.155
Art 9(2) . . . 324n.151, 324n.154, 326n.158
Art 11(2) 325n.157
Art 12(1) 324n.150

Art 12(2) 325n.155, 326n.158
Art 13 . . . . 310n.94, 325n.156
Art 13(1) 325n.157
Art 15 . . . . 310n.93, 325n.156, 328
Art 16(1) 324n.152
Art 35(1) 274–75, 366n.269
Art 35(2) 370–71, 377n.317
Art 35(3) 343n.213, 367n.271, 367n.272, 369n.281, 373–74, 376–77
Art 36 . . . . 371n.296
Art 37 383
Art 37(1) 380, 380n.331
Art 37(2) 381
Art 36 372
Art 38(2) 388n.350
Art 39 . . . . 326–27n.159
Art 39(1) 384n.337, 386n.340
Art 39(2) 384n.337
Art 43(2) 310n.95
Arts 48–67 . . . . 277, 280n.20
Art 48 309
Art 49(1) 301, 303–4n.75, 306n.81, 307
Art 49(2) 307n.83
Art 49(3) 274n.4, 277, 280n.20, 301n.67, 319n.136, 331n.169, 334n.178, 337n.184, 347n.224, 357n.252, 373n.302, 391n.351, 395n.366
Art 50(1) 315n.118
Art 50(1)(b) 332n.175
Arts 51–58 . . . . 342n.207
Art 51 . . . . 312n.97, 340–41, 369n.285, 398n.386
Art 51(2) 307n.82, 309n.88
Art 51(3) 312, 315n.121
Art 51(4)(b) 369–70
Art 51(4)(c) 369–70
Art 51(5)(b) 337
Art 51(6) 395nn.367–68
Art 52 . . . . 320n.143, 322–23, 370
Art 52(1) 395n.369
Art 52(2) 309n.88, 319–20
Art 52(4)(b) 369n.283, 370n.287
Art 53 . . . . 168n.29
Art 53(a) 395n.373
Art 53(c) 395n.370, 395n.373
Art 54(4) 395n.371
Art 55 . . . . . . 367nn.271–72, 369n.281, 373–74, 376–77, 378n.323
Art 55(1) 377n.317
Art 55(2) 395n.372
Art 56 279–80
Art 56(4) 395n.374

Art 57 . . . . 281n.21, 339, 340–41,
        358–59, 358n.255, 392
Art 57(1) 338n.191, 391, 392
Art 57(2)–(3) 280–81
Art 57(2) 352–53, 392
Art 57(2)(a) 338n.187
Art 57(2)(a)(i) 331, 338n.188
Art 57(2)(a)(ii) 334, 338n.189
Art 57(2)(a)(iii) 280n.19, 337n.184,
        338n.187, 345n.220
Art 57(2)(b) 338n.190, 347–48
Art 57(2)(c) 351, 352n.238
Art 57(3) 334, 335
Art 57(4) 278
Art 58 . . . . 280–81, 281n.21,
        357, 358–59, 358n.255
Art 58(a) 357, 359n.260, 360n.263
Art 58(b) 357, 359n.259, 360n.262
Art 58(c) 357, 360n.264
Art 66(8) 386n.343
Art 85 . . . . 342n.211
Art 85(3)(c) 280n.19
Art 86 . . . . 342n.211
Art 91 . . . 112n.400, 124n.443, 308n.87
Art 93 290–91
Annex I 386–87
    Ch III 328n.164, 387n.344
    Ch IV 328n.164, 387n.344
    Art 1 . . . . 327–28, 327n.163
    Arts 6–9 . . . . 384n.337, 387n.344
    Art 8 . . . . 328n.165
    Art 9(2) 328n.164, 387n.344
    Art 10 . . . . 387n.344
    Art 10(2) 328n.166
    Art 98 . . . . 328n.167
Protocol Additional to the Geneva
    Conventions of 12 August 1949,
    and Relating to the Protection
    of Victims of Non-International
    Armed Conflicts (Protocol II)
    (adopted 8 June 1977, entered
    into force 7 December 1978)
    1125 UNTS 609 . . . . 14n.42, 295,
        324–25, 394–95n.360
    Art 1(1) 295n.60
    Art 3(10) 335n.182
    Art 4 . . . . 312n.98
    Art 11(1) 325n.155
    Art 12 . . . . 386n.343
    Art 13(1) 281n.21
    Art 13(3) 312
Protocol Additional to the Geneva
    Conventions of 12 August 1949,
    and Relating to the Adoption of
    an Additional Distinctive Emblem
    (Protocol III) (adopted 8 December
    2005, entered into force 14 January
    2007) 45 ILM 558 327
Genocide Convention *see* Convention
    on the Prevention and Punishment
    of the Crime of Genocide
Hague Convention (IV) respecting
    the Laws and Customs of War on
    Land and its annex: Regulations
    concerning the Laws and Customs
    of War on Land (adopted 18
    October 1907, entered into
    force 26 January 1910) 205
    CTS 277 . . . . 275–76n.12, 370n.291
    Art 3 . . . . 112n.400
    Art 22 . . . . 274n.6, 366n.269
    Art 23(b) 380n.331, 380n.332, 383
    Art 23(f) 384–85n.338, 386n.343
    Art 26 351
Hague Convention (V) respecting
    the Rights and Duties of Neutral
    Powers and Persons in Case
    of War on Land (adopted 18
    October 1907, entered into force
    26 January 1910) 400n.390
    Art 11 . . . . 137n.488
    Art 20 . . . . 400n.390
Hague Convention (VII) relating
    to the Conversion of Merchant
    Ships into War-Ships (adopted 18
    October 1907, entered into force
    26 January 1910) 275–76n.12
Hague Convention (VIII) relative
    to the Laying of Automatic
    Submarine Contact Mine
    (adopted 18 October 1907,
    entered into force 26 January
    1910) 205 CTS 331 . . . . 275–76n.12
Hague Convention (XIII) concerning
    the Rights and Duties of Neutral
    Powers in Naval War (adopted
    18 October 1907, entered into
    force 26 January 1910)
    205 CTS 395 . . . . 400n.390
Hague Convention for the Protection
    of Cultural Property in the
    Event of Armed Conflict
    (adopted 14 May 1954, entered
    into force 7 August 1956) 249
    UNTS 240 . . . . 168n.29
    Art 1(a) 168n.29
    Art 4(4) 395n.365
    Art 17(3) 386n.343

Hague Declaration (IV, 3) on the Use of Bullets Which Expand or Flatten Easily in the Human Body (29 July 1899) 366n.267
    Art 23(e) 370–71
Inter-American Treaty of Reciprocal Assistance (adopted 2 September 1947, entered into force 3 December 1948, as amended 26 July 1975) 21 UNTS 77
    Art 3 .... 261n.359
Interim Agreement between the United States of America and the Union of Soviet Socialist Republics on Certain Measures With Respect to the Limitation of Strategic Offensive Arms (adopted 26 May 1972, entered into force 3 October 1972) 50 ILM 342
    Art V 83n.306
International Convention on Civil Aviation (signed 7 December 1944, entered into force 7 April 1947) 15 UNTS 295 70
    Art 1 .... 26n.103
    Art 3 .... 172n.45
    Art 17 .... 87n.323, 292n.51
International Telecommunication Convention (as amended 6 November 1982, entered into force 1 January 1984) 1531 UNTS 2
    Art 38(1) 188–89
International Telecommunication Union, 'Radio Regulations' (adopted as amended 15 September 2020, entered into force 1 January 2021) 186, 200
    Preamble, para 0.4 .... 185n.91
    Art 1.64 .... 185n.92
    Art 1.166 .... 187n.101
    Art 1.167 .... 187n.101
    Art 1.168 .... 187n.101
    Art 1.169 .... 186n.93, 187n.100
    Art 4.18 .... 187n.102
    Art 15 .... 185n.91
    Art 15.1 .... 186n.95, 189n.111
    Art 15.2 .... 186n.95, 189n.111
    Art 15.22 .... 185n.91
    Art 37 .... 328n.166
    Art 40 .... 328n.166
    Art 59 .... 328n.166
ISS Agreement *see* Agreement Among the Government of Canada, Governments of Member States of the European Space Agency, the Government of Japan, the Government of the Russian Federation, and the Government of the United States of America Concerning Cooperation on the Civil International Space Station
Liability Convention *see* Convention on International Liability for Damage Caused by Space Objects
Montevideo Convention *see* Convention on Rights and Duties of States
Moon Agreement *see* Agreement governing the Activities of States on the Moon and Other Celestial Bodies
New START Treaty *see* Treaty between the United States of America and the Russian Federation on Measures for the Future Reduction and Limitation of Strategic Offensive Arms
North Atlantic Treaty (adopted 4 April 1949, entered into force 24 August 1949) 34 UNTS 243
    Art 5 261–62
Outer Space Treaty *see* Treaty on Principles Governing the Activities of States in the Exploration and Use of Outer Space, Including the Moon and Other Celestial Bodies
Partial Nuclear Test Ban Treaty, PNTB *see* Treaty Banning Nuclear Weapon Tests in the Atmosphere, in Outer Space and Under Water
Registration Convention *see* Convention on Registration of Objects Launched into Outer Space
Rescue and Return Agreement *see* Agreement on the Rescue of Astronauts, the Return of Astronauts and the Return of Objects Launched into Outer Space'
Rome Statute of the International Criminal Court (adopted 17 July 1998, entered into force 1 July 2002) 2187 UNTS 90 .... 327n.162

Art 8(2)(b)(xx) 371n.293
Art 8(2)(b)(xi) 380n.332, 383n.336
Art 8(2)(b)(xxiv) 327n.162
Art 8(2)(d) 294n.57
Art 8(2)(e)(ii) 325n.155, 327n.162
Art 8(2)(e)(ix) 380n.332, 383n.336
Art 25(3)(e) 189n.113
Art 25(3)(f) 383n.336
Security Treaty between Australia, New Zealand, and the United States of America (adopted 1 September 1950, entered into force 29 April 1952) 131 UNTS 83
   Art IV 261n.359
St Petersburg Declaration 1868
   Preamble 309
Statute of the International Court of Justice (26 June 1945) 1 UNTS 295
   Art 38(1)(b) 18n.56
Strategic Arms Limitation Talks (SALT) *see* Treaty Between the United States of America and the Union of Soviet Socialist Republics on the Limitation of Strategic Offensive Arms Together with Agreed Statements and Common Understandings Regarding the Treaty (SALT II)
The Artemis Accords: Principles for Cooperation in the Civil Exploration and Use of the Moon, Mars, Comets, and Asteroids' (13 October 2020) 47–48, 165–66, 169
   s 9 . . . . 169n.35
   s 10(1) 48n.170
   s 10(2) 48nn.170–71, 101n.378
   s 11 . . . . 174n.57
   s 11(1) 165n.18
   s 11(6) 165n.18
   s 11(7) 165n.19
   s 11(7)(a) 165n.19
   s 11(7)(b) 165n.19
   s 11(11) 165n.20
Tlatelolco Treaty *see* Treaty for the Prohibition of Nuclear Weapons in Latin America and the Caribbean
Treaty Banning Nuclear Weapon Tests in the Atmosphere, in Outer Space and Under Water (entered into force 10 October 1963) 480 UNTS 43 (Partial Nuclear Test Ban Treaty, PNTB) 15–16n.47, 71, 80, 110n.394, 366–67
   Art I 79, 80
   Art I(a) 367n.270
   Art I.1(b) 80
Treaty Between the United States of America and the Russian Federation on Measures for the Further Reduction and Limitation of Strategic Offensive Arms (United States–Russia) (adopted 8 April 2010, entered into force 5 February 2011)
   Art X 83n.306
   Art X(1)(b) 178n.68, 242n.283
Treaty Between the United States of America and the Union of Soviet Socialist Republics on the Elimination of Their Intermediate-Range and Shorter-Range Missiles (adopted 8 December 1987, entered into force 1 June 1988) 1657 UNTS 2
   Art XII 83n.306
   Art XII(1) 220n.229
Treaty Between the United States of America and the Union of Soviet Socialist Republics on the Limitation of Strategic Offensive Arms Together with Agreed Statements and Common Understandings Regarding the Treaty (SALT II) (signed 18 June 1979)
   Art XI.1(c) 72n.266
Treaty between the United States of America and the Union of Soviet Socialist Republics on the Reduction and Limitation of Strategic Offensive Arms (START I Treaty) (entered into force 5 December 1994) UN Doc CD/1192
   Art X(1)(b) 220n.229
   Art XII(1) 220n.229
Treaty for the Prohibition of Nuclear Weapons in Latin America and the Caribbean (Tlatelolco Treaty) (opened for signature 14 February 1967, entered into force 25 April 1969) 634 UNTS 281 74

xxviii   TABLE OF INTERNATIONAL AGREEMENTS AND TREATIES

Treaty of Mutual Cooperation and
  Security Between Japan and
  the United States of America
  (adopted 19 January 1960,
  entered into force 19 May 1960)
  11 UST 1632
  Art V 261n.359
Treaty on Conventional Armed Forces
  in Europe (adopted 19 November
  1990, entered into force 9
  November 1992) 2441 UNTS 285
  Art XV 83n.306
  Art XV(2).................... 178n.68
Treaty on Principles Governing
  the Activities of States in the
  Exploration and Use of Outer
  Space, Including the Moon and
  Other Celestial Bodies (opened
  for signature 27 January 1967,
  entered into force 10 October
  1967) 610 UNTS 205 .... 4, 35,
      49–50, 85–86, 121, 124–25, 154,
      165–66, 201, 274–75
  Preamble 19n.69, 23n.94, 36–37,
      49–52, 53–54
  preamble, cl 10 .... 50n.177
  Art I 35–37, 38, 40, 43nn.147–48,
      100n.376, 168–69
  Art I(1)........... 36n.121, 38–39n.133
  Art I(2).................... 35n.116
  Art I(3).................... 35n.117
  Art II..... 26n.104, 41, 41n.139, 43n.145,
      45, 47–48, 79, 100n.375, 101,
      168–69, 201–2, 293, 295
  Art III......... 11–12, 14n.40, 24n.100,
      36n.120, 40, 55–56, 68–69, 106,
      110n.395, 115, 116, 118, 166, 187n.98,
      191, 201n.155, 243, 250n.319, 251,
      273–74, 296–97, 366, 374–75
  Art IV..... 49–50, 51–52, 55–56, 63–64,
      65–70, 72, 74, 76–78, 109–10,
      135n.480, 149, 168–69, 208n.182,
      266n.373, 270–71, 366–67
  Art IV(1) 61, 63n.232, 71–72, 73,
      76–77, 78–79, 110n.394
  Art IV(2) 49n.173, 63–64, 65–66,
      67–68, 149, 165n.17
  Art V 19–20, 39–40, 129–30, 131,
      133, 134–35, 134n.473, 136, 137n.485
  Art V(2).................... 134n.473
  Art V(3).................... 136n.483
  Art VI....... 25–26, 46n.160, 96, 98–99,
      100n.369, 105, 106–7, 106n.381,
      107–8nn.386–87, 108n.388,
      108n.389, 108n.391, 109–14, 115,
      116, 118–20, 125, 136n.483, 186–87,
      187n.99, 234, 234n.273, 245–46,
      248n.312, 258–59, 291–92,
      296n.62, 308, 402
  Art VII 20–21, 95n.353, 96–97, 99,
      116n.412, 121n.427, 123n.441
  Art VIII 19–20, 23–24, 25, 42n.144,
      86–87, 86n.314, 89n.330, 90,
      90n.332, 92, 96, 98, 99–100,
      129n.450, 135–36, 147, 149–50,
      167–68, 234, 292n.50
  Art IX.... 12, 38n.131, 39–40, 107n.386,
      139–40, 140n.494, 142–44, 145,
      160n.4, 162, 170–72, 173, 174–76,
      174n.55, 174n.57, 177, 178–83,
      178n.69, 186n.93, 189n.113,
      224n.239, 246–47, 290n.46
  Art X......................... 39
  Art XI....................... 39–40
  Art XII 146–51, 161n.8, 164–65
  Art XIII 118, 119–20
  Arts XXII–XXVIII.............. 21–22
  Art IX...................... 183n.89
Treaty on the Limitation of
  Anti-Ballistic Missile Systems
  (US–USSR) (adopted 26 May
  1972, entered into force 3
  October 1972) 944 UNTS 13
  Art XII 83n.306
  Art XII(1).................... 220n.229
Treaty on the Prevention of the
  Placement of Weapons in Outer
  Space, the Threat or Use of Force
  against Outer Space Objects'
  (Draft, 16 June 2014)
  Art I(c)...................... 72n.266
Treaty on the Prohibition of
  Nuclear Weapons (adopted
  7 July 2017, entered into force
  22 January 2021)................81
  Art 1(a) 81n.300
  Art 1(d) 81n.301
  Art 1(g) 81n.302
UN Convention on the Law of the
  Sea (adopted 10 December 1982,
  entered into force 16 November
  1994) 1833 UNTS 3 ....44, 47n.168, 70
  Pt XI.......................... 44
  Art 29.................... 88–89n.328
  Art 56(2) 172n.46
  Art 58(3) 172n.46

Art 87 .... 45n.158
Art 87(2) 172n.46
Art 91 .... 292n.51
Art 91(1) 87n.322, 233n.268
Art 95 .... 89n.329
Art 98 .... 133n.471
Arts 133–149 .... 44n.151
Art 236 .... 88n.327, 235n.274
UNESCO Convention for the Protection of the World Cultural and Natural Heritage, 16 November 1972 (1037 UNTS 151) 168n.29
Vienna Convention on Diplomatic Relations (adopted 18 April 1961, entered into force 24 April 1964) 500 UNTS 95
Art 14(1)(b) 131n.458
Vienna Convention on the Law of Treaties (adopted 23 May 1969, entered into force 27 January 1980) 1155 UNTS 331 .... 4–5, 12–13, 19–20, 180

Art 18 .... 16n.50, 24n.99
Art 30(1) 10n.25
Art 31 .... 7, 9n.20, 76–77, 108n.390, 182–83n.86
Art 31(1) 50–51, 130n.452, 142n.508
Art 31(2) 21n.80, 50–51
Art 31(3) 9n.20, 20n.70, 23n.95, 182–83n.86
Art 31(3)(a) 142n.508
Art 31(3)(b) ... 7n.12, 54n.192, 142n.508
Art 31(3)(c) 11n.26
Art 32 .... 7, 108n.390
Art 53 .... 10n.23
Art 62 .... 13n.32
Art 73 .... 13n.33
Vienna Convention on the Law of Treaties Between States and International Organisations or Between International Organisations (opened for signature 21 March 1986) 25 ILM 543
Art 34 .... 119n.423

Other International Instruments

Helsinki Final Act of the Conference on Security and Co-operation in Europe (adopted 1 August 1975) 14 ILM 1292
    principle VI 191n.114, 193n.127
ICRC, 'Constraints under International Law on Military Operations in Outer Space during Armed Conflicts' (working paper submitted to the UN Open-Ended Working Group on Reducing Space Threats, 2022) UN Doc A/AC.294/2022/WP.4 . . . . 275n.9
ICRC, 'Guidelines on the Protection of the Natural Environment in Armed Conflict' (2020)
    para 16 . . . . 376n.312
    para 18 . . . . 378n.323, 379n.330
    para 30 . . . . 379n.326
    paras 35–40 . . . . 376n.313
    para 48 . . . . 373–74n.304, 374n.307
    paras 50–72 . . . . 376n.313
Organization of American States, 'Terrorist Threats to the Americas' (Twenty-Fourth Meeting of the Consultation of Ministers of Foreign Affairs, 21 September 2001) OAS Doc RC.24/RES.1/01 . . . . 257n.345
United Kingdom of Great Britain and Northern Ireland, 'Draft declaration of basic principles governing the activities of States pertaining to the exploration and use of outer space' (4 December 1962) UN Doc A/C.1/879 . . . . 171n.40
UN Secretary-General, 'Depositary Notification: Saudi Arabia—Withdrawal' (5 January 2023) UN Doc C.N.4.2023.TREATIES-XXIV.2 24
UN Secretary-General, 'Status of the Protocols Additional to the Geneva Conventions of 1949 and relating to the protection of victims of armed conflicts' (information submitted by France, 28 September 2012) UN Doc A/67/182/Add.1, 3. . . . 279n.18
UN Office of Outer Space Affairs, 'Status of International Agreements relating to Activities in Outer Space, 20 March 2023, A/AC.105/C.2/2023/CRP.3, as at 1 January 2023. . . . . 19n.66, 134n.476
UN Office of Outer Space Affairs, 'Space Debris Mitigation Guidelines' (January 2010) UN Doc ST/SPACE/49 . . . . 141n.502
World Trade Organization, United States: Definitive Safeguard Measures on Imports of Circular Welded Carbon Quality Line Pipe from Korea—Report of the Appellate Body (15 February 2002) WT/DS202/AB/R, para 259 . . . . 247n.307
WTO, United States: Transitional Safeguard Measure on Combed Cotton Yarn from Pakistan—Report of the Appellate Body (8 October 2001) WT/DS192/AB/R, para 120 . . . . 247n.307

INTERNATIONAL LAW COMMISSION

ILC, 'Draft Articles on the Effects of Armed Conflicts on Treaties, with Commentary' (2011)
    UN Doc A/66/10 70
    Art 3 70
    Art 7 78–79
    Art 14 . . . . 70n.257, 76
    Art 14(2) 251n.321
    Annex 78n.294
ILC, 'Draft Articles on the Law of Treaties with Commentaries' (1966) UN Doc A/CN.4/175, 247 . . . . . 201n.154

ILC, 'Draft Principles on the Protection of the Environment in Relation to Armed Conflicts' (20 May 2022) UN Doc A/CN.4/L.968
   Principle 13 . . . . .374nn.305–6
   Principle 14 . . . . 378n.322
ILC, 'First report on subsequent agreements and subsequent practice in relation to treaty interpretation by Mr Georg Nolte, Special Rapporteur' (19 March 2013) UN Doc A/CN.4/660 (First ILC Report) 8n.13
   para 98 .8nn.17–18
ILC, 'Fragmentation of International Law: Difficulties Arising from The Diversification and Expansion of International Law—Report of the Study Group of the International Law Commission' (13 April 2006) UN Doc A/CN.4/L.682 (ILC Fragmentation Report)
   para 19 . . . . 10n.23
   paras 344–345 . . . . 10n.25
ILC, 'Report on the Work of its 63rd Session' (26 April–3 June and 4 July–12 Aug 2011) UN Doc A/66/10, 194–95 . . . . 12n.31, 13n.34, 68–69
   Art 3 . . . . 124n.442
ILC, 'Responsibility of States for Internationally Wrongful Acts' UNGA Res A/Res/56/83 (adopted 28 January 2002) 116, 187n.99
   Art 4(1) 108n.388
   Art 6 . . . . 77n.289
   Art 7 . . . . 77n.290, 308n.87
   Art 8 . . . . 108n.388, 290–91n.47
   Art 11 . . . . 113n.402, 290–91n.47
   Art 14 . . . . 111n.398
   Art 20 . . . . 117n.415
   Art 21 . . . . 68–69, 117n.416, 251n.321
   Art 22 . . . . .68–69, 117n.417, 243
   Art 23 . . . . 68–69, 117n.418
   Art 24 . . . . 68–69, 117n.419
   Art 25 . . . . 68–69, 117n.420
   Art 30 . . . . 116n.414
   Art 30(b) 248n.317
   Art 31 . . . . 116n.409
   Art 31(2) 247n.309
   Art 34 . . . . 116n.410
   Art 35 . . . . 116n.411
   Art 36(1) 116n.412
   Art 36(2) 116n.412
   Art 37(1) 116n.413
   Art 37(3) 116n.413
   Art 48(1) 246
   Art 48(1)(a) 246–47
   Art 48(1)(b) 246–47
   Arts 49–54 . . . . 117n.417, 243
   Art 49(1) 245n.295, 247n.303
   Art 49, commentary para 1 . . . . 247n.303
   Art 49, commentary para 7 . . . . 248n.313
   Art 49, commentary para 9 . . . . 248n.315
   Art 49(3) 245n.298
   Art 50 . . . . 117n.417
   Art 50(1) 244n.290
   Art 50(1)(a) 245n.292
   Art 50(1)(b)–(d) 245n.293
   Art 51 . . . . 117n.417, 247n.307, 247n.310
   Art 51, commentary para 1 . . . . 247n.308
   Art 51, commentary para 6 . . . . 247n.311
   Art 51, commentary 7 . . . . 247n.308
   Art 52(1) 247n.303
   Art 52(2) 247n.303
   Art 53 . . . . 117n.417, 248n.316
   Art 54, commentary para 6 . . . . 246n.299
ILC, 'Second Report on subsequent agreements and subsequent practice in relation to the interpretation of treaties by Georg Nolte, Special Rapporteur' (26 March 2014) UN Doc A/CN.4/671
   para 44 . . . . 8n.19
   paras 45–48 . . . . 8n.16
ILC, 'Subsequent agreements and subsequent practice in relation to the interpretation of treaties: Texts and titles of draft conclusions 6 to 10 provisionally adopted by the Drafting Committee on 27 and 28 May and on 2 and 3 June 2014' (3 June 2014) UN Doc A/CN.4/L.833, Draft Conclusion 9(2) 9n.20, 142n.508, 182–83n.86
ILC, 'Topical Summary of the Discussion held in the Sixth Committee of the General Assembly during its Fifty-Fifth Session prepared by the Secretariat' (15 February 2001) UN Doc A/CN.4/513 para 175 . . . . 246n.300

UNITED NATIONS COMMITTEE ON PEACEFUL USES OF OUTER SPACE (UNCOPUOS)

UNCOPOUS 'Additional Report' (27 November 1963) UN Doc A/5549/ADD.1 . . . . 171n.43

UNCOPUOS, 'Note Verbale Dated 29 July 2003 from the Permanent Mission of the Netherlands to the United Nations (Vienna) Addressed to the Secretary-General' (22 August 2003) A/AC.105/806 . . . . 96n.358

UNCOPUOS, 'Note Verbale Dated 31 January 2017 From the Permanent Mission of China to the United Nations (Vienna) Addressed to the Secretary-General' (22 March 2017) ST/SG/SER.E/789 . . . . 94n.350

UNCOPUOS, 'Note Verbale Dated 27 March 2017 From the Permanent Mission of France to the United Nations (Vienna) Addressed to the Secretary-General' (1 August 2017) UN Doc ST/SG/SER.E/797 . . . . 97n.362

UNCOPUOS, 'Note Verbale Dated 12 December 2018 from the Permanent Mission of the Russian Federation to the United Nations (Vienna) Addressed to the Secretary-General' (4 January 2019) UN Doc ST/SG/SER.E/868 . . . . 94n.349

UNCOPUOS, 'Provisional Verbatim Record of the Fifty-Second Meeting' (12 February 1968) UN Doc A/AC.105/PV.52, 3–5 . . . 130n.454

UNCOPUOS, 'Survey of the Problem of Discretion Exercised by States in Interpreting Basic Legal Principles and Norms related to Safety and Security in Outer Space – Working paper submitted by the Russian Federation' (21 June 2018) UN Doc A/AC.105/2018/CRP.17, para 11 . . . . 179n.73

UNCOPUOS, 'Unedited Transcript of the 569th Meeting' (7 June 2007) UN Doc COPUOS/T.569, 13–14 . . . 180–81n.79

UNCOPUOS, 'Verbatim record of the Forty-Fourth meeting' (25 October 1962) UN Doc A/AC.105.PV.44, 22 . . . . . 171n.39

UNCOPUOS, 'Verbatim Record of the Twentieth Meeting' (10 October 1963) UN Doc A/AC.105/PV.20, 17–30 . . . . . 82n.305

UNCOPUOS, 'Verbatim record of the Twenty-First meeting' (10 October 1963) UN Doc A/AC.105/PV.21, 16 . . . . 171n.39

UNCOPUOS Legal Sub-Committee, 'Provisional Summary Record of the Twenty-Second Meeting' (26 April 1963) UN Doc A/AC.109/C.2/SR.22, 11 . . . . 171n.41

UNCOPUOS Legal Sub-Committee, 'Background Paper Prepared by the Secretariat: The Question of the Definition and/or the Delimitation of Outer Space' (7 May 1970) UN Doc A/AC.105/C.2/7 36–57 . . . . 28n.111
para 28 . . . . 28n.113
para 162 . . . . 28–29n.114

UNCOPUOS Legal Sub-Committee 'Matters Relating to the Definition and Delimitation of Outer Space: Replies of the International Institute of Space Law (IISL)' (4 April 2017) UN Doc A/AC.105/C.2/2017/CRP.29 . . . . 28n.112

UNCOPUOS Legal Sub-Committee, 'Registration of Space Objects: Harmonization of Practices, Non-registration of Space Objects, Transfer of Ownership and Registration/Non-registration of 'Foreign' Space Objects' (19 January 2006) UN Doc A/AC.105/867 . . . . 87n.321

UNCOPUOS Legal Sub-Committee, 'Report of the Legal Sub-Committee on the Work of its Fifth Session (12 July–4 August and 12–16 September 1966) to the Committee on the Peaceful Uses of Outer Space (16 September 1966) UN Doc A/AC.105/35, Annex III, 3 . . . . 147n.521

UNCOPUOS Legal Sub-Committee
'Report of the Legal Sub-
Committee on the work of its
second session (16 April–3 May
1963) to the Committee on the
Peaceful Uses of Outer Space'
(6 May 1963) UN Doc
A/AC.105/12. . . . . 139n.492
Annex I, p 2 . . . . 82n.305
UNCOPUOS Legal Sub-Committee,
'Report of the Secretariat:
Historical Summary on the
Consideration of the Question on
the Definition and Delimitation
of Outer Space' (18 January 2002)
UN Doc A/AC.105/769
para 25 . . . . 27n.106, 27n.108
UNCOPUOS Legal Sub-Committee,
'Responses to the set of
Questions provided by the Chair
of the Working Group on the
Status and Application of the Five
United Nations Treaties
on Outer Space' (10 April 2015)
UN Doc A/AC.105/C.2/2015/
CRP.11 . . . . 17n.54, 24n.97
UNCOPUOS Legal Sub-Committee,
'Responses to the set of
Questions provided by the Chair
of the Working Group on the
Status and Application of the
Five United Nations Treaties on
Outer Space' (23 March 2017)
UN Doc A/AC.105/C.2/2017/
CRP.6 . . . . 17nn.54–55, 19n.63
UNCOPUOS Legal Sub-Committee,
'Responses to the set of
Questions provided by the Chair
of the Working Group on the
Status and Application of the Five
United Nations Treaties on Outer
Space' (6 April 2018) UN Doc
A/AC.105/C.2/2018/CRP.12. . . 17n.54
UNCOPUOS Legal Sub-Committee,
'Promoting the Discussion
of the Matters Relating to the
Definition and Delimitation
of Outer Space with a View
to Elaborating a Common
Position of States Members of the
[UNCOPUOS]' (17 May 2017)
UN Doc A/AC.105/C.2/L.302
para 15 . . . . 27n.109

UNCOPUOS Legal Sub-Committee
'Provisional Summary Record of
the Twenty-Eighth Meeting'
(7 May 1963) UN Doc A/
AC.105/C.2/SR.28, 7 . . . . 170n.36
UNCOPUOS Legal Sub-Committee,
'Provisional Summary Record of
the Twenty-First Meeting'
(25 April 1963) 171n.41
UNCOPUOS Legal Sub-Committee,
'Provisional Summary Record of
the Twenty-Fourth Meeting'
(1 May 1963) UN Doc A/AC.105/
C.2/SR.24, 5 . . . . 170n.36, 171n.39
UNCOPUOS Legal Sub-Committee,
'Provisional Summary Record of
the Twenty-Second Meeting'
(26 April 1963) UN Doc A/
AC.105/C.2/SR.22, 11 . . . . 170n.36
UNCOPUOS Legal Sub-Committee,
'Status of International
agreements relating to activities
in outer space as at 1 January
2012' (12 March 2012) UN Doc
A/AC.105/C.2/2012/CRP.3 . . . . 19n.67
UNCOPUOS Legal Sub Committee,
'Status of International
agreements relating to activities
in outer space as at 1 January
2017' (23 March 2017) UN Doc
A/AC.105/C.2/2017/CRP.7 . . . . 22n.86
UNCOPUOS Legal Sub-Committee,
'Status of International
Agreements relating to activities
in outer space as at 1 January
2021' UN Doc A/AC.105/C.2/
2022/CRP.10 . . . . 44n.153
UNCOPUOS Legal Sub-Committee,
'Summary Record of the Eighty-
Ninth Meeting' (2 February 1968)
A/AC.105/C.2/SR.89, 3 . . . . . . 132n.465
UNCOPUOS Legal Sub-Committee,
'Summary Record of the Eighty-
Seventh Meeting' (2 February
1968) UN Doc A/AC.105/C.2/
SR.87 . . . . 130n.454
UNCOPUOS Legal Sub-Committee,
'Summary Record of the Eighty-
Sixth Meeting' (9 February 1968)
UN Doc A/AC.105/C.2/SR.86
(UNCOPUOS Legal
Sub-Committee Summary
Record 86) 130n.454

UNCOPUOS Legal Sub-Committee,
'Summary Record of the Fifty-
Eighth Meeting,' (20 October 1966)
A/AC.105/C.2/SR.58, 9 .... 131n.459
UNCOPUOS Legal Sub-Committee,
'Summary Record of the Forty-
Fourth Meeting' (30 November
1965) UN Doc A/AC.105/C.2/
SR.44, 8 .... 131n.458
UNCOPUOS Legal Sub-Committee,
'Summary Record of the
Seventeenth Meeting' (27 June
1963) UN Doc A/AC.105/C.2/
S.17, 4 and 6................ 171n.41
UNCOPUOS Legal Sub-Committee,
'Summary Record of the Seventieth
Meeting' (3 August 1966)
A/AC.105/C.2/SR.70, 3 .... 67n.248
UNCOPUOS Legal Sub-Committee,
'Summary Record of the Seventy-
First Meeting' (4 August 1966) UN
Doc A/AC.l05/C.2/SR.71, 24 ... 52n.183
UNCOPUOS Legal Sub-Committee,
'Summary Record of the Sixty-
Eighth Meeting' (21 October
1966) UN Doc A/AC.105/C.2/
SR.68, 10 .... 171n.44
UNCOPUOS Legal Sub-Committee,
'Summary Record of the Sixty-
Fifth Meeting' (22 July 1966) A/
AC.105/C.2/SR.65, 9 ..... 66–67n.245
UNCOPUOS Legal Sub-Committee,
'Summary Record of the Sixty-
Fourth Meeting' (24 October
1966) UN Doc A/AC.l05/C.2/
SR.64, 3 .... 37n.124
UNCOPUOS Legal Sub-Committee,
'Summary Record of the
Sixty-Second Meeting' (19 July
1966) UN Doc A/AC.105/C.2/
SR.62, 2–3 .... 201n.156
UNCOPUOS Legal Sub-Committee,
'Summary Record of the Sixty-Sixth
Meeting' (21 October 1966) UN
Doc A/AC.105/C.2/SR.66....... 39n.137
UNCOPUOS Legal Sub-Committee,
'Summary Record of the Sixty-
Third Meeting' (20 October
1966) UN Doc A/AC.105/C.2/
SR.63, 7 .... 37n.125
UNCOPUOS Scientific and Technical
Subcommittee, 'National Research
on Space Debris, Safety of Space
Objects with Nuclear Power Sources
on Board and Problems Relating to
Their Collision with Space Debris'
(2 November 2016) UN Doc
A/AC.105/C.1/111, 11–12..... 74n.277

UNITED NATIONS GENERAL ASSEMBLY (UNGA)

UNGA, 'A More Secure World: Our
Shared Responsibility, Report of
the High-level Panel on Threats,
Challenges and Change' (2
December 2004) UN Doc A/59/565
para 188 .... 254n.337
UNGA, 'Declaration on the
Inadmissibility of Intervention
in the Domestic Affairs of States
and the Protection of Their
Independence and Sovereignty'
(21 December 1965) UNGA Res
2131 (XX)
para 1 .... 191n.114
UNGA, 'Declaration of Legal Principles
Governing the Activities of States
in the Exploration and Use of
Outer Space' (13 December 1963)
UN Doc A/RES/1962 (XVIII)
(1963 UNGA Declaration of Legal
Principles) 18, 37n.122, 41, 135
Para 2 .... 37n.124
para 5 .... 108n.391
para 6 .... 177n.66
para 7 .... 135n.481
UNGA, 'Declaration on International
Cooperation in the Exploration
and Use of Outer Space for the
Benefit and in the Interest of All
States, Taking into Particular
Account the Needs of Developing
Countries' (4 February 1997) UN
Doc A/RES/51/122....... 38, 43n.150
para 1 .... 38n.129
para 2 .... 38n.130
UNGA, 'Declaration on Principles of
International Law Concerning
Friendly Relations and Co-
operation Among States in
Accordance With the Charter
of the United Nations'
(24 October 1970)
A/RES/2625 (XXV) 85n.312, 195
principle 3, para 1 .... 191n.114

UNGA, 'Destructive direct-ascent anti satellite missile testing' (7 December 2002) UN Doc A/RES/77/41 ...... 140n.497, 176n.65

UNGA, 'Letter dated 16 June 1966 from the Permanent Representative of the Union of Soviet Socialist Republics to the United Nations Addressed to the Secretary-General' (16 June 1966) UN Doc A/6352)............ 82n.305, 109n.392

UNGA, 'Letter Dated 16 June 1966 from the Permanent Representative of the United States of America Addressed to the Chairman of the Committee on the Peaceful Uses of Outer Space' (17 June 1966) UN Doc A/AC.105/32............... 72n.267

UNGA, 'Letter Dated 11 July 1966 to the Chairman of the Legal Sub-committee by the Representative of the USSR (11 July 1966) UN Doc A/AC.105/C.2/L.13 .... 109n.392
Art 4......................... 72n.267

UNGA, 'In Larger Freedom: Towards Development, Security and Human Rights for All— Report of the Secretary General' (21 March 2005) UN Doc A/59/2005, para 124........ 254n.337

UNGA, 'No first Placement of Weapons in Outer Space' (2 December 2014) UN Doc A/RES/69/32, 5......... 61n.225

UNGA, 'Official compendium of voluntary national contributions on the subject of how international law applies to the use of information and communications technologies by States submitted by participating governmental experts in the Group of Governmental Experts on Advancing Responsible State Behaviour in Cyberspace in the Context of International Security established pursuant to General Assembly resolution 73/266' (13 July 2021) UN Doc A/76/136 ....193n.120

UNGA, 'Official Seal and Emblem of the United Nations' (7 December 1946) UN Doc A/RES/92(I)... 388n.348

UNGA, 'Principles Governing the Use by States of Artificial Earth Satellites for International Direct Television Broadcasting' (10 December 1982) UNGA Res 37/92 principle A1................. 191n.116

UNGA, 'Principles Relevant to the Use of Nuclear Power Sources in Outer Space' (23 February 1993) UN Doc A/RES/47/68 .... 74n.276

UNGA, 'Recommendations on National Legislation Relevant to the Peaceful Exploration and Use of Outer Space' (11 December 2013) UN Doc A/RES/68/74 ....115n.406
para 2 .... 107n.386, 115

UNGA, 'Report of the Group of Governmental Experts on Advancing Responsible State Behaviour in Cyberspace in the Context of International Security' (14 July 2021) UN Doc A/76/135 ....218–19n.225

UNGA, 'Report of Group of Governmental Experts on further practical measures for the prevention of an arms race in outer space' (April 2019) UN Doc A/74/77
para 30 .... 274n.5

UNGA, 'Report of the Committee on the Peaceful Uses of Outer Space, Sixtieth Session' (7–16 June 2017)UN Doc A/72/20, 15, para 103.................. 145n.518

UNGA, 'Report of the Conference on the Committee on Disarmament Volume 1' (1976) UN Doc A/31/27 .... 376n.316
para 327..................... 368n.277

UNGA, 'Report of the Working Group on National Legislation Relevant to the Peaceful Exploration and Use of Outer Space on the Work Conducted Under its multi-year Workplan' (3 April 2012) UN Doc A/AC.105/C.2/101 .... 115n.406

UNGA, 'Safety Framework
for Nuclear Power Source
Applications in Outer Space'
(19 May 2009) UN Doc
A/AC.105/934, 1 . . . . 74n.275
UNGA, 'Standing mandate for a
General Assembly debate when
a veto is cast in the Security
Council', (26 April 2022)
UNGA Res 76/262 . . . . . . 263–64n.363
UNGA, 'Summary record of the 13th
meeting' (Comments by the
representative of Sweden (Mr
Lundvist) speaking on behalf of
the Nordic countries (Denmark,
Finland, Iceland, Norway, and
Sweden, 7 November 2008) UN
Doc A/C.6/63/SR.13
para 32 . . . . 279n.18
UNGA, 'USSR Proposal: Declaration
of the Basic Principles governing
the Activities of States Pertaining
to the Exploration and Use of
Outer Space' (6 June 1962) UN
Doc A/AC.105/C.2/L.1 . . . . . . 171n.38
para 7 . . . . 108n.391
para 8 . . . . 82n.304
UNGA, 'USSR: Revised Draft
Agreement on the Rescue of
Astronauts in the Event of
Accident or Emergency Landing'
(23 October 1964) A/AC.105/
C.2/L.2/Rev. 2
Annex I, 4 . . . . 133n.469
UNGA First Committee
(3 December 1963) UN
Doc A/C.1/SR.1343, 171 . . . . . 171n.44
UNGA First Committee,
'Prevention of an Arms Race in
Outer Space' (14 Nov 2022) UN
Doc A/77/383, 23 . . . . .175n.63
UNGA First Committee, 'Summary
Record of the 1346th Meeting'
(5 December 1963) UN
Doc A/C.1/SR.1346, 189 . . . . . . 18n.61
UNGA First Committee, 'Summary
Record of the 1422nd Meeting' (20
December 1965) UN Doc A/C.1/
SR.1422, 429 (remarks of the US
Ambassador Charles Yost) 53n.185
UNGA First Committee, 'Summary
Record of the 1492nd Meeting'
(17 December 1966) UN Doc A/
C.1/S.R.1492, 428, para 7 . . . . 148n.525
UNGA First Committee, 'Verbatim
Record of the Fourteen Hundred
and Ninety-Second Meeting'
(27 January 1967) A/C.1/
PV.1492, 16 . . . . .37–38n.126
UNGA First Committee, 'Verbatim
Record of the Thirteen Hundred
and Forty Second Meeting'
(2 December 1963) UN Doc
A/C.1/PV.1342 . . . . 18n.61
UNGA First Committee, 'Verbatim
Record of the Twelve Hundred
and Eighty-Ninth Meeting'
(3 December 1962) UN Doc
A/C.1/PV. 1289, 13 . . . 53n.185, 82n.304
UNGA Res 377 (V) (3 November
1950) UN Doc A/RES/5/377
(Uniting for Peace) 263n.360
UNGA Res 1348 (XIII) (13 December
1958) (Question of the Peaceful
Use of Outer Space) 37n.122
UNGA Res 1721 (XVI) (20 December
1961) (International Co-operation
in the Peaceful Uses of Outer
Space) 37n.122, 41n.140, 52n.184
UNGA Res 1884 (XVIII) (17 October
1963) 71–72, 76–77
UNGA Res 2222 (XXI) (1966) 16n.49
UNGA Res 3314 (XXIX) (14
December 1974) UN Doc
A/RES/3314 (Definition of
Aggression Resolution) 205n.165
Art 3(a) 205–6n.171
Art 3(c) .205–6n.171
Art 3(e) .205–6n.171
Art 3(f) .205–6n.171
UNGA Res 32/84 (12 December 1977)
UN Doc A/RES/32/84 . . . . 73n.270
UNGA Res 38/80 (1983) UN Doc
A/RES/38/80
para 5(c) 27n.107
UNGA Res 47/68 (14 December
1992) UN Doc A/RES/47/68
Principle 3(1)(a) 140n.498
UNGA Res 51/37 (10 December 1996)
UN Doc A/RES/51/37 . . . . 73n.270
UNGA Res 51/56 (9 January 1997)
UN Doc A/RES/51/56, 1 . . . . . 66n.241
UNGA Res 54/44 (23 December 1999)
UN Doc A/RES/54/44 . . . . 73n.270

UNGA Res 75/36 (2021) UN Doc
   A/76/77 .... 375n.309
UNGA Sixth Committee, 'Summary
   Record of the 13th meeting'
   (28 February 2020) UN
   Doc A/C.6/74/SR.13 .... 243n.285

UNITED NATIONS SECURITY COUNCIL

UNSC, 'Commission for
   Conventional Armaments'
   (18 August 1948) UN
   Doc S/C.3/32/Rev.1, 2......... 73n.269
UNSC, 'Identical letters dated 8
   September 2015 from the
   Permanent Representative of
   France to the United Nations
   addressed to the Secretary-General
   and the President of the Security
   Council' (9 September 2015)
   UN Doc S/2015/745 .... 257n.346
UNSC, 'Letter dated 24 July 2015 from
   the Charge d'affaires a.i. of the
   Permanent Mission of Turkey
   to the United Nations addressed
   to the President of the Security
   Council' (24 July 2015)
   UN Doc S/2015/563 .... 257n.346
UNSC Res 678 (29 November 1990)
   UN Doc S/RES/678
   para 2 .... 267n.379, 268n.382
UNSC Res 1973 (17 March 2011)
   UN Doc S/RES/1973
   para 4 .... 269n.384, 293n.53
UNSC Res 2270 (2016) UN
   Doc S/RES/2270 .... 266n.373
   Preamble
   para 1 .... 266n.374
   para 11 .... 266n.374
   Annex 2.9................... 266n.374
UNSC Res 2310 (23 September
   2016) UN Doc
   S/RES/2310 .... 80n.297

National Instruments

AUSTRALIA

Criminal Code Act 1995 (Cth)
   s 268.70 .... 317n.133
   s 268.125 .... 317n.133
Space Activities Act 1998 (Cth) ... 107n.385
   pt 2 s 8 .... 28n.112
   pt 3, div 6 .... 163n.13

DENMARK

Executive Order (Bekendtgorelse)
   no 552 of 31 March 2016
   pt 4 s 7 .... 143n.511

FINLAND

63/2018 Act on Space Activities (Laki
   avaruustoiminnasta)
   s 10 .... 143n.511

JAPAN

Basic Space Law (Law No 43 of 2008)
   (enacted 21 May 2008, effective
   27 August 2008)
   Art 14 .... 57n.202

LUXEMBOURG

Law of July 20 2017 on the Exploration
   and Use of Space Resources
   (English Translation) (13 July 2017)
   Art 1 .... 46n.163

NIGERIA

National Space Research and
   Development Agency Act
   (2010) Cap. (9)
   pt 3, s 9(4) 143n.511

SOUTH AFRICA

Space Affairs Act 1993 .... 107n.385

UKRAINE

Law of 15 November 1996, Ordinance
   of the Supreme Soviet of Ukraine
   on Space Activity (Vidomosti
   Verkhovoni Rady Ukrainy, 1997 p 2)
   Art 9 .... 143n.511

UNITED ARAB EMIRATES

Federal Law No (12) of 2019 ...... 46n.164

UNITED KINGDOM

Outer Space Act 1986 .... 107n.385, 144n.517
   Preamble 143n.510
   Art 5(2)(e)(i) 143n.510
   Art 13(1) 143n.510
   Sch 1(a), para 14 .... 143n.510

UNITED STATES OF AMERICA

18 USC § 7(6) 87–88n.325
Commercial Space Launch
   Competitiveness Act, 51 USC
   § 51303 (2015) 46n.162, 131n.457
Military Commissions Act of 2009, 10
   USC § 948(a)(7) 317n.134
National Aeronautics and Space
   Administration Authorization
   Act 1970, Pub L 91-119
   18 November 1969
   s 8 .... 42n.141
National Defense Authorization Act
   for Fiscal Year 2012 .... 317n.134
Restatement (Third) of Foreign
   Relations Law in the United States
   (American Law Institute 1987)
   §1.02 .... 18n.61
   § 383 .... 202–3n.159
   § 402 .... 85n.313
   § 402, comment e 87n.321
   § 402, comment h 87n.324
   § 404 .... 85n.313
   § 905 .... 202–3n.159

Introduction

Goal of the *Manual*

1. This *Manual* is the result of a multi-year effort by a group of dedicated participants from across the globe who brought together their expertise in the law and technology related to military space activities and operations. Their objective was to identify, clarify, and succinctly articulate the extant rules of international law that apply to military space activities and operations, to explain the basis for those rules, and to delineate the areas of legal uncertainty that remain. The goal of the *Manual* is to provide assistance to those called upon to apply international law in contexts of strategic decision-making, policy-setting, and/or military activities and operations in space. More broadly, it is designed to assist military and civilian government personnel, space operators, practitioners, members of international organizations and non-governmental organizations (NGOs) involved in military space activities and operations, and other interested observers. It is hoped that the *Manual* may become a useful and reliable reference tool for aiding governments and military forces to avoid miscalculations or strategic error, to advance peaceful cooperation in space, and to help provide a safer and more predictable framework for military space activities and operations during times of peace, tension, and, if necessary, armed conflict.

Background of the *Manual*

2. Space is an area of increasing contemporary military, governmental, commercial, and other activities. As the scope and significance of military space activities continue to expand, the strategic importance of space is becoming universally acknowledged. Indeed, NATO not too long ago declared outer space to be an 'operational domain' for the alliance.[1] Such recognition follows that already made by many individual States, along with corresponding and expanding military space

---

[1] NATO, 'London Declaration: Issued by the Heads of State and Government participating in the meeting of the North Atlantic Council in London 3–4 December 2019' (Press Release, NATO 4 December 2019) art 6 ('We have declared space an operational domain for NATO, recognising its importance in keeping us safe and tackling security challenges, while upholding international law') [https://perma.cc/KA25-UYAF].

activities by States.[2] These developments reflect the inescapable fact that many terrestrially based military activities rely heavily upon space capabilities. These include satellite communications; position, navigation, and timing (PNT) functionality; environmental monitoring; meteorology; and intelligence, surveillance, and reconnaissance (ISR). Accordingly, the loss or degradation of such space-based services would represent a key strategic vulnerability. Yet no comprehensive examination of the application of international law to actions affecting these critical space-based capabilities or related military space operations has been available. This is in spite of the fact that understanding how the existing space treaty regime and general international law apply to establish boundaries, freedoms, and restraints for an ever-expanding range of actual and potential military space activities has now become a critical imperative. The *Woomera Manual* project was created to help answer that imperative and provide the needed comprehensive, objective, and universal examination of the application of international law to military space activities and operations. The project is spearheaded by the University of Adelaide (Australia), the University of Exeter (United Kingdom), the University of Nebraska College of Law (United States), and the University of New South Wales–Canberra (Australia) but was also joined by representatives from many other universities across the globe. Additionally, the *Woomera Manual* benefited greatly by the addition of numerous government lawyers (acting in their personal capacities), academics, NGOs, as well as technical experts. In addition, the *Woomera Manual* underwent an extensive process of peer review. Importantly, as discussed below, the draft manuscript was submitted to the foreign ministries of States by the Dutch Ministry of Foreign Affairs and the Editorial Board then received comments on the Manuscript from the representatives of States during State Consultations hosted by the Dutch Ministry of Foreign Affairs, assisted by the Dutch Ministry of Defence, at The Hague, 1–3 June 2022. Extensive written comments were also submitted by some States following State Consultations. These valuable State comments significantly shaped all the Rules in the *Manual*.

---

[2] Australian Department of Defence, 'Annual Report 19-20' (Commonwealth of Australia 2020) 96 [https://perma.cc/8UPG-CYTE] ('Space is becoming an increasingly congested and contested environment. Defence recognises the importance of this environment as both an essential enabler of military operations and a warfighting domain in its own right'); Stephen M McCall, 'Space as a Warfighting Domain: Issues for Congress' (US Congressional Research Service 10 August 2021) [https://perma.cc/Z2SE-AFPB] ('The United States is in the midst of making significant changes to policy on protecting national security pertaining to outer space. Military strategists increasingly consider space to be a warfighting domain—a location where offensive and defensive military operations take place—similar to air, land, and sea'); see generally Rule 3: Peaceful Purposes in Outer Space, paras 10–17 (detailing the growth of military space activities by States, including China, France, India, Japan, Russia, the United States, and others); see also Brian Weeden and Victoria Samson (eds), 'Global Counterspace Capabilities: An Open Source Assessment' (Secure World Foundation 2022) [https://perma.cc/3SJK-XUVS] (assessing the growth of the counterspace capabilities of numerous States).

Military Activity vs Military Operation

3. The *Manual* aims to articulate and clarify, to the extent possible, international law applicable to all military space activities. Military activities have a wide scope and include any action undertaken by military forces[3] relating to space, including the launching, orbiting, and recovery of space objects as well as the conduct of routine communications, data transmission, monitoring, and reconnaissance procedures. These activities would encompass the ground, link, and space segments of such activities, whether undertaken during times of peace or otherwise. The term 'military activity' as used in the *Manual* is a broader term than the term 'military operation', which is also used in the *Manual*. The International Committee of the Red Cross notes that the term military operation 'should be understood to mean movements, manoeuvres and actions of any sort carried out by armed forces with a view to combat'[4] and includes 'all movements and acts related to hostilities that are undertaken by armed forces'.[5] The military manuals of States use similar terminology.[6] Hence, for the purposes of this *Manual*, the term 'military space operation' is a subset of 'military space activities' and the law of armed conflict, as examined and applied in Part III, is relevant to all such operations.[7]

Organization of the *Manual*

4. The *Manual* is divided into three thematic Parts. Part I deals with routine military activities in space in peacetime (not related to an ongoing armed conflict) and focuses on international law, particularly the space law regime, as it applies to these military activities.[8] Part II focuses on military activities that occur in a time of tension or crisis, addressing activities that occur along a continuum of unfriendly acts that may be taken by States (including those that relate to the threat or use of force) and appropriate lawful responses to those actions. This Part places an additional emphasis on obligations and rights under the United Nations Charter regime.

---

[3] Where relevant, the Rules in this *Manual* also apply to a State's space activities that are characterized as 'intelligence activities' or involve space activities performed by a State's intelligence agencies.

[4] International Committee of the Red Cross, *Commentary on the Additional Protocols of 8 June 1977 to the Geneva Conventions of 12 August 1949* (Claude Pilloud and others (eds), Martin Nijhoff 1987) para 2191.

[5] ibid para 1875.

[6] See eg United Kingdom Ministry of Defence, 'The Joint Service Manual of the Law of Armed Conflict' (Joint Service Publication 383, United Kingdom Joint Doctrine and Concepts Centre 2004) para 5.32. fn 187 (pointing out that the phrase military operations 'has a wider connotation than "attacks" and would include the movement or deployment of armed forces').

[7] The application of the law of several Rules in Part III emphasizes the broad scope of military operations governed by the Rules (and the related protections afforded the civilian populations by the law of armed conflict) by referring to military space operations that occur 'from, to or within space'.

[8] Where appropriate, the status of these Rules during a time of armed conflict, and their relationship with different legal regimes, is also discussed. See Introduction to Part I.

Part III deals with military space operations that take place during an armed conflict, with an emphasis on the application of the law of armed conflict and its relationship with the space law regime and other relevant rules of international law. Notwithstanding the basic structure described above, some concepts find application in multiple parts and are dealt with accordingly.

5. Throughout the *Manual*, the terms 'space' and 'outer space' are used interchangeably and, unless otherwise noted, these terms also include the Moon and other celestial bodies. As discussed in the Note on Outer Space vs Airspace (Delimitation of Outer Space), international law has not defined the lowest altitude above the surface of the Earth at which the legal regime of space begins to apply. In addition, unless otherwise noted, the terms 'terrestrial domain' and 'Earth' both refer to the land, maritime, and aerial domains of Earth, as well as cyberspace to the extent it manifests in or applies to each of these domains.

6. The foundational cornerstone of the space law regime is the Outer Space Treaty[9] (abbreviated as 'OST') which is examined throughout this *Manual* and serves as the basis for Rules 1–18 set forth in Parts I and II. As discussed in Overview of the Space Law Regime, all the leading spacefaring States are parties to the OST and virtually all the other States involved in space activities are parties or Signatories to this Treaty. This allows for a consistency of approach in ascertaining the nature of treaty obligations applicable to contemporary military space activities and operations. Most or all of these treaty-based rules are likely also to have achieved the status of rules of customary international law (see Overview of the Space Law Regime).

Foundational Emphasis on State Practice

7. The *Woomera Manual* summarizes and, as appropriate, analyses and clarifies, the *lex lata* as found in the two primary sources of international law: treaty law and customary international law. In light of the central importance that States play in the development of public international law with respect to these sources, reliance must be placed on State practice and the views of Governments. Thus, State practice is foundational in four key respects in the *Woomera Manual*. First, State practice, coupled with the critical requirement of *opinio juris*, that is, State compliance with rules out of a sense of legal obligation, creates customary international law. Second, State practice in implementing international agreements, like the OST, may represent agreement by States in the authoritative interpretation of ambiguous terms in those agreements under the Vienna Convention on the Law of

---

[9] Treaty on Principles Governing the Activities of States in the Exploration and Use of Outer Space, Including the Moon and Other Celestial Bodies (opened for signature 27 January 1967, entered into force 10 October 1967) 610 UNTS 205 (OST).

Treaties. Third, State practice in the negotiation of international agreements found in the travaux préparatoires, that is, the official record of negotiation, may be used to help interpret ambiguous terms in an international agreement under the Vienna Convention on the Law of Treaties. Fourth, even when there is not yet widespread acceptance of a possible rule of customary international law or agreed interpretation of an international agreement, State practice can be instructive in identifying developing trends that may be shaping the contours of international law.

8. Accordingly, as a key drafting principle, the focus of the *Woomera Manual* is heavily upon identifying and incorporating relevant State practice in the interpretation and application of the sources of international law. While there are volumes of commentary on space law written by important academic writers and NGOs that certainly assisted the research undertaken for this project, the fact remains that States are the primary drivers of international law. Hence, in addition to drawing on the valuable comments provided by States during State Consultations, particular research attention was paid to State practice in implementing relevant treaties; the travaux préparatoires of relevant treaties; official statements made by States and actions taken by States in the context of military space activities; the official positions taken by States in military manuals and official policy statements; other available data and reports regarding activities by States in and related to space; and summaries and discussions of State practice provided by non-State entities active in this field and by some commentators. The manner in which State practice is evaluated and applied in this *Manual* is further explained in the section Methodology of *Manual*.

State Consultations

9. During the period 1–3 June 2022, the Government of the Netherlands facilitated a process of State Consultations in The Hague at which the Editorial Board presented the draft manuscript for State consideration. Twenty-four countries as well as the International Committee of the Red Cross participated and provided comments on the draft of the *Manual*. The countries that were represented at this consultation were as follows:

Australia	Guyana	New Zealand
Austria	Israel	Poland
Canada	Italy	Romania
Côte d'Ivoire	Japan	South Africa
Denmark	Kuwait	United Arab Emirates
Ecuador	Luxembourg	United Kingdom
France	Malaysia	United States of America
Germany	The Netherlands	Zimbabwe

10. The consultations were hosted at the Dutch Ministry of Foreign Affairs in The Hague and were extremely useful in clarifying key points that assisted in the revision of the *Manual*. State representatives identified areas of uncertainty in the law applicable to outer space, suggested helpful revisions, and volunteered additional examples of State practice to supplement the *Manual*'s content. They were supportive of the approach taken by the *Manual* in highlighting State practice to assist in ascertaining existing or emerging legal interpretations.

11. Following these State Consultations, many significant changes were made to the draft manuscript of the *Manual* and these are reflected in the text and sometimes also expressly identified in the footnotes. The Editorial Board acknowledges that participation in this event did not signify formal State endorsement of the content. At the same time, it was clear that States characterized the *Manual* as a highly useful and constructive project and provided comments in good faith on the structure of the *Manual* aiming to articulate existing law as clearly as possible.

12. The Editors also want to express their deep gratitude to the Government of the Netherlands, particularly Ms Wieteke Theeuwen and Lieutenant Colonel Duco le Clerq, whose strenuous efforts enabled the success of these State Consultations.

Collective Work

13. This *Manual* is the result of collective work over several years in which many contributors provided extensive, original, and valuable comments that shaped the content of the *Manual*. Extensive comments from States as part of State Consultations further significantly shaped the content of the *Manual*. The Editors then prepared the final version of the text. While not all the contributors can be committed to the formulation of each point in the *Manual* or every element of its structure and approaches, all the contributors shared the goal of providing the best possible exposition of the international law applicable to military space activities and operations, grounded in extant law and the practice of States.

Why is the *Manual* Called the *Woomera Manual*?

14. Finally, a word on the title of the *Woomera Manual*. The name is drawn from the town of Woomera, South Australia. Woomera has a long association with multinational space activities, and it was the site from which Australia become one of the first countries to design and launch its own satellite when the WRESAT satellite was launched in 1967.[10] Notably, this satellite was partially designed and

---

[10] Defence Science and Technology Group, 'WRESAT—Weapons Research Establishment Satellite' (Australian Department of Defence 2022) [https://perma.cc/4KC6-V85M].

constructed in the University of Adelaide. Woomera served as a British, US, European, and Australian centre for space operations throughout the 1960s and 1970s. Woomera is itself an Australian Aboriginal word in the Dharug language (of the Eora people, traditional custodians of the Sydney area) for a traditional Aboriginal spear-throwing device. The word was chosen as the name of the rocket range because a key purpose of a woomera was to enable much greater distance and accuracy in throwing a spear.

Methodology of the *Woomera Manual*
Interpretive issues

The drafting process for the *Woomera Manual* addressed several interpretative issues that required close attention and are worthy of some exposition in this brief review of the *Manual*'s methodology.

1.

State practice and its relevance regarding treaty interpretation

Throughout the *Manual*, numerous treaties that apply to military activities and operations are examined. The provisions of such instruments have been interpreted following the requirements of Articles 31 and 32 of the 1969 Vienna Convention on the Law of Treaties,[11] which includes a focus on the text itself and the context of the treaty, subsequent State practice in implementing the treaty, and, as a supplementary means of interpretation, the travaux préparatoires.

2.

Many military space activities are undertaken against a backdrop of State secrecy and high security classification, not least because of national security considerations and the technical capabilities being developed and deployed. Hence, States are not always forthcoming in public statements concerning their actions or non-actions related to military operations in space, including the legal basis for those actions. Despite this intermitttent reticence to publicly espouse legal positions, a State's actions and the corresponding reactions by other States may nonetheless convey legal meaning. As noted above, the subsequent practice of the States that are parties to a treaty, such as the OST, is a recognized basis of interpretation.[12]

3.

Interpretation based on State practice implementing treaties has been the subject of an International Law Commission (ILC) study, seeking to define its capacity and

4.

---

[11] Vienna Convention on the Law of Treaties (adopted 23 May 1969, entered into force 27 January 1980) 1155 UNTS 331 (VCLT).
[12] ibid art 31(3)(b) ('There shall be taken into account, together with the context: ... (b) any subsequent practice in the application of the treaty which establishes the agreement of the parties regarding its interpretation.').

reach better.[13] The Commission noted that relevant State practice includes 'official statements concerning the treaty's meaning, protests against non-performance, or tacit consent to statements or acts by other parties'.[14] According to the ILC, the State practice need not consist of a repeated pattern of high frequency but can also include single events, although of course such single events need to be weighted contextually for their evidentiary value.[15] In this regard, the *Woomera Manual* strives to identify as many forms of State practice as possible with respect to the interpretation of the terms of relevant treaties.

5. The ILC observed that while the threshold for finding relevant State practice was high under a relevant Treaty (such as the OST), there need not be a universal convergence of State practice to discern authentic meaning.[16] Descriptions distilled from international judicial fora regarding such a threshold were described as being a 'vast majority view',[17] 'emerging consensus',[18] or a 'discernible pattern'[19] that can be identified. The task is to find a common understanding that has accorded generally accepted meaning to a term. Importantly, it was also noted in the study that a contrary view of a single State does not undermine the efficacy of a conclusion of subsequent State practice.

The central role of State practice in the methodology of the *Manual*

6. Unlike other works, the methodology of this *Manual* is not based on the differing opinions of experts about what international law could or should be. Instead, it is based primarily on the examination of the foundation of international law: the practice of States. Research focused on the statements and conduct of States, including the positions taken by States in the travaux préparatoires, that is, evidence of the negotiating and drafting history of treaties, and the actions of States in implementing those treaties, thus serves as the basis for explaining existing international law, as well as examining the contours of its ongoing development. Where

---

[13] International Law Commission, 'First report on subsequent agreements and subsequent practice in relation to treaty interpretation by Mr Georg Nolte, Special Rapporteur' (19 March 2013) UN Doc A/CN.4/660 (First ILC Report).

[14] ibid para 110.

[15] ibid para 109 ('If, however, the concept of subsequent practice is divulged from a possible agreement between the parties, as it is recognized by international adjudicatory bodies, frequency is not a necessary element of the definition of the concept of "subsequent practice"').

[16] International Law Commission, 'Second Report on subsequent agreements and subsequent practice in relation to the interpretation of treaties by Georg Nolte, Special Rapporteur' (26 March 2014) UN Doc A/CN.4/671 (Second ILC Report) 21, paras 45–48.

[17] First ILC Report (n 13) para 98.

[18] ibid para 98.

[19] Second ILC Report (n 16) para 44.

this approach reveals significant alternate paths, they are noted in the *Manual*. Where State practice on a particular point is unclear or unsettled, that also is noted and discussed. In the same vein, for much of its content, the *Manual* relies on comments that were provided to the Editorial Board by the representatives of States during State Consultations.

The significance—or lack thereof—of State silence or inaction

In examining the subsequent practice of States under a treaty like the OST as a means of interpretation of that treaty with respect to military space activities and operations, as well as the development of customary international law, it is important to assess not only the actions and the official statements of those States but also to consider the possibility that their non-actions or silence constitute tacit consent with respect to the actions of another State or the acceptance that a breach of international law by that other State has not occurred.[20] However, it should also be noted that the legal significance of the silence of States in reacting to the statements or actions of other States—particularly during the development of a rule of customary international law or in the subsequent practice of States, under a treaty that reflects their agreement regarding the interpretation of that treaty—remains a subject of much debate and should be evaluated with caution.[21] For example, one State at State Consultations noted that in addition to legal considerations, there may be a number of non-legal considerations (such as policy, security, operational, or diplomatic concerns) that may factor into whether a State may decide to stay silent, choose not to act, or choose not to acknowledge publicly how it acts. Another State noted that where States have been silent, this may in fact indicate that States accept that there is not a breach of international law, but is not necessarily conclusive on this point. Nonetheless, in some contexts, States who are parties to an agreement who consistently fail to assert rights or demand performance of obligations that appear to be owed to them under specific provisions

7.

---

[20] It should be noted that Article 31(3) of the VCLT provides that in interpreting a treaty, 'there shall be taken into account, together with the context: ... (b) any subsequent practice in the application of the treaty which establishes the agreement of the parties regarding its interpretation'. The International Law Commission has noted that such an agreement under Article 31 'need not be legally binding' and that '[s]ilence on the part of one or more parties can constitute acceptance of the subsequent practice when the circumstances call for some reaction'. International Law Commission, 'Subsequent agreements and subsequent practice in relation to the interpretation of treaties: Texts and titles of draft conclusions 6 to 10 provisionally adopted by the Drafting Committee on 27 and 28 May and on 2 and 3 June 2014' (3 June 2014) UN Doc A/CN.4/L.833, Draft Conclusion 9(2).

[21] In this regard, one State at State Consultations noted that 'State practice in terms of positive actions provides a useful guide to the interpretation of the law. However, greater caution should be exercised when seeking to interpret the absence of actions or omissions, including the absence of public statements. While it may be the case that the absence of statements indicates that States do not consider an action a breach of international law, such a conclusion does not inevitably or necessarily follow. There may be other reasons why States decide not to make public statements.'

of that agreement may do so in a way that has legal significance.[22] For this reason, the *Manual* seeks to identify practice by States, particularly by States who are parties to the OST, in which provisions of the OST are invoked—or not invoked—in circumstances where these provisions and other obligations under international law are implicated.

Lex specialis and interpretative approaches

8. There were a number of general interpretative rules that guided work on the *Woomera Manual*. First, it was accepted that a peremptory norm will prevail over a contradictory norm which is not *jus cogens*.[23] Second, no a priori hierarchy exists as between customary and treaty norms,[24] with the exception of *jus cogens* norms. Third, obligations under the UN Charter will prevail over all other obligations stemming from any other international agreement (UN Charter Article 103), though it is acknowledged that there is no clear consensus on whether obligations under the UN Charter will prevail over States' customary obligations.[25]

9. It is an unavoidable feature of contemporary international law that multiple legal regimes can apply to a single legal question. International law is a decentralized and diffuse legal system, arising from multiple independent sources. Accordingly, different areas of international law are often developed in isolation from other areas of international law, so that two different rules of law from different areas may

---

[22] The context in which States choose to remain silent in the face of repeated, apparent violations of mutually binding legal obligations deserves examination and may be legally significant. For example, one State at State Consultations asserted that the representatives of a State might choose to remain silent with respect to some possible violations of the OST because it 'did not want to set a precedent'. Yet a State that chooses silence in order to 'not set a precedent' may be foregoing an opportunity to help set a legal threshold for a violation of an obligation under the OST. In fact, not acting actually *is* setting a precedent.

[23] VCLT (n 11) art 53; International Law Commission, 'Fragmentation of International Law: Difficulties Arising from The Diversification and Expansion of International Law—Report of the Study Group of the International Law Commission' (13 April 2006) UN Doc A/CN.4/L.682 (ILC Fragmentation Report) para 19.

[24] Although it can also be argued in some cases that 'relevant norms deriving from a treaty will prevail between the parties over norms deriving from customary law'. ibid paras 79–81, 85. 'Problems arising from a succession of codification on a particular subject' (1995) 66(I) Institute of International Law Yearbook: Preparatory Works 15, 248. This may be particularly true with respect to newer sources of law prevailing over older ones or agreements between States that establish special means of settlement regarding specific claims. See *Case Concerning Military and Paramilitary Activities in and against Nicaragua (Nicaragua v US)* (Merits) [1986] ICJ Reps 14, para 274 ('In general, treaty rules being lex specialis, it would not be appropriate that a State should bring a claim based on a customary-law rule if it has by treaty already provided means for settlement of a such a claim.').

[25] Charter of the United Nations (adopted 26 June 1945, entered into force 24 October 1945) 1 UNTS XVI, art 103; VCLT (n 11), art 30(1). In this regard, see the ILC Fragmentation Report (n 23) paras 344–345 (noting that '[o]pinions on whether also customary law is covered are split' but ultimately concludes that 'it seems sound to join the prevailing opinion that Article 103 should be read extensively—so as to affirm that charter obligations prevail also over United Nations Member States' customary law obligations').

both appear to apply to the same set of facts, with different apparent outcomes. The problem thus requires reconciliation of the apparent conflict.

10. The *Woomera Manual* methodology accepted that despite the imprecise relationships between potentially applicable legal rules, there is an obligation to attempt to accommodate all legal regimes in as coherent and harmonious a manner as possible.[26] Interpretative maxims such as *lex posterior*,[27] *lex specialis derogate legi generali*,[28] and *lex posterior generalis non derogat priori specialis*[29] at times offered a helpful means for ordering the priority of two (or more) applicable but misaligned or even contradictory rules of international law. However, it is not always clear how these maxims or any other interpretative maxim can automatically and decisively apply to a given instance of ambiguity. The ILC has identified the limited utility of such tools in some circumstances.[30] In short, there is no meta-rule of interpretation that conclusively settles potential conflict in application and/or meaning in every given circumstance. Therefore, resolution of potential legal conflicts needs to be addressed on a case-by-case basis. It is likely that, in any given situation, different interpretive tools may be relevant to resolving the interaction of different legal regimes. Such choices are necessarily guided by broader considerations as to best fit and most faithful accommodation of competing treaty/customary international law goals.

11. In respect of military space operations, it is clear that by virtue of Article III of the OST, general international law relating to the use of force, specifically the UN Charter, applies alongside existing space treaty law. In the context of armed conflict in outer space, it is also clear that the law of armed conflict, both in terms of treaty law as well customary international law, applies to regulate such armed conflict. This, however, necessarily raises a potential conflict of competing rights and obligations. Both space law and the law of armed conflict have generally been classified as *lex specialis* with respect to the *lex generalis* of public international law at large. Thus, the question becomes which of the two *lex specialis* regimes (ie the law of

---

[26] *Case Concerning the Right of Passage over Indian Territory (Portugal v India)* (Judgment: Preliminary Objections) [1957] ICJ Reps 125, 142 ('it is a rule of interpretation that a text emanating from a Government must, in principle, be interpreted as producing and intended to produce effects in accordance with existing law and not in violation of it'); VCLT (n 11) art 31(3)(c).

[27] 'Later law', signifying that 'in general, a later law is presumed to supersede a prior, conflicting law on the same subject'; Aaron X Fellmeth and Maurice Horwitz, 'Lex posterior' in *Guide to Latin in International Law* (online edn, OUP 2011) <https://www.oxfordreference.com/view/10.1093/acref/9780195369380.001.0001/acref-9780195369380-e-1281>.

[28] ibid 'Special laws repeal general laws'; 'Lex specialis derogat legi generali', <https://www.oxfordreference.com/view/10.1093/acref/9780195369380.001.0001/acref-9780195369380-e-1303>.

[29] ibid 'A later, general law does not repeal an earlier, specialized law'; ibid 'Lex posterior generalis non derogat priori specialis', <https://www.oxfordreference.com/view/10.1093/acref/9780195369380.001.0001/acref-9780195369380-e-1283>.

[30] Such maxims are detailed with significant specificity and their relationship to international legal reasoning reviewed in ILC Fragmentation Report (n 23) 30–99 (Lex Specialis) and 115–28 (Lex Prior/Posterior).

armed conflict or space law) supersedes the other in cases where the two might not be mutually compatible.

The *jus ad bellum* and military space operations

12. The question of reconciliation of the *jus ad bellum* with the space law regime also raises challenging issues. In this regard, the drafters of *the Woomera Manual* took note of the views of the ILC regarding the priority to be accorded the rights of national and collective self defence.[31] Hence, this *Manual* takes the approach that all relevant obligations in the OST and the other space treaties need to be accommodated to the greatest extent in every context involving military space activities and operations unless the exercise of rights under Article 51 of the UN Charter and the space treaty regime is incompatible. At this point of incompatibility, then Article 51 rights have priority. Importantly, incompatibility is not the same as inconvenience. Furthermore, the circumstances where incompatibility may be manifested must, consistent with the goal of accommodation of all applicable legal regimes, necessarily be confined to a narrowly understood set of circumstances.

13. In addition to defining incompatibility narrowly, as will be examined throughout this *Manual*, not all rights and obligations contained within the OST are equal and hence some may more easily yield to Article 51 rights. Thus, when acting in individual or collective self-defence, obligations under Article IX of the OST concerning prior consultations regarding potentially harmful interference with the activities of other States might be more easily superseded by Article 51 self-defence rights than others. On the other hand, there exist specific prohibitions in the OST regarding the placement in orbit and installation and stationing of nuclear weapons and other weapons of mass destruction on celestial bodies and in space. These specific prohibitions provide a much greater challenge in regard to determining the appropriate *lex specialis* and, as is discussed in the relevant commentary, an extremely nuanced approach needs to be adopted when navigating this reconciliation analysis.

The law of armed conflict and space

14. The effect of armed conflict on the application and interpretation of applicable treaties (and by extension customary international law) to military space operations is an issue that requires careful navigation. As a matter of practical utility, the performance of peacetime space related treaty obligations between belligerents is

---

[31] International Law Commission, 'Report on the Work of its 63rd Session' (26 April–3 June and 4 July–12 Aug 2011) UN Doc A/66/10, 194–95 (Report of the ILC on its 63rd Session).

necessarily compromised. How might this be understood from a methodological perspective? Under existing principles of treaty interpretation, a view may be taken that an armed conflict constitutes a fundamental change of circumstances or that it represents a supervening event that makes performance of inconsistent obligations impossible, and hence excuses observance of pre-existing rights and obligations under international law. The Vienna Convention on the Law of Treaties outlines these two concepts of fundamental change of circumstances and impossibility of performance and may thus supply the answer to the conundrum of performance in an armed conflict.[32] Ironically, however, the Vienna Convention was drafted on the basis that it did not apply (or need not apply) to armed conflict.[33] However, the ILC, in its study 'The Effects of Armed Conflict on Treaties', expressly includes these grounds in the draft articles.[34]

15. Despite this apparent ambiguity of meaning with either interpretation, the effect is the same. The ILC focuses on the *lex specialis* argument for the law of armed conflict having priority[35] to apply not only to specific interpretation of treaty terms but to underpin the general ordering of regimes. Hence, where there is unavoidable contradiction in obligations between peacetime and *in bello* rights/obligations, then *lex specialis* applies to give the rules of the law of armed conflict priority. Accordingly, despite space law being sometimes characterized as the *lex specialis* for space activity in a general sense, it must specifically yield to the extent necessary for rights and obligations under the law of armed conflict to be observed in a time of armed conflict from, to or within space. This conclusion reached by the ILC is consistent with the approach adopted in the *Woomera Manual*.

16. While it is clear that the law of armed conflict would apply to suspend incompatible obligations[36] owed under existing treaties between two (or more) belligerents engaged in armed conflict from, to, or within space, the separate and equally important question of the continuing rights of other States in space also needs to be properly clarified. The position taken in the *Woomera Manual* is that in relation to all other third-party States and their entities, international space law generally retains its full legal application. Notwithstanding this conclusion, it is possible that, depending on all the circumstances prevailing at the time, the law of armed conflict can still affect third-party rights under the Space Treaty regime.[37]

---

[32] VCLT (n 11) art 62.
[33] ibid art 73.
[34] Report of the ILC on its 63rd Session (n 31) 197–98.
[35] ibid 182 (Comment 4 to art 2(b) states: 'The use of this definition [armed conflict] is without prejudice to the rules of international humanitarian law, which constitute the lex specialis governing the conduct of hostilities').
[36] ibid 185 (Comment 2 to art 3 states: 'While the leading judgments on this matter are not always models of clarity, it has become evident that, under contemporary international law, the existence of an armed conflict does not ipso facto put an end to or suspend existing agreements, although a number of them may indeed lapse or be suspended on account of their nature.').
[37] ibid 182 (Comment 5 to art 2).

17. With respect to the law of armed conflict, it is evident that only one treaty governing the law of armed conflict expressly refers to space, namely the 1977 Convention on the Prohibition of Military or Any Other Hostile Use of Environmental Modification Techniques.[38] Despite this absence of express application of the rules of the law of armed conflict to space in existing treaties, there are general legal obligations contained within agreements such as the 1949 Geneva Conventions[39] as well as other relevant treaties that would necessarily apply to armed conflict in all contexts, including those occurring in space. Hence, common Article 2 of the four 1949 Geneva Conventions apply to 'all cases of declared war or any other armed conflict which may arise between two or more of the High Contracting Parties' without any geographical limitation expressly stated. Additionally, many rules of customary international law related to the law of armed conflict are not domain-specific and thus also apply to armed conflicts occurring from, to, or within outer space, despite having been originally formulated in land, sea, or air contexts.[40] The International Court of Justice has broadly stated that the law applicable to armed conflict 'applies to all forms of warfare and to all kinds of weapons, those of the past, those of the present and those of the future'.[41] Such a sweeping statement provides a firm foundation to accept that the law of armed conflict does apply to space and would provide the same protections afforded to humanity that it does in other domains. While this general proposition is not seriously doubted, it nonetheless raises the more specific and additional question of how the law would apply where the legal framework and physical realities of the space environment raise issues that may be fundamentally different from those found in the terrestrial environment. It should also be noted that some rules under the law of armed conflict are domain-specific and would not automatically apply in space. Some exceptions to such domain-specific rules, including rules found in specific articles in Additional Protocol I,[42] are discussed in the Introduction to Part III. In addition, one area of

---

[38] Convention on the Prohibition of Military or any other Hostile Use of Environmental Modification Techniques (adopted 10 December 1976, entered into force 5 October 1978) 1108 UNTS 151.

[39] Geneva Convention for the Amelioration of the Condition of the Wounded and Sick in Armed Forces in the Field of August 12, 1949 (opened for signature 12 August 1949, entered into force 21 October 1950) 75 UNTS 31 (GC I); Geneva Convention for the Amelioration of the Condition of Wounded, Sick and Shipwrecked Members of Armed Forces at Sea of August 12, 1949 (opened for signature 12 August 1949, entered into force 21 October 1949) 75 UNTS 85 (GC II); Geneva Convention relative to the Treatment of Prisoners of War of August 12, 1949 (opened for signature 12 August 1949, entered into force 21 October 1950) 75 UNTS 135 (GC III); Geneva Convention relative to the Protection of Civilian Persons in Time of War of August 12, 1949 (opened for signature 12 August 1949, entered into force 21 October 1950) 75 UNTS 287 (GC IV) (collectively 'Geneva Conventions').

[40] See OST art III (requiring States to carry on activities in the exploration and use of outer space, including the Moon and other celestial bodies, in accordance with international law).

[41] *Legality of the Threat or Use of Nuclear Weapons* (Advisory Opinion) [1996] ICJ Reps 226, para 86.

[42] Protocol Additional to the Geneva Conventions of 12 August 1949, and relating to the protection of victims of armed conflicts (Protocol I) (adopted 8 June 1977, entered into force 7 December 1978) 1125 UNTS 3 (AP I). See also explicit domain-specific restrictions in Non-International Armed Conflict on domain restrictions found in Protocol Additional to the Geneva Conventions of 12 August 1949, and Relating to the Protection of Victims of Non-International Armed Conflicts (Protocol II) (adopted 8 June 1977, entered into force 7 December 1978) 1125 UNTS 609 (AP II).

law related to armed conflict, the law of neutrality, is closely linked with terrestrial domains (particularly maritime) and comprises mainly domain-specific rules. The extension of all these rules to space thus raises complex and challenging issues (see Rule 48: Neutrality in Space).

The *Woomera Manual* process focuses on those obligations of the law of armed conflict that may apply to space by way of direct treaty application, or otherwise through corresponding obligations contained within customary international law. Additionally, in determining this application, a limited use of the mechanism of analogy was also applied to determine whether some particular rules of the law of armed conflict could apply to armed conflict in space. The jurisprudence of the Permanent Court of International Justice in the *Lotus* case,[43] subsequently followed by the International Court of Justice,[44] was noted where it was recognized that only precedents of practice offering a close analogy may be taken into account for the determination of a customary rule of international law governing the case under consideration.

18.

Overview of the Space Law Regime

'Space Law'

'Space law' is a term that encompasses a wide variety of different types of rules, regulations, and laws—both international and domestic—that apply to the vast array of space activities. This *Manual* specifically examines public international law applicable to military space activities and operations. The primary focus in Part I of this *Manual* is on the Outer Space Treaty[45] (the OST) and the other 'space treaties'[46] that implement and elaborate on the OST. Other international agreements and rules of international law relevant to space activities are also evaluated.[47] Part II

1.

---

[43] *The Case of the S.S. 'Lotus' (France v Turkey)* PCIJ Series A No 10, para 52.
[44] See eg *the North Sea Continental Shelf Cases (Germany v Denmark; Germany v Netherlands)* (Merits) [1969] ICJ Reps 3, para 79 and the *Reparation for Injuries Suffered in the Service of the United Nations* (Advisory Opinion) [1949] ICJ Reps 174, 182 (where the court decided it could not make an analogy from the 'traditional rule of diplomatic protection').
[45] The OST (n 9).
[46] The following four other space treaties are examined in the text below: Agreement on the Rescue of Astronauts, the Return of Astronauts and the Return of Objects Launched into Outer Space' (adopted 19 December 1967, entered into force 3 December 1968) 672 UNTS 119 ('Rescue and Return Agreement' or 'ARRA'); Convention on International Liability for Damage Caused by Space Objects (adopted 29 November 1971, entered into force 1 September 1972) 961 UNTS 187 ('Liability Convention'); Convention on Registration of Objects Launched into Outer Space (adopted 12 November 1974, entered into force 15 September 1976) 1023 UNTS 15 ('Registration Convention'); Agreement governing the Activities of States on the Moon and Other Celestial Bodies (adopted 5 December 1979, entered into force 11 July 1984) 1363 UNTS 3 ('Moon Agreement'). Only 18 States are parties to the less successful Moon Agreement, which contains problematic provisions in the view of numerous States and does not itself reflect customary international law.
[47] Examples of other international agreements relevant to space activities examined in this Part include: Treaty Banning Nuclear Weapon Tests in the Atmosphere, in Outer Space and Under Water

then provides additional emphasis on the UN Charter and its effects on military space activities. Part III then concentrates on the provisions of the law of armed conflict that are most applicable in space.

The Basic Legal Framework: The Outer Space Treaty

2. This *Manual* takes a rules-based approach to military space activities and operations and each of the rules in the following sections of Part I is based on Articles of the OST. This is particularly appropriate since the OST itself is regarded as 'the basic framework on international space law'.[48]

3. The OST was considered by the Legal Sub-Committee of the UN Committee on the Peaceful Uses of Outer Space (UNCOPUOS) in 1966, adopted by the UN General Assembly later that year,[49] opened for signature in January 1967, and entered into force in October 1967. A State that is a party to the OST is of course bound to abide by its terms in good faith and a State that is a Signatory but has not yet become a party is obligated to refrain from acts that defeat the object and purpose of the Treaty until that State makes its intention clear not to become a party to the Treaty.[50] There are no known cases of any State that is a party to the OST expressing an intention to withdraw from the Treaty, nor any Signatory indicating its intention not to become a party.

4. Currently there are 114 States that are parties to the OST, with an additional 22 having signed the Treaty but not yet ratified it.[51] The number of parties has

---

(entered into force 10 October 1963) 480 UNTS 43 (Partial Nuclear Test Ban Treaty) in Rule 5: Weapons of Mass Destruction; Agreement Among the Government of Canada, Governments of Member States of the European Space Agency, the Government of Japan, the Government of the Russian Federation, and the Government of the United States of America Concerning Cooperation on the Civil International Space Station (signed 29 January 1998, entered into force 27 March 2001) 41 ILM 1481 ('The ISS Agreement') in Rule 7: Jurisdiction. The body of public international law is also supplemented by some voluntary, non-binding, technical guidelines, such as the Inter-Agency Space Debris Coordination Committee (IADC) 'IADC Space Debris Mitigation Guidelines, Revision 1' (September 2007) IADC-02-01 and The Committee on Space Research's (COSPAR) Planetary Protection Policy, both examined in Rule 14: Avoidance of Harmful Contamination.

[48] UN Office of Outer Space Affairs, 'The Treaty on Principles Governing the Activities of States in the Exploration and Use of Outer Space, including the Moon and Other Celestial Bodies' (UNOOSA 2022) [https://perma.cc/S826-XJCW].
[49] UNGA RES 2222 (XXI) (1966).
[50] VCLT (n 11) art 18 ('A State is obliged to refrain from acts which would defeat the object and purpose of a treaty when: (a) it has signed the treaty or has exchanged instruments constituting the treaty subject to ratification, acceptance or approval, until it shall have made its intention clear not to become a party to the treaty.').
[51] See United Nations, Office of Disarmament Affairs, Treaties Database, Outer Space Treaty, Participants, Treaty Status Page, https://treaties.unoda.org/t/outer_space/participants (last accessed 15 August 2023).

continued to grow in recent years.⁵² Importantly, all major spacefaring States are parties to the OST, as are virtually all other States involved in space activities.⁵³ The space domain thus enjoys the benefit of a widely accepted and legally binding agreement that can serve as a framework for interaction, unlike some other areas of important strategic competition between major powers (such as cyberspace) that have no foundational international agreement.

The Outer Space Treaty as Customary International Law

Although an overwhelming majority of States that participate in space activities are legally bound by the terms of the OST as parties to that Treaty, States that are not parties to the OST are likely nonetheless also obligated to abide by most or all its substantive rules under customary international law. This view has been expressed by numerous States⁵⁴ as well as by numerous scholars.⁵⁵ The conclusion that a rule is binding on States as a matter of customary international law is a significant one and must be based first on evidence of the

5.

---

⁵² Eleven States have become parties to the OST since 2015: Azerbaijan (2015); Paraguay (2016); Nicaragua (2017); Malta (2017); Armenia (2018); Slovenia (2019); Bahrain (2019); Bosnia and Herzegovina (2020); Oman (2022); Croatia (2023); and Panama (2023), ibid.

⁵³ ibid One exception is the Islamic Republic of Iran, which is however a Signatory to the OST.

⁵⁴ See eg UNCOPUOS Legal Sub-Committee, 'Responses to the set of Questions provided by the Chair of the Working Group on the Status and Application of the Five United Nations Treaties on Outer Space' (10 April 2015) UN Doc A/AC.105/C.2/2015/CRP.11 ('The German delegation is of the opinion that the general principles of the Outer Space Treaty (OST) have become international customary law since almost all States conducting activities in outer space have ratified the OST and act according to its provisions.'); UNCOPUOS Legal Sub-Committee, 'Responses to the set of Questions provided by the Chair of the Working Group on the Status and Application of the Five United Nations Treaties on Outer Space' (23 March 2017) UN Doc A/AC.105/C.2/2017/CRP.6 ('In the view of the Austrian delegation, the general principles contained in the Outer Space Treaty can be regarded as customary international law....'); UNCOPUOS Legal Sub-Committee, 'Responses to the set of Questions provided by the Chair of the Working Group on the Status and Application of the Five United Nations Treaties on Outer Space' (6 April 2018) UN Doc A/AC.105/C.2/2018/CRP.12 ('In the opinion of the Czech Republic the general principles of the Outer Space Treaty can be considered as forming part of international customary law due to the wide adherence to it by the international community in the conduct of space activities. Both aspects, *opinio juris* and State practice, are fulfilled....').

⁵⁵ See eg Francis Lyall and Paul B Larsen, *Space Law: A Treatise* (Ashgate Publishing Limited 2009) 54, 70–80; Peter Stubbe, *State Accountability for Space Debris* (Koninklijke Brill 2017) 77–78. Other scholars describe the OST in terms of its constitutional, foundational, or 'magna carta'-like status. See generally, Frans von der Dunk (Rapporteur), 'Legal Aspects of Neo Threat Response and Related Institutional Issues: Final Report' (Secure World Foundation 9 Feb 2010) [https://perma.cc/47BP-AN9K]; Maurice N Andem, 'The Outer Space Treaty as the Magna Charta of Contemporary Space Law: A Brief Reflection' in International Institute of Space Law of the International Astronautical Federation (ed), *Proceedings of the Forty-Seventh Colloquium on the Law of Outer Space* (American Institute of Aviation and Aeronautics 2004) 292. It should be cautioned, however, that one State during State consultation expressed the view that there is not a sufficient basis for asserting that most of the OST's substantive rules are customary international law. At the same time, several States have also noted that 'an opinion or practice objecting to or dissenting from these principles [the general principles contained in the OST] by states which are not party to the Outer Space Treaty does not seem to be identifiable'. See eg Remarks by Austrian Delegation, 'Responses to the set of Questions provided by the Chair of the Working Group' (23 March 2017) UN Doc A/AC.105/C.2/2017/CRP.6 (n 54).

18   INTRODUCTION

'general practice'⁵⁶ of States, and on *opinio juris sive necessitatis*.⁵⁷ The widespread participation in the OST of virtually all States involved in space activities also lends support to this finding, as well as the fact that all the major spacefaring States are parties to the OST. With respect to the latter point, the International Court of Justice (ICJ) has observed that 'States whose interests are specially affected' play a particularly important role in the determination of whether some rule of customary international law has arisen.⁵⁸ In addition, as noted by one State, 'an opinion or practice objecting to or dissenting from these principles by states which are not party to the Outer Space Treaty does not seem to be identifiable'.⁵⁹

6. The conclusion that the content of the OST is binding on States as a matter of customary international law is significantly bolstered by the OST's origins. The OST was largely based on the Declaration of Legal Principles Governing the Activities of States in the Exploration and Use of Outer Space, which was unanimously adopted by the UN General Assembly in 1963.⁶⁰ A strong argument can be made that States generally regarded all the important principles of the 1963 Declaration as already having achieved the status of customary international law, even before the OST was drafted in 1966.⁶¹ The subsequent codification of those principles in the OST further advanced their development as rules of customary international law binding on all States.⁶²

7. As noted by one State, 'these principles [in the OST] have already been reflected in the unanimously adopted GA Resolution ... Such an unanimous approval is an

---

⁵⁶ Statute of the International Court of Justice (26 June 1945) 1 UNTS 295, art 38(1)(b).
⁵⁷ *North Sea Continental Shelf Cases* (n 44) para 77 ('Not only must the acts concerned amount to a settled practice, but they must also be such, or be carried out in such a way, as to be evidence of a belief that this practice is rendered obligatory by the existence of a rule of law requiring it. The need for such a belief, i.e., the existence of a subjective element, is implicit in the very notion of the *opinio juris sive necessitatis*.').
⁵⁸ ibid para 73.
⁵⁹ Responses to Questions on Status and Application of the Five UN Treaties on Outer Space on the Status and Application of the Five United Nations Treaties on Outer Space', 2017 (Germany) (n 54) 3.
⁶⁰ UNGA 'Declaration of Legal Principles Governing the Activities of States in the Exploration and Use of Outer Space' (13 December 1963) UN Doc A/RES/1962(XVIII) (1963 UNGA Declaration of Legal Principles)
⁶¹ See eg UNGA First Committee, 'Summary Record of the 1346th Meeting' (5 December 1963) UN Doc A/C.1/SR.1346, 189 (The Canadian Delegate stated that 'the legal principles contained in it reflected international law as it was currently accepted by Member States'); UNGA, 'Verbatim Record of the Thirteen Hundred and Forty Second Meeting' (2 December 1963) UN Doc A/C.1/PV.1342, 12 (Statement by the US Delegate: 'We believe these legal principles reflect international law as it is accepted by the Members of the United Nations'); ibid 42 (Statement by the Soviet Delegate, 'The Soviet Union, for its part, will also respect these principles contained in this declaration if unanimously adopted.'). *Restatement (Third) of Foreign Relations Law in the United States* (American Law Institute 1987) §1.02, n 2 ('Outer Space Declaration, for example, might have become law even if a formal treaty had not followed, since it was approved by all, including the principal 'space powers'). See Bin Cheng, *Studies in International Space Law* (OUP 1997) 142–49.
⁶² Lyall and Larsen (n 55) 54 ('Even though it can be argued that some of the principles [the OST] enunciates were already part of international custom, their incorporation in a treaty confirmed their status as between the parties. Further, as we will argue, the principles of the OST may now properly be said to have become customary, and hence binding on all states.').

indication of *opinio juris sive necessitatis* when accompanied by concomitant practice. A large majority of states, including all major space faring nations, have ratified the Outer Space Treaty and conduct their space activities in accordance with the above-mentioned principles.'[63]

Agreement on the Rescue and Return of Astronauts

Ninety-nine States are currently parties to Agreement on the Rescue and Return of Astronauts (ARRA),[64,65] with an additional 23 having signed the Agreement but not yet ratified it.[66] The number of States becoming parties to the Agreement has continued to increase over the last decade.[67] There are no cases of withdrawal or even known expressed intentions to withdraw, suggesting a continuing and indeed growing relevance of, and adherence to, the legal regime established by this Agreement.

8.

The States that are parties to the ARRA effectively include all the major spacefaring States and most other States involved in space activities. In addition, given that the Agreement includes obligations resting upon any State possibly confronted with (another State's) astronauts or space objects, it is important to note that the parties to the Agreement also include most States who might in such cases have the actual capacity to comply with the obligations in space under the ARRA to assist astronauts in distress and repatriate them, as well as to handle space objects appropriately.[68] Moreover, the ARRA is generally considered to present an elaboration, and as relevant thereby the appropriate interpretation, of Article V (as for astronauts) and Article VIII (as for space objects) of the OST.[69] Pursuant to the Vienna Convention on the Law of Treaties, the interpretation of these Articles in the OST

9.

---

[63] Responses to the set of Questions on Status and Application of the Five UN Treaties on Outer Space, 2017 (23 March 2017) UN Doc A/AC.105/C.2/2017/CRP.6 (Austria) (n 54) 5.

[64] For an examination of the application of the Agreement on the Rescue and Return of Astronauts to military space activities, see Rule 13: Astronauts and Personnel of a Spacecraft.

[65] ARRA (n 46).

[66] See UN Office of Outer Space Affairs, 'Status of International Agreements relating to Activities in Outer Space, 20 March 2023, A/AC.105/C.2/2023/CRP.3, as at 1 January 2023, [https://perma.cc/UT3B-88TG]...

[67] See UNCOPUOS Legal Sub Committee, 'Status of International agreements relating to activities in outer space as at 1 January 2012' (12 March 2012) UN Doc A/AC.105/C.2/2012/CRP.3 (listing only 88 States as parties to the ARRA).

[68] See ARRA (n 46) arts 1–5. The reasoning here is again consistent with the ICJ's observations in the *North Sea Continental* case regarding the importance of specially affected States. Note, however, that if an astronaut crashes onto land or sea, any State in the world could be in a position to assist.

[69] ibid Preamble ('Desiring to give further concrete expression to the rights and obligations contained in the [OST]'); see also Marboe, Neumann, and Schrogl, 'The 1968 Agreement on the Rescue of Astronauts, the Return of Astronauts and the Return of Objects Launched into Outer Space' in Stephan Hobe, Bernhard Schmidt-Tedd, and Kai-Uwe Schrogl (eds), *Cologne Commentary on Space Law*, vol II (Wolters Kluwer Deutschland GmbH 2013) 26.

20   INTRODUCTION

should take into account '(a) any subsequent agreement between the parties regarding the interpretation of the treaty or the application of its provisions; [and] (b) any subsequent practice in the application of the treaty which establishes the agreement of the parties regarding its interpretation'.[70]

10. The reasons above suggest the default conclusion that the ARRA by and large reflects customary international law.[71] No dissenting practice by States that are not parties to the ARRA has been identified, no evidence of a persistent objector[72] to the regime that it has established can be found, and certainly no evidence of the emergence of contrary practice on the part of a group of States.

11. For the above reasons, the possibility for States that are not parties to the ARRA (and, possibly, the OST) to validly argue that they can legally speaking freely depart from its provisions is very limited. The default assumption should be that its substantive regime[73] reflects customary international law.

The Liability Convention

12. Currently 98 States are parties to the Liability Convention,[74,75] with an additional 19 having signed the Convention but not yet ratified it.[76] The number of States becoming parties to the Convention has continued to increase over the last decade.[77] There are no cases known of withdrawal or even expressed intentions to withdraw, suggesting a continuing and indeed growing relevance of and adherence to the legal regime established by it.

13. As is the case for the ARRA, the States that are parties to the Liability Convention effectively include all the major spacefaring States and most of those States with space activities potentially giving rise to damage and liability issues in space, constituting

---

[70] VCLT (n 11) art 31(3).
[71] Notwithstanding this default conclusion, it must also be noted that to this point there is very little State practice in implementing the provisions of the ARRA in specific cases.
[72] A persistent objector is a State that consistently objected to a rule of customary international law during the rule's formation and afterwards and is thus itself generally considered to not bound to observe that rule. *Fisheries Case* (*UK v Norway*) (Judgment) [1951] ICJ 116, 131 (noting that the rule in question in that case 'would appear to be inapplicable as against Norway inasmuch as she has always opposed any attempt to apply it to the Norwegian coast'); *Asylum Case* (*Colombia v Peru*) (Judgment) [1950] ICJ 266, 277–78.
[73] Note that the formal and procedural clauses found in the ARRA arts 7–10, dealing with such issues as signature, ratification, accession, amendment, and withdrawal, would not be included in the parts of the agreement reflecting customary international law.
[74] For an examination of the application of the Liability Convention to military space activities, see Rule 12: International Liability for Damages Caused by Space Objects.
[75] Liability Convention (n 46).
[76] See 'Status of International Agreements relating to Activities in Outer Space' (n 66).
[77] See 'Status of International Agreements relating to Activities in Outer Space' (n 67) (listing 88 States as parties to the Liability Convention).

the main subject matter of the Convention's legal regime and consistent again the with importance of specially affected States noted by the ICJ in the *Continental Shelf* case.[78] Moreover, the Liability Convention is generally considered to present an elaboration, and as relevant thereby the appropriate interpretation, of (in particular) Article VII of the OST.[79] Pursuant to the Vienna Convention on the Law of Treaties, the interpretation of this Article in the OST should take into account '(a) any subsequent agreement between the parties regarding the interpretation of the treaty or the application of its provisions; [and] (b) any subsequent practice in the application of the treaty which establishes the agreement of the parties regarding its interpretation'.[80]

14. The reasons above suggest a default conclusion that the substantive provisions of the Liability Convention likely reflect customary international law.[81] No dissenting practice by States that are not parties to the Convention has been identified, no evidence of a persistent objector can be found, and certainly no evidence of the emergence of contrary practice on the part of any group of States.

15. The main area where such a default conclusion would not be valid concerns the procedural aspects of the Liability Convention, as opposed to the substantive ones. While any interpretation of Article VII of the OST that would substantially deviate from the elaboration of the Liability Convention would be very hard to uphold, issues such as *jus standi* and claims procedures, including the possible establishment of a Claims Commission, are not addressed in Article VII of the OST. These procedural rules were specifically developed for the Liability Convention only, and by that token should not be viewed as merely an elaboration or interpretation of OST Article VII.

16. In conclusion, there is a strong argument that States that are parties to the OST but not to the Liability Convention would be bound by the latter at least as to its substantive regime[82] on liability, as elaborating the provisions of the former. To that extent, and based on the discussion of the OST above, the substantive provisions of

---

[78] *North Sea Continental Shelf Cases* (n 44) paras 73–74. However, it should also be noted that the States that could be the victims of damage on earth caused by the crash of space objects could in theory include every State on Earth.

[79] See Liability Convention (n 46) Preamble; see also Lesley Jane Smith, Armel Kerrest, and Fabio Tronchetti, 'The 1972 Convention on International Liability for Damage Caused by Space Objects' in Hobe, Schmidt-Tedd, and Schrogl (eds), *Cologne Commentary on Space Law*, vol II (n 69) 98.

[80] VCLT (n 11) art 31(2).

[81] Notwithstanding this default conclusion, it should also be noted that to this point there is very little State practice in implementing the provisions of the Liability Convention in specific cases. For one example, see Rule 12: International Liability for Damage Caused by Space Objects, n 441 and related text, regarding the claim by Canada against the Union of Soviet Socialist Republics for damage caused by Soviet satellite Cosmos 954 in 1978.

[82] Note that, of course, the formal clauses of arts XXII–XXVIII, dealing with such issues as the possibility of IGOs to become de facto parties to the Convention, signature, ratification, accession, amendment, and withdrawal, would not be included in the parts of the Convention reflecting customary international law.

The Registration Convention

17. Currently, 74 States are parties to the Registration Convention,[83,84] with an additional three having signed the treaty.[85] The number of parties continues to increase (with 11 States joining in the last five years).[86] There are no known cases of withdrawal or even expressed intentions to withdraw, suggesting a continuing and indeed growing relevance of and adherence to the legal regime established by it.

18. States that are parties to the Registration Convention include all the major spacefaring powers and most States with any significant activity in outer space potentially giving rise to registration requirements, constituting the main subject matter of the Convention's legal regime.[87]

19. On the other hand, the number of States that are parties to the Registration Convention is far fewer than the number of States that are parties to the OST, the ARRA, and the Liability Convention. This is at least partly due to the relatively limited number of States that have launch capabilities and/or their own satellite that would trigger relevant obligations under the Convention.[88] However, in light of the fact that registration of space objects supports the implementation of other space law regime requirements—in particular registration of space objects helps identify potentially liable States for purposes of the Liability Convention[89]—it is still notable that a majority of States of the world have not signed up to the Convention.

---

[83] The Registration Convention (n 46).

[84] For an examination of the application of the Registration Convention to military space activities, see Rule 8: Registration of Space Objects.

[85] See UNOOSA, 'Status of International Agreements relating to Activities in Outer Space', (online database) <https://www.unoosa.org/oosa/en/ourwork/spacelaw/treaties/status/index.html> accessed 22 March 2023.

[86] See UNCOPUOS Legal Sub Committee, 'Status of International agreements relating to activities in outer space as at 1 January 2017' (23 March 2017) UN Doc A/AC.105/C.2/2017/CRP.7 (listing 63 States as parties to the Registration Convention).

[87] See United Nations, Office of Disarmament Affairs, Treaties Database (n 51).

[88] Pursuant to the Registration Convention (n 46) arts I(a), II–V, only launching States would qualify as States of registry directly subject to the Convention's legal regime. However, it is possible for almost any State to 'procure' a launch—making it a launching State—and the number of States with satellites in space is also steadily increasing. See 'Satellite Database' (Union of Concerned Scientists, 8 June 2023) https://www.ucsusa.org/resources/satellite-database (listing and providing details on more than 5,465 operational satellites currently in orbit around Earth).

[89] The identification of the launching State(s) of space objects is fundamental to both the Registration Convention and the determination of the international liability of States for damages caused by space objects (see Rule 12: International Liability of States for Damages caused by Space Objects).

20. In addition, the many 'loopholes' or 'escape clauses' in the Registration Convention as to its core obligations should warn against any quick conclusion that the Convention reflects clear-cut rules of customary international law lending themselves to uniform application. For example, Article II, which deals with national registration obligations, speaks about 'an appropriate registry', the contents of which 'shall be determined by the State of registry'.[90] Article IV, addressing States' obligations with respect to the international register, speaks about information to be provided 'as soon as practicable', optionally 'from time to time' and respectively 'to the greatest extent feasible and as soon as practicable'.[91] Indeed, State practice has been noticeably haphazard when it comes to complying with the actual requirements that the Convention *did* impose, sometimes even with a noticeable trend of diminishing compliance being noticed.[92] The Registration Convention also lacks any real transparency function, requiring States to indicate only the 'general function of the space object'.[93] Other limitations as well as additional challenges facing the Registration Convention are discussed in Rule 8: Registration of Space Objects.

21. Conversely, as is the case with the ARRA and Liability Conventions, it should be noted that the Registration Convention is generally considered to present an elaboration, and as relevant thereby the appropriate interpretation, of (in particular) Article VIII of the OST.[94] Pursuant to the Vienna Convention on the Law of Treaties, the interpretation of this Article in the OST should take into account '(a) any subsequent agreement between the parties regarding the interpretation of the treaty or the application of its provisions; [and] (b) any subsequent practice in the application of the treaty which establishes the agreement of the parties regarding its interpretation'.[95] However, this inference is considerably weaker than it is for the ARRA and the Liability Convention, since many States that are parties to the OST are not parties to the Registration Convention.

22. In sum, it would seem too early to conclude that the details of the Registration Convention, even as for the substantive parts only,[96] would comprehensively constitute an interpretation of Article VIII of the OST qualifying as customary

---

[90] Registration Convention (n 46) art II(1), (3).
[91] ibid art IV. Note also that the data required pursuant to art IV(1) are fairly limited, including merely a line on 'General function of the space object', art IV(1)(e).
[92] See eg Yoo Lee, 'Registration of Space Objects: ESA Member States' Practice' (2006) 22 Space Policy 42.
[93] Registration Convention (n 46) art IV(1)(b)(e). See discussion in Rule 8: Registration of Space Objects, paras 7 and 8..
[94] ibid Preamble.
[95] VCLT (n 11) art 31(3).
[96] Again, as with the Liability Convention, the formal clauses of arts VII–XII of the Registration Convention, dealing with such issues as the possibility of international governmental organizations becoming de facto parties to the Convention, signature, ratification, accession, amendment, and withdrawal would not be included in the parts of the Convention reflecting customary international law in any event.

international law binding also upon States not parties to the Registration Convention. Only the general principle of registration, with a generic obligation to somehow register space objects domestically and to inform the UN Secretary-General in very general terms, might rise to the level of being reflective of customary international law.[97]

The Moon Agreement

23. In spite of its drafting in the UNCOPUOS, which included the major spacefaring States, to date the Moon Agreement[98] has been ratified by only 18 States, including none of the major spacefaring countries (except Australia and Kazakhstan).[99] The opposition of the other major spacefaring States to the Moon Agreement, or hesitation towards signing it, may be based on several factors, but in particular the opposition to clauses pertaining to the 'common heritage of mankind' and its consequences for exploration and use of Moon resources. This widespread and sustained opposition pre-empts any possibility of the Agreement as a whole being seen as reflective of customary international law. Only those clauses in the Moon Agreement that restate clauses found in the OST can be regarded as such, but not any obligations or rights unique to the Moon Agreement itself.[100]

24. With respect to military space activities and operations, it is of particular importance to note that several restrictions on military activities found in the Moon Agreement are not found in the OST and do not reflect customary international law. For example, the Moon Agreement employs broad and undefined terms not found in the OST by prohibiting 'any other hostile act or threat of hostile act on the moon'.[101]

---

[97] In this regard, some States have explicitly noted that they regard the duty to register space objects under art VIII of the OST as accepted as customary international law. See eg Responses to Questions on Status and Application of the Five UN Treaties on Outer Space, 2015 (Germany) (n 54) 3; Hobe, Schmidt-Tedd, and Schrogl (eds), *Cologne Commentary*, vol II (n 69) 239 (noting that '[t]he general obligation to register space objects is one of those universally accepted principles').

[98] The Moon Agreement (n 46).

[99] See (n 66). One party to the Moon Agreement, Saudi Arabia, announced its decision to withdraw from the Moon Agreement in 2023. UN Secretary-General, 'Depositary Notification: Saudi Arabia—Withdrawal' (5 January 2023) UN Doc C.N.4.2023.TREATIES-XXIV.2 ('The action shall take effect for Saudi Arabia on 5 January 2024'). France and India, two major spacefaring countries, are among the Signatories, but since both have indicated over the last decades that they are unlikely to ratify the Agreement, it is even questionable whether these States could still be held to the obligation not to 'defeat the object and purpose' of the Agreement under applicable treaty law (see VCLT (n 11) art 18).

[100] For example, art 2 of the Moon Agreement (n 46) reaffirms the mandate found in Article III of the OST, stating that '[a]ll activities on the moon, including its exploration and use, shall be carried out in accordance with international law, in particular the Charter of the United Nations'.

[101] Moon Agreement (n 46) art 3(2).

Note on Legal Connections Between States and a Space Object

1. Space operators and military planners considering an action involving a satellite or other object in space should be aware of the legal connections that may exist between multiple States and a space object under the space law regime. Unlike the maritime and aerial domains, space objects do not possess the 'nationality' of any State and are not governed by the widely accepted international agreements that apply to ships and aircraft. Several Rules in this *Manual*, including those referenced in the following paragraphs, help explain the possible legal connections between States and space objects under the more complex space law regime. These legal connections are important in many ways, including the determination of which State has responsibility for a particular space object and its actions, the determination of which State exercises jurisdiction and control over a particular space object, and the determination of which State(s) are internationally liable for damages caused by a particular space object. It is important to note that these and other legal connections with a particular space object may involve multiple States. Other links between States and a particular space object, such as the services that a satellite provides to its users, are significant to note but may not correspond with recognized international legal connections between those States and that space object.

2. One important legal connection between a State and a space object is registration (see Rule 8: Registration of Space Objects). Under Article VIII of the OST, the State of Registry exercises jurisdiction and control over the space object and personnel thereof, although there are also other jurisdictional issues to bear in mind regarding the activities of States, persons, and corporations in space (see Rule 7: Jurisdiction). While registration represents an important legal connection between a space object and a particular State, not all space objects are registered and there may also be other significant or more important legal connections between a particular space object and States other than the State of Registry.

3. In particular, under Article VI of the OST, States bear international responsibility for national activities in outer space, including the Moon and other celestial bodies, whether such activities are carried on by governmental agencies or by non-governmental entities (see Rule 10: Responsibility of States for National Activities in Outer Space). If a particular space object is part of a State's national space activities, that State is also responsible for assuring that the space object's activities are carried out in conformity with the OST and international law and is further required to exercise authorization and continuing supervision over it.[102]

---

[102] As noted in Rule 10: Responsibility of States for National Activities in Outer Space, national space laws regulating space activities (making those space activities 'National Activities in Outer Space') generally apply authorization and supervision regimes to both space activities conducted by nationals (entities and natural persons) regardless of where undertaken, and space activities conducted from national territory, regardless of who undertakes them.

It is important to note that the State that is responsible for a space object may not necessarily be the State of Registry. The responsibility of a State for a space object under Article VI is a fundamental link between a State and a space object under the space law regime. It is also a fundamental link between a State and its nationals (both natural and juridical) and their activities in space.

4. The State(s) that qualify as a launching State of a particular space object also maintain an important international legal connection with that object. For example, each launching State is liable for the damages caused by the space object (see Rule 12: International Liability for Damage Caused by Space Objects). Further, one of the launching States generally becomes the State of Registry (see Rule 8: Registration of Space Objects). It should also be noted that even if a launching State is not the State of Registry of a space object, that State may have national laws asserting jurisdiction over, and regulating, a space object if it is launched from its territory.

5. While ownership of a space object may be important, particularly under the laws of the State or nationals of the State that own the object, it is not the most significant legal connection between a State and a space object and does not make the clear allocation of international legal responsibilities associated with the connections noted above (see Rule 9: Ownership of Objects in Space).

6. The users of the services provided by a satellite or other space object may have significant legal connections with that satellite or space object under contracts governed by the domestic law of States and may be of significant concern to those States. However, these States may lack an international legal connection with that satellite on a basis that is recognized by the space law regime.

Note on Outer Space vs Airspace (Delimitation of Outer Space)

1. Under customary international law, as reflected in treaties such as the Convention on International Civil Aviation, States hold 'complete and exclusive sovereignty' over the airspace above their territories.[103] Outer space is not subject to claims of sovereignty[104] and therefore it forms the vertical frontier of these national territories. However, there is no agreed international legal delimitation of this frontier.[105]

---

[103] International Convention on Civil Aviation (signed 7 December 1944, entered into force 7 April 1947) 15 UNTS 295 art 1.

[104] OST (n 9) art II.

[105] Notwithstanding the lack of an agreed international legal definition, various corporations may recognize space tourists with astronaut wings or other awards. (Note in this regard that space tourists are regulated as 'space flight participants' and not categorized as 'astronauts' under the laws of States with such *regulations*—see Rule 13: Astronauts and Personnel of a Spacecraft). However, these awards (and other awards for 'space' travel by private entities and even government agencies) do not constitute a basis for a State's official delimitation of the boundary of outer space.

International law does not define any precise delimitation of the boundary between airspace and outer space. Neither the five treaties dealing with outer space issues, nor the Convention on International Civil Aviation, do so and the practice and *opinio juris* of States has, thus far, failed to coalesce around a customary international law definition.

2. The Legal Sub-Committee of the UN Committee on the Peaceful Uses of Outer Space (UNCOPUOS) began considering the question of the definition and delimitation of outer space in 1967 and has heard and considered diverse views and proposals on this issue from many States.[106] However, in spite of many meetings dedicated to this question and the establishment by the UN General Assembly of a Working Group in 1984 to address this issue,[107] the UNCOPUOS Legal Sub-Committee concluded in 2002 that '[n]o agreements on substantive legal issues relating to the definition and delimitation of outer space are apparent'.[108] Since that time, as noted by a UNCOPUOS Legal Sub-Committee Working Group in 2017, it has become clear that 'the absence of agreement on such an important legal issue has created a deadlock in the Legal Sub-Committee, which has not been able to conceive a proper solution for this question'.[109]

3. Since the definition and delimitation of outer space issue was placed on the agenda of the Legal Sub-Committee in 1967, two main, conflicting approaches have crystallized: one 'supporting a clear delimitation of the frontier between airspace and outer space based on scientific or commonly accepted criteria, reflecting the "spatialist" approach'; the other considering that such delimitation is unnecessary or even impossible and therefore that activities performed in those areas should be assessed in congruence with their respective objectives, reflecting the 'functionalist' approach'.[110]

4. The spatialist approach to the definition and/or the delimitation of outer space has long been characterized by a wide range of proposals based on a variety of criteria. As described in a background paper prepared by the Secretariat of the UNCOPUOS Legal Sub-Committee, the criteria referred to most often are:

   A. Demarcation based upon the equation of the upper limit of national sovereignty with the concept of 'atmosphere';

---

[106] UNCOPUOS Legal Sub-Committee, 'Report of the Secretariat: Historical Summary on the Consideration of the Question on the Definition and Delimitation of Outer Space' (18 January 2002) UN Doc A/AC.105/769 (UNCOPUOS Historical Summary Delimitation Question) para 25 [https://perma.cc/FF78-GJS2].
[107] UNGA Resolution 38/80 (1983) UN Doc A/RES/38/80, para 5(c).
[108] UNCOPUOS Historical Summary Delimitation Question (n 106) para 25.
[109] UNCOPUOS Legal Sub-Committee, 'Promoting the Discussion of the Matters Relating to the Definition and Delimitation of Outer Space with a View to Elaborating a Common Position of States Members of the [UNCOPUOS]' (17 May 2017) UN Doc A/AC.105/C.2/L.302 para 15 [https://perma.cc/B9P5-P9XG].
[110] ibid.

B. Demarcation based on the division of atmosphere into layers (the atmosphere which surrounds the earth is divided by scientists into several layers and each layer has different characteristics);
C. Demarcation based on the maximum altitude of aircraft flight (theory of navigable air space);
D. Demarcation based on aerodynamic characteristics of flight instrumentalities (the 'von Karman line');
E. Demarcation according to the lowest perigee of an orbiting satellite;
F. Demarcation based up on the earth's gravitational effects;
G. Demarcation based on effective control;
H. Demarcation based upon the division of space into zones;
I. Demarcation based on a combination of various spatial approaches and other proposals; and
J. The question in general of fixing a boundary between air space and outer space.[111]

5. Some States have chosen to use one of the spatialist methods listed above to establish the limits of their airspace or their definition of outer space. For example, a few States have chosen to demarcate the limits of their airspace based on aerodynamic characteristics of flight instrumentalities, utilizing the von Karman line (the altitude at which a craft has to fly faster than orbital velocity to achieve sufficient aerodynamic lift) to set their limit at the somewhat arbitrary line of 100 kilometres (km).[112] Most States, however, have not defined outer space.[113]

6. As noted in the Background Paper prepared by the Secretariat of the UNCOPUOS Legal Sub-Committee, '[d]ifficulties in finding reliable physical or technological criteria for the solution of the problem of an upper limit of state sovereignty have been often cited to substantiate a functional approach to the regulation of activities in the space above the earth'.[114] The functional approach thus makes a distinction

---

[111] UNCOPUOS Legal Sub-Committee, 'Background Paper Prepared by the Secretariat: The Question of the Definition and/or the Delimitation of Outer Space' (7 May 1970) UN Doc A/AC.105/C.2/7 36–57 (Background Paper on Delimitation) [https://perma.cc/8HZT-R43D].

[112] See UNCOPUOS Legal Sub-Committee 'Matters Relating to the Definition and Delimitation of Outer Space: Replies of the International Institute of Space Law (IISL)' (4 April 2017) UN Doc A/AC.105/C.2/2017/CRP.29 (IISL Replies) 1 ('At the national level, several States decided to adopt the spatial approach and defined outer space as the area above an altitude above 100 km. Examples include Australia (1998), Kazakhstan (2012), and, most recently, Denmark (2016).'). In this regard, see Space Activities Act 1998 (Cth) pt 2 s 8 (Austl.) [https://perma.cc/VE3K-LUYV] (providing that 'launch a space object means launch the object into an area beyond the distance of 100 km above mean sea level, or attempt to do so').

[113] See IISL Replies to UNCOPUOUS Legal Subcommittee (n 112) 1; Background Paper on Delimitation (n 111) para 28 ('The attitude of States toward the definition of outer space can be characterized as one of substantial restraint as far as public pronouncements on the substance of the matter are concerned.').

[114] Background Paper on Delimitation (n 111) para 162; US Statement, Definition and Delimitation of Outer Space and the Character and Utilization of the Geostationary Orbit, Legal Sub-Committee of

between aeronautical and astronautical activities and generally denies the need for demarcation between air space and outer space. Proponents of the spatialist approach point to 'the advantage of providing greater legal certainty for actors'.[115]

From a practical standpoint, the lack of an agreed, international legal delimitation and definition of outer space means that a legal adviser should be aware that States may apply different definitions or approaches in determining whether a particular activity takes place 'in space'. However, the lack of such an internationally agreed definition has not to this point impeded international cooperation in outer space.

7.

the United Nations Committee on the Peaceful Uses of Outer Space at its 40th Session in Vienna from April' (2001) Digest of US Practice in International Law 721 [https://perma.cc/829B-TNYG] (arguing that '[w]hatever definition or delimitation were ultimately agreed upon would by its nature be arbitrary at worst, or, at best, be constrained by the current state of technology' and that 'defining or delimiting outer space is not necessary', that 'the lack of a definition or delimitation of outer space has not impeded the development of activities in either sphere', and that because technological advances are likely to continue, 'it would be dangerous for the Legal Sub-Committee to agree to an artificial line between air space and outer space, when it cannot predict the consequences of such a line').

[115] IISL Replies to UNCOPUOUS Legal Subcommittee (n 112) 1.

PART I
MILITARY SPACE ACTIVITIES DURING PEACETIME

Introduction

1. Part I deals primarily with routine civilian and military activities in space in peacetime (not related to an armed conflict) and focuses on international law, particularly the space law regime, as it applies to these military activities. Section 1 contains Rules concerning general freedoms and restrictions related to the use of outer space; Section 2 contains Rules concerning the responsibilities of States for national activities in outer space, the responsibilities of international organizations, and the international liability of States for damage caused by space objects; and Section 3 contains Rules concerning other obligations, including those related to Astronauts and Personnel of a Spacecraft, Avoidance of Harmful Contamination, and Visits to Facilities on the Moon and Other Celestial Bodies.

2. Because space is a congested and increasingly competitive domain, a better understanding and application of the basic Rules set forth in Part I of this *Manual* is an essential component in providing a safer and more predictable space ecosystem, reducing uncertainty and miscalculation, and managing the risk that competition could lead to conflict.

3. Although the Rules in this section primarily address space activities during peacetime, numerous Rules also provide some overview commentary on the reconciliation of those Rules based on the space law regime with the exercise of the right of self-defence by States, the exercise of belligerent rights by States, and the protection of the civilian population from hostilities during an armed conflict. The Rules governing such hostilities are examined in Part III, which addresses the application of the law of armed conflict/international humanitarian law to outer space.

SECTION 1
FREEDOMS AND RESTRICTIONS RELATED TO THE USE OF OUTER SPACE

Rule 1
Freedom of Use, Access, Exploration, and Scientific Investigation and Principles of Cooperation

Consistent with principles of cooperation, a State has a right to freely use and explore, and to freely engage in scientific investigation in outer space, including the Moon and other celestial bodies, and to freely access all areas of the Moon and other celestial bodies. Subject to specific limitations in the OST, States enjoy these rights without distinction between military and civilian activities.

Overview of Legal Basis of Rule

1. This Rule is based on the foundational 'free use principle' of the OST which provides that 'Outer space, including the Moon and other celestial bodies, shall be free for exploration and use by all States without discrimination of any kind, on a basis of equality and in accordance with international law, and there shall be free access to all areas of celestial bodies'.[116] The OST further provides that there shall be 'freedom of scientific investigation in outer space, including the Moon and other celestial bodies, and States shall facilitate and encourage international co-operation in such investigation'.[117] Under the broad subsidiary right of freedom of access, there is also no prohibition on a State exercising its right of free navigation through space and all States have rights of passage through space without interference.[118]

2. It has been noted that the free use principle found in Article I 'provides the international legal basis for all activity in outer space' and thus 'serves as the point of

---

[116] OST (n 9) art I, cl 2. Note, however, that freedom of access is limited by 'reciprocity' requirements in Article XII of the OST with respect to visiting stations, installations, equipment, and space vehicles on the Moon and other celestial bodies. See Rule 15: Visits to Facilities on the Moon and Other Celestial Bodies.
[117] ibid art I, cl 3.
[118] See eg 'National Space Policy of the United States of America' (US White House, 28 June 2010) 3 [https://perma.cc/3KZE-MX4S] ('The United States considers the space systems of all nations to have the rights of passage through, and conduct of operations in, space without interference.').

departure for any argument in favour of a particular use of outer space'.[119] However, the OST does impose some specific obligations and limitations on States with respect to the right of free use of space, as will be discussed shortly. The only explicit legal restrictions in the OST regarding the military use of space pertain to: specified military establishments and activities on the Moon or other celestial bodies (see Rule 4: Restrictions on Specified Military Establishments and Activities on Celestial Bodies); placing weapons of mass destruction in orbit around Earth or stationing or installing them in space or on the Moon or other celestial bodies (see Rule 7: Weapons of Mass Destruction); and limitations found in international law (particularly the United Nations Charter and its prohibition on the use of force) which are made applicable by the OST to all activities in the exploration and use of outer space, including the Moon and other celestial bodies.[120]

The Free Use Principle and International Cooperation

3. Like other freedoms and rights granted in the OST, the free use principle must be read in the context of various limitations or considerations, beginning with the requirement that space must be used on the basis of non-discrimination and equality in accordance with international law. The exploration and use of outer space, including the Moon and other celestial bodies, is further subject to the requirement that it be carried out 'for the benefit and in the interests of all countries, irrespective of their degree of economic or scientific development, and shall be the province of all mankind'.[121] The free use principle found in Article I of the OST is thus initially accompanied by four undefined principles in Article I itself:

   A. The principle of non-discrimination;
   B. The principle of equality in accordance with international law;
   C. The requirement that any use be carried out for the benefit and in the interests of all countries; and
   D. The recognition that space is the province of all mankind.

4. Although all the principles in Article I are legally binding (because they are found in the text and not only in the Preamble of the OST), the precise content of any obligations imposed by the vague principles accompanying the free use principle in Article I is unclear. For this reason, recourse to the travaux préparatoires is useful in discerning the intent of the parties with respect to this language. Most of the principles elaborating on free use that are found in Article I were drawn

---

[119] Canada, 'Terminology Relevant to Arms Control and Outer Space' (Working Paper Conference on Disarmament, 16 July 1986) CD/716, CD/OS/WP.15 (Canada, 'Terminology Relevant to Arms Control and Outer Space') 6.
[120] OST (n 9) art III.
[121] OST (n 9) art I, cl 1.

from prior UN General Assembly resolutions, particularly the 1963 Resolution entitled 'Declaration of Legal Principles Governing the Activities of States in the Exploration and Use of Outer Space'.[122] However, during the negotiation of the OST, the Soviet delegation proposed an additional requirement: that space should be used by all States 'without discrimination of any kind'.[123] The US delegation initially opposed this language, but withdrew its objections after supporters of the Soviet proposal 'insisted that this explicit non-discrimination language corresponds to a most favored nation clause which is necessary to assure cooperation among nations in space exploration'.[124] Further discussion of the non-discrimination clause, which was viewed as corresponding to the principle of equality, established that the equality referred to in Article I did not refer to 'de facto' equality but rather merely 'the absence of discrimination between states'.[125]

5. It is thus difficult to interpret the principles accompanying freedom of use in Article I as imposing any novel obligation on States to ensure the substantive de facto equality of States in the use or exploration of space or to share specific resources, programmes, or equipment in the use or exploitation of space. Rather, these provisions are better viewed as leaving space open to all nations and prohibiting discriminatory conduct. In endorsing the Soviet proposal regarding the language that was ultimately adopted in Article I, the United States declared that agreed language 'make[s] clear the intent of the treaty that outer space and celestial bodies are open not just to the big powers or the first arrivals, but shall be available to all, both now and in the future'.[126]

---

[122] UNGA Resolution 1962 (XVIII) Declaration of Legal Principles (n 60) ('Recognizing the common interest of all mankind in the progress of the exploration and use of outer space for peaceful purposes' and '[b]elieving that the exploration and use of outer space should be carried on for the betterment of mankind and for the benefit of States irrespective of their degree of economic or scientific development'). The UN General Assembly had previously recognized the 'common interest of mankind in outer space' and expressed the desire to 'promote energetically the fullest exploration and exploitation of outer space for the benefit of mankind'. Question of the Peaceful Use of Outer Space, UNGA Res 1348 (XIII) (13 December 1958). It had also expressed the belief that the 'exploration and use of outer space should be only for the betterment of mankind and to the benefit of States irrespective of the stage of their economic or scientific development'. International Co-operation in the Peaceful Uses of Outer Space, UNGA Res 1721 (XVI) (20 December 1961).
[123] Paul G Dembling and Daniel M Arons, 'The Evolution of the Outer Space Treaty' (1967) 33 Journal of Air Law and Commerce 419, 430 (discussing the consideration by member States of the UNCOPUOS Legal Sub-Committee of the Soviet draft of Article I.).
[124] ibid; UNCOPUOS Legal Sub-Committee, 'Summary Record of the Sixty-Fourth Meeting' (24 October 1966) UN Doc A/AC.l05/C.2/SR.64, 3 (The Hungarian delegate, speaking in support of the Soviet proposal that was ultimately adopted, stated that the non-discrimination clause 'corresponded to the most-favoured-nation clause' and that it also 'corresponded to the formula "on a basis of equality" in para 2 of the Declaration of Legal Principles, while being more categorical and eliminating all possibility of discrimination.').
[125] UNCOPUOS Legal Sub-Committee, 'Summary Record of the Sixty-Third Meeting' (20 October 1966) UN Doc A/AC.105/C.2/SR.63, 7 (The Romanian delegate, speaking in support of the Soviet draft, further noted that even if the words 'on a basis of equality' covered the same ground as 'without discrimination of any kind,' it was preferable to prohibit discrimination explicitly.).
[126] UNGA, 'First Committee Verbatim Record of the Fourteen Hundred and Ninety-Second Meeting' (27 January 1967) A/C.1/PV.1492, 16. During hearings before the US Senate, Ambassador Goldberg clarified that the OST did not require US communications satellites to be available for the benefit of

6. In determining the legal requirements associated with international cooperation and the extent to which the free use principle is informed by the accompanying imprecise principles in Article I, it is important to refer to UN General Assembly Resolution 51/122, often referred to as the 'Benefits Declaration'.[127] This resolution, adopted by consensus by the UN General Assembly at its 1996/1997 session, is widely regarded as providing 'an authoritative interpretation of the cooperation principle in Article I of the Outer Space Treaty'.[128] Although the resolution affirms that international cooperation in the exploration and use of outer space is to be 'carried out for the benefit and in the interest of all States, irrespective of their degree of economic, social or scientific and technological development, and shall be the province of all mankind', it emphasizes the freedom and discretion of each sovereign State in deciding precisely how this cooperation will take place.[129] It affirms that 'States are free to determine all aspects of their participation in international cooperation in the exploration and use of outer space on an equitable and *mutually acceptable* basis'.[130] The principles set forth in the Benefits Declaration are equally applicable to another provision in the OST which requires that States engaged in the exploration and use of outer space 'shall be guided by the principle of cooperation and mutual assistance',[131] although a State's freedom is bounded by the obligation to show 'due regard to the corresponding interests of all other States Parties to the Treaty'[132] (see Rule 17: Due Regard).

7. The Benefits Declaration (or Resolution) demonstrates how States have asserted their freedom to determine the precise contours of cooperative endeavours with other States in space and how the obligation to cooperate under the OST represents a duty of conduct and not of achieving a particular result. Indeed, State practice regarding Article I and its obligations to 'use space for the benefit and in the interests of all countries, irrespective of their degree of economic or scientific development' and to treat space as the 'province of all mankind' has generally been characterized by the insistence on the State's freedom of action and not as establishing specific or concrete restrictions on the free use principle.[133]

---

all countries and commented that Article I was a statement of 'general goals' that would require separate international agreements to cover the use of particular satellites. 'Treaty on Outer Space: Hearings Before the Committee on Foreign Relations United States Senate on Executive D, 90th Congress, First Session, March 7, 13 and April 12, 1967' (US Government Printing Office 1967) 31–37.

[127] UNGA, 'Declaration on International Cooperation in the Exploration and Use of Outer Space for the Benefit and in the Interest of All States, Taking into Particular Account the Needs of Developing Countries' (4 February 1997) UN Doc A/RES/51/122 (UN Benefits Declaration) [https://perma.cc/E9RY-C2NF].
[128] Marietta Benkö and Kai-Uwe Schrog, 'History and Impact of the 1996 UN Declaration on 'Space Benefits' (1997) 13 Space Policy 139.
[129] UN Benefits Declaration (n 127) para 1.
[130] ibid para 2 (emphasis added).
[131] OST (n 9) art IX.
[132] ibid.
[133] Stephan Hobe, Bernhard Schmidt-Tedd, and Kai-Uwe Schrogl (eds), *Cologne Commentary on Space Law: Outer Space Treaty*, vol I (Wolters Kluwer Deutschland GmbH 2009) 37 ('Opposed to any establishment of a concrete legal regime, the subsequent State practice with regard to Article I paragraph 1

Consistent with each sovereign State's freedom of action in space and its discretion in deciding precisely how its cooperation in space will take place, other provisions of the OST encourage various types of cooperation but do not impose mandatory obligations or sharing requirements on military or civilian activities.[134] For example, in order to promote international cooperation in the exploration and use of outer space, including the Moon and other celestial bodies, Article X of the OST provides that States 'shall consider on a basis of equality any requests by other States Parties to the Treaty to be afforded an opportunity to observe the flight of space objects launched by those States', but also importantly adds that '[t]he nature of such an opportunity for observation and the conditions under which it could be afforded *shall be determined by agreement between the States concerned*'.[135]

Similarly, Article XI of the OST provides that a State shall 'inform the Secretary-General of the United Nations as well as the public and the international scientific community' of the nature, conduct, locations and results of its activities in outer space, but only 'to the greatest extent feasible and practicable'.[136] This ambiguous language in Article XI regarding State compliance when 'feasible and practicable' was viewed by the Soviet delegation in the OST negotiations as generally requiring the reporting of activities in outer space and on celestial bodies only on a *voluntary* basis.[137] The Soviet delegation further drew a 'sharp distinction' between the voluntary reporting requirement in Article XI and the 'comparatively unequivocal obligation' imposed on States in reporting phenomena discovered which could

8.

9.

---

of the Outer Space Treaty shows an insistence on the State's freedom of action, particularly with regard to the sharing of benefits derived from space activities, rather than any concrete elaboration of clauses limiting the freedom of action of States.'). Although the phrase 'common province of mankind' introduces provisions addressing the legal regulation of a common space, it can be distinguished from similar phrases such as 'common heritage of mankind' which is found in art XI of the Moon Agreement and is viewed in that specific treaty regime as carrying obligations related to the sharing of resources. Nonetheless, the phrase 'common province of mankind' conveys, along with other terms found in art I of the OST, the 'interest of all mankind to enable the participation of non-space-faring and developing States in the exploration and use of outer space'. ibid 27.

[134] For example, State A cannot be prohibited from launching a military communications satellite into orbit, nor can State A be required to share with other States photo imagery taken by any of its military satellites (see Rule 3: Peaceful Purposes in Outer Space, discussing widespread and increasing military activities in space which are consistent with the term peaceful purposes; see also Rule 6: Military Space Activities and Intelligence Collection).

[135] OST (n 9) art X (emphasis added). This is sometimes referred to as the 'Observation' and 'Information' clause. Notwithstanding the explicitly voluntary nature of cooperation addressed in art X, one State at State Consultations noted that art X should be highlighted because of its potential for States to justify and safely conduct proximity operations and that this might prove to be important for current pressing security challenges in outer space.

[136] ibid art XI.

[137] Dembling and Arons (n 123) 441 (noting further 'the unequivocal refusal of the Soviet delegation to accept any provision requiring mandatory reporting to the Secretary-General'); UNCOPUOS Legal Sub-Committee, 'Summary Record of the Sixty-Sixth Meeting' (21 October 1966) UN Doc A/AC.105/C.2/SR.66 (UNCOPUOS Legal Sub-Committee Summary Record 66) 6–7 (remarks of Soviet representative Morozov).

constitute a danger to the life or health of astronauts under Article V and the 'mandatory' consultations required in advance of an event that would cause potentially harmful interference under Article IX of the OST.[138]

Specific Limitations or Restrictions on the Free Use Principle

10. The free use principle is thus a key part of the generally permissive OST legal framework governing both military and civilian activities in outer space and on the Moon and other celestial bodies. Particular importance may thus be attached to the specific limitations or restrictions imposed on activities set forth in the OST provisions that follow Article I. In addition to the key obligation under Article III of the OST to comply with international law, including the UN Charter, these limitations or restrictions on the free use principle addressed in other Rules in this *Manual* include:

> Rule 2: Non-Appropriation of Outer Space and Celestial Bodies;
> Rule 3: Peaceful Purposes in Outer Space, as a derivative of UN Charter obligations;
> Rule 4: Restrictions on Specified Military Establishments and Activities on Celestial Bodies;
> Rule 5: Weapons of Mass Destruction;
> Rule 10: Responsibility of States for National Activities in Outer Space;
> Rule 12: International Liability for Damage Caused by Space Objects;
> Rule 13: Astronauts and Personnel of a Spacecraft;
> Rule 14: Avoidance of Harmful Contamination;
> Rule 15: Visits to Facilities on the Moon and Other Celestial Bodies;
> Rule 17: Due Regard;
> Rule 18: Harmful Interference.

---

[138] Dembling and Arons (n 123) 436. The Soviet draft incorporating a voluntary rather than a mandatory approach to the submission of information on space activities prevailed with respect to art XI despite efforts by the United States and its supporters 'to embody in treaty form a principle that had already become a hallmark of the United States space program: a requirement that there be full dissemination of scientific and technical information for peaceful purposes'. Dembling and Arons (n 123) 443.

Rule 2
Non-Appropriation of Outer Space and Celestial Bodies

Outer space, including the Moon and other celestial bodies, is not subject to national appropriation by claim of sovereignty, by means of use or occupation, or by any other means.

The legality of the exploitation or extraction of resources in outer space, including on the Moon and other celestial bodies, is unsettled.

Overview of Legal Basis of Rule

1. This Rule is based on the 'non-appropriation principle' which is a foundational principle of space law and enshrined in Article II of the Outer Space Treaty (OST). It provides: 'Outer space, including the Moon and other celestial bodies, is not subject to national appropriation by claim of sovereignty, by means of use or occupation, or by any other means.'[139] The principle emerged as one of the first fundamental rules of space law, with its origins in Resolutions passed by the UN General Assembly in the early 1960s, particularly Resolution 1962, 'Declaration of Legal Principles Governing the Activities of States in the Exploration and Use of Outer Space'.[140]

2. The only example of an action by a State related to the potential appropriation of celestial bodies based on the presence of humans on a celestial body is the first landing on the Moon by the US Apollo 11 on 20 July 1969. This landing and the first

---

[139] OST (n 9) art II. The term 'occupation', as used in the OST, is not synonymous with the term 'occupation' as used in international humanitarian law.

[140] 1963 UNGA Declaration of Legal Principles (n 60) ('The General Assembly ... [s]olemnly declares that in the exploration and use of outer space States should be guided by the following principles: ... Outer space and celestial bodies are not subject to national appropriation by claim of sovereignty, by means of use or occupation, or by any other means.'); International Co-operation in the Peaceful Uses of Outer Space (n 122) ('Commends to States for their guidance in the exploration and use of outer space the following principles: ... Outer space and celestial bodies are free for exploration and use by all States in conformity with international law and are not subject to national appropriation....'); both resolutions were adopted by the General Assembly without controversy and without a vote. Even earlier in the space age, President Eisenhower had proposed to the UN General Assembly that '[w]e agree that celestial bodies are not subject to national appropriation by any claims of sovereignty'. US State Dept, 'Address by President Dwight Eisenhower to the UN General Assembly' (22 September 1960) [perma.cc/9FE4-JH27].

walk on the Moon were accompanied by the planting of a US flag on the Moon's surface. Importantly, however, the US law that mandated the choice of flags for this occasion provided '[t]his act is intended as a symbolic gesture of national pride in achievement and is not to be construed as a declaration of national appropriation by claim of sovereignty'.[141]

3. One important subset or category of measures included in the non-appropriation principle is the prohibition of national appropriation by 'claim of sovereignty'.[142] Sovereignty is a fundamental principle in international law and international relations. It generally refers to the supreme authority of a State within a territory, including a State's right to exclude any other State from that territory.[143] Claims to sovereignty under traditional mechanisms of international law (*inter alia* by occupation and prescription, accretion, cession, conquest) are not recognized in outer space or on celestial bodies.

4. In as much as there can be no sovereign territory in outer space or on celestial bodies, principles based on sovereignty over territory are inapplicable in space. A State on whose registry an object is launched and carried into outer space does, however, retain jurisdiction and control over such object (and over any personnel thereof) while in outer space or on a celestial body[144] (see Rule 8: Registration of Space Objects and Rule 7: Jurisdiction).

Unsettled Status of Resources in Outer Space, Including Celestial Bodies

5. History unfortunately demonstrates that disputes over resources, particularly with respect to competing claims, can lead to conflict among States which could implicate military responses in the context of space. The legal status of exploitation of natural resources from the Moon, asteroids, and other celestial bodies is unsettled. The OST contains no explicit references to the exploitation of natural resources in outer space. Thus, although various articles of the OST discussed above are highly

---

[141] National Aeronautics and Space Administration Authorization Act 1970 Pub L 91-119 18 November 1969 s 8.

[142] It should be emphasized that the term 'non-appropriation' involves a broader prohibition than just a claim of sovereignty since it encompasses not only such a claim of sovereignty but also appropriation by means of use or occupation, or by any other means.

[143] See *Island of Palmas Case (United States v Netherlands)* (1928) II RIAA 829, 838. ('Sovereignty in the relations between States signifies independence; Independence in regard to a portion of the globe is the right to exercise therein, to the exclusion of any other State, the functions of a State.'); see also Samantha Besson, 'Sovereignty' in Rüdiger Wolfram (ed), *Max Planck Encyclopedias of Public International Law* (online edn April 2011) [perma.cc/RSD8-556B] ("The principle of sovereignty refers to 'the supreme authority within a territory' and constitutes a 'pivotal principle of modern international law.').

[144] OST (n 9) art VIII.

relevant to this issue, no special legal regime is established by the OST to govern the extraction, ownership, and utilization of natural resources in outer space, including the Moon and other celestial bodies. This leaves States, and the non-governmental entities (including companies) which they supervise and for which they are responsible, with a broadly permissive OST framework in this area and subject to no specific resource-related prohibitions. While the scope of the strict prohibitions imposed by the non-appropriation principle (making 'the Moon and other celestial bodies not subject to national appropriation by claim of sovereignty, by means of use or occupation, or by any other means')[145] is unclear, it does not explicitly extend to natural resources.[146] In this regard, there is considerable disagreement among States regarding the right, under international law, to extract, own, and utilize natural resources in space, leading to calls for multilateral negotiations to develop an international agreement to resolve these issues and establish an appropriate space mining or resource exploitation regime.[147]

The OST broadly mandates that 'outer space, including the Moon and other celestial bodies, shall be free for exploration and use by all States without discrimination of any kind', adding that this shall be done 'on a basis of equality and in accordance with international law, and there shall be free access to all areas of celestial bodies'.[148] The OST further provides that the exploration and use of outer space, including the Moon and other celestial bodies, 'shall be carried out for the benefit and in the interests of all countries, irrespective of their degree of economic or scientific development, and shall be the province of all mankind'.[149] The legal impact of these broad, undefined conditions on the 'use' of outer space is unclear. Like many other parts of the OST, the precise interpretation of these conditions is left to subsequent State practice in the application of the Treaty or by other international law making. In 1996, a UN General Assembly Resolution addressing these conditions contained a declaration on international cooperation, but emphasized the discretion of each sovereign State in deciding how to cooperate with other States in implementing these conditions: 'States are free to determine all aspects of their participation in international cooperation in the exploration and use of outer space on an equitable and mutually acceptable basis.'[150]

6.

---

[145] OST (n 9) art II.
[146] As noted by one State at State Consultations, '[i]n the OST, there is the non-appropriation principle, on the one hand; and the principle of freedom of exploration and use of space and celestial bodies, on the other, while the exact scope of these principles is not altogether clear when it comes to the exploitation of space resources'. It further noted that the exploitation of space resources is 'highly controversial between States'.
[147] One State at State Consultations commented that '[w]e read Art. I OST as a limitation of the freedom of exploration and use, which at least prohibits national monopolization and appropriation. The exact scope, however, is ambiguous and should be subject to multilateral negotiations.' It went on to state that '[we are] firmly of the opinion that the recovery and use of space resources should be governed by an international agreement'.
[148] OST (n 9) art I.
[149] ibid.
[150] UN Benefits Declaration (n 127).

7. Notwithstanding the broad and permissive framework established by the OST with respect to the 'use' of outer space, some States have argued that the language in the OST translates into a requirement for a benefit-sharing regime for space mining activities similar to the framework found in Part XI of the UN Law of the Sea Convention (UNCLOS).[151] The UNCLOS legal framework is an internationally regulated system to exploit the resources of the area which are managed as part of the 'common heritage of mankind'.[152] This resembles the legal framework found in the Moon Agreement, in which the Moon and its natural resources are declared to be 'the common heritage of mankind' and the States parties to that agreement 'undertake to establish an international regime, including appropriate procedures, to govern exploitation of the natural resources of the Moon as such exploitation is about to become feasible'.[153]

8. No international legal benefit-sharing regime has been implemented for the exploitation of resources on the Moon and other celestial bodies, notwithstanding arguments advanced by some States based on the 'common heritage of mankind' principle in the Moon Agreement and UNCLOS, or on other concepts such as 'universal heritage' or '*res communis*'.[154] In this regard, the provisions of the poorly subscribed Moon Agreement do not constitute rules of customary international law and UNCLOS provisions relating to international regulation of resources and benefit-sharing do not apply to the Moon or other celestial bodies.

9. The US position on space resource utilization dates back several decades. In 1979, US Secretary of State Cyrus Vance articulated what was at that point already a

---

[151] United Nations Convention on the Law of the Sea (adopted 10 December 1982, entered into force 16 November 1994) 1833 UNTS 3 (UNCLOS) arts 133–149.

[152] ibid art 36.

[153] Agreement governing the Activities of States on the Moon and Other Celestial Bodies (adopted 5 December 1979, entered into force 11 July 1984) 1363 UNTS 3 (Moon Agreement) arts 11(1), 11(5). See Overview of the Space Law Regime, paras 23–24. It should be noted, however, that the Moon Agreement does not reflect customary international law and only 18 States are parties to the Treaty (and no major spacefaring or space-technology States, except Australia and Kazakhstan). UN Committee on Peaceful Uses of Outer Space (UNCOPUOS) Legal Sub-Committee, 'Status of International Agreements relating to activities in outer space as at 1 January 2021' UN Doc A/AC.105/C.2/2022/CRP.10*. It should be noted that one party to the Moon Agreement, Saudi Arabia, announced its decision to withdraw from that agreement in 2023. See UN Treaty Collection, Outer Space, https://treaties.un.org/Pages/ViewDetails.aspx?src=IND&mtdsg_no=XXIV-2&chapter=24&clang=_en ('On 5 January 2023, the Government of Saudi Arabia notified the Secretary-General of its decision to withdraw from the Agreement with effect from 5 January 2024 in accordance with article 20 of the Agreement.').

[154] There is no international consensus regarding these terms. As noted in 2017 by the US Representative to the UNCOPUOS Legal Sub-Committee in discussions related to the exploration, exploitation and utilization of space resources, '[w]e have heard the phrases global commons, common heritage of mankind, universal heritage, and res communis, in relation to outer space. These may be important concepts in international law, but they are not part of the Outer Space Treaty. Likewise, we have heard repeated reference to the Moon Agreement, but as we all know, that agreement is not widely ratified and its provisions do not reflect, and have not been incorporated into, customary international law.' UNCOPUOS, Legal Sub-Committee (56th Session)' Remarks of the US Representative Audio Recording (28 March 2017) <https://icms.unov.org/CarbonWeb/public/oosa/speakerslog/dc656751-ffce-4b22-977e-a0244f55010e> last accessed 29 March 2023.

long-standing US interpretation, that the non-appropriation principle 'applies to the natural resources of celestial bodies only when such resources are "in place"'.[155] He went on to state that the prohibition in the OST on national appropriation does not limit 'ownership to be exercised by States or private entities over those natural resources which have been removed from their "place" on or below the surface of the Moon or other celestial bodies' and that such removal of resources 'is permitted by the article contained in the 1967 Outer Space Treaty which states, *inter alia*, that '[o]uter space, including the Moon and other celestial bodies, shall be free for exploration and use by all States'.[156]

10. Not only does this position correspond with the approaches taken by some other States in distinguishing 'natural resources in place' from areas of celestial bodies generally (eg that distinction is even made in the Moon Agreement)[157] but it also clearly distinguishes laying a claim to mineral resources merely by discovering them and then attempting to preclude others from harvesting them (which would in the view of most States amount to appropriation of the area at issue prohibited by Article II of the OST). A comparison could also be drawn with fishing on the high seas: no individual or State can 'reserve' the fish resources in a certain part of the high seas, as that would be tantamount to the exercise of territorial sovereignty, but once the fish are caught, they are validly owned by the fishing crew.[158]

11. While the United States argues that the OST does not preclude the utilization of space resources that are not 'in place', that is, following extraction, it acknowledges that the OST clearly 'shapes the manner in which space resource utilisation activities may be carried out'.[159] Such activities may not, of course, be structured around sovereignty, ownership, or property rights in celestial bodies or resources in place, since such actions would violate the non-appropriation principle. Furthermore,

---

[155] Marian L Nash, 'Contemporary Practice of the United States Relating to International Law' [1994] American Journal of International Law 418, 422. The 'in place' language refers to resources in their unextracted form, ie forming part of or under the surface of the Moon or other celestial body prior to extraction or refinement.

[156] ibid 423.

[157] The Moon Agreement makes this distinction when it prohibits 'natural resources in place' from becoming the property of any State, see Moon Agreement (n 46) art 11(3). This restriction is of course subject in the Moon Agreement to the creation of a contemplated international regime to govern the exploitation of the natural resources of the Moon.

[158] Although, as noted by a State at State Consultations, the freedom of fishing on the high seas is explicitly covered by international law under Article 87 of UNCLOS (n 151).

[159] Brian Egan (Legal Adviser, US Department of State), 'The Next Fifty Years of the Outer Space Treaty' (Galloway Symposium on Critical Issues in Space Law, Washington DC 7 December 2016) [https://perma.cc/7AAR-M7J3] (Egan further notes, however, that '[t]o say that the Treaty does not preclude private ownership of resources extracted from a celestial body is not to suggest that the Treaty provides a comprehensive international regime for space resource utilization activities. At this stage, we see neither a need nor a practical basis to create such a regime.'). Also note US legal requirements in para 12, making the rights of US nationals to possess, own, transport, use, and sell the asteroid resource or other space resources subject to being obtained in accordance with the international obligations of the United States.

with respect to the companies engaged in space resource extraction, States bear international responsibility under the OST for national activities in outer space (even when carried on by non-governmental entities), for assuring that national activities are carried out in conformity with the OST, and for exercising 'authorization and continuing supervision' over the activities of non-governmental entities.[160]

12. Private firms are now moving forward, planning and preparing operations to explore and utilize space resources.[161] At the same time, some States have begun authorizing such operations and conveying rights under their respective laws to their nationals with respect to the ownership, use, transfer, and sale of natural resources extracted from outer space. For example, the 2015 US Commercial Space Launch Competitiveness Act provides space resource rights to US citizens, stating that '[a] United States citizen engaged in commercial recovery of an asteroid resource or a space resource under this chapter shall be entitled to any asteroid resource or space resource obtained, including to possess, own, transport, use, and sell the asteroid resource or space resource'.[162] The 2017 Luxembourg Law on the Exploration and Use of Space Resources states that '[s]pace resources are subject to appropriation'.[163] Along similar lines, a 2019 United Arab Emirates Law provides that 'the conditions and controls relating to permits for the exploration, exploitation and use of Space Resources, including their acquisition, purchase, sale, trade, transportation, storage and any Space Activities aimed at providing logistical services in this regard shall be determined by a decision issued by the Council of Ministers or whomever it delegates'.[164] In 2021, Japan became the fourth country to pass a law dedicated to the exploitation of space resources, allowing private businesses to extract and own mineral and other resources collected outside Earth.[165]

13. However, some States have criticized such national authorizations of space resource extraction as being inconsistent with the OST, others have protested that an agreed multilateral approach is more appropriate than national legislation, and others

---

[160] OST (n 9) art VI.
[161] Egan (n 159) ('Government space agencies are not alone in contemplating the utilization of resources found in celestial bodies to support deep space missions. Private firms have announced ambitious plans to develop parts of a deep space infrastructure to utilize space resources—water and minerals, for example—by converting them into fuel, and even manufacturing spacecraft in space.').
[162] See eg US Commercial Space Launch Competitiveness Act, 51 USC § 51303 (2015) (these rights are subject, however, to being 'obtained in accordance with applicable law, including the international obligations of the United States').
[163] Government of the Grand Duchy of Luxembourg, Law of July 20 2017 on the Exploration and Use of Space Resources (English Translation) (13 July 2017) [https://perma.cc/C3TG-G7PC] art 1.
[164] United Arab Emirates, Federal Law No (12) of 2019 (issued on 19 December 2019) [https://perma.cc/5RW8-VU79] art 18.
[165] Jeff Foust, 'Japan Passes Space Resources Law' (Alexandia, *Space News* 17 June 2021) [https://perma.cc/887G-54GY] ('The bill, formally known as the Law Concerning the Promotion of Business Activities Related to the Exploration and Development of Space Resources, grants Japanese companies permission to prospect for, extract and use various space resources. Companies that wish to do so must first obtain permission from the Japanese government.').

expressed have concerns about giving too much power to private enterprises or favouring one State's companies over the companies of another.[166] Echoing many of these sentiments, the Director General of the Russian Space Agency Roscosmos noted, in response to Japan's enactment of space resources legislation, that 'the matter of regulation of these mining activities is still a very thorny issue' and called for a 'system of regulations' to address these issues at an international level, rather than national laws on space resources legislation.[167] With respect to such criticism of national authorizations in this area, it is of course important to note that even if a State authorizes, under its own laws, nationals to extract, own, possess, and sell resources extracted from asteroids and other celestial bodies, such laws apply in space only to those persons and objects which are subject to that State's jurisdiction (see Rule 9: Jurisdiction).

14. An example of the increasing willingness of some States to embrace an interpretation of the OST that permits the extraction and utilization of space resources (while not explicitly addressing ownership) can be found in the 'Artemis Accords,' a set of non-legally binding, multilateral political commitments to the principles of cooperation in the civil exploration and use of the Moon, Mars, comets, and asteroids for peaceful purposes.[168] On 13 October 2020, eight States (later joined by numerous additional States)[169] announced that they joined the Artemis Accords, which specifically provide that, since 'the utilization of space resources can benefit

---

[166] See United Nations Committee on the Peaceful Uses of Outer Space, Legal Sub-Committee (56th Session) Remarks by Brazilian, Iranian and Russian Representatives, Audio Recordings (28 March 2017) <https://icms.unov.org/CarbonWeb/public/oosa/speakerslog/ecdbee63-c7d8-4267-a070-34155faed934>; United Nations Committee on the Peaceful Uses of Outer Space, Space Law Symposium (27 March 2017) <https://icms.unov.org/CarbonWeb/public/oosa/speakerslog/534cdc53-8532-4163-b4fc-ccb952f609a9>.

[167] 'Japan passes space resources law' (n 50) (This article further notes that Dmitry Rogozin, the Director General of Roscosmos, argued that 'Russia believes that states mustn't adopt any laws and regulations on a unilateral basis because space is our common heritage and belongs to everyone', he said. 'We consider the United Nations as ... suitable to discuss these issues.').

[168] 'The Artemis Accords: Principles for Cooperation in the Civil Exploration and Use of the Moon, Mars, Comets, and Asteroids' (13 October 2020) [https://perma.cc/PCD3-SWCY] (the Artemis Accords). One State at State Consultations emphasized that the Artemis Accords are not an appropriate framework for future activities on the Moon and instead suggested the following: 'Considering the substantial body of work of the international community with regards to establishing legal frameworks for activities outside of national sovereignty in the past, it is only logical to build on these achievements and discuss how and to what extent existing legal frameworks such as the regime to regulate the exploration and mining of the deep seabed in UNCLOS as well as the 1979 Moon Agreement can be modified and utilized as blueprints for the exploitation of space resources.'

[169] The original eight Signatory States are Australia, Canada, France, Italy, Japan, Luxembourg, the United Arab Emirates, the United Kingdom, and the United States. As of May 2023, numerous additional States have joined the Artemis Accords, including Bahrain, Brazil, the Czech Republic, Colombia, France, India, Israel, Mexico, New Zealand, Poland, the Republic of Korea, Romania, Singapore, and Ukraine. See, NASA, 'The Artemis Accords', at https://www.nasa.gov/specials/artemis-accords/index.html. One additional State, Saudi Arabia, joined the Artemis Accords on 14 July 2022, and announced its decision to withdraw from the Moon Agreement on 5 January 2023. See UN Treaty Collection (n 153). Saudi Arabia's withdrawal marks the first such withdrawal by a State from any of the five outer space treaties.

humankind by providing critical support for safe and sustainable operations', the Signatories 'emphasize that the extraction and utilization of space resources, including any recovery from the surface or subsurface of the Moon, Mars, comets, or asteroids, should be executed in a manner that complies with the Outer Space Treaty and in support of safe and sustainable space activities'.[170] The Signatories further affirm that 'the extraction of space resources does not inherently constitute national appropriation under Article II of the Outer Space Treaty, and that contracts and other legal instruments relating to space resources should be consistent with that Treaty'.[171] As part of this effort, the US National Aeronautics and Space Administration (NASA) has announced that its 'Lunar Surface Innovation Initiative will develop and demonstrate technologies to use the Moon's resources to produce water, fuel, and other supplies as well as capabilities to excavate and construct structures on the Moon'.[172]

---

[170] The Artemis Accords (n 168) s 10, paras 1 and 2.
[171] ibid s 10, para 2.
[172] NASA, 'Overview: In-Situ Resource Utilization Using Space-Based Resources for Deep Space Exploration' (NASA, 3 April 2020) [https://perma.cc/E3BE-G9DS] (NASA further notes that 'the farther humans go into deep space, the more important it will be to generate products with local materials, a practice called in-situ resource utilization (ISRU).').

Rule 3
Peaceful Purposes in Outer Space

A State that engages in the exploration and use of outer space shall comply with international law, including the UN Charter's obligation to not engage in the unlawful threat or use of force, and thus shall engage in only the peaceful (i.e., non-aggressive) exploration and use of outer space.

Overview of Legal Basis of Rule

With respect to the exploration and use of space generally, the phrase 'peaceful purposes' is not defined in the Outer Space Treaty (OST) and is prominently placed in the preamble of the OST. Notably, Article IV of the OST contains the phrase 'exclusively peaceful purposes', a phrase which is functionally defined and made applicable by Article IV only to specified military activities on the Moon and other celestial bodies[173] (see Rule 4: 'Restrictions on Specified Military Establishments and Activities on Celestial Bodies). As will be discussed shortly with respect to the application of the phrase 'peaceful purposes' to the exploration and use of space generally, the OST drafters' intentional placement of the phrase in the Preamble—and not in the text—was significant since a preambular phrase does not by itself impose legally binding obligations on States, as a textual provision does. As for the meaning of the phrase, some commentators continue to echo the sentiments of some States—expressed at the dawn of the space age—when they argue that the phrase peaceful purposes should be defined as 'non-military', that space should be disarmed or demilitarized, and that this interpretation of peaceful purposes should extend to space generally. This hope, however, was not realized by the States drafting the OST, as evidenced by both the text of the OST and its travaux préparatoires discussed below. In addition, the subsequent practice of States that are parties to the OST has effectively demonstrated a rejection of an interpretation of the phrase peaceful purposes—or any other phrase in the OST—as generally

1.

---

[173] The phrase 'peaceful purposes' is found in two places in the *text* of the treaty, in Article IV, para 2. Significantly, art IV, para 2, applies only to '[t]he Moon and other celestial bodies' but does not apply to 'outer space' generally. The first sentence of art IV, para 2, provides '[t]he Moon and other celestial bodies shall be used by all States Parties to the Treaty exclusively for peaceful purposes'; later in that paragraph, in contrast to those military activities that are specifically prohibited in para 1, para 2 states 'the use of military personnel for scientific research or for any other peaceful purposes shall not be prohibited'.

banning military activities in space.[174] The subsequent extensive practice of States further demonstrates a growing consensus that explicitly or effectively defines the phrase peaceful purposes as emphasizing compliance with UN Charter obligations, notably the obligation to not engage in an unlawful threat or use of force (see Rule 21: Use of Force; Rule 22: Threat of Force) or what has increasingly been referred to as 'aggressive' uses in space. Thus, during State Consultations, a State emphasized that a legitimate act of self-defence (see Rule 26: Self-Defence) is not inconsistent with peaceful purposes.

Peaceful Purposes as a Preambular Phrase

2. As discussed in paragraph 4, some States involved in the drafting of the OST strongly preferred the phrase 'peaceful purposes' to be applied to space generally as a binding obligation in the text of the OST. However, it was ultimately placed in the Preamble to the OST, where it supports the expression of goals and aspirations of the parties who recognize 'the common interest of all mankind in the progress of the exploration and use of outer space for peaceful purposes' and state the desire 'to contribute to broad international co-operation in the scientific as well as the legal aspects of the exploration and use of outer space for peaceful purposes'.

3. Because the reference to the peaceful purposes—as applied to space generally—is found in the Preamble to the OST, it is recognized as a source of interpretation of the text.[175] It is important to note, however, that while the preamble of a treaty is significant in the treaty's interpretation and outlines the reasons motivating the parties to conclude the treaty (with words in the OST such as 'recognizing' and 'desiring'), the preamble usually sets forth only goals and objectives and generally 'does not contain legal norms and does not have immediate legal significance'.[176] As indicated in the last clause of the Preamble to the OST, the provisions which the contracting States 'agreed on' are to be found only in the 'following' Articles.[177] Preambular material may, pursuant to Article 31(2) of the Vienna Convention on the Law of Treaties, be used for the purpose of interpreting treaty provisions, in this case the provisions of the OST. Similarly, it is part of the analysis required under Article 31(1) to interpret a treaty in the light of its object and purpose. It does not, however, convey substantive legal obligations and, as will be discussed, the widely recognized international understanding of the phrase 'peaceful purposes' does not mean 'non-military'. Both points help explain the general unwillingness

---

[174] Note, however, that some military activities are explicit banned in space under the OST (see eg Rule 5: Weapons of Mass Destruction).
[175] VCLT (n 11) art 31, para 2.
[176] Claude Schenker, 'Practice Guide to International Treaties' (Federal Department of Foreign Affairs, Switzerland 2015) para 46 [https://perma.cc/X2B4-F3FH].
[177] OST (n 9) preamble, cl 10.

of States, over the more than 50 years since the OST was concluded, to officially invoke 'peaceful purposes' in arguing that a particular military activity in space has contravened the OST.[178]

As indicated by the travaux préparatoires of the OST, the decision to not apply the phrase 'peaceful purposes' to space in the text and instead place it in the Preamble was a conscious one that had the support of both the United States and the Soviet Union and their respective allies. The unwillingness of these States to agree to apply the phrase 'peaceful purposes' to space generally and place it in the text (beyond its application just to the Moon and other Celestial Bodies in Article IV) was strongly criticized by some States during the consideration of drafts of the OST in the Legal Sub-Committee of the UN Committee on Peaceful Uses of Space (UNCOPUOS)[179] and in the final review of the proposed draft treaty in the First Committee of the United Nations General Assembly.[180] For States that viewed the phrase 'peaceful purposes' as meaning 'non-military', the consequences of not placing it in the text and applying it to space was clear. For example, in analysing and criticizing the final draft text of the OST, the representative of Brazil to the First Committee felt that this exclusion of the phrase from the text meant that 'the draft treaty thus allowed the non-peaceful or military use of outer space'.[181] The explicit obligation imposed on States to use the Moon and other celestial bodies exclusively for peaceful purposes while not including any reference to 'outer space' in Article IV also prompted the representative of India to suggest that 'there might seem to be reason for concluding that outer space could be used for non-peaceful purposes'.[182] In spite of

4.

---

[178] Even when States have strongly condemned particular military actions by States in space, such as the destructive ASAT tests by China in 2007 and by India in 2019 (and earlier ASAT tests by the United States and the Soviet Union during the Cold War), they have refrained from claiming that such actions constituted a violation of a legal obligation based on the phrase peaceful purposes.

[179] For example, the representative of India on the UNCOPUOS Legal Sub-Committee argued that the failure by the space powers to extend the application of the phrase peaceful purposes in the draft text of the OST beyond just the Moon and other celestial bodies to include space generally meant that, in a sense, the document 'ran counter to the whole history of the question in the United Nations'. UNCOPUOS Legal Sub-Committee Summary Record 66 (n 137) 6 (remarks of Mr Rao, India).

[180] In considering the draft OST from the Legal Sub-Committee of UNCOPUOS, '[t]he representatives of Austria, Brazil, Ceylon, Cyprus, India, Kenya, Mexico, and the United Arab Republic expressed regret that, according to the draft treaty, only the celestial bodies were to be used exclusively for peaceful purposes and that this requirement was not applicable generally to outer space'. UNGA 'The Peaceful Uses of Outer Space' (1966) UN Yearbook United Nation (UNYB) 32, 39.

[181] ibid. The Brazilian representative further argued that this loophole was contrary to the principles set forth in earlier, broader General Assembly resolutions which had emphasized the peaceful use of outer space. These comments left the representative of Pakistan expressing only a 'hop[e]' that this failure to reference outer space did not mean that outer space could be used for other than for peaceful purposes. ibid.

[182] ibid. The phrase 'exclusively for peaceful purposes' carries with it the similar obligation not to engage in aggressive uses of space and, for purposes of Article IV of the OST, also some restrictions on specific military activities. See Rule 4: Restrictions on Specified Military Establishments and Activities on the Moon and Other Celestial Bodies. UNCOPUOS Legal Sub-Committee Summary Record 66 (n 137). Mr Rao observed that since the OST was intended to govern the exploration and use of outer space as well as the Moon and other celestial bodies, the omission of outer space in art 4 left open the possibility of 'non-peaceful' uses of otherwise 'neutral' technology, such as 'orbit[ing] military bases as well as scientific laboratories'. ibid.

52   RULE 3 PEACEFUL PURPOSES IN OUTER SPACE

these perspectives, the peaceful purposes concept was not extended to outer space generally in Article IV, nor was it included in any other part of the text, and was instead included in the aspirational language of the Preamble to the OST.[183]

5. Confronted with the failure by States in UNCOPUOUS to extend the concept of peaceful purposes to space generally by including it among the legally binding obligations of the text of the OST, some State representatives to the First Committee of the UN General Assembly reviewing the final draft of the OST chose to emphasize the obligations of States to comply with their obligations under the UN Charter to not take any action contrary to the maintenance of peace and security.[184] This position is consistent with the now common interpretation held by many States (discussed in paragraphs 6 and 10–12) that the concept of peaceful purposes, when it does apply to space activities, reflects compliance with UN Charter obligations and requires non-aggressive conduct.

US and Soviet Views of Peaceful Purposes During the Negotiation of the OST

6. The United States and the Soviet Union led their respective groups of allied States in the Cold War era negotiations that resulted in the conclusion of the OST. These two States thus played highly prominent roles in the drafting of the OST. For its part, the United States had made its position on the phrase 'peaceful purposes' clear even before the United States and the Soviet Union submitted their first drafts of the treaty on 16 June 1966. As stated on 20 December 1965 by the US representative to the United Nations First Committee:

> [s]ince the beginning of the space age, the United States had constantly endorsed the principle that space should be used for peaceful purposes. In that context, 'peaceful' meant non-aggressive rather than non-military... There was no

---

[183] Proposals to include straightforward words of obligation regarding the application of the Peaceful Purposes Principle to outer space as a whole were made by some delegations in sessions of the UNCOPUOS Legal Sub-Committee, but these proposals were not adopted. See eg UNCOPUOS Legal Sub-Committee, 'Summary Record of the Seventy-First Meeting' (4 August 1966) UN Doc A/AC.105/C.2/SR.71, 24 [https://perma.cc/N43G-QJJU] (the Iranian Representative proposed the inclusion of this simple, obligatory, textual language in an early working group draft: 'The exploration and use of outer space, the moon and other celestial bodies shall be carried on for peaceful purposes.' Similarly, the representative of Argentina stated that the fundamental principle that the exploration and use of outer space and celestial bodies should be for peaceful purposes 'should have been stated in the first article of the treaty'); UNCOPUOS Legal Sub-Committee Summary Record 66 (n 137) 3 (remarks of Mr Ruda, Argentina).

[184] See UNGA, 'The Peaceful Uses of Outer Space' (n 180) (The representative from Austria noted that 'since the activities of States must be carried out in accordance with international law, including the United Nations Charter, any action contrary to the maintenance of peace and security would be inconsistent with the purpose of the draft treaty'. Similarly, the representative from Sweden expressed the view that 'the Charter obligations to maintain peace and security and to live together peacefully were also binding upon States with regard to their activities in outer space').

practical dividing-line between military and non-military uses of space: United States and Soviet astronauts had been members of their countries' armed forces; a navigation satellite could guide a warship as well as a merchant ship; communication satellites could serve military establishments as well as civilian communities. The question of military activities in space could not be divorced from the question of military activities on Earth. The test of any space activity must therefore be not whether it was military or non-military but whether it was consistent with the Charter and other obligations of international law.[185]

While the United States clearly stated its position that the phrase 'peaceful purposes' referred to non-aggressive conduct and the US delegation to the UNCOPUOS Legal Sub-Committee also voted to place that phrase (as applicable to outer space generally) in the Preamble and not the text, the Soviet delegation to the UNCOPUOS Legal Sub-Committee took a different approach—but ultimately reached essentially the same result. On the diplomatic front, the Soviet Union and its allies were vocal proponents of a ban on military uses of space.[186] Yet at the same time, it was a well-known fact that both the United States and the Soviet Union had already launched satellites into space for military purposes (particularly reconnaissance satellites).[187] Any examination of a ban on such satellites would have thus raised controversial issues. The Soviet delegation avoided this discussion by arguing that, as a procedural matter, the non-military use of space was inseparably linked to broader, general demilitarization talks which were taking place in another UN body, namely the Conference on Disarmament.[188] Thus, in spite of its demilitarization rhetoric, the Soviet Union ultimately supported applying the phrase peaceful purposes in the text only to celestial bodies in the Article IV of the OST and limiting its application to space to aspirational references in the Preamble. This was done despite protests and appeals for reconsideration by other States.[189]

7.

---

[185] UNGA First Committee, 'Summary Record of the 1422nd Meeting' (20 December 1965) UN Doc A/C.1/SR.1422, 429 (remarks of the US Ambassador Charles Yost). Similarly, in 1962 the US representative to the United Nations First Committee said: 'It is the view of the United States that outer space should be used only for peaceful—that is, non-aggressive and beneficial—purposes.' See also UNGA First Committee, 'Verbatim Record of the Twelve Hundred and Eighty-Ninth Meeting' (3 December 1962) UN Doc A/C.1/PV. 1289, 13.
[186] UNCOPUOS Legal Sub-Committee Summary Record 66 (n 137) 7 (during the preparatory work of the OST in the UNCOPUOS Legal Sub-Committee, the Soviet representative (Mr Morozov) stated that the Soviet Union was 'naturally in favour of a total ban on the use of outer space for military purposes').
[187] Dembling and Arons (n 123) 419.
[188] UNCOPUOS Legal Sub-Committee Summary Record 66 (n 137) (in deferring an Indian proposal to extend the peaceful purposes language in the draft OST to outer space generally, the Soviet representative sought to 'avoid being sidetracked into discussions of too general a nature' and referred the Indian representative to 'discussions in the Disarmament Committee regarding the question of banning the use of space for military purposes').
[189] See UNCOPUOS Legal Sub-Committee Summary Record 66 (n 137) 6–7 (statements by the Indian and Iranian delegates); UNCOPUOS Legal Sub-Committee Summary Record 71 (n 183) 10–19 (statements by the Austrian, Japanese, Brazilian, and Mexican delegates).

Importantly, however, these protests and appeals were not reflected in the final draft of the OST and are thus not the law governing outer space today.

8. The decision by the Soviets to agree to exclude the reference to peaceful purposes in space from the text of the OST left them with a position that effectively corresponded with the US interpretation: that military activities in space are not prohibited if they are 'non-aggressive' in accordance with UN Charter obligations and not in violation of any specific restrictions found in any other applicable treaty. This position—rejecting any ban on the military use of space—is also later reflected in the views of prominent Soviet scholars regarding the broad scope of permissible military activities in space and the regrettable absence of a demilitarization regime in space.[190]

9. National space legislation of the Russian Federation, the successor State to the USSR, currently contains numerous references to 'military space technology' and at the same time provides that one of the '[m]ain tasks of space activity under the jurisdiction of Russian Federation shall be ... ensuring defense capabilities of Russian Federation'.[191] Such references and goals are consistent with a State's right under the UN Charter to engage in self-defence, but are inconsistent with any argument that the 'non-militarization' of space is required by the concept of 'peaceful purposes'.

Subsequent State Practice Rejecting a 'Non-Military' Interpretation of Peaceful Purposes in Space in Favour of a 'Non-Aggressive' Interpretation

10. The subsequent practice of Parties in implementing a treaty is fundamentally important in interpreting phrases in a treaty.[192] In this regard, widespread, extensive, and continuous State practice involving diverse military space activities—dating back to the dawn of the space age—gives clear meaning to the concept of

---

[190] See Y Kolossov, 'Notions of "Peaceful" and "Military" Space Activities' in *Proceedings of the Twenty-Fifth Colloquium on the Law of Outer Space* (n 55) 117, 118 (noting that 'military aggressive activities are illegal according to international law and are regarded as a crime against international peace which gives rise to international responsibility ... [in contrast] non-aggressive military activities in outer space have been limited, but not banned. Such activities might include the use of missiles to repel acts of aggression, the use of various space objects (communications, navigation, meteorological satellites, etc.) ....'); Gennady Zhukov and Yuri Kolossov, *International Space Law* (Boris Belitzky tr, Praeger Publishers 1984) 59 (noting that in the absence of an agreement establishing a total demilitarization of space, 'international documents refer to the exploration and use of outer space for peaceful purposes exclusively merely as a goal to be pursued').

[191] 'Selected Examples of National Laws Governing Space Activities: Russian Federation' (United Nations Office for Outer Space Affairs) art 3 [https://perma.cc/NG7J-V9YR].

[192] VCLT (n 11) art 31, para 3(b) ('There shall be taken into account, together with the context ... (b) any subsequent practice in the application of the treaty which establishes the agreement of the parties regarding its interpretation ....').

peaceful purposes and removes any doubt about the lawfulness of non-aggressive military activities in space. Military satellites used by many States are a particularly powerful example of State practice. Satellites are fundamentally important to modern military operations and support essential military functions, including: global communications; positioning, navigation, and timing services; environmental monitoring; space-based intelligence, surveillance, and reconnaissance; and warning services for commanders. These important space capabilities help explain why so many satellites now orbiting Earth are military satellites.[193]

Although many commentators and some States early in the space era strongly supported the idea of a demilitarized space domain and viewed the phrase 'peaceful purposes' through that lens, the subsequent practice of States demonstrates that the 'non-military' interpretation of peaceful purposes has not prevailed in the international community. This point was highlighted in a working paper that was submitted by the Canadian delegation to the UN Conference on Disarmament as early as 1986. The paper evaluated the views of States concerning key words, phrases, and terms related to arms control and outer space and included an examination of the meaning of the phrase 'peaceful purposes'. After noting that the peaceful purposes requirement applies only to celestial bodies and not to Earth orbit or space generally, the Canadian delegation observed that Article III of the OST, which does apply to Earth orbit, 'requires states to conduct space activities in accordance with international law, including the United Nations Charter under which defensive or non-aggressive military activity is permissible'.[194] On this basis, the Canadian delegation concluded that it 'seems clear that the drafters of the Outer Space Treaty intended to restrict military activities only to the extent expressed in Article IV' and that the drafters 'merely required in Article III 'compliance by states with international law and the UN Charter, which do not prohibit military activities but aggression or a threat to, or breach of the peace'.[195] The Canadian delegation further argued that the practice of States provides clear support for the restrictive, non-aggressive interpretation of peaceful purposes as States continue to give clear meaning to this concept of peaceful purposes by their actions. While this was true when space was dominated by just a few space powers, this approach is supported even more clearly now by overwhelming State practice in the current space environment. As discussed in the following paragraphs, extensive, growing, and diverse military activities in, and military uses of, space by States continues in practice to reject defining the peaceful purposes as 'non-military'. Some States also

11.

---

[193] See 'Satellite Database', Union of Concerned Scientists, (n 88) (although military users of civilian imagery and communications satellites may be difficult to identify and classified missions may also mean that many 'government' satellites may also serve military purposes ones, the United States, Russia, and China alone have hundreds of satellites with designated military users/operators).
[194] Canada, 'Terminology Relevant to Arms Control and Outer Space' (n 119).
[195] ibid (also suggesting that some military satellites, such as those used for verification of arms control purposes, advanced the cause of world peace and were 'inherently stabilizing').

12. For example, France is the home of Europe's largest space programme which boasts a long history of both civil and military space activities, including the first French satellite in space, which was successfully launched in 1965. In 2019, the President of France announced the creation of a space command within France's Air Force, stating that the command would 'ensure our defense of space within space'.[196] He further added that the new space command would help to 'better protect our satellites, including in an active way'.[197] An incident in 2016 involving alleged intrusive actions by a Russian Luch-Olymp satellite against a French–Italian satellite had highlighted French concerns about the need for better defensive capabilities in space and prompted the French Minister of Defence to remark that '[we do] not want to embark on a space arms race,' but '[w]e will conduct a reasoned "arsenalization"'.[198] To support such efforts, the French military spending programme for 2019–2025 has earmarked €3.6 billion ($4.06 billion) for investments and renewal of French satellites.[199] Such French investments in military space technologies, growing French military space activities, and the key role that France plays in the European Space Agency (ESA) are all consistent with the interpretation of the phrase 'peaceful purposes' adopted by both the ESA and the European Defence Agency (EDA). As indicated by the Chief Executive of the EDA and the Director General of the ESA, the security initiatives of the ESA that are governed by that Agency's convention 'must be provided for exclusively peaceful purposes, a provision which has been interpreted under international law as non-aggressive uses of outer space'.[200]

---

[196] Norimitsu Onishi, 'France Nudges Europe Into Space Race, Where It Lags Behind' *NY Times* (New York, 18 July 2019) [https://perma.cc/3UMA-KQH8] (also quoting the President of the French Space Agency as saying, 'We already had a strong military program in space, ... [s]o it was logical to have a more structured organization.') The article further notes the call in 2018 by the US President for the establishment of a space force as a sixth branch of the American armed force, the creation by Russia of its own space command in 2011, and the identification of space by China as a critical part of its military strategy in a 2015 white paper on defence.

[197] 'France to Create New Space Defence Command in September' *BBC News* (London, 13 July 2019) [http://perma.cc/QH7X-Z6EY].

[198] Timothy Compston, 'Space Wars' *Intersec* (24 October 2019) [https://perma.cc/K948-P8JV].

[199] 'France to Create Space Command Within Air Force: Macron' *Reuters* (13 July 2019) [https://perma.cc/XHN4-633Z].

[200] Jorge Domecq (Chief Executive of the European Defence Agency) and Johann-Dietrich Wörner (Director-General of the European Space Agency), 'Space and Security: Crucial Synergies for European Citizens' (2017) European Defence Matters [https://perma.cc/V6SJ-M9QH]; See also 'The European Union and ESA: The Need for Closer Working Relations' (ESA 20 June 2002) [https://perma.cc/7HQ3-KDUU] ('It seems, on rereading the wording 'for exclusively peaceful purposes' in Article II of the Agency's convention ... that it no longer has the meaning intended at the time by the founders in the context of the Cold War. The concept has evolved a great deal over 30 years. For us today, it basically comes down to 'non-aggressive"').

In February 1970, Japan joined the list of countries to orbit a satellite around the Earth and has continued to actively develop its space programme since that time. In 1969, the same year in which Japan's space agency was established, the Japanese Diet adopted a resolution that effectively forbade any military use of space.[201] In 2008, however, the Japanese Diet enacted the Basic Space Law which explicitly authorized the State of Japan to 'take necessary measures to promote Space Development and Use to ensure international peace and security *as well as to contribute to the national security of Japan*'.[202] The effect of this legislation was to recognize the reality of ongoing military uses of space, lift the ban on the use of military technology in space, and bring Japan's interpretation of 'peaceful purposes' in line with the prevailing interpretation of the phrase as 'non-aggressive'.[203] The 2008 Basic Law thus authorized the Japanese Government to undertake a variety of surveillance, security, and military support functions in space.[204] A recent paper published by the Japanese Ministry of Defense Ministry and the Self Defense Forces (SDF) outlining goals, guidelines, and 'means to achieve objectives of defense' includes measures to strengthen important space capabilities and related joint, cross-domain operations.[205] It further notes that the SDF will establish and maintain a unit that 'specializes in space domain missions' and that it will 'strengthen its posture for joint operations in order to conduct persistent monitoring of situations in space, and to ensure superiority in use of space at all stages from peacetime to armed contingencies through such means as mission assurance and disruption of opponent's command, control, communications and information'.[206]

13.

---

[201] Paul Kallender, 'Japan's New Dual-Use Space Policy The Long Road to the 21st Century' (Center for Asian Studies November 2016) 17 (noting that 'Until 2008, Japanese space policy was uniquely wedded to a 1969 Peaceful Purposes Resolution (PPR) that forbad any military use of space … The National Diet's June 1969 adoption of the PPR strictly limited the development of space capabilities to "peaceful purposes only" (*heiwa no mokuteki ni kagiri*) and to an anti-militaristic principle that went beyond the United Nation's 1967 Outer Space Treaty').

[202] 'Basic Space Law (Law No 43 of 2008)' (Japan) (enacted 21 May 2008, effective 27 August 2008) art 14, [https://perma.cc/RJ7Z-3E3N] (emphasis added).

[203] Setsuko Aoki, 'Challenges for Japan's Space Strategy' (World Security Network 26 June 2008) [https://perma.cc/GMF5-JMXE] (noting that '[w]hile the term "peaceful purposes" has internationally been understood as "non-aggressive" from the advent of the space age, the same term has been interpreted as "non-military" in Japan.… The Basic Space Law, therefore, changes the interpretation of "peaceful purposes" from "non-military" to "non-aggressive" as understood by the rest of the world.'); Maeda Sawako, 'Transformation of Japanese Space Policy: From the 'Peaceful Use of space' to 'the Basic Law on Space' (2009) 7 The Asia-Pacific Journal 1 [https://perma.cc/HR7P-KKPV] (noting that 'after two decades of inconsistency between "the Principle of peaceful use of space" and the reality of militarized space activity, the new Japanese space law enacted in 2008 lifted the ban on the use of space technology for military purposes.… Japanese space policy reformed in 2008 implies the vision of the meaning of "peaceful" use from "non-military" use to "non-aggressive" use').

[204] Jessica West (ed), *Space Security 2009* (Space Security Index 2009) 60 [https://perma.cc/4DDB-5M8L] (noting that the Basic Law of 2008 'is based on the common interpretation of the Outer Space Treaty that allows for military use of space for peaceful purposes … and allows the deployment of satellites by the Ministry of Defense for non-aggressive purposes, including surveillance and military support functions, with possible early applications being missile warning, signals intelligence, and communications').

[205] Japanese Ministry of Defense, 'Defense of Japan 2019' (2019) 470 [https://perma.cc/R5D9-BZBH].

[206] ibid.

Other Examples of State Practice Showing Diverse and Growing Military Space Activities

14. A growing number of States are pursuing and/or expanding their military activities in space to enable them to improve protection and defence of their assets in space or to address other national security concerns.[207] The United Kingdom is such a State. It has a long history of space activities, becoming in 1962 the third nation after the Soviet Union and the United States to have a satellite in orbit. It operates a large number of both civil and military communications satellites, Earth observation satellites, and scientific and exploration spacecraft.[208] In its 2022 Defence Space Strategy, the UK Ministry of Defence stated that:

> [s]pace enables our ability to command and control globally, provide surveillance, intelligence and missile warning, as well as support deployed Joint forces ... UK Defence will be at the heart of Allied space efforts, providing resilience and complementarity in our joint pursuit for a safe and secure space domain ... we will help to prevent conflict, deter escalation, optimise resources and enhance mission assurance and resilience.[209]

    Toward these ends, and to 'both protect and defend the UK's equities in space and the services derived from space assets', the UK Ministry of Defence has stated that 'we will invest an extra £1.4bn in Defence space technologies over the next 10 years. This is in addition to the £5bn we are investing in Skynet satellite communications over a similar timeframe.'[210]

15. From modest beginnings in the 1990s, the space programme of the People's Republic of China has made impressive strides, becoming just the third nation to launch a human into space in 2003. Since that time, Chinese space activities have steadily grown and expanded. Although China has a significant military space programme, it has not produced a publicly available, fully articulated national space military policy. However, the Information Office of the State Council of the People's Republic of China published a white paper on China's Military Strategy in 2015 which clearly recognized that outer space has become one of the 'new commanding

---

[207] It may also be noted that no practice can be identified in which a State has engaged in military activities in outer space for the stated purposes of taking a 'counter-measure'—ie taking an action that they regard themselves as an action that would ordinarily be illegal but is made legal by being a response to a prior illegal act of another State.

[208] Aerospace Technology, 'The 10 Countries Most Active in Space' (21 December 2015) [https://perma.cc/E2V6-WNPZ] (further noting that 'the UK is one of the largest monetary contributors to the European Space Agency').

[209] UK Policy paper, 'National Space Strategy', p 6, February 2022 [https://perma.cc/3DW8-AA9U].

[210] UK Ministry of Defence, 'Defence Space Strategy: Operationalising the Space Domain' [https://perma.cc/4BCZ-WUTW] (also noting that the 'UK Space Command will lead our approach to space operations, Force Generation and capability programmes, supporting the government and Joint Commanders in standing Defence tasks, overseas operations and contingent functions').

heights in strategic competition among all parties' and that China will 'deal with security threats and challenges in [the outer space] domain, and secure its space assets to serve its national economic and social development, and maintain outer space security'.²¹¹ Another white paper issued by the Information Office of the State Council of the People's Republic of China in 2016 on 'China's space activities' chose not to equate the phrase 'peaceful purposes' with 'non-military', but noted only that it adheres to the principle of the use of outer space for peaceful purposes and 'opposes the weaponization of or an arms race in outer space'.²¹² China's 'vision' to 'build China into a space power in all respects' does, however, include efforts 'to effectively and reliably guarantee national security'.²¹³ Such efforts have in the past notably included an anti-satellite (ASAT) weapon test against one of its own weather satellites in 2007, creating a cloud of more than 3,000 pieces of space debris.²¹⁴

Although the Government of India took the view during the negotiation of the OST that the concept of peaceful purposes should exclude military activities and that space should be demilitarized, its own ASAT test in 2019 clearly demonstrated its desire to develop military space capabilities and become a 'space power'.²¹⁵ Responding to international criticism of its ASAT test, the Indian Government further argued that 'India is not in violation of any international law or Treaty to which it is a Party or any national obligation' and noted that '[t]he Outer Space Treaty prohibits only weapons of mass destruction in outer space, not ordinary weapons'.²¹⁶ After its ASAT test on 27 March India insisted that it was 'against the weaponization of Outer Space and supports international efforts to reinforce the safety and security of space-based assets'. India is continuing to develop and organize its military space capabilities.²¹⁷

16.

---

²¹¹ 'China's Military Strategy' *Xinhua* (26 May 2015) [https://perma.cc/86PM-FMFD].
²¹² State Council, People's Republic of China, 'Full Text of White Paper on China's Space Activities in 2016' *China Daily* (Beijing, 28 December 2016) [https://perma.cc/86PM-FMFD].
²¹³ ibid.
²¹⁴ Brian Weeden, '2007 Chinese Anti-Satellite Test Fact Sheet' (Secure World Foundation, 23 November 2010) [https://perma.cc/3V9G-DJDG] (further noting that much of the debris from the destruction of this Fengyun 3C weather satellite 'will remain in orbit for decades, posing a significant collision threat to other space objects in Low Earth Orbit (LEO)').
²¹⁵ Bibhudatta Pradhan and Archana Chaudhary, 'Modi Says Satellite Destruction Shows India is Now a "Space Power"' *Bloomberg News* (New York, 27 March 2019) [https://perma.cc/K5X6-5NW2] (further noting the announcement in a televised address by Prime Minister Modi to the nation that '[o]ur scientists used an anti-satellite missile to bring down a live satellite, 300 kilometers away in space', and that 'India had joined the U.S., Russia and China in an elite group of nations that have the capability to target satellites').
²¹⁶ ibid.
²¹⁷ 'Defence Space Agency to Come Up at Bengaluru' *Business Standard* (15 May 2019)('Soon after it successfully carried out an anti-satellite test, India is setting up its military space agency headquartered at Bengaluru ... the tri-services Space agency is likely to command all the space assets of the three services including the A-SAT capability, which can be used to destroy enemy space-based satellites and other assets.').

17. Through their legislation, regulations, policy statements, programmes, or activities, many other States continue to give meaning to the phrase 'peaceful purposes' in outer space by launching or operating military satellites, establishing military and national security space agencies, placing space programmes under the jurisdiction of military and defence organizations, or by planning to engage in such military and national security space activities in the future. For example, the United Arab Emirates National Space Strategy 5.1.1 aims to 'develop and acquire appropriate capabilities and technologies to enable various national security activities in times of peace, crisis, and conflict';[218] the Nigerian National Space Policy states that 'there shall be a Defence Space Command which would facilitate and implement the Defence and security aspects of the National Space Policy and Programmes 2001 for the enhancement of national security and development';[219] in a statement emailed on 8 November 2018 to the Chinese news agency Xinhua, Ethiopian Prime Minister Abiy's office stated that '[c]onsidering the context of modern warfare (land, air, seas, cyber and space), a defense force that can readily meet this context is in the process of being built' and that in addition to other programmes, Ethiopia's defence forces law 'will in future also include Cyber Security and Space Force considerations';[220] and the Director General of the Israeli Space Agency has noted that '[s]ince the beginning of the 1980s, the State of Israel's space activity has been the result of a national security need'.[221] Consistent with this stated national security need, on 6 July 2020, the Defense Minister of Israel hailed the launch of the Ofek-16 military reconnaissance satellite into orbit as an 'extraordinary achievement for the defense establishment, for the defense industries as a whole, and for Israel Aerospace Industries in particular'.[222] On 22 April 2020, the Revolutionary Guard Corps of the Islamic Republic of Iran announced that it successfully launched the country's first military reconnaissance satellite.[223]

---

[218] United Arab Emirates, 'National Space Policy of the United Arab Emirates' (UAE Government September 2016) 5.1.1. [https://perma.cc/F3P8-MLL3].
[219] Nigerian Defense Security Administration, 'History of the DSA' (Nigerian Defence Space Administration 2022) [https://perma.cc/5RTY-VQPT], (noting that the National Assembly of the Federal Republic of Nigeria established the Nigerian Defense Space Administration to, *inter alia*, '[d]evelop and operate military Space Technologies').
[220] 'Ethiopia Mulls Creating Space, Cyber Commands as Part of Defence Reforms' (Spacewatch Africa) [https://perma.cc/4SYL-AMHE].
[221] Avi Blasberger (Director General of the Israeli Space Agency) 'Director General's Message' (Israel Space Agency) [https://perma.cc/M7VC-5Z55] (stating that '[s]ince the beginning of the 1980s, the State of Israel's space activity has been the result of a national security need').
[222] 'The Israel Ministry of Defense and IAI Have Successfully Launched the Ofek 16 Satellite—Which Has Begun its Orbit in Space' (Israeli Aerospace Industries 6 July 2020) [https://perma.cc/5F64-7FVB] (further noting that the Ofek 16 is 'an electro-optical reconnaissance satellite with advanced capabilities' and that its development was enabled by 'the great experience gained by the defense establishment in the production of earlier satellites in the Ofek series, which have been produced and launched since the year 1988').
[223] 'Iran's Revolutionary Guards "Successfully Launch Military Satellite"' *BBC News* (London, 22 April 2020) [https://perma.cc/7ZGC-WJHT] (quoting the Revolutionary Guard Corps commander-in-chief, Maj-Gen Hossein Salami, as saying that the force had taken 'a major step in promoting the scope of [its] strategic information capabilities' and that '[t]oday, we are looking at the Earth from the

No General Ban on Weapons

As correctly noted by the Government of India in 2019, 'the Outer Space Treaty prohibits only weapons of mass destruction in outer space, not ordinary weapons'.[224] Furthermore, the precise drafting of the prohibition in Article IV, paragraph 1 only bans States from placing weapons of mass destruction (WMDs) in orbit around the Earth, installing them on celestial bodies, or stationing them in outer space in any other manner. The OST thus does not ban the use of outer space for the transit of ballistic missiles carrying nuclear warheads, a use which was not unfamiliar to the space powers and other States drafting the OST (see Rule 5: Weapons of Mass Destruction). With no other explicit prohibitions, States remain free to deploy other types of weapon systems in space,[225] although some uses of these weapons are of course restricted by the United Nations Charter, other international agreements, and other applicable rules of international law. For example, weapons that are by nature indiscriminate, or of a nature to cause superfluous injury or unnecessary suffering, are prohibited (see Rule 32: Distinction; Rule 42: Means and Methods of Warfare Generally). It is also important to note that while the testing of weapons is explicitly banned on the Moon and other celestial bodies, conventional weapons are not banned on the Moon and other celestial bodies under the OST.[226] However, there are other international agreements that ban specific conventional weapons[227] as well as agreements banning the possession and use of weapons of mass destruction. These agreements are not limited in their application to any specific domain (see Rule 5: Weapons of Mass Destruction).

18.

---

sky, and it is the beginning of the formation of a world power'); 'Iran Launches its First Military Satellite' *Al Jazeera* (Doha, 22 April 2020) [https://perma.cc/Z9KV-TYEB].

[224] Pradhan and Chaudhary (n 215).

[225] Aleksandr Klapovskiy and Vladimir Yermakof, 'Russia and the Outer Space Treaty' in Ajey Lele (ed), *Fifty Years of the Outer Space Treaty* (Institute for Defence Studies & Analyses 2017) 106 ('However, one should not forget that the OST fully bans only WMD in outer space. Regrettably, many "loopholes" in the ISL [international space law] regarding other types of weapons remain unaddressed. Therefore, conceptually, we need to bear in mind that, from a legal point of view, outer space remains unprotected from attempts of turning it into a new arena of military confrontation. Theoretically, non-WMD weapons may be placed into outer space any moment and become weapons of an actual prompt and clandestine use with a global outreach.'). In the absence of any legally binding obligation to prevent the placement of non-WMD weapons in space, some efforts in the United Nations General Assembly have focused on 'encourag[ing] all States, especially space-faring nations, to consider the possibility of upholding as appropriate a political commitment not to be the first to place weapons in outer space'. UNGA, 'No first Placement of Weapons in Outer Space' (2 December 2014) UN Doc A/RES/69/32, 5.

[226] See Rule 4: Restrictions on Specified Military Establishments and Activities on Celestial Bodies. It should also be noted that the 18 States that are parties to the Moon Treaty are subject to additional restrictions with respect to military activities on the Moon, including the prohibition of '[a]ny threat or use of force or any other hostile act or threat of hostile act on the moon' and the use of the Moon to 'engage in any such threat in relation to the earth, the moon, spacecraft, the personnel of spacecraft or man-made space objects'. Moon Agreement (n 46) art 3(2).

[227] See eg Convention on Prohibitions or Restrictions on the Use of Certain Conventional Weapons Which May be Deemed to be Excessively Injurious or to Have Indiscriminate Effects (and Protocols) (10 October 1980) 1342 UNTS 137.

19. It is also important to note that, as observed by the Canadian Government, although the phrases 'weaponization' and 'militarization' have been widely used in a political context, they 'are even more ambiguous ... and are not used in space law and do not even appear to have any generally accepted meaning in political discussions'.[228]

---

[228] Canada 'Terminology Relevant to Arms Control and Outer Space' (n 119) 14.

Rule 4
Restrictions on Specified Military Establishments and Activities on Celestial Bodies

A State shall use the Moon and other celestial bodies exclusively for peaceful purposes (i.e., it shall engage in only non-aggressive uses) and shall not engage in the following specified military activities on the Moon and other celestial bodies: the establishment of military bases, installations and fortifications; the testing of any type of weapons; and the conduct of military manoeuvres.

Overview of Legal Basis of Rule

1. This Rule is based on Article IV, paragraph 2 of the Outer Space Treaty (OST). The growing consensus view of the phrase 'peaceful purposes' refers to non-aggressive actions consistent with the requirements of the UN Charter (see Rule 3: Peaceful Purposes in Outer Space). The term 'exclusively peaceful purposes'[229] is effectively defined by the contents of the one paragraph in Article IV of the OST to which it applies, where it adds restrictions on specific military establishments and activities while continuing to require non-aggressive uses of space (ie compliance with UN Charter obligations).[230] Thus, the establishment of military bases, installations and fortifications, the testing of any type of weapons, and the conduct of military manoeuvres on celestial bodies are explicitly forbidden.[231] While the testing of weapons on the Moon and other celestial bodies is explicitly prohibited, weapons themselves are not banned by the OST, unless they involve the stationing or installing of weapons of mass destruction,[232] are an integral part of a 'fortification'; are integral to the conduct of military 'manoeuvres'; are stored in sufficient quantity at a particular location to constitute a military 'base', 'installation', or 'fortification'; or are

---

[229] The term 'exclusively peaceful purposes' is not defined or explained in the OST and is made applicable only to the test of art IV(2).

[230] OST (n 9) art IV, para 2 ('[t]he Moon and other celestial bodies shall be used by all States Parties to the Treaty exclusively for peaceful purposes').

[231] ibid. At State Consultations, one State noted that it would not regard the specified military activities in art IV 'as necessarily inconsistent with the use of space for peaceful purposes—for example, these activities could be lawful military activities in self-defense'.

[232] OST (n 9) art IV, para 1.

present for the purpose of 'testing'.[233] It is important in this regard to also note that military personnel and equipment are not completely banned on the Moon and other celestial bodies. Instead, the remainder of Article IV provides that '[t]he use of military personnel for scientific research or for any other peaceful purposes shall not be prohibited'.[234] The use of any equipment or facility necessary for the peaceful exploration of the Moon and other celestial bodies shall also not be prohibited.[235]

2. One view suggested by some commentators is that Article IV, paragraph 2, essentially imposes a demilitarization regime for the Moon and other celestial bodies and allows only specified military activities to occur there.[236] The better view adopted by this *Manual* and supported by the drafting history of Article IV, the analysis of the text of that Article provided shortly, and the meaning of the term 'peaceful purposes' as examined in Rule 5: Weapons of Mass Destruction, concludes that the obligation in Article IV paragraph 2 to use the Moon and other celestial bodies for 'exclusively peaceful purposes' does not impose any restrictions on military activities on the Moon and other celestial bodies beyond those activities which are explicitly prohibited in Article IV, as long as those activities are non-aggressive (ie do not involve the unlawful threat or use of force under the UN Charter).

---

[233] For example, art IV does not prohibit an astronaut from carrying a personal side arm. One such weapon would not, by itself, transform the location or facility where the astronaut lives and works into a military base, installation, or fortification. If the astronaut possesses numerous weapons, or if the astronaut leaves weapons behind when leaving the Moon, then it may be possible to argue that the location or facility where the weapons are held has become a 'military base, installation or fortification'. The OST does not define what constitutes a military base, installation, fortification, or what constitutes military manoeuvres.

[234] It should also be noted that the lawful exercise by a State of its inherent right of self-defence is a non-aggressive act consistent with the term 'peaceful purposes'. See eg United States Department of Defense, 'Department of Defense Law of War Manual' (December 2016 edn, US DoD 2015) (US DoD Law of War Manual) para 14.10.4 ('lawful military activities in self-defense (eg missile early warning, use of weapon systems) would be consistent with the use of space for peaceful purposes, but aggressive activities that violate the Charter of the United Nations would not be permissible'). For further discussion of the self-defence issue, see para 9.

[235] ibid. See further discussion of military equipment on the Moon, para 7.

[236] This view would hold that limiting the phrase 'exclusively for peaceful purposes' to the listed prohibitions in art IV(2) of the OST would deprive the provision of any effect. However, the text of art IV(2) does in fact impose significant additional obligations on States in the form of the specific stated restrictions on military activities, packaged in this article in this way by the States drafting the OST. Even if this result is viewed as rendering nugatory the word 'exclusively'—in what would ordinarily be a disfavoured approach to treaty interpretation—such a result is sometimes unavoidable based on the complex negotiations of the text of a particular treaty (particularly using modified provisions from another treaty, in this case the Antarctic Treaty (see paras 4–6). It is thus unclear what, if anything, the word 'exclusively' adds to the meaning peaceful purposes. In fact, the term 'peaceful purposes' and 'exclusively peaceful purposes' have sometimes been used interchangeably to mean the same thing: the non-aggressive use of space. See eg Domecq and Wörner (n 200) (noting that under the second article of ESA's Convention, ESA security initiatives 'must be provided for exclusively peaceful purposes, a provision which has been interpreted under international law as non-aggressive uses of outer space').

Inapplicability of the Moon Agreement to States That Are Not Parties to It

3. Some confusion on the part of writers in interpreting the international law applicable to military activities on the Moon and other celestial bodies is due to the inappropriate interposition of terms found in the Moon Agreement.[237] The Moon Agreement does not reflect customary international law and thus is binding on only the 18 States that are Parties to that Treaty. Notably, those 18 States do not include any of the major spacefaring or space-technology States, except Australia and Kazakhstan.[238] Under Article 3 of the Moon Agreement, which also uses the term 'exclusively peaceful purposes', significant, broad, undefined restrictions are imposed on military activities on the Moon and other celestial bodies and those constraints are different and more restrictive than those found in the OST. For example, under the Moon Agreement, States are prohibited from engaging in any 'hostile act or threat of hostile act on the Moon' and are further broadly prohibited 'to use the Moon in order to commit any such act or to engage in any such threat in relation to the Earth, the moon, spacecraft, the personnel of spacecraft or man-made space objects'.[239] As noted, these restrictions and similar concepts are not found in the OST or in customary international law, but are nonetheless sometimes mistakenly attributed by writers to be part of the legal regime now generally governing military activities on the Moon.

The Nature of the List of Prohibited Military Activities in Article IV and the Travaux Préparatoires of the Outer Space Treaty

4. One view of the restrictions on military establishments and activities found in Article IV, paragraph 2, might suggest that these restrictions are only *examples* of prohibited conduct and that the phrase 'exclusively for peaceful purposes' should be read expansively to prohibit all military activities and personnel except those engaged in non-military scientific research. However, this interpretation is impossible to reconcile with both the widely accepted understanding of the term 'peaceful purposes' (see Rule 3: Peaceful Purposes in Outer Space) and the drafting choices made by the States who constructed paragraph 2 of Article IV. Any argument that the list of prohibited military establishments and activities should be

---

[237] Moon Agreement (n 46).
[238] 'Status of International Agreements relating to Activities in Outer Space' (n 51). France and India signed the Moon Agreement in 1980 and 1982, respectively, but have never ratified it to become parties to the Treaty. See the Overview of the Space Law Regime, paras 23–34 for further examination of the Moon Agreement.
[239] Moon Agreement (n 46) art 3(2).

viewed as merely exemplary (and not exhaustive) is undermined by the fact that the prohibited military establishments and activities in question are not preceded by any words or phrases presupposing that they were meant to represent generic enumerations. Hence, the phrases 'such as' and *'inter alia'* are missing, even though the original model text clearly used by the drafters for the text of paragraph 2 of Article IV included both of these phrases. This important decision by the drafting States becomes apparent when one examines the negotiating history of Article IV, an article which was modelled after Article I of the 1961 Antarctic Treaty.[240]

5. The Antarctic Treaty, which had entered into force just a few years before the drafting of the OST, has been described by the UN General Assembly as a treaty requiring the 'the demilitarization of the continent'.[241] Significantly, however, while most of the language found in the second paragraph of Article IV of the OST is indeed identical to the language found in Article I of the Antarctic Treaty, Article I of the Antarctic Treaty goes much further in banning military activities by first prohibiting 'any measures of a military nature'.[242] Not only is this important phrase missing, but two signals that precede the list of explicitly banned military activities in the Antarctic Treaty are also absent. Thus, the drafters of the OST chose to *exclude* from the OST the following italicized key phrase and two signals that would have been used to indicate a generic, non-exhaustive list of military activities: 'There shall be prohibited, *inter alia*, any *measures of a military nature, such as* ....'[243]

6. The key words in Article I of the Antarctic Treaty which were excluded from the OST, had they been adopted, would have made the explicitly banned military establishments and activities in the OST clearly represent merely examples or illustrations of prohibited conduct and establishments. Obviously, however, that was not the approach chosen by the drafters of the OST. Unlike Article I of the Antarctic Treaty, Article IV of the OST thus does not 'demilitarize' the Moon and other celestial bodies by banning '*inter alia* measures of a military nature', and then listing prohibited military activities after the words 'such as'.[244] Instead, the OST simply prohibits three types of specified military activities, without the additional language which serves to identify these prohibitions as merely examples of intended demilitarization.[245] Furthermore, as noted, the OST does not contain the more restrictive language on military activities that is found in the Moon Agreement.

---

[240] The Antarctic Treaty (signed 1 December 1959, entered into force 23 June 1961) 402 UNTS 71.
[241] See eg UNGA Resolution 51/56 (9 Jan 1997) UN Doc A/RES/51/56, 1 [https://perma.cc/9MQA-9G5K] ('Recognizing that the Antarctic Treaty, which provides, inter alia, for the demilitarization of the continent ....').
[242] The Antarctic Treaty (n 240) art I.1.
[243] ibid (emphasis added).
[244] ibid.
[245] As noted by the US Representative on the UNCOPUOS Legal Sub-Committee, only 'certain restrictions on military activities in the Antarctic Treaty should be applied to activities on celestial bodies',

Military Equipment on the Moon

In evaluating the broad intended scope of permissible military activities on the Moon and other celestial bodies in paragraph 2 of Article IV, it is again instructive to turn to the travaux préparatoires of the OST. One of the most contentious issues in the negotiation of Article IV concerned the proposal by the United States to include an exception for '[t]he use of any equipment or facility necessary for peaceful exploration of the Moon and other celestial bodies'.[246] Stating that '[f]or any country engaging in space activity, military personnel, facilities and equipment played an indispensable role and would continue to be an essential part of future space programs', the United States argued in the UNCOPUOS Legal Sub-Committee that all types of equipment, including military equipment, should be permitted on celestial bodies.[247] The Soviet Union and its allied States initially strongly opposed the US proposal, arguing that it was inconsistent with the requirement that celestial bodies be used exclusively for peaceful purposes.[248] Representatives of these States further argued that any exception for the use of military equipment on celestial bodies 'would, by implication, leave a loop-hole for non-peaceful activities'.[249] Ultimately, however, these arguments did not prevail and the unmodified US proposal was adopted, leaving the criticized so-called loopholes and inconsistencies in the legal fabric of Article IV, paragraph 2. In light of this, it is difficult to argue that paragraph 2 prohibits the use of equipment on the Moon or other celestial bodies based solely on the equipment's military origins, prior military use, or possible military applications.[250] It can also be strongly argued, based on the travaux préparatoires, that the undefined term 'scientific research' in paragraph 2 does not exclude the possibility of research that has potential

7.

UNCOPUOS Legal Sub-Committee 'Summary Record of the Sixty-Fifth Meeting' (22 July 1966) A/AC.105/C.2/SR.65, 9 (UNCOPUOS Legal Sub-Committee Summary Record 65).

[246] OST (n 9) art IV, para 2.
[247] UNCOPUOS Legal Sub-Committee Summary Record 65 (n 245) 9 (remarks of Mr Goldberg, United States).
[248] UNCOPUOS Legal Sub-Committee 'Summary Record of the Seventieth Meeting' (3 August 1966) A/AC.105/C.2/SR.70, 3 [https://perma.cc/8AMR-86V4] (remarks of Mr Morozov, USSR) (arguing that the placement of military equipment on celestial bodies 'might result in activities which would run directly counter to the principle of the use of celestial bodies exclusively for peaceful purposes'). Regarding the perceived 'inconsistency' of the US approach with peaceful purposes, see UNCOPUOS Legal Sub-Committee Summary Record 71 (n 183) 21–22 (remarks Mr Partli, Hungary); ibid 24 (remarks of Mr Jarozek, Poland).
[249] UNCOPUOS Legal Sub-Committee Summary Record 71 (n 183) 12 (remarks of Mr Dashtseren, Mongolia). Similarly, the Soviet representative had previously argued that 'if the use of military equipment in outer space was allowed, the essence of the treaty would be distorted and a loophole would be created for evading one of its fundamental provisions'. UNCOPUOS Legal Sub-Committee Summary Record 65 (n 245) 11 (remarks of Mr Morozov, USSR).
[250] It should be noted that many types of equipment in space have military utility and that military equipment may have a lawful purpose in support of a State's inherent right to engage in self-defence.

military applications.²⁵¹ With respect to weapons, the OST prohibits weapons of mass destruction, the testing of weapons more generally, as well as any weapon that would be an integral part of a military installation or military manoeuvres. Furthermore, under customary and treaty law, many prohibitions and limits on weapons, as well as on means and methods of warfare, are applicable to outer space, including the Moon and other celestial bodies.

8. Although the Moon is specifically referenced elsewhere in the OST, it is not expressly included in the first paragraph of Article IV or in the second sentence of the second paragraph of Article IV. However, there is no indication in the travaux préparatoires that the States drafting the OST intended to exclude the Moon from these provisions. Furthermore, by referring repeatedly to 'the Moon and other celestial bodies' in its title and Articles, the text of the OST makes it clear that the Moon is included in the notion of celestial bodies. It would also be counterintuitive to permit an interpretation of the text that allowed installation or stationing of weapons of mass destruction on the Moon and not on other celestial bodies. This drafting error (ie omitting the word 'Moon' in these passages of Article IV) highlights the difficult context in which the Article was drafted and how the end result must be cautiously interpreted: some words may have been lost or their meaning displaced in the negotiation and conclusions of the final draft of the text.

Self-Defence and Armed Conflict

9. In accordance with Article III of the OST, a State retains its inherent right to self-defence under the UN Charter with respect to activities in space,²⁵² as well as the corresponding right to possess the instruments and weapons necessary to exercise

---

²⁵¹ In successfully making its case before the Legal Sub-Committee for the inclusion in OST art IV para 2 of the broad term 'any equipment' (without the exclusion of military equipment), the United States argued that 'man could not have penetrated outer space and survived in that hostile environment unless he had been able to draw upon the benefits of all research, civilian or military, involving both personnel and equipment'. UNCOPUOS Legal Sub-Committee Summary Record 65 (n 245) 9 (remarks of Mr Goldberg, United States). This focus on research is significant, as the United States also argued that much of the equipment used in outer space 'had been developed through military research' and referred to the rockets that carried astronauts into space as an example of this practice. UNCOPUOS Legal Sub-Committee Summary Record 70 (n 248) 6 (remarks of Mr Goldberg, United States). The United States further argued that the reliance on military research for these rockets 'could not, however, be said to constitute a violation of the principle of the peaceful uses of outer space'. ibid. Similarly, the representative of the United Kingdom argued that '[t]he fact that a piece of equipment owed its origin to military development should not preclude its use for peaceful purposes foreseen by the Treaty and apparent to all as peaceful purposes'. UNCOPUOS Legal Sub-Committee Summary Record 71 (n 183) 5 (remarks of Mr Darwin, United Kingdom).

²⁵² OST (n 9) art III ('States Parties to the Treaty shall carry on activities in the exploration and use of outer space, including the Moon and other celestial bodies, in accordance with international law, including the Charter of the United Nations ....'). A complete ban on all weapons in a particular place would greatly diminish the right of a State to exercise the right to self-defence there. A State at State Consultations noted in this regard that a State may always agree to not position or use weapons in a particular place. However, whether such a ban or restriction prevails over a State's right to engage in self-defence is a complicated issue to be assessed on a case-by-case basis, in accordance with the methodology discussed in this Rule and in the Methodology of *Manual*.

that right of self-defence. As is discussed in the commentary to Rule 5: Weapons of Mass Destruction (which focuses upon the WMD prohibitions contained in the first paragraph of Article IV) there is authority for this inherent right of self-defence to supersede an otherwise applicable treaty provision incompatible with that right. Such a proposition is expressly accepted by the ILC in the draft Articles on the Effects of Armed Conflicts on Treaties[253] and follows from normal canons of interpretation, especially in view of the likely *jus cogens* nature[254] of the inherent right of self-defence (see Methodology of *Manual*). While there is yet no State practice that has invoked Article 51 of the UN Charter to supersede an obligation under Article IV of the OST, it is likely that such invocation would be exercised in only the narrowest of circumstances.[255] There is an expectation under international law that all obligations arising from whatever source are to be accommodated and observed to the greatest extent (see Methodology of *Manual*). However, consistent with the right of self-defence which requires that the elements of necessity and proportionality are properly met, there exists the possibility that a State may supersede inconsistent treaty or customary international law obligations relevant to the positioning and use of nuclear weapons where there is no other reasonable option available to that State. While a treaty provision that is intended to apply even in armed conflict (such as rules about treatment of prisoners of war) will not be superseded during an armed conflict, the provisions of the OST do not carry indicia that they were intended to continue to apply in armed conflict. Hence in the context of the prohibitions contained in the second paragraph of Article IV, a State invoking its right to self-defence in conformity with the UN Charter, would, for example, be legally able to conduct military manoeuvres, establish military bases, installations, and fortifications as well as test weapons in a case where such restrictions would effectively prevent a State from exercising the right of self-defence.[256]

---

[253] International Law Commission, 'Report on the Work of Its 63rd Session' (26 April–3 June and 4 July–12 Aug 2011) UN Doc A/66/10, 175–211. As noted by a State in State Consultations, self-defence is also a circumstance precluding wrongfulness, so that even if the right to self-defence does not supersede another rule of international law, it can excuse a violation of that rule. See ILC, 'Responsibility of States for Internationally Wrongful Acts' UNGA Res A/Res/56/83 (adopted 28 January 2002) (ILC Articles on State Responsibility) art 21 ('The wrongfulness of an act of a State is precluded if the act constitutes a lawful measure of self-defence taken in conformity with the Charter of the United Nations.').

[254] The possible *jus cogens* status of the right of self-defence is disputed. However, even if it is merely an 'inherent' right and not *jus cogens*, it should be sufficiently important to supersede treaty rules that are not specific to an armed conflict. Whether this inherent right supersedes a particular provision in a treaty is a question that must be resolved on a case-by-case basis.

[255] A representative of a State at State Consultations expressed a non-official view that art IV of the OST is neither superseded by art 51 of the Charter of the United Nations nor by the law of armed conflict because art IV is an obligation owed to the international community as a whole and meant for the benefit of humankind and hence cannot be superseded in general by rules regulating conflicts between two States or more (*erga omnes*). At a minimum, this State representative suggested that the principles of necessity and proportionality would create a high threshold for utilizing the Moon and other celestial bodies in the exercise of the right of self-defence due to the *erga omnes* status of art IV.

[256] At State Consultations, one State noted that it would not regard the specified military activities in art IV 'as necessarily inconsistent with the use of space for peaceful purposes—for example, these activities could be lawful military activities in self-defense'.

10. The ILC Draft Articles on the Effects of Armed Conflicts on Treaties also expressly recognizes that the law of armed conflict is the *lex specialis* in a situation in which there is a resort to armed force between States, as determined however on a case-by-case basis.[257] Hence inconsistent treaty obligations outside of the law of armed conflict will yield to the lawful rights and obligations that are exercised in a time of armed conflict (see Methodology of *Manual*). This does not mean that treaties such as the OST are suspended *in toto*; rather, the ILC recognized that other treaties such as the OST would largely continue to apply. However, where there is a direct conflict with specific provisions of the law of armed conflict, then such latter provisions will have priority in application. In the context of Article IV, this would mean that lawful belligerent rights of attack and capture of military objectives on celestial bodies could be exercised. Correlatively, so too would the humanitarian obligations apply under the law of armed conflict regarding the protection of civilians and civilian objects. While the law of armed conflict will generally have priority in a time of armed conflict, the extent to which space law rights and obligations yield to the law of armed conflict would need to be interpreted and reconciled on a case-by-case basis (see Methodology of *Manual*).

11. The OST is a multilateral treaty, so a belligerent that seeks to suspend the operation of part of the treaty vis-à-vis opposing belligerent(s) may also simultaneously be compromising the rights of other treaty parties that are not involved in the armed conflict. This dilemma may also be presented by the application of other multilateral treaties, such as the 1982 Law of the Sea Convention[258] and the 1944 Convention on International Civil Aviation, during a time of armed conflict.[259] As the exposition in the *San Remo Manual on the Law of Naval Warfare*[260] and the *HPCR Manual on International Law Applicable to Air and Missile Warfare*[261] reflects, the peacetime rights under these treaties of parties that are not involved in the conflict are subject to belligerent rights that may be exercised by States engaged in armed conflict under the *lex specialis* law of armed conflict.

---

[257] Report of the ILC on its 63rd Session (n 31) 181 (also noting that an armed conflict includes a 're-sort to armed force between governmental authorities and organized armed groups'). While Article 3 of the ILC Report states that 'the existence of an armed conflict does not ipso facto terminate or suspend the operation of treaties: (a) as between States parties to the conflict or (b) as between a State party to the conflict and a State that is not', art 14 further provides that '[a] State exercising its inherent right of individual or collective self-defence in accordance with the Charter of the United Nations is entitled to suspend in whole or in part the operation of a treaty to which it is a party insofar as that operation is incompatible with the exercise of that right'.
[258] UNCLOS (n 151).
[259] International Convention on Civil Aviation (n 103).
[260] International Institute of Humanitarian Law, *San Remo Manual on International Law Applicable to Armed Conflicts at Sea* (Louise Doswald-Beck, ed, CUP 1995).
[261] Program on Humanitarian Policy and Conflict Research at Harvard University, *HPCR Manual on International Law Applicable to Air and Missile Warfare* (CUP 2013).

Rule 5
Weapons of Mass Destruction

(a) Every State is prohibited from:
  i. Placing in orbit around the Earth any objects carrying nuclear weapons or any other kinds of weapons of mass destruction,
  ii. Installing nuclear weapons or any other kinds of weapons of mass destruction on celestial bodies,
  iii. Stationing nuclear weapons or any other kinds of weapons of mass destruction in outer space in any other manner.
(b) In addition, each party to the Treaty Banning Nuclear Weapon Tests in the Atmosphere, in Outer Space and Under Water (the PNTB Treaty)[262] is obligated to prohibit, to prevent, and not to carry out any nuclear weapon test explosion, or any other nuclear explosion, at any place under its jurisdiction and control beyond the limits of the atmosphere, including outer space.

Overview of Legal Basis of Rule

1. Subpart (a) of this Rule derives from Article IV, paragraph 1 of the Outer Space Treaty (OST). Article IV, paragraph 1 requires each party 'not to place in orbit around the Earth any objects containing nuclear weapons or any other kinds of weapons of mass destruction [WMD], install such weapons on celestial bodies, or station such weapons in outer space in any other manner'. Article IV, paragraph 1 is a codification of UN General Assembly Resolution 1884 of 1963.[263] Prior to Resolution 1884, both the United States and the Soviet Union, the only two States which had the capacity to do so, had announced their desire to conclude an agreement banning the orbiting of objects carrying nuclear weapons, and later the United States further proposed to add refraining from stationing or installing any objects carrying nuclear weapons or other WMDs in outer space.[264] After the

---

[262] Treaty Banning Nuclear Weapon Tests in the Atmosphere, in Outer Space and Under Water (entered into force 10 October 1963) 480 UNTS 43 (the 'PNTB' Treaty). This treaty is also known as the 'Limited Nuclear Test Ban Treaty'.
[263] UNGA Res 1884 (XVIII) (17 October 1963).
[264] US Department of State, 'OST Narrative' (Bureau of International Security and Nonproliferation) [https://perma.cc/FLP4-RQR2]. See also 'Address by President Dwight Eisenhower to the UN General Assembly' (n 140).

conclusion of the OST, relevant practices of States active in space have also been widespread and consistent in conformity with the content of this Rule; there is no contrary State practice or *opinio juris*. The legal basis for subpart (b) of this Rule is explained in paragraphs 18–24.

Place in Orbit Around the Earth, Install on Celestial Bodies, and Station in Outer Space

2. The OST does not define 'place in orbit'. There is no definitive evidence of State practice or *opinio juris* as to its precise meaning. However, relevant State practice indicates a general agreement that the prohibition includes a bar against placing a nuclear weapon in full orbit around the Earth, but does not apply to a temporary transit of space, such as via a long-range ballistic missile en route to a terrestrial target.[265] State practice reveals no consensus on how Article IV would apply to a nuclear weapon placed into a fractional orbit or suborbital flight.[266]

3. The OST also does not contain a definition of 'install' or 'station'. At a rather late stage of the negotiations for the OST, the terms 'install' and 'station' were still used interchangeably in the different drafts or in statements of governments.[267] The meanings of all three terms are very similar. They all presuppose a certain sense of permanence or fixation, requiring more than mere presence or transition, although it must be noted that nothing in space is truly 'stationary' or fixed in location, except in relationship to something else—all objects are travelling through space at high speed. The prohibition against 'stationing' WMD in space would go beyond the prohibition against placing those weapons into orbit

---

[265] US DoD Law of War Manual (n 234) para 14.10.3.1.

[266] The US believes that art IV prohibits only a nuclear weapon in full orbit around the Earth, not including fractional orbit or suborbital flight, see DoD Law of War Manual (n 234) para 14.10.3.1. Russia and China, in their Draft PPWT, took a different approach, and proposed that a weapon is 'placed in outer space' even if it only 'follows a section of' Earth orbit 'before leaving this orbit'. However, it is unclear whether this definition reflects Russian and China's understanding of the term 'place in orbit around the Earth' in art IV(1) of the OST, see 'Treaty on the Prevention of the Placement of Weapons in Outer Space, the Threat or Use of Force against Outer Space Objects' (Draft, 16 June 2014) art I(c) [perma.cc/48YR-TCA8]. Note also that art IX.1(c) of the Strategic Arms Limitation Talks (SALT) II Treaty prohibits fractional orbit bombardment systems, which suggests that those two States believed that the OST did not already prohibit it. Treaty Between the United States of America and the Union of Soviet Socialist Republics on the Limitation of Strategic Offensive Arms Together with Agreed Statements and Common Understandings Regarding the Treaty (SALT II) (signed 18 June 1979) art XI.1(c).

[267] 'Letter Dated 11 July 1966 addressed to the Chairman of the Legal Sub-Committee by the Representative of the USSR' (11 July 1966) UN Doc A/AC.105/C.2/L.13, art 4 of Draft Treaty; 'Letter Dated 16 June 1966 from the Permanent Representative of the United States of America Addressed to the Chairman of the Committee on the Peaceful Uses of Outer Space' (17 June 1966) UN Doc A/AC.105/32.

around the Earth by, for example, prohibiting placing those weapons in orbit around the Sun.[268]

4. Although the Moon is specifically referenced elsewhere in the OST, it is not expressly included in paragraph 1 of Article IV. However, there is no indication in the travaux préparatoires that the States drafting the OST intended to exclude the Moon from this provision. Furthermore, by referring repeatedly to 'the Moon and other celestial bodies' in its title and Articles, the text of the OST makes it clear that the Moon is included in the notion of celestial bodies. It would also be counterintuitive to permit an interpretation of the text that allowed installation or stationing of WMD on the Moon and not on other celestial bodies.

5. These prohibitions in the OST are only on the placement, installation, and stationing of nuclear weapons and other WMD in outer space. They do not cover the use or testing of such weapons in outer space (see Rule 4: Restrictions on Specified Military Establishments and Activities on Celestial Bodies). Nor do they apply to weapons other than WMD. However, the use of such weapons during armed conflicts shall in any case be subject to the rules and principles of international humanitarian law (IHL) and other applicable international legal rules.

Nuclear Weapons and Other Weapons of Mass Destruction

6. This Rule prohibits the stationing of nuclear weapons and other kinds of weapons of mass destruction in outer space. There is no definition of 'weapons of mass destruction' in the OST. However, in 1948, the UN Commission for Conventional Armaments (CCA) defined WMD as 'atomic explosive weapons, radio-active material weapons, lethal chemical and biological weapons, and any weapons developed in the future which have characteristics comparable in destructive effect to those of the atomic bomb or other weapons mentioned above'.[269] Subsequent UN documents repeatedly referred to this definition.[270]

7. While the negotiating history of the OST provides no further indication to the definition of WMD, the US lead negotiator, when answering questions at the subsequent US Senate ratification hearings, explained that the term included '[b]acteriological, any type of weapons which could lead to the same type of catastrophe that a nuclear weapon could lead to'.[271] In later hearings, the US Deputy

---

[268] It is also worth noting for context that placing a weapon in a Lagrange Point would very likely be considered to be 'stationing' it in space. A Lagrange Point is a point where a smaller object holds its position relative to two larger celestial bodies.
[269] UNSC, 'Commission for Conventional Armaments' (18 August 1948) UN Doc S/C.3/32/Rev.1, 2.
[270] See eg UNGA Res 32/84 (12 December 1977) UN Doc A/RES/32/84; UNGA Res 51/37 (10 December 1996) UN Doc A/RES/51/37; UNGA Res 54/44 (23 December 1999) UN Doc A/RES/54/44.
[271] Hearings Before US Senate Foreign Relations Committee on the OST (n 126) 23.

74   RULE 5 WEAPONS OF MASS DESTRUCTION

Secretary of Defence further explained that it would include 'chemical and biological weapons ... or any weapon which might be developed in the future which would have the capability of mass destruction such as that which would be wreaked by nuclear weapons'.[272] These explanations are in line with the CCA definition in that they all include certain specific weapons, as well as future weapons the effects of which are comparable to those of nuclear weapons.

8. The term 'WMD' in the OST thus includes at least chemical, biological, and radiological weapons, as well as nuclear weapons, and also includes future weapons that have comparable large-scale deadly or destructive effects.

9. According to the Judgement of the International Court of Justice (ICJ) in the *Nuclear Weapons* Advisory Opinion, nuclear weapons are explosive devices whose destructive force results from the fusion or fission of the atom.[273] The Treaty for the Prohibition of Nuclear Weapons in Latin America (Tlatelolco Treaty) also provides a useful definition at Article V, namely 'a nuclear weapon is any device which is capable of releasing nuclear energy in an uncontrolled manner and which has a group of characteristics that are appropriate for use for warlike purposes'.[274]

10. This Rule does not preclude nuclear power sources (NPS) in space. NPS have been used in space since 1961. They have been used, for example, in interplanetary missions to the outer limits of the Solar System, for which solar panels were not suitable because of the long duration of the mission at great distances from the Sun.[275] The placement and use of nuclear power sources in space is not prohibited under international law.[276] The Scientific and Technical Subcommittee of COPUOS has a Working Group on the Use of Nuclear Power Sources in Outer Space, which works on NPS-related issues. The main concern of these works has been the contamination owing to launch failure or failure during operations in orbit.[277] As long as

---

[272] ibid 100.
[273] *Nuclear Weapons* (Advisory Opinion) (n 41) para 35.
[274] Treaty for the Prohibition of Nuclear Weapons in Latin America and the Caribbean (Tlatelolco Treaty) (opened for signature 14 February 1967, entered into force 25 April 1969) 634 UNTS 281. International law and practice sometimes differentiate between a 'nuclear weapon' and a 'nuclear explosive device' (with the latter category including so-called peaceful nuclear explosives used for non-weapons purposes, such as civil engineering). More recent arms control agreements have dealt with both categories collectively, by regulating or banning 'nuclear weapons and other nuclear explosive devices'. Subject to para 14 of this Rule, there is no basis for interpreting art IV of the OST to permit States to place a 'nuclear explosive device other than a nuclear weapon' into orbit. The Comprehensive Test Ban Treaty Glossary defines the latter as 'any nuclear weapon or other explosive device capable of releasing nuclear energy, irrespective of the purpose for which it could be used'.
[275] UNGA 'Safety Framework for Nuclear Power Source Applications in Outer Space' (19 May 2009) UN Doc A/AC.105/934, 1.
[276] ibid; UNGA 'Principles Relevant to the Use of Nuclear Power Sources in Outer Space' (23 February 1993) UN Doc A/RES/47/68.
[277] UNCOPUOS Scientific and Technical Subcommittee, 'National Research on Space Debris, Safety of Space Objects with Nuclear Power Sources on Board and Problems Relating to Their Collision with Space Debris' (2 November 2016) UN Doc A/AC.105/C.1/111, 11–12.

such power sources do not constitute nuclear explosive devices they do not fall within the scope of this Rule.[278]

11. Chemical weapons are toxic chemicals that can cause death, temporary incapacitation, or permanent harm to humans or animals through chemical action, as well as their precursors, and munitions and devices designed to deliver such toxic chemicals.[279] Toxic chemicals and precursors, where intended for purposes not prohibited under the CWC,[280] are not prohibited as chemical weapons as long as the types and quantities are consistent with such purposes.

12. Toxic chemicals, such as liquid propellants and coolants, are widely used in the space industry and likely will be used in future missions of resource extraction. One example is hydrazine, which is a highly toxic chemical used in deep space missions as a propellant. For space missions that last for several years, propellants might be brought in storage to outer space or otherwise manufactured in space and/or on celestial bodies. In these cases, these chemicals are not being used for their toxic properties and do not constitute chemical weapons and are thus not prohibited under the CWC as long as their type and quantity are consistent with their stated purposes.

13. Biological weapons refer to weapons that employ microbial or other biological agents, or toxins whatever their origin or method of production, of types and quantities that have no justification for prophylactic, protective, or other peaceful purposes.[281]

14. The issue of planetary defence is an ongoing and speculative matter of consideration within space law. To that end, it is not discussed in this *Manual*. However, where a nuclear explosive device is specifically designed and used to deflect an asteroid to avoid its collision with the Earth, then such action does not violate this Rule. In such a situation, the nuclear device does not qualify as a weapon because it is not used, intended, or designed to cause death of, or injury to persons, nor damage to, or destruction of objects of an adverse party (see Rule 42: Means and Methods of Warfare Generally).[282]

---

[278] During State Consultations, one State noted that this Rule would not prohibit a nuclear power source that provided power for a non-nuclear weapon in space.

[279] Convention on the Prohibition of the Development, Production, Stockpiling and Use of Chemical Weapons and on Their Destruction (adopted 3 September 1992, entered into force 29 April 1997) 1974 UNTS 317 (CWC) art II.

[280] According to CWC, such purposes include: industrial, agricultural, research, medical, pharmaceutical, or other peaceful purposes; protective purposes, namely those purposes directly related to protection against toxic chemicals and to protection against chemical weapons; military purposes not connected with the use of chemical weapons and not dependent on the use of the toxic properties of chemicals as a method of warfare. ibid art II (9).

[281] Convention on the Prohibition of the Development, Production and Stockpiling of Bacteriological (Biological) and Toxin Weapons and on their Destruction (adopted 10 April 1972, entered into force 26 March 1975) 26 UNTS 163 (BWC) art I.

[282] There are however differing opinions on whether the use of a nuclear explosive device is allowable for the purpose of Planetary Defence. An alternative view is that the inherent nature of such a device

Applicability of Article 51 National/Collective Self Defence

15. The legal rights of all OST parties are generally inseparable. As such, any action that limits the rights of a State Party and is inconsistent with the OST is generally not allowable. Therefore, a question arises as to whether a State is entitled to suspend a general obligation owed to other parties to an international agreement as a part of a lawful action of individual or collective self-defence (hereinafter 'self-defence') under Article 51 of the UN Charter.[283] Article 14 of the ILC Draft Articles on the Effects of Armed Conflicts on Treaties (ILC Draft Articles) reflects this Article 51 right in context and provides: 'A State exercising its inherent right of individual or collective self-defence in accordance with the Charter of the United Nations is entitled to suspend in whole or in part the operation of a treaty to which it is a Party insofar as that operation is incompatible with the exercise of that right.' While an easily stated proposition, there is ambiguity in the scope and application of this general pronouncement. The manner and scope of an Article 51 right superseding an incompatible treaty obligation is not fully canvassed by the ILC. This raises a number of questions, including, how does such a right of self-defence, which itself may be considered *jus cogens*,[284] apply in the face of specific prohibitions concerning, *inter alia*, the placement, installation, and stationing of weapons of mass destruction around Earth, within space and on celestial bodies? To date, there is no State practice that has settled this issue, however, two approaches would appear to be available when undertaking this reconciliation exercise and they are detailed below:

> A. First, it might be argued that Article 51 cannot override the prohibitions contained in Article IV, paragraph 1 of the OST under any practical circumstances, as States ceded any right to place, station, or install WMD in orbit or on celestial bodies as a means of self-defence.[285] This argument would be based upon an assessment of the object and purpose of the OST as permitted under Article 31 of the VCLT[286] which establishes that the prohibition on the placement of WMD in orbit, the stationing of them in space and/or installation on a celestial body are central obligations of this treaty. Moreover,

makes it permanently a weapon (and as such, prohibited by the OST and PNTB) regardless of its use for Planetary Defence. See David A Koplow, 'Exoatmospheric Plowshares: Using a Nuclear Explosive Device for Planetary Defense Against an Incoming Asteroid' (Georgetown University Law Center 2018) [https://perma.cc/GTD6-8ZYJ].

[283] See discussion in Methodology of *Manual* regarding these obligations owed to other parties to an international agreement, particularly the OST.
[284] The right of self-defence is explicitly described as an 'inherent right' under art 51 of the UN Charter (n 25).
[285] This approach may be argued with respect to a conflict between the OST and a right established under another treaty, but it may be particularly difficult to reconcile with international law if self-defence is *jus cogens*.
[286] VCLT (n 11).

in using such specific language in the OST, the parties should be understood to have intended that these obligations would be durable, applying even if a State determined that its national self-defence would be assisted by acting contrary to Article IV. Significantly, the issue of banning nuclear weapons was a specific goal of the OST negotiations[287] and the Treaty effectively implemented (largely verbatim) General Assembly Resolution 1884 (XVIII) (17 October 1963) that expressly called upon States to 'refrain from placing in orbit around the Earth objects carrying nuclear weapons or other kinds of weapons of mass destruction, installing such weapons on celestial bodies, or stationing such weapons in outer space'. Hence, just as the ICJ concluded that a 'per se' unlawful weapon cannot be lawfully employed even in national self-defence,[288] it could be argued that Article 51 should not allow for the deployment of a weapon system in a manner expressly prohibited under the OST. Moreover, Article IV, paragraph 1 should not fall within this category of self-defence exception as it is not possible to suspend this obligation for one State without limiting the rights of other parties to the treaty. This is an obligation owed *erga omnes partes*, or in the words of the ILC, an obligation established for the 'protection of a collective interest' for all State parties.[289] As the ILC has recognized, such collective interests can be manifested in setting 'general standards of protection'.[290] It is notable that the ILC itself uses a 'nuclear free zone treaty' as an instance of an obligation owed *erga omnes partes* and hence such example has obvious resonance here. In short, the placement of nuclear weapons or other WMD in space would inevitably affect the fundamental rights of the other State Parties under the OST and undermine a central provision of this treaty.

B. Secondly, it might be argued that Article 51 rights will, if necessary, prevail over inconsistent treaty provisions such as those contained in Article IV. This interpretation is based upon both the conclusion of the ILC Draft Articles and the ICJ *Nuclear Weapons* Advisory Opinion. This opinion contemplated that while the use of such weapons systems was 'scarcely reconcilable' with the law of armed conflict,[291] it was potentially lawful where a State's survival was at stake.[292] In such circumstances, the deployment of nuclear weapons

---

[287] Dembling and Arons (n 123) 427.
[288] *Nuclear Weapons* Advisory Opinion (n 273) para 39.
[289] ILC Articles on State Responsibility (n 253) 126, para 6; see also *Application of the Convention on the Prevention and Punishment of the Crime of Genocide (The Gambia v Myanmar)* (Provisional Measures: Order of 23 January 2020) para 41 (Court noting the 'common interest' that States have in observing the Genocide Convention and the right for any Party to invoke the responsibility of another State under that particular Treaty) [https://perma.cc/A4Y6-VMDB]; since art IV also represents customary international law the obligation would also generally flow to all States, even those not party to the treaty.
[290] ILC Articles on State Responsibility (n 253) 127, para 7.
[291] *Nuclear Weapons* Advisory Opinion (n 273) para 95.
[292] ibid paras 96–97.

in orbit may be a lawful incident of the right of self-defence, which is an inherent, if not *jus cogens*, right. However, such a determination must also acknowledge and accommodate potentially incompatible treaty provisions to the greatest extent possible. In this case-by-case analysis, the standard of incompatibility is stringent. It requires far more than a simple determination that an action in violation of a treaty might provide some assistance in self-defence, which is itself governed by requirements of necessity and proportionality. Rather, it requires that to otherwise breach an important *erga omnes partes* obligation between parties to an agreement, such as those contained within Article IV regarding the placement, stationing, and/or installation of nuclear weapons (or in this case, also an *erga omnes* obligation based on a rule of customary international law), a State has no other reasonable option available (as a manifestation of the *jus ad bellum* requirements of necessity and proportionality) to it to exercise the right of self-defence. In such narrow circumstances, the general obligations contained in Article IV regarding the placement, stationing, and/or installation of nuclear weapons must yield to the more fundamental right of self-defence to the limited extent necessary to realize that right properly.

16. As the right of national self-defence is characterized as being 'inherent' within the Charter, the same taxonomy of considerations would apply in the context of customary international law. Hence, if the prohibitions concerning the placement, stationing, and/or installation of nuclear weapons were accepted as customary international law, such prohibitions would also be subject to the same reasoning regarding rights of national and collective and self-defence as outlined above.

Applicability in Armed Conflicts

17. Article IV, paragraph 1 of the OST would continue to apply during armed conflict, including during an armed conflict that extended into space. The existence of an armed conflict does not *ipso facto* terminate or suspend the operation of treaties or customary rules.[293] According to Article 7 of the ILC Draft Articles on the Effects of Armed Conflicts on Treaties, there is a presumption that multilateral law-making treaties continue in operation, in whole or in part, during armed conflict.[294] However, in their statements on this issue, both the United States and the United Kingdom noted the possibility that certain provisions of such treaties might be inoperative between belligerents.[295] As outlined earlier in the analysis of possible options regarding the right of self-defence, the ICJ *Nuclear Weapons*

---

[293] Report of the ILC on its 63rd Session (n 31) art 3.
[294] ibid art 7 and annex.
[295] ILC Report on its 63 Session (n 257) 122.

Advisory Opinion did not conclude definitively that the use of nuclear weapons were unlawful where survival of a State was at stake. While, according to the Court, such use is 'scarcely reconcilable' with the requirements of the law of armed conflict, it is evident that there are circumstances where the use of nuclear weapons might be lawful. The use of such weapons between belligerent naval fleets on the high seas is one possibility, the targeting of massed armies and armour in an open desert is another, and the use in space is potentially yet another. In such circumstances, given the relative absence of civilian populations and civilian objects, the usual questions of distinction and proportionality, in particular, might be resolvable. Hence, if such use is conceivable and potentially lawful in accordance with the ICJ determination relating to the permissible defensive use of nuclear weapons in extreme circumstances, then the provisions of Article IV, paragraph 1 might yield to the stringent application of the law of armed conflict. This would mean that the actions of placing such nuclear weapons in orbit, stationing them in space and/or installing them on a celestial body may be justified if necessary for their employment, in accordance with the law of armed conflict.

Testing Nuclear Weapons in Space for States that are Parties to the Partial Nuclear Test Ban Treaty

18. Subpart (b) of this Rule is derived from Article I of the PNTB,[296] under which each party undertakes 'to prohibit, to prevent, and not to carry out any nuclear weapon test explosion, or any other nuclear explosion, at any place under its jurisdiction and control ... beyond [the limits of the atmosphere], including outer space'.

19. This treaty has been joined by 125 parties, including most of the States that are active in space and that possess nuclear weapons (although notably not by China or France). It is not clear whether the contents of the Treaty represent customary international law. No State has conducted a nuclear explosive test in space for decades, and none is known to have expressly reserved the option to do so.

20. Each PNTB party is obligated not only to refrain from conducting a nuclear explosion in space, but also to prohibit and prevent others from doing so, at any place under the State's jurisdiction and control. Since Article II of the OST prohibits States from asserting sovereignty over space, it is not clear what 'jurisdiction' would refer to in this context. A State may well exercise at least temporary 'control' over a specified location in space, and therefore incur an obligation to prohibit and prevent nuclear explosions by anyone there. The PNTB also obligates each party 'to refrain from causing, encouraging, or in any way participating in, the carrying out' of any of the prohibited nuclear explosions.

---

[296] PNTB Treaty (n 262).

80   RULE 5 WEAPONS OF MASS DESTRUCTION

21. Although the PNTB is often referred to as a 'test ban' treaty, Article I specifies that the prohibition applies more broadly to 'any nuclear weapon test explosion, or any other nuclear explosion'. Therefore, the treaty prohibits all nuclear explosions in space, regardless of their avowed or real purpose, type, or motive. The discussion above, concerning whether the OST's prohibitions would apply to a nuclear explosive device that was placed into Earth orbit for non-weapons applications such as to divert an asteroid, is therefore irrelevant here.

22. Some might argue that a hypothetical nuclear explosion that was conducted in a chamber drilled deep into the interior of the Moon or another celestial body could be characterized as being detonated 'underground' (and thereby permitted under the PNTB) rather than 'in outer space' (and thereby prohibited.) However, PNTB Article I.1(b) also prohibits a nuclear explosion in any environment 'if such explosion causes radioactive debris to be present outside the territorial limits' of the State conducting the explosion. So even that hypothetical nuclear explosion inside a celestial body would be prohibited.

23. The PNTB would be supplemented and largely superseded by the Comprehensive Nuclear Test Ban Treaty (CTBT), which would ban nuclear explosions for any purpose in any environment, including underground. The CTBT has been negotiated, signed by 184 States, and ratified by 168, but it is not yet in force because it requires ratification by 44 designated States before it can enter into force for any State, and only 38 of those 44 have ratified. Nonetheless, Article 18 of the Vienna Convention on the Law of Treaties specifies that during the interval between signature and entry into force of a treaty, a Signatory State is required 'to refrain from acts which would defeat the object and purpose' of the treaty. In this connection, the UN Security Council affirmed in 2016 that a nuclear weapon test explosion or any other nuclear explosion would defeat the object and purpose of the CTBT. Such an explosion, in space or at any other location, would therefore be illegal for any of the CTBT's Signatory States.[297]

24. It is important to note that the PNTB was not intended to prohibit the use of nuclear weapons in armed conflicts.[298] However, it is clear that the use of nuclear weapons during armed conflicts shall in any case be subject to the rules and principles of IHL and other applicable international legal rules.

---

[297] 'Joint Statement on the Comprehensive Nuclear-Test-Ban Treaty by the Nuclear Nonproliferation Treaty Nuclear-Weapon States' (Joint Statement issued by governments of China, France, Russia, United Kingdom, and United States, September 2016) [https://perma.cc/Q78F-QMV6]; UNSC Res 2310 (23 September 2016) UN Doc S/RES/2310.

[298] See Statement of Hon Dean Rusk (US Secretary of State) 'Nuclear Test Ban Treaty: Hearings before the Committee on Foreign Relations of the United States Senate, 88th Congress' (1st Session, US Gov Printing Office 1963) 13 (noting that '[t]his treaty does not affect the use of nuclear weapons in war. It has to do with nuclear weapon testing in time of peace.').

Treaty on the Prohibition of Nuclear Weapons

25. States that are parties to the Treaty on the Prohibition of Nuclear Weapons[299] are obligated, *inter alia*, not to: '[d]evelop, test, produce, manufacture, otherwise acquire, possess or stockpile nuclear weapons or other nuclear explosive devices';[300] '[u]se or threaten to use nuclear weapons or other nuclear explosive devices';[301] and '[a]llow any stationing, installation or deployment of any nuclear weapons or other nuclear explosive devices in its territory or at any place under its jurisdiction or control'.[302] These prohibitions would apply in space as well as elsewhere.

---

[299] Treaty on the Prohibition of Nuclear Weapons (adopted 7 July 2017, entered into force 22 January 2021) [https://perma.cc/M858-D8RW].
[300] ibid art 1(a).
[301] ibid art 1(d).
[302] ibid art 1(g).

Rule 6
Military Space Activities and Intelligence Collection

Military space activities for the purpose of collecting intelligence from, to, and within space are not prohibited, unless the specific means or methods of collection violate applicable international legal obligations.

Overview of Legal Basis of Rule

1. Among the earliest uses of outer space were military space activities whose purpose was the collection of intelligence from reconnaissance satellites in outer space.[303] Although there was some dispute early in the space age about the lawfulness of such intelligence collection,[304] this disagreement has long been tacitly settled.[305] Many States are now engaged in various types of intelligence collection in space, thus exercising what they view as one of their rights under the Outer Space Treaty

---

[303] See 'Surveillance' (*Encyclopedia Astronautica*) [https://perma.cc/47GU-9WWV] (detailing the numerous types of surveillance and reconnaissance satellites that have been deployed in space, including Russian and US military surveillance and reconnaissance satellites deployed in the earliest part of the space age); Paul B Stares, *The Militarization of Space: U.S. Policy, 1945–1984* (Cornell University Press 1985) 53, 135.

[304] Compare the Soviet Union's proposal at the UN Legal Sub-Committee in June 1962 for basic principles that included, *inter alia*, '[t]he use of artificial satellites for the collection of intelligence information in the territory of foreign states is incompatible with the objectives of mankind in its conquest of outer space' (UNGA 'USSR Proposal' (6 June 1962) UN Doc A/AC.105/C.2/L.1, para 8) with Ambassador Gore's speech to the First Committee of the UN on 3 December 1962: 'One of the consequences of these factors is that any nation may use space satellites for such purposes as observation and information gathering. Observation from space is consistent with international law, just as observation from the high seas.' UNGA First Committee, 'Verbatim Record of the Twelve Hundred and Eighty-Ninth Meeting' (n 185) 13.

[305] The Soviet Union's proposed rule regarding intelligence collection by satellites being 'incompatible with the objectives of mankind' was included in their successive treaty drafts as late as April 1963 (see UNCOPUOS 'Report of the Legal Sub-Committee on the work of its second session (16 April–3 May 1963) to the Committee on the Peaceful Uses of Outer Space' (6 May 1963) UN Doc A/AC.105/12, Annex I, p 2) but was removed as of 1966 (see UNGA 'Letter dated 16 June 1966 from the Permanent Representative of the Union of Soviet Socialist Republics to the United Nations Addressed to the Secretary-General' (16 June 1966) UN Doc A/6352). See also the Soviet Union delegate's speech to the UN Subcommittee on Outer Space on 9 September 1963, in which the Soviet Union's customary obligations to espionage satellites were noticeably omitted (UNCOPUOS 'Verbatim Record of the Twentieth Meeting' (10 October 1963) UN Doc A/AC.105/PV.20, 17–30). See also Ward Wright, 'United Nations Group Fails to Gain Accord on Space Use Rule' (20 May 1963) 78(20) Aviation Week & Space Technology 129, quoted in Stares (n 303).

(OST) (see Rule 1: Freedom of Use, Access, Exploration, Scientific Investigation, and Principles of Cooperation). Furthermore, various arms control treaties even contain clauses that obligate each Party not to interfere with satellites performing intelligence collection activities for verification purposes, commonly referred to as 'national technical means of verification of the other Party' or NTMs.[306]

2. Intelligence is not a term defined in international law. For the purposes of this Rule, intelligence is defined as the product that results from collecting, processing, integrating, evaluating, analysing, and interpreting information related to the activities, intent, and capabilities of foreign nations, hostile or potentially hostile forces, or areas of actual or potential operations.[307]

State Practice Related to Intelligence Collection in Space

3. States collect intelligence from, to, and in space. Intelligence collection from space may include, for example, imagery (photographs, infrared, and Synthetic Aperture Radar (SAR)) and electronic (signals and measurement and signature intelligence). Intelligence collection in space may include various space situational awareness (SSA) systems,[308] and intelligence collection into space may likewise include various SSA systems.

---

[306] See eg provisions in arms control treaties addressing the protection of national technical means for verification, including: the Treaty Between the United States of America and the Russian Federation on Measures for the Further Reduction and Limitation of Strategic Offensive Arms (United States–Russia) (adopted 8 April 2010, entered into force 5 February 2011) art X ('each Party undertakes ... not to interfere with the national technical means of verification of the other Party operating in accordance with this Article'); the Treaty on the Limitation of Anti-Ballistic Missile Systems (US–USSR) (adopted 26 May 1972, entered into force 3 October 1972) 944 UNTS 13 art XII; Interim Agreement between the United States of America and the Union of Soviet Socialist Republics on Certain Measures With Respect to the Limitation of Strategic Offensive Arms (adopted 26 May 1972, entered into force 3 October 1972) 50 ILM 342, art V; Treaty Between the United States of America and the Union of Soviet Socialist Republics on the Elimination of Their Intermediate-Range and Shorter-Range Missiles (adopted 8 December 1987, entered into force 1 June 1988) 1657 UNTS 2, art XII; Treaty on Conventional Armed Forces in Europe (adopted 19 November 1990, entered into force 9 November 1992) 2441 UNTS 285, art XV.

[307] States provide different definitions of this term. See eg Office of the Chairman of the Joint Chiefs of Staff, 'DOD Dictionary of Military and Associated Terms' (US Dept of Defence, 2020) 107 (defining intelligence as 'the product resulting from the collection, processing, integration, evaluation, analysis, and interpretation of available information concerning foreign nation, hostile, or potentially hostile forces or elements, or areas of actual or potential operations'); UK Ministry of Defence, *Joint Doctrine Publication 2-00: Understanding and Intelligence Support to Joint Operations* (3rd edn, Change 1, Development, Concepts and Doctrine Centre 2011) [https://perma.cc/7VW9-GKRJ] Lexicon-7 (defining intelligence as '[t]he directed and co-ordinated acquisition and analysis of information to assess capabilities, intent and opportunities for exploitation by leaders at all levels' and collection as 'the exploitation of sources by collection agencies and the delivery of the information obtained to the appropriate processing unit for use in the production of intelligence').

[308] Space Situational Awareness (SSA) refers to keeping track of objects in orbit and predicting where they will be at any given time. See Space Foundation Editorial Team, 'The Space Briefing Book' (The Space Foundation 2019) 19; See also European Space Agency, 'Space Situational Awareness Program Overview' [https://perma.cc/5YE3-BAPY] (noting that SSA includes 'SST—Space surveillance and tracking of objects in Earth orbit (Watching for active and inactive satellites, discarded launch stages

4. At the outset of the space age, intelligence collection in and from space supporting military space activities was conducted exclusively by sovereign States. However, non-military and commercial entities now routinely collect intelligence from, to, and in space in support of military space activities.[309] Military, non-military, and commercial space intelligence collection are captured by the Rule—the determining factor is the nature of the activity, not the entity that carries it out. Indeed, commercial space entities now routinely sell imagery (optical and SAR) and signals collection to governments.[310] States may place limits upon collection by entities over whom they assert jurisdiction,[311] but this has no impact on the lawfulness of the intelligence collection activities under international law.

---

and fragmentation debris that orbit the Earth)', 'SWE—Space weather (Monitoring conditions at the Sun and in the solar wind, and in Earth's magnetosphere, ionosphere and thermosphere, that can affect space-borne and ground-based infrastructure or endanger human life or health)', and 'NEO—Near-Earth objects (Detecting natural objects that can potentially impact Earth and cause damage')).

[309] See eg Airbus, 'Universal Registration Document 2020' (Registration Document, Autoriteit Financiële Markten, 26 March 2021) 47, 50; Christopher J Scolese, 'Testimony of Dr. Christopher J. Scolese, Director—National Reconnaissance Office' (Speech, House Armed Services Committee, Subcommittee on Strategic Forces Hearing on 'Fiscal Year 2022 Space Priorities and Posture', 24 May 2021) 11; Defence Intelligence Agency, 'Challenges to Security in Space' (Report DIA_F_01403_A, January 2019) 8; AllSource Analysis, 'AllSource Analysis Wins NGA Contract to Identify and Monitor North Korean Military Facilities' (Press Release, 11 September 2019) [https://perma.cc/4KWY-SERE]; Joint Chiefs of Staff, 'Space Operations' (Joint Publication 3-14, United States Government, 26 October 2020) II-4, I-5; Lockheed Martin, 'Enhanced Geospatial Intelligence for UK Armed Forces' (News Release, 1 September 2015), [https://perma.cc/MT7K-UETE].

[310] See eg Jon Powers, 'National Reconnaissance Office Renews Contract With Planet Federal' (Media Release, Planet Labs PBC, 15 July 2021) [https://perma.cc/5LK4-943Q]; National Geospatial-Intelligence Agency, 'NGA Awards New Planet Contract, Leverages High-Revisit Imagery and Automated Processing' (Press Release, 3 October 2018) [https://perma.cc/37UM-7FJX]; MAXAR, 'Maxar Technologies Awarded Study Contract with U.S. National Reconnaissance Office for Commercial Imagery Capabilities' (Press Release, 3 June 2019) [https://perma.cc/4G6Y-ZYEW]; MAXAR, 'MDA to Provide RADARSAT-2 Information to Meet Critical and Complex Challenges for Land and Maritime Monitoring' (Press Release, 26 March 2018) [https://perma.cc/6NJC-FEMJ]; Black Sky, 'BlackSky Awarded NRO Contract for Commercial Imagery to Support U.S. Government Mission Needs' (Media Release, 3 June 2019) [https://perma.cc/F4TV-FG72].

[311] See, generally UNOOSA, 'National Space Law' (Online database 2022) <https://www.unoosa.org/oosa/en/ourwork/spacelaw/nationalspacelaw/index.html> accessed 29 March 2023.

Rule 7
Jurisdiction

A State retains jurisdiction and control over its registered space objects and over any personnel thereof and also jurisdiction over all its nationals, both natural and juridical, while in space or on celestial bodies, as well as jurisdiction on other recognised bases under international law over other persons, space objects and activities.

Overview of Legal Basis of Rule

1. Jurisdiction and the exercise of control over a State's territory are both fundamental manifestations of the notion of sovereignty.[312] Customary international law recognizes several bases for States to exercise prescriptive jurisdiction; that is, the power of a State to prescribe conduct through the passage of laws and regulations. Most importantly, these bases include territoriality and nationality but may also include the protective principle, universality, and in some limited circumstances, the passive nationality principle (nationality of the victim).[313] In space, given the absence of national territories, territorial jurisdiction issues are not present. Also,

---

[312] 'Sovereignty in the relations between States signifies independence. Independence in regard to a portion of the globe is the right to exercise therein, to the exclusion of any other State, the functions of a State.' *Island of Palmas Case* (n 143). The primacy of a State's jurisdiction over its own domestic affairs is explicitly recognized in the United Nations Charter. See UNGA, Charter of the UN Nations (signed 26 June 1945, entered into effect 24 October 1945) 1 UNTS XVI, art 2(7) ('Nothing contained in the present Charter shall authorize the United Nations to intervene in matters which are essentially within the domestic jurisdiction of any state ….'). Consistent with a State's exclusive jurisdiction of over its domestic affairs and the UN Charter, States similarly have a 'duty not to intervene in matters within the domestic jurisdiction of any state'. UNGA, 'Declaration on Principles of International Law Concerning Friendly Relations and Co-operation Among States in Accordance With the Charter of the United Nations' (24 October 1970) A/RES/2625 (XXV).

[313] *Restatement (Third) of Foreign Relations Law in the United States* (n 61) § 402, § 404 (noting that a State has jurisdiction to prescribe based on territoriality (conduct that takes place within its territory; relates to the status of persons, or interests in things, present within its territory, and; conduct outside its territory that has or is intended to have substantial effect within its territory); nationality (the activities, interests, status, or relations of its nationals outside as well as within its territory); protective principle (certain conduct outside its territory by persons not its nationals that is directed against the security of the State or against a limited class of other State interests); passive personality principle (exceptional basis of jurisdiction based on the nationality of the victim, increasingly accepted as applied to terrorist and other organized attacks on a State's nationals by reason of their nationality); and universal jurisdiction (for certain offences recognized by the community of nations as of universal concern, such as piracy, slave trade, attacks on or hijacking of aircraft, genocide, war crimes, and perhaps certain acts of terrorism).

while natural juridical persons are subject to their respective State's nationality jurisdiction, the space law regime does not recognize a 'nationality' of space objects. However, international law also recognizes that a State may exercise jurisdiction over objects and persons pursuant to an international agreement. For example, with respect to activities in outer space, the Outer Space Treaty (OST) establishes a legal framework which provides that the State of Registry has jurisdiction and control over a space object and over any personnel thereof (as discussed below).[314] Similarly, with respect to other activities, States turned to familiar bases of jurisdiction in drafting an agreement to establish a legal framework to define their jurisdiction and control with respect to their respective elements in the International Space Station (the ISS) and their nationals.[315] Thus, the basic rule that emerged for the ISS is that 'each partner shall retain jurisdiction and control over the elements it registers ... and over personnel in or on the Space Station who are its nationals'.[316]

Jurisdiction of States in Space

2. Although the OST prohibits a State from asserting claims of sovereignty over outer space, including the Moon and other celestial bodies, it clearly reaffirms the reach of one aspect of a State's jurisdiction into space by explicitly providing in Article VIII that '[a] State Party to the Treaty on whose registry an object launched into outer space is carried shall *retain* jurisdiction and control over such object, and over any personnel thereof, while in outer space or on a celestial body'.[317] This Article does not, however, provide that the State of Registry has *exclusive* jurisdiction to regulate the space object and personnel thereof, and any related interactions, in the sense that other States might assert concurrent prescriptive jurisdiction on another basis (such as nationality).[318] However, the jurisdiction of the State of Registry under Article VIII will override the personal jurisdiction of the national State of

---

[314] It is also possible the national laws of a State may assert jurisdiction over all space objects launched from that State's territory, regardless of the space object's officially recognized registration status under art VIII (see generally, UNOOSA, 'National Space Law' (n 311)).

[315] ISS Agreement (n 47).

[316] ibid art 5. In some circumstances, an affected ISS Partner State may also exercise criminal jurisdiction over an alleged perpetrator (representing a convention-based example of an application of the passive nationality principle of jurisdiction). ibid art 22.5.

[317] OST (n 9) (emphasis added). The jurisdiction of the State of Registry over the space object clearly extends not only to persons while they are on board, but also when they are outside the space object. See Cheng, *Studies in International Space Law* (n 61) 416 (noting that '[t]he substitution of the word "thereof" for "thereon", which was the expression used in paragraph 7 of General Assembly resolution 1962, was intended to make this point explicit').

[318] For example, another State might assert prescriptive jurisdiction on the basis of the nationality of a person located on another State's space object. Such shared or concurrent jurisdiction is reflected in art 22 of the ISS Agreement, which grants primary jurisdiction to prosecute an astronaut to the State of nationality and secondary jurisdiction to prosecute the perpetrator is granted to both (i) the State of the victim, and (ii) the State that owns the flight element where the crime took place (or where criminal damage occurred to the flight element). ISS Agreement (n 47) art 22.

the individuals on a space object, 'at least insofar as the concrete power of implementation and enforcement (jurisdiction) is concerned'.[319]

Nationality jurisdiction is founded on the theory that a sovereign State has jurisdiction over its nationals regardless of their location, since '[n]ationality serves above all to determine that the person upon whom it is conferred enjoys the rights and is bound by the obligations which the law of the State in question grants to or imposes on its nationals'.[320] A State may also ascribe nationality to corporations,[321] vessels,[322] and aircraft[323] (although in the two latter cases, a State's authority might best be described as a special and independent type of jurisdiction associated with specific international legal regimes governing maritime and aerial activities).[324] As noted, the OST recognizes that States retain their jurisdiction over objects in space on the basis of the space object's State of Registry under Article VIII, but *not* on the basis of the space object's 'nationality'.[325]

3.

---

[319] Cheng, *Studies in International Space Law* (n 61) 415.

[320] *Nottebohm Case (Liechtenstein v Guatemala)* (Judgment) [1955] ICJ Reps 1, 20. Although this case relates to persons and not to objects and is addressing an individual's nationality for purposes of a State asserting diplomatic protection on behalf of its national, it also made the general observation that the specific requirements for nationality jurisdiction are established by each State under its own laws. As noted in the text above, space objects are subject to their own jurisdictional regime under the OST and are not treated as 'persons' for purposes of nationality jurisdiction. However, persons may be made the subject of a State's jurisdiction wherever they are located, including in space.

[321] After observing that a State may assert diplomatic protection only on behalf of one of its own nationals, the International Court of Justice held that 'the traditional rule attributes the right of diplomatic protection of a corporate entity to the State under the laws of which it is incorporated and in whose territory it has its registered office. These two criteria have been confirmed by long practice and by numerous international instruments.' *Case Concerning The Barcelona Traction, Light and Power Company, Limited (Belgium v Spain)* (Judgment) [1970] ICJ Repo 3, 42. See also *Restatement (Third) of Foreign Relations Law in the United States* (n 61) § 402, comment e ('The nationality principle is applicable to juridical as well as to natural persons. For the purposes of this section, the nationality of a corporation or comparable juridical entity is that of the state under whose law it is organized.'). With respect to space activities, the German Government has observed that '[i]n practice, however, there are a number of legal problems in the determination of the nationality of companies and organizations. As far as clarity in the registration system is concerned, the criterion should be clear and unambiguous. The criterion of the registered seat of such legal entities can be applied to any company or organization— whether national or international.'); UNCOPUOS Legal Sub-Committee, 'Registration of Space Objects: Harmonization of Practices, Non-registration of Space Objects, Transfer of Ownership and Registration/Non-registration of 'Foreign' Space Objects' (19 January 2006) UN Doc A/AC.105/867 ('UNCOPUOS Registration of Space Objects'). [https://perma.cc/57M9-HWW6] (Reply of Germany).

[322] UNCLOS (n 151) art 91.1 ('Every State shall fix the conditions for the grant of its nationality to ships, for the registration of ships in its territory, and for the right to fly its flag. Ships have the nationality of the State whose flag they are entitled to fly.').

[323] International Convention on Civil Aviation (n 103) art 17 ('Aircraft have the nationality of the State in which they are registered.').

[324] *Restatement (Third) of Foreign Relations Law* (n 61) § 402, comment h.

[325] The OST does not use the word 'nationality' for the exercise of jurisdiction by the State of registration over registered space objects. In practical terms, this jurisdiction and control by a State may sometimes resemble nationality jurisdiction and, like nationality, art 2 of the Registration Convention (n 46) permits only one State to be the State of Registry for a space object. However, unlike ships or planes, space objects do not have the nationality of the State whose flag they are entitled to fly or the nationality of the State in which they are registered (as provided for ships and planes under applicable international conventions). States have, however, enacted domestic laws specifically extending their jurisdiction to space objects that they register under the OST. See eg 18 USC § 7(6), 'Special maritime and territorial jurisdiction of the United States defined' ('The term "special maritime and territorial jurisdiction of

4. States are increasingly attempting to regulate the activities of nationals and convey rights and impose obligations on them under national laws with respect to space activities. For example, some States, including the United States, have enacted laws that authorize activities by their nationals or convey rights to their nationals with respect to the ownership of, or interests in, natural resources extracted from outer space, while other States have criticized such assertions of nationality jurisdiction on a variety of bases (see Rule 2: Non-Appropriation of Outer Space and Celestial Bodies).

5. A government may be able in its own courts, as well as in those of other States, to assert immunity from various non-contractual claims with respect to its space activities and space objects that are owned and operated by that government. This type of 'sovereign immunity' means that a government cannot be sued for public liability in its own courts or, except if otherwise dictated pursuant to international law, the courts of other States.[326] However, space law recognizes no concept of 'sovereign immunity' like the legal status that the law of the sea attaches in the marine environment to a 'warship, naval auxiliary, other vessels or aircraft owned or operated by a State and used, for the time being, only on government non-commercial service'.[327] Space objects, including military space objects, technically lack the 'nationality' of a State, operate in a different environment and under different rules, and cannot meet the legal requirements for a warship imposed by the law of the sea.[328] However, while a warship on the high seas has 'complete immunity from

the United States", as used in this title, includes ... [a]ny vehicle used or designed for flight or navigation in space on the registry of the United States pursuant to the [OST]'.). Some States may also enact laws that apply to space objects that are launched from their territory, regardless of the object's State of registration.

[326] 'Sovereign immunity' is defined as 'preclud[ing] litigant from asserting an otherwise meritorious cause of action against a sovereign or a party with sovereign attributes unless sovereign consents to suit'. Henry Campbell Black (ed), *Black's Law Dictionary* (5th edn, West Publishing Company 1979) 1252; *West's Law and Commercial Dictionary in Five Languages: Definitions of the Legal and Commercial Terms and Phrases of American, English, and Civil Law Jurisdictions* (vol II, West Publishing Company 1983) 552 (referring to *Principe Compania Naviera, S.A. v Board of Com'rs of Port of New Orleans*, 333 F. Supp. 353, 355 (1971); *Union Oil Co. of California v Basalt Rock Co.*, 30 Cal. App.2d 317, 319–20 (1939); and *Fidelity Coal Co. v Diamond*, 310 Ill. App. 387 (1941)).

[327] UNCLOS (n 151) art 236. Similarly, space objects are unlike maritime vessels and aircraft where the right of sovereign immunity can be claimed under customary international law for State owned or operated vessels and aircraft engaged in government non-commercial service. See US Department of the Navy, 'The Commander's Handbook on the Law of Naval Operations' (August 2017 edn, US Office of the Chief of Naval Operations 2007) (US Commander's Handbook of Naval Operations) paras 2.1.1 and 2.4.2.

[328] UNCLOS (n 151) art 29 (UNCLOS defines a warship as 'a ship belonging to the armed forces of a State bearing the external marks distinguishing such ships of its nationality, under the command of an officer duly commissioned by the government of the State and whose name appears in the appropriate service list or its equivalent, and manned by a crew which is under regular armed forces discipline'). In addition to the absence of sovereign immunity discussed above, other legal requirements for a warship imposed by the law of the sea cannot be met by a space object. For example, art 29 of UNCLOS (n 151) requires that a warship have the nationality of the flag State and bear 'the external marks distinguishing such ships of its nationality'. Space objects technically have no 'nationality', registration for space objects does not include a required specification of any particular military status (see Rule 8:

the jurisdiction of any State other than the flag State',[329] the State of Registry of a space object under the OST does retain 'jurisdiction and control over such object, and over any personnel thereof, while in outer space or on a celestial body'.[330] In practice, this means that the State of Registry may exclude all individuals, entities, or representatives of any other State from a space object unless authorized by the State of Registry, including any related efforts by other States to implement concrete measures of enforcement jurisdiction on the space object.[331]

Registration of Space Objects), and there are no required 'markings' for space objects (and of course conventional 'markings' also present challenges in the space environment).

[329] UNCLOS (n 151) art 95.
[330] OST (n 9) art VIII.
[331] See Cheng, *Studies in International Space Law* (n 61) 415 ('The quasi-territorial jurisdiction of the State of registry overrides, therefore, the personal jurisdiction of the national State of the individuals, at least insofar as the concrete power of implementation and enforcement (jurisdiction) is concerned.'). During State consultation, States did not resist this characterization of the concrete powers of the State of registry but found the term 'quasi-territorial jurisdiction' misleading and problematic under the Space Law regime and therefore this term is not used in this *Manual*.

Rule 8
Registration of Space Objects

A State, or one of the States, that launches a space object into Earth orbit or beyond, including a space object used in military space activities or operations, shall register that space object by means of an entry in an appropriate registry which it shall maintain and must furnish to the Secretary-General of the United Nations specified information concerning each space object carried on its registry.

Overview of Legal Basis of Rule

1. This Rule is based on Article VIII of the Outer Space Treaty (OST), as implemented by the Registration Convention.[332] The launching State that registers a space object is referred to as the State of Registry. Each State of Registry is also required, as soon as practicable, to furnish to the Secretary-General of the United Nations specified information concerning each space object carried on its registry.[333] The OST and the Registration Convention make no distinction between military and civil space objects. Importantly, if an object is sent only on a sub-orbital flight, it need not be registered since it is not a space object launched into Earth orbit or beyond. Similarly, missiles and other military space objects that follow a ballistic trajectory before returning to Earth, detonating, or impacting a target in space need not be registered.

---

[332] This obligation applies to States that are parties to the Registration Convention (n 46). Under art II(1), a launching State 'shall register the space object by means of an entry in an appropriate registry which it shall maintain'. See Overview of the Space Law Regime, paras 17–22, for an examination of the status of the Registration Convention and the customary international law status of the generic registration requirement in art VIII of the OST.

[333] Under art IV(1) of the Registration Convention (n 46), each State of Registry is required to 'furnish to the Secretary-General of the United Nations, as soon as practicable, the following information concerning each space object carried on its registry: (a) name of launching State or States; (b) an appropriate designator of the space object or its registration number; (c) date and territory or location of launch; (d) basic orbital parameters, including: (i) nodal period; (ii) inclination; (iii) apogee; (iv) perigee, and; (e) general function of the space object'. Under this art V, the State of Registry has a specific obligation to include information regarding any space object which is marked with a designator or registration number or both.

The Space Law Registration Regime

Seventy-four States are currently parties to the Registration Convention, including all the major spacefaring States.[334] The United Nations Office for Outer Space Affairs (UNOOSA) reports that '[t]o date over 88% of all satellites, probes, landers, crewed spacecraft and space station flight elements launched into Earth orbit or beyond have been registered with the Secretary-General'.[335] While this may be an impressive percentage, it still leaves a significant number of unregistered space objects in these categories.[336] In addition, a very large number of mostly unregistered space debris objects orbit Earth.[337] Space debris poses an increasing risk to both military and civilian space activities.[338]

The failure by some States to register all their space objects raises several difficulties, including nuanced compliance problems and unsettled legal issues which will be discussed shortly. These problems and issues may present challenges for military and civilian lawyers assessing the legal connection of a particular State to a particular space object. They also highlight the importance of legal connections other than registration that may be present between a State and a space object. A brief review of these different possible legal connections is provided in Note: Legal Connections between States and a Space Object. In addition to registration, another critical legal connection focuses on the State that has 'international responsibility' for a space object as part of its national activities in space (see Rule 10: Responsibility of States for National Activities in Outer Space). Furthermore, a State that qualifies as a launching State will remain liable for damages caused by the space object that it launched (see Rule 12: International Liability for Damage Caused by Space Objects). Other legal connections, such as the ownership or use

---

[334] UNOOSA, 'Status of International Agreements relating to Activities in Outer Space' (Online database, 2023) <https://www.unoosa.org/oosa/en/ourwork/spacelaw/treaties/status/index.html> last accessed 23 March 2023. An additional three States are Signatories to the Registration Convention.

[335] United Nations Office for Outer Space Affairs, 'United Nations Register of Objects Launched into Outer Space' (5 July 2021) [https://perma.cc/ZNS6-D6RA].

[336] As of 6 March 2023, the UN Online Index of Objects Launched into Outer Space listed 15,189 space objects (approximately 89% of which are registered). 'Online Index of Objects Launched into Outer Space' (UNOOSA). https://www.unoosa.org/oosa/osoindex/search-ng.jspx?lf_id=; See 'Satellite Database', Union of Concerned Scientists, (n 88) for details regarding registered space objects.

[337] The UN Registry of Objects Launched into Outer Space thus includes only a small fraction of the total objects in orbit around Earth. The rest are space debris objects, nearly all of which are not registered by any State. NASA notes that there are '[m]ore than 27,000 pieces of orbital debris... are tracked by the Department of Defense's global Space Surveillance Network (SSN) sensors'. Marc Garcia 'Space Debris and Human Spacecraft' (NASA 2021) [https://perma.cc/5QJV-3LTZ] (further noting that there are 'approximately 100 million pieces about 0.4 inches (or one millimeter) and larger' orbiting the Earth). The European Space Agency estimates that there are 1 million debris objects from 1 to 10 cm in size orbiting the Earth. 'Space Debris by the Numbers' (ESA 11 July 2022) [https://perma.cc/VV5A-YLWU].

[338] The ESA notes that '[a]ny of these objects can cause harm to an operational spacecraft. For example, a collision with a 10-cm object would entail a catastrophic fragmentation of a typical satellite, a 1-cm object would most likely disable a spacecraft and penetrate the ISS shields, and a 1-mm object could destroy sub-systems on board a spacecraft.' European Space Agency, 'How Many Space Debris Objects are Currently in Orbit?' (European Space Agency) [https://perma.cc/T7ZY-UKC5].

of a space object, may be important in some respects (particularly under domestic laws and contracts governed by domestic law) but does not provide the clear and unambiguous links to a State under international law that are established by references to the launching State.[339]

Registration Challenges

4. Registration is the clearest and often the most important legal link between a State and a space object. The State of Registry exercises jurisdiction and control over the space object under Article VIII of the OST (see Rule 7: Jurisdiction). However, as previously noted, not all space objects are registered and there are some important unsettled legal issues related to registration. At the outset, it is important to note that while the space law regime recognises that a State of Registry retains its jurisdiction and control over its space objects under Article VIII of the OST, this authority is not on the basis of the space object's 'nationality', as is the case with ships and aircraft[340] (see Rule 7: Jurisdiction). Furthermore, as previously noted, registration may not be the only important link between a State and a space object.

5. One challenge under the existing space law registration regime is presented by the question of precisely what kind of space objects must be registered. Registration information provided by States may comprise several different categories of space objects, including both functional and non-functional objects (that are produced during or just after launch).[341] In practice, however, many States of Registry provide information only on functional objects, while also often excluding information on 'foreign objects' (payloads).[342] In practice, States may also not provide

---

[339] 'Registration of Space Objects: Harmonization of Practices, Non-registration of Space Objects, Transfer of Ownership and Registration/Non-registration of "Foreign" Space Objects' (n 321) 4 ('While the reference to a launching State with respect to a particular space object creates a clear and unambiguous allocation of responsibilities vis-à-vis the general public, a reference to the State of the owner of a space object does not fulfil these requirements.').

[340] The OST does not use the word 'nationality' for the exercise of jurisdiction over registered space objects. In practical terms, this jurisdiction and control by a State resembles nationality jurisdiction in many respects (see Rule 7: Jurisdiction). However, unlike ships or planes, space objects do not have the nationality of the State whose flag they are entitled to fly or the nationality of the State in which they are registered (as provided for ships and planes under applicable international conventions—which also require a 'genuine link' between a State and a ship with that State's nationality). Similarly, space objects are not governed by the same restrictions and regulations that govern naval vessels or aircraft under widely accepted, applicable international conventions.

[341] Article I(b) of the Registration Convention (n 46) does specify that the term 'space object' includes 'component parts of a space object as well as its launch vehicle and parts thereof'.

[342] Niklas Hedman (UNOOSA), 'Registration of Space Objects with the United Nations' (UN/China/APSCO Workshop on Space Law, Beijing, China, November 2014) [https://perma.cc/G3U8-6LGH] (noting, for example, that China generally registers functional objects only, although sometimes registers objects built and/or launched by China on behalf of foreign client; France registers functional objects, upper stages and payload adapters from the launch vehicle; India registers functional objects and upper stages of launch vehicles; Japan registers functional objects only; the Russian Federation functional objects only; and the United States registers functional objects and upper stages and some secondary objects deriving from the launch. Prior to 2008, the United States registered all its objects

information on changes in the status of objects, including information on active de-orbiting or decaying objects[343] and changes in ownership.

6. While registration information for a space object is required to include the basic orbital parameters (nodal period, inclination, apogee, and perigee),[344] it is only a voluntary option to update that information throughout the lifetime of the space object.[345] Consequently, the initial orbital parameters with which an object was registered are not necessarily indicative of the current orbital parameters of the object. Therefore, an object with given orbital characteristics may or may not be the object that has a registry entry associated with that orbit, and the absence of an object in a registered orbit does not necessarily mean the object no longer exists or is not functional.

Lack of Transparency

7. Another challenge under the existing space law registration regime is the lack of any requirement for providing detailed information on the functions or purpose of a space object.[346] While the Registration Convention requires that certain basic types of information must be provided by the State registering a space object, UNOOSA processes these submissions without conducting a review of their contents to confirm or challenge their accuracy or propriety.[347] Some States have

in orbit deriving from a launch, including new objects tracked from breakups of previously registered space objects. None of these States register foreign objects/payloads.).

[343] Article IV(3) of the Registration Convention (n 46) requires that '[e]ach State of registry shall notify the Secretary-General of the United Nations, to the greatest extent feasible and as soon as practicable, of space objects concerning which it has previously transmitted information, and which have been but no longer are in earth orbit'.
[344] Registration Convention (n 46) art IV(1).
[345] ibid art IV(2) ('Each State of registry may, from time to time, provide the Secretary-General of the United Nations with additional information concerning a space object carried on its registry.').
[346] The Registration Convention (n 46) requires that States indicate only the 'general function of the space object'. ibid art IV(1)(b)(e). It should be noted that, with respect to space objects that perform military functions, this is another example of how the space registration regime differs from the Law of the Sea regime and its rules governing warships (which establish clear legal distinctions for warships based on their stated military/State functions and also mandate clear markings indicating this status on warships).
[347] UNOOSA supports broad participation in its registration regime and has not made intrusive inquiries into registration information submitted by States. For example, although UNOOSA has stated that it strives to implement UN Security Council decisions, including those relating to measures aimed at restricting the development of ballistic missile-related weapons by the Democratic People's Republic of Korea (DPRK), it nonetheless has elected to register DPRK submissions of satellites which were launched by rockets that could also serve as ballistic missiles. See 'Statement by Simonetta Di Pippo, Director, UNOOSA' (59th Session of the Committee on the Peaceful Uses of Outer Space, Vienna, 8–17 June 2016) [https://perma.cc/UU7R-RLYZ] ('The [DPRK] on 25 April 2016 submitted, in accordance with article IV of the Registration Convention, an official registration of the satellite Kwangmyongsong-4, which was launched by the Democratic People's Republic of Korea on 7 February 2016. The Office, in acting on behalf of the Secretary-General, has issued the registration submission as document ST/SG/SER.E/768.').

thus chosen to describe satellites that perform specific military and intelligence functions in very general or vague terms, as evidenced by the lack of such detailed or revealing descriptions in many entries in the UNOOSA Online Registry of Objects Launched Into Space.[348] Operating under the general guidelines of the Registration Convention, States have often rejected transparency in the registration process with respect to the specific mission, functions, or capabilities of space objects, particularly those associated with the military entities of States.[349] It should be noted that the Registration Convention does not establish a definite time requirement/deadline for each State of Registry to furnish information concerning each space object to the Secretary-General of the United Nations, other than 'as soon as practicable'.[350] In addition, the Registration Convention contains no enforcement measures or compliance procedures.

8. One particular aspect of transparency concerns the possibility of identifying a space object as exclusively dedicated to civilian use in order to protect the civilian population and civilian objects against the effects of attacks.[351] Although such an action is not required by the space law registration regime as developed in the OST and the Registration Convention, the parties to an armed conflict are obligated, to the maximum extent feasible, to take necessary precautions to protect the civilian population, individual civilians and civilian objects under their control against the dangers resulting from military operations in or related to outer space (see Rule 41: Precautions Against the Effects of Attack). Such precautions could include considering the identification of space objects that are specially protected or exclusively dedicated to civilian use. However, it should also be noted that under current technological limitations and State practice, there is no marking system in place

---

[348] UN Online Index (n 336).

[349] For example, the 'general function' statement on a Russian submission on 4 January 2019 was, 'Space object intended for assignments on behalf of the Ministry of Defence of the Russian Federation.' UNCOPUOS, 'Note Verbale Dated 12 December 2018 from the Permanent Mission of the Russian Federation to the United Nations (Vienna) Addressed to the Secretary-General' (4 January 2019) UN Doc ST/SG/SER.E/868. Other submissions by major spacefaring States with acknowledged military space programmes similarly show few designations of military or defence functions for many space objects associated with military organizations and instead generically refer only to 'communications', 'earth observation', or 'research'.

[350] Registration Convention (n 46) art IV(1). In practice, this information may be provided years after the launch of a space object. For example, on 22 March 2017, China submitted registration information for 56 space objects launched between January 2014 and August 2016. UNCOPUOS, 'Note Verbale Dated 31 January 2017 From the Permanent Mission of China to the United Nations (Vienna) Addressed to the Secretary-General' (22 March 2017) ST/SG/SER.E/789.

[351] ICRC 'Constraints under International Law on Military Operations in, or in Relation to, Outer Space during Armed Conflicts' (Working Paper submitted in response to UNGA Res 76/231 and UNGA Res 76/230, 3 May 2022) [https://perma.cc/666L-VLF4] 5–6 ('Measures that could be considered [to protect civilians and civilian objects against the effects of military operations in, or in relation to, outer space] include … working towards identifying space systems serving specially protected objects like hospitals and objects indispensable to the survival of the civilian population, such as drink water installations and supplies, and irrigation networks. If a space object is exclusively dedicated to civilian use, the State of registry should register it as such, clearly indicating its protected status under IHL.'

that identifies space objects based on their exclusively civilian or specially protected status (see Rule 45: Improper Use of Markings).

Which State is the State of Registry?

9. Multiple States may qualify as a launching State for a particular space object.[352] This presents the possibility that: one launching State might be the State which launched a space object; another launching State (or multiple States) may have 'procured' the launch of that space object; another launching State may be the State from whose territory that space object was launched; and yet another launching State may be the State from whose facility that space object was launched. Deciding which State(s) qualifies as a 'launching State' is a key determination for purposes of both registration and liability (see Rule 12: International Liability for Damage Caused by Space Objects). Yet the complexity of the registration structure (with the possibility of a multitude of launching States and uncertainty over which one of those States will assume registration responsibility) may often result in 'a non-registration' of space objects.[353] In addition to the challenges that are inherent in a regulatory regime that is based on multiple launching States, the German Government has noted that a further source of divergent registration practice is the 'non-harmonized interpretation of the term "launching State".[354] This lack of a harmonized approach has been created in part by the fact that 'there is no common understanding about the wording "procuring the launch"'.[355] For example, there is no clear consensus that a State 'procures the launch' of a space object if a company that is a national of that State procures the launch in another State. Without a harmonized interpretation of such terms, it may be challenging unambiguously to connect some space objects with all the appropriate, accountable States. Further challenges regarding the identification of the launching State for registration purposes may be presented by the

---

[352] A 'launching state' is defined as: (i) a State which launches a space object; (ii) a State which procures the launching of a space object; (iii) a State from whose territory a space object is launched; and (iv) a State from whose facility a space object is launched. Registration Convention (n 46) art I(a).

[353] 'Registration of Space Objects: Harmonization of Practices, Non-registration of Space Objects, Transfer of Ownership and Registration/Non-registration of "Foreign" Space Objects' (n 321) 4 (further suggesting that 'a general back-up solution for registration is needed in cases of missing consensus on registration' and that '[a] practical solution could be to oblige the host country if there is no other agreement for the satellite'). Unfortunately, there is no State consensus on such a proposed back-up solution and the prospect of permanent liability for any damages caused by a space object under art VII of the OST may diminish the eagerness of some States to declare themselves be a launching State for registration purposes.

[354] ibid.

[355] ibid. While the German Government has further argued that '[i]n the case of an in-orbit delivery, the relevant State of the customer (who will be the first owner of the satellite after the in-orbit delivery) should be regarded as launching State in the sense of "procuring the launch," there is currently no consensus on the registration of space objects that are transferred or delivered in-orbit'.

increasingly common deployment of satellites by the International Space Station or from other space stations.[356]

10. Where two or more States qualify as the launching State with respect to any space object, they shall jointly determine which one of them shall register the object under the Registration Convention.[357] In practice, this requirement has led to some disagreements among launching States regarding which State has the responsibility to register a particular space object, particularly when private corporations procure the launch of a space object. For example, two communication satellites, designated NSS-6 and NSS-7, were built by Lockheed Martin Commercial Space Systems (a US corporation) for New Skies International NV (a Dutch corporation), launched in 2002 from French territory (with launch services provided by Arianespace SA, a French corporation), and delivered in orbit to New Skies. The Government of the Netherlands objected to its name being placed next to entries for NSS-6 and NSS-7 on the UNOOSA Online Index of Objects Launched into Outer Space, indicating that information in these entries about the Netherlands had 'been obtained from other sources and had not been communicated to the United Nations in conformity with the Registration Convention'.[358] The Government of the Netherlands stated that it was not the 'launching State', 'State of Registry', or 'launching authority' for the purposes of the Liability Convention or the Registration Convention.[359] In spite of the role played by a Dutch company in arguably 'procuring' the launch of these satellites, the Government of the Netherlands rejected being designated as a launching State or the State of Registry, although it stated that it bore 'international responsibility for their operation in accordance with article VI [of the OST]' and had 'jurisdiction and control over them in accordance with article VIII [of the OST]'.[360]

Changes in Ownership and Registration of Space Objects

11. Each State of Registry must also notify the Secretary-General of the United Nations, to the greatest extent feasible and as soon as practicable, of space objects concerning which it has previously transmitted information, and which have been but no longer are in Earth orbit.[361] However, neither the Registration Convention

---

[356] For example, a single company (Nanoracks, with its main headquarters in the United States) offers commercial satellite deployment services and has deployed more than 200 satellites from the International Space Station as of the end of 2020. 'ISS Satellite Launch Services' (Nanoracks Official Website) [https://perma.cc/8H7D-P2VL] See also Jean-François Mayence, 'QB 50: Legal Aspects of a Multinational Small Satellite Initiative' in Irmgard Marboe (ed), *Small Satellites* (Brill 2016) 195–210.

[357] Registration Convention (n 46) art II(2).

[358] UNCOPUOS, 'Note Verbale Dated 29 July 2003 from the Permanent Mission of the Netherlands to the United Nations (Vienna) Addressed to the Secretary-General' (22 August 2003) A/AC.105/806.

[359] ibid.

[360] ibid.

[361] Registration Convention (n 46) art IV(3).

nor the OST contain any requirement for a State to report a change in ownership of an operating (in-orbit) space object from one State to another State. In fact, neither agreement make any mention of transfers of ownership or registration between States of in-orbit space objects. Although some States have previously argued that registration transfers of in-orbit space objects are not permitted, there is at least one example of a State agreeing to make such an in-orbit transfer of registration. The State notified UNOOSA and UNOOSA recorded that State's submission.[362] Changing the State of Registry of a space object to a State that was not one of the launching States presents a particular challenge, since the registration of space objects according to the Registration Convention is reserved exclusively to launching States. A related challenge concerns the issue of liability for any damage caused by a transferred object, given that the prevailing obligation under Article VII of the OST rests exclusively with the launching State(s) of the object.

---

[362] In 2014 Airbus Defence and Space agreed to sell its in-orbit SPOT 7 optical Earth observation satellite to Azerbaijan's Azercosmos space agency. Subsequently, the Government of France, the State of Registry of SPOT 7, informed the United Nations that the SPOT 7 satellite had been 'transferred to and registered by Azerbaijan in December 2016 and was therefore removed from the French National Register'. UNCOPUOS, 'Note Verbale Dated 27 March 2017 From the Permanent Mission of France to the United Nations (Vienna) Addressed to the Secretary-General' (1 August 2017) UN Doc ST/SG/SER.E/797.

Rule 9
Ownership of Space Objects

The ownership of both civilian and military objects launched into outer space, including objects landed or constructed in outer space or on a celestial body, and of their component parts, is not affected by their presence in outer space or on a celestial body or by their return to the Earth.

Overview of Legal Basis of Rule

1. The text of this Rule is drawn from Article VIII of the Outer Space Treaty (OST).[363] It does not create any new ownership rights but instead affirms that the ownership status of an object (and its contents) which is launched into space is not affected or changed merely because of its presence in space. A military object is treated the same way as other objects under this Rule.

Legal Issues Related to Ownership of Space Objects

2. It is important to note that ownership is only one possible legal connection between a State and a space object, and it usually is not the most important one for purposes of space law (see Note: Legal Connections between States and a Space Object).[364] Although an object or component thereof may be owned by a government or by a person or corporation under the laws of the State of their nationality, a different State may have 'international responsibility' for the object if the object is part of a 'national activity' for which that State is responsible under Article VI of the OST (see Rule 10: Responsibility of States for National Activities in Outer Space); a different State may qualify as a 'launching State' of the space object, with various related legal obligations, including liability for damages caused by the space object (see Rule 12: International Liability for Damage Caused by Space Objects); one of the launching States may also qualify as the State of Registry, with the right to

---

[363] OST (n 9) art VIII.
[364] As noted by the German Government, '[w]hile the reference to a launching State with respect to a particular space object creates a clear and unambiguous allocation of responsibilities vis-à-vis the general public, a reference to the State of the owner of a space object does not fulfil these requirements'. 'Registration of Space Objects: Harmonization of Practices, Non-registration of Space Objects, Transfer of Ownership and Registration/Non-registration of 'Foreign' Space Objects' (n 321) 4.

exercise jurisdiction and control over the object and personnel thereof based on its registration (see Rule 8: Registration of Space Objects); and finally, different States may have other jurisdictional rights over the object and persons onboard based on other factors (see Rule 7: Jurisdiction).

3. If an object, including its component parts, which is launched into outer space is found beyond the limits of the State Party to the Treaty on whose registry it is carried, it shall be returned to that State Party, which shall, upon request, furnish identifying data prior to its return.[365] Accordingly, the owner of the object may not be the State of Registry and hence has no immediate entitlement to the return of that object.

4. The right of ownership of an object, which is established under the national laws of relevant States, extends to both natural and juridical persons (eg corporations) and to governments, if national laws so provide. If there is any dispute or uncertainty regarding the ownership of an object prior to its launching into space, the launching of that object into space does not change or resolve those disputes or uncertainties. National laws will also dictate the circumstances in which ownership ceases and in which the property is abandoned. Moreover, in a time of armed conflict, the ownership of military property transfers to the belligerent party that lawfully captures such property in accordance with the law of armed conflict.[366]

5. It is important to note that the ownership in space of an object by a person or corporation under the laws of State X does not interfere with the jurisdiction of State X to exercise legal control over ownership of rights to that property, including determining how to regulate that object and how to transfer ownership of the object. An object in space may also be sold or transferred to a different owner pursuant to the applicable laws of the States involved the transaction, although the sale or transfer of an object does not change the international legal responsibilities of a launching State with respect to that object under Article VII of the OST, nor the State of Registry under Article VIII of the OST or the Registration Convention (see Rule 8: Registration of Space Objects).

6. Ownership of objects which are 'landed' on a celestial body '[are] not affected by their presence in outer space'.[367] Objects which are 'constructed' on celestial bodies are also 'not affected by their presence in outer space',[368] presumably leaving any

---

[365] ibid.
[366] See Canadian Office of the Judge Advocate General 'Law of Armed Conflict at the Operational and Tactical Levels' (Canadian National Defence 2001) (Canadian Joint Doctrine Manual) para 622 ('All enemy public movable property captured on a battlefield is known as "booty" and becomes the property of the capturing state.'); US DoD Law of War Manual (n 234) para 5.17; German Federal Ministry of Defence, 'Law of Armed Conflict Manual' (Joint Service Regulation ZDv 15/2, 2013) (German Law of Armed Conflict Manual) para 553.
[367] OST (n 9) art VIII.
[368] ibid.

ownership questions focused on the laws of the States that are involved in the construction activities. Those elements that go into the construction which as such are launched into outer space would still be owned by whoever was their owner back on Earth, including if those elements originated from multiple States. Elements taken from *in-situ* resources, however, are a different matter as they are not addressed by Article VIII, OST, and/or the Registration Convention—see paragraph 9.

7. The construction of an object on a spacecraft or on another object in outer space is not directly addressed by Article VIII of the OST. However, construction activities on a space object clearly take place under the jurisdiction and control of the space object's State of Registry and are thus governed by the State of Registry's laws.[369] An example of the application of relevant State laws to creation/invention activities onboard a space object under the jurisdiction of a State can be found in the international legal framework governing the creation of intellectual property on the International Space Station (the ISS).[370] The ISS Agreement assigns inventorship based on the jurisdiction of a 'Partner State' over a specific 'Space Station flight element,' meaning that the invention activity 'shall be deemed to have occurred only in the territory of the Partner State of that element's registry.'[371]

8. Several items have already been constructed on board space objects by using additive or '3D printing.'[372] Three-dimensional (3D) printing using materials from asteroid material on Earth has also been demonstrated as practical[373] and several States are also exploring or planning to build objects or facilities on celestial bodies using *in-situ* space resources.[374] These activities present new questions about the legal status of such items 'constructed' in space using space resources. For example, using resources from celestial bodies in 3D printing could be viewed as violating the 'non-appropriation' principle in the OST[375] or, under another view, could be permitted under the 'free use principle.'[376] Other questions, yet to be answered, may be raised about the machinery launched into space which then produces

---

[369] It is also possible that such activities undertaken by nationals from another State would also presumably qualify as 'national activities in outer space' of that State under OST (n 9) art VI.

[370] ISS Agreement (n 47) D.II.4.2.

[371] ibid art 21, para 2 ('Subject to the provisions of this Article, for purposes of intellectual property law, an activity occurring in or on a Space Station flight element shall be deemed to have occurred only in the territory of the Partner State of that element's registry, except that for ESA-registered elements any European Partner State may deem the activity to have occurred within its territory.').

[372] Phil Goldstein, 'NASA Turns to 3D Printing to Help Astronauts Abroad the International Space Station' (*FedTech*, 24 October 2018) [https://perma.cc/5T3U-E3TA].

[373] Mike Wall, 'Asteroid-Mining Company 3D-Prints Object from Space Rock Metals' [https://perma.cc/HME2-Z86C]

[374] 'Building a Lunar Base with 3D Printing' (The European Space Agency, 31 January 2013) [https://perma.cc/5XC8-UE3K] ('Setting up a lunar base could be made much simpler by using a 3D printer to build it from local materials.'); 'Russia Plans to Use 3D printing, Lunar Dust to Create Moon Base—Roscosmos' (Moscow, Tass, 6 July 2019) [https://perma.cc/NA7L-CF6F]; Thomas, 'China Reveals Plans to 3D Print Houses on the Moon's Surface' (http://www.3ders.org, accessed 15 January 2019) [https://perma.cc/J8XH-Y8GA].

[375] OST (n 9) art II.

[376] ibid art I.

from *in-situ* resources certain elements of the objects constructed in space. For example, it is not clear that the ownership of the machinery (such as 3D printers or mining equipment) that produces elements of constructed objects on a celestial body determines (or even relates to) the ownership of those constructed objects. Such questions await relevant State practice under existing agreements or under new agreements to be concluded in the future. In this regard, as part of the 'Artemis Accords' (discussed shortly), NASA has announced that its Lunar Surface Innovation Initiative 'will develop and demonstrate technologies to use the Moon's resources to produce water, fuel, and other supplies as well as capabilities to excavate and construct structures on the Moon'.[377]

There currently is no global acceptance of what the legal regime applicable to mined resources is/should be. The right to extract, own and sell resources from asteroids and other celestial bodies is thus controversial. However, some States, including the United States, Luxembourg, and the United Arab Emirates, have explicitly recognized in their national legislation the right to appropriate these resources, the authority to license space mining operations, or the right of their citizens to possess, own, transport, use, and sell these resources. In addition, several States have joined 'the Artemis Accords' (a set of non-legally binding, multilateral political commitments to the principles of cooperation in the civil exploration and use of the Moon, Mars, comets, and asteroids for peaceful purposes) in which the Signatories affirm that 'the extraction of space resources does not inherently constitute national appropriation under Article II of the Outer Space Treaty, and that contracts and other legal instruments relating to space resources should be consistent with that Treaty'.[378]

9.

---

[377] NASA, 'Overview: In-Situ Resource Utilization Using Space-Based Resources for Deep Space Exploration' (n 172) 3.
[378] The Artemis Accords (n 168) s 10, para 2.

SECTION 2
RESPONSIBILITY AND LIABILITY

Rule 10
Responsibility of States for National Activities in Outer Space

A State bears international responsibility for all its national activities in outer space, including military space activities, whether such activities are carried on by governmental or non-governmental entities, and is required to ensure the conformity of such activities with international law as well as to authorise and continuously supervise them.

Overview of Legal Basis of Rule

1. This Rule is derived from Article VI of the Outer Space Treaty (OST), which provides in its relevant parts, that:

> States Parties to the Treaty shall bear international responsibility for national activities in outer space, including the Moon and other celestial bodies, whether such activities are carried on by governmental agencies or by non-governmental entities, and for assuring that national activities are carried out in conformity with the provisions set forth in the present Treaty. The activities of non-governmental entities in outer space, including the Moon and other celestial bodies, shall require authorization and continuing supervision by the appropriate State Party to the Treaty.[379]

2. This commentary examines six major elements of this Rule raised by its application to military activities: (i) the concept of attribution of 'international responsibility'; (ii) the concept of '*national* activities in outer space'[380] for which such responsibility arises and the inclusion of activities of 'non-governmental entities' in this context; (iii) the inclusion of 'military activities' in this context; (iv) questions related to the special attribution rule of Article VI as it applies to non-governmental entities with respect to the threat or use of force and armed conflict; (v) the requirement of 'authorization and continuing supervision'; and (vi) the concept of 'the legal consequences of an internationally wrongful act, including reparation'.

---

[379] OST (n 9) art VI.
[380] ibid (emphasis added).

International Responsibility

3. The **first major element** to be addressed concerns the attribution of 'international responsibility', noting that the term of art in modern public international law is 'State responsibility'. Logically, 'international responsibility' can be interpreted only as 'responsibility under international law', that is in the context of the international community of States, as opposed to responsibility in a domestic legal context. 'State responsibility' likewise focuses on what essentially is the accountability of States for applying the rules of international law applicable between them.[381]

4. The State responsibility in Article VI refers to 'assuring that national activities are carried out in conformity with the provisions set forth in the present Treaty', which, through Article III (requiring all relevant activities to be 'in accordance with international law'), effectively means in conformity with international law in toto. This would essentially equate with the doctrine of State responsibility in general public international law, which arises if an internationally wrongful act has been committed. This is further discussed in the section on Reparation for an Internationally Wrongful Act.

National Activities in Space

5. The **second major element** of the Rule is identifying the '*national* activities in outer space',[382] for which a State bears 'international responsibility' and, specifically, the extent to which it bears responsibility for activities conducted by 'non-governmental entities'. Neither Article VI nor the subsequent space treaties elaborates these terms or concepts further.

6. However, many States have enacted and implemented national space legislation that includes a regime of authorization and supervision (alternatively called licensing, permission, or approval) of space activities of 'non-governmental entities' so as to comply with Article VI.[383] This State practice, given its manifestation by way of domestic law thereby serves as the most authoritative interpretation of the term '*national* activities in outer space'.[384] Since States are held responsible for such

---

[381] The term 'international responsibility' also effectively extends the term 'State responsibility' to include 'responsibility of international organizations' within the limits indicated by the last sentence of Article VI: 'When activities are carried on in outer space, including the Moon and other celestial bodies, by an international organization, responsibility for compliance with this Treaty shall be borne both by the international organization and by the States Parties to the Treaty participating in such organization'. ibid.

[382] ibid.

[383] See 'National Space Law Collection' (online database, UNOOSA) <http://www.unoosa.org/oosa/en/ourwork/spacelaw/nationalspacelaw/index.html> accessed 23 March 2023; 'National Space Legislations' (online database, ESA) [https://perma.cc/7JWY-9AZY].

[384] OST (n 9) art VI (emphasis added).

national activities in outer space, those are the activities that they will naturally subject to such a regime of authorization and continuing supervision (see paragraphs 15–19), which conversely means that the scope of their authorization and supervision regimes points to their respective interpretation of Article VI in this respect.

Analysing the national space legislation adopted in over two dozen States around the world, the overwhelming majority of States with such a national space law regulating space activities applies its authorization and supervision regime to both space activities conducted by nationals (entities and natural persons) regardless of where undertaken, and space activities conducted from national territory, regardless of who undertakes them, which is very often extended moreover to vehicles registered with the State at issue.[385] In other words, the most authoritative interpretation of 'national activities' would be activities either conducted by nationals or from national territory, including most likely also activities conducted from domestically registered ships and aircraft.[386] Alternative formulations of national space activities are neither consistent with State practice nor the travaux préparatoires of the OST.[387]

7.

---

[385] See eg Australia, 'Space Activities Act 1998' (Federal Registration of Legislation) [https://perma.cc/EUW9-39DE]; Phillippe Clerc and Julien Mariez (trs), 'LOI no 2008-518 du 3 juin 2008 relative aux operations spatiales' 34 Journal of Space Law [https://perma.cc/T7J2-V52Q]; Faculty of International Law and the National Center for Remote Sensing, Air, and Space Law (trs), 'Chinese Law: Registration, Launching and Licensing Space Objects' [2008] 33 Journal of Space Law 437 [https://perma.cc/4WCX-6RVG]; 'Selected Examples of National Laws Governing Space Activities: Norway' (UNOOSA 2021) [https://perma.cc/PR8T-TGAA]; 'Selected Examples of National Laws Governing Space Activities: Russian Federation' (UNOOSA 2021) [https://perma.cc/Y5NN-D8LS]; 'Selected Examples of National Laws Governing Space Activities: Sweden' (UNOOSA 2021) [https://perma.cc/6939-GXUR]; 'Space Affairs Act (South Africa, 1993)' [https://perma.cc/V4ES-JPUD]; United Kingdom, 'Outer Space Act 1986' [https://perma.cc/5ABX-7JD4]; [US] National and Commercial Space Program, 51 USC §§ 10101-71301 (2010) [https://perma.cc/5ZLJ-CTPS].

[386] See para 17, noting how para 2 of UN General Assembly Resolution 68/74 supports this interpretation by emphasizing that the launching State and State responsible for national activities should ascertain national jurisdiction over space activities carried out from territory under its jurisdiction and/or control and should 'issue authorizations for and ensure supervision over space activities carried out elsewhere by its citizens and/or legal persons established, registered or seated in territory under its jurisdiction and/or control'. Note that one view raised during State Consultations is that the term 'national activities' does not necessarily include all activities undertaken by a State's nationals. Yet it is hard to see how the activities of nationals would not be included in 'national activities' under art VI in order to ensure that all entities in outer space comply with international law and all the key rules of the space law regime. For example, as noted by one State, the duty of 'due regard' under art IX of the OST imposes 'due diligence obligation upon states over the conduct of their nationals and vessels, with the view to ensuring that their conduct do not prejudice the rights and interests of other states'. Republic of the Philippines, 'The Duty of "due regard" as a foundational principle of responsible behaviour in space' (6 May 2022) UN Doc A/AC.294/2022.WP (Advanced Unedited working paper) ('Philippines working paper') para 11.1.

[387] One State representative at State Consultations offered an unofficial argument for an alternative definition of 'national space activities' as including only space activities that can be attributed to a State according to customary international law rules. This alternative, however, would make art VI superfluous as simply restating customary international law and would supplant the special attribution regime of art VI envisioned by the drafters of the OST with the Articles on State Responsibility. In this light, the suggested alternative is difficult to reconcile with the primary obligation in art VI that States

8. The first part of the concept 'National Activities in Outer Space', with respect to attribution, is straightforward: in outer space as elsewhere, a State is responsible for internationally wrongful acts conducted in whole or in part by its 'governmental agencies'.[388]

9. The next part of the concept of 'National Activities in Outer Space' (which makes States responsible for the activities of 'non-governmental entities') is unique in international law. Following standard rules of treaty interpretation and the ordinary meaning of the words in the text, the phrase '*whether* such activities are carried on by governmental agencies *or* by non-governmental entities'[389] to which international space law responsibility applies should leave little doubt. Consequently, each State is directly responsible for all the space acts of its non-governmental entities—even if the non-governmental entity acts without the knowledge of the government or acts beyond the scope of its licence or authorization (but see discussion in paragraph 14 regarding the involvement of non-governmental agencies in actions related to the threat of use of force or during an armed conflict).

10. This interpretation is confirmed by an examination of the preparatory work of the OST.[390] During the negotiations that led to the OST, the Soviet Union sought to restrict the scope of permissible activities in space exclusively to government entities.[391] Eventually, the Soviet Union compromised to the extent of accepting in the treaty one permissive reference to space activities carried out by non-governmental entities (such as corporations), on the condition that all activities of such entities would be subsumed under (direct) responsibility of the State

---

bear international responsibility for national activities in outer space 'whether such activities are carried on by governmental agencies or by non-governmental entities'.

[388] Note that this would follow both from the specific clause of art VI and from the general theory of State responsibility in public international law. See ILC Articles on State Responsibility (n 253) art 4.1. ('The conduct of any State organ shall be considered an act of that State under international law, whether the organ exercises legislative, executive, judicial or any other functions, whatever position it holds in the organization of the State, and whatever its character as an organ of the central government or of a territorial unit of the State.' Along similar lines, art 8 provides: 'The conduct of a person or group of persons shall be considered an act of a State under international law if the person or group of persons is in fact acting on the instructions of, or under the direction or control of, that State in carrying out the conduct.').

[389] OST (n 9) art VI (emphasis added).

[390] See VCLT (n 11) art 32 (providing that 'recourse may be had to supplementary means of interpretation, including the preparatory work of the treaty and the circumstances of its conclusion, in order to confirm the meaning resulting from the application of Article 31, or to determine the meaning when the interpretation according to article 31: (a) leaves the meaning ambiguous or obscure; or (b) leads to a result which is manifestly absurd or unreasonable').

[391] Article VI is based on Principle 5 of the UNGA Resolution 1962 (XVIII) Declaration of Legal Principles (n 60), which is in all-important respects essentially identical to the text of art VI. The original Soviet position in the drafting work of this resolution was that 'all activities ... shall be carried out solely and exclusively by States'. UNGA 'USSR Proposal: Declaration of the Basic Principles governing the Activities of States Pertaining to the Exploration and Use of Outer Space' (6 June 1962) UN Doc A/AC.105/C.2/L.1 para 7.

concerned.[392] An analysis of the travaux préparatoires confirms that this is the major reason for explicit inclusion of the term 'non-governmental entities' and related conditions in Article VI. The resulting language in the OST makes a State just as responsible for the activities of non-governmental entities as it is for its own activities in outer space, as long as those qualify as '*national* activities in outer space'.[393]

11. The last part of the concept of 'national activities in outer space' is the scope of the term 'national', with a view to what *categories* of (activities of) 'non-governmental entities' a particular State might consequently be held responsible for. This leads to the question of whether this Rule applies to make States responsible for some or all 'military space activities' that are conducted by non-governmental entities. Thus, the **third major element** of the Rule relates to answering the question: to what extent does the preceding discussion apply to 'military space activities'?

Military Space Activities

12. Military space activities encompass a wide range of activities of a military nature that may be conducted by a variety of entities. These activities are clearly encompassed within the concept of 'national activities in outer space'. Under the OST, a State has the right to explore and use outer space, including the Moon and other celestial bodies, to engage freely in scientific investigation, and to have free access to all areas of celestial bodies (see Rule 1: Freedom of Use, Access, Exploration, Scientific Investigation, and Principles of Cooperation). These freedoms are extended under the OST to all types of activities in space and no distinction is made between military space activities and other space activities. Military activities have been present in space from the beginning of the space age and only certain military space activities are prohibited by the OST. These prohibitions are found in Article IV and apply to specific military establishments and activities on the Moon and other celestial bodies (see Rule 4: Restrictions on Specified Military Establishments and Activities on Celestial Bodies) and with respect to weapons of mass destruction

---

[392] The Soviet compromise language that was adopted by the General Assembly is thus essentially identical to the text of Article VI of the OST. See UNGA 'Letter Dated 16 June 1966 From the Permanent Representative of the Union of Soviet Socialist Republic to the United Nations Addressed to the Secretary-General' (16 June 1966) UN Doc A/6352; UNGA 'Letter Dated 11 July 1966 to the Chairman of the Legal Sub-committee by the Representative of the USSR (11 July 1966) UN Doc A/AC.105/C.2/L.13 (with reference to UN Doc A/6352); see also Bin Cheng, 'Article VI of the 1967 Space Treaty Revisited: "International Responsibility, 'National Activities", and "The Appropriate State"' (1998) 26 Journal of Space Law 7, 14 (Noting that the result of this compromise is that 'non-governmental national space activities are assimilated to governmental space activities. This assimilation and consequently the assumption by the contracting States of direct States responsibility for non-governmental space activities is a fundamental innovation which the Treaty has introduced into international law.').

[393] OST (n 9) art VI (emphasis added).

(see Rule 5: Weapons of Mass Destruction).[394] Any breach of these prohibitions in peacetime by a governmental or nongovernmental entity would trigger responsibility of a relevant State or States under Article VI as discussed above. Note that it is possible that more than one State will bear responsibility for the same activity in outer space—many space activities are conducted by nationals of several States, or by nationals of one State operating from the territory of another, and possibly even involving space objects registered with a third State.

13. Military space activities, like other space activities, must be carried out in accordance with international law, including the Charter of the United Nations.[395] Consistent with UN Charter obligations addressing the threat or use of force, as well as the related concept of 'peaceful purposes' under the OST, military space activities must be non-aggressive (see Rule 3: Peaceful Purposes in Outer Space). However, with respect to these obligations under the UN Charter and also under the law of armed conflict, several important questions are addressed below regarding the attribution to States of military activities conducted by non-governmental entities.

The *Jus ad Bellum*, the *Jus in Bello*, and Attribution to States of the Conduct of Non-Governmental Entities

14. **The fourth major element** also relates to the scope of what is included in military space activities, but focuses on whether particular activities by a non-governmental entity involving the threat or use of force (relating to the *jus ad bellum*) will result in the attribution of responsibility to a particular State under Article VI, and whether particular activities by a non-governmental entity during an armed conflict will also result in the attribution of responsibility to a particular State (relating to the *jus in bello* and also the law of neutrality).

The *jus ad bellum*

A. Although Article VI provides that a State is internationally responsible for all breaches of international obligations by a non-governmental entity that is suitably connected with that State, Article VI raises special concerns with

---

[394] Under art IV, para 1, of the OST, a State is prohibited from placing WMD's in orbit around the Earth, installing such weapons on celestial bodies, or stationing such weapons in outer space in any other manner; under art IV, para 1, a State is prohibited from establishing military bases, installations and fortifications, testing of any type of weapons, and conducting military manoeuvres on the Moon or other celestial bodies. A State is further obligated to prohibit, to prevent, and not to carry out, any nuclear weapon test or explosion in outer space and under water under the PNTB Treaty (n 262).

[395] OST (n 9) art III.

respect to possible contemporary uses of force. To automatically apply the special attribution regime in Article VI in this area would make a State responsible for any violations by any of its nationals or non-governmental entities of the prohibition on the threat or use of force and the attendant consequences, including the activation of the right to self-defence against that State in cases where the activity by the non-governmental entity reaches the level of an 'armed attack'.[396] However, in light of the factors noted below, it is not consistent with existing international law to interpret the scope of Article VI to make the actions of a non-governmental entity automatically the responsibility of a particular State with respect to the threat and use of force as addressed by Articles 2(4) and 51 of the United Nations Charter (ie in circumstances where existing attribution rules of international law would not make the State responsible).

B. During the more than 50 years that States have engaged in space activities since the conclusion of the OST, international law has continued to develop, particularly with respect to the use of force and the right of self-defence under the UN Charter. International law, as articulated by the International Court of Justice, now clearly recognizes the prohibition against the use of force as a peremptory norm and clearly establishes a threshold/burden of proof for attribution when a State invokes the right to use of force in self-defence.[397] Against this backdrop, and in light of the pre-eminence of UN Charter obligations over the obligations of Members of the United Nations under any other international agreement,[398] there is no State practice which supports an attribution rule based on Article VI that would supersede the 'effective control' requirements articulated by the International Court of

---

[396] This would reflect the strictest possible interpretation of the view originally espoused by the Soviet Union during UNGA diplomacy in the run up to OST negotiations. Hobe, Schmidt-Tedd, and Schrogl (eds), *Cologne Commentary*, vol I (n 133).

[397] See *Nicaragua v US* (Merits) (n 24) para 190 (noting that State practice with respect to the 'principle of the prohibition of the use of force expressed in art 2, para 4, of the Charter of the United Nations' indicates that it is 'not only a principle of customary international law but also a fundamental or cardinal principle of such law'). In addition, even when conduct on the part of a State involving the use of force is alleged, the ICJ has determined that the State making such an allegation must, with respect to both the armed attack itself and its attribution, discharge 'the burden of proof of the facts showing the existence of such an attack'. *Case Concerning Oil Platforms (Islamic Republic of Iran v United States of America)* (Merits) [2003] ICJ 4, para 57 (holding that 'if at the end of the day the evidence available is insufficient to establish that the missile was fired by Iran, then the necessary burden of proof has not been discharged by the United States').

[398] UN Charter (n 25) art 103. ('In the event of a conflict between the obligations of the Members of the United Nations under the present Charter and their obligations under any other international agreement, their obligations under the present Charter shall prevail.'). Along similar lines, those provisions of the OST and other space law treaties that are inconsistent with exercise of the right of self-defence as reflected in Article 51 of the UN Charter would be inapplicable to the extent of such inconsistency. See ILC Articles on State Responsibility (n 253) 14 ('A State exercising its inherent right of individual or collective self-defence in accordance with the Charter of the United Nations is entitled to suspend in whole or in part the operation of a treaty to which it is a party insofar as that operation is incompatible with the exercise of that right.').

Justice with respect to the attribution of the actions of a non-governmental entity to a State when those actions related to a use of force.[399]

C. This conclusion appears to be particularly appropriate in light of the vast and continuing expansion of non-government entities in space, a domain that was dominated exclusively by State activities when the OST was negotiated and entered into force over 50 years ago. To apply such an attribution rule automatically now with respect to the use of force, in the increasingly complex and competitive space domain, might increase the risk of armed conflict occurring in space instead of promoting peace and security. Any default rule attributing the conduct of a non-governmental entity to a State with respect to the use of force outside existing criteria for such attribution under international law would also present new dangers in light of dramatic and profound technological developments which have transformed and expanded the capabilities of non-governmental entities to engage in harmful actions in space, particularly through new damaging cyber capabilities.

Particular aspects of the *jus in bello*

D. There is insufficient State practice to allow a definitive resolution of the relationship between the special rule of attribution contained in Article VI of the OST and the legal test for attribution of conduct to a State for aspects of the law of armed conflict. It is clear that, during armed conflict, a State 'shall be responsible for all acts committed by persons forming part of its armed forces'.[400] In addition, in respect of the conduct of a non-governmental entity during armed conflict, State responsibility arises where a State exercises effective control over such entity.[401] In the absence of effective control, or

---

[399] For such conduct alleged to violate the prohibition on the use of force to give rise to legal responsibility of a State, it would in principle have to be proved that that State involved had 'effective control' of the operations of the non-State actor (or in this case, a 'non-governmental actor') in the course of which the alleged violations were committed. See *Nicaragua v US* (Merits) (n 24) 115.

[400] Convention (IV) respecting the Laws and Customs of War on Land and its annex: Regulations concerning the Laws and Customs of War on Land (adopted 18 October 1907, entered into force 26 January 1910) 205 CTS 277 (Hague Convention IV) art 3; Protocol Additional to the Geneva Conventions of 12 August 1949, and relating to the Protection of Victims of International Armed Conflicts (Protocol I) (adopted 8 June 1977, entered into force 7 December 1978) 1125 UNTS 3 (Additional Protocol I) art 91.

[401] *Nicaragua v US* (Merits) (n 24) para 115 (finding that in order for the conduct of a paramilitary force 'to give rise to legal responsibility of the United States, it would in principle have to be proved that that State had effective control of the military or paramilitary operations in the course of which the alleged violations [of the law of armed conflict] were committed'); *Case Concerning Application of the Convention on the Prevention and Punishment of the Crime of Genocide (Bosnia and Herzegovina v Serbia and Montenegro)* (Merits) [2007] ICJ Reps 43, para 401 ('Genocide will be considered as attributable to a State if and to the extent that the physical acts constitutive of genocide that have been committed by organs or persons other than the State's own agents were carried out, wholly or in part, on the instructions or directions of the State, or under its effective control.'); Jean-Marie Henckaerts and Louise Doswald-Beck (eds), *ICRC, Customary International Humanitarian Law, Vol 1: Rules* (CUP 2005) Rule 149(c) ('A State is responsible for violations of international humanitarian law attributable to

other special situations,[402] a State would not be responsible for the conduct of a non-governmental entity in the context of armed conflict.[403] However, if the special attribution mandated by Article VI of the OST were to apply in this situation, a State could be found to be automatically responsible for the conduct of a non-governmental entity that violates the law of armed conflict, even if the State had no prior knowledge of the non-governmental entity's illegal actions or indeed had taken all reasonable steps to try to repress such conduct. If Article VI of the OST were to attribute the conduct of a non-governmental entity to the State in these circumstances, it could give rise to manifestly absurd results and serve to enlarge the participation of States in armed conflicts in space—with potentially devastating consequences for international peace and security. However, the fortunate and welcome absence of an armed conflict in space to this point means that there is no State practice interpreting the application of Article VI in these circumstances.

Neutrality

E. There is also insufficient State practice, and no consensus on applicable law, to allow a definitive resolution of the relationship between the special rule of attribution contained in Article VI of the OST and the legal test for attribution of conduct to a State for the actions of a national or a non-governmental entity that violate the law of neutrality. First it must be noted that while the fundamental aspects of the law of neutrality appear to apply to military space operations during an international armed conflict (see Rule 48: Neutrality in Space), the precise scope of neutrality obligations in space is unsettled. Furthermore, the specific types of conduct by space objects that could violate a neutral State's obligations are unsettled, as is the determination of which parts of the law of neutrality are specific to domains other than space. Notwithstanding these uncertainties, to the extent that the law of neutrality does apply to space the automatic attribution of actions by a non-governmental entity in space to a State that results in the loss of that State's neutrality risks unnecessarily expanding conflicts in space and would

---

it, including ... violations committed by persons or groups acting in fact on its instructions, or under its direction or control.').

[402] A well-accepted example is conduct adopted by a State: *United States Diplomatic and Consular Staff in Tehran* (*United States v Iran*) [1980] ICJ Reps 3, para 74; ILC Articles on State Responsibility (n 253) art 11.

[403] It should be noted, however, that if the space object causes damage to another space object in an incident that is not connected to the armed conflict, the launching State remains liable for damages caused by the space object and may be required to make full reparation if the non-governmental entity was at fault for an internationally wrongful act. See Rule 12: International Liability for Damage Caused by Space Objects.

be inconsistent with both the goals of the UN Charter and the object and purpose of the OST in advancing the peaceful use and exploration of space. Thus, it would be the case with respect to violations of the law of armed conflict by non-governmental actors on Earth or in space, a State would presumably be required to exercise effective control over a non-governmental entity to have that entity's actions in space attributed to it—with the resulting loss of that State's neutrality.

Authorization and Continuing Supervision of Space Activities Carried Out by Non-Governmental Entities

15. The **fifth major element** of Article VI is the requirement of 'authorization and continuing supervision' of space activities carried out by 'non-governmental entities', a requirement that is consistent with, and provides an implementation mechanism for, the appropriate State's acceptance of responsibility. This requirement does not supplant or replace a State's primary obligation of responsibility for national activities in space under Article VI.[404]

16. The regime of authorization and continuing supervision of non-governmental entities is directly linked to national space legislation which many States have enacted and implemented so as to comply with Article VI.[405] National space legislation thus includes a regime of authorization and supervision (which may also be referred to as licensing, permission, or approval) of space activities of 'non-governmental entities' so as to comply with Article VI. However as outlined in paragraph 7, a State will bear international responsibility for non-governmental entities, even in circumstances where they do not abide by an existing licensing and authorization regime.

17. As previously noted, a State that adopts a national space law typically applies its authorization and supervision regime to both space activities conducted by nationals (entities and natural persons) regardless of where undertaken, and space activities conducted from national territory, regardless of who undertakes them, which is very often extended moreover to vehicles registered with the State at issue. Thus,

---

[404] See Cheng, 'Article VI of the 1967 Space Treaty Revisited' (n 393) 26 (noting that interpreting art VI for non-governmental space activities as consisting of no more than what is expressly laid down in the latter part of the article (assuring compliance with the terms of the OST and subjecting such activities to authorization and continuing supervision) would 'dispense with the first part of the sentence altogether. It would also be contrary to the history of the treaty'); Peter Stubbe, *State Accountability for Space Debris: A Legal Study of Responsibility for Polluting the Space Environment and Liability for Damage Caused by Space Debris* (Brill Nijhoff 2018) 96 (noting that the obligation to authorize and supervise '[o]nly covers one part of Art. VI OST. The first half of Article VI, sentence 1, of the OST, additionally and equally important, provides for a modified attribution of state responsibility.').

[405] See National Space Activities, paras 5–11.

this is the subject matter to which the authorization and continuing supervision regimes applies.

Such an interpretation would also be in line with paragraph 2 of United Nations General Assembly Resolution 68/74, which states: **18.**

> The State, taking into account its obligations as a launching State and as a State responsible for national activities in outer space under the United Nations treaties on outer space, should ascertain national jurisdiction over space activities carried out from territory under its jurisdiction and/or control; likewise, it should issue authorizations for and ensure supervision over space activities carried out elsewhere by its citizens and/or legal persons established, registered or seated in territory under its jurisdiction and/or control....[406]

In short, Article VI sets out a specialized regime for the attribution of breaches of international law related to activities in outer space such that States bear international responsibility for activities in outer space that they themselves conduct, as well as for those activities conducted by persons or entities with their respective nationalities, conducted from their respective national territories, or conducted from their registered ships, aircraft, space objects and other vehicles. **19.**

Reparation for an Internationally Wrongful Act

When it comes to the **sixth major element**, the concept of 'reparation' which essentially concerns the legal consequences once international responsibility has actually been incurred, analysis moves beyond Article VI, since this Article itself does not indicate what a particular State should do in order to redeem a violation of the OST and more broadly of international space law in general for which it is considered responsible. **20.**

However, Article III does provide that 'States Parties to the Treaty shall carry on activities in the exploration and use of outer space, including the moon and other celestial bodies, in accordance with international law'. This clause is generally interpreted to mean that general rules of international law apply to outer space and space activities unless contradicted or superseded by specific rules of space law, qualifying to that extent as *lex specialis* to the *lex generalis* of general public international law. **21.**

---

[406] UNGA, 'Recommendations on National Legislation Relevant to the Peaceful Exploration and Use of Outer Space' (11 December 2013) UN Doc A/RES/68/74; see also UNGA, 'Report of the Working Group on National Legislation Relevant to the Peaceful Exploration and Use of Outer Space on the Work Conducted Under its multi-year Workplan' (3 April 2012) UN Doc A/AC.105/C.2/101.

22. Given that the analysis has essentially equated the 'international responsibility' of Article VI for the purpose of the present Rule with the 'State responsibility' of general public international law, straightforward treaty interpretation of Article III would make the general rules of public international law applicable to 'State responsibility' applicable also to 'international (space law) responsibility'. The general rules of public international law on 'State responsibility', originating in the *Chorzow Factory* case[407] and most recently codified in the ILC Articles on Responsibility of States for internationally wrongful acts,[408] provide that once such responsibility arises, it needs to be redeemed by providing 'reparation'.[409] Reparation can take three forms:[410] restitution,[411] compensation,[412] and satisfaction,[413] individually or in combination. The substance of such reparation of course has to be determined with reference to the substance and character of the international wrongful act and, if necessary, seising courts or arbitral tribunals to that end or exercising appropriate diplomatic mechanisms.

23. Once responsibility for an internationally wrongful act arises, the State that is responsible for the internationally wrongful act is also under an obligation to cease that act, if it is continuing, and to offer appropriate assurances and guarantees of non-repetition, if circumstances so require.[414] This obligation

---

[407] *Case Concerning the Factory at Chorzów (Germany v Poland)* (Merits) PCIJ Series A No 17 (holding that, as a general principle of international law, reparation is to be made for violations of international law and that a State is responsible for the acts of government organs or officers).

[408] ILC Articles on State Responsibility (n 253). The final text with commentary and apparatus is in James Crawford, *The International Law Commission's Articles on State Responsibility: Introduction, Text and Commentaries* (CUP 2002).

[409] ILC Articles on State Responsibility (n 253) art 31.

[410] ibid art 34 ('Full reparation for the injury caused by the internationally wrongful act shall take the form of restitution, compensation and satisfaction, either singly or in combination, in accordance with the provisions of this chapter.').

[411] ibid art 35 ('A State responsible for an internationally wrongful act is under an obligation to make restitution, that is, to re-establish the situation which existed before the wrongful act was committed', provided it is 'not materially impossible' and 'does not involve a burden out of all proportion to the benefit deriving from restitution instead of compensation').

[412] ibid art 36(1) ('The State responsible for an internationally wrongful act is under an obligation to compensate for the damage caused thereby, insofar as such damage is not made good by restitution.' Article 36(2) further states that the compensation 'shall cover any financially assessable damage including loss of profits insofar as it is established.') It is important to note that compensation for international wrongful acts under this Rule must be distinguished from compensation for liability for damages caused by space objects under art VII of the OST, which is addressed by Rule 12: International Liability for Damage Caused by Space Objects.

[413] ibid art 37(1) ('The State responsible for an internationally wrongful act is under an obligation to give satisfaction for the injury caused by that act insofar as it cannot be made good by restitution or compensation.' Article 37(2) further provides that '[s]atisfaction may consist in an acknowledgement of the breach, an expression of regret, a formal apology or another appropriate modality' and art 37(3) states that '[s]atisfaction shall not be out of proportion to the injury and may not take a form humiliating to the responsible State.').

[414] ibid art 30.

is in addition to the obligation that the responsible State is under to make full reparation for the injury caused by the internationally wrongful act. There are also six recognized, limited circumstances precluding the wrongfulness of an act of a State: consent,[415] self-defence,[416] countermeasures,[417] force majeure,[418] distress,[419] and necessity.[420]

---

[415] ibid art 20 ('Valid consent by a State to the commission of a given act by another State precludes the wrongfulness of that act in relation to the former State to the extent that the act remains within the limits of that consent.').

[416] ibid art 21 ('The wrongfulness of an act of a State is precluded if the act constitutes a lawful measure of self-defence taken in conformity with the Charter of the United Nations.').

[417] ibid art 22 ('The wrongfulness of an act of a State not in conformity with an international obligation towards another State is precluded if and to the extent that the act constitutes a countermeasure taken against the latter State in accordance with chapter II of part three [of the ILC Articles on State Responsibility (arts 49–54)].'). In particular, countermeasures shall not affect the following obligations: '(a) the obligation to refrain from the threat or use of force as embodied in the Charter of the United Nations; (b) obligations for the protection of fundamental human rights; (c) obligations of a humanitarian character prohibiting reprisals; (d) other obligations under peremptory norms of general international law'. ibid art 50. Furthermore, countermeasures must be 'commensurate with the injury suffered, taking into account the gravity of the internationally wrongful act and the rights in question' and 'shall be terminated as soon as the responsible State has complied with its obligations ... in relation to the internationally wrongful act'. ibid arts 51 and 53.

[418] ibid art 23 ('The wrongfulness of an act of a State not in conformity with an international obligation of that State is precluded if the act is due to force majeure, that is the occurrence of an irresistible force or of an unforeseen event, beyond the control of the State, making it materially impossible in the circumstances to perform the obligation.' However, this preclusion does not apply if 'the situation of force majeure is due, either alone or in combination with other factors, to the conduct of the State invoking it; or ... the State has assumed the risk of that situation occurring').

[419] ibid art 24 ('The wrongfulness of an act of a State not in conformity with an international obligation of that State is precluded if the author of the act in question has no other reasonable way, in a situation of distress, of saving the author's life or the lives of other persons entrusted to the author's care.' However, this preclusion does not apply if 'the situation of distress is due, either alone or in combination with other factors, to the conduct of the State invoking it; or ... the act in question is likely to create a comparable or greater peril').

[420] ibid art 25 ('Necessity may not be invoked by a State as a ground for precluding the wrongfulness of an act not in conformity with an international obligation of that State unless the act: (a) is the only way for the State to safeguard an essential interest against a grave and imminent peril; and (b) does not seriously impair an essential interest of the State or States towards which the obligation exists, or of the international community as a whole.' Furthermore, 'necessity may not be invoked by a State as a ground for precluding wrongfulness if: (a) the international obligation in question excludes the possibility of invoking necessity; or (b) the State has contributed to the situation of necessity'.).

Rule 11
Responsibility of International Organizations

When activities, including military space activities, are carried on in space by an international organization, responsibility for compliance with the OST and international space law in general shall be borne both by the international organization and by each State that is a party to the OST that is a member of that organization.

Overview of Legal Basis of Rule

1. This Rule is based on the final sentence of Articles VI and XIII of the Outer Space Treaty (OST).

2. Article VI of the OST is viewed as part of the *lex specialis* of the space law regime with reference to the broad concept of State responsibility as developed under the *lex generalis* of public international law (see Rule 10: Responsibility of States for National Activities in Outer Space; and Methodology of *Manual*).

Legal Issues Related to the Responsibility of International Organizations

3. The responsibility under this Rule specifically pertains to ensuring the compliance of space activities with the OST and, pursuant to Article III of the OST, this responsibility appropriately extends to compliance of such activities with *all* international law applicable to outer space. The specific obligation under the OST for international organizations, or respectively their member States, to bear international responsibility for violations of the UN Charter and violations of the law of armed conflict raises untested legal questions (see paragraphs 8 and 9).

4. The OST contains no mechanism through which an international organization may expressly declare its acceptance of the rights and obligations under the OST.[421]

---

[421] Such mechanisms are included in the Registration Convention, the Liability Convention, and the Rescue and Return Agreement, where they serve to assist Member States of international organizations by providing a speedy and efficient mechanism for handling respective rights and obligations.

The travaux préparatoires of the OST reveals that the lack of such a mechanism in is due largely to the position taken by the Soviet Union in the negotiations of the text of Article VI: the Soviet representative indicated that his country was 'categorically opposed to the idea that international organizations should not be responsible for their activities in space unless they had made a declaration to that effect', but at the same time the USSR 'could not agree that such organizations should be placed on a footing of equality with parties to the treaty, which were sovereign States'.[422]

While it may be argued under general international law that treaties do not bind international organizations without their consent,[423] the *lex specialis* of space law, founded on the OST (including Article VI), sets forth a different responsibility regime that is applicable to both States and international organizations. Article XIII of the OST further establishes a framework for States to conduct space activities in conjunction with international organizations, that is, intergovernmental organizations,[424] by requiring that '[a]ny practical questions arising in connection with activities carried on by international intergovernmental organizations in the exploration and use of outer space ... shall be resolved by the States Parties to the Treaty either with the appropriate international organization or with one or more States members of that international organization, which are Parties to this Treaty'.

5.

Taken together, relevant clauses in Articles VI and XIII of the OST clarify that States always retain at least a residual responsibility for ensuring that international organizations of which they form part will comply with international space law. Articles VI and XIII of the OST thus ensure that the responsibility for space activities conducted in the context of an intergovernmental organization is shared between that organization and its member States in order to allow third parties to address the organization to the extent that the organization has the capacities

6.

Such mechanisms do not, however, allow States to evade their individual responsibilities for national space activities conducted under the auspices or as a part of an international organization. It should be noted that, according to their terms, these international agreements apply only to an international organization if the majority of the members of that international organization are parties to the Outer Space Treaty and only if the international organization declares its acceptance of the resulting rights and obligations.

[422] UNCOPUOS Legal Sub-Committee Summary Report 70 (n 248) 6 (Regarding the responsibility of both international organizations and the States participating in it, Mr Morozov (Soviet Representative) also asked the members to recall similar language in connection with 'the compromise reached when the draft Declaration of Legal Principles Governing the Activities of States in the Exploration and Use of Outer Space had been prepared').
[423] Vienna Convention on the Law of Treaties Between States and International Organisations or Between International Organisations (opened for signature 21 March 1986) 25 ILM 543, art 34 ('A treaty does not create either obligations or rights for a third State or a third organisation without the consent of that State or that organisation.').
[424] OST (n 9). Article XIII focuses only on international *intergovernmental* organizations, while sentence 3 of art VI refers to 'international organisations'. This is because art XIII is not suitable for international *non-governmental* organizations, since those organizations are not composed of participating States that are capable of bearing international responsibility in addition to the international organization.

and legal competences to ensure compliance with the rules of the OST—while at the same time precluding the possibility that member States may escape ultimate responsibility to the extent the organization does not have such capacities and competences.[425]

7. Thus, in general, the choice between holding the organization itself responsible for any violation of the OST or holding its member States responsible for any violation of the OST should be made on the basis of whether the organization is capable of itself ensuring that proper reparation will be provided for the violation and decides to do so or whether the Member States respectively need to take up their responsibility to ensure such reparation will be provided.[426]

8. Article 2(4) of the UN Charter explicitly imposes on individual Members of the United Nations the obligation to refrain from the threat or use of force, making individual States the primary focus of international responsibility in this area. In this regard, the responsibility of individual States with respect to the use of force involves special requirements (see Rule 10: Responsibility of States for National Activities in Outer Space, paragraph 13).

9. The UN Charter does not recognize the right of international organizations, as such, to engage in self-defence. Only States ('Members of the United Nations') are recognized as having the right to use force in self-defence under Article 51. Regional organizations can facilitate collective self-defence by States in space in response to armed attacks (see Rule 27: Collective Self-Defence) and regional organizations can also engage in enforcement measures in space, if authorized by the UN Security Council (see Rule 28: Collective Security Measures). Responsibility for violations of the law of armed conflict similarly resides primarily with the individual States making up an international organization and will be subject to special requirements (see Rule 10: Responsibility of States for National Activities in Outer Space, paragraph 13). As noted, these issues raise untested legal questions with respect to military space activities.

---

[425] These provisions have thus been described as a mechanism that prevents a State Party to a treaty from circumventing its responsibilities and hiding 'behind a corporate veil by transferring the responsibility for its activities to an international intergovernmental organisation'. Hobe, Schmidt-Tedd, and Schrogl (eds), *Cologne Commentary*, vol I (n 133) 215.

[426] *Case Concerning the Factory at Chorzów* (n 407) 17 (holding that, as a general principle of international law, reparation is to be made for violations of international law and that a State is responsible for the acts of government organs or officers); See also Rule 10: Responsibility of States for National Activities in Outer Space, paras 20–23.

Rule 12
International Liability for Damage Caused by Space Objects

A State that launches or procures the launching of an object into outer space and a State from whose territory or facility an object is launched is internationally liable for damage to another State or to its natural or juridical persons by such object or its component parts on the Earth, in air space or in outer space.

A launching State is absolutely liable to pay compensation for damage caused by its space object on the surface of the Earth or to aircraft in flight. In the event of damage being caused to a space object of one launching State or to persons or property on board such a space object by a space object of a launching State, the launching State shall be liable only if the damage is due to its fault or the fault of persons for whom it is responsible.

This Rule applies to both military and civilian space objects. The only limited exceptions to this Rule relate to qualifying damage caused by actions connected with an armed conflict, conducted in accordance with the law of armed conflict.

Overview of Legal Basis of Rule

1. This Rule is based on the Outer Space Treaty (OST) and the Liability Convention,[427] under which a State that launches or procures the launching of an object into outer space, including the Moon and other celestial bodies, and a State from whose territory or facility an object is launched, is internationally liable for damage to another State or to its natural or juridical persons by such object or its component parts anywhere, including on the Earth, in air space, or in outer space, including the Moon and other celestial bodies.[428] This international liability must be distinguished from liability under any private contractual relationships and from State responsibility for national activities (see Rule 10: Responsibility of States for National Activities in Outer Space).

---

[427] OST (n 9) art VII; Liability Convention (n 46) art II. See Overview of The Space Law Regime, paras 12–16, examining the Liability Convention and the likely status of its substantive provisions as customary international law.

[428] Liability Convention (n 46) arts I(c), II–V.

The Space Law Liability Regime

2. Under the Liability Convention,[429] which implements the OST, a launching State is 'absolutely liable' to pay compensation for damage caused by its space object on the surface of the Earth or to aircraft flight.[430] However, the Convention further provides that:

> exoneration from absolute liability shall be granted to the extent that a launching State establishes that the damage has resulted either wholly or partially from gross negligence or from an act or omission done with intent to cause damage on the part of a claimant State or of natural or juridical persons it represents.[431]

3. In the event of damage being caused elsewhere than on the surface of the Earth to a space object of one launching State or to persons or property on board such a space object by a space object of another launching State, the latter shall be liable only if the damage is due to its fault or the fault of persons for whom it is responsible.[432]

4. Whenever two or more States jointly launch a space object, they shall be jointly and severally liable for any damage caused.[433]

Exceptions, Procedures, and Precedents

5. The provisions of the Liability Convention do not apply to damage caused by a space object of a launching State to nationals of that launching State or to foreign nationals during such time as they are participating in the operation of that space object from the time of its launching or at any stage thereafter until its descent, or during such time as they are in the immediate vicinity of a planned launching or recovery area as the result of an invitation by that launching State.[434]

6. Procedures and requirements for presenting claims for compensation for damage caused by a space object on the surface of the Earth or to aircraft flight are provided in the Liability Convention.[435] A claim for compensation for damage under Liability Convention must be presented by a State to a launching State through

---

[429] Paragraphs 2–6 are based on the application of rules found in the Liability Convention.
[430] Liability Convention (n 46) art II.
[431] ibid art VI(1). This limitation is subject to that requirement that '[n]o exoneration whatsoever shall be granted in cases where the damage has resulted from activities conducted by a launching State which are not in conformity with international law'). ibid art VI(2).
[432] ibid art III.
[433] ibid art V. The Liability Convention further provides that '[a] launching State which has paid compensation for damage shall have the right to present a claim for indemnification to other participants in the joint launching' and that '[a] State from whose territory or facility a space object is launched shall be regarded as a participant in a joint launching', art III(2)–(3).
[434] ibid art VII(b).
[435] ibid arts VII–XXXIII.

diplomatic channels.[436] A State has one year from the 'date of the occurrence of the damage or the identification of the launching State which is liable' to present a claim.[437] If no settlement of a claim can be reached by the parties through diplomatic negotiations, the parties must establish a Claims Commission at the request of either party.[438] However, the decision of the Claims Commission is legally binding only if the parties so agree.[439] Alternatively, a State may also pursue a claim 'in the courts or administrative tribunals or agencies of a launching State'[440] but cannot do this at the same time as pursuing the claim through diplomatic channels.

The absence, to date, of accidents involving space objects that have been the subject of international claims means that there is very little State practice regarding the implementation of the OST liability provision and the Liability Convention. To date, only one opportunity, involving damage on Earth, has been clearly presented: the 1978 crash of the nuclear-powered Soviet satellite Cosmos 954 in Canadian territory. In that case, the Canadian Government filed a claim for damages through diplomatic channels. Although the Soviets refrained from discussing the OST and the terms and procedures of the Liability Convention in the ensuing diplomatic negotiations, the Soviet Union ultimately agreed to a monetary settlement with the Canadian Government. The Protocol prepared by the Canadian Government that accompanied the settlement broadly invoked the obligations found in the OST, the Liability Convention, and general principles of international law.[441]

7.

---

[436] ibid art IX. Article X(1) further provides that '[a] claim for compensation for damage may be presented to a launching State not later than one year following the date of the occurrence of the damage or the identification of the launching State which is liable'.
[437] ibid art X(1).
[438] ibid art XIV (providing that 'within one year from the date on which the claimant State notifies the launching State that it has submitted the documentation of its claim, the parties concerned shall establish a Claims Commission at the request of either party').
[439] ibid art XIX(2).
[440] ibid art XI (2).
[441] Canada invoked the Liability Convention and general principles of international law in submitting a claim for damages related to this incident through diplomatic channels to the Soviet Union. See 'Canada: Claim Against the Union of the Soviet Socialist Republics for Damage Caused by Soviet COSMOS 954' (1979) 18 ILM 889, 899–930. The Soviet Union did ultimately settle the claim by paying $3 million (Canadian) of the $6 million in costs presented by the Canadian Government, but the diplomatic negotiations leading to this settlement do not reveal how the substantive provisions of the Liability Convention may be applied and the parties did not resort to the procedures specified in the Liability Convention. The Protocol of settlement that was signed by the two States stated that it represented the 'full and final settlement of all matters connected with the disintegration of the Soviet satellite Cosmos 954'; the Canadian claim accompanying the Protocol (but not part of the Protocol) stated that the settlement was founded on the liability of the Soviet Union under art VII of the OST, art II of the Liability Convention, and also on 'general principles of international law'. See 'Canada–Union of Soviet Socialist Republics: Protocol on Settlement of Canada's Claim for Damages Caused by 'COSMOS 954' (1981) 20 ILM 689, art I. The Canadian claim accompanying the Protocol of settlement stated that '[t]he standard of absolute liability for space activities, in particular activities involving the use of nuclear energy, is considered to have become a general principle of international law' and noted that '[a] large number of states, including Canada and the Union of Soviet Socialist Republics, have adhered to this principle as contained in the 1972 Convention on International Liability for Damage caused by Space Objects'). ibid paras 15, 20, and 22.

Military Space Activities and Damage to Space Objects Generally

8. Neither the OST nor the Liability Convention makes any distinction between civilian and military purposes for which space objects may be used. Thus, in principle space objects involved in military activities that cause damage would, pursuant to Articles II and III of the Liability Convention, trigger the liability of their launching State(s) (but see paragraphs 9–11). Similarly, the launching State(s) of space objects involved in military activities would, pursuant to Article II of the Liability Convention, be entitled to claim compensation for such space objects being damaged (but see paragraphs 9–11).

Military Space Activities and Damage to Space Objects During an Armed Conflict

9. During an armed conflict, the mere existence of hostilities does not *ipso facto* terminate or suspend the operation of the Outer Space Treaty or the Liability Convention as between belligerent parties or between a belligerent party and a third State.[442] However, the rules imposing liability may be inapplicable during armed conflict, to the extent that those rules are incompatible with the law of armed conflict. This means that a belligerent State would not be liable for any damage lawfully inflicted (on Earth or in space) in the course of hostilities against the other belligerent or a third party.[443] In such a case, the belligerent's privilege would supersede the space liability regime insofar as the law of armed conflict serves as the *lex specialis* displacing ordinary civil liability—provided that the attack in question was lawful. If the attack violated the rules of armed conflict, there are legal consequences under the law of armed conflict and potentially also under the OST and the Liability Convention. Another view, expressed during State consultation and also shared by the ICRC, is that while the law of armed conflict is *lex specialis* between the belligerent parties, the specifics of a space environment should lead to space law (and the space liability regime) being *lex specialis* rather than the law of armed conflict for all third parties to the conflict, holding the conflict parties liable for all their potential damages to third parties after the OST. To the extent that damage is caused by a space object during an armed conflict that has

---

[442] Report of the ILC on its 63rd Session (n 31) art 3.
[443] Article 91 of Additional Protocol I, for example, provides that 'a Party to the conflict which violates the provisions of the Conventions or of this Protocol shall, if the case demands, be liable to pay compensation. It shall be responsible for all acts committed by persons forming part of its armed forces.' Additional Protocol I (n 400).

no nexus to that armed conflict, the space liability regime would continue to apply between the belligerents and third States with respect to that space object.[444]

Damage caused by a space object of, launched by, or operated by, a non-governmental entity gives rise to liability of the launching State(s) of that space object under the OST and Liability Convention. This space liability regime exists in conjunction with, but is separate from, a broader legal regime referred to as international responsibility for national activities in space (see Rule 10: Responsibility of States for National Activities in Outer Space).[445] It should thus be noted that liability for damages caused by a space object is the particular focus of this Rule and that liability attaches to the launching State(s) of the space object, regardless of the status of the space object as governmental or non-governmental and regardless of who is responsible for the space object as one its national activities in space under Article VI of the OST.

10.

Just as the usual rules about liability are suspended between the belligerents (as the launching States of space objects) during an armed conflict, it is also suspended between the non-governmental entities of those belligerent States[446]—to the extent that the damages in question are caused or suffered by non-governmental entities in connection with the armed conflict.

11.

UN Security Council Enforcement Measures

The space liability regime is superseded when the UN Security Council adopts enforcement measures under Chapter VII of the UN Charter, to the extent that it may frustrate those enforcement measures (see Rule 27: Collective Self-Defence). In such situations, the obligation to implement UN Security Council resolutions will prevail over any obligations under the space liability regime to pay compensation for damage.[447]

12.

---

[444] In principle, the space law liability regime would also continue to apply between the non-governmental entities of the belligerents, to the extent that damages are not connected in any way with the armed conflict in question.
[445] Article VI of the OST provides that 'each State bears "international responsibility" for all its national activities in outer space, including military space activities, whether such activities are carried on by governmental or non-governmental entities, and with respect to the latter, is required to ensure the conformity of such activities with international law as well as to authorize and continuously supervise them'. OST (n 9).
[446] It is also suspended as between one belligerent State and the other belligerent State's non-governmental entities—to the extent that the damages in question are caused or suffered by non-governmental entities in connection with the armed conflict.
[447] Article 25 of the UN Charter provides that 'all Members of the United Nations agree to accept and carry out the decisions of the Security Council in accordance with the present Charter' and art 103 provides that '[i]n the event of a conflict between the obligations of the Members of the United Nations under the present Charter and their obligations under any other international agreement, their obligations under the present Charter shall prevail'. UN Charter (n 25).

SECTION 3
OTHER OBLIGATIONS

Rule 13
Astronauts and Personnel of a Spacecraft

(a) A State must render all possible assistance to military and civilian personnel of a spacecraft in the event of accident, distress, emergency landing, or unintended landing, and must safely and promptly return such persons to representatives of the relevant launching authority.

(b) A State is required to immediately inform other States or the Secretary-General of the United Nations of any phenomena that it discovers in outer space, including the Moon and other celestial bodies, which could constitute a danger to the life or health of military or civilian astronauts.

Overview of Legal Basis of Rule

1. This Rule is derived from Article V of the Outer Space Treaty (OST)[448] and the Agreement on the Rescue and Return of Astronauts (ARRA)[449] and reflects humanitarian considerations. The Preamble to the ARRA notes the provisions in the OST on the rescue and return of astronauts and expresses the desire 'to develop and give further concrete expression to these duties'.[450]

Personal Scope of Application

2. Article V of the OST uses the term 'astronauts' exclusively. In contrast, while the ARRA explicitly refers to astronauts in its title and Preamble, the term 'personnel of a spacecraft' is used in its operative provisions. Unfortunately, the drafters of the ARRA neglected to use the term astronaut anywhere in the text.[451] This

---

[448] OST (n 9).
[449] Agreement on the Rescue of Astronauts, the Return of Astronauts and the Return of Objects Launched into Outer Space' (adopted 19 December 1967, entered into force 3 December 1968) 672 UNTS 119 (ARRA).
[450] ibid. This language strongly suggests that the ARRA should be regarded as a 'further amplification of existing legal duties prescribed by Articles V and VIII of the [OST] and not an initial imposition of the obligations already binding upon the patties to the Outer Space Treaty'. Paul G Dembling and Daniel M Arons, 'The Treaty on Rescue and Return of Astronauts and Space Objects' (1968) 9 William and Mary Law Review 630, 642 fn 48. See Overview of The Space Law Regime, paras 8–11, examining the ARRA and its likely status as customary international law.
[451] The arguably sloppy drafting of the ARRA is often attributed to the extraordinary rush associated with its conclusion. See eg Cheng, *Studies in International Space Law* (n 61) 285 ('The 1968 Astronauts

omission has raised questions regarding the meaning of these two terms. Neither term is defined in international space law and it is questionable whether an 'ordinary meaning' can be readily afforded terms such as 'astronaut'.[452] For example, the Russian text of the OST is as authentic as the English text and the term used therein, *kosmonavt* or 'cosmonaut', is understood as not dependent on the duties performed by the personnel of a spacecraft.[453] That 'astronauts' and 'personnel of a spacecraft' have the same meaning can be drawn from the title and Preamble to the ARRA. The use of 'astronaut' in the title and Preamble would be nonsensical if the term 'personnel of a spacecraft' was intended to mean something different. The travaux préparatoires to the ARRA supports this conclusion given the extent to which the two terms were used interchangeably by the delegates.[454] While there have been suggestions that the phrase 'astronaut' is narrower in scope, potentially only applying to the pilot or co-pilot of a space vehicle, these two terms should generally be considered as synonymous.[455] This Commentary will therefore use these terms interchangeably.

3. Given the emergence of commercial space tourism, a key issue is whether such persons would fall within the scope of this Rule. One purposive construction would point towards the Rule applying to *all* persons involved in *any* space flight given its underlying humanitarian character. However, while space tourism was not discussed during the drafting of the OST or ARRA, the fact that Article V of the OST describes astronauts as 'envoys of mankind' might suggest that space tourists—as mere passengers on a commercial flight—should be excluded from the scope of this Rule.

4. There is at least some State practice to support this conclusion. The 'International Space Station [ISS] Principles' distinguish between a

Agreement may be said to provide a classic object lesson in how not to make a treaty ... the haste in which the final text was prepared and rushed through the United Nations resulted in a very poorly conceived and drafted instrument ....').

[452] See VCLT (n 11) art 31(1) ('A treaty shall be interpreted in good faith in accordance with the ordinary meaning to be given to the terms of the treaty in their context and in the light of its object and purpose.').
[453] Zhukov and Kolossov (n 190) 74.
[454] See eg UNCOPUOS, 'Provisional Verbatim Record of the Fifty-Second Meeting' (12 February 1968) UN Doc A/AC.105/PV.52, 3–5 (Mr Wyzner, Poland); UNCOPUOS Legal Sub-Committee, 'Summary Record of the Eighty-Sixth Meeting' (9 February 1968) UN Doc A/AC.105/C.2/SR.86 (UNCOPUOS Legal Sub-Committee Summary Record 86), 15 (Mr Prandler, Hungary); and COPUOS Legal Sub-Committee, 'Summary Record of the Eighty-Seventh Meeting' (2 February 1968) UN Doc A/AC.105/C.2/SR.87, 5 (Mr Chuluunbaatar, Mongolia) (describing the 'objective' of the ARRA as guaranteeing the safety of *astronauts*).
[455] See Frans Von der Dunk (ed), *Handbook of Space Law* (Edward Elgar Publishing 2015) 80 (noting that the two terms 'were generally considered to be synonymous, with "personnel" perhaps pointing to a bit more precisely to their standard role of employees in the service of a space agency tasked with specific operational duties'); cf M Lachs, *The Law of Outer Space* (A.W. Sijthoff Int Pub Co 1972) 79, 89 n 4.

professional astronaut and a 'spaceflight participant'.[456] US domestic legislation similarly draws a distinction between a 'space flight participant' and the crew of a launch or re-entry vehicle.[457] Therefore, while there is no definitive position at present, the emerging view is that persons with responsibilities for the operation of the spacecraft or with professional duties in outer space should be considered 'personnel of a spacecraft', whereas mere participants in space flight should not. Given the nature of space travel and exploration at the dawn of the space age, persons with such responsibilities, professional duties and training are also much more likely to be the type of individuals that States had in mind when they crafted the rights and obligations contained in the OST and ARRA.

Envoys of Mankind

5. Article V of the OST opens by proclaiming that States *'shall regard astronauts as envoys of mankind in outer space'*. At an early stage of the negotiations of the draft OST, there were suggestions that this provision could mean that astronauts are entitled to the privileges and immunities of diplomatic envoys.[458] However, based on the travaux préparatoires of the OST and State practice, it is generally accepted that this portion of Article V has mere symbolic value.[459] At the same time, the label of 'envoys of mankind' may reinforce the above conclusion that Article V, OST, and Articles 1–4, ARRA, were not meant to address humans present in outer space for their own private purposes, whether employment in the service of a private operator or enjoyment of the spaceflight as such.

---

[456] Multilateral Crew Operations Panel (MCOP), 'Principles Regarding Processes and Criteria for Selection, Assignment, Training and Certification of ISS (Expedition and Visiting) Crewmembers, Multilateral Crew Operations Panel' (Revision A, UNOOSA November 2001)s 3 [http://perma.cc/LQ8N-3MHY].

[457] US Commercial Space Launch Competitiveness Act (n 162), 51 USC § 50902.

[458] UNCOPUOS Legal Sub-Committee, 'Summary Record of the Forty-Fourth Meeting' (30 November 1965) UN Doc A/AC.105/C.2/SR.44, 8 (Mr Ustor, Hungary). On the status of diplomatic 'envoys', see Vienna Convention on Diplomatic Relations (adopted 18 April 1961, entered into force 24 April 1964) 500 UNTS 95, art 14(1)(b).

[459] During the negotiation of the OST, the Soviet representative indicated that he believed the term 'envoy of mankind' as used in art V was nothing more than 'the expression used in the article to justify the legal obligations it laid down'. UNCOPUOS Legal Sub-Committee, 'Summary Record of the Fifty-Eighth Meeting,' (20 October 1966) A/AC.105/C.2/SR.58, 9. See also Vladlen S Vereshchetin, 'Astronauts', *Max Planck Encyclopedias of Public International Law* (OUP January 2006) s A(4) ('It is generally admitted that ... qualifying astronauts as "envoys of mankind", entails moral rather than legal consequences and does not provide astronauts with a special legal personality or supra nationality.'); Cheng, *Studies in International Space Law* (n 61) 460, 507 (noting that it was soon recognized that the term envoy of mankind 'was no more than a figure of speech without really any legal significance' and that the term 'has not appeared in any subsequent multilateral treaties on space sponsored by the United Nations').

Rescue on Sovereign Territory

6. The four conditions that trigger a State's obligation to rescue personnel of a spacecraft are accident, distress, emergency landing, or unintended landing.[460] Where such personnel land in the sovereign territory or territorial waters of a State under these conditions, that State is legally obligated to 'immediately take all possible steps to rescue them and render them all necessary assistance'.[461] This need to provide 'all possible assistance' means the rescue effort of a State must equate to its best effort. Although several space missions have returned to Earth with a tragic loss of life, to date there is no State practice related to the rescue or return of astronauts under this Rule.

7. If assistance by the launching authority would 'contribute substantially' to rescue efforts, the launching authority is required to 'cooperate' with the relevant State.[462] The term 'launching authority' refers to the State or international organization responsible for launching the space vehicle.[463] Any joint rescue operation is subject to the direction and control of the territorial State, which is required to act in close and continuing consultation with the launching authority.[464]

8. In the unlikely event that the launching authority and territorial State disagree over the ability of the former to enter the sovereign territory of the latter as part of a rescue mission, the territorial State is entitled to refuse access.[465] However, that State would itself remain under a duty to provide 'all possible assistance'. Further, the State performing a rescue operation must inform the launching authority and

---

[460] ARRA (n 46) art 2 provides that '[i]f, owing to accident, distress, emergency or unintended landing, the personnel of a spacecraft land in territory under the jurisdiction of a Contracting Party, it shall immediately take all possible steps to rescue them and render them all necessary assistance'. These four conditions are sometimes referred to as the four conditions of distress.

[461] ibid. The Swedish delegate stated that 'he assumed that the expression "all possible steps" in the first sentence of article 2 meant action within the limits of the facilities at the contracting [territorial] parties' disposal'. UNCOPUOS Legal Sub-Committee Summary Report 86 (n 391) 20 (Mr Blix, Sweden).

[462] ARRA (n 46).

[463] ibid art 6. Note that the term 'launching authority' not only refers to the State responsible for launching but also 'an international intergovernmental organization is responsible for launching, provided that that organization declares its acceptance of the rights and obligations provided for in this Agreement and a majority of the States members of that organization are Contracting Parties to this Agreement and to the [OST]'. ibid.

[464] ibid art 2.

[465] In proposing the language now found in art 2 of the ARRA that makes it the responsibility of the launching authority to cooperate with the State on whose territory the landing has occurred, the French delegate stressed that 'it would be for the launching authority to give its cooperation to the sovereign state, and not the other way around'. UNCOPUOS Legal Sub-Committee, 'Summary Record of the Eighty-Ninth Meeting' (2 February 1968) A/AC.105/C.2/SR.89, 3 (Mr Deleau, France). The US delegate agreed, noting that 'the territorial authority would have the final say in the matter' (Mr Reis, US) ibid 4. Delegates from Mexico, the United Arab Emirates, Iran, and India all expressed their support for this position. ibid.

the Secretary-General of the UN of the steps being taken and what progress is being made.[466]

Rescue Elsewhere on Earth

If it is discovered that the personnel of a spacecraft have landed on the high seas, or in any other place on Earth not under the territorial jurisdiction of a State, States 'in a position to do so' must assist, if necessary, in any search and rescue operations.[467] Given that Article V of the OST demands 'all possible assistance' in the event of an emergency landing on the high seas, the phrase 'assistance' in Article 3 of the ARRA should be read as 'all possible assistance'. Whether States are in a position to assist in any specific case will depend on their technological capabilities and the geographical position of their aircraft or vessels vis-à-vis those personnel in distress.[468]

9.

A proposal to require the relevant launching authority to direct any rescue effort when taking place outside sovereign territory was rejected during the negotiations leading to the ARRA.[469] Therefore, a State in a position to assist may do so without approval from the State that acted as launching authority. Nevertheless, any State performing such a rescue must inform the launching authority and the Secretary-General of the UN of the steps being taken and their progress.[470] Insofar as this Rule concerns rescue on the high seas, it is in addition to the long-established duty to assist persons in distress at sea under customary international law.[471]

10.

Rescue in Outer Space

Where personnel of a spacecraft have alighted on the Moon under conditions of distress, or any other celestial body, States that are in a position to do so must extend assistance in search and rescue operations for such personnel.[472] All possible

11.

---

[466] ARRA (n 46) art 2.
[467] ibid art 3.
[468] The obligation in art 3 was viewed in the travaux préparatoires as the same found in art 2, ie 'all possible action', meaning 'action within the limits of the facilities at the contracting [territorial] parties' disposal'. UNCOPUOS Legal Sub-Committee Summary Record 86 (n 455) (Mr Blix, Sweden).
[469] For the proposal, see 'USSR: Revised Draft Agreement on the Rescue of Astronauts in the Event of Accident or Emergency Landing' (23 October 1964) A/AC.105/C.2/L.2/Rev. 2 (USSR: Revised Draft ARRA) Annex I, 4. See in this regard para 9 above regarding the launching authority's obligation to give its cooperation to the sovereign State in rescue efforts.
[470] ARRA (n 46) art 3.
[471] See eg UNGA, Convention on the High Seas (adopted 29 April 1958, entered into force 30 September 1962) 450 UNTS 11, art 12; and UNCLOS (n 151) art 98.
[472] ARRA (n 46) art 3. During the negotiations leading to the ARRA, France queried whether the expression 'any other place not under the jurisdiction of any State' would include outer space (see

assistance must also be provided by fellow astronauts to personnel of a spacecraft in orbit who are suffering distress.[473] The extent to which States will be in a position to assist personnel of a spacecraft experiencing distress, at present, is clearly heavily circumscribed. However, to the extent such rescue efforts take place, the State providing assistance must inform the launching authority and the Secretary-General of the UN of the steps being taken and the progress of the rescue mission.[474]

12. The Moon Agreement provides that, in the event of an emergency involving threat to human life, States Parties may use the equipment, vehicles, installations, facilities, or supplies of other States Parties on the Moon.[475] Few States are parties to the Moon Agreement[476] and none of its provisions have attained the status of rules of customary international law, thus the use of other States' supplies would still presumptively require consent. This is not unsurprising given that the astronauts of other States may themselves depend on existing supplies of oxygen, water, etc to sustain their own lives in the austere environment of the Moon. However, more broadly, under this Rule and Article V of the OST, the astronauts of one State shall render all possible assistance to fellow astronauts of another State in the event of accident, distress, emergency landing, or unintended landing.

Return of Personnel

13. Once a State has found personnel of a spacecraft after an emergency landing, that State must 'safely and promptly' return all such personnel to representatives of the launching authority for the relevant spacecraft. Although Article V of the OST provides that personnel should be returned 'to the State of registry' of their space vehicle, Article 4 of the ARRA refines this requirement by clarifying it is sufficient

---

UNCOPUOS Legal Sub-Committee Summary Report 86 (n 461) 13 (Mr Deleau, France)). It was generally accepted that it would (see eg ibid 7 (Mr Reis, United States)).

[473] OST (n 9) art V ('In carrying on activities in outer space and on celestial bodies, the astronauts of one State Party shall render all possible assistance to the astronauts of other States Parties.'). It is generally accepted that art V, para 2 of the OST acts to fill the gaps in the wording of art 3 of the ARRA (see eg Eilene Galloway, 'Agreement on the Rescue of Astronauts, the Return of Astronauts and Return of Objects Launched into Outer Space: Analysis and Background Data' (Staff Report Prepared for the use of the Committee on Aeronautical and Space Sciences, US Senate, 90th Congress, 2d session, 16 July 1968) 12.
[474] ARRA (n 46) art 3.
[475] Moon Agreement (n 46) art 12(3).
[476] Only 18 States have ratified or acceded to the Moon Agreement (and one of those States, Saudi Arabia, indicated its intention to withdraw in 2023) See 'Status of International Agreements Relating to Activities in Outer Space as at 1 January 2023, [https://perma.cc/UT3B-88TG]; Overview of the Space Law Regime, paras 23–24. None of the major spacefaring or major space-technology States are parties to the Moon Agreement (except Australia and Kazakhstan).

to return rescued personnel to 'representatives' of the launching authority (eg to officials at the appropriate embassy).[477]

Subject to the discussion below, this Rule imposes an unconditional obligation on States to return the personnel of a spacecraft after successful search and rescue operations. During the formulation of the ARRA, the Soviet Union sought to make the duty of return contingent on the launching authority having complied with the 'Declaration of Legal Principles'.[478] If this position had been adopted, the State on whose territory an emergency landing occurred could refuse to return the astronauts if that State determined said astronauts had been involved in various activities it considered contrary to the Declaration. However, the Soviet proposal was rejected.[479]

14.

The obligation to return astronauts is not contingent on the launching State paying compensation for any damage caused by the landing a space vehicle (see Rule 12: International Liability for Damage Caused by Space Objects). It also makes no difference whether the downed personnel of a spacecraft are in the military service of the launching authority. See, however, paragraphs 18–21 regarding the effect of armed conflict on this obligation. The OST contains no prohibition on military personnel in outer space (see Rule 3: Peaceful Purposes in Outer Space) and explicitly permits military personnel to be present on the Moon and other celestial bodies.[480] Downed military personnel must, therefore, be safely and promptly returned to a representative of the launching authority. However, the *intentional* landing of a spacecraft in foreign territory would fall outside this Rule if not taking place under conditions of distress.

15.

Jurisdiction and Control

Article VIII of the OST provides that the right of jurisdiction and control over a space object and 'any personnel thereof', irrespective of nationality, belongs to the State in which the spacecraft is registered[481] (see Rule 7: Jurisdiction). Article VIII only applies where the personnel of a spacecraft are located in outer space, or on a

16.

---

[477] See eg UNCOPUOS Legal Sub-Committee Summary Record 86 (n 455) 8 (Mr Reis, United States).
[478] USSR: Revised draft ARRA (n 46) Annex I, art 5. The Declaration of Legal Principles (n 60) was adopted by the General Assembly in its resolution 1962 (XVIII) of 13 December 1963.
[479] UNCOPUOS Legal Sub-Committee Summary Record 87 (n 454) 10 (Mr Marschik, Austria) (describing draft art 4 of the ARRA as an 'absolute obligation' of return). See also UNCOPUOS Preliminary Verbatim Record 52 (n 454) 66 (Mr Reis, United States) (where draft art 4 is said to 'repeat' art V of the OST, the latter of which is 'absolute and unconditional').
[480] OST (n 9) art IV; Hearings Before US Senate Foreign Relations Committee on the OST (n 126) 22.
[481] Article 7 of the Declaration of Legal Principles refers to 'personnel therein'. This was changed to 'thereof' in art VIII of the OST to make clear the provision applied to personnel outside and inside the space object. See Cheng, *Studies in International Space Law* (n 61) 458.

celestial body. General international law rules governing the exercise of jurisdiction by States thus apply where personnel of a spacecraft are on Earth. With respect to shared jurisdiction over space objects while in space, Article VIII does not remove the right of States to conclude, *inter se*, appropriate additional agreements on jurisdiction and control over space objects and any personnel thereof[482] (see Rule 7: Jurisdiction).

Reports on Any Phenomena Discovered in Space Which Could Constitute a Danger to the Life or Health of Astronauts

17. States are required to immediately inform other States or the Secretary-General of the United Nations of 'any phenomena that they discover in outer space, including the Moon and other celestial bodies, which could constitute a danger to the life or health of astronauts'.[483]

Effect of Hostilities

18. Between belligerent States, the obligation to rescue personnel of a spacecraft would not apply during an armed conflict.[484] This obligation would not, however, be suspended or otherwise restricted between a belligerent party and a third State. Nonetheless, the standard of 'all possible assistance' as contained in Article V of the OST is contextual and during an armed conflict the capacity of a belligerent to devote resources to any rescue operation may be dramatically reduced.

---

[482] For example, the International Space Station Agreement provides that each State Partner shall retain jurisdiction and control over the elements of the ISS that it registers, over personnel in or on the Space Station who are its nationals, and over other individuals in designated circumstances involving criminal misconduct. ISS Agreement (n 47) arts 2 and 22.

[483] OST (n 9) art V, para 3. The OST makes this requirement applicable to States Parties to the OST. Citing both the obligation under the OST to inform UN Secretary-General of any phenomena in space which could constitute a danger to the life or health of astronauts and the responsibility of the United States under Article VI of the OST for the conduct of private US companies in space, the Chinese Government stated in 2021 that it had informed the UN Secretary-General that 'Starlink satellites launched by SpaceX of the US had two close encounters with the China Space Station in July and October this year respectively when Chinese astronauts were working there' and called on the United States to 'respect international order in space based on international law, take prompt measures to prevent such incidents from recurring, and act responsibly to safeguard the safety of in-orbit astronauts'. 'Foreign Ministry Spokesperson Zhao Lijian's Regular Press Conference on December 28, 2021' (Embassy of China in the US 2021) [https://perma.cc/EMS5-K6B7].

[484] There is however a customary rule of international law applicable in a time of armed conflict that provides: 'Whenever circumstances permit, and particularly after an engagement, each party to the conflict must, without delay, take all possible measures to search for, collect and evacuate the wounded, sick and shipwrecked without adverse distinction.' Henckaerts and Louise Doswald-Beck (eds), *Customary International Humanitarian Law*, Vol 1: Rules (n 402) 398, Rule 109.

19. A more difficult legal issue is the extent to which the obligation to return personnel of a spacecraft would continue to apply after the onset of an armed conflict.[485] In an international armed conflict, for example, the law of armed conflict permits belligerents to detain prisoners of war (POWs) until the cessation of active hostilities,[486] and to intern civilians for such time as it is 'absolutely necessary' for the security of the State.[487] Neutral States are also obligated to intern able-bodied combatants found on their territory until the end of the conflict.[488] The special protections for medical and religious personnel under the law of armed conflict may also be relevant (See Rule 38: Medical Units and Religious Personnel).

20. To date there has been no State practice concerning the detention of a belligerent party's military astronauts and personnel as prisoners of war during a time of armed conflict. There is a potential contradiction between peacetime obligations to promptly return military astronauts and belligerent rights to detain such military members as prisoners of war. Consistent with the approach of the International Law Commission (ILC),[489] the law of armed conflict will likely act as the *lex specialis* in this instance (see Methodology of *Manual*). The effect of this interpretation would be that military personnel are not required to be promptly returned to the State of Registry or representatives of the launching authority due to their status under the law of armed conflict. This could be said to comport with the fact that military personnel, even where astronauts or personnel, are above all else members of the armed forces and can be assigned to roles focused on harming the enemy at any time. An alternative view expressed by some States during State consultation would be that military astronauts engaging in purely scientific activity should have some unique status under this Rule. Accordingly, under this approach they should be returned under the space law regime. States could agree upon such a status in the future but have not yet done so. Civilian personnel of a spacecraft, however, would still need to be returned by a neutral State and could only be interned by an opposing belligerent where 'absolutely necessary' for the security of the State.

---

[485] In peacetime, there are obligations contained within art V of the OST and art 4 of the ARRA to, respectively, return 'astronauts' promptly to the State of registration and 'personnel of a spacecraft' promptly to representatives of the launching authority.

[486] Geneva Convention Relative to the Treatment of Prisoners of War of 12 August 1949 (signed 8 December 1949) 75 UNTS 135 (GC III), art 118.

[487] Geneva Convention Relative to the Protection of Civilian Persons in Time of War of 12 August 1949 (signed 8 December 1949) 75 UNTS 287, arts 42 and 132.

[488] Convention (V) respecting the Rights and Duties of Neutral Powers and Persons in Case of War on Land (adopted 18 October 1907, entered into force 26 January 1910) art 11; 'San Remo Manual on International Law Applicable to Armed Conflicts at Sea' (12 June 1994), para 168 (extending this obligation beyond land warfare).

[489] Report of the ILC on its 63rd Session (n 31), commentary to art 2, para 4 ('the rules of international humanitarian law ... constitute the *lex specialis* governing the conduct of hostilities').

21. In according priority to rights and obligations under the law of armed conflict concerning the detention of military astronauts as POWs under the Third Geneva Convention,[490] it is still possible to accommodate international space law rights in one context. Article 21 of the Third Geneva Convention permits the release and return of POWs under conditions of parole.

---

[490] GC III (n 486).

Rule 14
Avoidance of Harmful Contamination

In the conduct of space activities, including military space activities, a State shall avoid harmful contamination of outer space and adverse changes in the environment of the Earth resulting from the introduction of extraterrestrial matter.

Overview of Legal Basis of Rule

1. This Rule addresses two related obligations. The first is the need to avoid 'forward contamination' of outer space. The second is, in essence, the need to avoid 'backward contamination' of the Earth. The text of this Rule derives from Article IX of the Outer Space Treaty (OST).[491] For a discussion of related issues regarding the protection of the environment during an armed conflict, see Rule 43: Natural Environment.

2. It is important to note that Article IX of the OST does not distinguish between military and civilian activities in outer space. This Rule therefore applies to military space activities. For the broader requirement of due regard for the interests of other States in the exploration and use of outer space, see Rule 17: Due Regard.

Harmful Contamination of Outer Space

3. The reference to outer space in this Rule should be read to include the Moon and other celestial bodies, in keeping with the wording in Article IX of the OST. Therefore, the duty to avoid harmful contamination applies to space beyond the Earth's environment. The obligation in Article IX refers to 'studies' of outer space and 'exploration' thereof. The development of the scope of this provision reveals that in 1963, the UN General Assembly accepted that only 'research' on celestial bodies needed to avoid harmful contamination.[492] By the time of the Treaty's final draft language the scope of the prohibition had extended beyond just 'research' to 'exploration'.[493] The expansive added language of 'exploration' thus represented an

---

[491] OST (n 9) art IX.
[492] UNGA, 'The Peaceful Uses of Outer Space' (n 180) 33.
[493] ibid 38.

4. The term 'harmful contamination' is not defined in the OST or otherwise within the broader corpus of international space law. What is evident, nonetheless, is that there must be both 'contamination' of outer space and that this must reach the threshold of being 'harmful'. The term 'contamination' is wide enough to include the introduction of terrestrial matter[494] (or potentially also energy) to outer space, or the proliferation of such matter through activities in space. Some support for this assessment can be found in Article 7(1) of the Moon Agreement,[495] which refers to 'harmful contamination' of the Moon through the introduction of 'extra-environmental matter'. The term 'contamination' also encompasses living organisms. Thus, by way of example, the introduction of tardigrades to the surface of the Moon[496] or the creation of 'space debris' as a result of an anti-satellite weapons test[497] would both fall potentially within the term 'contamination'. A separate question is whether such acts would rise to such a level as to be considered 'harmful'.

5. In the absence of any treaty definition, guidance for the interpretation of the term 'harmful' can be gleaned from its ordinary meaning, that is, causing or capable of causing damage. State practice tends to support the view that this harm must at least be significant. For example, the Principles Relevant to the Use of Nuclear Power Sources in Outer Space, adopted by the UN General Assembly, stipulates that the design and use of space objects with nuclear power sources should not cause 'significant contamination of outer space'.[498] In addition, the United States, China, and India (as well as the Soviet Union during the Cold War) have all conducted destructive anti-satellite weapons tests that, to varying degrees, have created considerable amounts of debris in space that risk causing severe damage. Yet, these cases have not seen States invoke this section of Article IX of the OST.[499]

---

[494] In the sense that any contamination which would result in harm to a State's experiments or programs is to be avoided under art IX of the OST, space debris should be regarded as a form of harmful contamination. See Hobe, Schmidt-Tedd, and Schrogl (eds), *Cologne Commentary*, vol I (n 133) 177.

[495] Moon Agreement (n 46) art 7(1).

[496] Daniel Oberhaus, 'A Crashed Israeli Lunar Lander Spilled Tardigrades on the Moon' *Wired* (5 August 2019) [https://perma.cc/L275-34RM].

[497] See eg UNGA 'Destructive anti-ascent anti-satellite missile testing' (7 December 2002) UN Doc A/RES/77/41 in which the General Assembly, '[c]oncerned by the impact of destructive direct-ascent anti-satellite missiles on the long-term sustainability of the outer space environment' and '[c]oncerned that the use of destructive anti-satellite systems might have widespread and irreversible impacts on the outer space environment, ... Calls upon all States to commit not to conduct destructive anti-ascent anti-satellite missile tests' and '[c]onsiders such a commitment to be an urgent, initial measure aimed at preventing damage to the outer space environment'. See additional discussion of this UN General Assembly Resolution in Rule 17: Due Regard).

[498] UNGA Resolution 47/68 (14 December 1992) UN Doc A/RES/47/68, Principle 3(1)(a).

[499] The one possible exception is a statement made by former Japanese Prime Minister, Shinzo Abe, that China's ASAT test on its Feng Yun 1C polar orbit weather satellite in 2007. However, the reported rationale behind Prime Minister Abe's statement that the test failed to comply with the OST appears

It is vital to understand that this Rule does not *prohibit* harmful contamination of outer space. Instead, it is an obligation to *avoid* such detrimental effects. The Rule is, therefore, limited to requiring States to take steps to avoid harmful contamination. This inescapably gives States latitude in interpretation. Indeed, the German Federal Foreign Office has opined that the OST's provisions on harmful contamination 'have proven to be of little practical importance in their current form'.[500] In keeping with the wording of the OST, it appears that adverse changes to the environment of Earth are also not prohibited per se under this Rule, as States are only required to avoid such environmental changes. This necessary distinction thus serves to materially weaken the effect of the legal regime on 'backward contamination' of the Earth. Outside the legally binding framework of the OST, a number of countries have chosen to voluntarily adhere to guidelines set forth by the Committee on Space Research (COSPAR)[501] on the issue of biological and organic contamination. Parallels with respect to space debris can be seen through the voluntary, non-binding international mitigation measures elaborated as guidelines by the Inter-Agency Space Debris Coordination Committee (IADC).[502]

6.

Adverse Changes in the Environment of the Earth

The issue of 'backward contamination' of our planet is addressed in this Rule by the obligation to avoid adverse changes in the environment of the Earth by the introduction of extraterrestrial matter. The OST does not define what is meant by the terms 'adverse changes' or 'extraterrestrial matter'. Since 'matter' is generally understood to be anything that has mass, extraterrestrial organisms are likely included within its scope. However, photons (light) and other forms of energy within the electromagnetic spectrum that do not have the requisite mass do not fall within the bounds of the obligation. This means, for example, that adverse changes in the environment of Earth resulting purely from military space-based uses of the electromagnetic spectrum are not covered by this Rule.

7.

to be based on the art IX obligation to undertake consultations in advance and not on the creation of 'harmful contamination'. See James Clay Moltz, *Asia's Space Race* (CUP 2011) 231.

[500] 'Space Law' (German Federal Foreign Office) [https://perma.cc/UU8X-DHNR].
[501] The National Scientific Institutions of many States, including Brazil, China, France, Russia, Saudi Arabia, and the United States are members of COSPAR: 'National Scientific Institutions' (*Committee on Space Research (COSPAR)*, 10 April 2019) [https://perma.cc/3PN7-XA4Y].
[502] Inter-Agency Space Debris Coordination Committee (IADC) 'IADC Space Debris Mitigation Guidelines, Revision 1' (September 2007) IADC-02-01 [https://perma.cc/72EW-4M5H]. These IADC guidelines later served as the basis for the Space Debris Mitigation Guidelines of the Committee on the Peaceful Uses of Outer Space (Space Debris Mitigation Guidelines). UNOOSA, 'Space Debris Mitigation Guidelines' (January 2010) UN Doc ST/SPACE/49 [https://perma.cc/THF2-4N2L].

8. The ordinary meaning of the word extraterrestrial is 'originating, situated, or occurring outside the Earth or its atmosphere'.[503] When considered in light of the requirement for the *introduction* of extraterrestrial matter to Earth, the reintroduction of matter originating from Earth appears to fall outside Article IX of the OST. Support for this view can be extrapolated from no State having claimed that the return to Earth of spacecraft triggers consideration of Article IX. The best example of this is Canada's *Claim against the USSR for Damage Caused by Soviet Cosmos 954*.[504] Indeed, after the deposit on Canadian territory of hazardous radioactive debris from the Cosmos 954 satellite, the Canadian Statement of Claim relied upon the USSR's clear obligation to compensate for damage under the Liability Convention rather than pursuing possible alternative causes of action.[505] This is despite Cosmos 954 carrying on board a uranium enriched nuclear reactor, radioactive debris being spread over 'a large area of Canadian territory' and its breakup rendering part of that territory 'unfit for use'.[506]

9. What degree of change to the environment of Earth would be considered adverse is unclear from relevant treaty law, but it is likely that significant detrimental effects would be a reasonable determinative threshold.

Appropriate Measures

10. States Parties to the OST are required, 'where necessary', to adopt 'appropriate measures' for the purpose of avoiding harmful contamination of outer space and adverse changes in the environment of the Earth by introducing extraterrestrial matter'.[507] None of these terms are further defined in the OST. There is insufficient State practice to demonstrate 'subsequent practice establishing the agreement of the parties'[508] regarding what constitutes 'appropriate measures' for the purpose of avoiding harmful contamination under Article IX of the OST and at what point those measures are 'necessary'.[509] Similarly, there is insufficient State practice to

---

[503] See eg *Webster's II New College Dictionary* (Houghton Mifflin Co 1995) 398.
[504] Canadian Claim Against USSR for Damage Caused by COSMOS 954 (n 441) 899.
[505] It should be noted, however, that the Canadian Government necessarily framed its complaint against the USSR in this matter under the liability framework explicitly contemplated in arts II and XII of the Liability Convention in order to receive compensation for damages caused by the crash.
[506] Canadian Claim Against USSR for Damage Caused by COSMOS 954 (n 441) 905.
[507] OST (n 9) art IX.
[508] VCLT (n 11) art 31(1); see also International Law Commission (ILC), 'Subsequent agreements and subsequent practice in relation to the interpretation of treaties' (3 June 2014) UN Doc A/CN.4/L.833 2 draft conclusion 9 ('1. An agreement under article 31, paragraph 3 (a) and (b), requires a common understanding regarding the interpretation of a treaty which the parties are aware of and accept. Though it shall be taken into account, such an agreement need not be legally binding. 2. The number of parties that must actively engage in subsequent practice in order to establish an agreement under art 31 para 3(b), may vary. Silence on the part of one or more parties can constitute acceptance of the subsequent practice when the circumstances call for some reaction.').
[509] Although not explicitly implementing art IX of the OST or made applicable to activities in outer space, the duty to establish environmental impact assessment procedures is consistent with appropriate

establish any rule of customary international law in this area. However, the domestic legislation and licensing requirements of some States do require space operators to avoid harmful contamination of space to comply with international obligations in this area, even though these requirements do not explicitly refer to Article IX of the OST. For example, with respect to the launching and operation of space objects and the carrying on of other activities in outer space by persons connected to the United Kingdom, the laws of the United Kingdom confer licensing and other powers on government officials 'to secure compliance with the international obligations of the United Kingdom' and state that a licence may contain conditions requiring the licensee to conduct operations in such a way as to 'prevent the contamination of outer space or adverse changes in the environment of the earth'.[510] Other States have adopted somewhat similar national legislation and licensing requirements, seeking to promote the avoidance of harmful contamination of space without explicitly referring to Article IX or to international obligations.[511]

Voluntary, Non-Binding Guidelines That May Be Relevant to Regulatory Frameworks for National Space Activities

Some voluntary, non-binding guidelines have been developed by international governmental and non-governmental organizations that address the need to avoid the harmful contamination of outer space. For example, COSPAR's Planetary

11.

---

measures to avoid harmful contamination of the environment. See eg Convention on Environmental Impact Assessment in a Transboundary Context (25 February 1991) 1989 UNTS 309 art 2(1) ('The parties shall, either individually or jointly, take all appropriate and effective measures to prevent, reduce and control significant adverse transboundary environmental impact from proposed activities.').

[510] Outer Space Act 1986 (United Kingdom) Preamble and art 5(2)(e)(i) [https://perma.cc/GX2S-UNXL]. Article 13(1) para 14 of sch 1(a) further provides that a licence under the Act may be granted subject to 'conditions requiring the licensee to conduct the licensee's activities in such a way as ... to prevent the contamination of outer space or adverse changes in the environment of the earth'.

[511] See eg National Space Research and Development Agency Act (2010) Cap. (9) pt 3 s 9(4) (Nigeria) ('A licence may, in particular, contain conditions ... (e) requiring the licensee to conduct operations in such a way as to (i) prevent the contamination of outer space or cause adverse changes in the environment of the earth'.); Executive Order (*Bekendtgørelse*) no 552 of 31 March 2016 pt 4 s 7 (Denmark) (requiring that '[s]pace activities must be performed with due consideration for the surrounding environment' and operators may be required to provide a description 'the potential environmental impact in outer space of the space activity' and 'measures to minimise the impact on the environment on the Earth, in the atmosphere and in outer space'); 63/2018 Act on Space Activities (*Laki avaruustoiminnasta*) s 10 (Finland) ('In its application for authorisation of space activities, the operator shall assess the environmental impacts of the activities on the earth, in the atmosphere and in outer space, and present a plan for measures to counter and reduce adverse environmental impacts.'); Ukraine Law of 15 November 1996, Ordinance of the Supreme Soviet of Ukraine on Space Activity (*Vidomosti Verkhovnoi Rady Ukrainy*, 1997 p 2) art 9 ('The following shall be prohibited in connection with the conduct of space activity in Ukraine: The presenting of a direct threat to the life and health of human beings and the causing of damage to the environment; The violation of international norms and standards regarding pollution of outer space.').

Protection Policy[512] supports practices by national space agencies such as NASA, the European Space Agency (ESA), and the Japan Aerospace Exploration Agency (JAXA) on the avoidance of biological and organic contamination of both outer space and the Earth.[513] ESA notes that COSPAR 'has formulated a planetary protection policy to guide compliance with the United Nations Outer Space Treaty'.[514] JAXA refers to COSPAR's Planetary Protection Policy and associated requirements 'as a reference standard for spacefaring nations and in guiding compliance with Article IX of the UN Outer Space Treaty'.[515] It is important to note, however, that while some States regard COSPAR's Planetary Protection Policy as a useful reference standard and a guide to compliance with OST obligations, there is no consensus among States Parties to the OST that this policy and its related requirements represent 'appropriate measures' that are 'necessary' to implement Article IX of the OST.

12. The Space Debris Mitigation Guidelines of the Committee on the Peaceful Uses of Outer Space (COPUOS)[516] may also be viewed as supporting efforts to avoid harmful contamination of space with respect to debris. In addition, the IADC Space Debris Mitigation Guidelines may be included in many State licensing requirements.[517] UNCOPUOS has noted that both these Guidelines, together with the European Code of Conduct for Space Debris Mitigation, International Organization for Standardization standard 24113:2011 ('Space systems: space

---

[512] G Kminek and others, 'COSPAR's Planetary Protection Policy' (COSPAR December 2017) [https://perma.cc/KY83-RCGX].

[513] See Office of Safety & Mission Assurance (OSMA), 'Planetary Protection' (NASA 2021) [https://perma.cc/P8FX-9LJE]. See also OSMA, 'Biological Planetary Protection for Human Missions to Mars' (NID 8715.129, NASA 9 July 2021) [https://perma.cc/ZC48-ADNP] (noting that NASA has been 'a key participant and advocate for the development of internationally accepted protocols to prevent backward and forward contamination, including the guidelines for 'Human Missions to Mars' in the [COSPAR] planetary protection policy').

[514] ESA, 'Planetary Protection' (ESA) [https://perma.cc/X56A-JPBF] (further noting that 'ESA has adopted this policy and acts on behalf of its Member States to ensure that the requirements are met for all missions the Agency is flying or contributing to').

[515] Japan Aerospace Exploration Agency (JAXA), 'Contributing to the International Planetary Protection Policy for Martian Moon Exploration' (JAXA 6 September 2019) [https://perma.cc/PQ9M-PLXX].

[516] 'Space Debris Mitigation Guidelines' (n 503).

[517] See examples of State practice in UNCOPUOS, 'Compendium of Space Debris Mitigation Standards Adopted by States and International Organizations' (UNCOPUOS 17 June 2021) 8, 17, 74 [https://perma.cc/N436-6SU2]: Australia's Space (Launches and Returns) Act 2018 provides that '[a]pplications for the launch of an Australian space object overseas or a launch to space from Australia include consideration of the space environment, including space debris ... A debris mitigation strategy must: Be based on an internationally recognised guideline or standard for debris mitigation'; the Canadian Space Agency (CSA) 'adopted the IADC Space Debris Mitigation Guidelines in 2012 to mitigate the potential creation of space debris generated from its projects, missions and activities ... The IADC Space Debris Mitigation Guidelines will apply to all CSA projects, missions and activities'; the UK's Outer Space Act 1986 provides that 'in assessing a mission proposed by a licence applicant ... during the safety review, applicants will be obliged to demonstrate compliance/conformance with existing norms/best practices in relation to measures such as the IADC Space Debris Mitigation Guidelines, Space Debris Mitigation Guidelines of the Committee, and the growing body of international standards relating to debris'.

debris mitigation requirements') and International Telecommunication Union (ITU) recommendation ITU-R S.1003 ('Environmental protection of the geostationary-satellite orbit') are used by some States 'as reference points in their regulatory frameworks for national space activities'.[518]

Civilian and Military Activities Encompassed by Rule

13. Both civilian and military space activities are encompassed by this Rule. While no measures can be identified that have been adopted by States explicitly pursuant to Article IX to require military forces to avoid harmful contamination of outer space, there is significant military practice regarding protection of the natural environment which could apply to space, particularly during armed conflict[519] (see Rule 43: Natural Environment).

Effect of Hostilities on Status of Rule

14. The obligation to avoid harmful contamination of outer space and adverse changes in the environment of the Earth resulting from the introduction of extra-terrestrial matter continues to apply to the extent that it is compatible with the existence of hostilities conducted in accordance with the law of armed conflict (see Rule 43: Natural Environment).

---

[518] UNGA 'Report of the Committee on the Peaceful Uses of Outer Space, Sixtieth Session' (7–16 June 2017) UN Doc A/72/20, 15, para 103.

[519] Note, however, the efforts by some States to explicitly apply the principles found in art IX of the OST to military space activities. See eg US Secretary of Defense 'Tenets of Responsible Behavior in Space' (Memorandum, US DoD, 7 July 2021) (directing DoD Components to 'conduct space operations consistent with the following Tenets of Responsible Behavior' including to '[o]perate in, from, to and through space with due regard to others and in a professional manner, limit the generation of long-lived debris, avoid the creation of harmful interference, maintain safe separation and safe trajectory, communicate and make notifications to enhance the safety and stability of the domain').

Rule 15
Visits to Facilities on the Moon and Other Celestial Bodies

Subject to prior notice and consultations, a State is permitted to visit all stations, installations, equipment and space vehicles of another State on the Moon and other celestial bodies on the basis of reciprocity. This includes facilities being used by military personnel or in which military personnel are present, on the Moon and other celestial bodies.

Overview of Legal Basis of Rule

1. This Rule derives from Article XII of the Outer Space Treaty (OST):

   All stations, installations, equipment and space vehicles on the Moon and other celestial bodies shall be open to representatives of other States Parties to the Treaty on a basis of reciprocity. Such representatives shall give reasonable advance notice of a projected visit, in order that appropriate consultations may be held and that maximum precautions may be taken to assure safety and to avoid interference with normal operations in the facility to be visited.

Facilities vs Space Objects

2. The 'facilities' referred to in this Rule are all 'stations, installations, equipment and space vehicles' on the Moon and other celestial bodies. The umbrella term 'facilities' is used in this commentary to refer to such 'stations, installations, equipment and space vehicles' as may be present on the Moon and/or other celestial bodies in light of that term's usage in the last sentence of Article XII. This Rule only applies to facilities on the Moon and other celestial bodies, it does not apply to objects in outer space itself[520] or to space objects generally.

---

[520] India suggested that art 6 of the draft under consideration, the provision which was to become art XII of the OST, should refer to outer space as well as celestial bodies but that proposal was not adopted. See UNCOPUOS Legal Sub-Committee Summary Record 64 (n 124) 7.

Alongside Article XII and its reference to facilities, Article VIII of the OST provides that a State Party 'on whose registry an object launched into outer space is carried shall retain jurisdiction and control over such object, and over personnel thereof, while ... on a celestial body'. Accordingly, registered space objects while on a celestial body are subject to the prescriptive and the exclusive enforcement jurisdiction of the State of Registry (see Rule 8: Registration of Space Objects). The interaction between Article VIII and Article XII is not clearly articulated in the Treaty and no attempt is made to clearly distinguish between jurisdictional rights applicable to an Article VIII 'object' on a celestial body or an Article XII 'facility'. Moreover, there is no elaboration in the Treaty, nor in the negotiating history that delineates when a space 'object' under Article VIII may become a 'facility' under Article XII and thus be subject to the rights of reciprocal visitation.

The Travaux Préparatoires and the Term 'Reciprocity'

To date, there has been no establishment of facilities on the Moon or a celestial body that could serve as the basis of a physical visit where Article XII could have been invoked. Accordingly, to better understand the meaning of Article XII, recourse must be made to the negotiating history of the provision. The negotiating history of Article XII of the OST reveals an important debate over different approaches to the issue of visits. On the one hand, the original US draft of Article XII was framed liberally so as to allow 'open access at all times'[521] to stations, installations, equipment, and space vehicles on the Moon and celestial bodies by representatives of State Parties to the OST. This view was consistent with the existing visit and inspection regime contained within the Antarctic Treaty.[522] On the other hand, a more restrictive view was presented by the Soviet Union that provided conditions regarding such visits. The Soviet proposal sought to make visits on the basis of reciprocity and also included a requirement for an independent agreement as to the timing of a visit in order to ensure maximum precautions could be taken to assure safety and non-interference with the normal operations of the facility.[523] Ultimately, the United States accepted the proposed Soviet condition for visits on the basis of 'reciprocity', as opposed to 'access at all times', as reflected in the final version of Article XII. A requirement for a prior agreement was replaced by the language now found in Article XII specifying that 'representatives shall give reasonable advance notice of a projected visit, in order that appropriate consultations

---

[521] UNCOPUOS Legal Sub-Committee, 'Report of the Legal Sub-Committee on the Work of its Fifth Session (12 July–4 August and 12–16 September 1966) to the Committee on the Peaceful Uses of Outer Space (16 September 1966) UN Doc A/AC.105/35, Annex III, 3.
[522] The Antarctic Treaty (n 240) art VII; UNCOPUOS Summary Record 63 (n 125) 6.
[523] UNCOPUOS Legal Sub-Committee Summary Record 64 (n 124) 8–10.

may be held and that maximum precautions may be taken to assure safety and to avoid interference with normal operations in the facility to be visited'.

5. The precise meaning of the term 'reciprocity' was discussed at length during the negotiation of Article XII by States on the UNCOPUOS Legal Sub-Committee. Questions were discussed such as whether a State's right to visit would be capped by the number of facilities that it maintained on the Moon or other celestial bodies, and whether facilities would be open for reciprocal visits by others (and what the term 'reciprocal' meant). One State representative questioned whether a State that had only one such facility on the Moon would be entitled to visit five facilities of another State, or whether a State that had no facilities on the Moon would have the right to conduct any visits at all.[524] There was considerable discussion of these interpretations of reciprocity under Article XII,[525] but the leading view appeared to be that States are entitled to the right of reciprocal visitation to the stations, installations, equipment and space vehicles of other States, irrespective of the number of such facilities and irrespective of whether the visiting State has its own facilities.

6. A fundamental reciprocity issue was highlighted by the representative of the United Kingdom who noted that there were two different possible types of reciprocity: 'one whereby each State had a right to take the initiative in gaining access to a station on a celestial body, as provided in the treaty, and another whereby a State must grant a similar right to others only if it itself wishes to conduct inspections'.[526] Although the Soviet representative did not clarify which of these two types of reciprocity he was referring to,[527] the Soviet amendment that introduced the concept of reciprocity to Article XII 'suggested to several delegations that if a particular nation, which controls a station on a celestial body, has no desire to inspect the stations ... of other nations, it is under no obligation to permit visitors from other stations to enter its own stations'.[528]

7. With respect to the US interpretation of the term reciprocity, the US delegate stated that '[r]epresentatives of a State Party to the Treaty conducting activities on

---

[524] ibid 5 (it was speculated by the Italian representative that where one State Party had five installations on a celestial body, and another State Party only had one, then the exercise of reciprocity could mean that only one of the five installations could be visited; the Italian representative further noted that 'conditions of reciprocity would exist only for countries which had actually conducted space activities').
[525] ibid 8; UNGA First Committee 'Summary Record of the 1492nd Meeting' (17 December 1966) UN Doc A/C.1/S.R.1492, 428, para 7.
[526] ibid 9 (further noting that 'it would be advisable to ascertain which type of reciprocity the Soviet representative had in mind').
[527] ibid 8 (the Soviet representative simply noted that '[t]he Soviet text was entirely clear concerning the principle of reciprocity. Reciprocity should be understood in the traditional sense of the word in international law.').
[528] Dembling and Arons (n 123) 449; During the negotiation of art XII, the Japanese representative, responding to the issues—particularly those raised in the context of reciprocity—summarized the discussions by stating that he 'shared the doubts of the representatives of Italy, Canada, and Lebanon concerning the Soviet proposal'. UNCOPUOS Legal Sub-Committee Summary Report 64 (n 124) 8.

celestial bodies should have the right of access to the stations, installations, equipment and space vehicles of another State party on a celestial body, regardless of whether the second State had ever claimed or exercised a right of access itself'.[529] He further stated that 'the United States was prepared to include reciprocity in its text if the above-mentioned interpretation was universally shared and if the other provisions in the article were consistent with the idea of reciprocity'.[530] Although the US delegate cautioned that '[a]ccess should not be conditional, and the notion of prior agreement implied a sort of veto on it',[531] the text of Article XII ultimately did in fact contain conditions ('prior notice', 'consultations', and 'reciprocity' for visits) and the US proposal for 'open access at all times' for visits was not adopted.

8. This Rule relates to '[a]ll stations, installations, equipment and space vehicles on the Moon and other celestial bodies' as expressed in Article XII. This would include any facilities meeting these definitions that are being used by the military. While Article IV of the OST prohibits the establishment of military bases, installations, and fortifications, mere military use of facilities or military personnel being present in facilities on the Moon and other celestial bodies is not prohibited, subject to the restrictions on military activities in Article IV, paragraph 2 of the OST (see Rule 4: Restrictions on Specified Military Establishments and Activities on Celestial Bodies).

9. A distinction may be made between the legal regimes applicable to a space object under Article VIII and a facility on a celestial body under Article XII, the latter being subject to reciprocal visits and various procedural and substantive requirements. During the treaty negotiations, the representative of India sought to include a provision to the OST that extended reciprocal rights of visitation to 'platforms' in space.[532] This proposition was rejected, thus ensuring that there was a qualitative difference between space objects in space or on a celestial body (to which Article VIII rights applied) and a facility on a celestial body (to which Article XII applied). While there is necessary overlap concerning jurisdictional rights, there is a difference concerning the exercise of rights of visitation. In establishing the difference between a space object under Article VIII and a facility under Article XII, it is evident that the wording of Article XII envisages an element of permanence and ongoing operational capacity for a facility. The listing of 'stations,

---

[529] UNCOPUOS Legal Sub-Committee Summary Report 70 (n 248) 6–7 (the US delegate stated what he regarded as the correct interpretation of reciprocity as follows: 'if the first State has denied access to representatives of the second State then the latter was not required on the principle of reciprocity to grant access to representatives of the first State' and further added that this interpretation was 'a well-established principle of law, and that was why the United States delegation thought that no mention of reciprocity was needed'.).
[530] ibid.
[531] ibid.
[532] ibid 7 (the Indian Representative, Mr Krishna Rao, is referring to Article 6 of the draft, which became art XII in the OST.).

installations, equipment and space vehicles' suggests a relatively inclusive list of purposeful structures and related equipment dedicated to ongoing operational activity. Additionally, the requirement not to impede 'normal operations' and to ensure the 'safety' of personnel engaged in such operations, reinforces the ordinary meaning of these terms, thus pointing to a particular functionality associated with more than temporary activity on a celestial body.

Procedures Related to Visits

10. Visits under this Rule require 'reasonable advance notice' to undertake consultations. Consultation requires good faith dialogue to establish the timing and requirements of a visit. The question of how much advance notice would be required must be determined on the basis of the circumstances ruling at the time. Article XII's reference to consultations is predicated upon the need to ensure 'that maximum precautions may be taken to assure safety and to avoid interference with normal operations in the facility to be visited' and this directly reflects the treaty negotiation consensus that access is not absolute and that the right of visit is subject to serious considerations of safety and non-interference with normal operations.[533] Accordingly, in taking 'maximum precautions' a State could impose numerous conditions and limitations to ensure the safe conduct of any visit and the prevention of interference with normal operations. Hence a visit under this Rule may not necessarily entitle the visiting State to access all areas of a facility. Rather, it is possible that those representatives from the visiting State, when granted access, may visit only those areas that have been cleared for visit. Such restrictions would be agreed upon during consultations as would the timing of a visit and would be part of the 'maximum precautions' a State is entitled to take to assure safety and avoid interference with the normal operations of the facility.

11. The term 'visit' is not defined in the OST. It is nonetheless notable that the term used in the Antarctic Treaty, which was initially in contemplation during the negotiations of Article XII,[534] allows for an unlimited right of open access to all 'stations, installations and equipment' anywhere within Antarctica and a corresponding right of 'inspection' of those same facilities at 'all times'. Similar absolute access rights as proposed by the United States during the OST negotiations were not accepted. More particularly, rights of 'inspection' as opposed to reciprocal 'visit' are not included within the wording of Article XII. Accordingly, while there is a reciprocal right of visit to facilities on the Moon and other celestial bodies, such a right is necessarily limited by considerations of safety and non-interference with normal

---

[533] ibid 8–9 (where comments from the Soviet, Japanese, and Italian representatives reinforced this point.).
[534] UNCOPUOS Legal Sub-Committee Summary Report 63 (n 125) 6.

operations as well as a functional limit regarding activities that may be undertaken during the course of a visit that do not thus constitute an inspection. The Soviet delegate to the negotiation of Article XII of the OST noted that there was a danger in using the Antarctic Treaty too closely as an analogy, stating that 'one could not automatically apply conditions which were appropriate to one set of circumstances to an entirely different situation. It was true that outer space, like Antarctica, could be considered a no man's land, but there the similarity ended.'[535]

12. The precise contours of the application of this Rule during an armed conflict remain to be established by State practice. However, it seems likely that the 'right of visits' regime under this Rule would be suspended between belligerents during an armed conflict because such visits are incompatible with the armed conflict (see Methodology of *Manual*). As between a neutral/third party and a belligerent, the right of visit would continue, but the restrictions to avoid interference with the visited facility's operations may become stricter or more developed.

---

[535] ibid 10.

PART II
MILITARY SPACE ACTIVITIES DURING TIMES OF TENSION AND CRISIS

Introduction

Overview of the Legal Framework

1. The space law rules discussed in this *Manual* are principally designed to operate during times of peace and to advance peaceful uses of space.[1] Together with other international legal obligations, particularly those found in the UN Charter, these rules provide a framework for the peaceful cooperation of States in exploring and using space. Disputes between States related to space activities are governed by the same overall obligations in the UN Charter that govern States in other domains, notably the obligation of all Member States to first 'settle their international disputes by peaceful means in such a manner that international peace and security, and justice, are not endangered'.[2]

2. As space becomes more congested and the varied interests of States related to the use and exploration of space continue to grow, the risk of disputes arising among States increases. It is in the interest of all States that such disputes do not lead to armed conflict and this means that understanding and observing the existing international law governing the space domain becomes even more critical during times of tension and crisis. Determining the appropriate response by a State to unfriendly actions in space by another State is vitally important during times of tension and crisis to avoid, wherever possible, miscalculations or misinterpretations of the law that could lead to unnecessary conflict. This determination by a State must begin with an accurate legal characterization of the other State's unfriendly act and must then be followed by an assessment of appropriate, legally available, responses.

---

[1] It should be noted that the space law rules discussed in this *Manual* continue to apply during an armed conflict unless they impede a State's right of self-defence (exercised in conformity with the UN Charter) or cannot be harmonized with the rights and obligations of a State under the law of armed conflict.
[2] Charter of the United Nations (adopted 26 June 1945, entered into force 24 October 1945) 1 UNTS XVI (UN Charter) art 2(4).

Section 1
Legal Obligations and Prohibitions of Particular Relevance During Times of Tension and Crisis

3. Section 1 of Part II of the *Manual* contains Rules dealing with rights, obligations, and prohibitions that may be particularly relevant during what may be referred to as times of tension and crisis. This phraseology of 'times of tension and crisis' carries with it no particular legal significance or definitional boundary in itself. Rather it is used to merely describe the legal regime that is of particular importance in circumstances that are not routine military activities in space but are not yet taking place during a time of armed conflict. These rules are important in appropriately characterizing the legal status of unfriendly actions by States, evaluating legally appropriate responses, and understanding important rights and obligations.

4. Rule 17: Due Regard, Rule 18: Harmful Interference (as set forth in the Outer Space Treaty (OST)),[3] and Rule 19: ITU Harmful Radio Interference all serve as the basis of common space law obligations and prohibitions that apply at all times but are of particular importance during times of tension and crisis. Rule 16 on Zones explains how zones in space or on celestial bodies may, if properly declared and maintained in observance of other States rights under the OST, may offer an opportunity to better implement these obligations.

5. Rule 20: Non-Intervention Principle, Rule 21: Use of Force, Rule 22: Threat of Force, and Rule 23: Armed Attack comprise a set of rules regarding wrongful conduct in space, including notably actions that involve the threat or use of force. Important analysis found in Rule 21: Use of Force and in Rule 23: Armed Attack also address counterspace weapon systems that can temporarily or partially disrupt, interfere with, or degrade the functions of satellites and other space objects. This analysis is important in distinguishing between unfriendly acts that do, and do not, constitute a use of force or that do not rise to the level of an armed attack.

Section 2
Response Actions

6. Section 2 of Part II of the *Manual* examines appropriate response actions, by individual States and collectively by States, regional organizations, and the United Nations, to the unfriendly actions and internationally wrongful acts of States discussed above, including those that involve the use of force.

---

[3] Treaty on Principles Governing the Activities of States in the Exploration and Use of Outer Space, Including the Moon and Other Celestial Bodies (opened for signature 27 January 1967, entered into force 10 October 1967) 610 UNTS 205 (OST).

7. In responding to unfriendly acts by other States in space or in any other domain, Article 33(1) of the UN Charter lists a variety of means available for States to resolve disputes peacefully. Article 2(3) of the UN Charter requires that States first seek resolution of a dispute by these peaceful means if the continuance of the dispute is likely to endanger the maintenance of international peace and security. Further, some procedures, means, or measures for peaceful settlement of disputes are found in international agreements governing specific activities or potential disputes. For example, with respect to space activities, the OST provides for international consultations if a State has reason to believe that an activity or experiment planned by it or its nationals in outer space would cause potentially harmful interference with activities of other States Parties in space or if a State has reason to believe that an activity or experiment planned by another State Party in space would cause potentially harmful interference (see Rule 18: Harmful Interference). Similarly, the OST and Liability Convention establish requirements, standards, and procedures to compensate States for the damages caused by space objects based on the international liability of the space object's launching State (see Rule 12: International Liability for Damage Caused by Space Objects).

8. In addition to the specific rules in the space law regime which govern certain types of disputes, a State is also generally responsible under international law for internationally wrongful acts that can be attributed to that State. These include violations of obligations under applicable international agreements, such as the OST. With respect to attribution, it should be noted that the OST establishes a special attribution regime that makes States bear international responsibility for national activities in outer space, whether such activities are carried on by governmental agencies or by non-governmental entities (including private companies), and for assuring those national activities are carried out in conformity with the OST and international law (see Rule 10: Responsibility of States for National Activities in Outer Space). Recourse to appropriate tribunals or other available adjudicative or resolution procedures is left to the States that are parties to the dispute—either pursuant to any applicable international agreements or on a mutually agreed basis.

9. In addition to the response options discussed above, important response options relevant to military activities in space are discussed in the following rules in this section—Rule 24: Retorsion, Rule 25: Countermeasures, Rule 26: Self-Defence, Rule 27: Collective Self-Defence, and Rule 28: Collective Security Measures.

10. If an armed conflict in space does occur, or if an armed conflict in any other domain extends to space, it is critical that the rules governing armed conflicts are well understood and carefully applied to prevent unnecessary harm to the civilian population and non-belligerents. These rules on international law, referred to as the law of armed conflict, are discussed in the context of military space operations in Part III.

SECTION 1
LEGAL OBLIGATIONS AND PROHIBITIONS OF PARTICULAR RELEVANCE DURING TIMES OF TENSION AND CRISIS

Rule 16
Zones

A State may designate particular zones around its space objects or otherwise in space or on celestial bodies. However, such designation shall not limit the rights that any other State has under international law; impose any additional legal obligations upon other States; violate any other rule under international law, including the non-appropriation principle; nor confer additional rights upon the designating State.

Overview of Legal Basis of Rule

1. The declaration and establishment of zones is not per se prohibited by international law, including international space law. Conversely, there is no express or direct authority in the OST or in any other treaty that specifically provides for the declaration and establishment of a zone in space, although an appropriate designation of a zone under this Rule could be consistent with the free use of space (see Rule 1: Freedom of Use, Access, Exploration, and Scientific Investigation and Principles of Cooperation). However, if a zone is designated in space or on a celestial body, its legal characteristics must be clearly stated in order to not infringe on the rights of other States. In addition to all other international legal obligations, a State designating a zone in space must specifically ensure compliance with its obligations to respect of free use and exploration of space by other States (see Rule 1: Freedom of Use, Access, Exploration, and Scientific Investigation and Principles of Cooperation); the non-appropriation of space and celestial bodies (see Rule 2: Non-Appropriation of Outer Space and Celestial Bodies); due regard for the corresponding interests of other States (see Rule 17: Due Regard); the duty to consult with other States if a State has reason to believe that an activity planned by it or its nationals would cause potentially harmful interference with activities of other States (see Rule 18: Harmful Interference); and any other applicable obligations under the OST. The establishment of zones in space must also conform to applicable obligations set forth in the International Telecommunication Union (ITU) Constitution and Regulations (see Rule 19: ITU Harmful Radio Interference). It is important to also note that the establishment of zones in space is unlike the establishment of zones in the air, land, and sea contexts, which are based on international legal rights associated with territorial sovereignty and/or on applicable conventions governing the air and sea domains. Thus, the general application of

analogies based on other domains to explain or designate zones in space is problematic. In addition, to the extent that zones are sometimes established in these other domains to exclude other States from areas around military bases, those circumstances are not present in space owing to the absence of military bases, installations, or fortifications on celestial bodies (see Rule 4: Restrictions on Specified Military Establishments and Activities on Celestial Bodies), except in the most limited circumstances during an armed conflict.

The Mechanics of Zones in Space

2. Physically, objects in space are in constant motion, making location-based zones particularly challenging to delineate. Given the orbital mechanics of space activity, a State declaring such a zone must address the likelihood that other States' space objects may have difficulty avoiding such a zone. Any outer space-based zone (also sometimes referred to as a 'volume' to highlight its three-dimensional nature) should be assessed relative to a fixed point of reference, such as an object or coordinates. As a hypothetical example, State A designates a 500 metre (m) warning/buffer zone around its nuclear command, control, and communications (NC3) satellite directed at on-orbit, close-approach satellites. Such a zone would not exist in a fixed location, given the NC3 satellite's constant orbit around Earth and Earth's constant rotation around the sun; however, a three-dimensional 500 m span around the NC3 satellite would be sufficiently defined to form a cognizable zone.

Establishment of Safety-Based Manoeuvre Zones

3. In outer space, unlike in the maritime environment, there are currently few guidelines or legally binding rules that dictate how objects must manoeuvre or establish priority among them.[4] To date, although some general rules do exist in space under the OST, no States have objected on international legal grounds to another State's satellite approaching one of their own. This is true despite some serious public protests on other grounds.[5] For example, the Russian Luch-Olymp satellite has provocatively approached multiple satellites for unknown purposes and generated

---

[4] The only legally binding space law rules in this area are the general and not well-developed obligations found in art IX of the OST (n 3) relating to due regard and harmful interference (see Rule 17: Due Regard and Rule 18: Harmful Interference). It is possible, however, that these obligations could be used as the foundation for the declaration of related warning or safety zones.

[5] See eg Sandra Erwin, 'Raymond Calls Out Russia For "Threatening Behavior" in Outer Space' *Space News* (Washington DC, 10 February 2020) [https://perma.cc/Y7SJ-LSGU]; Caroline Kelly and Barbara Starr, 'Space Force Says Russian Satellites are Following American Satellite' *CNN* (Atlanta, 11 February 2020) [https://perma.cc/C9NN-87NR]; WJ Hennigan, 'Exclusive: Strange Russian Spacecraft Shadowing U.S. Spy Satellite, General Says' *Time* (New York, 10 February 2020) [https://perma.cc/MX5L-5S6M].

protests from other States, but no assertions of violations of international law have been made by any State.[6] Thus, until such time as States invoke provisions of the OST or any other applicable international legal obligations with respect to the establishment of zones or States agree to some other legally binding regime, any declared zone (for safety purposes or otherwise) may be respected as a matter of practicality and comity, but not as a matter of international law (unless mandated by the UN Security Council as a enforcement action under Chapter VII of the UN Charter).[7] Although a State ordinarily has no express legal right to exclude others from access to any part of space or a celestial body,[8] it may prudentially warn other States that their unexplained entry into a particular designated location in space during a specified time interval may result in the declaring State taking actions that carry adverse consequences. Such declarations must themselves be based upon acceptable grounds of international law, such as self-defence or lawful countermeasure in accordance with its rights under existing law.

4. To date, no publicly available evidence exists regarding the establishment by a State of a safety zone in space. Regarding a safety-based zone in space established pursuant to an intergovernmental agreement, the Multilateral Control Board of the International Space Station (ISS) has established International Rendezvous System Interoperability Standards to enable 'on-orbit crew operations, rendezvous and docking/berthing and collaborative endeavours utilizing different spacecraft in deep space'. These standards include zones and corridors for operations within an ISS approach sphere which are consistent with this Rule. As articulated by NASA, a 4 kilometre (km) by 2 km notification 'Approach Ellipsoid' and a 200 m 'Keep-Out Sphere' around the ISS are designed to provide procedures for commercial craft (typically resupply for the ISS) attempting to dock with the ISS, in order to ensure the safety of the ISS. They do not purport to be more broadly applicable to

---

[6] Brian Weeden and Victoria Samson (eds), 'Global Counterspace Capabilities: An Open Source Assessment' (Secure World Foundation April 2022) 2-11 to 2-12 [https://perma.cc/3SJK-XUVS]. However, such approaches are not without concern. In 2018, the French Minister of Defence criticized the Luch-Olymp approach of a French-Italian secure communication satellite as 'espionage' (a crime under domestic law only)—'France Accuses Russia of Spying on Military from Space' *Reuters* (Toulouse, 7 September 2018) [https://perma.cc/HAB2-HPT4]. The United States has expressed concern over the Luch-Olymp satellite and other close approach satellites, though the concern focused on its potential for future interference with satellites, not about its inspection capacity: Maddy Longwell, 'State Department Concerned over Russian Satellite's Behavior' *C4ISRNet* (14 August 2018) [http://perma.cc/AMZ7-MYCM]; Erwin (n 5) (describing the approach as 'concerning' and 'threatening').

[7] There are, however, some examples of States enacting legislation which authorizes the designation of zones in space for ensuring the safety of space activities. See eg Russia's domestic space law, within the 'space objects' section, which provides for special rules 'within the zone minimally necessary for ensuring safety of space activity' that 'shall be binding for Russian and foreign organizations and citizens'. United Nations Office for Outer Space Affairs (UNOOSA) (tr), 'Selected Examples of National Laws Governing Space Activities: Russian Federation—Decree No. 5663-1 of the Russian House of Soviets' art 17.5. [https://perma.cc/4MVY-6QYR]. Note, however, that art 17.5 also provides that '[t]he rights of jurisdiction and control over space objects, as well as of ownership thereof *shall not affect the legal status of the area of outer space or the surface or subsoil of a celestial body occupied by it*' (emphasis added).

[8] Access to facilities on the Moon and other celestial bodies may, however, be restricted for safety purposes consistent with the rules set forth under art XII of the OST (n 3).

any other craft in these zones, and there are no assertions of an enforcement mechanism for these areas.

5. A properly designated space zone may also serve as a communication tool for space-faring States similar to a Notice to Airmen (NOTAM) or Notice to Mariners (NOTMAR), in the respective domains of operations, by informing other craft of potential hazards from the declaring State's use of outer space. Such warning may be a legitimate tool for States, particularly in the context of any duty to warn under the due regard requirement of Article IX of the OST (Rule 17: Due Regard), to avoid harmful interference under Article IX of the OST (Rule 18: Harmful Interference), or as mitigation for fault under applicable liability regimes (Rule 12: International Liability for Damages Caused by Space Objects). For example, if a State chooses to conduct conventional weapons testing or potentially harmful military operations in outer space, the establishment of a zone may be appropriate to communicate parameters of the operation so as to avoid interference with the operation and harm to other States. Similarly, if a State was to de-orbit a satellite, providing notice and a warning with the zone of descent to States with satellites in subjacent orbits would be reasonable. However, it must be emphasized that the declaration of any such zone does not confer any additional rights or enforcement remedies on the declaring State, or restrict the rights of any other State.

Establishment of Warning Zones for Identification, Self-Defence, and Other Communication Purposes

6. Without prejudice to any obligations under the OST, particularly the obligation not to appropriate or assert sovereignty over any part of space, certain aspects of a terrestrial-based zone might extend into outer space. For example, the concept of a Space Defence Identification Zone (SpaDIZ), an identification zone contiguous with the subjacent State's airspace, akin to a terrestrial Air Defence Identification Zone (ADIZ) extending into space, might be considered viable if fully consistent with the requirements of the OST and supported by State practice.[9] An ADIZ is a zone 'established in international airspace adjacent to national airspace by which States establish reasonable conditions of entry into their territory'.[10] Such an identification zone would be premised on a State's fundamental national security interest in protecting its territorial sovereignty, and could not constitute any claim of appropriation or sovereignty over the zone itself.[11] Accordingly, the zone has no

---

[9] Such a zone may share some characteristics of a terrestrial-based ADIZ but cannot infringe on the rights of any State under the OST.

[10] Harvard University Program on Humanitarian Policy and Conflict Research, *HPCR Manual on International Law Applicable to Air and Missile Warfare* (CUP 2013) (AMW Manual) 295.

[11] See General Counsel of Department of Defense, *Department of Defense Law of War Manual* (rev edn, United States Department of Defense 2016) (US DoD Law of War Manual) para 14.2.4.1.

relevance for an aircraft (or spacecraft) that is transiting the zone with no intent to enter the declaring State's airspace.[12] In principle, such an identification zone might be feasible in space with respect to space objects intending to enter the national airspace (or territory) of a subjacent State. However, no State has designated such a SpaDIZ or similar construct emanating from its territory to date,[13] therefore no State practice currently supports the legal validity of such a zone in space.

7. Another type of zone in outer space, one which does not emanate from sovereign territory, could be based on self-defence, particularly defence of space objects (Rule 26: Self-Defence). Broadly, military and national defence/security activities are permissible uses of outer space (Rule 1: Freedom of Use, Access, Exploration, and Scientific Investigation and Principles of Cooperation and Rule 3: Peaceful Purposes in Outer Space). A State may assert its right of self-defence with respect to its space objects and systems, subject to Article 51 of the UN Charter (see Rule 26: Self-Defence).[14] A State may elect to designate a warning zone in order to deter potentially threatening space craft from approaching its objects, as an extension of its right of self-defence. For instance, a State might declare that a deliberate approach by another space object within a specified distance of a particularly important satellite would raise a point of significant concern in their decision-making calculus of whether an armed attack may be imminent. The designation

---

[12] Thus, the scope of application of such a zone is limited to aircraft seeking entry into a State's sovereign territory or airspace and failure to provide ADIZ identification may result in only the State's refusal of consent to enter national airspace. On the other hand, the Peoples Republic of China (PRC) apparently seeks to assert broader rights in its designated ADIZ. On 23 November 2013, the PRC established what it called 'the East China Sea Air Defense Identification Zone' (ECS ADIZ). Later, the PRC Ministry of National Defense (MND) issued rules for the ECS ADIZ that 'apply generally to aircraft flying in the ECS ADIZ, regardless of whether the aircraft intends to enter the PRC's airspace. The rules require flight plan identification, radio identification, transponder identification, and logo identification.' Ian E Rinehart and Bart Elias, 'China's Air Defense Identification Zone (ADIZ)' (CRS Report, US Congressional Research Service 2015) 7. The rules further warn that 'China's armed forces will adopt defensive emergency measures to respond to aircraft that do not cooperate in the identification or refuse to follow the instructions'. 'Announcement of the Aircraft Identification Rules for the East China Sea Air Defense Identification Zone of the People's Republic of China' *China Daily* (Beijing, 23 November 2013) [perma.cc/Z9QU-WLJF]. These Chinese Air Defense Identification Zones have been protested on international legal grounds by other States; see eg Ministry of Foreign Affairs of Japan, 'Statement by the Minister for Foreign Affairs on the announcement on the 'East China Sea Air Defense Identification Zone' by the Ministry of National Defense of the People's Republic of China' (24 November 2013) [https://perma.cc/R69J-6JNH] ('The announced measures unduly infringe the freedom of flight in international airspace, which is the general principle of international law, and will have serious impacts on the order of international aviation.').
[13] States have passed domestic laws regulating re-entry of spacecraft. See eg *Space (Launches and Returns) Act 2018* (Cth) pt 3, div 6 (Australia).
[14] See, generally, the French Ministry for the Armed Forces, 'Space Defence Strategy—Report of the "Space" working group' (Report, Pôle création Bureau des éditions 2019) 2.1.1.1 (stating as a defence objective 'to be able to defend our space interests in space against unfriendly, wrongful or aggressive acts, in accordance and in compliance with international law'); US Dept of Defense, 'Directive 3100.01—Space Policy' (reissue, 4 November 2016) (US DoD Space Policy 2016) para 4.b ('The sustainability and stability of the space environment, as well as free access to and use of space, are vital to U.S. national interests. Purposeful interference with U.S. space systems, including their supporting infrastructure, will be considered an infringement of U.S. rights.').

of such a sphere within which a State would regard its space object as possibly subject to an imminent armed attack does not, by itself, confer any enforcement right on the State. In such a case, the zone is merely a communication tool for a State to convey both internally (to forces) and externally (to adversaries) when it perceives that an armed attack or illegal use of force *might be* imminent, and at which point the State would have to consider forcible or non-forcible means to address the threat, consistent with the spectrum of options available under international law. Any incursion of the zone is not automatically a trigger for an assertion of the right of self-defence; it is merely a line from which the declaring State would raise the possibility of asserting a right of self-defence. However, no State practice to date supports this type of declaration. It is important to note that a State explicitly declaring a 'keep out zone' is legally problematic, as such a declaration would be inconsistent with other States' legal rights to use space for free navigation. However, a properly designated 'warning zone' as described in this paragraph does not infringe on those rights in the same way because such zones are not exclusionary.

8. For example, State A designates a fixed-distance warning zone around its space craft (A-1), which it has notified the world community is headed to a Lagrange point to conduct various military activities. States A and B are not involved in an armed conflict but are in a period of heightened tension. State B launches a craft (B-1) assessed by State A to have destructive intercept capabilities, which approaches A-1. State A reminds State B of the designated zone, the sensitivity of the mission, and State A's view of a threat from B-1. When B-1 approaches within the stated zone around A-1, A-1, perceiving an imminent attack, employs defensive force that destroys B-1. In this case, the violation of the zone itself did not provide State A with any additional legal authority for the use of force. Instead, any legal justification for State A's actions must be founded on the proper exercise of its inherent right of self-defence under Article 51 of the UN Charter. The anticipated imminent armed attack against A-1 by B-1, with the zone violation as a critical data point in State A's determination, would serve here as the basis for A's actions in self-defence.

Establishment of Zones on the Moon or Other Celestial Bodies

9. Regarding zones on the Moon or other celestial bodies, there have been no designations by States of zones to demonstrate State practice on the matter (although see the discussion of the Artemis Accords in paragraph 10). While the above considerations would apply to zones on celestial bodies, such zones also require consideration under Article XII of the OST (see Rule 15: Visit to Facilities on the Moon and Other Celestial Bodies). In peacetime, under Article XII of the OST, the visitation of facilities (to include stations, installations, equipment, and space vehicles) requires

notification and allows 'maximum precautions may be taken to assure safety and to avoid interference with normal operations' (see Rule 15: Visit to Facilities on the Moon and Other Celestial Bodies). As practice develops, such precautions may include zones in furtherance of the safety or preservation of normal operations of such a facility, thereby providing a basis for zones unique to celestial bodies.

On 13 October 2020, eight States (subsequently followed by numerous other States)[15] announced that they joined the 'Artemis Accords', a set of non-binding, intergovernmental political commitments to 'principles for international cooperation and partnership in civil space exploration'.[16] The Signatories state that they intend, *inter alia*, to use their experience under the Accords 'to contribute to multilateral efforts to further develop international practices, criteria, and rules applicable to the definition and determination of safety zones[17] and harmful interference'.[18] These safety zones, which could exist in space or on celestial bodies, are applicable under the Accords only to the extent that 'the Signatories intend to provide notification of their activities and commit to coordinating with any relevant actor to avoid harmful interference'.[19] The Signatories to the Accords further commit 'to respect the principle of free access to all areas of celestial bodies and all other provisions of the Outer Space Treaty in their use of safety zones'.[20] The non-legally binding status of the Accords (replete with words like 'should' and 'intend to') and their explicit tie to only Signatories and civil space limit what can be drawn from them. Thus, the relevance of the Artemis Accords in establishing a precedent for other States in the designation of any type of zone in space is not clear. Nonetheless, the US Department of State has noted that the nations that have joined the Artemis Accords 'are setting an important standard for international cooperation in outer space'.[21] However, it should also be noted that the Preamble to the Accords clearly couches the Accords within the Signatories' intended compliance

10.

---

[15] As of 30 March 2023, a total of 24 States have joined the Artemis Accords. See para 13, Rule 2: Non-Appropriation of Outer Space and Celestial Bodies.
[16] 'The Artemis Accords: Principles for Cooperation in the Civil Exploration and Use of the Moon, Mars, Comets, and Asteroids' NASA (13 October 2020) [https://perma.cc/PCD3-SWCY]. For additional discussion of the Artemis Accords, see para 13, Rule 2: Non-Appropriation of Outer Space and Celestial Bodies. See generally, NASA, 'The Artemis Accords' <https://www.nasa.gov/specials/artemis-accords/index.html> accessed 27 March 2023.
[17] It should be noted that these 'safety zones' are not intended to ensure the safety of any military bases, installations, and fortifications, or the conduct of military manoeuvres on celestial bodies and thus do not implicate the restrictions found in art IV(2) of the OST.
[18] ibid s 11, para 6. Such safety zones are intended to support 'deconfliction of space activities' as the Signatories 'reaffirm their commitment to the Outer Space Treaty, including those provisions relating to due regard and harmful interference'. ibid s 11 para 1.
[19] ibid s 11, para 7. The Signatories further state their intention that '[t]he size and scope of the safety zone, as well as the notice and coordination, should reflect the nature of the operations being conducted and the environment that such operations are conducted in' and that '[t]he size and scope of the safety zone should be determined in a reasonable manner'. ibid s 11, paras 7(a) and (b).
[20] ibid s 11, para 11.
[21] Office of the Spokesperson (US State Dept), 'France Becomes Twentieth Nation to Sign the Artemis Accords' (Media Note, US State Department 7 June 2022) [https://perma.cc/DD3S-RDZ7].

with the OST (particularly the concepts of due regard and harmful interference avoidance), presenting the view of the Signatory States that safety zones, limited in these ways, may legally fit within the rights and obligations enumerated in the OST.

Establishment of Zones under Chapter VII of UN Charter

11. As the UN Charter applies to State activities in space pursuant to Article III of the OST, the UN Security Council, pursuant to its authority under Chapter VII of the UN Charter to use armed force to restore international peace and security,[22] could impose an enforceable 'keep-out', 'no-approach', or 'no-transit' zone in space, akin to the air-based 'no-fly zone' (notwithstanding the physical differences of travel through air and space). Obligations imposed on States by the UN Security Council under Chapter VII of the UN Charter are binding on all States and as such, prevail over obligations under any other international agreement, including the OST.[23]

Possible Establishment of Zones during Armed Conflict

12. Special rules might apply to the declaration of zones during an armed conflict. In domains other than space, and subject to some restrictions under other legal regimes, belligerents are authorized under customary international law to exercise control over the immediate area of military operations to include (where necessary) the exclusion of non-belligerents from the area of operations even in international airspace or on the high seas.[24] These concepts might be extended in the future to the space domain as well, based generally on a belligerent's overall right to take measures necessary to accomplish a legitimate military purpose, irrespective of the domain of operation.[25] The declaration of a zone in the immediate area of

---

[22] UN Charter (n 2) art 41.
[23] ibid arts 25 and 103.
[24] See *Oxford Manual on the Laws of Naval Warfare* (Institute of International Law 1913) art 50; 'Rules concerning the Control of Wireless Telegraphy in Time of War and Air Warfare' (The Hague, 1923) art 30; Louise Doswald-Beck (ed), *San Remo Manual on International Law Applicable to Armed Conflicts at Sea* (CUP 1995)(San Remo Manual) Rule 106; AMW Manual (n 10) Rules 106B and 107.
[25] See International Committee of the Red Cross, *Commentary on the Additional Protocols of 8 June 1977 to the Geneva Conventions of 12 August 1949* (Claude Pilloud and others (eds), Martin Nijhoff 1987) (*Commentary on the Additional Protocols*) para 1389 ('the necessity for measures which are essential to attain the goals of war and which are lawful in accordance with the laws and customs of war'); *United States v List (The Hostage Case)* Case No 7 [1948] *reprinted in Trials of War Criminals Before the Nuremberg Military Tribunals Under Control Council Law No. 10* (United States Government Printing Office 1950) vol XI, 1230 ('Military necessity permits a belligerent, subject to the laws of war, to apply any amount and kind of force to compel the complete submission of the enemy....'); Ministry of Defence, 'The Joint Service Manual of the Law of Armed Conflict' (Joint Service Publication 383, United Kingdom Joint Doctrine and Concepts Centre 2004) (United Kingdom LOAC Manual) para 2.2.3; US Department of the Navy, 'The Commander's Handbook on the Law of Naval Operations' (August 2017 edn, US Office of the Chief of Naval Operations 2007) (US Commander's Handbook

operations in outer space (including the Moon and other Celestial Bodies) during armed conflict does not eliminate other obligations within the zone owed by belligerents to neutrals (see eg Rule 17: Due Regard), subject to the law of armed conflict. State practice for such a zone in outer space is undeveloped, so no definition of 'immediate area of operations' or the scope of enforcement mechanisms in a space context can be further determined. In addition, the articulation and definition of 'immediate area of operations' and any enforcement mechanisms would suffer from the challenges of physics, constant motion, and other space-specific factors.[26]

13. In designating any zone in space during an armed conflict, a State is constrained by all the requirements of the law of armed conflict, including military necessity. That is, a belligerent cannot declare a zone simply because it wants to do so—there must be a rationale that is clearly related to effective war-fighting and the legitimate exercise of its belligerent rights. That rationale may also be more difficult or complex to establish in the void of space. Furthermore, a State is legally required to take into account the potential practical impacts of that designation on other States and the rights that those States have under the OST. In particular, the scope of a zone in an immediate area of military operations during armed conflict is constrained by the facts prevailing at the time; any designated zones beyond such immediate area of operations are subject to the restrictions ordinarily imposed by this Rule and by the OST. Practical considerations are also likely to be highly relevant to States in designating zones, including the potential difficulty of third parties even being capable of avoiding the designated zone. In this regard, it was noted by a State during State Consultations that the restricted manoeuvrability of many satellites argues for the primary applicability of the non-appropriation principle (that would prohibit appropriating an area of space by designating a zone imposing obligations on other States), even during an armed conflict.

Zones on Celestial Bodies for the Protection of Space Heritage Sites

14. While the OST prohibits the national appropriation of outer space, the Moon, or celestial bodies, Article VIII confirms that the State of Registry retains jurisdiction

---

of Naval Operations) para 7.8 (naval zones are 'based on a belligerent's right to attack and destroy its enemy, its right to defend itself without suffering from neutral interference, and its right to ensure the security of its forces').

[26] It should be noted here that military planners and responsible authorities should exercise care and be aware that many satellites of neutral States may have little or no ability to manoeuvre to avoid entry into the declared zone (in contrast to land and naval warfare, where there may be a presumption that a neutral State can affirmatively decide to stay out of such a zone).

and control over any object launched into outer space 'while in outer space or on a celestial body'.[27] For example, the United States registered the Lunar Module from the Apollo 11 mission (the 'Eagle')[28] and retains jurisdiction and control over it on the surface of the Moon. It is important to note, however, that this registration does not cover the 'site' of the Moon landing, only the hardware located there. If an object such as the Eagle and its component parts are properly designated, they arguably could qualify as protected 'cultural property' in space—although this would be a significant and untested extension of the protection of cultural property located on Earth.[29] There is no time limit on a State's jurisdiction and control of a space object.

15. Any designation by a State of safety or protective zones around an object in space or on a celestial body must not impose legal restrictions that exceed the limitations of the OST framework in regulating the freedom of other States to explore and use space and access celestial bodies (see Article IV of the OST and Rule 1: Freedom of Use, Access, Exploration, and Scientific Investigation and Principles of Cooperation). A recent effort by the US National Aeronautics and Space Administration (NASA) involves a series of 'recommendations' to spacefaring entities on how to protect and preserve the historic and scientific value of US Government lunar artefacts.[30] NASA does not, however, suggest that it is in any way attempting to establish any binding obligations on other States. Instead, NASA has articulated, in detail, various recommended restrictions and procedures related to US Government space assets on the lunar surface, noting that representatives of commercial entities have approached NASA 'out of respect for hardware ownership, and a sincere desire to protect general scientific and historic aspects of these sites'.[31] Recommended restrictions and procedures include voluntary 'exclusion

---

[27] OST (n 3) art VIII.
[28] Registration Convention. Information Furnished in Conformity with General Assembly Resolution 1721 B (XVI) by States Launching Objects into Orbit or Beyond (12 February 1970).
[29] A number of treaties, which generally are explicitly restricted in their scope to the territories of States, are intended to establish special protection of cultural property and sites and may apply both in peacetime and in armed conflict. See eg Convention for the Protection of Cultural Property in the Event of Armed Conflict, The Hague, 249 UNTS 215 (14 May 1954); UNESCO Convention for the Protection of the World Cultural and Natural Heritage, 16 November 1972 (1037 UNTS 151); Additional Protocol I, art 53 (prohibiting the commission of 'any acts of hostility directed against the historic monuments, works of art or places of worship which constitute the cultural or spiritual heritage of peoples … to use such objects in support of the military effort [and] to make such objects the object of reprisals'). The possible extension of some of these protections, particularly under art 1(a) of the 1954 Hague Convention on Cultural Property, to 'movable property' that is of 'great importance to the cultural heritage of every people'—but is located in space or on celestial bodies—is unsettled. The ICRC takes the position that State practice establishes the following rule (among other rules protecting cultural property, broadly defined) as a norm of customary international law applicable in both international and non-international armed conflicts: 'Special care must be taken in military operations to avoid damage to buildings dedicated to religion, art, science, education or charitable purposes and historic monuments unless they are military objectives.' Rule 38, ICRC CIHL Study; see also Rules 39–41.
[30] 'NASA Recommendations to Space-Faring Entities: How to Protect and Preserve the Historic and Scientific Value of U.S. Government Lunar Artifacts' (NASA 20 July 2011) [https://perma.cc/45DS-V8LH].
[31] ibid 5.

zones', for example around the Apollo 11 and 17 landing sites, with recommended 'boundary areas into which visiting spacecraft should not enter'.[32] While such actions would not amount to a 'claim of sovereignty' on the surface of the Moon, any attempt by a State to impose such restrictions as legal obligations on other States would violate Article II of the OST as occupation of space by that State and would violate Article I of the OST by impeding the free use of space and the rights of other States under the OST. NASA notes, however, that the document 'does not represent mandatory USG or international requirements; rather, it is offered to inform lunar spacecraft mission planners interested in helping preserve and protect lunar historic artifacts and potential science opportunities for future missions'.[33]

The 'Artemis Accords' are a set of non-legally binding, multilateral political commitments to the principles of cooperation in the civil exploration and use of the Moon, Mars, comets, and asteroids for peaceful purposes.[34] Among other objectives, the Signatories to the Accords state their intention 'to preserve outer space heritage, which they consider to comprise historically significant human or robotic landing sites, artefacts, spacecraft, and other evidence of activity on celestial bodies in accordance with mutually developed standards and practices' and to use their experience 'to contribute to multilateral efforts to further develop international practices and rules applicable to preserving outer space heritage'.[35] It is important to emphasize, however, that the Artemis Accords do not purport to establish legally binding obligations that infringe on the rights of other States in space but instead state objectives and intentions related to facilitating efforts to develop future standards and practices.

16.

---

[32] ibid 9, 17.
[33] ibid 5.
[34] The Artemis Accords (n 16).
[35] ibid sec 9.

Rule 17
Due Regard

A State shall conduct all of its space activities, including military space activities, with due regard to the corresponding interests of other States.

Overview of Legal Basis of Rule

1. This Rule is derived from Article IX of the Outer Space Treaty (OST). It is designed to ensure that States exercise their freedom of exploration and use of outer space, including the Moon and other celestial bodies, in a manner that does not prejudice the interests of other States and of the international community as a whole in their exploration and peaceful uses of outer space.[36] As such, the obligation to exercise due regard is intended as a means of balancing the rights and interests of many States in the exploration and use of outer space. This Rule applies to all activities in space, including military space activities, although it does not apply between belligerents during an armed conflict (see paragraph 9).[37]

Origins of Due Regard in Space

2. The phrase 'due regard' in the context of the OST was first suggested during the 1962–1963 drafting of a proposed General Assembly resolution by the UNCOPUOS Legal Sub-Committee. The June 1962 draft put forward by the Soviet Union included a requirement that 'any measures that might in any way hinder' use of space by other States 'shall be permitted only after prior discussion of, and

---

[36] See eg United Nations Committee on the Peaceful Uses of Outer Space (UNCOPUOS) Legal Sub-Committee, 'Provisional Summary Record of the Twenty-Second Meeting' (26 April 1963) UN Doc A/AC.105/C.2/SR.22, 11 (Japan stating that '[f]reedom in the use of outer space should be recognized in so far as it did not prejudice the interests of other States in the peaceful uses of outer space'); UNCOPUOS Legal Sub-Committee, 'Provisional Summary Record of the Twenty-Fourth Meeting' (1 May 1963) UN Doc A/AC.105/C.2/SR.24, 5 (Morocco stating that 'the interests of each nation and of the international community as a whole must be protected against any abuse'); UNCOPUOS Legal Sub-Committee (2nd Session) 'Provisional Summary Record of the Twenty-Eighth Meeting' (7 May 1963) UN Doc A/AC.105/C.2/SR.28, 7 (Czechoslovakia considering that 'freedom to be limited, to the extent that the activities of one country should not endanger those of others in outer space').

[37] During State Consultations, one State recommended that this Rule should emphasize the cessation of the due regard principle between belligerents during an armed conflict, stating that 'this is critical for the planning and execution of military space activities'.

agreement upon, such measures between the countries concerned'.[38] This was interpreted by some delegations as imposing an unacceptable right of 'veto' over the space activities of other States.[39] The United Kingdom put forward its own proposed resolution in December 1962; this included a somewhat less direct obligation to consider the concerns of other States, specifying that the freedom to conduct activities in space 'shall be exercised by all States with due regard to the interests of other States in the exploration and use of outer space, and to the need for consultation and co-operation between States in relation to such exploration and use'.[40] This formulation received support from several delegations in the Legal Sub-Committee,[41] after which the United Kingdom proposed that it be incorporated into the Soviet draft to 'avoid the difficulties seen by her delegation and other in paragraph 6 of the Soviet draft, which seemed to impose a veto on activities in outer space'.[42] This suggestion and a modified form of this proposed wording then informed the agreed final draft resolution presented to the General Assembly,[43] which subsequently became the relevant part of the agreed version of Article IX of the OST and was thus substantively unchanged. Some delegations expressed the view that the obligation of giving 'due regard' to other States' space activities derived from 'the duty of States to co-operate with each other, which was laid down [in the UN Charter], and to the fundamental idea that outer space should be used and explored for the benefit of mankind'.[44] While an argument can be made that the due regard principle may be considered to be strictly linked to the other rights and obligations contained in Article IX, the principle would have less impact than

---

[38] United Soviet Socialist Republic, 'USSR Proposal' (6 June 1962) UN Doc A/AC.105/C.2/L.1.

[39] See eg UNCOPUOS, 'Verbatim record of the twenty-first meeting' (10 October 1963) UN Doc A/AC.105/PV.21, 16 (Mr Hay, Australia); UNCOPUOS Legal Sub-Committee, 'Provisional summary record of the twenty-fourth meeting' (1 May 1963) UN Doc A/AC.105/C.2/SR.24, 11 (Ms Gutteridge, United Kingdom); see also the discussion of the US delegate regarding their parallel consultation proposal and the undesirability of a 'veto' power: UNCOPUOS, 'Verbatim record of the forty-fourth meeting' (25 October 1962) UN Doc A/AC.105.PV.44, 22.

[40] United Kingdom of Great Britain and Northern Ireland, 'Draft declaration of basic principles governing the activities of States pertaining to the exploration and use of outer space' (4 December 1962) UN Doc A/C.1/879.

[41] See eg UNCOPUOS Legal Sub-Committee, 'Provisional summary record of the twenty-first meeting' (25 April 1963) 6 (Mr Tremblay, Canada); UNCOPUOS Legal Sub-Committee, 'Provisional summary record of the twenty-second meeting' (26 April 1963) UN Doc A/AC.109/C.2/SR.22, 11 (Mr Matsui, Japan); UNCOPUOS Legal Sub-Committee, 'Summary record of the seventeenth meeting' (27 June 1963) UN Doc A/AC.105/C.2/S.17, 4 and 6 (Mr Fedorenko USSR); ibid 8 (Ms Gutteridge, United Kingdom).

[42] UNCOPUOS Legal Sub-Committee, 'Provisional summary record of the twenty-fourth meeting' (1 May 1963) UN Doc A/AC.105/C.2/SR.24, 11 (Ms Gutteridge, United Kingdom).

[43] The fourth session of the Legal Sub-Committee had closed without a consensus as to the proposed resolution. The final negotiations occurred informally between September 1963 and a single meeting convened on 22 November 1963 as the fifth session of the UNCOPUOS. Ultimately, the language proposed by the United Kingdom was incorporated, as had been suggested (see UNCOPOUS 'Additional Report' (27 November 1963) UN Doc A/5549/ADD.1).

[44] UNCOPUOS Legal Sub-Committee, 'Summary Record of the Sixty-Eighth Meeting' (21 October 1966) UN Doc A/AC.105/C.2/SR.68, 10 (Mr Gotlieb, Canada); see also UNGA First Committee (3 December 1963) UN Doc A/C.1/SR.1343, 171 (Mr Golemanov, Bulgaria).

it would carry as a separate free-standing or standalone provision. This *Manual* assesses the text of Article IX and State Practice favour the broader interpretation of due regard as a standalone obligation (see discussion in paragraph 5).

Due Regard and Maritime Analogies

3. The phrase 'due regard' is used in several other treaties from the mid-twentieth century.[45] The obligation of due regard is one also owed in the maritime environment and finds expression in multiple provisions within the Law of the Sea Convention.[46] These provisions and related maritime jurisprudence may offer practical guidance in clarifying the application of due regard in outer space (see paragraph 4). The Permanent Court of Arbitration in the maritime context has determined that what is required in observing 'due regard' is dependent on the facts in each situation and must be determined by reference to 'the extent of the anticipated impairment, the nature and the importance of the activities contemplated by [the State] and the availability of alternative approaches'.[47] In essence, the case law that exists in the maritime context establishes the general proposition that due regard obligations require a State to consider seriously the lawful rights and interests of another State in areas where those States have competing rights and interests.[48]

4. In a paper submitted to the UN General Assembly in May 2022 on the topic of the 'duty of due regard' in space, the Government of the Philippines emphasized that '[i]nterpretations of the application of the duty of 'due regard' arising from law of sea jurisprudence could offer practical guidance in the context of clarifying the application of the same duty in outer space'.[49] Drawing on law of the sea jurisprudence, the Philippines notes that while the content of the obligation of due regard 'does not constitute a blanket limit on state conduct, it also does not permit states to merely note other states' rights and still do as they wish'.[50] Much like its

---

[45] Convention on International Civil Aviation (signed 7 December 1944, entered into force 7 April 1947) 15 UNTS 295, art 3; UNGA, Convention on the High Seas (adopted 29 April 1958, entered into force 30 September 1962) 450 UNTS 11, art 26(3); see also the early United States proposal for the Rescue and Return Agreement, providing that 'the action of States should be governed by humanitarian concern and with a due regard for scientific needs'—see UN Doc A/AC.105/C.2/L.3.
[46] United Nations Convention on the Law of the Sea (opened for signature 10 December 1982, entered into force 16 November 1994) 1833 UNTS 3 (UNCLOS), arts 56(2), 58(3), and 87(2).
[47] *In the Matter of the Chagos Marine Protected Area Arbitration (Mauritius v United Kingdom)* (Award) [2015] PCA 2011-03, para 519.
[48] ibid; *South China Sea Arbitration (Philippines v China) (Award)* [2016] PCA 2013-19; *In the Matter of the Arctic Sunrise Arbitration (Netherlands v Russia) (Award on the Merits)* [2015] PCA 2014-02, para 328.
[49] Republic of the Philippines, 'The Duty of "due regard" as a foundational principle of responsible behaviour in space' (Advanced Unedited working paper, 6 May 2022) UN Doc A/AC.294/2022.WP.12 [https://perma.cc/H533-QVFQ] ('Philippines Working Paper') para 11.1.
[50] ibid (also discussing the application of due regard in the maritime context and effectively supporting the extension of the Permanent Court of Arbitration's general reasoning of 'due regard' to the space context, ie that the obligations stemming from the duty of due regard would depend on 'the

application in the maritime context, the specific content of the due regard obligation in space is viewed by the Philippines as encompassing, *inter alia*, 'a conscious balancing of rights and interests', which 'should involve two dimensions: first, between and among spacefaring nations; and second between a spacefaring nation and the wider international community'.[51]

Interpreting Due Regard and Its Significance

It is not entirely clear whether the placement of 'due regard' within Article IX of the OST imposes a standalone obligation, whether the due regard provision relates to the specific requirement to avoid harmful contamination (see Rule 14: Avoidance of Harmful Contamination), or whether the provision relates to the specific requirement for consultation on potentially harmful interference (see Rule 18: Harmful Interference). However, the plain text of Article IX supports the view that the duty of due regard is a stand-alone obligation, since the first sentence of that Article contains several direct obligations: 'States Parties to the [OST] shall be guided by the principle of co-operation and mutual assistance and shall conduct all their activities in outer space, including the Moon and other celestial bodies, with due regard to the corresponding interests of all other States Parties to the Treaty.' A broad, stand-alone obligation of due regard can play a key role in advancing the peaceful exploration and use of outer space under the OST and also serve as a foundation for future cooperative activities in space (see paragraph 8). One State at State Consultations emphasized these points and noted that 'due regard is an obligation of its own', while acknowledging that 'its scope and exact meaning [may be] unclear and still await an internationally accepted interpretation'. As noted, the Philippines also takes a broad view of the scope of the due regard obligation in outer space (implicitly as an overarching, standalone rule), even stating that '[t]he duty of "due regard" imposes a "due diligence obligation" upon states over the conduct of their nationals and vessels, with the view to ensuring that their conduct do[es] not prejudice the rights and interests of other states'.[52] Another State notes that the OST 'provides the core international regulatory framework for all activities in outer space' and that its various obligations include a broad requirement '[t]hat States Parties must conduct all activities in outer space with due regard to the interests of all countries'.[53]

5.

nature of the rights and duties involved, their importance, the extent of the anticipated impairment, the nature and importance of the activities contemplated, and the availability of alternative approaches').

[51] ibid paras 9 and 11.
[52] ibid para 11.
[53] New Zealand Foreign Affairs and Trade, 'Norms, Rules and Principles of Responsible Behaviours in Space' (Submission to United Nations Office for Disarmament Affairs Open-Ended Working Group on reducing space threats through norms, rules and principles of responsible behaviours, May 2021) 3.

6. It has been suggested by some writers that due regard could contribute to, or help to determine, the level of fault of a launching State with respect to the liability of that State for damages caused by a space object.[54] While this is a reasonable interpretation of both the OST and the concept of fault in liability, no supporting State practice on this point exists.

7. Many States have stressed the importance of elaborating the content of the due regard obligation in the OST to reduce growing threats to space systems.[55] Upholding and elaborating the duty of due regard in the conduct of activities in outer space is also viewed as not only essential to reducing threats to space systems but also to promoting responsible behaviour in space generally.[56] In addition, due regard has served as a foundational principle in new international cooperative activities, such as the Artemis Project.[57]

8. During an armed conflict, the duty to exercise due regard ceases between belligerents. The obligation of due regard continues to apply as between a belligerent and third parties/neutral States, subject to the requirements of the law of armed conflict, just as the obligations with respect to the treatment of civilians and civilian property continue to apply.

Due Regard and Destructive Anti-Satellite Tests

9. As noted in other Rules in this *Manual* (see Rule 14: Avoidance of Harmful Contamination and Rule 18: Harmful Interference), destructive anti-satellite (ASAT) tests that generate long-lasting and hazardous debris have become a serious concern for the international community. Although such tests continue to be strongly criticized by many States,[58] it is difficult to find official statements by

---

[54] Irmgard Marboe (ed), *Soft Law in Outer Space: The Function of Non-binding Norms in International Space Law* (Bohlau Verlag 2012) 137 (noting that States have a duty to exercise due regard by engaging in reasonable efforts to avoid harm to other countries and their citizens and that 'a violation of that duty may give rise to a claim based on fault liability').

[55] 'Open-ended working group on reducing space threats through norms, rules and principles of responsible behaviours', Chair's Summary of discussions under agenda items 5 and 6(a)' (Advance Unedited, 20 May 2022) UN Doc A/AC.294/2022/3, para 8; ('Many delegations considered that specific requirements that follow from the principle of due regard, as contained in article IX of the Outer Space Treaty, should be elaborated in the context of reducing threats related to space systems.').

[56] Philippines Working Paper (n 49) para 11.2.

[57] The Artemis Accords (n 16). Section 11 of the legally non-binding Artemis Accords addresses the concept of 'due regard' in the context of 'deconfliction of space activities' and deals with 'due regard' in situations of actual or potential harmful interference, as addressed in art IX of the OST ('The Signatories acknowledge and reaffirm their commitment to the [OST], including those provisions relating to due regard and harmful interference' and that 'consistent with Article IX of the [OST], a Signatory authorizing an activity under these Accords commits to respect the principle of due regard'). For more information on the Artemis Project, see Rule 2: Non-Appropriation of Outer Space and Celestial Bodies, para 13.

[58] With respect to a Russian ASAT missile test on 15 November 2021, against its own Kosmos 1408 satellite that generated a sizeable cloud space debris, see Chelsea Gohd, 'Russian Anti-Satellite Missile

governments invoking a failure to show due regard under Article IX of the OST with respect to these irresponsible and dangerous tests. However, in response to such tests, and building upon the foundation of its announced 'Tenets of Responsible Behavior in Space' (in which the US Department of Defense instructed its components to, among other things, conduct space operations consistent with the tenet to 'operate in, from, to, and through space with due regard to others and in a professional manner'),[59] the United States announced on 18 April 2022 its intention 'not to conduct destructive, direct-ascent anti-satellite (ASAT) missile testing'.[60] Other States soon joined the United States by accepting its invitation to make similar commitments.[61] On 13 October 2022, the United States (on behalf of itself and ten other countries)[62] submitted a draft resolution entitled 'Destructive direct-ascent anti-satellite missile testing' to the First Committee of the UN General Assembly, which the Committee approved and sent to the General Assembly.[63] On 7 December 2022, the UN General Assembly approved the resolution by a recorded vote of 155 in favour to 9 against and 9 abstentions.[64] This Resolution explicitly recalls that 'pursuant to its article IX, States parties to the Treaty shall conduct

---

Test Draws Condemnation from Space Companies and Countries' (*Space.com*, 10 August 2022) [https://perma.cc/2HDU-RKF3]. For its part, the Russian Federation stated that the test 'was conducted in strict conformity with international law, including the 1967 Outer Space Treaty' and that 'the debris it produced did not create any threat and does not pose any obstacles or difficulties to the functioning of orbital stations and spacecraft, or to other space activities'. 'Comment by Foreign Ministry Spokeswoman Maria Zakharova on aspects of the space activities of Russia and other states' (The Ministry of Foreign Affairs of the Russian Federation, 16 November 2021) [https://perma.cc/RWN4-MCHF].

[59] US Secretary of Defense 'Tenets of Responsible Behavior in Space' (Memorandum, US DoD, 7 July 2021).

[60] 'White House Fact Sheet: Vice President Harris Advances National Security Norms in Space' (The [US] White House, 18 April 2022) [https://perma.cc/8FN9-HD4E] (noting that 'Vice President Kamala Harris announced that the United States commits not to conduct destructive, direct-ascent anti-satellite (ASAT) missile testing' and that 'this commitment addresses one of the most pressing threats to the security and sustainability of space, as demonstrated by Russia's November 2021 destructive direct-ascent ASAT missile test. The People's Republic of China conducted a similar test in 2007.').

[61] Marcia Smith, 'U.S.-Led ASAT Test Moratorium Gains Ground' (*Spacepolicyonline.com*, 3 November 2022) [https://perma.cc/7ARG-M8KB] (noting that Australia, Canada, Germany, Japan, the New Zealand, the United Kingdom, South Korea, and Switzerland had accepted the US invitation and made similar commitments to not conduct such tests).

[62] Subsequently, Albania, Australia, Belgium, Bosnia and Herzegovina, Bulgaria, Croatia, Cyprus, Czechia, Denmark, Estonia, Fiji, Finland, France, Georgia, Greece, Hungary, Iceland, Italy, Kiribati, Latvia, Lithuania, Luxembourg, the Marshall Islands, Monaco, Montenegro, the Netherlands, North Macedonia, Norway, Palau, Poland, Portugal, Romania, Singapore, Slovakia, Slovenia, Somalia, Sweden, Switzerland, Timor-Leste, Tonga, and Türkiye joined in sponsoring the draft resolution.

[63] UN General Assembly, Report of the First Committee, 'Prevention of an Arms Race in Outer Space' (14 Nov 2022) UN Doc A/77/383, 23 (draft resolution A/C.1/77/L.62, entitled 'Destructive direct-ascent anti-satellite missile testing'). The First Committee approved the draft Resolution by a recorded vote of 154 to 8, with 10 abstentions.

[64] UN Press Release, 'General Assembly Adopts over 100 Texts of First, Sixth Committees Tackling Threats from Nuclear Weapons, International Security, Global Law, Transitional Justice', 7 December 2021, GA/12478. The nine votes against the resolution against were made by Belarus, Bolivia, Central African Republic, China, Cuba, Iran, Nicaragua, Russian Federation, and Syria; the nine abstentions were India, Lao People's Democratic Republic, Madagascar, Pakistan, Serbia, Sri Lanka, Sudan, Togo, and Zimbabwe.

all their activities in outer space with due regard for the corresponding interests of all other States parties' and '[c]alls upon all States to commit not to conduct destructive direct-ascent anti-satellite missile tests'.[65] While a 'call' by the UN General Assembly does not represent a legal obligation incumbent on States, the significant number of States voting to approve this Resolution may be instructive regarding an emerging consensus on the scope of the term 'due regard' under Article IX of the OST as it might apply with respect to destructive ASAT tests.

---

[65] Destructive direct-ascent anti-satellite missile testing, UNGA Res 77/41 (7 December 2022).

Rule 18
Harmful Interference

(a) A State shall undertake appropriate international consultations before proceeding with any national activity in outer space that it has reason to believe would cause potentially harmful interference with the peaceful exploration and use of outer space by other States.

(b) A State shall request consultations, should it have reason to believe that another State's national activity in outer space would cause potentially harmful interference with its own peaceful exploration and use of outer space.

Overview of Legal Basis of Rule

1. This Rule is based on Article IX of the Outer Space Treaty (OST) and draws from the 1963 Declaration of the Legal Principles Governing the Activities of States in the Exploration and Use of Outer Space.[66] This Rule was designed to implement, at least in part, the obligation of due regard with respect to the peaceful exploration and use of outer space by other States[67] (see Rule 17: Due Regard).

Application of Rule

2. This Rule does not proscribe harmful interference with the peaceful exploration and use of outer space by other States. Rather, it creates an affirmative obligation for a State to 'undertake appropriate international consultations' when it has reason to believe that its national space activity would cause potentially harmful

---

[66] UNGA Res 1962 (XVIII) (13 December 1963) GAOR 18th Session Supp 15, para 6 ('If a State has reason to believe that an outer space activity or experiment planned by it or its nationals would cause potentially harmful interference with activities of other States in the peaceful exploration and use of outer space, it shall undertake appropriate international consultations before proceeding with any such activity or experiment.').

[67] UNCOPUOS Legal Sub-Committee Summary Record 68 (n 44), 3 (USSR), 8 (Bulgaria) (the Bulgarian representative noted that 'the Soviet draft provided for the appropriate international consultations as machinery for applying the provisions contained in Article VIII [of the Soviet draft]'); see Paul Dembling and Daniel Arons, 'The Evolution of the Outer Space Treaty' (1967) 33 The Journal of Air Law and Commerce 419, 440 ('Article IX of the OST was taken from Article VIII of the USSR draft and from Article 10 of the US draft. The Soviet version was in turn a reiteration of Paragraph 6 of the Declaration of Legal Principles. Article IX of the Treaty closely follows the text of the Soviet version.').

interference with peaceful space activities of other States. In contrast, States are prohibited from causing harmful interference to the radio services or communications of other States in certain circumstances (see Rule 19: ITU Harmful Radio Interference). This Rule is without prejudice to the duty not to interfere with satellites that are part of the 'national technical means' (NTM) of verification under bilateral arms control treaties.[68]

3. This Rule applies to activities and experiments (both military and non-military) that are planned or directly conducted by a State, and also to any activity or experiment planned or conducted by that State's nationals in outer space.[69] More broadly, a State is responsible for all of its 'national activities in outer space' (see Rule 10: Responsibility of States for National Activities in Outer Space, paragraphs 3–5) and thus a State will have obligations under this Rule with respect to potentially harmful interference caused by a satellite launched, controlled, or operated by a private company of that State, or under a licence issued by that State, or for which that State is otherwise responsible as a national activity in outer space.

4. Paragraph (b) of the Rule confirms that this obligation creates a corresponding right on the part of the potentially affected State to request consultations, which is also derived from Article IX of the OST.[70] During the negotiation of Article IX of the OST in the Legal Sub-Committee of the UN Committee on the Peaceful Uses of Outer Space, the Soviet delegate described the obligations related to harmful interference as a 'double guarantee' and noted that when the right to request consultations is invoked, it would be compulsory to comply with such an initiative in opening international consultation.[71]

Broad Meaning of the Term 'Harmful Interference'

5. For the purpose of this Rule, 'harmful interference' has a broad meaning. In other contexts, such as the ITU and domestic communications and spectrum

---

[68] See eg Treaty between the United States of America and the Russian Federation on Measures for the Future Reduction and Limitation of Strategic Offensive Arms (adopted 8 April 2010, entered into force 5 February 2011) 50 ILM 342 (New START Treaty) art X(1)(b) [https://perma.cc/J7EP-6K4X]; Treaty on Conventional Armed Forces in Europe (adopted 19 November 1990, entered into force 9 November 1992) 2441 UNTS 285, art XV(2).

[69] OST (n 3) art IX ('If a State Party to the Treaty has reason to believe that an activity or experiment planned by it *or its nationals in outer space*....') (emphasis added)).

[70] ibid art IX ('A State Party to the Treaty which has reason to believe that an activity or experiment planned by another State Party in outer space, including the Moon and other celestial bodies, would cause potentially harmful interference with activities in the peaceful exploration and use of outer space, including the Moon and other celestial bodies, may request consultation concerning the activity or experiment.').

[71] UNCOPUOS Legal Sub-Committee Summary Record 68 (n 44) 9 (USSR representative Morozov stated that 'the text being drafted was not a resolution or declaration, but a treaty having compulsory force and that it would therefore be compulsory to comply with the request for which it provided'.)

management laws or regulations, harmful interference refers to encumbrances on the use of the electromagnetic spectrum (see Rule 19: ITU Harmful Radio Interference).[72] However, the same term used in Article IX of the OST suggests a broader meaning in light of the object and purpose of that treaty, which relates to the peaceful exploration and use of outer space. No State policy statements appear to support a reading of Article IX confining it exclusively to radio frequency interference as outlined in the ITU.[73] Rather, given history of this provision in the OST and the OST's broader purpose, the OST definition appears to include the ITU definition as well as other types of interference. This includes interference through physical means, such as risking collision with other space objects, as well as non-physical measures that impede or preclude other States' peaceful use and exploration of outer space. Furthermore, this broader interpretation is consistent with the travaux préparatoires related to Article IX of the OST.[74]

Appropriate Consultations and State Practice

6. This Rule requires 'appropriate consultations' in the event of potentially harmful interference. Neither the text of the OST nor State practice specify the circumstances or the manner in which such consultations are to be conducted, leaving the particulars to the States' discretion. However, the travaux préparatoires relating to Article IX suggest that at the very least, the provision of information is required regarding activities or experiments which might interfere with other States' space activities.[75] It would be reasonable also to assume that the provision of this information has to be timely and sufficient so as to enable other States to respond in an appropriate way to protect their own space activities. The duty to undertake

---

[72] See Constitution and Convention of the International Telecommunication Union (adopted 22 December 1992, entered into force 1 July 1994) 1825-26 UNTS 3 (ITU Constitution) (n 90) 1003 (defining harmful interference as '[i]nterference which endangers the functioning of a radionavigation service or of other safety services or seriously degrades, obstructs or repeatedly interrupts a radiocommunication service operating in accordance with the Radio Regulations').

[73] See eg UNCOPUOS, 'Survey of the Problem of Discretion Exercised by States in Interpreting Basic Legal Principles and Norms related to Safety and Security in Outer Space – Working paper submitted by the Russian Federation' (21 June 2018) UN Doc A/AC.105/2018/CRP.17, para 11 ('This term covers all situations'); US DoD Law of War Manual (n 11) para 14.10.5; US DoD Space Policy 2016 (n 14) para 4(b) ('Purposeful interference with U.S. space systems, including their supporting infrastructure, will be considered an infringement of U.S. rights.').

[74] UNCOPUOS Legal Sub-Committee Summary Record 68 (n 44) 5 (USSR clarifying that 'the provision of information concerning the *potentially harmful effects* of an activity or experiment must certainly be compulsory' (emphasis added)). USSR Proposal 1962 (n 38) para 6 (proposing the requirement of prior discussion and agreement for 'the implementation of any measures that might *in any way hinder* the exploration or use of outer space for peaceful purposes by other countries' (emphasis added)).

[75] UNCOPUOS Legal Sub-Committee Summary Record 68 (n 44) 7 (the USSR representative observing that this rule is intended to obligate every State Party to 'to transmit to other parties information on activities or experiments which might interfere with their own activities').

consultations does not carry with it any requirement or mandate for a particular outcome. Despite this, it is likely that questions of any alleged fault causing damage in space may have regard to the positions adopted by relevant parties in the course of such a consultation under Article IX.

7. It is unclear what constitutes 'harmful' with respect to the nature of interference triggering consultations, given the absence of any openly available State practice of initiating or requesting consultations. Several incidents involving possible claims of harmful interference have occurred, but they have not triggered requests for consultations under Article IX. For example, to date no State has publicly requested consultations regarding potentially harmful interference involving unwanted rendezvous and proximity operations (RPOs) that may present a risk of collision, nor has any State informed other States of an RPO that it had reason to believe would cause potentially harmful interference. Instead, unwanted and provocatively close RPOs have prompted strong protests by States, but not yet on grounds involving violation of any international legal obligations.[76]

8. Similarly, even when States have engaged in activities that created large amounts of space debris which might have given reason to believe would cause potentially harmful interference with other States' space activities, no consultations have been held or requested under Article IX of the OST.[77] In 2007, China destroyed its own weather satellite with a ground-based ASAT kinetic kill vehicle at an altitude of approximately 863 km, creating several thousand pieces of debris that could potentially interfere with other States' use of low Earth orbit for many years.[78] No consultation took place, although some States criticized China on various grounds for this operation.[79] In 2008, the United States destroyed one of its satellites at

---

[76] For example, after a Russian Luch-Olymp satellite made a close approach to a French-Italian satellite in 2017 in an apparent attempt to intercept communications or for other unknown purposes, French Minister of the Armed Forces Florence Parly did not claim that the Russian satellite had engaged in potentially harmful interference but instead stated that '[a]ttempting to listen to your neighbors is not only unfriendly, it's an act of espionage': *Reuters* 7 September 2018 (n 6).

[77] One State during State Consultations stated the following: 'Destructive testing of anti-satellite missiles (that is testing which creates space debris) could cause irreversible, permanent interferences for a wide variety of space systems and applications. Due to the inherent risk and unpredictability of collision and permanent damage to the space environment, it can be argued that destructive anti-satellite testing, may—depending on the specific effects—constitute harmful interference.'

[78] See Brian Weeden, '2007 Chinese Anti-Satellite Test Fact Sheet' (Secure World Foundation, 23 November 2010) [https://perma.cc/KN64-L9T9].

[79] See UNCOPUOS, 'Unedited Transcript of the 569th Meeting' (7 June 2007) UN Doc COPUOS/T.569, 13–14 (UK expressing concerns about the 'lack of international consultation before the test was carried out.'); 'Japan's Abe Charges China Satellite Test Illegal' (*Space Daily*, 31 January 2007) [https://perma.cc/QRS7-G5FL] (Japan's Prime Minister said of the operation: 'I believe it would not be in compliance with basic international rules such as the Outer Space Treaty.' It should be noted, however, that Japan did not officially identify any specific articles in the OST that were allegedly violated by China in its 2007 ASAT test; Ambassador Donald A Mahley (US Acting Deputy Assistant Secretary for Threat Reduction, Export Controls), 'The State of Space Security' (Remarks delivered at the Space Policy Institute, The George Washington University, Washington DC, 24 January 2008) [https://perma.cc/5RH8-4PPK] ('To date, we have not received satisfactory answers to our questions concerning China's motivations for the test, the nature of their pre-test analysis on the risk of debris endangering spacecraft,

approximately 247 km altitude with an ASAT, although each piece of the debris created as a result is assessed to have re-entered the atmosphere within the following 18 months, thus no longer posing a threat to future space activities.[80] Six days before the mission, the United States notified the international community of its plan to destroy the satellite, but the United States explicitly stated that the strike did not 'meet the standard' to trigger any consultation under Article IX of the OST.[81] No assertions by any State to contradict this statement are known. In 2019, India launched a PDV-Mk II missile to strike a satellite in orbit at approximately 280 km, creating approximately 250 pieces of debris at various altitudes—with some ascending to 2,200 km and posing a risk to numerous space activities.[82] Asserting that it did not anticipate lasting debris (and, arguably, harmful interference), India explicitly denied any violation of international law.[83] No international consultations appear to have occurred before the mission, nor did any State request appropriate consultations or complain afterwards about their absence. This was also the case with respect to a destructive ASAT test by the Russian Federation in

---

and China's plans for future anti-satellite testing.'); see also UNCOPUOS, 'Information furnished in conformity with the Treaty on Principles Governing the Activities of States in the Exploration and Use of Outer Space, including the Moon and Other Celestial Bodies—Note verbale dated 3 December 2021 from the Permanent Mission of China to the United Nations (Vienna) addressed to the Secretary-General' (6 December 2021) UN Doc A/AC.105/1262, in which China claimed that Starlink satellites launched by SpaceX of the United States had two close encounters with the China Space Station in 2021 and China invoked art V (the duty to inform UN Secretary-General of any phenomena in space which could constitute a danger to the life or health of astronauts) and art VI (that States Parties shall bear international responsibility for national activities in outer space, even when carried on by non-governmental entities and are responsibility for ensuring conformity with the OST)—but China did not invoke art IX of the OST or suggest that any harmful interference requiring consultations had occurred. For the US response, see John Feng, 'China Says U.S. Ignored Complaints After Space Station Near Misses In Orbit' *Newsweek* (New York, 10 February 2022) at https://www.newsweek.com/china-says-us-ignored-e-mail-complaints-space-station-starlink-near-misses-orbit-1677993 ('a State Department spokesperson said the U.S. Space Force "did not estimate a significant probability of collision" between the space station and any Starlink spacecraft—or it would've sent a "close approach notification" to a Chinese point of contact').

[80] See Brian Weeden, 'Through a Glass, Darkly: Chinese, American, and Russian Anti-satellite Testing in Space' (Secure World Foundation, 17 March 2014) 26 [https://perma.cc/XSC2-X9C8]. Several factors could indicate that the action taken by the United States in 2008 was different from the Russian, Chinese, and Indian ASAT operations, including that the stated intention of the United States was not to conduct an ASAT weapons test, but rather to take the action as a means to address a safety concern presented by the possibility that the satellite in question might crash to the ground with its toxic hydrazine propellant tank intact. Further to that point, the United States noted that the missile in question had not been developed as an ASAT weapon but had been repurposed for this effort.

[81] NASA Office of Public Affairs, 'Reentry of U.S. Satellite' (Remarks by US Deputy National Security Advisor James Jeffrey, Transcript, 14 February 2008) [https://perma.cc/5UC2-56RZ] ('While we do not believe that we meet the standard of Article IX of that treaty that says we would have to consult in the case of generating potentially harmful interference with other activities in space, we do believe that it is important to keep other countries informed of what is happening.').

[82] See Caleb Henry, 'India ASAT Debris Spotted above 2,200 Kilometers, Will Remain a Year or More in Orbit' *Space News* (Colorado Springs, 9 April 2019) [https://perma.cc/B9ZJ-XFV8].

[83] Government of India, Ministry of External Affairs, 'Frequently Asked Questions on Mission Shakti, India's Anti-Satellite Missile Test Conducted on 27 March 2019' (27 March 2019) [https://perma.cc/JCF9-B6LX].

2021, which generated a large and long-lasting debris field.[84] In addition, prior to these recent incidents, both the Soviet Union and the United States conducted destructive ASAT tests during the Cold War without any State making an allegation of harmful interference or requesting consultations and without either the United States or the Soviet Union notifying other States of potentially harmful interference.[85] This State practice demonstrates, at least to this point, that States do not consult prior to engaging in specific debris-causing events, leaving uncertain the standard as to when States must engage in consultations for purposes of Article IX of the OST.[86]

---

[84] On 15 November 2021, the Russian Federation conducted a destructive test of a direct-ascent anti-satellite missile against one of its own satellites, generating sharp criticism from other States but no invocation of art IX or other provisions of the OST. See eg Antony J Blinken, US Secretary of State, 'Russia Conducts Destructive Anti-Satellite Missile Test' (Press Statement, 15 November 2021) [https://perma.cc/SNM2-8LNH] ('The long-lived debris created by this dangerous and irresponsible test will now threaten satellites and other space objects that are vital to all nations' security, economic, and scientific interests for decades to come.'); 'Russian Anti-Satellite Missile Test Draws Condemnation' *BBC News* (London, 16 November 2021) [https://perma.cc/NK7G-5LYE] (quoting UK Defence Secretary Ben Wallace as saying that the test 'shows a complete disregard for the security, safety and sustainability of space' and that 'the debris resulting from this test will remain in orbit putting satellites and human spaceflight at risk for years to come'). The German Government stated that '[t]he Federal Government is deeply concerned by Russia's test of a ground-based anti-satellite missile on 15 November 2021, which destroyed one of Russia's own satellites. The destruction of the satellite in low Earth orbit created a large amount of debris which will be detrimental to the free and unimpeded use of outer space for all countries for years to come. The test and the resulting debris will also expose the astronauts on board the International Space Station to additional risks. This irresponsible behaviour entails a high risk of miscalculations and escalation.' 'The Federal Foreign Office on the destructive test of a ground-based anti-satellite missile by Russia' (German Federal Foreign Office, 16 November 2021) [https://perma.cc/ZM3E-MWPU]. However, rather than invoking art IX of the OST, the German Federal Foreign Affairs Office noted that '[t]he test highlights ... the urgent need for the international community to agree on rules for the peaceful and sustainable use of space and measures to build confidence and security'. ibid.

[85] In an event possibly foreshadowing the demand for an art IX consultation provision, the United States conducted an experiment from 1961–1963 called 'Project Westford' which involved launching millions of copper wires or needles into orbit to facilitate global radio communications. In response to protests from the Soviet Union and other States, as well as various groups of scientists regarding the potential hazards of this project and its contamination of space, the US Ambassador to the United Nations, Adlai E Stevenson, ultimately stated that 'the United States intends to continue to consult on experiments of this type and to avoid any harmful side effects in carrying out all space activities': 'Statement on Project West Ford' (1963) 49 US State Department Bulletin 1252, 107. With respect to the conduct of debris-generating ASAT tests, it should be noted that on 18 April 2022 the United States announced its intention not to conduct further destructive, direct-ascent ASAT missile testing; other States have since joined the United States in making similar commitments, and on 13 October 2022, the United States (on behalf of itself and 10 other countries) submitted a draft resolution to the First Committee of the UN General Assembly entitled 'Destructive direct-ascent anti-satellite missile testing', which was approved by the General Assembly on 7 December 2022, by a recorded vote of 155 in favour to 9 against and 9 abstentions. See Rule 17: Due Regard, para 9.

[86] One State at State Consultations suggested that missing public State practice is not necessarily an indicator that States think a certain behaviour or activity is lawful or unlawful, arguing that for policy reasons States might choose to articulate their opinions in private or, especially with regards to art IX OST, choose not to set precedents or blame another State publicly for an illegal action when there is no set interpretation. The representative of this State further suggested that a State may remain silent because of security reasons related to a particular incident. Pointing to the Vienna Convention on the Law of Treaties, another State cautioned against relying on any conclusion based on the instances of State inaction (related to the highlighted instances above) to draw conclusions as to whether the legal standard in art IX of the OST was engaged or is uncertain. Yet such silence by States (or criticism that does not invoke legal terms or provisions of the OST) may nonetheless have legal significance (see Methodology

9. Although there have been ambiguous or unconfirmed reports of various types of limited actions involving electronic, cyber, and high energy laser capabilities against satellites, to date there is no publicly available evidence that such incidents have resulted in any State undertaking international consultations before proceeding with these actions under Article IX of the OST, nor that any State has requested consultations based on its belief that these actions would cause potentially harmful interference. Similarly, although there is considerable evidence that States have engaged in jamming electronic communications to and from satellites (see Rule 19: ITU Harmful Radio Interference and Rule 21: Use of Force), to date there is no publicly available evidence that these actions have resulted in any State invoking its rights under Article IX of the OST with respect to harmful interference.

10. Cumulatively, State practice to date indicates that no State has ever invoked Article IX and engaged in any relevant consultations. A State that has found itself in a situation that potentially implicated Article IX of the OST may have chosen to not invoke that article and engage in related consultations for many reasons, including: (i) it did not believe that any of its potentially harmful actions in space would cause harmful interference under Article IX of the OST;[87] (ii) it disregarded Article IX; or (iii) it chose not to invoke Article IX for political, policy, security, or other reasons not publicly revealed.[88] It thus remains an open question whether the continuing failure by States to invoke Article IX is due to diverse internal decisions by States that have no legal significance or whether this inaction by States reflects a common understanding that there is an increasingly high threshold for what constitutes harmful interference under Article IX.[89]

---

of *Manual*). In this regard, art 31(3) of the Vienna Convention on the Law of Treaties provides that in interpreting a treaty, 'there shall be taken into account, together with the context: ... (b) any subsequent practice in the application of the treaty which establishes the agreement of the parties regarding its interpretation'. The International Law Commission has noted that such an agreement under art 31 'need not be legally binding' and that '[s]ilence on the part of one or more parties can constitute acceptance of the subsequent practice when the circumstances call for some reaction'. UN General Assembly, International Law Commission Report, para 9, UN Doc A/CN.4/L.833 (3 June 2014).

[87] Similarly, in the case of a victim State, that State may have considered that the actions of another State, including actions involving debris-causing damage to its own satellites, did not rise to the level of harmful interference under art IX.

[88] One State at State Consultations suggested rephrasing the paragraph as follows:

Cumulatively, State practice to date appears to indicate that States have not yet conducted consultations under Article IX of the OST. However, this does not imply that: (1) States do not believe that any the potentially harmful actions in space would cause harmful interference under Article IX of the OST; (2) States disregarded Article IX; or (3) States considered that actions in space, including actions involving debris-causing damage to their own satellites, have not risen to the level of harmful interference under Article IX. States have, however, stated concerns that certain activities, namely destructive anti-satellite missile testing, is detrimental to the free and unimpeded use of outer space for all states.

[89] Some States suggest, as one did during State Consultations, that they may have chosen to not invoke art IX of the OST because they 'did not want to set a precedent'. Yet a State that chooses silence in order to 'not set a precedent' may be foregoing an opportunity to help set a legal threshold for harmful interference. In fact, not acting actually *is* setting a precedent.

Application During an Armed Conflict

11. During an armed conflict in which a State's military space activities are likely to cause harmful interference with other States' space activities, the obligation to consult set forth in this Rule will not apply between belligerent States. While the obligation to undertake such consultations with neutral or other States continues to apply, the specifics of such consultations are likely to differ depending on the circumstances prevailing at the time, including humanitarian and military considerations such as operational security, risk to forces, and mission accomplishment. For example, a State may consider consultations inappropriate when such consultations could reveal sensitive military plans, capabilities, or activities.

Rule 19
ITU Harmful Radio Interference

(a) Under the Constitution and Regulations of the International Telegraphic Union (ITU) and subject to paragraph (b), a State shall not cause, and must ensure that its operating agencies do not cause, harmful interference to ITU-compliant radio services or communications, including communications from, to, or within outer space, of any State.

(b) A State retains its entire freedom under the ITU Constitution and Regulations to utilize its military radio installations, but must, so far as possible, comply with ITU obligations relative to giving assistance in case of distress and to preventing any of its installations used for military communications, including communications to, from, or within outer space, from causing harmful interference.

(c) This ITU-based rule does not preclude the application of other international legal obligations relative to the use by a State of any part of the electromagnetic spectrum in military space operations.

Overview of Legal Basis of Rule

1. This Rule is based on Article 45 of the ITU Constitution,[90] as well as relevant sections of the ITU Radio Regulations.[91] Among the variety of telecommunication stations covered by the ITU Instruments is a 'space station', which is defined as a 'station located on an object which is beyond, is intended to go beyond, or has been beyond, the major portion of the Earth's atmosphere'.[92] Thus, ITU

---

[90] ITU Constitution (n 72). As of January 2021, 193 States are party to the ITU Constitution: see International Telecommunication Union, 'List of Member States' <http://www.itu.int/online/mm/scripts/gensel8> accessed 26 March 2023.

[91] For example, the ITU Radio Regulations essentially restate the harmful radio interference rule in its preamble:

> All stations, whatever their purpose, must be established and operated in such a manner as not to cause harmful interference to the radio services or communications of other Members or of recognized operating agencies, or of other duly authorized operating agencies which carry on a radio service, and which operate in accordance with the provisions of these Regulations.

International Telecommunication Union, 'Radio Regulations' (adopted as amended 15 September 2020, entered into force 1 January 2021) (ITU Radio Regulations) preamble, para 0.4. Moreover, art 15 of the Radio Regulations states that '[i]t is essential that Member States exercise the utmost goodwill and mutual assistance in the application of the provisions of Article 45 of the Constitution and of this Section to the settlement of problems of harmful interference'. ITU Radio Regulations, art 15.22.

[92] ibid art 1.64.

regulations apply to communications to, in, and from outer space. These include radiocommunications between ground stations and space objects, and among space objects, which can be used for a variety of military purposes such as telemetry, command and control, satellite-based Internet services, and global navigation satellite systems.

Application of Rule

2. This Rule is limited to interference with the use of a certain portion of the electromagnetic spectrum, and therefore does not extend to other types of space-based interference, such as interference using other parts of the electromagnetic spectrum, undertaking unsafe, intrusive rendezvous and proximity operations, or engaging in activities that block or otherwise interfere with optical sensors in satellites.[93] This Rule applies regardless of whether the harmful radio interference is intentional, accidental, or incidental. Although some States have specifically objected to 'purposeful' interference with space objects as an infringement of their rights,[94] the intent of the interfering State is not relevant to this Rule.

3. The obligation not to cause harmful interference requires that '[t]ransmitting stations shall radiate only as much power as is necessary to ensure a satisfactory service'.[95] If there are numerous satellites in close proximity, the radiocommunications of each one should only be as strong as to ensure a satisfactory service; higher power levels beyond assigned parameters, although possibly advantageous to the operation of the satellite, may be a violation of this obligation if they harmfully interfere with the transmission of other satellites that are operating in compliance with the ITU Radio Regulations.

4. States Parties must also ensure that their operating agencies, which are recognized or duly authorized by the State, do not cause harmful interference.[96] This positive obligation requires States to take all necessary and practicable steps to ensure that harmful interference is not caused by their operating agencies.[97] For example, if a private space company is recognized or duly authorized by the State to operate a large constellation of communications satellites, that State would have

---

[93] The ITU regulates only a specific portion of the electromagnetic spectrum, which currently includes all radio waves and microwaves but does not extend to infrared waves, ultraviolet radiation, or other higher frequencies. ibid art 1.169 (focusing on 'radionavigation service' or 'radiocommunication service'). As stated in para 9, the harmful use by a State of any part of the electromagnetic spectrum, including radio waves and microwaves, may also violate or implicate other international legal obligations, including the duty to avoid harmful interference under art IX of the OST (n 3).
[94] See eg US DoD Space Policy 2016 (n 14) para 4b.
[95] ITU Radio Regulations (n 91) arts 15.1, 15.2.
[96] ITU Constitution (n 72) art 45(2).
[97] ibid arts 6(2), 45(3).

the obligation to adequately regulate all aspects of its use of radio frequencies—including the power, timing, and directionality of the frequencies—so that it would not cause harmful interference to the radio services of other States. In addition, if a non-governmental entity (including a private space company) is part of a particular State's 'national activities in outer space', that State bears international legal responsibility under Article VI of the OST for the conduct of the non-governmental entity and for assuring that the entity's actions are carried out in conformity with the OST and any other applicable international legal obligations.[98] ITU obligations generally, not only in the context of space communications but also with respect to international non-satellite communications, are part of these international legal obligations for which a State may be held responsible.[99]

ITU defines harmful interference as '[i]nterference which endangers the functioning of a radionavigation service or of other safety services or seriously degrades, obstructs or repeatedly interrupts a radiocommunication service operating in accordance with the Radio Regulations'.[100] This is differentiated from other types of radio frequency interference, which do not qualify as harmful and are, therefore, not prohibited under this Rule.[101] The Radio Regulations specifically prohibit '[a]ny emission capable of causing harmful interference to distress, alarm, urgency or safety communications on the international distress and emergency frequencies established for these purposes by these Regulations'.[102] Interference must rise to the level of endangering the function of a service, or must seriously degrade or obstruct or repeatedly interrupt a service in order to trigger this Rule. Consider, for example, the French protest in 2009 (and subsequently) of satellite jamming by Iran against BBC Persia, Voice of America, and other Western media broadcasts from a French EUTELSAT satellite—protests which were squarely based upon

5.

---

[98] See Rule 10: Responsibility of States for National Activities in Outer Space, and OST (n 3) art VI. Pursuant to art III of the OST, international law is made applicable to all activities in space.

[99] After the conduct of a non-governmental entity is attributed to a State under art VI of the OST (n 3), the State in question is subject to the general rules of international law governing State responsibility for violations of international legal obligations and accompanying determinations of fault and appropriate reparations or other means of satisfaction for these violations. See Rule 10: Responsibility of States for National Activities in Outer Space; ILC, 'Responsibility of States for internationally wrongful acts' UNGA Res A/Res/56/83 (adopted 28 January 2002) (ILC Articles on State Responsibility).

[100] ITU Constitution (n 72) Annex para 1003. See also ITU Radio Regulations (n 91) art 1.169.

[101] The ITU Radio Regulations distinguish the following types of interference:
   Interference—The effect of unwanted energy due to one or a combination of emissions, radiations, or inductions upon reception in a radiocommunication system, manifested by any performance degradation, misinterpretation, or loss of information which could be extracted in the absence of such unwanted energy (art 1.166);
   Permissible Interference—Observed or predicted interference which complies with quantitative interference and sharing criteria contained in these Regulations or in ITU-R Recommendations or in special agreements as provided for in these Regulations (art 1.167);
   Accepted Interference—Interference at a higher level than that defined as permissible interference and which has been agreed upon between two or more administrations without prejudice to other administrations (art 1.168).

[102] ibid art 4.18. See also ITU Constitution (n 72) art 48(2) ('military installations must, so far as possible, observe statutory provisions relative to giving assistance in case of distress').

the requisite interference prohibited by the ITU.[103] Similarly, in 2014, EUTELSAT and ARABSAT operators protested against jamming originating from Ethiopia, providing relevant data to the ITU.[104] Such jamming could fall foul of the obligation not to cause harmful radio interference due to persistent interruption of the signal.[105] On the other hand, if the interference merely weakened the television signal or caused some minor degradation or loss of information for brief periods, it would not constitute 'harmful' interference contemplated under this Rule.

Exemption for Military Radio Installations

6. Paragraph (b) of the Rule recognizes the entire freedom that ITU Member States retain under ITU regulations with regard to military radio installations, which are exempted from various obligations within the ITU framework.[106] While the ITU Constitution does not define 'military radio installations', it is the nature of the installation itself that determines the scope of exemption, not the content or purpose of the radio communication that is transmitted via the installation.[107] Hence military ground stations that transmit signals to military satellites would clearly constitute a 'military radio installation'. Alternatively, the exemption may not apply if a military communication transmitted via a satellite transponder leased from a commercial company caused harmful interference with the radio services of other States. This reading is consistent with the purpose of the ITU Constitution to promote the use of telecommunication services with a view to facilitating peaceful relations and to coordinate efforts to eliminate harmful interference between radio stations of different countries.[108] It is also noted that the reference to 'military

---

[103] See Cesar Jaramilo (ed), *Space Security Index 2013* (Spacesecurity.org 2013) 86; ibid 156; Peter B de Selding, 'France Seeks ITU Help To Halt Satellite Signal Jamming by Iran' *Space News* (Paris, 8 January 2010)[perma.cc/PH88-RFQQ].

[104] Peter B de Selding, 'Eutelsat Blames Ethiopia as Jamming Incidents Triple' *Space News* (Paris, 6 June 2014) [perma.cc/SW3Z-43P2].

[105] See UN Office for Outer Space Affairs, *Highlights in Space 2010* (United Nations 2011) 100 ('Iran's jamming of signals led the French regulators (ANF) to ask the International Telecommunication Union (ITU) to intervene with the Iranian government, to persuade Tehran to stop jamming satellite signals from the BBC World Service's Persian-language broadcasts into Iran.').

[106] ITU Constitution (n 72) arts 6(1), 48(1). It is not within the mandate of the Radio Regulations Board to make decisions with reference to art 48 of the ITU Constitution. 'Report on the Implementation of the Strategic Plan and the Activities of the Union for 2018–2019 (ITU Annual Progress Report)' (International Telecommunications Union, 18 April 2019) ITU Doc C19/35-E, 15.

[107] At the 2015 World Radiocommunication Conference (WRC-15), it was reported that 15 States requested application of art 48 on the grounds that the satellite networks were used for the purpose of national defence, military, or governmental use. 'Report of the Director on the Activities of the Radiocommunication Sector—Part 2: Experience in the Application of Radio Regulatory Procedures and Other Related Matters' (WRC-15, ITU 2015) ITU Doc CMR15/4(Add.2)(Rev.1)-E, para 3.2.4.3. However, it has been decided that art 48 does not encompass stations used for governmental purposes in general. Lilian Jeanty, 'The Radio Regulations Board and WRC-19' (*ITU News*, 24 October 2019) [perma.cc/GW6Y-D5AY].

[108] ITU Constitution (n 72) arts 1(1)(e), 1(2)(b).

radio installations of their army, navy and air forces' was replaced when the ITU Constitution superseded the International Telecommunication Convention in 1992.[109] This means that the exemption applies to any radio installations of military nature, regardless of the organizational designation of the governmental agency in command.

7. However, even in such cases, States must, so far as possible, follow ITU obligations relative to 'giving assistance in case of distress and to the measures to be taken to prevent harmful interference'.[110] Such other obligations include ITU Regulations which state that '[a]ll stations are forbidden to carry out unnecessary transmissions, or the transmission of superfluous signals, or the transmission of false or misleading signals, or the transmission of signals without identification' (with certain exceptions).[111] Paragraph (b) of the Rule exempts States from abiding by this prohibition to the extent that it is not practically possible to prevent the unnecessary transmissions, or the superfluous, false, misleading, or unidentified signals being emitted via a military radio installation due to the nature of the military operation, such as jamming and spoofing. The assessment of what is practically possible under the attendant circumstances may take account of the sovereign right to stop or cut off any private communications which may appear dangerous to the security of the State or contrary to its laws, to public order, or to decency.[112]

8. This exemption applies reciprocally, which means that military installations operating outside ITU Radio Regulations are not entitled to invoke ITU protections, such as protection against harmful interference.

Application of Other International Legal Obligations

9. This Rule does not preclude the application of other international legal obligations relative to the use by a State of any part of the electromagnetic spectrum in military space operations. For example, these obligations may relate to harmful interference under the OST or radio communications inciting genocide contrary to the Genocide Convention and the International Criminal Court Statute.[113]

---

[109] Compare, for example, International Telecommunication Convention (as amended 6 November 1982, entered into force 1 January 1984) 1531 UNTS 2, art 38(1).
[110] ITU Constitution (n 72) art 48(2).
[111] ITU Radio Regulations (n 91) arts 15.1 and 15.2.
[112] ITU Constitution (n 72) art 34.
[113] OST (n 3) art IX; Convention on the Prevention and Punishment of the Crime of Genocide (adopted 9 December 1948, entered into force 12 January 1951) 78 UNTS 276, art 3(c); Rome Statute of the International Criminal Court (adopted 17 July 1998, entered into force 1 July 2002) 2187 UNTS 90, art 25(3)(e).

Application of Rule During Armed Conflict

10. During an armed conflict, this Rule does not apply between belligerents. The rule continues to apply and prohibit radio harmful interference by the belligerents with ITU-compliant radio services or communications of other countries, except to the extent that it is incompatible with military space operations conducted in accordance with the law of armed conflict.

Rule 20
Non-Intervention Principle

A State shall not engage in any activity, including a military space activity, directed against another State that constitutes a violation of the non-intervention principle.

Overview of Legal Basis of Rule

1. The non-intervention principle, which is set forth in many international instruments,[114] is a rule of customary international law and a corollary to the principle of the sovereign equality of States.[115] As such, this principle extends to activities in outer space, including military space activities, pursuant to Article III of the OST.[116] For purposes of this Rule, prohibited intervention may include the use of space assets by a State against another State in space or on Earth, as well as the use by a State of assets in any other domain against another State in space.

2. The International Court of Justice (the ICJ) has broadly stated this Rule in the following terms: 'The principle of non-intervention involves the right of every

---

[114] See eg Declaration on Principles of International Law concerning Friendly Relations and Co-operation among States in accordance with the Charter of the United Nations, UNGA Res 2625 (XXV) (24 October 1970) (Friendly Relations Declaration) principle 3, para 1; Helsinki Final Act of the Conference on Security and Co-operation in Europe (adopted 1 August 1975) 14 ILM 1292 (Helsinki Final Act) principle VI; Declaration on the Inadmissibility of Intervention in the Domestic Affairs of States and the Protection of Their Independence and Sovereignty, UNGA Res 2131 (XX) (21 December 1965) (Declaration on the Inadmissibility of Intervention) para 1; Convention on Rights and Duties of States (adopted 26 December 1933, entered into force 26 December 1934) 165 LNTS 19, art 8.

[115] *Case Concerning Armed Activities on the Territory of the Congo (Democratic Republic of the Congo v Uganda)* (Judgment) [2005] ICJ Rep 168 (*Armed Activities in the Congo* Judgment) para 162; *Case Concerning Military and Paramilitary Activities in and against Nicaragua (Nicaragua v United States of America)* (Merits) [1986] ICJ Rep 14 (*Nicaragua* Judgment) para 202. One State has observed in the cyber context that '[t]he general concept of sovereignty by itself does not provide a sufficient or clear basis for extrapolating a specific rule of sovereignty or additional prohibition for cyber conduct going beyond that of non-intervention'. Attorney-General of the United Kingdom, the Rt Hon Suella Braverman, 'International Law in Future Frontiers' (Speech, Chatham House, 19 May 2022) [https://perma.cc/E2CZ-BFN4].

[116] The principle of non-intervention has also been directly applied to space by the UN General Assembly. See eg Principles Governing the Use by States of Artificial Earth Satellites for International Direct Television Broadcasting, UNGA Res 37/92 (10 December 1982) principle A1 ('Activities in the field of international direct television broadcasting by satellite should be carried out in a manner compatible with the sovereign rights of States, including the principle of non-intervention.'). To date, no State practice could be identified regarding the explicit application by a State of the principle of non-intervention to space activities consistent with this UN General Assembly resolution.

sovereign State to conduct its affairs without outside interference; though examples of trespass against this principle are not infrequent, the Court considers that it is part and parcel of customary international law.'[117] However, there is less precision regarding precisely what constitutes the affairs of every sovereign State that it has a right to conduct 'without outside interference'. In addition, unless the use of force is involved, the precise definition of the required key element of prohibited intervention—coercion—is unsettled (as discussed in paragraph 4). Notwithstanding the multiplicity of declarations by States accepting the principle of non-intervention, concrete examples of State practice in this area that do not involve the use of armed force are difficult to find, for several reasons. One is that the rhetoric of States and others is often used inconsistently and imprecisely in international political disputes, mixing the language of 'intervention' with different forms of 'interference', improper derogation of sovereignty, or other unwelcome conduct, making it difficult to determine whether a specific legal complaint about 'intervention' is really being asserted. Second, States very rarely make an official, unambiguous assertion about illegal intervention (sometimes, perhaps because States want to preserve the legal right to undertake a similar type of action themselves), so there are very few concrete examples of adjudication and resolution of this legal standard that do not involve the use of armed force. It is thus not surprising that several States have concluded that there is a lack of consensus about the scope, reach, or boundaries the principle of non-intervention,[118] as well as discord about the possible application of the principle in any particular situation.

Matters Which Each State Is Permitted, by the Principle of State Sovereignty, to Decide Freely

3. The ICJ elaborated on the affairs that every sovereign State has a right to conduct without outside interference by stating that an intervention is prohibited if it is 'bearing on matters in which each State is permitted, by the principle of State sovereignty, to decide freely. One of these is the choice of a political, economic, social and cultural system, and the formulation of foreign policy.'[119] However, there are many interrelated conceptual approaches that States and international organizations have taken to describe those matters that States are permitted to decide freely

---

[117] *Nicaragua* Judgment (n 115) para 202.

[118] The Rt Hon Jeremy Wright QC MP (UK Attorney-General), 'Cyber and International Law in the 21st Century' (Speech, 23 May 2018) [https://perma.cc/Y9K2-22VN] (Speech by UK Attorney-General); Hon. Paul C Ney, Jr, 'DOD General Counsel Remarks at U.S. Cyber Command Legal Conference' (Speech, 2 March 2020) [https://perma.cc/55P5-CF3Z] (Speech by US DoD General Counsel) ('There is no international consensus among States on the precise scope or reach of the nonintervention principle....').

[119] *Nicaragua* Judgment (n 115) para 205.

and thus constitute the target of prohibited intervention.[120] The result has been considerable ambiguity and uncertainty about the precise operational parameters of the principle. For example, the Friendly Relations Declaration refers to those things involving 'the exercise of a State's sovereign rights'[121] and some States similarly refer to 'matters of an inherently sovereign nature'[122] or 'matters of government which are at the heart of a state's sovereignty, such as the freedom to choose its own political, social, economic and cultural system'.[123] Another approach refers to matters that are within the 'exclusive competence' of a State.[124] A related term is the 'reserved domain' (domaine réservé)[125] which some States also use in defining the target of prohibited intervention.[126] Other international instruments, including the UN Charter, refer to matters that are 'within the domestic jurisdiction of a State',[127] while one State simply refers to a State's 'core functions'.[128] The advent of damaging cyber capabilities has led some States to highlight specific areas, activities, or sectors that are critical to a State's sovereignty and that are clearly within

---

[120] See UNGA, Official compendium of voluntary national contributions on the subject of how international law applies to the use of information and communications technologies by States submitted by participating governmental experts in the Group of Governmental Experts on Advancing Responsible State Behaviour in Cyberspace in the Context of International Security established pursuant to General Assembly resolution 73/266 (13 July 2021) UN Doc A/76/136 (Official Compendium of National Contributions); Cyber Law Toolkit, 'Prohibition of intervention' [https://perma.cc/45KH-VL6Z].

[121] Friendly Relations Declaration (n 114) (also stating that 'armed intervention and all other forms of interference or attempted threats against the personality of the State or against its political, economic and cultural elements, are in violation of international law').

[122] Submission by Australia, Official Compendium of National Contributions (n 120) 16 ('the ability to control, decide upon or govern matters of an inherently sovereign nature.').

[123] Speech by the Rt Hon Jeremy Wright, UK Attorney-General (n 115).

[124] This term is consistent with the French text of the Covenant of the League of Nations ('une question que le droit international laisse à la compétence exclusive') and the Charter of the United Nations ('des affaires qui relèvent ... de la compétence nationale d'un État').

[125] Regarding the definition of domaine réservé, see Submission by Estonia, Official Compendium of National Contributions (n 120) 76 (describing examples of a nation's domaine réservé for purposes of the non-intervention principle as 'national democratic processes such as elections, or military, security or critical infrastructure systems'). The concept of domaine réservé is described by States and scholars in different ways, but generally refers to a State's internal affairs, ie a sphere of activity that is 'not, in principle, regulated by international law'. *Nationality Decrees Issued in Tunis and Morocco* (Advisory Opinion) [1923] PCIJ Reps Ser. B No 4, 24. For a discussion of different views regarding the term domaine réservé and a State's inherently sovereign functions for purposes of the non-intervention principle, see also NATO Cooperative Cyber Defence Centre of Excellence, *Tallinn Manual 2.0 on the International Law Applicable to Cyber Operations* (Michael N Schmitt ed, 2nd edn, CUP 2017) (Tallinn Manual 2.0) para 22 of the commentary to Rule 4.

[126] See eg Finnish Ministry for Foreign Affairs, 'International law and cyberspace—Finland's national positions' (English edn, 19 October 2020) (Finnish Position Paper) [https://perma.cc/CT9Y-MMY6] ('Hostile interference by cyber means may also breach the customary prohibition of intervention in the internal affairs of another State, provided that it is done with the purpose of compelling or coercing that State in relation to affairs regarding which it has free choice (so-called domaine réservé).'); Submission by Germany, Official Compendium of National Contributions (n 120) 34 ('for State-attributable conduct to qualify as a wrongful intervention, the conduct must (1) interfere with the *domaine réservé* of a foreign State and (2) involve coercion').

[127] UN Charter (n 2) art 2(7); Helsinki Final Act (n 114) Principle VI.

[128] Speech by US DoD General Counsel (n 118) (referring to the 'international law prohibition on coercively intervening in the core functions of another State (such as the choice of political, economic, or cultural system)').

that State's domestic jurisdiction. For example, one State notes that interference by digital means in its internal or external affairs 'which causes or may cause harm to [its] "political, economic, social and cultural system, may constitute a violation of the principle of non-intervention".[129] Another State suggests that a non-exhaustive list of four of the most significant sectors that are vulnerable to disruptive cyber conduct (and areas thus subject to prohibited intervention) are energy security, essential medical care, economic stability, and democratic processes.[130]

The Key Element of Coercion

4. As noted by the ICJ, an intervention is wrongful 'when it uses methods of coercion' to affect a State's protected choices, 'which must remain free ones'.[131] Unfortunately, there is no clear definition in State practice of the term 'coercion'. As noted by one State, '[t]he precise definition of coercion, and thus of unauthorised intervention, has not yet fully crystallised in international law. In essence it means compelling a state to take a course of action (whether an act or an omission) that it would not otherwise voluntarily pursue.'[132] Varied definitions are offered by other States.[133]

---

[129] See eg République Française Ministère des Armées, 'International Law Applied to Operations in Cyberspace' (DICoD / Pôle Éditions, October 2019)(French Position Paper) 7 [https://perma.cc/2LBH-3JRE].

[130] Speech by UK Attorney-General, the Rt Hon Suella Braverman (n 115) (listing the following examples of covert cyber operations by a foreign State which would coercively restrict or prevent the provision of essential medical services or essential energy supplies and would breach the rule on non-intervention, understanding that every case needs to be assessed on its facts: 'disruption of systems controlling emergency medical transport (e.g., telephone dispatchers); causing hospital computer systems to cease functioning; disruption of supply chains for essential medicines and vaccines; preventing the supply of power to housing, healthcare, education, civil administration and banking facilities and infrastructure; causing the energy supply chain to stop functioning at national level through damage or prevention of access to pipelines, interchanges, and depots; or preventing the operation of power generation infrastructure').

[131] *Nicaragua* Judgment (n 115) para 205. The Friendly Relations Declaration (n 114) also states that the purpose of the unlawful intervention is to 'coerce another State in order to obtain from it the subordination of the exercise of its sovereign rights and to secure from it advantages of any kind'.

[132] Submission by the Netherlands, Official Compendium of National Contributions (n 120) 57; Speech by UK Attorney-General, the Rt Hon Suella Braverman (n 115) ('While the precise boundaries of coercion are yet to crystallise in international law, we should be ready to consider whether disruptive cyber behaviours are coercive even where it might not be possible to point to a specific course of conduct which a State has been forced into or prevented from taking.').

[133] See eg Submission by Australia, Official Compendium of National Contributions (n 120) 5 ('coercive means are those that effectively deprive or are intended to deprive the State of the ability to control, decide upon or govern matters of an inherently sovereign nature'); New Zealand Ministry of Foreign Affairs and Trade, 'The Application of International Law to State Activity in Cyberspace' (Position Paper, 1 December 2020)(New Zealand Position Paper) [https://perma.cc/RJG8-AGBX] (defining coercive as 'an intention to deprive the target state of control over matters falling within the scope of its inherently sovereign functions ... Coercion can be direct or indirect and may range from dictatorial threats to more subtle means of control.'); Submission by Germany, Official Compendium of National Contributions (n 120) 34 ('coercion implies that a State's internal processes regarding aspects pertaining to its *domaine réservé* are significantly influenced or thwarted and that its will is manifestly bent by the foreign State's conduct').

Whatever the term's precise definition, one State cautions that 'as is widely accepted, the element of coercion must not be assumed prematurely'.[134]

Coercion and Armed Intervention

5. The paradigm or most obvious case of unlawful intervention involves military or armed intervention.[135] As noted by the ICJ, 'the element of coercion, which defines, and indeed forms the very essence of, prohibited intervention, is particularly obvious in the case of an intervention which uses force, either in the direct form of military action, or in the indirect form of support for terrorist or subversive armed activities within another State'. Similarly, as noted by one State, '[a]lthough there is no clear definition of the element of coercion, it should be noted that the use of force will always meet the definition of coercion. Use of force against another state is always a form of intervention.'[136] Thus, because that a State's national defence is an exercise of its sovereign rights (or a core function, or a matter within its exclusive competence, or domaine réservé etc), military space activities such as those involving the collection and use of satellite imagery for national defence are examples of matters that fall within that State's exercise of sovereign rights. Thus, a use force by State A against State B's military assets in space is likely to constitute a violation by State A of the non-intervention principle, even if that use of force does not rise to the level of an armed attack (see Rule 21: Use of Force and Rule 23: Armed Attack).

6. Actions that constitute an 'indirect use of force' may also constitute a violation of the non-intervention principle. For example, the Friendly Relations Declaration refers to acts of intervention which 'organize, assist, foment, finance, incite or tolerate subversive, terrorist or armed activities directed towards the violent overthrow of the regime of another State, or interfere in civil strife in another State'.[137] The ICJ in the *Nicaragua* Judgment also found that 'the support given by the United States ... to the military and paramilitary activities of the *contras* in Nicaragua, by financial support, training, supply of weapons, intelligence and logistical support, constitute[d] a clear breach of the principle of non-intervention'.[138]

---

[134] ibid 34.
[135] A related difficult and especially common situation may be the apparent 'threat' of armed intervention on Earth, which could also involve threats presented by space assets. However, a 'show of force' involving military capabilities on Earth or in space will not be sufficiently coercive to be illegal, unless— in a manner similar to the threat of force—a more specific and definite threat or demand is present, along with coercive intent or purpose on the part of a capable State in directing military actions against another State. See Rule 22: Threat of Force.
[136] Submission by the Netherlands, Official Compendium of National Contributions (n 120) 57.
[137] The International Court of Justice has found that this provision is declaratory of customary international law: *Armed Activities in the Congo* Judgment (n 115) para 162.
[138] *Nicaragua* Judgment (n 115) para 242.

7. Thus, it is possible for a State to violate the non-intervention principle through military space activities that support an indirect use of force on Earth through the provision of some form of assistance to rebels, insurgents, or other armed groups seeking the violent overthrow of the government of another State (or violent breakaway of a region of that State). Consider, for example, State A using its satellites and related military space systems to provide significant support to armed rebels operating inside State B, by providing them with weather data, communications, and intelligence, surveillance, and reconnaissance (ISR) data. This support by State A, to armed rebels seeking to change the political system of State B, would constitute an indirect use of force and an act of prohibited intervention by State A. This use by State A of its military assets in space in support of an armed insurgency on Earth may thus constitute a violation of the non-intervention principle even if these actions do not rise to the level of a direct use of force or an armed attack in space against State B.[139]

Non-Forcible Prohibited Intervention or Just Unwanted Interference?

8. Below the threshold of armed intervention, there is debate about what non-forcible actions may constitute prohibited intervention, displaying the necessary element of coercion. In this regard, there are few official, unambiguous statements or protests by States that specific acts against them constitute unlawful intervention. One of the reasons underlying this problem is the reality of frequent efforts by States to influence each other's policies and decisions with actions that are perceived as unfriendly but do not constitute coercion and prohibited intervention. For example, State leaders often use the term 'intervention' in a loose, political fashion to refer to unfriendly or obnoxious behaviour, rather than in a strict legal fashion to refer to a violation of a particular legal right. Therefore, it can be unclear whether a state is referring to a violation of this specific legal rule or making a broader political point.[140] The key element in distinguishing prohibited intervention from such diverse types of alleged interference and other unfriendly but lawful actions is the ambiguous term coercion. Repeated criticism by a State of another State, no matter how harsh, and persistent attempts in communications with that other State to obtain certain desired reactions from that State are unlikely to qualify as coercion and

---

[139] A more difficult case for unlawful intervention is posed by a situation in which State A engages in disrupting the satellite communications of a State B that are being used by the police of State B that are merely engaged in riot control and addressing civil disturbances.

[140] See eg Associated Press, 'Spain Recalls Nicaragua Ambassador after "Interference" Jibe', *US News* (Madrid, 11 August 2021) [https://perma.cc/6BXC-B23E] (noting that Spain recalled its ambassador to Nicaragua after what Spain described as 'incendiary remarks' in a statement sent by the Nicaraguan foreign ministry that denounced Spain for 'cynical and continual meddling, interference and intervention in our internal affairs, inappropriate of democratic governments').

prohibited intervention.¹⁴¹ Diplomatic actions, even if they are resented or perceived as unfriendly, punitive, or applying pressure on a State, are also unlikely, by themselves, to be illegal coercion. Similarly, the broadcast of unwanted information by radio or TV to a State's population or unfriendly postings on the Internet about that State and its officials—including those relayed via satellites—may often be described as unacceptable interference by the targeted State. As noted by one State, '[t]he fact that behavior attributed to another State is unwelcome, irresponsible, or indeed hostile, does not mean that it is also unlawful. A core element of the non-intervention rule is that the offending behavior must be coercive.'¹⁴² Even radio or TV broadcasts or Internet postings—again via satellite transmissions—that the targeted State may describe as inciting violence or civil unrest may involve subjective judgments regarding the content of the information about which States may disagree. Harder cases may be presented by other factual scenarios. Consider an attempt by State A to incite violence and trigger an uprising against the government of State B by broadcasting false news (via satellite transmissions) that the government of State B is planning an assassination of the iconic leader of an ethnic group. It must be noted that examples of specific acts in which a State has officially and explicitly invoked the non-intervention principle in such circumstances are difficult to identify.

Non-Forcible Prohibited Intervention: Economic Disruptions?

9. Various types of interference that may appear to be highly coercive, particularly in the economic realm, do not constitute prohibited intervention, even if the use of such means is intended to influence outcomes in, or conduct with respect to, a matter reserved for exercise of the target State's sovereign rights. For example, the Nicaraguan government complained about various types of economic pressure applied by the United States against Nicaragua (including a trade embargo, trade quotas, and efforts to prevent international financial organizations from approving loans to Nicaragua) but the ICJ was 'unable to regard such action on the

---

¹⁴¹ Submission by Germany, Official Compendium of National Contributions (n 120) 34 ('Even harsher forms of communication such as pointed commentary and sharp criticism as well as (persistent) attempts to obtain, through discussion, a certain reaction or the performance of a certain measure from another State do not as such qualify as coercion.'). Speech by UK Attorney-General, the Rt Hon Suella Braverman (n 115) ('All States have the freedom to make their views known about processes in other countries—delivering hard, sometimes unwelcome messages, and drawing attention to concerns. This is part and parcel of international relations ... It is this coercive element that most obviously distinguishes an intervention prohibited under international law from, for example, more routine and legitimate information-gathering and influencing activities that States carry out as part of international relations.').
¹⁴² Speech by UK Attorney-General, the Rt Hon Suella Braverman (n 115).

economic plane as is here complained of as a breach of the customary-law principle of non-intervention'.[143]

10. Notwithstanding various types of economic pressure that do not constitute prohibited intervention, several States have made statements suggesting that certain cyber actions, in extremis, directed against the economies or financial systems of a State could violate the non-intervention principle. For example, one State has argued that 'the use by a State of cyber activities to ... significantly disrupt the functioning of a States' [sic] financial systems would constitute a violation of the principle of non-intervention'.[144] Another State official has argued that covert cyber operations by a foreign State which coercively interfere with free and fair electoral processes would constitute a prohibited intervention.[145] Less severe actions that cause limited harmful economic effects to a State, for example a military space activity that disrupts satellite communications essential for financial transactions or other business activities, appear unlikely, even when done with coercive intent, to constitute a violation of the non-intervention principle unless perhaps that harm can be said to extend to the larger 'economic system' of the targeted State.[146]

Non-Forcible Prohibited Intervention: A State's Electoral Processes

11. There is no shortage of declarations by States indicating that they believe various actions, particularly cyber activities, that deliberately cause significant damage to, or loss of functionality in, a state's critical infrastructure may violate the non-intervention principle.[147] Some of these actions might also qualify as an unlawful use of force (see Rule 21: Use of Force). In recent years, as many States have emphasized that their electoral processes are within the exercise of their sovereign rights or domaine réservé, they have also indicated that some non-forcible actions against these electoral processes may constitute a violation of the non-intervention principle. Yet there is also a wide range of views regarding what type of interference in a State's electoral process constitutes prohibited intervention and the key element

---

[143] *Nicaragua* Judgment (n 115) para 245.

[144] Submission by Australia, Official Compendium of National Contributions (n 120) 5 (this conclusion is subject to meeting the two elements of a prohibited intervention, ie (i) coercive means, and (ii) intervention in matters that a State is permitted by the principle of State sovereignty to decide freely).

[145] Speech by UK Attorney-General, the Rt Hon Suella Braverman (n 115) (further noting that, although every activity needs to be assessed on its facts, specific examples of these activities could include: 'operations that disrupt the systems which control electoral counts to change the outcome of an election; or operations to disrupt another State's ability to hold an election at all, for example by causing systems to malfunction with the effect of preventing voter registration').

[146] 2019 French Position Paper on International Law Applied to Cyberspace (n 129) 7 ('Interference by digital means in the internal or external affairs of France, i.e. interference which causes or may cause harm to France's ... economic ... system, may constitute a violation of the principle of non-intervention.')

[147] See Official Compendium of National Contributions (n 120).

of coercion. On one end of the spectrum, some States have established a relatively high bar for finding a violation of the non-intervention principle in this area.[148] Whether cyber methodologies or other systems employed in military space activities are currently capable of preventing States from holding an election, altering the results of an election, or intervening in the operation of legislative bodies is subject to developing technological capabilities and debate—but theoretically such measures employed by military space activities could violate the non-intervention principle.[149] Other military space capabilities, such as transmitting radio signals for the purpose of manipulating the broadcasting of national election campaigns in State, while clearly within the capacity of current technologies, are lower on the spectrum and are not likely to reach the threshold for prohibited intervention.

Even on the lower end of the spectrum, a few States have declared that various types of information or misinformation directed at a State to influence public opinion in the electoral process is enough to constitute a violation of the non-intervention principle.[150] The transmission of such misinformation by digital/cyber means to engineer public opinion in elections and the dissemination by digital/cyber means

---

[148] See eg Submission by Australia, Official Compendium of National Contributions (n 120) 5 ('The use by a State of cyber activities to prevent another State from holding an election, or manipulate the electoral system to alter the results of an election in another State, intervene in the fundamental operation of Parliament ... would constitute a violation of the principle of non-intervention.'); New Zealand Position Paper (n 133) para 10 ('Examples of malicious cyber activity that might violate the non-intervention rule include: a cyber operation that deliberately manipulates the vote tally in an election or deprives a significant part of the electorate of the ability to vote.'); Submission by United States, Official Compendium of National Contributions (n 120) 140 ('A cyber operation by a State that interferes with another country's ability to hold an election or that manipulates another country's election results would be a clear violation of the rule of non-intervention.'); Speech by UK Attorney-General, the Rt Hon Suella Braverman (n 115) ('covert cyber operations by a foreign State which coercively interfere with free and fair electoral processes would constitute a prohibited intervention ... every activity needs to be assessed on its facts, but such activities could include: operations that disrupt the systems which control electoral counts to change the outcome of an election; or operations to disrupt another State's ability to hold an election at all, for example by causing systems to malfunction with the effect of preventing voter registration').

[149] But see para 9 regarding the frequent efforts by States to influence each other's and decisions with actions that are perceived as unfriendly but do not constitute coercion and prohibited intervention.

[150] See eg Armed Forces Cyberspace Center, 'Declaration of General Staff of the Armed Forces of the Islamic Republic of Iran Regarding International Law Applicable to the Cyberspace', reported at 'General Staff of Iranian Armed Forces Warns of Tough Reaction to Any Cyber Threat' *Nournews* (August 2020) [https://perma.cc/DBT4-MZSY] ('Measures like cyber manipulation of elections or engineering the public opinions on the eve of the elections may be constituted of the examples of gross intervention ... sending mass messages in a widespread manner to the voters to affect the result of the elections in other states is also considered as the forbidden intervention.'); Submission by Norway, Compendium of National Contributions (n 120) 68–69 (although noting that it is 'aware that there are differences of opinion as to where the threshold for breach [of the non-intervention principle] lies', Norway states that 'unduly influencing public opinion through the dissemination of confidential information obtained through cyber operations ("hack and leak"), would be in violation of the prohibition of intervention'). It should be noted that in recent years several States that have strongly criticized these types of interference (via social media and other means of influence) have generally criticized such actions as irresponsible or unlawful, but to this point have refrained from explicitly characterizing them as prohibited intervention—see eg 'Reckless campaign of cyber attacks by Russian military intelligence service exposed' (United Kingdom National Cyber Security Centre, 3 October 2018) [https://perma.cc/QV9B-YEU3].

of private information obtained through cyber operations are examples of interference that lie within existing technological capabilities that are capable of being employed in military space activities.

Other Regimes Regulating Interference

13. This Rule is also distinguished from various forms of interference with space activities of that are regulated specifically under relevant treaties, particularly under the OST (see Rule 18: Harmful Interference) and under ITU regulations (see Rule 19: ITU Harmful Radio Interference). In some circumstances, such forms of interference could rise to the level of intervention prohibited under customary international law, depending on the circumstances or even a threat or use of force (see Rule 21: Use of Force).

14. Note also that under legal regimes that apply in some regional contexts, a principle of non-interference may be applied to situations that involve non-coercive interference that would otherwise be lawful under the general international law.[151] To date, no State practice could be identified regarding the application of these regimes to space activities, including the transmission via satellite of unwelcome transmissions of information.

15. This Rule applies exclusively to relations between States. It does not address an action by an international organization as a prohibited intervention. However, it should be noted that the United Nations is subject to a specific provision in the UN Charter prohibiting it from intervening in matters that are essentially within the domestic jurisdiction of a State, except when it is taking enforcement measures under Chapter VII of the UN Charter.[152] However, given the fact that the UN does not at this time have or operate its own satellite or any other space assets, this specific rule has limited application in the space context. Military space operations that are undertaken pursuant to enforcement measures authorized under Chapter VII of the Charter (addressed in Rule 28: Collective Security Measures) are exempt from this prohibition, as noted above.

---

[151] See eg Constitutive Act of the African Union (adopted 11 July 2000, entered into force 26 May 2001) 2158 UNTS 3, art 4(g) (establishing for the Union and its members the broad principle of 'non-interference by any Member State in the internal affairs of another'); Charter of the Association of Southeast Asian Nations (adopted 20 November 2007, entered into force 15 December 2008) art 2(e) (requiring ASEAN and its Member States to act in accordance with the broad principle: of 'non-interference in the internal affairs of ASEAN Member States'.).

[152] UN Charter (n 2) art 2(7).

Rule 21
Use of Force

A State shall not engage in activities, including military space activities, that constitute a use of force against another State, in violation of the UN Charter.

Overview of Legal Basis of Rule

1. This Rule is based on Article 2(4) of the UN Charter,[153] and is also reflective of customary international law.[154] This Rule applies to any activity in the exploration and use of outer space, including the Moon and other celestial bodies, in accordance with the explicit requirement in the Outer Space Treaty (OST) that all such activities be conducted in accordance with international law and the United Nations Charter.[155] The travaux préparatoires of the OST further indicate that this reference to the UN Charter was included to ensure that the use and exploration of outer space would not jeopardize international peace and security.[156]

The UN Charter Regime and the Use of Force

2. The reference in Article 2(4) of the UN Charter to 'the territorial integrity and political independence' of a State was not intended by the drafters of the UN Charter to limit the geographical scope of the Article 2(4). Instead, an examination of the

---

[153] UN Charter (n 2) art 2(4), which reads: 'All Members shall refrain in their international relations from the threat or use of force against the territorial integrity or political independence of any State, or in any other manner inconsistent with the Purposes of the United Nations.'

[154] The prohibition of the use of force may also be regarded as a *jus cogens* or peremptory norm. For example, the ICJ has noted that the prohibition on the use of force 'is frequently referred to in statements by State representatives as being not only a principle of customary international law but also a fundamental or cardinal principle of such law' and that both parties in the case before the Court recognized the prohibition as '*jus cogens*'. Nicaragua Judgment (n 115) para 190. The International Law Commission has also expressed the view that 'the law of the Charter concerning the prohibition of the use of force in itself constitutes a conspicuous example of a rule in international law having the character of *jus cogens*', ILC, 'Draft Articles on the Law of Treaties with Commentaries' (1966) UN Doc A/CN.4/175, 247. However, the *jus cogens* status of self-defence is disputed. See discussion in Methodology of Manual.

[155] OST (n 3) art III. Note that further issues raised by the application of the OST and the legal connection between a State and a space object for purposes of the use of force and an armed attack is discussed in Rule 23: Armed Attack, paras 15–20.

[156] See UNCOPUOS Legal Sub-Committee 'Summary Record of the Sixty-Second Meeting' (19 July 1966) UN Doc A/AC.105/C.2/SR.62, 2–3 (United Arab Republic) 4 (Canada).

travaux préparatoires of the Charter demonstrates that this reference to territorial integrity or political independence was intended to emphasize the equal sovereignty of states (especially the weaker or smaller ones).[157] In addition, it seems clear from the travaux préparatoires that the final sentence of Article 2(4) requiring States to refrain from the use of force 'in any other manner inconsistent with the purposes of the United Nations' was intended to state the prohibition on the interstate use of force in the broadest possible terms.[158] Therefore, the fact that there is no sovereign State territory in space (because Article II of the OST prohibits national appropriation of space, such as by a claim of sovereignty) does not restrict the coverage of Article 2(4) of the UN Charter. Although a State does not exercise 'sovereignty' over a space object under the space law regime, it may in some cases be legally invested with the right to exercise jurisdiction and control over a space object and might thus be able to invoke on this basis (among other possible legal connections with the space object) the prohibition under Article 2(4) in response to a use of force against that space object and also respond in self-defence if that use of force qualifies as an armed attack (see Rule 23: Armed Attack, paragraphs 15–20, discussing the legal connection between a State and a space object for purposes of the use of force and determining the victim of an armed attack).

3. There are two universally accepted exceptions to the prohibition of the threat or use of force: the right of individual or collective self-defence under Article 51 of the UN Charter (see Rule 26: Self-Defence and Rule 27: Collective Self-Defence) and collective enforcement action authorized by the UN Security Council under Chapter VII of the UN Charter (Rule 28: Collective Security Measures). The use of force in, from, or through outer space in accordance with either of these exceptions is lawful.

4. The term 'use of force' is not defined in the UN Charter. However, in its origins and traditional application, Article 2(4) is generally accepted as referring to the use of 'armed' or 'physical' force.[159] This interpretation is confirmed by

---

[157] See Ian Brownlie, *International Law and the Use of Force by States* (OUP 1963) 267 (noting that this language was 'not intended to be restrictive, but, on the contrary, to give more specific guarantees to small states and that it cannot be interpreted as having a qualifying effect').

[158] United Nations Information Organization, 'Documents of the United Nations Conference on International Organization (vol 6, San Francisco, 1945) (UNCIO Docs) 335 (The US delegate stated that the words were intended to convey 'in the broadest terms an absolute all-inclusive prohibition').

[159] See eg 'Independent International Fact-Finding Mission on the Conflict in Georgia' (vol II, Council of European Union 2008) 242 (the 'prohibition of the use of force covers *all physical force* which surpasses a minimum threshold of intensity' (emphasis added)); ILA Committee on Use of Force, 'Final Report on Aggression and the Use of Force' (Sydney Conference, ILA 2018) (ILA Final Report) [https://perma.cc/U9YN-CNQP] ('Article 2(4) is generally accepted as referring to the use of "armed" or "physical" force'); Bruno Simma and others (eds), *The Charter of the United Nations: A Commentary* (vol I, 3rd edn, OUP 2012) 209 ('the travaux préparatoires of the UN Charter illustrate the fact that only military force is the concern of the prohibition of the use of force ... Also, the prevailing international practice of states and international practice treats only incidents involving military force as falling under the prohibition of the use of force and thereby confirms its narrow reading.'); 'Unilateral Remedies' in *Restatement of the Law Third: The Foreign Relations Law of the United States* (vol 2, American Law Institute 1987) § 905, 383 ('Article 2(4) prohibits the threat or use of military force.'); Avra Constantinou,

examining the travaux préparatoires of the UN Charter, its text, and State practice in implementing the Charter. For example, during the drafting of UN Charter, proposals by some States to include economic measures as a form of force were explicitly rejected by the conference (no matter how damaging, harmful, or destructive the consequences).[160] This decision is reflected in the UN Charter itself, which explicitly focuses on particular instruments and modalities (and not consequences or effects) as it categorizes the 'complete or partial interruption of economic relations' as a measure 'not involving the use of armed force'.[161] In this regard, it should be noted that the terms 'force' and 'armed force' are used interchangeably in the UN Charter.[162] The widely accepted focus of the Charter on armed, physical force is further confirmed by the list of examples in the Charter of other modalities or measures (in addition to economic measures) that do *not* ordinarily constitute the use of force, such as the 'complete or partial interruption of telegraphic, radio, and other means of communication'[163] (see paragraphs 12–13).

The Traditional Approach on the Use of Armed Force and the Emerging 'Effects-Based' Approach

5. Statements by several States in recent years which potentially expand the definition of the use of force in future conflicts to encompass purely cyber actions based primarily on their damaging effects (ie death, injury, or damage equivalent/similar to the results of physical, armed force) are discussed in paragraphs 15–22. Several States at State Consultations further noted that this 'effects-based' approach has

---

The Right of Self-Defence under Customary International Law and Article 51 of the UN Charter (Bruylant 2000) 36–37 (noting the correlation between arts 2(4) and 51 of the Charter in that 'they both deal with armed force only'); Leland M Goodrich, *Charter of the United Nations: Commentary and Documents* (3rd edn, CUP 1969) 70 ('While it is not explicitly stated, it can be presumed that the word "force" as used in [art 2(4)] means only "armed force" ').

[160] At the San Francisco Conference, the Delegate from Brazil proposed an amendment that the use of economic coercion be included under the prohibition of the use of force in art 4(2), which was rejected by a vote of 26 to 2. UNCIO Docs (n 158) vol 6, 334, vol 3, 252–53; Brownlie (n 157) 266. Although various types of economic pressure do not constitute a use of force, some States have suggested that certain coercive cyber actions, in extremis, directed against the economies or financial systems of a State, could violate the non-intervention principle (see Rule 20: Non-Intervention Principle).

[161] Article 41 sets forth those measures not involving the use of armed force that the Security Council may decide to employ under its Chapter VII powers 'to give effect to its decisions'.

[162] In addition to the reference to measures not involving armed force in art 41, one of the goals stated in the preamble of the UN Charter is 'to ensure, by the acceptance of principles and the institution of methods, that *armed force* shall not be used, save in the common interest' (emphasis added). Along similar lines, art 44 provides that when the Security Council has 'decided to use Force', it shall turn to Members to provide 'armed forces' in fulfilment of the obligations assumed elsewhere in Chapter VII. See Tom Ruys, 'The Meaning of "Force" and the Boundaries of the Jus Ad Bellum: Are "Minimal" Uses of Force Excluded from UN Charter Article 2(4)?' (2014) 108 American Journal of International Law 159, 163.

[163] UN Charter (n 2) art 41.

been increasingly recognized by States as extending beyond purely cyber actions to encompass other actions that may not involve the physical use of armed force.[164] However, as noted by one State at State Consultations, 'this does not mean that the effects-based approach would replace the traditional approach where armed force is utilized'. Indeed, as discussed below, these two approaches should be regarded as complementary, depending on the circumstances. While the effects-based approach may be useful in some situations, it also has limitations in other circumstances where the traditional focus on armed, physical force is more appropriate. For example, a missile fired at a satellite that misses that satellite and causes no damaging effects may nonetheless constitute a use of force or an armed attack. In another context, military forces may engage in a use of force (including in an act of aggression, as discussed below) by the unauthorized entry of its military forces into the territory of another State, without necessarily causing any damage. In other cases, damage may be caused by a missile fired during a military space operation, but if that missile was fired accidentally, unintentionally, or due to a technical malfunction, it may not constitute a use of force (see further discussion of accidents, mistakes, and other non-intentional acts with respect the use of force and an armed attack in Rule 23: Armed Attack, paragraph 20). Finally, even if the effects-based approach is applied, the assessment of effects is still based on damages that are equivalent to those caused by traditional, physical, armed force. Thus, harmful effects caused by cyber operations that resemble theft (including exfiltration of data), acts of espionage, economic measures, actions resulting in purely monetary losses, misinformation, or psychological operations are not likely to be equivalent to the loss of human life, injury, or damage to property caused by the use of armed physical force (see also paragraph 19). Furthermore, even if such damages do occur, it may be difficult to establish the proximate cause of such damages in the absence of a direct link to the use of physical, armed force; for example, acts of deception taken by State A that could result in actions taken by State B that result in damages to State B's space assets, but the proximate cause of these damages cannot be clearly linked to the State A's acts of deception because of numerous intervening actions and actors.

6. The Charter's foundational, traditional focus on physical, armed force is further reinforced by the subsequent practice of States in implementing the Charter. For example, the Definition of Aggression Resolution, which states that 'aggression is

---

[164] For example, as discussed in para 23, one State at State Consultations noted that non-kinetic means employing the electro-magnetic spectrum (like jamming) that temporarily or partially interfere with the functioning of early warning systems may be considered by some States to amount to a use of force because of the potential effects on a State's critical national defence systems (particularly to defend against a nuclear attack), even though such electronic measures are not ordinarily considered to be a use of force. This State further noted that this was a good example of how the traditional armed force approach might be expanded in some circumstances to encompass an effects-based approach. However, another State argued that the UN Charter and the nature of outer space (especially the dual-use of space assets) demands an effects-based approach.

the most serious and dangerous form of the illegal *use of force*', also confirms that an act of aggression 'means the use of *armed force*' (including the unauthorized presence of military forces on another State's territory or a blockade of another State by naval forces, without reference to causing any damage).[165] Along similar lines, the Friendly Relations Declaration, adopted by the General Assembly on 24 October 1970,[166] interprets the principle that States shall refrain from the threat or use of force by focusing on measures that presume the use of armed force and forcible actions.[167] The prohibition on the use of force has also been recognized by the International Court of Justice (ICJ) to include 'indirect' force, at least where a State arms rebel or insurgent groups in another State (which in the context of the *Nicaragua* case, included military assistance to the 'Contra' rebels 'in the form of the provision of weapons or logistical or other support').[168]

As the ICJ made clear in the *Nicaragua* case—with respect to a State providing arms to an insurgent movement in another State—that an action does not necessarily require damage, injury or death to constitute an use of force.[169] While the test for finding an armed attack may be determined by 'scale and effects' and must be distinguished as one of 'the most grave forms of the use of force',[170] the term 'scale and effects' (used by the ICJ in contrasting a 'frontier incident from an armed attack') is not the test that has been used by the ICJ to find a use of force. In fact, a use of force is not necessarily required to result in physical damage or injury at all, although such effects may often accompany a use of force.[171]

7.

---

[165] UNGA Res 3314 (XXIX) (14 December 1974) UN Doc A/RES/3314 (Definition of Aggression Resolution) (emphasis added). The examples of aggression provided in the Resolution further illustrate this point by focusing primarily on the use of the 'armed forces of a State'—by invasion, attack, bombardment, blockade, or by the unauthorized presence of a State's armed forces on another State's territory. Brownlie (n 157) 209; ILA Final Report (n 159) 4.
[166] Friendly Relations Declaration (n 114).
[167] When interpreting the prohibition of the threat or use of force, the Declaration deals solely with military or armed force, but when it addresses the obligation to not intervene in matters within the domestic jurisdiction of another State, it includes the use of economic, political, or any other types of measures to coerce another State. By doing so, it has been noted that 'the Declaration underlies the fact that the scope of Art. 2(4) is restricted to armed force'. Brownlie (n 157) at 209; ILA Final Report (n 159) 4 (noting how the generally accepted view that art 2(4) refers to the use of 'armed' or 'physical' force is 'confirmed in the list of examples appearing in the Friendly Relations Declaration'); Dino Kritsiotis, 'Topographies of Force' in Michael N Schmitt and Jelena Pejic (eds), *International Law and Armed Conflict: Exploring the Fault Lines* (Brill 2007) 67–68 (observing that the Friendly Relations Declaration 'demonstrates the conscious effort of the General Assembly in October 1970 to frame an understanding of the prohibition of intervention that was more expansive in nature than the prohibition of force'). For its part, the ICJ has chosen to determine the scope of the prohibition of use of force under customary international law by referring to the Friendly Relations Declaration without mentioning the paragraph on intervention which addresses the prohibition of economic, political or any other type of measures to coerce another State. *Nicaragua* Judgment (n 115) para 191.
[168] ibid para 195.
[169] ibid para 228 (concluding that 'the arming and training of the contras can certainly be said to involve the threat or use of force against Nicaragua').
[170] ibid paras 191 and 195.
[171] For example, the Definition of Aggression Resolution includes numerous examples of aggression ('the most serious and dangerous form of the illegal use of force') which need not involve any physical damage or injury but instead focus on the invasion, occupation, or unauthorized presence

Counterspace Weapon Systems and Capabilities

8. While there are many different ways to categorize counterspace weapons and capabilities,[172] several major, broad categories can be identified,[173] beginning with those that most clearly correspond to application of armed, physical force upon which the UN Charter's prohibition of the use of force was founded. Thus, the first major and familiar category of counterspace weapons consist of those weapons that rely upon one type of physical force, commonly referred to as kinetic energy systems.[174] These weapons rely on the energy of motion, that is, the velocity of objects, to deliver significant mass to destroy targets.[175] In space, these weapons can include missiles, projectiles, or any other object that can be shot, manoeuvred, or launched from Earth, celestial bodies, or from other objects in space. One example of this type of counterspace weapon is a kinetic kill weapon (or vehicle), such as a direct-ascent ASAT weapon that strikes a satellite on a trajectory that intersects the

---

of armed forces on the territory of another State, naval blockades, and the placing of a State's territory at the disposal of an aggressor. See Definition of Aggression Resolution (n 165) arts 3(a), (c), (e), and (f). As noted by one scholar regarding State practice on this point: 'No one can seriously contest, for instance, that a large-scale territorial incursion by military forces of a neighboring state—such as the Russian troop deployment in the Crimea in early 2014—can be characterized as a use of force in the sense of Article 2(4), even if no single shot had been fired, and even if the incursion were to end (for example, under political pressure of the international community) without any actual hostilities.' Ruys (n 162) 189.

[172] This Rule includes a discussion of both counterspace 'weapons' and 'capabilities' (such as capabilities along the electro-magnetic spectrum and cyber capabilities) because the means employed by a State to engage in a use of force is not required to be categorized as a 'weapon'. One State at State Consultations suggested that the 'use of force can be defined as the application of armed force against the personality of another State that results in physical damage to or destruction of the property of another State, or degradation of the functionality of a space object of another State, or personal injury to the nationals of another State. And hence, is a combination of capabilities and effects. Those capabilities, however, do not need to be designated weapons, but rather could be achieved by a variety of means taking into account the specifics of space.'

[173] See Todd Harrison and others, 'Space Threat Assessment 2020' (Center for Strategic & International Studies 2020) (2020 CSIS Threat Assessment) 2–5 (listing and examining four major, broad categories of counterspace weapons: (i) Kinetic Physical; (ii) Non-Kinetic Physical, consisting mainly of directed energy weapons; (iii) Electronic and; (iv) Cyber).

[174] Although the term 'kinetic' is a popular political, social, and even military colloquialism with many different meanings, as an official military term it is best defined as 'relating to actions that involve the forces and energy of moving bodies, including physical damage to or destruction of targets through use of bombs, missiles, bullets, and similar projectiles'. US Air Force, 'Air Force Supplement to the Department of Defense Dictionary of Military and Associated Terms' (US Air Force Doctrine Document 1-02, updated 6 January 2012, 11 January 2007) 45–46; 'Kinetic, *adj.* and *n.*', definition A(2)(a), *Oxford English Dictionary* (online edn, OUP 2022) <www.oed.com/> accessed 22 February 2022 (defining kinetic as 'of, pertaining, or relating to, motion; due to or resulting from motion' and kinetic energy as 'the power of doing work possessed by a moving body by virtue of its motion'). The concept of kinetic energy is a particularly important concept in outer space, where objects in motion at extremely high speeds that have enormous destructive capabilities do not need explosive warheads like bombs or missiles used in terrestrial applications.

[175] David Wright, Laura Grego, and Lisbeth Gronlund, *The Physics of Space Security: A Reference Manual* (American Academy of Arts and Sciences 2005) 5, fn 1 ('Weapons that destroy by direct impact are called kinetic kill weapons. The kinetic energy of the fast-moving weapon and/or target provides the energy to destroy the target.').

targeted space object without placing the interceptor into orbit.[176] Unlike a direct-ascent weapon, a co-orbital ASAT weapon is first placed into orbit and can then be manoeuvred to strike or damage its target.[177] These weapon systems are not unlike other weapons long associated with physical, armed force and are clearly encompassed by the prohibition of the use of force when employed by a State against a target. While they can cause great damage, a missile or other projectile intentionally fired at an object or person in space that happens to miss its intended target nonetheless may qualify as a use of force, a threat of force, or an armed attack[178] (see Rule 23: Armed Attack).

A sub-category of counterspace weapons that are commonly associated with the terrestrial application of the use of force include rockets, missiles, shells, and other delivery systems that are able to destroy a target not by the kinetic energy of their own velocity but instead by the stored chemical energy of conventional explosives or other components that propel fragments or other objects with great force.[179] Nuclear weapons, which possess several types of destructive capabilities (both kinetic and non-kinetic) can also be included in this category, although they have a different application in space than in other domains.[180] The use of these weapons, as well as other weapons of mass destruction (WMDs) that rely on the physical properties of toxic chemicals or dangerous pathogens and toxins, can clearly constitute a use of force under Article 2(4) and were unfortunately familiar to the

9.

---

[176] 2020 CSIS Threat Assessment (n 173) 3 (further noting that '[b]allistic missiles and other missile defense systems can also be modified to act as direct-ascent ASAT weapons, as long as they have sufficient power to reach the target satellite's orbit'). Direct-ascent weapons are those that 'use ground, air-, or sea-launched missiles with interceptors that are used to kinetically destroy satellites through force of impact but are not placed into orbit themselves': Weeden and Samson (n 6) xxxi.

[177] Co-orbital weapons are defined as weapons that 'are placed into orbit and then maneuver to approach the target to attack it by various means'. Weeden and Samson (n 6) xxxi. Some co-orbital weapons may contain explosives, but those explosives are used to generate fragments and increase the chance of a kinetic impact, not to generate blast effects as the latter do not exist in the vacuum of space. Chemical sprays could be used to coat optics, solar panels, or sensitive instruments to reduce or destroy their functionality. Co-orbital weapons may also employ robotic arms which are capable of manipulating another space object and changing its orbit or otherwise making it unable to function properly. Although in this situation the space object may not be damaged, the action by a robotic arm which permanently makes that space object unable to function properly may constitute a use of force.

[178] As noted, physical damage, death, or injury is not necessarily a requirement for a use of force, although such damaging effects are usually associated with a use of force and those effects are usually intended by the user.

[179] Bob Preston and others, *Space Weapons, Earth Wars* (Project Airforce, RAND 2002) 24 [https://perma.cc/E9VP-3AHB]. It should be noted, however, that in terrestrial applications, the kinetic impact of shrapnel or other objects is accompanied by destructive blast effect—which is not present in space.

[180] While nuclear, chemical, and biological weapons rely on radioactive isotopes, toxic chemicals, and deadly pathogens and toxins, and can be classified to that extent as physical, non-kinetic weapons, they have enormous destructive power—and nuclear weapons generate not only nuclear radiation but also tremendous heat and blast shockwaves, releasing kinetic energy. To the extent, however that nuclear weapons rely solely on blast effects, they have little or no application in space (since explosions do not generate blast effects in space). As counterspace weapons, nuclear weapons can create a dangerous high radiation environment in space and can also generate a destructive electromagnetic impulse.

framers of the UN Charter.[181] The possession, deployment, transfer, or use of nuclear weapons and other WMDs may also violate other treaty and customary international law obligations[182] (see Rule 5: Weapons of Mass Destruction).

10. Another major category of counterspace weapon consists of 'directed energy weapons' which are able to direct destructive energy to their targets without transporting significant mass.[183] 'Directed energy' is an umbrella term covering technologies that produce concentrated electromagnetic energy and atomic and subatomic particles.[184] Counterspace weapons that rely on directed energy include high-energy lasers, high-powered microwave weapons, and electromagnetic pulse (EMP) weapons.[185] Since they travel at the speed of light and are able to cause damage without relying on kinetic energy, these weapons have many potential applications in space. While they are generally part of significant technological advancements since the UN Charter was signed in 1945 and substitute different types of electromagnetic radiation for more conventional weapons employing armed force, they can potentially destroy or seriously damage targets in space. For example, they are capable of damaging critical components of space objects, such as solar panels and optical lenses. The use of these weapons to destroy or permanently damage another State's assets in space would appear to generally fall within the prohibition on the use of force in Article 2(4), although to date there are no

---

[181] *Nuclear Weapons* Advisory Opinion [1996] ICJ Rep 226, 266 (unanimously ruling that '[a] threat or use of force by means of nuclear weapons that is contrary to Article 2, paragraph 4, of the United Nations Charter and that fails to meet all the requirements of Article 51, is unlawful'). To the extent that nuclear, chemical, or biological weapons are described as 'non-kinetic', the harmful physical properties of radioactive isotopes, chemicals, pathogens, and toxins must be distinguished from data transmitted by often harmless, non-kinetic cyber capabilities.

[182] In particular, in the context of the space law regime, States are prohibited from placing in orbit any objects carrying nuclear weapons or any other kinds of WMDs, installing such weapons on celestial bodies, or stationing such weapons in outer space in any other manner. OST (n 3) art IV. The use of chemical and biological weapons is also strictly prohibited by the law of armed conflict.

[183] Preston and others (n 179) 24. These weapons are also sometimes classified as a subset of 'Physical, Non-Kinetic Weapons'. 2020 CSIS Threat Assessment (n 173) 3. It should be noted, however, that while light does not have mass, particles do. Particle-beam weapons are nonetheless sometimes also classified as directed energy weapons. A particle-beam weapon uses a high-energy beam of subatomic particles to damage the target by disrupting its atomic or molecular structure.) See generally, Bahman Zohuri, *Directed-Energy Beam Weapons* (ebook, Springer Nature Switzerland 2019) 309–21.

[184] US Joint Chiefs of Staff, 'Joint Publication 3-13.1—Electronic Warfare' (8 February 2012) I-1, I-2 [https://perma.cc/2HJ7-86NN] (further noting that broad range of wavelengths known as the electromagnetic spectrum includes radio waves, microwaves, infrared, visible light, ultraviolet, X-rays, and gamma-rays, classified in order of decreasing wavelength and increasing energy and frequency). It is important to also note that laser radiation—like all light—is also a form of electromagnetic radiation. Directed energy weapons are thus generally defined as weapons that 'use focused energy, such as laser, particle, or microwave beams to interfere or destroy space systems': Weeden and Samson (n 6) xxxi.

[185] An electromagnetic pulse (EMP) is a short but powerful burst of electromagnetic radiation that can be created by several means. A High Altitude EMP is 'a near-instantaneous electromagnetic energy field that is produced in the atmosphere by the power and radiation of a nuclear explosion, and that is damaging to electronic equipment over a very wide area, depending on power of the nuclear device and altitude of the burst'. See Clay Wilson, 'High Altitude Electromagnetic Pulse (HEMP) and High Power Microwave (HPM) Devices: Threat Assessments' (CRS Report, Congressional Research Service 2008) p 6 [https://perma.cc/DXU3-ZRLE].

clear, corroborated reports of States employing these weapons against other States in space.

11. Several directed energy weapon systems, including high-energy lasers and high-powered microwave weapons, also have the capability to temporarily or partially disrupt, interfere with, or degrade the functions of satellites when lower levels of energy are used. For example, while a high-powered microwave weapon may cause permanent damage to electrical circuits and processors when operated at higher power levels, at lower levels of power, this same weapon or another version of it can also be used to temporarily disrupt a satellite's electronics and corrupt data stored in memory.[186] Similarly, a laser that can cause permanent damage at higher power can also temporarily blind/overwhelm (or 'dazzle') the optical sensors of a satellite at lower power.[187] These technological capabilities, similar in that they all employ different parts of the electromagnetic spectrum, can thus partially or temporarily disable satellites by disrupting, degrading, or interfering with their communications or other functions. An examination of the legal status of these actions and whether they constitute a use of force must address, among other things, measures employing the electromagnetic spectrum that temporarily jam or otherwise interfere with communications to or from space systems; the provisions of the UN Charter dealing with measures that interrupt communications; and extensive State practice related to electronic jamming.

Electronic Measures Using the Radio Frequency Part of the Electromagnetic Spectrum: Jamming

12. Another major category of counterspace weapons or capabilities consists of electronic measures that temporarily interrupt or interfere with communications to or from space systems, commonly referred to as jamming.[188] These measures, which use the RF region of the electromagnetic spectrum, are often employed in both space and terrestrial applications to interfere with communications. With respect to military space operations, receivers on a satellite (the uplinks) or on the ground station (the downlinks) can be negated by intruding signals.[189] Such electronic

---

[186] 2020 CSIS Threat Assessment (n 173) 3.
[187] ibid ('Lasers can be used to either temporarily "dazzle" or permanently blind mission-critical sensors.').
[188] These measures are often associated with 'electronic warfare', which in space concern weapons that 'use radiofrequency energy to interfere with or jam the communications to or from satellites'. Weeden and Samson (n 6) xxiii.
[189] Wright, Grego, and Gronlund (n 175) 112. Receivers can also be confused by false signals through a cyber technique called 'spoofing' (see para 21). Spoofing is sometimes classified as an electronic measure or a component of 'electronic warfare' because false signals are employed. However, because spoofing primarily involves the transmission of false or misleading data, it is included in the discussion of malicious cyber actions below.

measures represent an important capability relevant to military space operations, since satellites are likely to be highly dependent on electronic communications, as well as ground-based operations that may be harmed when those communications are interrupted. Although these electronic measures can temporarily impede or disrupt one aspect of the functionality of some satellites, they can also be completely reversible. Military space operations that use electronic measures to temporarily interrupt or interfere with communications *generally* do not, however, rise to the level of a use of force.[190] The starting point for legal analysis here begins with the UN Charter, which explicitly categorizes the 'complete or partial interruption of ... telegraphic, radio, and other means of communication' as measures 'not involving the use of armed force'.[191] This language appears to raise the presumption that electronic interruption of radio and other communication to, in, or through space, by itself, does not ordinarily violate the prohibition on the use of force.[192]

13. While it is possible to argue that the drafters of Article 41 of the UN Charter did not envision modern military communication systems and the concept of 'signals', such an argument fails to give due weight to the broad language of the Charter itself, the context in which it was drafted, and subsequent State practice. First, Article 41 itself uses broad, all-encompassing language by referring to 'telegraphic, radio, and *other means of communication*'.[193] Second, the language in Article 41 was adopted by States near the end of a world conflict in which the utility of transmitting and

---

[190] But see para 23 regarding particularly sensitive 'early warning' satellites and related command and control space systems, on which strategic nuclear stability and international peace and security depends.

[191] UN Charter (n 2) art 41. The plain meaning of the term 'communication' is a broad one, generally referring to 'the transmission or exchange of information' without restrictions as to the means that are used: 'Communication, *n.*' definition II(5)(b), *Oxford English Dictionary* (n 174). The phrase 'other means of 'communication' could thus be viewed as encompassing communication over computer networks, leaving the interruption of such communications as being generally outside the scope of the use of force prohibition. Such a conclusion would be consistent with the cyber incident in Estonia in 2007 that effectively shut down a wide variety of computer system communications among banks, universities, government agencies, and corporations across Estonia. See para 16.

[192] One State at State Consultations agreed with the presumption that electromagnetic interferences such as jamming in general do not reach the threshold necessary to constitute a use of force, but it did not believe that art 41 of the UN Charter was the basis for this presumption. Another State noted that while art 41 of the Charter may be a relevant consideration in making an assessment of whether an action constitutes a use of force, in light of all the technical developments since the drafting of the Charter, it may not be appropriate to conclude that the methods referred to in art 41 cannot constitute a use of force where they have the same or similar effects as kinetic methods. Another State emphasized that to completely rule out the possibility of some actions that temporarily interfere with or disrupt space communication could in fact constitute a use of force would create an unacceptable lacuna in the modern use of force framework.

[193] UN Charter (n 2) art 41 (emphasis added). The plain meaning of the term 'communication' is a broad one, generally referring to 'the transmission or exchange of information' without restrictions as to the means that are used: 'Communication, *n.*' definition II(5)(b), *Oxford English Dictionary* (n 174). The phrase 'other means of communication' could thus be viewed as encompassing communication over computer networks, leaving the interruption of such communications as being generally outside the scope of the use of force prohibition. Such a conclusion would be consistent with the cyber incident in Estonia in 2007 that effectively shut down a wide variety of computer system communications among banks, universities, government agencies, and corporations across Estonia. See para 16.

jamming radio communications, including even radio waves that guided remotely controlled weapons, was already well recognized by military forces.[194] Third, as detailed below, States appear to continue to take a permissive view of the legality of measures that interfere with modern military communications and it is difficult to find evidence of any State declaring such measures to be a use of force.[195]

State practice in implementing the UN Charter provides important guidance in interpreting Article 2(4) with respect to electronic measures that interfere with communications with space objects. In spite of extensive evidence of jamming by States directed against the uplinks and downlinks of other State's satellites,[196] the absence of an official protest or complaint by any State that such actions constitute a use of force helps support the conclusion that jamming is not usually a use of force for the purposes of Article 2(4).[197] In the case of jamming communications satellites (particularly global navigation satellite systems (GNSS) satellites), there is considerable contemporary State practice confirming that such acts are in fact being taken by States and that these acts have generated a variety of responses and legal complaints—but no protests or complaints based on those actions constituting a use of force. For example, the US reaction to its GNSS satellites being jammed in the region near North Korea in 2016 was not to assert that a use of force had been taken against the satellites in question but rather the US State Department issued a notice warning ships/aircraft in the vicinity of resulting navigational hazards.[198] Similarly, in 2016 the GNSS signals to an unmanned aerial vehicle (UAV) being used by the Organization for Security and Co-operation in Europe (OSCE) to monitor the ongoing conflict in Ukraine were jammed and as a result the UAV

14.

---

[194] For example, in 1943 the Germans developed a radio-controlled bomb known as the Ruhrstahl X-1. The Allies were able to develop electronic countermeasures that interfered with the radio communication, hence utilizing the electro-magnetic spectrum for counter-action, George Raynor Thompson and Dixie R Harris, *The Signal Corps: The Outcome (Mid 1943 Through 1945)* (US Army in WW II: The Technical Services, CMH Pub 1966) 302 [https://perma.cc/QQ6T-TMT2]. Also widely recognized at the time was a key remote-sensing tool (radar) that utilized pulses of high-frequency electromagnetic waves. Radar system were also, of course, subject to jamming and other electronic countermeasures.

[195] Several States at State Consultations cautioned against interpreting the silence of States as conveying assent in this and other areas (see discussion in Methodology of *Manual*), while not disagreeing that there is a growing practice of numerous States to engage in jamming and spoofing activities. Some States at State Consultations also emphasized that there may be particular circumstances in which States may be likely to regard electronic measures that interrupt critical military communications as a use of force.

[196] For numerous examples of jamming and jamming capabilities in the context of military activities and increasing 'electronic warfare', see Weeden and Samson (n 6). Examples of States jamming radio and television broadcasts are also particularly numerous. See Guilhem Penent (ed), *Governing the Geostationary Orbit: Orbital Slots and Spectrum Use in an Era of Interference* (Ifri 2014) [https://perma.cc/Z4XL-CLQK]; Stephanie Nebehay, 'UN Tells Iran to End Eutelsat Satellite Jamming' *Reuters* (Geneva, 26 March 2010) [https://perma.cc/QU5V-CVCR]; Selding (n 104).

[197] But see para 22 regarding special concerns about interference with particularly sensitive 'early warning' satellites and related command and control systems, on which strategic nuclear stability and international peace and security may depend.

[198] 'US Calls for Caution about Dangers of GPS Jamming by N. Korea' *The Korea Times* (Seoul, 11 April 2016) [https://perma.cc/AFK9-R325].

'began spinning uncontrollably and losing altitude' and apparently crashed. Yet there is no record of any State in the OSCE suggesting that these actions constituted a use of force.[199] After EUTELSAT, a major European satellite operator, filed numerous complaints with the International Telecommunication Union (ITU) regarding interference which appeared to be emanating from Iran in 2010, the ITU publicly condemned Iran for these actions and stated that 'in this case there is evidence that there is a deliberate attempt to block the satellite transmissions' and that Iran should 'eliminate it as a matter of highest priority'.[200] Although Iran was alleged to have violated treaty and other international legal obligations, the affected States did not allege that these continuing acts of jamming constituted a use of force.[201] In some cases, States have even claimed a right under international law to engage in electronic jamming, alleging that the various broadcasts they are responding to are 'illegal transmissions of radio and television'.[202]

Other Capabilities Across the Electromagnetic Spectrum That Temporarily Disrupt, Interfere with, or Degrade Space Systems

15. The presumption that electronic measures, such as jamming, that temporarily interfere with communications (including those between ground stations and satellites) do not generally constitute a use of force seems well founded on the basis of the UN Charter and the practice of States implementing the Charter. The implications of this presumption with respect to the partial or temporary disruption, interference with, or degrading of the functions of space objects may be significant across the entire electromagnetic spectrum, beyond just radio waves and radio communications. At the outset, a useful comparison might be made between the temporary electronic interruption of the communication functions of satellite by a jamming signal that swamps its receiver and the temporary disabling of a satellite's

---

[199] 'Spot Report by OSCE Special Monitoring Mission to Ukraine (SMM): SMM Long-Range Unmanned Aerial Vehicle Crashes Near Contact Line in Donetsk region' (*OSCE*, 19 April 2019) [https://perma.cc/9MVR-3MK7].
[200] Nebehay (n 196) (further noting that although 'Iranian authorities have been jamming foreign satellite broadcasts into their territory since late last year, with broadcasters such as the BBC and Deutsche Welle affected. Iran has not admitted it is sending out these signals....').
[201] Most legal protests against these actions have instead focused on the infringement of freedom of information and expression. See eg Michael de Rosen, 'Letter to Eutelsat Regarding Iranian Government's Jamming of Satellite Broadcasts' (*Human Rights Watch*, 25 June 2010) [https://perma.cc/B8FZ-VEWH] (noting that 'Ezatollah Zarghami, the head of the Islamic Republic of Iran Broadcasting (Iran's state-run broadcast company), publicly acknowledged that his government engages in jamming of foreign broadcast satellites. Reports indicate that Iran is increasingly relying on jamming of foreign media to stifle freedom of information and expression inside the country....').
[202] See eg 'Cuba Denies Jamming Broadcast' *BBC News* (London, 19 June 2003) [https://perma.cc/AQK2-W6AU] (quoting a statement by the Cuban Government that 'Cuba, within its rights, has interfered, interferes and will continue to interfere only the illegal transmissions of radio and television that the government of the United States makes to our country').

optical sensor by the overwhelming light of laser dazzling.²⁰³ These two potential weapon systems, when used to partially or temporarily disrupt, interfere with, or degrade satellite functions, are in fact sometimes both referred to as threats that are 'low-end, non-kinetic and reversible'.²⁰⁴ While there have been some reports and allegations of States using lasers in space against each other, reports of such incidents are fragmentary, uncorroborated, or ambiguous. To date, however, no State has ever claimed that any use of lasers in space has constituted a use of force. While microwave radiation can also partially or temporarily disrupt a satellite's electronics, to date there are no confirmed reports of any hostile use of microwave radiation in space. Unlike potential use of cyber capabilities (discussed below), the potential use of non-kinetic capabilities along the electromagnetic spectrum as weapons in space is a developing area that some States are not yet prepared to may constitute a use of force.²⁰⁵ However in view of the position taken by some States that cyber operations may amount to a use of force (as discussed below), it is at least arguable that non-kinetic methods utilizing the electromagnetic spectrum (eg jamming, lasers) could also amount to a use of force if the effects reached a level similar to the use of armed, physical or kinetic force.

Cyber Capabilities

16. Another category of counterspace weapons is based on cyber capabilities.²⁰⁶ Malicious cyber actions present many challenges for military space operations. Computer worms, viruses, logic bombs, and diverse assortments of malware, corrupted data, and hacking techniques are unlike other instruments, modalities, and measures that may involve the use of force. Rather than directing some destructive mass or energy at a target, malicious cyber acts involve the use or transmission of data to control or otherwise adversely affect computers, machine components, and connected systems or that adversely affect the data resident in or transmitted by these systems. While cyber actions clearly lie outside the physical, armed force on which the use of force prohibition in the UN Charter was founded and are not

---

²⁰³ Wright, Grego, and Gronlund (n 175) 125.
²⁰⁴ Kestutis Paulauskas, 'Space: NATO's Latest Frontier' (NATO Review, 13 March 2020) [https://perma.cc/7QHE-K4R8] (stating that '[t]hreats can be low end, non-kinetic and reversible, for example, jamming and spoofing of communication signals and laser-dazzling sensors').
²⁰⁵ While one State at State Consultations noted that although cyber operations can meet the threshold of a use of force in certain circumstances in and of themselves, that State has not announced a position on the use of other (non-kinetic) means that may amount to armed or physical force. This State noted that this is a developing area of law and State practice, and that it is an open question whether an effects-based approach could properly lead to a conclusion that using other non-kinetic counterspace weapons could amount to a use of force where they have the same or similar effects to armed, physical or kinetic force.
²⁰⁶ Cyber weapons 'use software and network techniques to compromise, control, interfere, or destroy computer systems'. Weeden and Samson (n 6) xxxi.

easily placed in any of the categories of counterspace weapons or capabilities described above, modern military systems (including space systems) are highly dependent on computers and States have thus recognized that their military systems may be damaged or destroyed by cyber actions. In addition, cyber actions may also achieve temporary, reversible effects that are similar to those caused by electronic jamming, lasers, or microwaves when those weapon systems interrupt or interfere with communications or disrupt or degrade other satellite other operations. Such cyber actions thus appear to share many characteristics of the electronic measures that are ordinarily excluded from the concept of a use of force under Article 41 of the UN Charter.

17. State practice to date regarding damaging but temporary, disruptive cyber actions appears to support the conclusion that Article 2(4) and the use of force prohibition is generally not implicated by such actions.[207] For example, in 2007, a massive 'distributed denial-of-service' action crippled Estonian banks, universities, government offices, and media outlets by flooding their computer systems with incoming traffic and knocking related Estonian websites offline.[208] As a result, an enormous amount of information was rendered inaccessible, many machines (like automated teller machines (ATMs)) were no longer able to function, and no communications or other actions could be accomplished through overwhelmed Estonian websites and related computer systems for the several days and in some cases for weeks. The impact of this cyber action went well beyond merely interrupting communications and instead included the temporary crippling of important government and commercial functions in Estonia. Although the Estonian Government appealed to the North Atlantic Treaty Organization (NATO) for assistance, the Estonian defence minister, Jaak Aaviksoo, observed that '[n]ot a single NATO defence minister would define a cyber-attack as a clear military action at present'.[209] While such highly disruptive cyber actions with damaging economic consequences

---

[207] Such a determination depends on the target and a holistic evaluation of the circumstances. For example, temporary disruption of key military systems may be part of, or a precursor to, a larger use of force in space or in other domains.

[208] Dimitar Kostadinov, 'Estonia: To Black Out an Entire Country—Part One' *INFOSEC* (1 October 2013) [https://perma.cc/4PAU-CVB9]. The source of this massive hostile action was difficult to attribute, as it originated from so many countries and involved many hijacked zombie computers and botnets.

[209] Ian Traynor, 'Russia Accused of Unleashing Cyberwar to Disable Estonia' *The Guardian* (Brussels, 17 May 2007). [https://perma.cc/YT8C-RQTZ]. This conclusion by NATO Defence Ministers came even after a spokesman for the Estonian Defence Minister compared the cyber 'attacks' against Estonia to those launched against America on 11 September 2001. This scenario was greatly complicated by the inability to clearly attribute this hostile cyber action to the Russian Government. It should also be noted that NATO has since observed that '[c]yber threats to the security of the Alliance are complex, destructive, coercive, and becoming ever more frequent' and that 'Allies recognise that the impact of significant malicious cumulative cyber activities might, in certain circumstances, be considered as amounting to an armed attack'. Brussels Summit Communiqué, issued by the Heads of State and Government participating in the meeting of the North Atlantic Council in Brussels, 14 June 2021 [https://perma.cc/TL2D-RA44] (further reaffirming that 'a decision as to when a cyber attack would lead to the invocation of Article 5 would be taken by the North Atlantic Council on a case-by-case basis').

could be characterized as cyber vandalism, cyber subversion, or cyber terrorism (or, in extreme situations involving the significant disruption of a State's financial or economic system, may even constitute illegal intervention, see Rule 20: Non-Intervention Principle), State practice to date has not established that any specific cyber actions have reached the threshold for a use of force. The E-Minister of Estonia ultimately described this 2007 cyber incident in Estonia not as a use of force but as a 'cyber riot'.[210]

18. Some weapons systems used during the Second World War, and a diverse assortment of modern weapon systems, are controlled remotely by electronic means and this phenomenon has now become a common aspect of many types of military technologies. Space technology is particularly dependent on remotely controlled systems, as few objects in space are actually piloted by humans present in spacecraft. If cyber capabilities, such as hacking into a computer system, enable an unauthorized State to take control of another state's space object or weapon and then direct it against another State's space systems, such an action would appear to clearly qualify as a use of force based on the hijacking and use of the weapon itself. This analysis is based on a basic recognition of the use of remote-control systems to operate many modern weapon systems and space technologies.[211] A closely related question is whether the hijacking of the satellite, by itself, qualifies as a use of force. Although it appears that no State has, to date, successfully undertaken such an activity or made such a claim, the ability to hijack a satellite by cyber means has clearly been demonstrated.[212] It is also possible that even the momentary unauthorized control of a satellite can effectively destroy it or render it useless, particularly if this moves the satellite out of its designated orbit.[213] In light of the unique characteristics of space technology, the space environment, and its dominant reliance on remotely controlled systems, a strong argument could be made that such an action represents more than mere interference and could rise to the level of a use of force. To date, however, no State practice exists on this point.

---

[210] See Andy Greenberg, 'When Cyber Terrorism Becomes State Censorship' *Forbes* (New York, 14 May 2008) [https://perma.cc/K6C3-3JHX].

[211] In contrast to overwhelming the receivers on a satellite or on the ground with intruding signals by jamming them or confusing or spoofing them with false signals, hijacking the control of a satellite is a much more difficult process. All satellites require a link to and from the ground to perform 'telemetry, tracking, and command' (TT&C) functions. See Wright, Grego, and Gronlund (n 175) 112 (further noting that '[t]he TT&C system operates the satellite and evaluates the health of the satellite's other systems; it is therefore essential. Although interfering with the TT&C channel could cause a great deal of damage, these channels are usually well protected [with encryption and encoding]).'

[212] See eg US-China Economic and Security Review Commission, '2011 Report to Congress' (US Government Printing Office, November 2011) p 216 [https://perma.cc/7GEW-KDFX] ('On October 22, 2008, Terra EOS [Earth observation system] AM–1, a National Aeronautics and Space Administration-managed program for earth observation, experienced nine or more minutes of interference. The responsible party achieved all steps required to command the satellite but did not issue commands.').

[213] See eg 'NASA Computers Hacked by Intruders' *Via Satellite* (1 December 2008) [https://perma.cc/6JEL-C58A]. (Reportedly, '[o]n one occasion, an American-German deep-space-peering satellite, ROSAT, was hacked and turned toward the sun to make it useless').

19. Cyber actions may employ computers, information systems, and data to mislead, confuse or deceive humans (including leaders of governments and military organizations, managers, and operators of machines and other technologies), transmit propaganda, and misinformation, or support psychological operations to subvert governments. These actions can also be accomplished by other, traditional means (radio, TV, publications, or other forms of communication) and do not by themselves constitute a use of force when they are part of a military operation. Labelling any of these information operations as a 'weapon' or colloquially referring to their use as an 'cyberattack' does not make their use qualify as a use of force.[214] The more that a malicious cyber action affecting a human operator resembles an information or psychological operation, the less likely that cyber action qualifies as a use of force.

20. Cyber actions may manipulate or destroy data in machines and computers in such a way as to cause permanent damage to connected systems or result in death, injuries, or destruction. These capabilities raise challenging questions regarding the use of force. As noted, an action against information transmitted by cyber means does not resemble the conventional, physical, or armed force which formed the basis of the use of force prohibition in the UN Charter. However, several States have, prospectively at least, taken the position that even though cyber actions are not traditional, physical instruments employed as armed force, they nonetheless could in some cases qualify as a use of force based on their similar effects. For example, the Government of the Netherlands has stated that it believes that 'cyber operations can fall within the scope of the prohibition of the use of force, particularly when the effects of the operation are comparable to those of a conventional act of violence covered by the prohibition'.[215] The Government of Australia has

---

[214] In analysing the legality of the threat or use of nuclear weapons, the ICJ observed that the UN Charter 'neither expressly prohibits, nor permits, the use of any specific weapon, including nuclear weapons' and that the provisions of the UN Charter will 'apply to any use of force, regardless of the weapons employed'. *Nuclear Weapons* Advisory Opinion (n 181) 244. However, this does not mean that any type of technology or action (including cyber technologies and information operations) can be categorized as a use of force merely by labelling that action as an 'attack' or the technology as a 'weapon'. Such an argument misreads both the UN Charter and the ICJ's opinion in this case. The specific highly destructive, physical capabilities of nuclear weapons as an instrument when employed as a use of force underlies this opinion, not a theory that any technique, device, or instrument that is referred to as a weapon qualifies as a use of force when it is employed. The ICJ explicitly states in this regard that, in order 'correctly to apply to the present case the Charter law on the use of force the Court, it is imperative for the Court to take account of the unique characteristics of nuclear weapons and in particular their destructive capacity, their capacity to cause untold human suffering, and their ability to cause damage to generations to come'. ibid.

[215] Submission by the Netherlands, Official Compendium of National Contributions (n 120) 58. See also Finnish Position Paper (n 126) (noting that 'most commentators agree that a cyberattack which is comparable to an armed attack in terms of its extent and impacts equates to an armed attack, and self-defence is justified as response' but also acknowledging that 'there is currently no established definition of a cyberattack that would amount to 'use of force' in the sense of art 2(4) of the UN Charter, or 'an armed attack' in the sense of art 51).

indicated that if the damage caused by a cyber operation is 'equivalent to a traditional armed attack, then the inherent right to self-defence is engaged'.[216] Along somewhat similar lines, the US Department of Defense (DoD) has concluded that 'cyber operations may in certain circumstances constitute uses of force within the meaning of Article 2(4) of the Charter of the United Nations and customary international law. For example, if cyber operations cause effects that, if caused by traditional physical means, would be regarded as a use of force under *jus ad bellum*, then such cyber operations would likely also be regarded as a use of force'.[217] The US position is nuanced, however, emphasizing that in assessing whether an event constitutes a use of force in or through cyberspace, 'we must evaluate factors including the context of the event, the actor perpetrating the action (recognizing challenging issues of attribution in cyberspace), the target and location, effects and intent, among other possible issues'.[218] NATO has also affirmed that 'cyber defence is part of NATO's core task of collective defence' but further notes that 'a decision as to when a cyber attack would lead to the invocation of Article 5 [on collective self-defence] would be taken by the North Atlantic Council on a case-by-case basis'.[219]

21. Based on the positions taken by several States regarding possible future conflicts, it may be argued that an interpretation of Article 2(4) is emerging—in the context of cyber operations and potentially in some other operations—that would be based more heavily on consequences and not on physical, armed force and associated weapon systems or instruments.[220] This view would hold that a military space

---

[216] Submission by Australia, Official Compendium of National Contributions (n 120) 6 (further noting that 'if a cyber activity—alone or in combination with a physical operation—results in, or presents an imminent threat of, damage equivalent to a traditional armed attack, then the inherent right to self-defence is engaged'). This Australian statement presumes, of course, that an armed attack represents the 'most grave form of the use of force' (see Rule 23: Armed Attack). The Government of France has also 'reaffirm[ed] that a cyberattack may constitute an armed attack within the meaning of Article 51 of the United Nations Charter, if it is of a scale and severity comparable to those resulting from the use of physical force' while also noting that '[i]n the light of these criteria, the question of whether a cyberattack constitutes armed aggression will be examined on a case-by-case basis having regard to the specific circumstances'. French Position Paper (n 129) para 1.2.1.
[217] US DoD Law of War Manual (n 11) para 16.3.1.
[218] Harold Hongju Koh, 'International Law in Cyberspace: Remarks as Prepared for Delivery to the USCYBERCOM Inter-Agency Legal Conference' (US Department of State, 18 September 2012) [https://perma.cc/QWA6-9M3F]. It should be noted that Mr Koh emphasized 'some clear-cut cases' of hostile cyber actions, such as a malicious computer code opening the gates of a dam and causing the same physical effects of a bomb breaking a dam and flooding a civilian population—while at the same time noting '[a]s you all know, however, there are other types of cyber actions that do not have a clear kinetic parallel, which raise profound questions about exactly what we mean by "force" '. Mr Koh further noted that only 'those cyber activities that *proximately* result in death, injury, or significant destruction would likely be viewed as a use of force' (emphasis added).
[219] NATO, 'Wales Summit Declaration: Issued by the Heads of State and Government Participating in the Meeting of the North Atlantic Council in Wales' (Press Release, 5 September 2014) para 72 [https://perma.cc/MAF4-GD9L].
[220] Tallinn Manual 2.0 (n 125) Rule 69 ('A cyber operation constitutes a use of force when its scale and effects are comparable to non-cyber operations rising to the level of a use of force.').

operation may constitute a use of force in the cyber context when it causes injuries or deaths of persons, or damage to or destruction of an object.[221] Although several States have indeed declared that future cyber actions resulting in effects similar to those caused by traditional physical uses of force or violence may qualify as a use of force prohibited under Article 2(4), there is not yet any official State practice unambiguously supporting this position with respect to any particular cyber incident.[222] Even in those situations in which hostile cyber actions have apparently resulted in significant permanent damage, no State has officially claimed, to date, that it has been the victim of a use of force or officially characterized those actions as a use of force.[223] Similarly, to date, no State has invoked Article 51 of the UN Charter and notified the UN Security Council that it has been a victim of an armed attack that was accomplished solely by cyber means. A few States have also objected to this interpretation that a cyber action can give rise to self-defence.[224] Cyber actions may also present great challenges in attributing conduct to States, and the proximate cause of damages associated with cyber incidents may be difficult to determine. The increasing frequency of State-sponsored malicious, damaging cyber actions that have not been characterized by any State as a use of force suggests that there may be a high threshold for such a finding or characterization.[225]

---

[221] ibid Rule 11, para 8 ('Acts that injure or kill persons or damage or destroy objects are unambiguously uses of force' while noting in Rule 13 that the required harm 'must be significant').

[222] Several States at State Consultations emphasized the difficulty in assigning legal significance to silence or inaction and pointed to the multitude of reasons that may, in practice, influence a State's determination on whether to make public comment on the consistency of the conduct of other States with international law. One State noted that while it may be the case that the absence of statements indicates that States do not consider an action a breach of international law, such a conclusion does not inevitably or necessarily follow.

[223] For example, even though the Iranian Government admitted that the so-called Stuxnet virus 'succeeded in creating problems for a limited number of our centrifuges', it did not characterize this hostile cyber act as a use of force or as an armed attack, but rather as 'a bad thing'. Mark Clayton, 'Stuxnet: Ahmadinejad Admits Cyberweapon Hit Iran Nuclear Program' *The Christian Science Monitor* (30 November 2010) [https://perma.cc/VP5U-3BJ8] (quoting the Iranian President, Mahmoud Ahmadinejad); 'Iran Accuses Siemens Over Stuxnet Virus Attack' TEHRAN (*Reuters*, 17 April 2011) [https://perma.cc/NCR3-D7PN] (quoting Gholamreza Jalali, head of Iran's civilian defence, as saying that '[t]his was a hostile act against us which could have brought major human and material damages had it not been encountered promptly').

[224] See eg Declaration by Miguel Rodríguez, Representative of Cuba, Final Session of Group of Governmental Experts on Developments in the Field of Information and Telecommunications in the Context of International Security. (New York, 23 June 2017) [https://perma.cc/CZY7-356N] 2 ('We consider unacceptable the formulations contained in the draft, aimed to establish equivalence between the malicious use of ICTs and the concept of "armed attack", as provided for in Article 51 of the Charter, which attempts to justify the alleged applicability in this context of the right to self-defense'). China and Russia have reportedly taken similar positions. See 'Dispute Along Cold War Lines Led to Collapse at UN Cyberwarfare Talks' *The Guardian* (London, 23 August 2017) [https://perma.cc/T36V-V38Y] ('Thirteen years of negotiations came to an abrupt end in June, it has emerged, because of the right to self-defence in the face of an attack.').

[225] Differing views with respect to this phenomenon point to the developing nature of international law related to hostile cyber acts. One State at State Consultations disagreed that the failure by any State to ever characterize a particular State-sponsored hostile cyber action as a use of force

One malicious cyber action that continues to be used extensively by States is   **22.**
the sending of false, misleading information through 'spoofing', particularly
with respect to transmitting false GNSS signals.[226] However, to date, no malicious act of spoofing has been publicly characterized as a use of force or an
armed attack by any State.[227] Thus, to date, the frequently occurring, temporary distortion of satellite communications by spoofing continues to be dealt
with by States inside a legal framework that does not involve a use of force
under the UN Charter, but instead in a manner similar to the treatment of the
frequent jamming of satellite communications. It is possible that even limited,
temporary spoofing may have adverse, indirect consequences for navigation
and transportation systems on Earth. These consequences may include inconvenience, delays, economic losses, and possibly even accidents or other occur-
rences that result in injury or loss of life. To date, no State has claimed that
the damages caused by a specific spoofing incident constitutes a use of force
or an armed attack. However, based on a purely effects-based cyber analysis,
serious damages that includes injury or loss of life that are clearly caused by
a spoofing incident could give rise to a claim of a use of force or an armed attack. Nonetheless, it may be difficult to establish in a particular incident or
accident that spoofing was the proximate cause of the accident and resulting
damages, particularly considering back-up or subsidiary navigation systems
that are available to many different types of aircraft, ships, and other transportation systems.

suggests that there may be a high threshold for such a finding or characterization. This State's view
was based on the many reasons that States may have to be reticent to take such a position. Another
view focuses on the many years of increasingly frequent and damaging State-supported cyber actions in which States have generally described these actions as only 'irresponsible' and not unlawful.
In addition, discord has accompanied efforts by States to agree on the precise legal characterization
of malicious, damaging cyber acts supported by States. To this point, such efforts have yielded only
general, recommended 'norms' of responsible behaviour. See 'Report of the Group of Governmental
Experts on Advancing Responsible State Behaviour in Cyberspace in the Context of International
Security' (14 July 2021) UN Doc A/76/135.

[226] Spoofing of GNSS signals is 'the broadcast of false signals with the intent that the victim receiver
will misinterpret them as authentic signals. The victim might deduce a false position fix, a false clock
offset, or both. A coordinated sequence of false position or timing fixes could induce dangerous behaviour by a user platform that believed the false fixes.' Mark L Psiaki and Todd E Humphreys, 'GNSS
Spoofing and Detection' (2016) 104(6) *Proceedings of the Institute of Electrical and Electronics Engineers*
1 [https://perma.cc/QZ97-66N2]. The authors further note how GPS spoofing has been used in a variety of malicious ways, including sending a hovering drone into an unplanned dive and steering a yacht
off course. For a detailed review of numerous recent examples of spoofing practices, apparently conducted by States, see generally Weeden and Samson (n 6).
[227] This is in spite of speculation with respect to several incidents involving the possibility of sophis-
ticated interference and spoofing of satellite-based command and control signals or GPS signals with
respect to military UAVs. See eg Weeden and Samson (n 6) 08–04 (discussing the downing in late 2011
of a stealthy US RQ-170 Sentinel UAV in Iran).

Early Warning Satellites and Related Command and Communication Systems

23. As discussed above, actions like the following may not ordinarily rise to the use of force: temporary disruption or interference with the communication systems or other functions of a space object by electronic jamming and spoofing; the temporary dazzling of a space object's optical sensors by laser; the partial or temporary disruption, degrading, or manipulating of a space object's functions by spoofing or cyber means; and the partial or temporary disruption or degrading of electronic systems by microwave radiation.[228] Some States may argue, however, that this conclusion should not apply to temporarily disrupting, interfering with, or degrading the functions of satellites that provide an early warning of nuclear ballistic missile launches, related command and communication systems, and hotline communications satellites links. This argument would be based on the irreplaceable and fundamental role these assets may play in alerting a State to a nuclear weapons attack. For example, satellites providing links to hotline communications may play an important role in averting an unintended crisis. The possibility also exists that a State might interpret interference with these capabilities as an incipient nuclear, armed attack posing an existential threat to that State. More broadly, these systems serve an important stabilizing function in maintaining international peace and security. In some cases, States have already thus shown a willingness to restrict any type of interference, including measures far less than the use of force, with respect to satellites that perform mutually beneficial, stabilizing verification functions related to arms control.[229] For example, over the course of many years, the United States and the Soviet Union/Russia recognized the important arms control functions that surveillance satellites could perform and entered into agreements to protect those satellites from any interference by the other party.[230] Similarly, early

---

[228] It should be noted, however, that because of the physical characteristics of the space environment, the use of some weapon systems to cause even the temporary loss of functionality of a satellite may result in its effective incapacitation or destruction by moving it out of its designated orbit and potentially destroying that satellite or rendering it permanently functionally useless, thus constituting a use of force.

[229] See eg Treaty on the Limitation of Anti-Ballistic Missile Systems (USA–USSR) (entered into force 3 October 1972) 944 UNTS 13, art XII(1); Treaty on the Elimination of their Intermediate-range and Shorter-range Missiles (USA–USSR) (entered into force 1 June 1988) 1657 UNTS 2, art XII(1); Treaty between the US and the USSR on the Reduction and Limitation of Strategic Offensive Arms (START I Treaty) (entered into force 5 December 1994) UN Doc CD/1192, art XII(1); New START Treaty (n 68) art X(1)(b) ('each Party undertakes ... not to interfere with the national technical means of verification of the other Party operating in accordance with this Article').

[230] This recognition was, however, accomplished via separate treaties, not as an interpretation of art 2(4). Thus, it could be argued that these two States felt it necessary to provide this explicit protection to NTM satellites because they did not think that art 2(4) was sufficient protection. In addition, although 'National Technical Means' was understood to denote relevant surveillance satellites, the protected satellites were never explicitly identified. Furthermore, the term 'interference' was not defined.

warning satellites and related command and communication systems play a fundamental, critical role in maintaining international peace and security, a reality explicitly recognized by several States and emphasized in their national security policies.[231]

---

[231] See Government of the Russian Federation, 'Russian Federation Military Doctrine' *Nezavisimaya Gazeta* (22 April 2000) released at 'Russia's Military Doctrine' (*Arms Control Association*) Section I.5 [https://perma.cc/B9RD-2PSZ] (noting that the 'main external threats' to Russia include 'actions aimed at undermining global and regional stability, not least by ... disrupting the functioning of strategic nuclear forces, missile-attack early warning, antimissile defense, and space monitoring systems'); Government of the Russian Federation, 'The Military Doctrine of the Russian Federation' (No Pr.-2976, 25 December 2014) released by the Embassy of the Russian Federation to the United Kingdom of Great Britain and Northern Ireland (tr), 'The Military Doctrine of the Russian Federation' (Press Release, 29 June 2015) Sec II.14.b [https://perma.cc/GD2S-VZ4P] (noting that the 'main military threats' to Russia include 'disruption [of] the functioning of its strategic nuclear forces, missile warning systems, systems of outer space monitoring'); Working Paper submitted by Canadian delegation to the Conference on Disarmament, 'Terminology Relevant to Arms Control and Outer Space' (16 July 1968) UN Doc CD/716, arguing that the use of military satellites for arms control verification is 'inherently stabilizing' and that '[w]ithout such an application of the use of military satellites for verification purposes, many significant international arms control agreements would not be possible. Other military uses of space (e.g. early warning, communications) can also be viewed as stabilizing'); Panel Discussion with Heather Wilson, US Secretary of the Air Force (Reagan National Defense Forum, 2 December 2017) 36.14 <https://www.c-span.org/video/?438064-2/national-security-space-strategy> accessed 22 February 2022, https://perma.cc/F7JL-CCRJ ('The United States heretofore has not had a declaratory policy with respect to space, but I think it's probably time as a country that we start to talk about this. That if one of our satellites, particularly our satellites that provide indication and warning of a missile launch, or that provide command and control for our national command authority, that if another country interferes with those satellites, that we would consider that to be a hostile act and we would respond. Not necessarily in the same domain, we respond across domains.').

Rule 22
Threat of Force

A State shall not engage in activities, including military space activities, that constitute a threat of force in violation of the UN Charter.

Overview of Legal Basis of Rule

1. This Rule is derived from the same sources of international law underlying the prohibition on the use of force (see Rule 21: Use of Force) and, therefore, equally applies to any activities in the exploration and use of outer space and is subject to the same exceptions. A threat of force is unlawful only when the execution of the threat would be unlawful; however, if the contemplated action would be lawful, then the threat to undertake that action would ordinarily be lawful too.[232] For example, if State A threatens to destroy military communications satellites of State B in the lawful exercise of the right of self-defence, this threat would not per se amount to a breach insofar as the threatened forcible action would comport with the restrictions that international law places on the exercise of the right of self-defence (see Rule 26: Self-Defence and Rule 27: Collective Self-Defence).

Application of Rule

2. An unlawful threat of force will occur only where there is a threat of a definite use of force. In the *Nuclear Weapons* Advisory Opinion, the International Court of Justice contrasted such a particular threat of force from the mere 'inference of preparedness' to use weapons (in the context of nuclear deterrence).[233] The Court explained that it is the 'credible' intention to use force, if necessary, that makes a policy of deterrence effective and that such credibility to use force in self-defence is not equivalent to an unlawful threat to use force.[234] In other words, a threat of the use of force must be sufficiently definite to amount to a threat. For this reason, the

---

[232] *Nuclear Weapons* Advisory Opinion (n 181) paras 47–48.
[233] ibid para 48.
[234] ibid ('Possession of nuclear weapons may indeed justify an inference of preparedness to use them. In order to be effective, the policy of deterrence, by which those States possessing or under the umbrella of nuclear weapons seek to discourage military aggression by demonstrating that it will serve no purpose, necessitates that the intention to use nuclear weapons be credible.')

existence of a national space defence policy, even if viewed as adversarial, would not be deemed as a breach of the prohibition unless it went so far as to make a definite threat of force against a State or States in violation of the UN Charter.

3. A threat necessarily involves a State's words and actions communicating, through any of several various methods, an intention to undertake an unlawful use of force.[235] What is required for a threat of force is that, in the totality of the circumstances, the actions of a State communicate an intention to undertake a definite, unlawful use of force.[236] A threat of force thus requires coercive intent or purpose on the part of a State in directing actions against another State.[237]

4. Accordingly, a State conducting research into ASAT technologies, developing missile defences or laser tracking stations, or developing an ASAT capability is not necessarily considered to be threatening the use of force. Similarly, the intentional placement of a weapon in space, including a satellite with co-orbital ASAT capabilities or with on-orbit servicing capabilities that could be used for hostile acts against other space objects, would not—on their own—amount to prohibited threats of force because they demonstrate only capacity and do not communicate an intent to use unlawful force. Further, the demonstration by a State of its military space capabilities, such as conducting an anti-satellite missile test against its own space object (whether this involves merely 'a close fly-by' or an actual impact) is not likely—of itself—to communicate an intent to undertake a particular unlawful use of force against another State and thus is unlikely to amount to an illegal threat of force. In this regard it should be noted that no State has objected to an anti-satellite weapon test by another State against its own space object on the basis that such a test is a threat or use of force.

---

[235] *Guyana v Suriname* (Award) [2007] PCA 2004-04, paras 435, 439, 484 ('The Tribunal is of the view that the order given by Major Jones to the rig [to leave the area or 'face the consequences'] constituted an explicit threat that force might be used if the order was not complied with' and '[t]he Tribunal finds that Surname's [sic] threat of force in a disputed area, while also threatening international peace and security, jeopardised the reaching of a final delimitation agreement.'). See also Brownlie (n 157) 364 (defining a threat as 'an express or implied promise by a government to resort to force conditional on non-acceptance of certain demands of that government').

[236] In particular, conducting military exercises near a State's border, patrolling waters off a State's coast with warships, and undertaking paratrooper exercises in proximity to another State, were held not to amount to a threat of force in *Nicaragua* Judgment (n 115) paras 92, 227.

[237] See eg Oliver Dörr and Albrecht Randelzhofer, 'Article 2(4)' in Simma and others (eds) (n 159) 218 ('the threat of force forbidden by Art. 2 (4) requires a coercive intent directed towards specific behaviour on the part of another State'); 'Letter dated 20 June 1995 from the Minister of Foreign Affairs of the French Republic' (20 June 1995) submitted to the ICJ in association with *Nuclear Weapons* Advisory Opinion (n 181) 25 [https://perma.cc/L339-4LHZ] (stating that the prohibition of the threat of the use of force must be targeted to coerce a state to act differently to how it would have freely chosen— 'coercition pour amener un Etat à une conduite ou à des actes différents de ceux qu'il pouvait librement choisir'); UN Special Committee on Principles of International Law concerning Friendly Relations and Co-operation among States, 'Summary Record of the 19th Meeting' (21 March 1966) UN Doc A/AC.125/SR.19, p 7 (Madagascar) (stating that the threat must be made 'for the purpose of intimidating a State into changing its policies').

5. However, it is possible that—considered in light of the surrounding circumstances—a variety of actions may communicate the intent to make an unlawful threat to use force. For example, the firing of an ASAT weapon by State A that passes very close to State B's satellite—but with no physical impact—may amount to a threat of force if a reasonable observer can conclude, given the totality of circumstances with respect to the relations between these States involved, that this action communicates to State B that an unlawful use of force would be directed against it.[238]

6. There is an inherent grey area regarding which combinations of circumstances can be properly viewed as a communication of an intent to undertake a particular unlawful use of force. As an example, the mere intentional placement of a potentially hostile object in proximity to the space object of another State[239] would not ordinarily amount to a threat of force (because it does not communicate a clear intent to undertake an unlawful use of force). Thus, positioning a satellite in low Earth orbit (LEO) to create repeating conjunctions (close approaches), or keeping a satellite in geostationary orbit (GEO) in proximity to another satellite (eg keeping a station 100 km away, and maintaining that spacing notwithstanding the target satellite's own station-keeping manoeuvres) would not—alone—ordinarily amount to a threat of force. However, other factors, such as conjunctions that create a serious risk of collision, may change this legal assessment. Another factor may arise in other contexts: if the close approach occurs at a time of increased tensions between the two States, then it is more likely to be (correctly) interpreted as a threat. In addition, the intentional placement of a space object in close proximity to sensitive ballistic missile early warning satellites and related command and communication systems (that may play a critical role in maintaining international peace and security and in averting a nuclear conflict),[240] may lead some States to conclude that there is a threat of a particular unlawful use of force. It is cautioned, however, that this Rule should not be applied as justification for establishing and enforcing an exclusion ('keep-out') zone around any particular space object or category of space objects (see Rule 16: Zones) or in any other manner that violates the freedom of use, exploration, and access in space (see Rule 1: Freedom of Use, Access, Exploration, and Scientific Investigation and Principles of Cooperation and Rule 2: Non-Appropriation of Outer Space and Celestial Bodies).

7. It is the threat of an unlawful use of force itself that is prohibited. Accordingly, it does not matter whether the threat achieves its intended outcome(s) (if any), nor

---

[238] The firing of an ASAT weapon that nearly hits a targeted satellite may, if it was intended to hit the targeted satellite, also constitute a use of force, and not just a threat of force (see Rule 21: Use of Force); it may, of course, be impossible for the operators of the targeted satellite to tell whether the attacker has missed accidentally or on purpose.

[239] Such placement, however, may constitute harmful interference or a violation of due regard under art IX of the OST (n 3). See Rule 17: Due Regard and Rule 18: Harmful Interference.

[240] See Rule 21: Use of Force, para 22.

whether the threatened conduct materializes. For example, if State A threatened to use a laser to damage State B's satellites that provide State B's military forces with positioning, navigation, and timing (PNT) signals, in an attempt to cause State B to cancel planned military exercises, this would amount to a breach, even if State B in fact went ahead with the exercises, and irrespective of whether State A in fact undertook the threatened activity.

8. There may be some basis to argue that there is no threat of force when a State makes a 'threat' but is manifestly lacking any capability to make good its threat, or where a State clearly has no intention of carrying out threats, such as threats that might be made for purely domestic political reasons. With respect to threats of aggression, the International Law Commission (ILC) has observed that a State must have 'good reason to believe' that an unlawful use of force against it is being 'seriously contemplated',[241] and that 'mere passing verbal excesses' was excluded.[242] For example, a threat by State A to 'obliterate all of State B's satellites' would not amount to an unlawful threat of force if it was known (with certainty) that State A had no capability to in fact carry out an attack that could inflict significant damage on any of B's satellites or that State's A's statements constituted purely excessive political rhetoric.

---

[241] *Report of the International Law Commission on the Work of its Forty-First Session* (UN GAOR Supp No 10, United Nations 1989) UN Doc A/44/10.
[242] ibid.

Rule 23
Armed Attack

A State shall not engage in an activity, including one that is from, to, or within space, that constitutes an armed attack in violation of the UN Charter.

Overview of Legal Basis of Rule

1. An 'armed attack' is a prohibited use of force and is referred to Article 51 of the UN Charter, which recognizes the inherent right of individual or collective self-defence 'if an armed attack occurs' against a UN Member (see Rule 26: Self-Defence). Article 51 reflects customary international law.[243] International law, including the UN Charter, is expressly made applicable to space by the OST.[244] An 'armed attack' thus represents a critically important prohibition in international law with respect to military space activities. This Rule is without prejudice to the right of a State to use force in response to an armed attack under Article 51 of the UN Charter or pursuant to a UN Security Council Resolution under Chapter VII of the UN Charter. It is important to note that this Rule and Rule 26: Self Defence address only the *jus ad bellum*, the circumstances under which it would be lawful (or not) to initiate an armed conflict. Other rules in this *Manual* deal with an 'attack' in the *jus in bello*, the law governing the conduct of hostilities (see Part III: Military Space Operations During Armed Conflict).

2. An 'incipient armed attack' is encompassed in the prohibition against an armed attack and is discussed in Rule 26: Self-Defence.

A 'Use of Force' Is the First Key Underlying Requirement in Identifying an 'Armed Attack'

3. While the term 'armed attack' is not defined in the UN Charter, it is generally understood to comprise the 'most grave forms of the use of force'.[245] This means that the use of force is a fundamental term in the context of military space activities and that the determination of what constitutes a 'use of force' is the first,

---

[243] *Nicaragua* Judgment (n 115) paras 176, 193.
[244] OST (n 3).
[245] *Nicaragua* Judgment (n 115) para 191.

foundational step in determining the existence of an armed attack in space or in any other domain (see Rule 21: Use of Force). The next step must address whether the use of force in question amounts to a 'most grave' form of the use of force (see 'gravity threshold', paragraphs 7–10).

4. Notwithstanding the widely held view articulated by the ICJ that there is a required gravity threshold for finding the existence of an armed attack, the United States has argued that 'the inherent right of self-defence *potentially* applies against *any* illegal use of force'.[246] In practice, however, in those instances in which the United States has resorted to the use of force in the exercise of self-defence, it has ordinarily done so on the basis of responding to what it has characterized as an armed attack under Article 51 of the UN Charter, without arguing that any use of force qualifies as an armed attack or that a low threshold for the use of force is sufficient.

5. Before undertaking an analysis of precisely what satisfies the 'gravity threshold' for an armed attack and then addressing other requirements for an armed attack, a determination must first be made regarding whether the underlying action in question constitutes a use of force. As discussed in Rule 21: Use of Force, the UN Charter's original, foundational focus on the prohibition of physical, armed force closely corresponds with many modern counterspace weapon systems that rely on kinetic energy to deliver significant mass to destroy targets. In space, these weapons can include missiles, projectiles, or any other object that can be shot, manoeuvred, or launched from Earth, space, celestial bodies, or from other objects in space.[247] These weapon systems include direct-ascent ASAT weapons that strike satellites on a trajectory that intersects the targeted space object without placing the interceptor into orbit, as well as co-orbital ASATs that are first placed into orbit and can then be manoeuvred to strike or damage targets in a variety of ways, including via robotic arms that are capable of manipulating other space objects to prevent them from functioning properly. In addition to conventional weapons, counterspace weapons and capabilities can include WMDs, particularly nuclear weapons, which possess enormous destructive power even in space. The use of any these weapon systems can clearly qualify as a use of force and an armed attack. Other types of counterspace weapons and capabilities are 'directed energy weapons',[248] which include high-energy lasers, high-powered microwave weapons, and electromagnetic

---

[246] US DoD Law of War Manual (n 11) para 1.11.5.2. (emphasis added).
[247] They are sometimes referred to as 'kinetic kill weapons' since 'the kinetic energy of the fast-moving weapon and/or target provides the energy to destroy the target'. Wright, Grego, and Gronlund (n 175) 5, fn 1. As discussed in Rule 21: Use of Force, weapons that rely on kinetic energy include both hit-to-kill mechanisms that collide with a target and also fragments and other materials that are propelled by explosive devices, both nuclear and conventional (although the blast effect created by nuclear weapons is not present in space, given the lack of atmosphere).
[248] 'Directed energy' is an umbrella term covering technologies that produce concentrated electromagnetic energy and atomic and subatomic particles (see Rule 21: Use of Force). Directed energy weapons are able to transfer destructive energy to targets without transporting significant mass.

pulse (EMP) weapons.[249] These weapons employ the destructive capabilities of different parts of the electromagnetic spectrum to cause physical damages similar to those caused by conventional, physical armed force. Considering that computer-dependent systems and complex technologies characterize most space activities, hostile cyber actions also represent a considerable threat to satellites and all military space activities, and several States have recognized that some cyber actions could constitute a use of force in any domain based on their ability to cause damaging effects that are equivalent to those caused by traditional, physical, armed force (see Rule 21: Use of Force, paragraphs 15–22). As discussed below, the emphasis that some States and commentators place on the severity of the effects of cyber actions places less focus on the nature or type of action involved. However, the damages caused by a cyber action must still be similar or equivalent to the type of damages caused by traditional, physical armed force to qualify as a use of force.

6. Many unfriendly or harmful actions that States engage in—such as adverse economic measures, espionage, theft/exfiltration of data, actions resulting in purely monetary losses, misinformation and psychological operations, and political and diplomatic pressure—do not, by themselves qualify as a use of force.[250] Similarly, the UN Charter lists various measures (in addition to economic measures) that do not constitute the use of armed force, such as electronic measures that result in the 'complete or partial interruption of telegraphic, radio, and other means of communication'.[251] Furthermore, State practice indicates that jamming radio signals has become a common practice employed by military forces[252] that has not, to date, been characterized by States as a use of force or an armed attack.[253] Thus, it is likely that the use of the RF part of the electromagnetic spectrum to temporarily or partially disrupt or jam communications with satellites, as well other similar types of interference with communications, will generally not qualify as a use of force or as an armed attack. Arguably, a similar approach may be generally appropriate with respect to other non-kinetic reversible counterspace weapons that employ other parts of the electromagnetic spectrum in low-energy mode that cause temporary

---

[249] As discussed in Rule 21: Use of Force, there is no confirmed hostile use of these capabilities in space against a State. One State at State Consultations, having previously noted that cyber operations can meet the threshold of use of force in certain circumstances in and of themselves, indicated that it has not yet stated a position on the use of other (non-kinetic) means that may not amount to armed or physical force. However, this State went on to note that this is a developing area of law and State practice and that it is an open question whether an effects-based approach could properly lead to a conclusion that using other non-kinetic counterspace weapons could amount to a use of force where they have the same or similar effects to kinetic/traditional armed force.
[250] See Rule 21: Use of Force, para 5.
[251] UN Charter (n 2) art 41. See discussion in Rule 21: Use of Force.
[252] See Rule 21: Use of Force, para 13. For a review of recent examples of jamming and growing international jamming capabilities, see generally Weeden and Samson (n 6).
[253] Observing that there may be many reasons why States decide not to make public statements, several States at State Consultations indicated that where States have been silent on issues (such as jamming), this may indicate that they accept that there is not a breach of international law but is not necessarily conclusive on this point.

or reversible effects (eg lasers for temporarily dazzling optical sensors of satellites and microwave radiation to temporarily or partially disrupt the electronic systems of satellites, see Rule 21: Use of Force), which is discussed below. Cyber actions transmitting data that temporarily or partially disrupts, interferes with, or degrades the functions of a satellite without causing permanent damage may also be appropriately included in this analysis as generally not constituting a use of force or an armed attack (see paragraph 12).

The 'Gravity Threshold'

7. In the *Nicaragua* case, the ICJ held that it is 'necessary to distinguish the most grave forms of the use of force (those constituting an armed attack) from other less grave forms'.[254] The precise requirements for meeting this gravity threshold remain unsettled. In distinguishing a damaging but ambiguous 'frontier incident' from an 'armed attack', the ICJ applied a 'scale and effects' test.[255] However, this test is ill-defined and the gap between a use of force and an armed attack may sometimes be rather narrow. In the *Oil Platforms* case, while reiterating the distinction between 'the most grave forms of the use of force' and 'other less grave forms',[256] the Court did not explicitly apply the 'scale and effects' test and acknowledged that a use of force against a single military platform or a single military ship could suffice to reach the gravity threshold required for an armed attack.[257]

8. Although the ICJ applied the 'scale and effects' test in the *Nicaragua* case to determine whether a particular use of force constituted an armed attack, it did not use that test to determine whether a use of force was present. However, some commentators have concluded that the 'scale and effects' test would also be 'appropriate' for deciding whether the damaging effects of a cyber action (or other type of action) constitutes a use of force if those damages are similar to the damages caused by the use of traditional, physical, armed force.[258] Nevertheless, caution must be exercised

---

[254] *Nicaragua* Judgment (n 115) para 191.
[255] ibid para 195 (holding that the operation in question 'because of its scale and effects, would have been classified as an armed attack rather than as a mere frontier incident had it been carried out by regular armed forces'). It remains unclear whether mere 'frontier incidents' may constitute an armed attack, although it has been suggested that a review of State practice 'indicates that small-scale border attacks involving the use of lethal force are not excluded from the concept of 'armed attack' and may give rise to the right of self-defence'. ILA Final Report (n 159).
[256] *Case Concerning Oil Platforms (Islamic Republic of Iran v USA) (Merits)* [2003] ICJ Rep 161 (*Oil Platforms* case) 187 para 51.
[257] ibid 195 para 72.
[258] Tallinn Manual 2.0 (n 125) Rule 11 ('A cyber operation constitutes a use of force when its scale and effects are comparable to non-cyber operations rising to the level of a use of force'); some States have adopted a similar test in determining whether an armed attack has occurred by asking whether the damaging effects of the cyber action are equivalent to those caused by traditional, physical, armed force. See Rule 21: Use of Force, paras 15–22.

in relying exclusively on such an effects-based approach. Although an armed attack generally does result in casualties or significant property damage, this is not always the case.[259] For example, in a military space operation, it is possible that a missile, kinetic kill vehicle, or some other projectile fired or launched at a space object that misses that object and causes no damage may, depending on the circumstances (as discussed below), qualify as a use of force and an armed attack. Similarly, if State X fires an ASAT at State Y's satellite, but State Y intercepts the ASAT before it can do any damage, that could still qualify as a use of force and an armed attack.[260]

9. Based on the above, the application of the gravity threshold for an armed attack may not always be an easy or clear test. Nonetheless, if a use of force occurs in space and the gravity threshold is applied to determine if the affected State is a victim of an armed attack, the focus will generally continue to be on whether the use of force in question has resulted in the physical damage, permanent disabling, or destruction of space objects and harm to persons and their property on Earth, along with an assessment of the degree or severity of the damage and harm. Thus, uses of force that result in or are intended to cause the physical destruction of satellites, move a satellite out of a functional orbit, or permanently disable or seriously damage satellites are likely to qualify as meeting the gravity threshold/scale and effects test.[261] If an effects-based test is applied, its primary focus would be on damages that are equivalent to those caused by physical armed forces and meet the scale and effects test for an armed attack. However, determining whether an armed attack has occurred must include consideration of more than just damages: each incident must be assessed on a case-by-case basis, taking into account all the relevant legal issues and circumstances.[262] Even though there is no national territory to invade or defend in space, space objects can clearly be subject to armed attack.[263] However, special attention must be focused on the challenging issue of the legal status of the

---

[259] See discussion in Rule 21: Use of Force, paras 5–7 (noting among other things, the invasion, occupation, or unauthorized presence of armed forces on the territory of another State, naval blockades, and the placing of a State's territory at the disposal of an aggressor can constitute 'the most serious and dangerous form of the illegal use of force', even if no shots are fired and no physical damage or injury occurs).

[260] As noted in para 19, it is also possible that even when physical damage is present, there may not be an armed attack if those damages are accidental, unintentional or the result of a mistake or mechanical failure. In addition, damages caused by cyber actions may present special challenges in determining that an armed attack has occurred (notwithstanding the presence of physical damages) due to difficulties in positively determining the source of the cyber action or incidents of sabotage in which the victim State chooses to not officially classify an action resulting in significant physical damages as an armed attack (see eg the STUXNET incident in Iran in 2010).

[261] But see discussion in para 19 on accidents, mistakes, and other non-intentional acts.

[262] The underlying use of force must be identified and, even in the case of cyber actions in which the importance of effects is emphasized, the context of the event must also be analysed, attribution of the actor perpetrating the event must be achieved, and the target and intent must be evaluated, among other possible issues. Koh (n 218).

[263] A use of force, including one that constitutes an armed attack, is not limited to an action directed at the territorial integrity or political independence of a State (see Rule 21: Use of Force).

space objects that are attacked (discussed in paragraphs 13–20). Several other key issues relevant to military space operations and armed attacks are discussed below.

Temporary or Partial Disruption, Interference with, or Degrading of the Functions of Space Objects

10. As discussed in Rule 21: Use of Force there are different versions of counterspace weapon systems and capabilities utilizing the electromagnetic spectrum that can be employed in low energy mode to temporarily or partially disrupt, interfere with, or degrade the functions of space objects. Data transmitted by cyber capabilities can achieve the same effects. Two different lines of legal analysis are presented for evaluating whether these types of actions constitute armed attacks against space objects. One analytical approach would focus on the nature of an action and the instruments used and suggest, based on the UN Charter, that the action does not ordinarily rise to a use of force. Under this analysis, even if the action could be regarded as a use of force, it may not be sufficiently grave to ordinarily be regarded as an armed attack. Another line of analysis, proposed by some commentators and adopted by some States primarily with respect to possible cyber actions, would apply an effects-based approach suggesting that temporary or partial disruptions, interference with, or degrading of the functions of a space object are not usually armed attacks because they fail to meet a scale and effects test. However, both lines of analysis must take into account the circumstances surrounding the action as well as the special importance or sensitivity of some critical military space systems (see paragraph 12).

Evaluating the Degree of Damage Caused to a Space Object

11. The assessment of the degree of damage caused to a space object may (but not always) influence the judgment about whether an armed attack has occurred. Although to date no State practice exists on this point, considerations in assessing the degree of damage caused by weapons employing traditional, physical armed force against a space object may include the impact on some services and outputs of the targeted space object on Earth, notably those related to military, security, and defence functions. The resulting damaging effects caused by such physical armed force on such essential services or outputs—to the extent that those effects are not too remote—may thus be a factor to consider in assessing the gravity of a use of force and in determining whether it constitutes an armed attack.[264] Under an

---

[264] During State Consultations, some States criticized the inclusion of various damaging effects, particularly those described as second- or third-order effects, or beyond, as appropriate factors in determining that an attack had occurred (in the *jus in bello* context) or that an armed attack had occurred (in

effects-based approach to the evaluation of the damaging effects of a cyber action or other non-kinetic capability directed against a space object, a 'scale and effects' test would be applied, provided that the damaging effects are equivalent to the damages caused by traditional, physical, armed force and that the non-kinetic action in question is the proximate cause of those effects.[265] Under both approaches, short-term or reversible effects not leading to any physical damage or injury—causing only inconvenience, irritations, or loss of non-essential satellite services—are likely to preclude a military space operation from being characterized as an armed attack in most but not all circumstances (see paragraph 12).

Circumstances in Which Temporarily or Partially Disrupting, Interfering with, or Degrading the Functions of Space Objects May Be an Armed Attack

12. There are many actions described above that do not ordinarily rise to the level of a use of force or an armed attack because they only temporarily disrupt, interfere with, or degrade the functions of space objects. However, as noted by States during State Consultations, such action could qualify as an armed attack depending on the circumstances, particularly if these actions occur during a time heightened tension and depending on the target. For example, some States may regard these actions to be particularly threatening if they are taken against their satellites that provide an early warning of nuclear ballistic missile launches, related command and communication systems, and hotline communications satellite links (see Rule 21: Use of Force, paragraph 23). This argument would be based on the unique stabilizing role these space objects and systems play in maintaining international peace and security, based on the fundamental function that these assets play in alerting a State to a nuclear weapons attack posing an existential threat to that State, and based on the value of hotline communication links that could help avert a conflict. In addition, even temporary interference with a State's satellites that perform other vital national security and defence functions may, in the totality of circumstances and in conjunction with other military actions being taken against that State (in space or in other domains) by another State, constitute an armed attack. A particular action

a *jus ad bellum* context). This criticism was based on the possibility that such effects may be remote—remote in the sense that, particularly in the space context, the effects of an armed attack might pass through layers of different actions, human responsibilities, and diverse complications (which may involve unexpected or intervening circumstances), leading to effects that are not the proximate result of the attack.

[265] One State at State Consultations noted that States taking an effects-based approach to the destruction or disabling of a satellite are likely to include some of the effects on Earth in their assessment in determining whether an armed attack has occurred.

taken during a time of international tension and crisis could also reasonably be interpreted differently from the same act occurring during a time of calm.

The Legal Connection Between a State and a Space Object for Purposes of the Use of Force and Determining the Victim of an Armed Attack

An important issue on which there is insufficient State practice to give a definitive, comprehensive answer is the nature of the legal connection that is required between a space object and a State in order for an action against that space object to amount to a use of force or armed attack against that State. At the outset it should again be noted that State practice in domains other than space indicates that a territorial nexus is not always required for finding a use of force (including a use of force that constitutes an armed attack), as demonstrated by cases involving attacks on embassies and warships where the emanations of a State are most clear.[266] In this regard, as noted, the ICJ concluded that it could 'not exclude the possibility that the mining of a single military vessel might be sufficient to bring into play the 'inherent right of self-defence'.[267] While commercial 'flagged' vessels possessing the nationality of the flag State[268] are also sometimes regarded as possessing a sufficient connection to the flag State to bring the right of self-defence into play,[269] mere ownership of a commercial ship by nationals of a particular State may not be enough to serve as a sufficient legal connection.[270] In contrast to actions against property owned by nationals, a State may have a more recognized connection with its nationals who are themselves attacked outside of that State's territory, particularly if they are attacked because of their nationality.[271]

13.

---

[266] ILA Final Report (n 159) 7.
[267] *Oil Platforms* case (n 256) para 72.
[268] UNCLOS (n 46) art 91(1) ('Every State shall fix the conditions for the grant of its nationality to ships, for the registration of ships in its territory, and for the right to fly its flag. Ships have the nationality of the State whose flag they are entitled to fly. There must exist a genuine link between the State and the ship.').
[269] For example, with regard to the 1975 *Mayaguez* incident, the United States indicated in a letter to the UN Secretary General that it 'reserved' the right to take 'such measures as may be necessary to protect the lives of American citizens and property, including appropriate measures of self-defence under Article 51 of the United Nations Charter'. Eleanor C McDowell, *Digest of United States Practice in International Law 1975* (Department of State Publication 8865, US Government Printing Office 1976) 779. Ambassador Scali wrote a similar letter later that day, to the UN Security Council President, ibid 779–80.
[270] See *Oil Platforms* case (n 256) para 64 (noting that 'the *Texaco Caribbean* [previously referred to by the Court as 'United States-owned'], whatever its ownership, was not flying a United States flag, so that an attack on the vessel is not in itself to be equated with an attack on that State').
[271] It is important to note, however, that there is no consensus that attacks against the nationals of a State may be included. ILA Final Report (n 159) p 18 (further noting that State practice demonstrates that this view is stronger 'if it is clear that the nationals have been targeted as a result of their nationality and are seen by their attackers as individual manifestations of their State').

14. The legal connection between a State and a space object that is required for determining a use of force and an armed attack against that State is more complicated in space than in other domains. Space objects are not 'flagged' and do not possess the nationality of States like ships or airplanes do (see Rule 7: Jurisdiction). Instead, a complex collection of potentially overlapping legal connections may exist between several States and a particular space object (see Note on Legal Connections Between States and a Space Object). An obvious legal connection between a space object and a State—and perhaps the closest to being 'flagged'—is registration, a status that explicitly confers jurisdiction and control on the State of Registry over the space object and 'any personnel thereof'.[272] Although a State does not strictly exercise 'sovereignty' over a space object under the space law regime, in those cases where it exercises jurisdiction and control over a space object under Article VIII of the OST it might be able to claim that it is a victim of an armed attack and assert the right of self-defence with respect to actions against that space object. Another critical and potentially even more important legal connection between a State and a space object, which is not found in any other domain, relies on the status of a space object as being part of a national activity in space for which a State is 'responsible' under the OST (see Rule 10: Responsibility of States for National Activities in Outer Space).[273] Yet another potentially significant and related connection is between a space object and its launching State(s), even if that State is not the State of Registry (see Rule 7: Jurisdiction and Rule 8: Registration of Space Objects).

15. At present, there is no State practice in space to assess or to apply in determining the sufficiency of a State's legal connection with a space object regarding an alleged armed attack against it and the exercise of self-defence. Although the registration of a space object by a State is a strong legal connection and may be sufficient, other legal relationships—particularly responsibility for the space object under Article VI of the OST, may be more important. Multiple legal connections with multiple States may be present simultaneously. The significance of these connections can only be resolved through relevant State practice or future agreements. In the simplest and clearest case, a space object would be launched by a State from its own territory, registered in that State, operated by that State, regulated as a national space activity that is the responsibility of that State under Article VI of the OST, and owned by that State. However, such a scenario is only one of many possible sets of legal connections between a space object and a State.

---

[272] OST (n 3) art VIII. In practice, this status also allows the State of Registry to exclude all individuals, entities, or representatives of any other State from a space object unless authorized by the State of Registry, including any related efforts by other States to implement concrete measures of enforcement jurisdiction on the space object (see Rule 7: Jurisdiction, para 2).

[273] OST (n 3) art VI. The overwhelming majority of States with national space legislation apply their space authorization and supervision regimes to space activities conducted/controlled by nationals (entities and natural persons) or from national territory, including most likely also activities conducted from domestically registered ships and aircraft.

16. In the case of a satellite performing military functions, a State that is reliant on those functions is very likely to maintain at least one of the several legal connections discussed above with that satellite. In addition, although ownership does not allocate international legal obligations and rights like the recognized legal connections discussed above under the space law regime (see Note on Legal Connections Between States and a Space Object and Rule 9: Ownership of Objects in Space), ownership of a space object by a State or by a State's military organization may implicate or indicate fundamental State interests. A satellite owned by a military or national security organization of a State may also be viewed by that State as an emanation or expression of its sovereignty, against which an action might amount to a use of force or armed attack.[274]

17. Another challenging problem concerns the relationship between a State that only uses the services of a commercial or other satellite that is registered or otherwise legally connected with another State. If State B merely uses the services of a satellite that is legally attributable/connected to State A (under any of the most important legal connections described above, particularly registration and responsibility), this does not give State B a legal right to exercise self-defence if the satellite is attacked by State C (absent any other connection between State B and State A's satellite). Thus, the mere use by State B of the services of State' A's satellite, absent any legal connection to State A's satellite, appears to be an insufficient basis for State B to invoke the right to use force in self-defence of State A's satellite. However, this does not prejudice the right of State A to request State B to exercise the right of collective self-defence (provided that State A first declares that it has been the victim of an armed attack and then requests State B's assistance in collective self-defence). In another scenario, if States B and C are belligerents in an armed conflict and the services of State A's satellite are being used for the military benefit of State B, it may be permissible under the law of armed conflict for State C to attack State A's satellite if it qualifies as a military objective (see Rule 34: Military Objectives).

18. At present, there is no international legal basis for a State that is affected by an attack on another State's satellite to be automatically entitled, solely on the basis of losing the benefits of that satellite's services, to exercise the right of self-defence. In addition, the OST neither grants nor recognizes any international legal status that is conferred on States by leases or other contractual relationships with private entities or other States, including leases or contracts regarding satellite services.

---

[274] It must again be remembered, however, that even a military space object does not possess 'nationality' and does not have the same emanations of sovereignty that are clearly associated with warships or military aircraft under applicable regimes governing the maritime and air domains (see Rule 7: Jurisdiction). The space law regime thus recognises no concept of 'sovereign immunity' like the legal status that the Law of the Sea attaches in the marine environment to a 'warship, naval auxiliary, other vessels or aircraft owned or operated by a State and used, for the time being, only on government non-commercial service'. UNCLOS (n 46) art 236.

Thus, in the absence of any State practice to date, a lease between a State and a private entity for military purposes/defence services provided by that private entity's satellite does not, without some international legal connection between that State and the satellite, appear to authorize the exercise of self-defence by that State of the space object if it is attacked. Some might argue that a State that has a lease for vital military services that are provided by another State's satellite might claim a right of self-defence if those vital defence functions are lost as a result of an armed attack on that other State's satellite, but this appears to present an untested and unsettled question that lies outside the existing space law regime.[275]

Accumulated Incidents Constituting an Armed Attack

19. The ICJ has implicitly recognized that although an isolated incident may not amount to an armed attack, if that incident originates from the same source and forms part of a series of coordinated attacks against a State, collectively they can amount to an armed attack.[276] The series of such incidents must be sufficiently connected to be considered as a whole, constitute a use of force, and be of sufficient gravity to constitute an armed attack.

Accidents, Mistakes, and Other Non-Intentional Acts

20. While States have expressed different views regarding whether intention is required for a use of force, there is considerable State practice relating to actions that could be characterized as a use of force which States have nonetheless refrained from treating as violating Article 2(4)—because those actions lacked deliberate character, especially in the case of accidental military incursions into a State's territory.[277] Not only do States usually refrain from shooting at those who accidentally violate their borders, States often criticize the State that does shoot in those circumstances.[278] Territory and border incursions are obviously not a concern in

---

[275] One State at State Consultations suggested that the possibility exists for a State to take an effects-based approach in finding an armed attack if destroying or suspending the functioning of *any* space object results in effects equivalent to Earth to a kinetic attack against that State.

[276] See *Nicaragua* Judgment (n 115) para 231 (addressing whether various incursions into the territories of Honduras and Costa Rica could be treated 'as amounting, singly *or collectively*, to an armed attack') (emphasis added); *Oil Platforms* case (n 256) para 64 (addressing whether the attack in question, 'either in itself *or in combination* with the rest of the "series … of attacks" … can be categorized as an 'armed attack' on the United States) (emphasis added); *Armed Activities in the Congo* Judgment (n 115) para 146 ('even if this series of deplorable attacks could be *regarded as cumulative in character*, they still remained non-attributable to the DRC') (emphasis added).

[277] For a collection and assessment of relevant State practice, see Ruys (n 162) 189 (noting that 'state practice reveals that, when faced with territorial incursions ostensibly or allegedly lacking hostile intent, territorial states often refrain from invoking the language of Article 2(4) or 51').

[278] A notable example was the condemnation by States of the USSR for shooting down KAL Flight 007 in 1983. See also Craig A Morgan, 'The Downing of Korean Air Lines Flight 007' (1985) 11 Yale

space. However, space is a dangerous and increasingly congested environment where small mistakes or miscalculations in complex orbits can lead to crashes or other accidents involving space objects travelling at incredible speeds. The possibility of mechanical error would also seem especially noteworthy in space because of the complex technologies involved and the harsh space environment. Space objects are also generally controlled by operators in distant locations and are heavily dependent on computers. In the foreseeable future, space objects may also be controlled by computers utilizing some degree of artificial intelligence, which might behave in ways that humans will not always foresee. It would thus seem that at a minimum, some allowance should be made in space for the possibility of considering a potentially destabilizing incident to be regarded as an accident, mistake, or a harmless act that lacks a deliberate or premeditated character rather than viewing it a use of force leading to unnecessary conflict.[279] It should also be noted that some unintentional acts, particularly those involving negligence, may carry legal consequences, such as liability to pay compensation (see Rule 12: International Liability for Damage Caused by Space Objects). Thus, even if the act does not rise to the level of a use of force, it may still be an internationally wrongful act. Finally, with respect to armed attacks, some State practice implicitly supports the view that hostile intent must be displayed to determine whether an armed attack has occurred,[280] while another view of State practice emphasizes that 'the existence of mistake or accident is highly relevant in deciding whether the use of force in self-defence is necessary'.[281]

Journal of International Law 231, 252 ('Most states and international organizations that indicated a position condemned the Soviet action as unjustified.').

[279] It should be noted, however, that a State whose rights are being violated may not know enough about the benign intentions of a particular space craft giving rise to that violation or that State may be unaware whether there has been an accident, an unauthorized action, or a malfunction. Some of the same factors that make space operations difficult and unpredictable may thus also render interpretation of another actor's ambiguous space actions difficult and uncertain. Especially in a time of crisis, the margin to excuse an accidental violation may be thin.

[280] Ruys (n 162) 172 (noting that 'on numerous occasions, states claiming to be the victims of armed attacks or attempting to justify forcible responses to territorial incursions stressed the premeditated or deliberate character of the initial attacks or provocations'); *Oil Platforms* case (n 256) para 64 (emphasizing the absence of the specific intention of harming the ship); *Nicaragua* Judgment (n 115) para 231 (questioning 'possible motivations' of cross-border incursions).

[281] ILA Final Report (n 159) 7 (describing this position as what 'may be the better view', but also noting that the Definition of Aggression Resolution, the case law of the ICJ, and State practice may be referred to in support of the argument that intent 'is a relevant factor for determining whether an "armed attack" has occurred').

SECTION 2
RESPONSE ACTIONS

Rule 24
Retorsion

A State may engage in military space activities that constitute retorsion.

Overview of Legal Basis of Rule

1. Retorsion is an 'unfriendly' but lawful act that an aggrieved State may adopt against another State. It is founded on the fundamental and sovereign right of a State to be free to engage in all actions which are not otherwise prohibited by international law. Retorsion must be distinguished from countermeasures (see Rule 25: Countermeasures) and belligerent reprisals (see Rule 47: Belligerent Reprisals) in that no legal justification is required for taking action in a manner consistent with all international obligations of the acting State. No rule of international law prohibits or prevents States from engaging in acts of retorsion involving military space activities or in response to unlawful or unfriendly acts committed in space. All military and civilian uses of outer space are presumed to be lawful unless otherwise prohibited under international law (see Rule 1: Freedom of Use, Access, Exploration, and Scientific Investigation and Principles of Cooperation).

Application of Rule

2. A retorsion is a reactionary act—one that is undertaken in response to a previous internationally wrongful act or unfriendly conduct. The only condition on a retorsion is that it is a lawful, but unfriendly, act in response to the act of another.[282] In other words, so long as the retorsion is compliant with existing treaty and customary obligations, there are no other requirements that need to be met. Thus, for example, if State A has been sharing various space launch services with State B, State A may terminate that sharing arrangement in response to State B's conduct

---

[282] Although the concept of retorsion focuses on actions taken in response to other actions, it should be noted that unfriendly but lawful actions may be taken at any time by a State, regardless of any other State's prior or subsequent actions.

of unfriendly, but lawful, military naval manoeuvres near State A's territorial sea. Likewise, the jamming of military signals in response to the conduct of freedom of navigation operations in disputed maritime zones might be considered an act of retorsion, unless such act violates any existing treaty or customary international law obligations.[283]

---

[283] Such jamming of signals may, under some circumstances, violate existing international legal obligations. It is possible that such jamming may constitute a breach of the principle of non-intervention (see Rule 20: Non-Intervention Principle) or harmful interference under the OST (see Rule 18: Harmful Interference), in which case the act could not be considered as retorsion. Some surveillance satellites that monitor compliance with obligations under arms control treaties 'national technical means of verification' are also protected from harmful interference pursuant to those treaties'. See eg New START Treaty (n 68) art X(1)(b). Some States may argue also argue that the jamming of signals to or from satellites that provide an early warning of nuclear ballistic missile launches, related command and communication systems, and hotline communications satellites links has the potential to amount to a threat or use of force (see Rule 21: Use of Force and Rule 22: Threat of Force).

Rule 25

Countermeasures

A State may take a countermeasure, including through military space activities, in response to an internationally wrongful act committed against it by another State.

Overview of Legal Basis of Rule

This Rule is based on Articles 22 and 49–54 of the ILC's Articles on State Responsibility.[284] These articles have achieved wide acceptance by many States as representative of customary international law.[285] Since international law is explicitly made applicable to activities in space under Article III of the OST, remedies available under general international law, including countermeasures, are also available in space and in relation to military space activities.[286] This Rule is without prejudice to the legality of actions taken by a State when authorized by a decision of the UN Security Council under Chapter VII of the UN Charter (see Rule 28: Collective Security Measures) or in the exercise of the State's inherent right of self-defence under Article 51 of the UN Charter (see Rule 26: Self-Defence and Rule 27: Collective Self-Defence).

1.

---

[284] ILC Articles on State Responsibility (n 99).
[285] See UNGA Sixth Committee, 'Summary Record of the 13th meeting' (28 February 2020) UN Doc A/C.6/74/SR.13 (recording the official position of a majority of States on the committee that all or most of the ILC Articles on State Responsibility represent customary international law—see eg statement by Finland (p 2) on behalf of the Nordic Countries (Denmark, Finland, Iceland, Norway, and Sweden) observing that the 'ILC draft articles had already become widely known and cited by lawyers, governments and legal institutions, most notably by the International Court of Justice. Adopted in 2001 ... the articles have only gathered more authority as a restatement of the law on State responsibility.'). The ILC Articles on State Responsibility are routinely applied as authoritative by international tribunals. See eg *Gabčíkovo-Nagymaros Project (Hungary v Slovakia)* (Judgment) [1997] ICJ Reps 7, para 50; *Archer Daniels Midland Company and Tate & Lyle Ingredients Americas, Inc v United Mexican States* (Award) [2007] ICSID Case No ARB(AF)/04/05 (*Archer Daniels* case) para 125; *Corn Products International Inc v United Mexican States* (Decision on Responsibility) [2008] ICSID Case No ARB(AF)/04/01, para 145; *Cargill Inc v United Mexican States* (Award) [2009] ICSID Case No ARB(AF)/05/02, para 382.
[286] Countermeasures may only be taken against a State in response to an internationally wrongful act committed by that State (see paras 2–3).

Requirements and Application

2. A countermeasure is an act taken by an injured State vis-à-vis the responsible State, which would otherwise constitute a violation of international law but is not wrongful because it is taken in response to a prior internationally wrongful act committed by the responsible State.[287] Therefore, this Rule authorizes a military space activity that would otherwise be in breach of an obligation incumbent on the injured State if it qualifies as a lawful countermeasure.

3. The term 'countermeasure' is a distinct legal concept under the law of State responsibility. It should be distinguished from the operational concept of countermeasures, such as the use of redundancy, camouflage, and frequency-hopping for communications channels (so-called passive countermeasures) or the use of internally hosted decoys and space-based defence systems (so-called active countermeasures).[288] This Rule refers only to countermeasures in the formal legal sense of the term. Countermeasures under this Rule should also be distinguished from related legal concepts, such as belligerent reprisals and retorsion.[289] Importantly, countermeasures are limited to non-forcible acts that are not associated with an armed conflict,[290] whereas 'belligerent reprisals' refers to acts, including the use of armed force, taken in the context of armed conflict that would violate the law of armed conflict but for the fact that they are responding to violations by the adversary party and meet certain stringent conditions (see Rule 47: Belligerent Reprisals). Acts of 'retorsion' refer to unfriendly but nevertheless lawful acts by the aggrieved State against another State (see Rule 24: Retorsion). As long as these acts are not inconsistent with any international obligations of the injured State, they do not qualify as countermeasures within the scope of this Rule.

4. There is no requirement under international law for countermeasures to be either in-kind or reciprocal in nature.[291] Accordingly, provided the relevant conditions are met, a State may engage in a military space activity as a countermeasure in response to a prior internationally wrongful act, regardless of the domain in which the act is committed or the means used to commit the act. For example, a State

---

[287] See eg Air Service Agreement of 27 March 1946 between the United States of America and France (1978) 18 RIAA 417, 443 para 81 ('Under the rules of present-day international law, and unless the contrary results from special obligations arising under particular treaties ... [a] State is entitled ... to affirm its rights through "countermeasures"'); *Gabčíkovo-Nagymaros* Judgment (n 285) para 82 ('wrongfulness [of a countermeasure] may be precluded on the ground that the measure so adopted was in response to [another State's] prior failure to comply with its obligations under international law').

[288] Office of the Chairman of the Joint Chiefs of Staff, 'DOD Dictionary of Military and Associated Terms' (US Department of Defense 2021) 52 (defining countermeasure as a 'form of military science that, by the employment of devices and/or techniques, has as its objective the impairment of the operational effectiveness of enemy activity').

[289] A point expressly noted in the ILC Articles on State Responsibility (n 99) 128.

[290] *Corfu Channel Case (United Kingdom v Albania)* (Judgment) [1949] ICJ Reps 244, para 35; *Nicaragua* Judgment (n 115) para 249; ILC Articles on State Responsibility (n 99) art 50(1).

[291] ILC Articles on State Responsibility (n 99) p 128.

may respond to a wrongful act committed in a terrestrial context with space-based countermeasures or may use land-based assets to take countermeasures in response to a wrongful act committed in space.

5. The use of force is prohibited as a means to conduct a countermeasure.[292] Also, countermeasures may not affect obligations for the protection of fundamental human rights, those of a humanitarian character, and other obligations under peremptory norms of international law, such as the prohibitions of aggression, slavery, genocide, racial discrimination, apartheid, and torture.[293] For example, under no circumstances may a State engage in a military space activity that would amount to or facilitate genocide, not even in response to a prior genocide committed by another State.[294]

6. There are six conditions that must be met in order for countermeasures to be justified. First, countermeasures must be taken only against a State responsible for a prior internationally wrongful act.[295] If the original act does not qualify as a breach of international legal obligations, then countermeasures are unavailable as a response option for the aggrieved State.[296]

7. Second, countermeasures must be directed only against the responsible State.[297] Countermeasures will not legitimize conduct inconsistent with the international obligations of the injured State vis-à-vis third States.[298] This requirement may be especially difficult to apply in space in view of the legal connections that are possible between a particular space object and several different States (see Note on Legal Connections Between States and a Space Object). Article VI of the OST provides that a State bears international responsibility for its national activities in outer space and for ensuring that those national activities are carried out in conformity with the OST (see Rule 10: Responsibility of States for National Activities in Outer Space). Thus, any space object that is part of a State's national activities in space is the internationally responsibility of that State for purposes of this Rule. It is

---

[292] ibid art 50(1)(a); *Guyana v Suriname* (n 235) para 446; *Nicaragua* Judgment (n 115) para 249; Submission by Australia, Official Compendium of National Contributions (n 120) 8; French Position Paper (n 129) 8. But see *Case Concerning Oil Platforms (Islamic Republic of Iran v USA)* (Merits—Judge Simma, separate opinion) [2003] ICJ Reps 161, paras 12–13.

[293] ILC Articles on State Responsibility (n 99) art 50(1)(b)–(d).

[294] *Application of the Convention on the Prevention and Punishment of the Crime of Genocide (Bosnia and Herzegovina v Serbia and Montenegro)* (Counter-claims—Order of 17 December 1997) [1997] ICJ Rep 243, para 35 ('in no case could one breach of the [Genocide] Convention serve as an excuse for another').

[295] ILC Articles on State Responsibility (n 99) art 49(1); *Gabčíkovo-Nagymaros* Judgment (n 285) para 83. (countermeasures must be 'taken in response to a previous international wrongful act of another State').

[296] *Naulilaa Case (Portugal v Germany)* (1949) 2 RIAA 1011, 1027 ('The first condition—sine qua non—of the right to exercise reprisals is a motive created by a preceding act which is contrary to the law of nations.').

[297] *Gabčíkovo-Nagymaros* Judgment (n 285) para 83.

[298] ILC Articles on State Responsibility (n 99) art 49, commentary para 3.

important to note that a State bears international responsibility for national activities in outer space 'whether such activities are carried on by governmental agencies or by non-governmental entities'.

8. Views are divided on the extent to which non-injured third States may come to the assistance of the injured State (the issue of 'collective countermeasures'), noting that the ILC considered the current state of the law on this point as 'uncertain'.[299] One view is that third States may engage only in conduct that is not otherwise unlawful (Rule 24: Retorsion) in support of the aggrieved State, meaning that only the injured State, and no other State, may lawfully engage in countermeasures under international law.[300] This view accords with the ICJ judgment in *Nicaragua*, where it held that '[t]he acts of which Nicaragua is accused ... could only have justified proportionate counter-measures on the part of the State which had been the victim of these acts'.[301] The other view is that non-injured States may also apply a countermeasure to support the State directly affected by the prior internationally wrongful act.[302] The latter position recognizes collective countermeasures as an important safeguard in particular for those States that lack the capacity to engage in military space activities themselves. As noted, cross-domain countermeasures are permissible, notably when an injured State may lack the capacity to respond with a countermeasure in a particular domain.

9. One State at State Consultations observed that most State space actors cannot effectively act in space alone and therefore rely on partnerships. Thus, the question of collective countermeasures is of critical practical importance to these States. In this regard, Article 48(1) of the ILC Articles on State Responsibility provides that '[a]ny State other than an injured State is entitled to invoke the responsibility of another State in accordance with paragraph 2 if: (a) the obligation breached is owed to a group of States including that State, and is established for the protection of a collective interest of the group; or (b) the obligation breached is owed to the international community as a whole'.

10. In addition to an uninjured State acting in support of an injured State, the free use of outer space might be viewed as an *erga omnes* obligation that is owed at least to the States Parties to the OST, and hence a group of States. Thus, as noted by a State at State Consultations, it could be argued that an infringement of the free use of

---

[299] ibid art 54, commentary para 6.
[300] See eg ILC, 'Topical Summary of the Discussion held in the Sixth Committee of the General Assembly during its Fifty-Fifth Session prepared by the Secretariat' (15 February 2001) UN Doc A/CN.4/513 para 175 (noting that several States expressed strong opposition to the notion of collective countermeasures); French Position Paper (n 129) 7; *Nicaragua* Judgment (n 115) para 211.
[301] *Nicaragua* Judgment (n 115) para 249.
[302] See Andrew Whyte (ed), 'President Kaljulaid at CyCon 2019: Cyber Attacks Should Not Be Easy Weapon' *ERR News* (Tallinn, 29 May 2019) [perma.cc/52RL-FTD2] ('Estonia is furthering the position that states which are not directly injured may apply countermeasures to support the state directly affected by the malicious cyber operation').

outer space as it is defined by the OST, especially by the due regard principle in Article IX of the OST, could lead to several States taking countermeasures alongside each other, that is, taking collective countermeasures, since they are directly affected by that infringement according to either Article 48(1)(a) or (b) of the ILC Articles on State Responsibility.

Third, the injured State must call upon the responsible State to fulfil its obligations of cessation and reparation, and notify the latter of the intention to take countermeasures.[303] This is because countermeasures must aim to induce the responsible State to comply with its relevant obligations.[304] The object of countermeasures is to restore a situation of legality between the affected States and bring to an end any violations of international law,[305] not to punish the responsible State. However, this procedural requirement may be waived when there is an urgent need to preserve the rights of the injured State.[306]

11.

Fourth, countermeasures must 'be commensurate with the injury suffered, taking into account the gravity of the internationally wrongful act and the rights in question'.[307] Disproportionate measures amount to retaliation and thus exceed the permissible object of countermeasures, potentially giving rise to responsibility on the part of the injured State.[308] Proportionality under the law of countermeasures should be distinguished from other legal standards and rules bearing the same name, which are referred to elsewhere in this *Manual*. In particular, it is distinct from proportionality as one of the requirements for the lawful use of force in self-defence (Rule 26: Self-Defence) and also from the obligation of proportionality in attack during an armed conflict (Rule 38: Proportionality in Attack).

12.

In this context, the notion of 'injury' should be understood broadly to include 'any damage, whether material or moral, caused by the internationally wrongful act of a State'.[309] The injured State is also obligated to take into account the gravity of the act of the responsible State and the rights in question.[310] In practice, this means that the injured State should take into account both quantitative and qualitative factors, such as the importance of the interest protected by the rule infringed and the seriousness of the breach.[311] This assessment must be done on a case-by-case

13.

---

[303] ILC Articles on State Responsibility (n 99) art 52(1). Note that there is no need to specify what measures will be taken.
[304] ibid art 49(1).
[305] ibid art 49, commentary para 1.
[306] ibid art 52(2).
[307] ibid art 51. See also, WTO, *United States: Transitional Safeguard Measure on Combed Cotton Yarn from Pakistan—Report of the Appellate Body* (8 October 2001) WT/DS192/AB/R, para 120; WTO, *United States: Definitive Safeguard Measures on Imports of Circular Welded Carbon Quality Line Pipe from Korea—Report of the Appellate Body* (15 February 2002) WT/DS202/AB/R, para 259; *Archer Daniels* case (n 285) paras 152 and 160.
[308] ILC Articles on State Responsibility (n 99) art 51, commentary paras 1 and 7.
[309] ibid art 31(2).
[310] ibid art 51.
[311] ibid art 51, commentary para 6; *Archer Daniels* case (n 285) para 155.

basis. Suppose, for example, that State A unlawfully caused harmful radio interference contrary to the *Convention of the International Telecommunication Union* (see Rule 19: ITU Harmful Radio Interference) with the broadcast from one of State B's satellites.[312] It would be disproportionate for State B to launch a cyber operation against State A's space command and control centre aimed at denying its use of space capabilities altogether. This is because the effects of the operation launched by State B in response would be significantly out of proportion to those caused by State A's wrongful act.

14. Fifth, countermeasures must, insofar as possible, be taken in such a way as to permit the subsequent resumption of performance of the relevant obligations. In other words, countermeasures should be temporary in character in line with their overall object.[313] A State may therefore be precluded from, for example, taking an action that would permanently degrade a satellite's function to transmit signals because the effects are not reversible.[314] However, the effects of countermeasures are required to be reversible only insofar as possible.[315] This means that if the injured State reasonably believed that it could induce the responsible State to comply with its obligations only by engaging in measures with potentially permanent effects, then this requirement would not bar such a course of action, provided it was not deemed disproportionate.

15. Sixth, countermeasures must be terminated as soon as the responsible State has complied with its obligations towards the injured State, as the justification for countermeasures will cease at that point.[316] Any unreasonable delay in termination amounts to a violation of international law by the originally injured State, which can trigger its international responsibility. At State Consultations, one State noted that, in the outer space domain, internationally wrongful acts that are ordinarily below the threshold of armed attack, such as jamming, can be turned on and off in an instant. Therefore, it is extremely difficult to assess whether the act ceased altogether or whether the jamming belongs to a larger pattern. The obligation of the perpetrator—to guarantee and ensure that the act will not be repeated—could be helpful in these situations to determine whether the act has actually ceased.[317]

---

[312] For purposes of clarifying State B's right to respond, the phrase 'State B's satellite' refers to a satellite that is the responsibility of State B under art VI of the OST and is ideally also registered to State B.

[313] ILC Articles on State Responsibility (n 99) art 49, commentary para 7.

[314] *Gabčíkovo-Nagymaros* Judgment (n 285) para 87 (because the purpose of countermeasures is 'to induce the wrongdoing State to comply with its obligations under international law ... the measure must therefore be reversible').

[315] ILC Articles on State Responsibility (n 99) art 49, commentary para 9 ('the duty to choose measures that are reversible is not absolute') and p 129 (countermeasures 'must be *as far as possible* reversible in their effects in terms of future legal relations between the two States' (emphasis added)).

[316] ibid art 53.

[317] See ILC Articles on State Responsibility (n 99) art 30(b).

16 This Rule is linked to Rule 24 on Retorsion because relevant actions by States may have points of similarity with both Rules, although an act of retorsion and a countermeasure are legally quite different. Whether an unfriendly action taken by State A against the satellite of State B implicates any countermeasures by State A—and thus would require compliance with applicable countermeasure procedures— depends on the characterization of the unfriendly act by State A as an 'internationally wrongful act'. For example, if the action by State A violates the obligation to show due regard (see Rule 17: Due Regard), State B may take an appropriate and proportionate countermeasure against the internationally wrongful act by State A in accordance with this Rule and applicable procedures. If, however, the unfriendly action taken by State A is lawful and does not violate the obligation to show due regard, State B is free to take any unfriendly, lawful action in response (see Rule 24: Retorsion), including a response similar to State A's original unfriendly action, without recourse to the procedures outlined in this Rule.

Rule 26
Self-Defence

A State may exercise its inherent right of individual self-defence against any activity, including an action from, to, or within space, that constitutes an armed attack, and its right of anticipatory self-defence against any activity that amounts to an imminent armed attack against it.

Overview of Legal Basis of Rule

1. Article 51 of the UN Charter recognizes the inherent right of individual or collective self-defence if an armed attack occurs against a UN member. The UN Charter and international law are explicitly made applicable to the exploration and use of outer space, including the Moon and other celestial bodies,[318] by the Outer Space Treaty (OST).[319] Article 51 also reflects customary international law.[320] For purposes of self-defence, an armed attack must meet the requirements detailed in Rule 23: Armed Attack and Rule 21: Use of Force. The exercise of the right of self-defence must also conform to the requirements of necessity and proportionality (see paragraphs 3–9). An armed attack under this rule includes an imminent armed attack (see paragraphs 10–14). Any exercise of self-defence remains subject to all the requirements set forth in Article 51 and remains subject to the primacy of any effective measures that may be imposed by the UN Security Council (see paragraph 18).

---

[318] With respect to the exercise of the right of self-defence on the Moon and other celestial bodies, see the discussion in Rule 4: Restrictions on Specified Military Establishments and Activities on Celestial Bodies.

[319] OST (n 3) art III. Article 51, like other parts of the UN Charter, is essential to the regulation of the use and exploration of space as well as the maintenance of international peace and security in space. See UNCOPUOS, 'Achievement of a uniform interpretation of the right of self-defence in conformity with the United Nations Charter as applied to outer space as a factor in maintaining outer space as a safe and conflict-free environment and promoting the long-term sustainability of outer space activities—Working paper submitted by the Russian Federation' (2 February 2015) UN Doc A/AC.105/C.1/2015/CRP.22, para 3 ('the exploration and use of outer space are regulated by the international law based on the UN Charter. Accordingly, the principle of self-defence itself is not an exception from the general context.').

[320] *Nicaragua* Judgment (n 115) paras 176, 193.

Application to Space

2. Non-aggressive military activities, including the lawful exercise of the right of self-defence, are fully consistent with the exploration and use of outer space for peaceful purposes (see Rule 3: Peaceful Purposes in Outer Space). In fact, a State's inherent right of self-defence is built into the space law regime through the explicit incorporation of the UN Charter in Article III of the OST. Furthermore, the application of any legal regime (including the OST) that does not carry indicia that it was intended to continue to apply in armed conflict is suspended to the extent that it would frustrate, in whole or in part, the ability of a State to take measures in the exercise of its inherent right to defend itself which are taken in conformity with the UN Charter[321] (see Methodology of *Manual*).[322]

Necessity

3. Under customary international law, the exercise of the right to self-defence is subject to the requirements of necessity and proportionality.[323] The long-established principle of necessity constrains measures taken in self-defence to only those that are required to achieve the legitimate ends sought and not otherwise prohibited by international law.[324] Furthermore, consistent with UN Charter obligations, various national military manuals recognize that the application of the necessity principle includes the requirement that the attack in question should be averted unless no reasonable alternative means of redress are available.[325]

---

[321] The application of the space law regime is suspended if it would frustrate the ability of the State, in whole or in part, to defend itself. See ILC, 'Draft Articles on the Effects of Armed Conflicts on Treaties, with Commentary' (2011) UN Doc A/66/10, art 14(2). With respect to internationally wrongful acts generally, it should also be noted that the '[t]he wrongfulness of an act of a State is precluded if the act constitutes a lawful measure of self-defence taken in conformity with the Charter of the United Nations'. ILC Articles on State Responsibility (n 99) art 21.

[322] For example, the law of armed conflict (including the rules on weapons and on means and methods of warfare) remains fully applicable in a situation of self-defence.

[323] *Nuclear Weapons* Advisory Opinion (n 181) para 41 ('The submission of the exercise of the right of self-defence to the conditions of necessity and proportionality is a rule of customary international law ... This dual condition applies equally to Article 51 of the Charter, whatever the means of force employed.').

[324] A famous, early expression of this principle is found in the exchange of diplomatic notes regarding the *Caroline* affair in 1837 in which the US Secretary of State Daniel Webster noted that an 'act justified by the necessity of self-defence, must be limited by that necessity, and kept clearly within it'. Letter from Daniel Webster to Lord Ashburton (27 July 1842) [https://perma.cc/3QF7-RN52].

[325] See eg US DoD Law of War Manual (n 11) 1.11.1.3 (further noting that 'in exercising the right of self-defense, diplomatic means must be exhausted or provide no reasonable prospect of stopping the armed attack or threat thereof'); Norwegian Defence University College, *Manual of the Law of Armed Conflict* (1st English edn, The Chief of Defence 2018)(Norwegian LOAC Manual) para 1.9 ('To be lawful, a state's use of armed force in self-defence against an armed attack must be necessary and proportionate. In practice, there must be no alternative means of protecting the state against the armed attack.'); Danish Ministry of Defence, *Military Manual on International Law Relevant to Danish Armed Forces in International Operations* (Jes Rynkeby Knudsen ed, Defence Command Denmark 2016) (Danish LOAC Manual) para 2.2.3 ('An act of self-defence must be necessary ... if it is assessed that a

4. With respect to the evaluation of what measures are necessary to support a claim of self-defence, the ICJ has held that 'since the requirement of international law that measures taken avowedly in self-defence must have been necessary for that purpose is strict and objective', there is no room left for any 'measure of discretion'.[326] While this may be true in the abstract, it has also been observed that 'in practice of course the assessment of the necessity of a particular action is far from straightforward, and can be undertaken only on the basis of the facts available at the time, but with a good faith assessment of those facts'.[327]

5. A key element in evaluating what measures are necessary for a State in order to exercise its right of self-defence concerns the legitimate aim of such measures.[328] A narrow view, consistent with the overall objectives of the UN Charter and the desire to reduce the possibility of excessive recourse to force by States, would allow only for stopping an ongoing attack. However, a much more widely accepted view also allows for preventing further attacks as a legitimate aim of measures necessary for a State's exercise of self-defence.[329]

Proportionality

6. If a use of force in self-defence is necessary, it must also meet the requirement of proportionality. In the *Nicaragua* case, the ICJ referred to a specific rule 'whereby self-defence would warrant only measures which are proportional to the armed attack and necessary to respond to it' as 'a rule well established in customary international law'.[330] Proportionality limits the use of force employed in response to an armed attack to what is required to repel or halt an attack or to prevent future attacks.[331] Care must be taken not to confuse the requirement of proportionality in this context, with that of proportionality in the context of countermeasures (Rule 25: Countermeasures) or under the law regulating the conduct of hostilities,

---

diplomatic effort will be capable of handling the dispute, it should be considered whether an act of self-defence is necessary.')

[326] *Oil Platforms* case (n 256) para 73.
[327] Elizabeth Wilmshurst (ed), 'Principles of International Law on the Use of Force by States in Self-Defence' (ILP WP 05/01, The Royal Institute of International Affairs 2005) (Chatham House Principles) 8 fn 11 [https://perma.cc/3J99-RKXG].
[328] It should be noted that the legitimate aims of self-defence do not include punishment, retribution, revenge or making an aggressor 'pay a price'.
[329] See ILA Final Report (n 159).
[330] *Nicaragua* Judgment (n 115) para 176.
[331] US DoD Law of War Manual (n 11) para 1.11.1.2 ('Proportionality involves a weighing of the contemplated actions with the justification for taking action. For example, the proportionality of the measures taken in self-defense is to be judged according to the nature of the threat being addressed. Force may be used in self-defense, but only to the extent that it is required to repel the armed attack and to restore the security of the party attacked.'). A State at State Consultations noted that 'the requirement of proportionality means that the actions must be in proportion to this attack in nature, size and intensity'.

which involve different considerations and evaluations (Rule 38: Proportionality in Attack).

7. Since the focus of proportionality is on is on what is required to repel or halt an armed attack or to prevent or deter future attack or threats, it does not require the defending State to match the same degree or type of force used in an armed attack.[332] Rather, the focus must be on the nature of the threat that is being addressed and the relationship of the actions taken in self-defence for the purpose of responding to that threat.[333]

8. Both the armed attack and the measures taken in the exercise of self-defence must be considered in their contexts to make a proper proportionality assessment. Thus, all actions taken by the aggressor State and the defending State related to the armed attack in question are to be assessed as a whole.[334] It is not valid, for example, to consider an armed attack on several satellites in isolation when those attacks are in fact the 'first shots' in a broader terrestrial campaign or part of a continuing series of attacks.[335] Similarly, it is not valid to consider only the defensive action by a defending State against one of the attacker's satellites, if the defending State is responding with a broader campaign that also involves terrestrial campaigns. It is the assessment of the actions taken by both parties as a whole that is the measuring stick for proportionality, not individual components of the armed attack on, or responses against, space objects.

9. Proportionality does not require actions taken in self-defence to be geographically bounded to the area or domain of the attack and can thus extend from terrestrial

---

[332] William H Taft IV (Legal Adviser, US Department of State) 'Self-Defense and the Oil Platforms Decision' (2004) 29 Yale Journal of International Law 295, 305 ('There is no requirement in international law that a State exercising its right of self-defense must use the same degree or type of force used by the attacking State in its most recent attack. Rather, the proportionality of the measures taken in self-defense is to be judged according to the nature of the threat being addressed. A proper assessment of the proportionality of a defensive use of force would require looking not only at the immediately preceding armed attack, but also at whether it was part of an ongoing series of attacks, what steps were already taken to deter future attacks, and what force could reasonably be judged to be needed to successfully deter future attacks.'); ILA Final Report (n 159) 12 ('[a] pure "equivalence of scale" approach to proportionality is incorrect: the preferred position is that the measures be balanced in light of the aims of the self-defence ... the legitimate aims in this context are to halt any ongoing attack and prevent the continuation of further attacks').
[333] US DoD Law of War Manual (n 11) 1.11.1.2 ('the proportionality of the measures taken in self defense is to be judged according to the nature of the threat being addressed.'); ILC, 'Addendum—Eighth report on State responsibility by Mr. Roberto Ago, Special Rapporteur—the internationally wrongful act of the State, source of international responsibility (part I)' (1980) UN Doc A/CN.4/318/Add.5-7, para 121 ('The requirement of the proportionality of the action taken in self-defence ... concerns the relationship between that action and its purpose, namely—and this can never be repeated too often—that of halting and repelling the attack ... It would be mistaken, however, to think that there must be proportionality between the conduct constituting the armed attack and the opposing conduct.').
[334] *Oil Platforms* case (n 256) para 77.
[335] Taft (n 332) 305 ('A proper assessment of the proportionality of a defensive use of force would require looking not only at the immediately preceding armed attack, but also at whether it was part of an ongoing series of attacks, what steps were already taken to deter future attacks, and what force could reasonably be judged to be needed to successfully deter future attacks.').

domains to space and vice versa. This is because the inherent right of self-defence extends to all domains to which the UN Charter applies, including space. Under Article 51, an appropriate and proportionate use of force in self-defence by a victim State in response to an armed attack by an aggressor in any domain may include actions against space objects of the aggressor State or other military operations against the aggressor State in space. Thus, for an aggressor State acting in a terrestrial domain, space is not a sanctuary from the lawful exercise of self-defence by a victim State. More generally of course, the lawful exercise of self-defence and all other non-aggressive military activities in space are fully consistent with the concept of peaceful purposes in the space law regime (see Rule 3: Peaceful Purposes in Outer Space), although all military activities and operations, including the exercise of the right of self-defence, must be harmonized with other applicable legal regimes to the extent possible.

Imminent Armed Attack and Anticipatory Self-Defence

10. The question of whether a State may engage in anticipatory self-defence to address an imminent armed attack has been much debated. A strict view of Article 51 of the UN Charter focuses on the wording of the English text which recognizes the inherent right of a State to engage in self-defence 'if an armed attack occurs' against a Member of the United Nations.[336] In accordance with this view, any pre-existing customary right to anticipatory self-defence did not survive the adoption of the UN Charter and the right of self-defence only arises if an armed attack 'occurs'. However, subject to the conditions discussed in this Rule, there appears to be long-standing, substantial, and growing support among States for the view that the right to self-defence under the UN Charter extends to a clearly indicated, imminent armed attack.[337] Furthermore, several States have expressed the view that self-defence against an imminent armed attack was part of customary international

---

[336] Although the English version of art 51 is the focus of most discussions in this area, the French version (and Spanish) appears to represent a more ambiguous requirement about the timing of the armed attack ('dans le cas où un Membre des Nations Unies est l'objet d'une agression armée'). If translated into English, this would mean '[i]n the case where a Member of the United Nations is *the object of an armed attack*' (emphasis added).

[337] See UNGA, 'A More Secure World: Our Shared Responsibility, Report of the High-level Panel on Threats, Challenges and Change' (2 December 2004) UN Doc A/59/565, para 188 ('a threatened State, according to long established international law, can take military action as long as the threatened attack is imminent, no other means would deflect it and the action is proportionate'); UNGA, 'In Larger Freedom: Towards Development, Security and Human Rights for All—Report of the Secretary General' (21 March 2005) UN Doc A/59/2005, para 124 ('Imminent threats are fully covered by Article 51, which safeguards the inherent right of sovereign States to defend themselves against armed attack. Lawyers have long recognized that this covers an imminent attack as well as one that has already happened.'). It should be noted, however, that not all States at the United Nations agreed with this assessment.

law before the adoption of the UN Charter and remains part of customary international law today.³³⁸

11. The traditionally accepted expression of the standard of imminence required in anticipatory self-defence is the 'Webster formula' contained in correspondence by US Secretary of State Webster to Lord Ashburton following the 1837 *Caroline* incident: a State is permitted to act when it can show a 'necessity of self-defence, instant, overwhelming, leaving no choice of means, and no moment for deliberation'.³³⁹

12. The right to respond with armed force to an imminent armed attack is generally referred to as anticipatory self-defence and that is the term used in this *Manual*. However, terminology in this area of law is itself a subject of debate and is not always used consistently. Other terms that are sometimes used in this area include 'pre-emptive' and 'preventive' self-defence. Although these terms are subject to different interpretations, they are often used in connection with measures claimed to be for purposes of defence against possible future attacks, even if those attacks are not certain to occur, or not judged to be imminent. Thus defined, the concepts of pre-emptive or preventive self-defence have no foundation in international law and could be easily abused, undermining the UN Charter regime.³⁴⁰ If such an interpretation of pre-emptive or preventive self-defence were to be applied in the context of military space activities, a direct-ascent ASAT could be attacked at any time even if there was no evidence of an imminent armed attack. Such an action would not be a lawful exercise of the right of self-defence.

---

³³⁸ House of Lords Debates 21 April 2004, vol 660, cols 370–371 (Lord Goldsmith, UK Attorney-General): 'It is clear that the language of Article 51 was not intended to create a new right of self-defence. Article 51 recognises the inherent right of self-defence that states enjoy under international law... It is not a new invention. The charter did not therefore affect the scope of the right of self-defence existing at that time in customary international law, which included the right to use force in anticipation of an imminent armed attack.'); US DoD Law of War Manual (n 11) para 1.11.5.1 ('Under customary international law, States had, and continue to have, the right to take measures in response to imminent attacks.'); George Brandis (Attorney-General of Australia) 'The Right of Self-Defence Against Imminent Armed Attack in International Law'(lecture given at TC Beirne School of Law, 25 May 2017) [https://perma.cc/A43Z-X8SJ] ('it is now recognised that customary international law permits self defence not only against an armed attack that has occurred but also against one that is imminent'); Danish LOAC Manual (n 325) para 2.2.3 ('States may exercise this right of self-defence in anticipation of an imminent armed attack. This is not an inherent right under the UN Charter but is recognised in customary international law.').
³³⁹ Webster (n 324). The Webster formulation in the *Caroline* incident has been cited and re-stated in numerous international proceedings. See eg judgment in *Trial of the Major War Criminals before the International Military Tribunal—Volume 1, Official Text in the English Language* (Secretariat of the International Military Tribunal 1947) 207 [https://perma.cc/HP55-ZWHB] (noting, after the defence had argued that Germany was compelled to attack Norway in a preventative action to forestall an Allied invasion, 'it must be remembered that preventive action in foreign territory is justified only in case of "an instant and overwhelming necessity for self-defense, leaving no choice of means, and no moment of deliberation"'.).
³⁴⁰ UK Attorney-General Lord Goldsmith (n 338) col 370 ('It is therefore the [United Kingdom] Government's view that international law permits the use of force in self-defence against an imminent attack but does not authorise the use of force to mount a pre-emptive strike against a threat that is more remote.').

13. An assessment of imminence must be made in good faith on the basis of sound evidence and that there must be a reasonable and objective basis for concluding that an armed attack is imminent.[341] This assessment must also take into account the nature of the threat and be applied with regard to the particular circumstances of each case, including the capabilities of the attacker and the possibility that the attack may come without further warning.[342] In this respect, one State's official but deceptive statement of its intention to conduct its space activity such as a test launch does not automatically deprive the potential target State of its right of self-defence if its good faith assessment of the evidence concludes that the space activity actually constitutes an imminent armed attack.

14. In space, one type of threat that deserves special attention in this area involves any threat to satellites that provide an early warning of nuclear ballistic missile launches, related command and communication systems, and hotline communications satellites links (see Rule 21: Use of Force, paragraph 23). The unique stabilizing function that these satellites and systems perform in maintaining international peace and security, the key role that they play in preventing a first use of nuclear weapons, and the catastrophic consequences of a conflict involving nuclear weapons mean that a State is likely to be justified invoking a lawful right to exercise self-defence against any adversary State posing an imminent threat of armed attack against those satellites and systems.[343]

'Non-State' Actors

15. Article 51 of the UN Charter does not specify that the armed attack that gives rise to the exercise of self-defence must be carried out by a State and thus the text leaves

---

[341] The Rt Hon Jeremy Wright (UK Attorney-General), 'The Modern Law of Self-Defence' (lecture given to International Institute for Strategic Studies, 11 January 2017) [https://perma.cc/2XUW-ALG5] ('states do need to be able to take necessary and proportionate action where there is clear evidence that armed attacks are being planned and directed against them, and where it is the only feasible means to effectively disrupt those attacks'); Australia Attorney-General Brandis (n 338) ('Australia's longstanding view is that there must be a reasonable and objective basis for determining that an attack is imminent. And this view can only be formed on the basis of all available evidence when the assessment is made … it is an assessment which must be carried out in "good faith and on the basis of sound evidence", the standard reflected in the Chatham House Principles [n 327]. Nothing less will establish a sufficient level of confidence to justify the use of force in self defence against an imminent armed attack.').

[342] Chatham House Principles (n 327) 8. The 'nature of the threat' that a State faces is arguably broad enough to include an assessment of the likely effects of the attack, so that a State threatened by a possible nuclear attack might justifiably respond sooner than a State threatened by conventional attack.

[343] See William H Taft IV (US State Department Legal Adviser) 'International Law and the Use of Force' (remarks given at Georgetown University Law Center Symposium, 27 October 2004) [https://perma.cc/NH83-DFLV] ('The right of self-defense could be meaningless if a state cannot prevent an aggressive first strike involving weapons of mass destruction. The right of self-defense must attach early enough to be meaningful and effective, and the concept of "imminence" must take into account the threat posed by weapons of mass destruction, the intentions of those who possess such weapons and the catastrophic consequences of their use.').

room for an interpretation that armed attacks can be carried out by non-State actors (actors that have no connection with any State).³⁴⁴ Although there are extensive legal debates over whether a State has a right to use force in self-defence against non-State actors outside its borders, there is considerable State practice, stretching back many years and especially since the 11 September 2001 terrorist attacks,³⁴⁵ which provides clear support for the claim of the right of self-defence on an extraterritorial basis against non-State actors. In particular, military actions by numerous States on Syrian territory against Daesh (ISIS, ISIL, or the so-called Islamic State) since 2015 have clearly demonstrated the willingness of numerous States to invoke the right of self-defence under Article 51 to conduct extraterritorial military operations against a non-state actor.³⁴⁶ Difficult legal questions continue to be raised, however, regarding the way that this right self-defence against a non-State actor is exercised, particularly when it involves actions on the territory of a third State that give rise to disputes over that that State's responsibilities and claims by that State that its sovereignty has been violated or that is the victim of the unlawful use of force.

16. Non-State actors also pose questions regarding the legal status of a continuing series of armed attacks and further imminent armed attacks. New types of threats,

---

³⁴⁴ This interpretation is clearly reflected in various national military manuals and State position papers that focus on the act (and not the actor) in defining the right to self-defence. See eg Danish LOAC Manual (n 325) para 2.2.3 ('Whether the attack is conducted by a State or a non-State actor has no effect the right of self-defence.'); US DoD Law of War Manual (n 11) para 1.11.5.4 ('The inherent right of self-defense, recognized in Article 51 of the Charter of the United Nations, applies in response to any "armed attack," not just attacks that originate with States.'). This approach is particularly true with respect to State's views regarding the possible actions of non-State actors in cyberspace. See eg Submission by Germany, Official Compendium of National Contributions (n 120) 43 ('Acts of non-State actors can also constitute armed attacks. Germany has expressed this view both with regard to the attacks by Al Qaeda and the attacks of ISIS.').
³⁴⁵ Military operations conducted by the United States in self-defence against al Qaeda in Afghanistan notably received support from many States. See eg NATO, 'Statement by the North Atlantic Council' (NATO Press Release, 12 September 2001) [https://perma.cc/W7MQ-TG8R]; Organization of American States, 'Terrorist Threats to the Americas' (Twenty-Fourth Meeting of the Consultation of Ministers of Foreign Affairs, 21 September 2001) OAS Doc RC.24/RES.1/01.
³⁴⁶ See ILA Final Report (n 159) 15, fn 95 cataloguing letters from numerous States to the UN Security Council in 2015 and 2016 reflecting a mixture of claims based on the right to engage in individual and collective self-defence (on behalf of Iraq) across borders against non-State actors (Daesh/ISIL forces) in Syria. These include letters to the Security Council by Canada, Turkey, the United Kingdom, the United States, Australia, France, Denmark, Norway, and Belgium. See eg UNSC, 'Identical letters dated 8 September 2015 from the Permanent Representative of France to the United Nations addressed to the Secretary-General and the President of the Security Council' (9 September 2015) UN Doc S/2015/745 ('In accordance with Article 51 of the Charter of the United Nations, France has taken actions involving the participation of military aircraft in response to attacks carried out by ISIL from the territory of the Syrian Arab Republic.'); UNSC, 'Letter dated 24 July 2015 from the Chargé d'affaires a.i. of the Permanent Mission of Turkey to the United Nations addressed to the President of the Security Council' (24 July 2015) UN Doc S/2015/563 ('The terrorist attack that took the lives of 32 Turkish citizens in Suruç on 20 July 2015 reaffirms that Turkey is under a clear and imminent threat of continuing attack from Daesh ... Individual and collective self-defence is our inherent right under international law, as reflected in Article 51 of the Charter of the United Nations. On this basis, Turkey has initiated necessary and proportionate military actions against Daesh in Syria ....').

258   RULE 26 SELF-DEFENCE

including those posed by terrorist/non-State armed groups, may mean that the concept of what constitutes an imminent armed attack will develop to meet these new circumstances and that a State may be able 'to act in self-defence in circumstances where there is evidence of further imminent attacks by terrorist groups, even if there is no specific evidence of where such an attack will take place or of the precise nature of the attack'.[347]

17. In a strictly legal sense, there cannot be a belligerent 'non-State actor' in space, at least under current conditions and under the existing space legal regime.[348] While non-governmental entities, including corporations and individuals, are engaged in space activities, these entities operate within a State-oriented space legal regime.[349] States bear international responsibility for national activities in outer space, 'whether such activities are carried on by governmental agencies or by non-governmental entities'.[350] Thus, as a national of a State or entity regulated by that State, a 'non-governmental entity' is viewed by the space law regime as the responsibility of a State (see discussion of nationals and national activities in outer space in Rule 10: Responsibility of States for National Activities in Outer Space). In this capacity, the State is also responsible for ensuring that the activities of these non-governmental entities are carried out in conformity with the OST and other international legal obligations and are subject to that State's required 'authorization and continuing supervision'.[351] Thus, although no national State territory exists in space, actors in space (governmental and non-governmental) are very much part of a State's responsibility. With respect to a particular satellite, space station, or other space object, there may be significant additional legal connections with several specific States (see Note on Legal Connections Between States and a Space Object). Besides the States responsible for these space objects under Article VI of the OST, States with other legal connections may include the State of Registration, which exercises jurisdiction and control over a space object and the personnel thereof (see Rule 8: Registration of Space Objects) and the launching State(s), which are

---

[347] UK Attorney-General Lord Goldsmith (n 338) col 370 ('It must be right that states are able to act in self-defence in circumstances where there is evidence of further imminent attacks by terrorist groups, even if there is no specific evidence of where such an attack will take place or of the precise nature of the attack.').

[348] Assets of States in space have been used to assist in targeting non-State armed groups on Earth and it is conceivable that non-State armed groups could acquire counterspace weapons and attack space assets of a State (see Rule 10: Responsibility for National Activities in Outer Space and Rule 30: Non-International Armed Conflicts). However, non-international armed conflicts cannot originate or take place solely in space (see Rule 30: Non-International Armed Conflicts).

[349] Even in situations in which space activities are carried out by an international organization, art VI of the OST (n 3) requires that when 'activities are carried on in outer space ... by an international organization, responsibility for compliance with this Treaty shall be borne both by the international organization and *by the States Parties to the Treaty participating in such organization*' (emphasis added).

[350] ibid. See also Rule 10: Responsibility of States for National Activities in Outer Space.

[351] ibid.

liable for damages caused by the space object (see Rule 12: International Liability for Damage Caused by Space Objects).

While space-based assets have been used to assist the military forces of States engaged in armed conflicts with non-State actors in other domains (see Rule 30: Non-International Armed Conflicts), current technological barriers to entry and the space law regime itself prevent belligerent non-State actors from operating independently in space. If, however, an organized armed group composed of terrorists, insurgents, or other non-State actors were somehow able to engage in an armed attack against a State in space, it would give rise to the right of self-defence by the victim State, since the UN Charter applies to all activities in space. Attribution of any State responsibility for such an armed attack in these circumstances would raise unprecedented and untested issues.

18.

Reporting and Termination of Defensive Measures

A State is required to report immediately any action, including a military space operation, that constitutes an exercise of the right of self-defence to the UN Security Council under Article 51 of the UN Charter. The failure to make such a report does not invalidate a State's lawful exercise of its right to engage in self-defence, although such a failure could nonetheless be viewed procedurally as contradicting its claim to be acting on the basis of self-defence.[352] In addition, under Article 51 of the Charter, a military space operation in self-defence must cease when 'the Security Council has taken measures necessary to maintain international peace and security'. The UN Charter does not specify what these measures might be, although the Security Council clearly has the power to restore international peace and security by imposing binding enforcement measures on all States pursuant to Chapter VII. Although the Security Council has not explicitly exercised its authority to divest a State of its right to continue to exercise its right of self-defence in a conflict, it can and has called for ceasefires prohibiting all further military action by any State, including by the defender.[353]

19.

---

[352] *Nicaragua* Judgment (n 115) para 235 ('[T]he United States has itself taken the view that failure to observe the requirement to make a report [under art 51] contradicted a State's claim to be acting on the basis of collective self-defence.').

[353] See eg Oscar Schachter, 'United Nations Law in the Gulf Conflict' (1991) 85 American Journal of International Law 452, 458–59 (discussing suspension of the right to use force in self-defence in the context of UN Security Council resolutions and measures during the 1990–1991 Gulf War and noting that '[s]ignificantly, no government contested the ultimate right of the Council to prohibit all military action by a state, even if defensive').

Rule 27
Collective Self-Defence

A State may exercise its inherent right of collective self-defence against any activity, including an action from, to, or within space, that amounts to an actual or imminent armed attack directed against another State upon request by the victim State.

Overview of Legal Basis of Rule

1. Article 51 of the UN Charter recognizes that the inherent right of self-defence covers both collective and individual self-defence, which is reflective of customary international law.[354] A State may exercise the right of collective self-defence when an armed attack, including a military space activity that amounts to an actual or imminent armed attack, is directed against another State, upon request by that victim State. This Rule thus encompasses two complementary rights. First, a State that is the victim of an armed attack has a right to seek assistance, and second, the other State or States have a right to act in assisting the victim State in its self-defence. All the requirements for the lawful exercise of the right of self-defence (Rule 26: Self-Defence) also apply to collective self-defence.

Requirements and Application

2. Under customary international law, a State may invoke the right of collective self-defence only when it has declared itself to be the victim of an armed attack and has requested assistance from other States.[355] For instance, consider a situation where State A's military communication satellite is subject to a persistent high-powered laser attack by a hostile actor that amounts to a use of force and an armed attack, but State A does not have technological capability to fend it off. If State A is the victim of an armed attack and declares itself to be a victim of an armed attack, it is entitled

---

[354] UN Charter (n 2) art 51; *Nicaragua* Judgment (n 115) para 193.
[355] *Nicaragua* Judgment (n 115) para 199 ('the Court finds that in customary international law ... there is no rule permitting the exercise of collective self-defence in the absence of a request by the State which regards itself as the victim of an armed attack'. The Court further noted that this requirement for a request for assistance by the victim State was 'additional to the requirement that such a State should have declared itself to have been attacked'.

to request State B for assistance. State B may then invoke the right of collective self-defence in conducting a military operation to assist State A in terminating the laser attack and helping to defend it against further attacks.

3. Subject to paragraph 4 below, collective self-defence requires that an explicit request for assistance must be made by the victim State.[356] Thus, another State may not invoke the right of collective self-defence to assist the victim State solely on the basis of its own assessment of the situation.

4. A special case of a request for assistance by a victim State may be accomplished through the operation of a pre-existing collective self-defence agreement. The manner in which the right of collective self-defence can be exercised under such a pre-existing agreement depends on the requirements and conditions set forth in that agreement. Some pre-existing collective security agreements, such as the NATO Treaty, may prescribe that an armed attack against one of its Member States shall be considered as an attack against them all and that each Member State shall assist the victim State in the exercise of collective self-defence.[357] However, it is important to carefully review the terms in these treaties and examine how these terms have been interpreted and implemented by their respective organizations. For example, Article V of the NATO Treaty requires each Member State only to take 'such action as it deems necessary' in assisting another Member State in collective self-defence.[358] Other collective security agreements[359] may contain similar or more ambiguous terms, histories of nuanced interpretations and implementation, and

---

[356] ibid para 232 ('It is also evident that if the victim State wishes another State to come to its help in the exercise of the right of collective self-defence, it will normally make an *express request* to that effect' (emphasis added).

[357] The North Atlantic Treaty (adopted 4 April 1949, entered into force 24 August 1949) 34 UNTS 243, art 5.

[358] ibid. (This action by States may include, but does not require, 'the use of armed force' to restore and maintain the security of the North Atlantic area.).

[359] See eg Security Treaty between Australia, New Zealand, and the United States of America (adopted 1 September 1950, entered into force 29 April 1952) 131 UNTS 83, art IV ('Each Party recognizes that an armed attack in the Pacific Area on any of the Parties would be dangerous to its own peace and safety and declares that it would act to meet the common danger in accordance with its constitutional processes.'); Treaty of Mutual Cooperation and Security Between Japan and the United States of America (adopted 19 January 1960, entered into force 19 May 1960) 11 UST 1632, art V ('Each Party recognizes that an armed attack against either Party in the territories under the administration of Japan would be dangerous to its own peace and safety and declares that it would act to meet the common danger in accordance with its constitutional provisions and processes.'); Inter-American Treaty of Reciprocal Assistance (adopted 2 September 1947, entered into force 3 December 1948, as amended 26 July 1975) 21 UNTS 77, art 3 ('The High Contracting Parties agree that an armed attack by any State against an American State shall be considered as an attack against all the American States and, consequently, each one of the said Contracting Parties undertakes to assist in meeting the attack in the exercise of the inherent right of individual or collective self-defense recognized by Article 51 of the Charter of the United Nations.'); Charter of the Organization of American States (adopted 30 April 1948, entered into force 13 December 1951, as last amended 10 June 1993) 119 UNTS 48, art 3(h)('An act of aggression against one American State is an act of aggression against all the other American States'), art 28 ('Every act of aggression by a State against the territorial integrity or the inviolability of the territory or against the sovereignty or political independence of an American State shall be considered an act of aggression against the other American States').

various required procedures. These must all be carefully examined to determine whether a State is authorized or obligated under any particular agreement to provide assistance in collective self-defence and whether such mechanisms serve as an effective substitute for an explicit request by the victim State for assistance in collective self-defence and whether further action is required by the treaty organization or by the victim State.

Rule 28
Collective Security Measures

(a) The United Nations Security Council has broad discretion in determining whether an activity, including a military space activity, constitutes a threat to the peace, breach of the peace, or act of aggression, and may impose enforcement measures on the responsible State under Chapter VII of the Charter of the United Nations.

(b) The United Nations Security Council may authorize military space activities for purposes of the maintenance of the international peace and security in accordance with the Charter of the United Nations.

Overview of Legal Basis of Rule

1. The UN Security Council has the primary responsibility under the UN Charter for the maintenance of international peace and security.[360] In this regard, the Security Council is responsible for determining 'the existence of any threat to the peace, breach of the peace, or act of aggression and shall make recommendations, or decide what measures shall be taken in accordance with Articles 41 and 42, to maintain or restore international peace and security'.[361] This means that, upon finding a threat to the peace, breach of the peace, or act of aggression, the Security Council can either make recommendations or decide to use its 'exceptional powers'[362] under Articles 41 and 42 to take actions which are referred to as 'enforcement measures'.[363] Enforcement measures can range from a wide array of non-forcible

---

[360] UN Charter (n 2) art 24(1). While the Security Council has primary responsibility in this area, under art 11 the General Assembly may also discuss 'any questions relating to the maintenance of international peace and security' and make recommendations. However, art 12 provides that '[w]hile the Security Council is exercising in respect of any dispute or situation the functions assigned to it in the present Charter, the General Assembly shall not make any recommendation with regard to that dispute or situation unless the Security Council so requests'. Under the 'Uniting for Peace Resolution', if General Assembly resolved that 'if the Security Council, because of lack of unanimity of the permanent members, fails to exercise its primary responsibility to act as required to maintain international peace and security ..., the General Assembly shall consider the matter immediately with the view to making recommendations to Members ... in order to restore international peace and security. If not in session, the General Assembly may meet using the mechanism of the emergency special session.' 'Uniting for Peace' UNGA Res 377 (V) (3 November 1950) UN Doc A/RES/5/377.

[361] UN Charter (n 2) art 39.

[362] *Prosecutor v Tadić* (Decision on the Defence Motion for Interlocutory Appeal on Jurisdiction) ICTY-94-1 (2 October 1995) (*Tadić* decision) para 31.

[363] United Nations, 'Maintain International Peace and Security' [perma.cc/W3VA-KCCM]. As noted, although it does not have the 'primary' responsibility for the maintenance of international

264   RULE 28 COLLECTIVE SECURITY MEASURES

actions under Article 41 (see paragraph 8) to forcible actions under Article 42 (see paragraphs 9–10). Before making recommendations or deciding upon enforcement measures, Article 40 provides that the Security Council may call upon the parties concerned to comply with 'provisional measures' as it deems necessary or desirable in order to prevent an aggravation of the situation (see paragraphs 2–3). Unlike a non-legally binding recommendation or a call for cooperation, an action by the Security Council which is styled as a 'decision' is a legally binding obligation which all UN Member States, 'agree to accept and carry out'.[364] Enforcement measures of any sort, including those involving military space activities, may not be taken by any State or regional organization unless authorized by the Security Council.[365]

Provisional Measures

2. The objective of provisional measures under Article 40 of the Charter is to 'prevent an aggravation of the situation'.[366] While the types of possible provisional measures that fall under Article 40 are not expressly enumerated in the UN Charter, Security Council practice shows numerous and diverse examples that include calling for, recommending, or demanding 'a withdrawal of armed forces, a cessation of hostilities, a conclusion or observance of a ceasefire or a creation of the conditions necessary for unimpeded delivery of humanitarian assistance'.[367] Provisional measures could thus include actions calling for or demanding the suspension of designated military space activities and the cessation of hostilities in space.

---

peace and security, the UN General Assembly is authorized under the UN Charter to discuss any questions relating to the maintenance of international peace and security and make recommendations. Furthermore, following the Russian invasion of Ukraine in February 2022, the UN General Assembly decided to automatically meet within 10 days if the veto is used in the Security Council by one of its five permanent members. See 'UN General Assembly mandates meeting in wake of any Security Council veto' (UN News 26 April 2022) [https://perma.cc/6TS5-P3PM]; UNGA, 'Standing mandate for a General Assembly debate when a veto is cast in the Security Council', UNGA Res 76/262 (26 April 2022).

[364] UN Charter (n 2) art 25.
[365] ibid art 53.
[366] ibid art 40 (further providing that 'measures shall be without prejudice to the rights, claims, or position of the parties concerned' and that the Security Council 'shall duly take account of failure to comply with such provisional measures').
[367] See 'Article 40—Provisional measures to prevent the aggravation of a situation' in UNSC, 'Repertoire of Security Council Practice' (online database, UNSC 2020) (UN Repertoire of UNSC Practice) <https://www.un.org/securitycouncil/content/repertoire/actions> accessed on 2 March 2020. The repertoire provides a comprehensive review of provisional measures adopted by the UN Security Council and 'outlines the decisions of the Council containing specific provisional measures that the Council called upon the parties to comply with in order to prevent an aggravation of the situation, and covers instances where the adoption of measures falling under Article 40 was discussed'.

Although Article 40 indicates that provisional measures to prevent the aggravation of a conflict are to be adopted prior to the imposition of enforcement measures under Articles 41 and 42, the practice of the Security Council 'reflects a more flexible interpretation of Article 40'.[368] In fact, in light of 'prolonged, complex and rapidly changing nature of conflicts' dealt with by the Security Council over many years, provisional measures have in some cases been 'imposed in parallel to the adoption of measures under Articles 41 and 42 of the Charter'.[369]

3.

Determination of Threat to the Peace, Breach of the Peace, or Act of Aggression

The Security Council decides what measures shall be taken in accordance with Articles 41 and 42 to maintain or restore international peace and security based on its determination that there exists a threat to the peace, breach of the peace, or act of aggression.[370] This determination is political in nature, as the Security Council is a political and not a judicial body and it is not required to provide a legal record or a legal rationale for its decisions. While an 'act of aggression' may be more amenable to a legal analysis since it has been defined by the UN General Assembly as 'the most serious and dangerous form of the illegal use of force',[371] a threat to peace is unquestionably a more political concept. As recognized in paragraph (b) of this Rule, the Security Council thus has enormous discretion in making this determination.[372]

4.

The great discretion afforded the Security Council in determining the existence of a threat to the peace, breach of the peace, or act of aggression means that its decisions could encompass responses to actions in any domain, including military space activities. For example, if the actions by one State against another State's military satellites involve a use of force (see Rule 21: Use of Force), the Security Council may determine that those actions constitute a threat of the peace, or act of aggression. Other types of actions in space, that do not constitute a use of force, may nonetheless also constitute a threat to the peace. For example, the Security Council could determine that the placement by a State of nuclear weapons in space may constitute such a threat, in a manner similar to the way the Security Council has previously affirmed that the 'proliferation of nuclear, chemical and biological weapons

5.

---

[368] United Nations, *Repertoire of the Practice of the Security Council—Supplement 2014-2015* (ST/PSCA/1/Add.19, United Nations 2018) 307 [perma.cc/5SBH-Q2VE].
[369] ibid.
[370] UN Charter (n 2) art 39.
[371] Definition of Aggression Resolution (n 165).
[372] *Tadić* decision (n 362) para 31 (noting, however, that in making this determination the Security Council does not have 'totally unfettered discretion, as it has to remain, at the very least, within the limits of the Purposes and Principles of the Charter').

[WMDs], as well as their means of delivery, constitutes a threat to international peace and security.[373] Similarly, use of space technologies, such as rockets that can function as ballistic missiles, may give rise to a threat to international peace and security and be the subject of the UN Security Council enforcement actions. For example, in 2016, the Security Council condemned the successful launch by the Democratic People's Republic of Korea (DPRK) of an Earth observation satellite since it used ballistic missile technology.[374] The Security Council reaffirmed that proliferation of WMDs and their means of delivery constitutes a threat to international peace and security, again banned further space launches by the DPRK that use ballistic missile technology, and decided on enforcement measures under Article 41 that included sanctions on the DPRK National Aerospace Development Administration.[375]

Enforcement Measures Generally

6. Upon finding a threat to the peace, breach of the peace, or act of aggression under Chapter VII of the UN Charter (see following paragraphs), the UN Security Council may exercise it exceptional powers to impose enforcement measures under Articles 41 and 42. These powers are 'coercive vis-à-vis the culprit State or entity' and are also 'mandatory vis-à-vis the other Member States'.[376] In the latter case, not only are Member States required to carry out the decisions of the Security Council (Article 25), but they are also under a specific obligation 'to carry out the decisions of the Security Council for the maintenance of international peace and security' (Article 48); to 'give the United Nations every assistance in any action it takes in accordance with the present Charter' (Article 2(5)); and to cooperate with each other 'in affording mutual assistance in carrying out the measures decided upon by the Security Council' (Article 49).

Regional Organizations

7. Regional arrangements, agencies, or organizations,[377] including those that operate under a collective security agreement such as NATO, may be utilized by the Security

---

[373] UNSC Res 2270 (2016) UN Doc S/RES/2270. Such an action would also separately be a violation of art IV of the OST (n 3) (see Rule 5: Weapons of Mass Destruction).

[374] ibid preamble para 11, para 1, Annex 2.9.

[375] ibid Annex 2.9. These measures included freezing the assets of various individuals and entities, including the DPRK National Aerospace Development Administration (based on that entity's involvement in the 'DPRK's development of space science and technology, including satellite launches and carrier rockets'.)

[376] *Tadić* decision (n 362) para 31.

[377] See UN Charter (n 2) art 52(1) ('Nothing in the present Charter precludes the existence of regional arrangements or agencies for dealing with such matters relating to the maintenance of international

ENFORCEMENT MEASURES NOT INVOLVING THE USE OF FORCE 267

Council in enforcement measures under Chapter VIII of the UN Charter.[378] Such measures may include military space activities undertaken by a regional organization and its member States and may utilize the space assets of member States and of the regional organizations. States participating in collective security activities as part of enforcement measures authorized by the Security Council (under Articles 41 or 42) are distinct from, but may complement, States exercising their inherent right of collective self-defence (under Article 51).[379] Enforcement measures authorized by the Security Council (often referred to as a type of 'collective security measure') and collective self-defence activities may both be performed by regional organizations operating under a collective security agreement (Rule 27: Collective Self-Defence).

Enforcement Measures Not Involving the Use of Force

8. Once a situation is recognized by the Security Council as constituting a threat to the peace, a breach of the peace, or an act of aggression, it may authorize and impose broad a range of forcible and non-forcible enforcement measures. Enforcement measures not employing the use of force under Article 41 often precede measures that employ the use of force Article 42. By invoking Article 41 of the UN Charter, the Security Council may 'decide what measures not involving the use of armed force are to be employed to give effect to its decisions, and it may call upon the Members of the United Nations to apply such measures'. According to Article 41, these measures may include 'complete or partial interruption of economic relations and of rail, sea, air, postal, telegraphic, radio, and other means of communication, and the severance of diplomatic relations'. It is important to note that this list is not exhaustive and that the Security Council has historically authorized a wide of variety measures, tailored to many different situations, that it concluded did not qualify as a 'use of force'[380] (see Rule 21: Use of Force). Even within the specific examples of measures that do not involve the use of force which are set forth

peace and security as are appropriate for regional action provided that such arrangements or agencies and their activities are consistent with the Purposes and Principles of the United Nations.').

[378] ibid art 53 ('The Security Council shall, where appropriate, utilize such regional arrangements or agencies for enforcement action under its authority. But no enforcement action shall be taken under regional arrangements or by regional agencies without the authorization of the Security Council....').

[379] For example, the Security Council imposed enforcement measures against Iraq for its invasion of Kuwait in 1990 and authorized Member States who were already 'cooperating with the Government of Kuwait' in collective self-defence to engage in enforcement measures under Chapter VII to implement Security Council resolutions against Iraq and to restore international peace and security in the area. UNSC Res 678 (29 November 1990) UN Doc S/RES/678, para 2.

[380] See UN repertoire of UNSC Practice (n 368) 'C. Article 41—Measures not involving the use of armed force' (which 'captures decisions of the Council imposing, modifying, exempting from or terminating measures under Article 41 and highlights issues that were raised in the Council's deliberations in connection with Article 41').

in Article 41, military space activities could be utilized by the Security Council to disrupt communication satellites as part of enforcement measures focused on the 'complete or partial interruption of ... telegraphic, radio and other means of communication'. Within the broad scope of its exceptional powers, the Security Council could also employ military space activities to assist in the implementation of enforcement measures in terrestrial domains that do not involve the use of force. For example, an enforcement action could utilize satellites to detect the shipping of prohibited items in implementing economic sanctions against a targeted State.

Enforcement Measures Involving the Use of Force

9. Military space activities that constitute a use of force (see Rule 21: Use of Force) may be employed by the Security Council as part of an enforcement action authorized under Article 42 of the UN Charter. While Article 42 provides that the Security Council 'may take such action by air, sea, or land forces as may be necessary to maintain or restore international peace and security', the Security Council may also take such action by space forces. Although to date there is no State practice on this point, the object and purpose of the UN Charter supports broad Security Council power to maintain or restore international peace and security. International courts assessing the Security Council's authority have also concluded that it has 'broad discretion in deciding on the course of action and evaluating the appropriateness of the measures to be taken'.[381]

10. Although the Security Council is authorized to employ a wide range of enforcement measures that it deems necessary to restore international peace and security, it may also impose whatever limitations it chooses to place on such measures, including limits on the scope and areas of military operations that are authorized in any enforcement measure. In some cases, after finding a threat to international peace, breach of the peace, or act of aggression, the Security Council has used all-encompassing language with respect to enforcement measures, authorizing 'all necessary measures' under Chapter VII of the UN Charter to restore international peace and security, thus encompassing both forcible and non-forcible measures of all types (which could include military space activities).[382] At the same time, the

---

[381] See eg *Tadić* decision (n 362) para 31 (further observing that that if a question arises 'as to whether the choice of the Security Council is limited to the measures provided for in Articles 41 and 42 of the Charter (as the language of Article 39 suggests), or whether it has even larger discretion in the form of general powers to maintain and restore international peace and security under Chapter VII at large', the answer to the latter question is 'one of course does not have to locate every measure decided by the Security Council under Chapter VII within the confines of Articles 41 and 42, or possibly Article 40').

[382] See eg UNSC Res 678 (n 379) para 2 (acting under Chapter VII of the Charter, the Security Council demanded that Iraq comply fully with prior resolutions regarding its invasion of Kuwait and authorized Member States cooperating with the Government of Kuwait 'to use all necessary means to uphold and implement [prior relevant resolutions] and to restore international peace and security in the area').

Security Council may impose restrictions or limits on the scope, objectives, or execution of enforcement measures.[383] For example, with respect to an enforcement action that was undertaken by military aircraft against Libya in 2011, the Security Council limited the scope and objective of that action by authorizing Member States 'to protect civilians and civilian populated areas under threat of attack in the Libyan Arab Jamahiriya, including Benghazi, while excluding a foreign occupation force of any form on any part of Libyan territory'.[384] It further decided to 'establish a ban on all flights in the airspace of the Libyan Arab Jamahiriya in order to help protect civilians'.[385] In a similar manner, the Security Council could authorize an enforcement measure under Chapter VII that employs only a restricted set of military space activities or utilizes the military space activities for a specific objective. The enforcement measures could also be directed at restricting the target State's military space activities.

Peacekeeping Operations

11. In fulfilling its primary responsibility for the maintenance of international peace and security, the Security Council may adopt a range of measures, including the establishment of UN peacekeeping operations. Although they were once viewed as primarily performing the function of monitoring ceasefires, modern peacekeeping operations are often multi-dimensional and are called upon to facilitate 'the promotion of national dialogue and reconciliation, protect civilians, assist in the disarmament, demobilization and reintegration of combatants, support the organization of elections, protect and promote human rights, and assist in restoring the rule of law'.[386] The legal basis for such action is primarily associated with Chapter VI of the UN Charter which deals with the 'Pacific Settlement of Disputes'.[387]

---

[383] See UN repertoire of UNSC Practice (n 367) 'D. Article 42—Other measures to maintain or restore international peace and security' (providing case studies that examine the Council's authorization of enforcement action under Chapter VII of the Charter.).

[384] UNSC Res 1973 (17 March 2011) UN Doc S/RES/1973, para 4.

[385] ibid. The Resolution also employed regional organizations to assist in these enforcement measures by '[a]uthoriz[ing] Member States that have notified the Secretary-General, acting nationally or through regional organizations or arrangements, and acting in cooperation with the Secretary-General, to take all necessary measures ... to protect civilians and civilian populated areas under threat of attack').

[386] United Nations Peacekeeping Best Practices Section, *UN Peacekeeping Operations—Principles and Guidelines* (United Nations 2008) 6 [perma.cc/4K3H-YDZ3].

[387] Chapter VI of the UN Charter does not specifically refer to peacekeeping operations but does provide in art 33 a broad framework for diverse measures that promote peace through agreed cooperation: 'the parties to any dispute, the continuance of which is likely to endanger the maintenance of international peace and security, shall, first of all, seek a solution by negotiation, enquiry, mediation, conciliation, arbitration, judicial settlement, resort to regional agencies or arrangements, or other peaceful means of their own choice'. In practice, however, the Security Council has not explicitly invoked Chapter VI when passing a resolution authorizing the deployment of a United Nations peacekeeping operation.

A peacekeeping operation may also involve regional arrangements and agencies in the maintenance of international peace and security under both Chapter VI and Chapter VIII of the UN Charter.[388] These operations are characterized by (i) consent of the parties, (ii) impartiality, and (iii) non-use of force (except in self-defence and defence of the mandate).[389] Usually this involves the consent of a host country on whose territory the peace operations take place, a situation which cannot occur in space owing to the absence of any sovereign territory. It is possible, however, for military space activities to support peace operations in terrestrial domains.[390] For example, pursuant to the mandate issued by the Security Council, UN peacekeepers monitoring a ceasefire could employ a remote sensing satellite at their disposal to monitor the movement of belligerent troops on Earth. To the extent peacekeepers conduct military space operations to implement their mandate, they must do so in a manner that complies with that mandate and peacekeeping requirements. As an example, peacekeepers would not be permitted to intercept signals from a military communications satellite used by one of the parties in dispute to share them with the other party, unless the mandate so stipulated.

Primacy of Enforcement Measures Over Conflicting International Agreements

12. Not only must a decision of the Security Council be carried out by all Members of the United Nations under Article 25 of the UN Charter but an obligation under the UN Charter (including one imposed by the Security Council) also prevails over any conflicting obligation Member States may have under other international agreements.[391] This applies to any obligation under space treaties. Thus, if the Security Council found that an asteroid was projected to have a catastrophic collision with Earth and that potential collision constituted a threat to international peace and security under Chapter VII of the UN Charter, it could decide to authorize the placement of nuclear weapons in orbit around Earth for planetary defence against

---

[388] In recent years, the Security Council has also adopted the practice of invoking Chapter VII of the Charter 'when authorizing the deployment of United Nations peacekeeping operations into volatile post-conflict settings where the State is unable to maintain security and public order', in part to 'remind the wider United Nations membership of their obligation to give effect to Security Council decisions'. *UN Peacekeeping Operations* (n 386) 14.

[389] United Nations, 'Principles of Peacekeeping' [perma.cc/K3DZ-ZC3L].

[390] Although there is no sovereign territory in space and no State practice on this point, in principle the Security Council could also authorize peacekeeping operations to occur at any location in space, based on the consent of States that are operating there.

[391] UN Charter (n 2) art 103.

PRIMACY OF UN CHARTER OBLIGATIONS 271

the asteroid threat, even though Article IV of the Outer Space Treaty prohibits such action (Rule 5: Weapons of Mass Destruction). All Members of the United Nations would thus consent and/or assist in carrying out this decision of the Security Council for the maintenance of international peace and security under Article 48 and afford each other mutual assistance in carrying out the measures decided upon by the Security Council under Article 49.

PART III
MILITARY SPACE OPERATIONS DURING ARMED CONFLICT

Introduction: Space, the Law of Armed Conflict, and General Protection from Hostilities

'Preserving a measure of humanity in the midst of an armed conflict'

1. If efforts at peacefully resolving a dispute fail and an armed conflict occurs in outer space, the interests of humanity demand that the law of armed conflict (LOAC), also referred to as international humanitarian law (IHL), be carefully and correctly applied to such a conflict.[1] As noted by the International Committee of the Red Cross (ICRC), 'IHL does not legitimize the use of force in outer space; nor does it encourage the militarization or weaponization of outer space. The sole aim of IHL is to preserve a measure of humanity in the midst of armed conflict, notably to protect civilians.'[2]

Applicability of the Law of War/International Humanitarian Law

2. Since the law of armed conflict is indisputably part of international law, its applicability to outer space can be confirmed by Article III of the Outer Space Treaty (OST), which requires that all activities in the exploration and use of outer space be conducted in accordance with international law. Furthermore, the International Court of Justice has observed that the established principles and rules of the law of armed conflict apply 'to all forms of warfare and to all kinds of weapons, those of the past, those of the present and those of the future'.[3] In addition, the four Geneva

---

[1] It is also referred to as the law of war. It should also be noted that the word 'humanity' is relevant even to uninhabited spacecraft and other locations where civilians may not be present.
[2] International Committee of the Red Cross, 'International Humanitarian Law and the Challenges of Contemporary Armed Conflicts' (ICRC 2019 Challenges of Armed Conflicts Report) 33 [perma.cc/Z7Z2-CF9N].
[3] *Legality of the Threat or Use of Nuclear Weapons* (Advisory Opinion) [1996] ICJ Rep 226 (*Nuclear Weapons* Advisory Opinion) para 86.

Conventions of 1949 explicitly state that they apply 'to all cases of declared war or any other armed conflict which may arise between two or more of the High Contracting Parties'.[4] Various military manuals and policy statements of States further confirm this broad application of the law of armed conflict to outer space, although some States disagree.[5]

3. In any armed conflict, the right of the parties to the conflict to choose means or methods of warfare (including those involving space and space associated capabilities) is not unlimited. This is a central tenet of the regulation of the conduct of hostilities, having been included in various formulations in the 1899 and 1907 Hague Regulations,[6] and Article 35(1) of Additional Protocol

---

[4] Protocol Additional to the Geneva Conventions of 12 August 1949, and relating to the protection of victims of armed conflicts (Protocol I) (adopted 8 June 1977, entered into force 7 December 1978) 1125 UNTS 3 (Additional Protocol I); 1949 Geneva Conventions I–IV, Common Article 2. The ICRC has further observed that 'Article 49(3) of Additional Protocol I shows that the Protocol's rules on the conduct of hostilities are meant to apply to all types of warfare that may affect civilians on land. This would include hostilities in outer space.' ICRC 2019 Challenges of Armed Conflicts Report (n 2) 33. Although some treaties are to be applied mainly or solely within a party's territory, the law of armed conflict is obviously intended to apply generally beyond such limitations and the concept of territory is not relevant in space.

[5] See eg US General Counsel of Department of Defense, 'Department of Defense Law of War Manual' (rev edn, United States Department of Defense 2016) (US DoD Law of War Manual) para 14.10.2 (as a State not party to Additional Protocol I, the United States adopts the position that 'law of war treaties and the customary law of war are understood to regulate the conduct of hostilities, regardless of where they are conducted, which would include the conduct of hostilities in outer space. In this way, the application of' the law of war to activities in outer space is the same as its application to activities in other environments, such as the land, sea, air, or cyber domains'); Australian Working Paper submitted to the Open-Ended Working Group on Reducing Space Threats Through Norms, Rules and Principles of Responsible Behaviour (UN OEWG on Reducing Space Threats)—2 February 2023—A/AC.294/2023/WP.14 [https://perma.cc/D6C9-H3T9] ('Australia maintains the position that international law, including the UN Charter, applies to the exploration and use of space . . . The application of international law in space includes international humanitarian law. Relevant rules of IHL include the principles of distinction, proportionality, and necessity, the requirement of precautionary measures, the prohibition of indiscriminate attacks, and the prohibition of using means and methods of warfare that cause superfluous injury. The recognition of this does not promote or pre-empt conflict in space. On the contrary, it reminds us that if conflict occurs in, from, and through outer space, there is existing international law which will apply to regulate the conduct of hostilities in the space domain.'); EU joint contribution on the works of the UN OEWG on Reducing Space Threats, 14 June 2023 [https://perma.cc/S6ZE-HECP] ('the EU and its Member States believe that the final OEWG report should reaffirm the main principles of international law applicable to Outer Space, including the applicability of UN Charter and international humanitarian law to outer space. This would reaffirm that States are subject to the rules regulating armed conflict, regardless of whether the conflict occurs on Earth or in Outer Space.'). It should be noted, however, that some governments' experts have expressed concern 'about engaging in a discussion on the application of international humanitarian law, since such a discussion might signal acceptance of the notion that armed conflict could be conducted in outer space'. UNGA, 'Report of Group of Governmental Experts on further practical measures for the prevention of an arms race in outer space' (April 2019) UN Doc A/74/77, para 30. Similarly, in commenting on a draft manuscript of the *Woomera Manual*, the representative of China at the UN OEWG on Reducing Space Threats argued that 'it is too early to conclude that IHL is truly applicable in space', UN OEGW on Reducing Space Threats, '5th Meeting, 3rd Session' (digital broadcast, 1 February 2023) <https://media.un.org/en/asset/k15/k15kmcfcvp> at 2:49:18 (last accessed 1 March 2023).

[6] Convention (IV) respecting the Laws and Customs of War on Land and its annex: Regulations concerning the Laws and Customs of War on Land (adopted 18 October 1907, entered into force 26 January 1910) 205 CTS 277 (Hague Convention IV) art 22 ('The right of belligerents to adopt means of injuring the enemy is not unlimited.').

I.⁷ It is also reflected in customary international law.⁸ The ICRC thus notes that 'the use of weapons in outer space, would not occur in a legal vacuum. It is constrained by existing law, notably the Outer Space Treaty, the UN Charter, and IHL rules governing means and methods of warfare.'⁹ This also means that while the law of armed conflict applies to the use of weapons and armed conflicts generally in space and has ultimate priority, it must nevertheless be reconciled to the greatest possible extent with any competing obligations of the parties concerned under treaty rules applicable to space activities, especially the Outer Space Treaty (see Methodology of the *Manual* and the discussion of *lex specialis*).

4. The law of armed conflict applies regardless of whether the resort to force under *jus ad bellum* was lawful.¹⁰ This principle is confirmed in Additional Protocol I, which reaffirms that 'the provisions of the Geneva Conventions of 12 August 1949 and of this Protocol must be fully applied in all circumstances to all persons who are protected by those instruments, without any adverse distinction based on the nature or origin of the armed conflict or on the causes espoused by or attributed to the Parties to the conflict.'¹¹

Rules Relevant to the Space Domain

5. Although the law of armed conflict is applicable to all operational domains including space, the application of some obligations under the law of armed conflict may be precluded in space when they are specific to a particular domain other than space. For example, the rules of international law specific to naval warfare or air warfare are not automatically applicable to military space operations.¹²

---

⁷ Additional Protocol I (n 4) art 35(1) ('In any armed conflict, the right of the Parties to the conflict to choose methods or means of warfare is not unlimited.').

⁸ *Nuclear Weapons* Advisory Opinion (n 3) paras 78–79 (affirming that the principle that 'States do not have unlimited freedom of choice of means in the weapons they use' is one of 'intransgressible principles of international customary law').

⁹ ICRC 2019 Challenges of Armed Conflicts Report (n 2) 33. For the ICRC's most recent statement on this issue, see ICRC, 'Constraints under International Law on Military Operations in Outer Space during Armed Conflicts' (working paper submitted to the UN Open-Ended Working Group on Reducing Space Threats, 2022) UN Doc A/AC.294/2022/WP.4. See also International Committee of the Red Cross, *Commentary on the Additional Protocols of 8 June 1977 to the Geneva Conventions of 12 August 1949* (Claude Pilloud and others, eds, Martin Nijhoff 1987)(*Commentary on the Additional Protocols*) 393, para 1389 (noting that within this framework, 'when the law of armed conflict does not provide for any prohibition, the Parties to the conflict are in principle free within the constraints of customary law and general principles').

¹⁰ ICRC 2019 Challenges of Armed Conflicts Report (n 2) 33 ('IHL applies to any military operations conducted as part of an armed conflict, including those occurring in outer space, regardless of whether or not the use of force is lawful under the UN Charter (*jus ad bellum*.').

¹¹ Additional Protocol I (n 4) preamble, para 5.

¹² See eg 1907 Hague Convention (VI) relating to the Status of Enemy Merchant Ships at the Outbreak of Hostilities (adopted 18 October 1907, entered into force 26 January 1910) 205 CTS 305; 1907 Hague Convention (VII) relating to the Conversion of Merchant Ships into War-Ships (adopted 18 October 1907, entered into force 26 January 1910); 205 CTS 139; 1907 Hague Convention (VIII)

Note on Rules of the Law of Armed Conflict with Limited Relevance to Space in the Foreseeable Future

6. This *Manual* does not provide a review of every rule that could arguably or potentially apply to imagined scenarios or actions in space. Instead, it addresses the rules of the law of armed conflict that have the most likely application to space in the foreseeable future. It focuses on rules of the greatest importance and that are related to the most important activities and operations in the space domain. It excludes those rules that: are difficult to realistically apply in the physical space environment; rely on legal structures that are not found in space (such as rules that rely solely on the nationality or ownership of a space object, based on analogies with vessels or aircraft); or await clarification by State practice in future settings, such as rules related to potential conflicts on celestial bodies when permanent facilities are present and permanent civilian populations reside there.

Note on Limited Discussion of Rules Addressing Non-International Armed Conflicts

7. For the reasons previously stated, this *Manual* primarily addresses the law of armed conflict with respect to military space operations as it relates to international armed conflicts. An international armed conflict occurs when the criteria of Common Article 2(1) of the Geneva Conventions of 1949 are met. Under this clause, an international armed conflict exists 'in all cases of declared war or of any other armed conflict which may arise between two or more of the High Contracting Parties, even if the state of war is not recognized by one of them' (see Rule 29: International Armed Conflict). To the extent that such a conflict exists, any space operations with a nexus to that conflict would be governed by the law of armed conflict, as addressed in this Part. In contrast, according to Common Article 3 of the Geneva Conventions of 1949, a non-international armed conflict refers to a situation in which an 'armed conflict not of an international character occurs in the territory of one of the High Contracting Parties' (see Rule 30: Non-International Armed Conflict).

8. Space assets have been used by States in connection with fighting non-international armed conflicts in terrestrial domains (eg by using satellites to relay signals to control remotely piloted aircraft engaged in terrestrial operations against terrorist groups). However, technological challenges currently make non-international armed conflicts in space unlikely, and it is legally problematic for a

---

relative to the Laying of Automatic Submarine Contact Mine (adopted 18 October 1907, entered into force 26 January 1910) 205 CTS 331.

non-international armed conflict to originate in space or take place exclusively in space (see Rule 30: Non-International Armed Conflict). The unique legal regime governing space currently presents numerous obstacles to the concept of a belligerent 'non-State' actor operating in space (as distinguished from the activities in space of 'non-governmental entities' that are the responsibility of States) (see Rule 10: Responsibility of States for National Activities in Outer Space). Some aspects of non-international armed conflicts that have only limited application to military space operations owing to (i) the constraints imposed by the space law regime with respect to such conflicts originating or occurring exclusively in space, and (ii) territorial restrictions under the law of armed conflict related to the establishment of a non-international armed conflict. However, to the extent that military space activities and military space assets may be used in conjunction with non-international armed conflicts on Earth, these issues are addressed.

Applicability of Additional Protocol I to Military Space Operations

9. Article 49(3) of Additional Protocol I states that the provisions of Section I of the Protocol (Articles 48–67) 'apply to any land, air or sea warfare which may affect the civilian population, individual civilians, or civilian objects on land. They further apply to all attacks from the sea or from the air against objectives on land but do not otherwise affect the rules of international law applicable in armed conflict at sea or in the air.' Regarding the application of the obligations in Articles 48–67 to military space operations, those obligations focus on actions 'which may affect the civilian population, individual civilians or civilian objects on land'. The better interpretation of these provisions would extend the protection to the civilian population, individual civilians, or civilian objects on land and elsewhere, regardless of where the warfare in question originates, even if military space operations were not a serious concern during the negotiation of Additional Protocol I. Otherwise, the ongoing extension of military operations from, to, or within space would leave an enormous and growing vacuum of legal obligations providing for the general protection of the civilian population and civilian objects both on Earth and in space. In light of growing civilian uses of space, the growing reliance of the civilian population of Earth on space assets, and the abundance of dual-use objects in space, this Manual takes the position that Articles 48–67 of Additional Protocol I should, where possible, be applied to military space operations. One State at State Consultations supported this view, focusing on the effects of space operations on the civilian population on Earth.[13]

---

[13] One State at State Consultations noted that, in its view, Additional Protocol I would apply to space activity with a connection to the territory of the State, which would include space-based attacks against land targets and to attacks against space-based assets that would affect the civilian population. In this

10. Similarly, regarding precautions on attacks, the logic and motivation behind the obligation in Article 57(4) (which provides that '[i]n the conduct of military operations at sea or in the air, each Party to the conflict shall, in conformity with its rights and duties under the rules of international law applicable in armed conflict, take all reasonable precautions to avoid losses of civilian lives and damage to civilian objects') support the application of these obligations to military space operations and the need to take all reasonable precautions in military space operations to avoid losses of civilian lives and damage to civilian objects on Earth or in space.

Status of the ICRC Study on Customary Humanitarian International Law

11. The ICRC has published a Study on Customary International Humanitarian Law (and maintains an accompanying Customary IHL database) in which it sets forth 161 rules that it has determined are norms of customary IHL, based on State practice and *opinio juris*.[14] It is a useful resource that is frequently cited in the commentary of Rules in Part III of this *Manual*. However, it is important to note that several States have expressed serious concerns regarding the Study's methodology and conclusions, both during State Consultations and in earlier written submissions and statements in various fora and publications.

12. For example, the United States has stated that 'it is important to make clear—both to the ICRC and to the greater international community—that, based upon the U.S. review thus far, the United States is concerned about the methodology used to ascertain rules and about whether the authors have proffered sufficient facts and evidence to support those rules'.[15] Similarly, while the United Kingdom noted that 'the Study is an impressive piece of research, and will be a very useful quarry for the future', it also stated that 'we at least will treat the Rules with some degree of reservation. Overall, we feel that they represent too much of what States should do, rather than what they actually do, i.e. they state not what the law is but what it should

---

State's view, this interpretation serves the purpose of the fundamental principles found in Additional Protocol I and is also consistent with the Martens clause. Additionally, to the extent any of the articles in Additional Protocol I reflect customary international law obligations, this State believed these obligations would not have the same territorial limitations as under Additional Protocol I and thus would apply to activities in outer space, regardless of whether there is a connection to the territory of the State.

[14] International Committee of the Red Cross, 'Customary Humanitarian International Law Databases' (Online Database, ICRC 2022) <https://ihl-databases.icrc.org/en/customary-ihl/v1> accessed 28 March 2023 (ICRC CIHL Study).
[15] 'Letter from John B. Bellinger, III, Legal Adviser, Department of State, & William J. Haynes II, General Counsel, Department of Defense, to Dr. Jacob Kellenberger, President, International Committee of the Red Cross, Regarding Customary International Humanitarian Law Study' [2007] International Legal Materials 514.

be.'¹⁶ Commenting on the International Law Commission's draft principles on protection of the environment in relation to armed conflicts, the Government of Israel stated that '[l]ike other States, Israel has serious reservations regarding the methodology applied in the ICRC Study on Customary Humanitarian Law, and consequently, regarding many of its conclusions. This methodology is inconsistent in many respects with the ILC's own conclusions on the identification of customary international law.'¹⁷

The ICRC's views of State practice, while useful, cannot themselves represent State practice. As France has simply noted, while '[t]he study constitutes a useful doctrinal work, ... it could not be used as such against States'.¹⁸ **13.**

Note on Space Objects Containing Dangerous Forces

In addition to the protection afforded to all civilian objects under the law of armed conflict, Article 56 of Additional Protocol I provides additional protection for works and installations containing dangerous forces, namely dams, dykes, and nuclear electrical generating stations. These protections prohibit attacks on such installations or on military objectives located near them, if such an attack may cause the release of dangerous forces and consequent severe losses among the civilian **14.**

---

¹⁶ Statement of FCO Legal Adviser at the Meeting of National Committees on International Humanitarian Law of Commonwealth States, 20 July 2005, reproduced at (2005) 76 BYIL 694, 695. See also Sixth Committee of the United Nations General Assembly, Summary record of the 13th meeting (comments from Representative of the United Kingdom (Ms Gladstone, UNGA 7 November 2008) UN Doc A/C.6/63/SR.13, para 61 (noting that '[w]hile her [Majesty's] Government recognized that there might be cases in which such law could supplement the extensive range of treaties in that field, it had reservations about volume I of the study. In particular, some of the examples provided were not, in its view, properly to be regarded as State practice for the purpose of the rules relating to the formation of customary international law. Furthermore, the study sometimes jumped too quickly to the conclusion that a rule had entered into the corpus of that law without sufficient evidence of State practice.').
¹⁷ Israel, 'Comments from the State of Israel on the International Law Commission's Draft Principles on the Protection of the Environment in Relation to Armed Conflicts as adopted by the Commission in 2019 on first reading' (submitted to 73rd Session of the International Law Commission, 2021) [https://perma.cc/S8YH-U8DV] para 108.
¹⁸ UN Secretary-General, 'Status of the Protocols Additional to the Geneva Conventions of 1949 and relating to the protection of victims of armed conflicts' (information submitted by France, 28 September 2012) UN Doc A/67/182/Add.1, 3. It is also clear that State views of the ICRC Study differ and that the Study has given rise to considerable debate. See Sixth Committee of the United Nations General Assembly, 'Summary record of the 13th meeting' (Comments by the representative of Sweden (Mr Lundvist) speaking on behalf of the Nordic countries (Denmark, Finland, Iceland, Norway, and Sweden, 7 November 2008) UN Doc A/C.6/63/SR.13, para 32 (noting that the ICRC Study 'would on the whole be very useful to States', but also observing that 'views clearly differed on the study on customary international humanitarian law conducted by ICRC'); ibid, comments by the representative of Tunisia (Mr Mansour) para 74 (noting how the Tunisian delegation had followed with interest 'the debate inspired by the 2005 publication of the ICRC study on customary international humanitarian law' and further observed that '[n]otwithstanding the development of customary international law, the clarification and possibly the development of the law applicable to non-international armed conflicts remained a major task to be undertaken'.

population.[19] Works and installations containing dangerous forces are not currently covered in this *Manual* and for the foreseeable future, no dams, dykes, or nuclear electrical generating stations are likely to be located in outer space or on celestial bodies. Notwithstanding this, in respect of the release of dangerous forces from objects located in space, nuclear energy is used as a power source in some spacecraft and various toxic chemicals are used for the propulsion and in other systems of spacecraft. Military space operations against such spacecraft would be subject, at a minimum, to the requirement in Rule 46: Constant Care, and the obligation to take precautions in attack (Section 3), including Rule 38: Proportionality in Attack.

Overview of Section 3: Precautions in Attack

15. The Rules in Section 3 of this Part encompassing precautions in attack are largely expressed in Article 57(2)–(3) and Article 58 of Additional Protocol I, which apply to international armed conflicts.[20] Customary international law applicable to international armed conflicts and possibly to non-international armed conflicts obliges all parties to an armed conflict, including those involved in military space operations, to take all feasible precautions in the planning, deciding, and carrying

---

[19] The customary international law status of this Article is the subject of disagreement. The ICRC takes the position that State practice has established this rule is a norm of customary international law applicable in both international and non-international armed conflicts. See ICRC CIHL Study (n 14) Rule 43. As previously noted, serious concerns have been expressed by some States about the methodology used in the ICRC CIHL Study. Some States have also expressed particular concerns about art 56 of Additional Protocol I. See eg US DoD Law of War Manual (n 5) para 5.13 ('The United States has objected to this article of AP I ... Insofar as Article 56 of AP I deviates from the regular application of the principles of distinction and proportionality, the U.S. view has been that it does not reflect customary international law applicable in international and noninternational armed conflicts.'); United Kingdom, 'Ratification (with Declarations and Reservations): United Kingdom of Great Britain and Ireland: Deposit of Instrument with Government of Switzerland: 28 January 1998' (2001) 2020 UNTS 75, 78 ('Re. Articles 56 and 85, paragraph 3 (c), the United Kingdom cannot undertake to grant absolute protection to installations which may contribute to the opposing Party's war effort, or to the defenders of such installations, but will take all due precautions in military operations at or near the installations referred to in paragraph 1 of Article 56 in the light of the known facts, including any special marking which the installation may carry, to avoid severe collateral losses among civilian populations; direct attacks on such installations will be launched only on authorization at a high level of command.'); France, 'Statement on Ratification of AP I', translated in Dietrich Schindler and Jiri Toman (eds), *The Laws Of Armed Conflicts: A Collection Of Conventions, Resolutions, And Other Documents* (tr, 4th edn, Martin Nijhoff Publishers 2004) 801 ('The Government of the French Republic cannot guarantee an absolute protection to the works and installations containing dangerous forces which may contribute to the opposing Party's war effort, or to the defenders of such installations, but will take all precautions referred to the provisions of Article 56, of Article 57, paragraph 2(a)(iii) and of paragraph 3(c) of Article 85 in order to avoid severe collateral losses among the civilian populations, including possible direct attacks.').

[20] As noted in paras 9–10 of this introduction, art 49(3) of Additional Protocol I states that arts 48–67 (which include those articles underlying the Rules in section 3 on precautionary measures in attack) are applicable to warfare on land, air, and sea and this Manual interprets Additional Protocol I as also extending to military space operations that may affect the civilian population, individual civilians, or civilian objects in any domain).

out of an attack, so as to avoid or minimize incidental loss to civilian life, injury to civilians, or damage to civilian objects ('harm').[21]

16. The obligations to take precautions applies to the planning, as well as to the execution of an 'attack'. These obligations manifest when an attack is contemplated, and a possible target is assessed as meeting the definition of a military objective (see Rule 34: Military Objectives). The obligation to take precautions in attack does not apply to military operations that do not constitute an attack within the meaning of the law of armed conflict, although the complementary obligation to take constant care to spare the civilian population does apply to such military operations that do not constitute an attack (see Rule 46: Constant Care).

17. The requirement to take precautions contains or relates to several obligations, which are detailed and further discussed in Section 3: Rule 36: Verification, Rule 37: Choice of Means and Methods of Attack, Rule 39: Suspension or Cancellation of Attack, Rule 40: Warnings, and Rule 41: Precautions Against the Effects of an Attack.

18. The scope of the obligation to take precautions in attack is broad with respect to the range of the military personnel to which it applies, and it may also extend over

---

[21] See *Prosecutor v Kupreškić* (Judgment) ICTY-95-16-T (14 January 2000) para 524 ('Such provisions [reflecting principles that to some extent are spelled out in Articles 57 and 58 of Additional Protocol I], it would seem, are now part of customary international law, not only because they specify and flesh out general pre-existing norms, but also because they do not appear to be contested by any State, including those which have not ratified the Protocol. Admittedly, even these two provisions leave a wide margin of discretion to belligerents by using language that might be regarded as leaving the last word to the attacking party.'). The precautionary measures in this Section are found in the military manuals of many States. See eg United Kingdom Ministry of Defence, 'JSP 383: The Joint Service Manual of the Law of Armed Conflict' (Joint Service Publication 383, United Kingdom Joint Doctrine and Concepts Centre 2004) (UK LOAC Manual) paras 2.5–2.5.3; Chief of Defence Staff (Canada), *Law of Armed Conflict at the Operational and Tactical Levels* (Office of Judge Advocate General 2001) (Canadian LOAC Manual) para 204.1, German Federal Ministry of Defence, 'Law of Armed Conflict Manual' (May 2013) (German LOAC Manual) para 3.412. The ICRC takes the position that State practice has established these precautions as norms of customary international law applicable in both international and non-international armed conflicts. ICRC CIHL Study (n 14) Rules 14–22 (but see Introduction to Part III, paras 11–13, noting that serious concerns have been expressed by some States about the methodology used in the ICRC CIHL Study); ILA Study Group on the Conduct of Hostilities in the 21st Century, 'The Conduct of Hostilities and International Humanitarian Law: Challenges of 21st Century Warfare' (2017) 93 International Law Studies 322, 372 ('The obligation to take all feasible precautions to avoid or minimize the risk to civilians resulting from military operations is a fundamental principle of the law of armed conflict.') However, with respect to non-international armed conflicts, the application of each of these precautionary measures as a matter of customary international law is likely but not clearly established. While none of these precautions are set forth in Additional Protocol II nor in Common Article 3 of the Geneva Conventions, the ICRC has nonetheless observed that art 13(1) of Additional Protocol II requires that 'the civilian population and individual civilians shall enjoy general protection against the dangers arising from military operations', and that 'it would be difficult to comply with this requirement without taking precautions in attack'. ICRC CIHL Study (n 14) Rule 15. The ICRC further notes that since the Tribunal in the *Kupreškić* case found the requirement to take precautions in attack to be customary international law because it specified and fleshed out general pre-existing norms, 'it can be argued indeed that the principle of distinction, which is customary in international and non-international armed conflicts, inherently requires respect for this rule'. ibid.

a considerable period of time. The obligation under Additional Protocol I thus applies to all military personnel engaged in military space operations, whether in senior command positions or lower level command and operator roles.[22] The specific obligation of a particular individual will be determined by both the nature of the specific precaution and the individual's authority regarding the attack itself.[23] For example, certain precautions will need to be taken by an operator employing kinetic-energy based weapons, directed energy weapons, cyber capabilities, robotic mechanisms, or other means or methods of warfare in an attack on a targeted space object, even after the decision to attack has been already made at more senior levels. The obligation is also continuous and ongoing, as it applies to the various steps throughout the planning and execution of an attack.

Feasibility

19. The precautions required are those that are 'feasible' (to include 'everything feasible' and 'all things feasible'); this standard should be understood as that which is practicable or practically possible taking into account all circumstances ruling at the time,[24] including humanitarian and military considerations.[25] The determination of what precautions would be considered 'feasible' is dependent on the context and must be made in good faith and based on the available information under the circumstances ruling at the time.[26] Thus, any assessment of whether a commander or operator should have taken a specific precaution must be made in light of the situation faced at the time the decision was made rather than based on hindsight.[27]

20. The military considerations relevant in assessing the 'feasibility' of a certain precaution include, *inter alia*, the urgency of the situation, the probability that the use of certain precautions would affect the success of the military mission; operational risks of exposing the forces to casualties or other security risks; the cost of

---

[22] *Commentary on the Additional Protocols* (n 9) para 2197 ('a large majority of the delegations at the Diplomatic Conference wished to cover all situations with a single provision').
[23] UK LOAC Manual (n 21) para 5.32.9.
[24] *Commentary on the Additional Protocols* (n 9) para 2198.
[25] US DoD Law of War Manual (n 5) para 5.2.3.2; UK LOAC Manual (n 21) para 5.32, fn 191; Bundesministerium der Verteidigung, 'Law of Armed Conflict Manual' (Joint Service Regulation (ZDv), German LOAC Manual (n 21) para 412; New Zealand Defence Force, *Manual of Armed Forces Law, Vol 4: Law of Armed Conflict* (2nd edn, New Zealand Defence Force 2017) (New Zealand LOAC Manual) para 2.2.10; Canadian LOAC Manual (n 21) G-L 6.
[26] *Commentary on the Additional Protocols* (n 9) para 2198 ('the interpretation [of feasible] will be a matter of common sense and good faith'); New Zealand LOAC Manual (n 25) paras 8.7.5–8.7.6; *Kupreškić* Judgment (n 21) 524 ('reasonable care must be taken in attacking military objectives so that civilians are not needlessly injured through carelessness'); US DoD Law of War Manual (n 5) para 5.2.3.2 ('The standard for what precautions must be taken is one of due regard or diligence, not an absolute requirement to do everything possible ... [f]easible precautions are those that are practicable or practically possible, taking into account all circumstances ruling at the time.').
[27] US DoD Law of War Manual (n 5) para 5.2.3.3; UK LOAC Manual (n 21) para 5.32.10.

taking the precaution, in terms of time, or other resources;[28] competing demands for means of warfare; and whether taking the precaution forecloses alternative courses of action.[29] The humanitarian considerations that have to be taken into account include the likelihood and degree of humanitarian benefit from taking the precaution.[30]

---

[28] See Danish Ministry of Defence, *Military Manual on International Law Relevant to Danish Armed Forces in International Operations* (Jes Rynkeby Knudsen, ed, Defence Command Denmark 2016) (Danish LOAC Manual) 317; 324; 327 ('Only feasible precautions must be taken. This brings an element of pragmatism to the process: parties to a conflict engaging in attacks undertake to do what can reasonably be required within the limits of the time and resources available and without exposing their own forces to unnecessary danger.'); New Zealand LOAC Manual (n 25) 8.7.6 ('They will usually be set in accordance with command, strategic and tactical considerations, as well as practical issues such as capability and resources, many of which the commander will be unable to change.').

[29] New Zealand LOAC Manual (n 25) para 8.7.6; US DoD Law of War Manual (n 5) para 5.2.3.2; Danish LOAC Manual (n 28) ch 8, para 3.4.2. For further discussion of these considerations, see Rule 36: Verification, para 4; Rule 37: Choice of Means and Methods of Attack, para 2.

[30] US DoD Law of War Manual (n 5) para 5.2.3.2.

SECTION 1
CHARACTERIZATION OF ARMED CONFLICT

Rule 29
International Armed Conflict

An international armed conflict exists whenever there is a resort to armed force between States, including when this takes place from, to, or within space, or in cases of declared war.

Overview of Legal Basis of Rule

1. It is generally accepted as a matter of customary international law that an international armed conflict occurs when the criteria of Common Article 2(1) to the Geneva Conventions of 1949 are met.[31] Under this clause, an international armed conflict exists 'in all cases of declared war or of any other armed conflict which may arise between two or more of the High Contracting Parties, even if the state of war is not recognized by one of them'.[32] To the extent that such an international armed conflict exists, even if it is primarily terrestrial in nature, any military space operations with a nexus to the conflict would be governed by the law of armed conflict (LOAC)/International Humanitarian Law (IHL).[33] Furthermore, Common Article 2 of the Geneva Conventions of 1949 contains no explicit spatial or geographical limitation on its ambit, and thus its operational scope includes space, subject to

---

[31] New Zealand LOAC Manual (n 25) para 5.3.1; German LOAC Manual (n 21) paras 133, 202, and 203; Harvard University Program on Humanitarian Policy and Conflict Research, *HPCR Manual on International Law Applicable to Air and Missile Warfare* (CUP 2013) (AMW Manual) r 1; US DoD Law of War Manual (n 5) para 3.3.1; UK LOAC Manual (n 21) ss 3.2–3.3; Canadian LOAC Manual (n 21) GL-9; Australian Department of Defence, *Law of Armed Conflict* (Defence Publishing Service 2006) (Australian LOAC Manual) 1.51; *Prosecutor v Tadić* (Decision on the Defence Motion for Interlocutory Appeal on Jurisdiction) ICTY-94-1-AR72 (2 October 1995) (*Tadić* decision) para 70.

[32] Geneva Conventions I–IV, Common Article 2 (n 4). For States that are Parties to Additional Protocol I, an international armed conflict will also exist where a people are fighting against colonial domination, alien occupation, or racist regimes in the exercise of its right of self-determination: Additional Protocol I (n 4) art 1(4).

[33] For example, a satellite that significantly supports and/or advances the military activities of a belligerent in the land, sea, air, or space theatres of operations is likely to have a sufficient nexus to the armed conflict to attract the law of armed conflict to the activities of the satellite. Separate but related issues concern the civilian or military character of the satellite, its relationship to a particular State or States (see Note on Legal Connections Between States and a Space Object), and issues of attribution and State responsibility (see Rule 10: Responsibility of States for National Activities in Outer Space). In addition, a satellite that by its nature, location, purpose, or use makes an effective contribution to military action in an armed conflict and whose total or partial destruction, capture, or neutralization, in the circumstances ruling at the time, offers a definite military advantage, constitutes a military objective under the law of armed conflict (see Rule 34: Military Objectives). Issues related to the status of a neutral State's satellite in these circumstances raise additional questions (see Rule 48: Neutrality in Space and Rule 10: Responsibility of States for National Activities in Outer Space).

any other applicable obligations of international law. Thus, where an international armed conflict exists, including one that takes place from, to, or within space, all relevant rules of the law of armed conflict relating to international armed conflict will apply.

2. Although treaty law does not define the term *armed conflict*, there must be a resort to armed force for a dispute between at least two States to be considered an international armed conflict.[34] This reasoning has been adopted by international tribunals[35] and appears in military manuals.[36] The 2016 Commentary to Geneva Convention I also confirms that armed conflicts, as referred to in Article 2(1), 'occur when one or more States have recourse to armed force against another State, regardless of the reasons for or the intensity of the confrontation'.[37] Thus, an international armed conflict exists from, to or within space when one or more States resort to the use of armed force against another State in space or against another State on earth with the use of space assets, whether that armed force originates from space or terrestrial domains (land, sea, and airspace) or is directed from space against targets in space or terrestrial domains.[38]

Threshold Requirement and Determination of the Existence of Armed Conflict

3. Another view would hold that there may not be any threshold requirements for the use of armed force in order to trigger an international armed conflict (such as the intensity or duration of the confrontation) and that 'any difference arising

---

[34] *Tadić* decision (n 31) para 70 ('We find that an armed conflict exists whenever there is a resort to armed force between States or protracted armed violence between governmental authorities and organized armed groups or between such groups within a State.').

[35] See in the International Criminal Tribunal for the former Yugoslavia (ICTY): *Prosecutor v Halilovic* (Trial Judgement) ICTY-01-48-T (16 November 2005) para 24; *Prosecutor v Galić* (Trial Judgement) ICTY-98-29-T (5 December 2003) para 9; in the International Criminal Court (ICC): *Prosecutor v Lubanga Dyilo* (Judgment) ICC-01/04-01/06-2842 (14 March 2012) (*Dyilo* ICC Judgment) paras 533 and 541; in the Special Court for Sierra Leone (SCSL): *Prosecutor v Taylor* (Trial Judgement) SCSL-03-01-T (18 May 2012) paras 563–566.

[36] Australian LOAC Manual (n 31) 1.51; Ministère de la Défense (French Ministry of Defence), *Manuel de Droit des Conflits Armés* (French Ministry of Defence 2012) (French LOAC Manual) 33; UK LOAC Manual (n 21) para 3.3.

[37] ICRC, *Commentary on the First Geneva Convention* (Knut Dörman and others, eds, CUP 2016) (2016 GC I Commentary) para 218. ICRC *Commentary on the Third Geneva Convention: Convention (III) relative to the Treatment of Prisoners of War* (CUP 2021) para 242 (making international humanitarian law applicable 'as soon as a State undertakes hostile military action(s) against another State'); see also US DoD Law of War Manual (n 5) 3.3.1 (using the term *if two or more States oppose one another*, rather than using any explicit reference to *resort to armed force*).

[38] The use of armed force against another State that gives rise to an international armed conflict has been defined broadly by the ICRC with respect to possible targets. See 2016 GC I Commentary (n 37) para 241 ('The existence of an international armed conflict is determined by the occurrence of hostilities against the population, armed forces or territory of another State . . . .'). This definition reasonably extends to and includes hostilities against a State's critical infrastructure, including its space assets.

between two States and leading to the intervention of armed forces is an armed conflict within the meaning of Article 2, even if one of the Parties denies the existence of a state of war. It makes no difference how long the conflict lasts, or how much slaughter takes place.'[39] This position has been adopted in the context of international criminal law jurisprudence[40] and by some States.[41] The Use of Force Committee of the International Law Association noted this ICRC position but, after carefully examining State practice in this area, 'found little evidence to support the view that the Conventions apply in the absence of fighting of some intensity'.[42]

4. It should be noted that the existence of an international armed conflict is a question of fact and is independent of the subjective views of the parties (even if one or both of the parties do not consider themselves to be in an armed conflict).[43]

5. Although the existence of an international armed conflict 'presupposes the involvement of the armed forces of at least one of the opposing States',[44] the involvement of the armed forces is not necessarily the sole factor (nor necessarily even a factor in every case) for determining the existence of an international armed conflict.[45] For

---

[39] Jean Pictet (ed), *Commentary on the Geneva Conventions of 12 August 1949, Vol 1: Geneva Convention for the Amelioration of the Condition of the Wounded and Sick in Armed Forces in the Field* (ICRC 1952) 32; 2016 GC I Commentary (n 37) paras 236–237: 'for international armed conflict, there is no requirement that the use of armed force between the Parties reach a certain level of intensity before it can be said that an armed conflict exists. Article 2(1) itself contains no mention of any threshold for the intensity or duration of hostilities ... Even minor skirmishes between the armed forces, be they land, air or naval forces, would spark an international armed conflict and lead to the applicability of humanitarian law.'

[40] In the ICTY: *Prosecutor v Delalić* (Trial Judgment) ICTY-04-83-T (15 September 1998) para 184 (see also para 208); *Tadić* decision (n 31) para 70; in the ICC: *Prosecutor v Lubanga Dyilo* (Decision on the Confirmation of Charges) ICC-01/04-01/06-083-tEN (29 January 2007) para 207. The SCSL used the definition of international armed conflict proposed by the ICTY in *Tadić* (see *Taylor* Trial Judgment (n 35) paras 563–566).

[41] See eg US DoD Law of War Manual (n 5) 3.4.2 (noting that 'the United States has interpreted "armed conflict" in Common Article 2 of the 1949 Geneva Conventions to include "any situation in which there is hostile action between the armed forces of two parties, regardless of the duration, intensity or scope of fighting"').

[42] See ILA Committee on the Use of Force, 'Final Report on the Meaning of Armed Conflict in International Law' in International Law Association Report of the Seventy-Fourth Conference, The Hague (International Law Association 2010) 2 [https://perma.cc/JLA5-SA4K].

[43] As noted, Common Article 2 of the Geneva Conventions states that an international armed conflict exists 'in all cases of declared war or of any other armed conflict which may arise between two or more of the High Contracting Parties, *even if the state of war is not recognized by one of them*' (emphasis added). The military manuals of States also emphasize this point. See eg US DoD Law of War Manual (n 5) para 3.4.2 ('Jus in bello rules apply when parties are actually conducting hostilities, even if the war is not declared or if the state of war is not recognized by them.').

[44] 2016 GC I Commentary (n 37) para 226 (noting that 'an armed conflict presumes the deployment of military means in order to overcome the enemy or force it into submission, to eradicate the threat it represents or to force it to change its course of action. When classic means and methods of warfare—such as the deployment of troops on the enemy's territory, the use of artillery or the resort to jetfighters or combat helicopters—come into play, it is uncontroversial that they amount to an armed confrontation between States and that the application of the Geneva Conventions is triggered.').

[45] ibid para 228 (noting that 'the question of "who" is involved in the armed opposition between States should not significantly affect the classification of the situation as an international armed conflict. When a State resorts to means and methods of warfare against another State, that situation qualifies

example, consider a case in which a State's civilian intelligence agency operates a satellite that is intentionally manoeuvred into another State's satellite and destroys it. The fact that it was a civilian organ of the State that conducted the operation (rather than a military organ) has no bearing on the characterization of the situation as an international armed conflict. Likewise, the involvement of the armed forces in a space operation does not necessarily transform a situation into an international armed conflict. For instance, a military unit manoeuvring a military satellite to come close to another satellite to observe its actions and potentially access its incoming and outgoing transmissions, without more, is unlikely to be considered an initiation of an international armed conflict.[46]

Attribution of State Responsibility in Space

6. With respect to the attribution of State responsibility for actions in outer space, the OST establishes a special attribution regime, discussed in paragraph 8. Under the law of armed conflict, as set forth in Article 93 of Additional Protocol I, a State 'shall be responsible for all acts committed by persons forming part of its armed forces'. In broader terms, the 2016 Commentary to Geneva Convention I states that '[t]he existence of an international armed conflict is determined by the occurrence of hostilities against the population, armed forces or territory of another State, carried out by State agents acting in an official capacity and under instructions or by other persons specifically instructed to carry out such hostilities by State agents or organs, and not done in error'.[47] However, a higher standard than 'specific

as an international armed conflict, irrespective of the organ within that State that has resorted to such means and methods.').

[46] However, in the *jus ad bellum* context, it is possible that the inferred actions and intent of the military satellite might, under some circumstances, be viewed by an adversary State as constituting a threat of a use of force, a use of force, or an armed attack, particularly if the targeted satellite is a sensitive early warning satellite or part of related command and control systems, on which strategic nuclear stability and international peace and security is said to depend. See Rule 21: Use of Force, para 22. It is also possible that the military satellite may have violated obligations under the Outer Space Treaty (the OST), such as a failure to show due regard—see Rule 17: Due Regard; UNGA, 'Treaty on Principles Governing the Activities of States in the Exploration and Use of Outer Space, Including the Moon and Other Celestial Bodies' (adopted 27 January 1967, entered into force 10 October 1967) 610 UNTS 205 (Outer Space Treaty or OST), art IX.

[47] 2016 GC I Commentary (n 37) para 241. With respect to State responsibility generally under international law, the ILC has concluded that 'the conduct of a person or group of persons shall be considered an act of a State under international law if the person or group of persons is in fact acting on the instructions of, or under the direction or control of, that State in carrying out the conduct'. ILC, 'Responsibility of States for internationally wrongful acts' UNGA Res A/Res/56/83 (adopted 28 January 2002) (ILC Articles on State Responsibility) art 8. Article 11 of the ILC Articles on State Responsibility also makes a State responsible for conduct 'to the extent that the State acknowledges and adopts the conduct in question as its own'. *United States Diplomatic and Consular Staff in Tehran (United States v Iran)* (Judgment) [1980] ICJ Reps 3 para 74 ('The approval given ... by the Ayatollah Khomeini and other organs of the Iranian State, and the decision to perpetuate them, translated continuing occupation of the Embassy and detention of the hostages into acts of that State. The militants, authors of the invasion

instructions' was established for attributing the actions of a paramilitary group to the United States by the International Court of Justice in the *Nicaragua* case where the Court concluded that 'it would in principle have to be proved that that State had effective control of the military or paramilitary operations' in question'.[48]

7. As previously noted, different State responsibility regimes may apply to different types of actors in various situations. With respect to space, a State bears international responsibility under Article VI of the OST for its national activities in space, whether such activities are carried on by governmental agencies or by non-governmental entities and for ensuring that all national activities are carried out in conformity with the OST (see Rule 10: Responsibility of States for National Activities in Outer Space). Article VI thus attributes responsibility to a State for the actions of its all individuals, corporations, and other non-governmental entities making up its national activities in space, although special considerations related to effective control of those entities may apply regarding the application of this Rule in the context of the law of armed conflict and also with respect to the threat or use of force (see Rule 10: Responsibility of States for National Activities in Outer Space).

8. In addition to determining which State is responsible for a space object under Article VI of the OST, additional complications may arise in determining which States may be parties to an international armed conflict when a State resorts armed force against another State's space object. For a discussion of this issue with respect to the use of force and armed attacks (see Rule 23: Armed Attack). The relationship between States and space objects is subject to multiple, overlapping legal connections (see Note on Legal Connections Between States and a Space Object), none of which may be independently determinative of status as a party to an international armed conflict. These legal connections include, *inter alia*: registration by a State of the space object; responsibility of a State for the space object as part of that State's national activities in space; the launching of the object by a State ('launching State' status); and although not an allocation of international rights and obligations like the above legal connections, ownership or use of the space object by a national of a State (including its juridical persons/companies) or by the State itself.

---

and jailers of the hostages, had now become agents of the Iranian State for whose acts the State itself was internationally responsible.').

[48] *Military and Paramilitary Activities in and against Nicaragua (Nicaragua v US) (Merits)* [1986] ICJ Reps 14 (*Nicaragua* case) para 115 (emphasis added). The 2016 GC Commentary acknowledges the decision in *Nicaragua* and notes that the level of control by a foreign State over the non-State armed group necessary to render an armed conflict international is 'debated', but concludes that 'the notion of control is central to the question of attribution of the actions of a non-State armed group to a State'. 2016 GC I Commentary (n 37) para 269.

9. Under the space law regime, a satellite can have only one State of Registry, although as many as four different States—or more—may qualify as a 'launching State'.[49] The status of a launching State is presumptively a prerequisite for a State to register a satellite (Rule 8: Registration of Space Objects).[50] However, whether a use of armed force against a satellite can trigger an international armed conflict between the State that resorts to the use of armed force and the satellite's State of Registry is less clear than it is in relation to the registry–nationality nexus for vessels and aircraft, since space objects do not possess a nationality like ships and aircraft.[51] While registry may be a key legal connection in making this assessment with respect to a satellite, other legal connections noted above may also be important. The significance of these other connections can be resolved only through additional relevant State practice. In the simplest and clearest case, a space object would be launched by one State from its own territory, registered in that State, operated by that State, regarded as a national space activity that is the responsibility of that State under Article VI of the OST, and owned by that State. Such a scenario is, however, only one of many possible sets of legal connections between a space object and a State.

10. Regarding the use of armed force against a satellite registered by an international organization, there is no consensus whether an international armed conflict would be initiated between the State that resorts to armed force and that international organization (or possibly, in an alternative scenario, by an international organization against a State[52] (see Rule 11: Responsibility of International Organizations)).

---

[49] There are four categories of States that potentially qualify as a 'launching State'. Article I of the Liability Convention defines a 'launching State' as (i) a State which launches a space object; (ii) a State which 'procures' the launching of a space object; (iii) a State from whose territory a space object is launched; (iv) and a State from whose facility a space object is launched. UNGA, 'Convention on International Liability for Damage Caused by Space Objects' (adopted 29 November 1971, entered into force 29 March 1972) 961 UNTS 187 (Liability Convention) art I. It is also possible that more than one State may qualify as a 'procuring State' (see Rule 8: Registration of Space Objects). In addition, it is possible, although not envisioned by the Registration Convention, that one State may transfer registration of a space object in orbit to another State that was not one of the original launching States (see Rule 8: Registration of Space Objects).

[50] OST (n 46) art VIII; UNGA, 'Convention on Registration of Objects Launched into Outer Space (adopted 6 June 1975, entered into force 15 September 1976) 1023 UNTS 15 (Registration Convention) art II; Liability Convention (n 49) art I.

[51] Convention on International Civil Aviation (adopted 7 December 1944, entered into force 4 April 1947) 15 UNTS 295 (Chicago Convention) art 17; *United Nations Convention on the Law of the Sea* (adopted 10 December 1982, entered into force 16 November 1994) 1833 UNTS 3 (UNCLOS) art 91.

[52] Under Chapter VIII of the UN Charter, the UN Security Council is authorized to use regional security organizations to implement Chapter VII enforcement actions to restore international peace and security; the resulting use of armed force against a State could thus in principle initiate an international armed conflict between the international organization and a State. See eg NATO, acting as a regional security organization on behalf of the UNSC, imposing a no-fly zone against Libya as part of an enforcement measure under UNSC Resolution 1973 (2011).

Accidents and Mistakes

11. Accidents and mistakes do not amount to a resort or recourse to armed force against another State giving rise to an international armed conflict[53] (see discussion of accidents, mistakes, and other non-intentional acts in Rule 23: Armed Attack). For example, a debris-causing event by a State that is neither intended, nor likely, to affect another State would not trigger the application of the law of armed conflict between the State responsible for this debris-causing event and any other States and would not have the effect of making those other States parties to the international armed conflict.

Terrestrial Domain Limitations

12. Common Article 2 also states that an international armed conflict will exist in situations of belligerent occupation, as that term is understood in the law of armed conflict, even when there is no resistance to the occupation.[54] In situations of armed conflict relating to space, space assets could facilitate acts of occupation taking place in the terrestrial domain. However, under Article II of the OST, outer space and celestial bodies are not subject to national appropriation by claim of sovereignty, by means of use or occupation, or by any other means. Consequently, it is not technically possible under the international space law regime to *occupy* (as the term is understood in the law of armed conflict) space or any area of a celestial body because only the sovereign territory of a State is subject to occupation.[55] Thus, to the extent the initiation of an international armed conflict by virtue of belligerent occupation is relevant to space operations, it is only so based on occupation of territory on the Earth.

---

[53] 2016 GC I Commentary (n 37) art 2 para 241 ('It is important, however, to rule out the possibility of including in the scope of application of humanitarian law situations that are the result of a mistake or of individual ultra vires acts, which—even if they might entail the international responsibility of the State to which the individual who committed the acts belongs – are not endorsed by the State concerned. Such acts would not amount to armed conflict.'); UK LOAC Manual (n 21) para 3.3.1.

[54] Geneva Conventions I–IV, Common Article 2 (n 4).

[55] It should also be noted that the subject of permanent civilian populations residing on celestial bodies lies outside the scope of this *Manual* and raises untested and unsettled questions under the space law regime and the law of armed conflict. Although OST (n 46) art II clearly states that a State may not subject space or celestial bodies to national appropriation by claim of sovereignty or by means of use or occupation, this does not mean that a State is physically prohibited from 'using' or 'occupying' a location (assuming that such use or occupation does not in any way constitute an attempt by that State to appropriate any area of space or a celestial body).

Rule 30
Non-International Armed Conflict

A non-international armed conflict exists whenever there is armed violence of sufficient intensity occurring between a State and one or more organized armed groups, or between organized armed groups in the territory of a State.

To the extent that a terrestrial non-international armed conflict that originates on the territory of a State involves military operations from, to, or within space, all relevant rules of the law of armed conflict relating to non-international armed conflicts apply to those operations.

Overview of Legal Basis of Rule

1. According to Common Article 3 of the Geneva Conventions of 1949, a non-international armed conflict (NIAC) refers to a situation in which an 'armed conflict not of an international character occurs *in the territory* of one of the High Contracting Parties' (emphasis added). In addition to this requirement, two supporting criteria must be met to establish that an armed confrontation, as set out in the Rule, is a NIAC: first, the hostilities must be of sufficient intensity[56] beyond 'situations of internal disturbances and tensions, such as riots, isolated or sporadic acts of violence or other acts of a similar nature';[57] and secondly, the armed group (or groups) involved must be sufficiently organized.[58] Collectively, these requirements are recognized under customary international law as defining a non-international armed conflict.[59]

---

[56] Jurisprudence by international criminal tribunals has clarified that the criterion is 'intensity' of violence. 'Duration' may be indicative of intensity but is not a requirement in itself. See Commentary to the Third Geneva Convention (n 37) para 461 ff. Although the 'intensity' of an armed conflict can be defined in different ways, one element which arguably constitutes its own criterion is the duration of a conflict and thus whether it could be described as a 'protracted' armed conflict. See *Tadić* decision (n 31) para 70 ('we find that an armed conflict exists whenever there is a resort to armed force between States or protracted armed violence government authorities and organized armed groups or between such groups within a State'.

[57] See Rome Statute of the International Criminal Court (adopted 17 July 1998, entered into force 1 July 2002) UNTS 2187 UNTS 88, art 8(2)(d) (distinguishing 'armed conflicts not of an international character' from such 'situations of internal disturbances and tensions').

[58] See *Milošević Case* (Decision on motion for judgment of acquittal) IT-02-54 (16 Jun 2004) paras 16–17; *Furundžija Case* (Trial Judgment) IT-95-17/1-T (10 December 1998) para 59, *Mucić et al.* (Trial Judgment) IT-96-21 (16 November 1998) para 183; UK LOAC Manual (n 21) para 15.3.1; ICRC, 2016 GC I Commentary (n 37) para 421.

[59] Canadian LOAC Manual (n 21) para 1702; German LOAC Manual (n 21) paras 1302–1303; Norwegian Defence University College, 'Manual of the Law of Armed Conflict' (1st edn, The Chief

As noted, Common Article 3 of the Geneva Conventions of 1949 limits a NIAC to a situation in which an armed conflict not of an international character occurs in the territory of one of the High Contracting Parties. For States that are parties to Additional Protocol II of the Geneva Conventions of 1949, an even more restrictive territorial limitation can be found for armed conflicts to which that instrument applies.[60] Because Article II of the OST prohibits States from appropriating any 'territory' in space or on a celestial body (see Rule 2: Non-Appropriation of Outer Space and Celestial Bodies), the restrictions under the law of armed conflict limiting NIACs to territories occurring 'in the territory' of a State appear to argue against the possibility of the establishment or origination of a NIAC in space.[61]

2.

Limitations Imposed by Space and by the Space Law Regime

Although military space operations and assets have supported terrestrial military operations involving existing NIACs and those military space operations have been governed by the rules of armed conflict applicable to NIACs, at the present time it is unlikely that a NIAC can originate in space or take place exclusively in space. This is based on both the practical and legal limitations. First, on a practical and technological basis, within the future time frame that this *Manual* operates, it is difficult to contemplate that non-State armed groups will be technologically capable of starting and waging an armed conflict entirely in space. However, as discussed in paragraph 4, it is perhaps possible to contemplate organized non-State armed groups in existing NIACs on Earth managing at some point in the foreseeable future to employ limited capabilities in space. Second, if a non-State organized armed group did have the technical capabilities to start and wage an armed conflict exclusively in space, it would be highly problematic from a legal perspective for a NIAC to originate in or occur exclusively in space. As noted, Common Article 3 explicitly refers to NIACs arising in the territory of a State that is a party to the Geneva Conventions of 1949. In addition, legal obstacles to establishing a NIAC in

3.

---

of Defence 2013) (Norwegian LOAC Manual) para 1.36; AMW Manual (n 31) r 2(a), nn 5–6; Michael N Schmitt, Charles HB Galloway, and Yoram Dinstein, *The Manual on the Law of Non-International Conflict with Commentary* (International Institute of Humanitarian Law 2006) para 1.1.1.

[60] Protocol Additional to the Geneva Conventions of 12 August 1949 and relating to the protection of the victims of non-international armed conflicts (Protocol II) (adopted 6 August 1949, entered into force 7 December 1978) 1125 UNTS 3, art 1(1). Protocol II is applicable only to NIACs that take place '*in the territory of a High Contracting Party*' between its armed forces and dissident armed forces or other organized armed groups that are 'under responsible command [and] *exercise such control over a part of its territory* as to enable them to carry out sustained and concerted military operations and to implement this Protocol' (emphasis added).

[61] It should be noted that while space objects may be under the jurisdiction and control of a State, this status does not make these objects 'territory' of that State for purposes of the Geneva Conventions of 1949.

space are presented by the existing space la regime. As noted in the Introduction to Part III, the space law regime is inherently State-focused. It is thus generally presumed that all satellites or other space objects are registered by a particular State, that each State remains responsible for all its national activities in space, and that a launching State is liable for damages caused by its space objects (see Rule 8: Registration of Space Objects; Rule 10: Responsibility of States for National Activities in Outer Space; Rule 12: International Liability for Damage Caused by Space Objects). Even a non-governmental entity, such as a corporation, remains the responsibility of a particular State as part of that State's national responsibilities in space.[62] For these reasons, a belligerent 'non-State' actor/'non-State' armed group in space is an anomaly under the space law regime.

4. Despite the inherent legal challenges and current practical and technological limitations of a NIAC originating in space (and not the territory of a State) or a NIAC taking place exclusively in space, it is possible to contemplate at some point in the future an exceptional case in which a non-State organized armed group in an existing NIAC on Earth could use cyber means to hijack or control an adversary State's satellites or use some other advanced ASAT technology to cause damages to a space object of that State.[63] If such a case were to arise as an extension of an existing NIAC on Earth between the victim State and the non-State organized armed group, it is possible—but unsettled—that the relevant rules of the law of armed conflict governing a NIAC would apply in light of the territorial limitations on NIACs. However, as noted with respect to current practice, the military assets of States in space that have been used in conjunction with attacks on non-State armed groups in existing NIACs in terrestrial domains continue to be governed by the rules of the law of armed conflict applicable to NIACs. However, it is more difficult to contemplate a NIAC originating in space.[64]

Other Geographic Limitations on Non-International Armed Conflicts

5. Notwithstanding the language found in Common Article 3 of the Geneva Conventions of 1949 limiting a NIAC to an armed confrontation occurring in the

---

[62] OST (n 46) art VI.
[63] One State at State Consultations suggested the possibility that a non-State-organized armed group that is a party to a NIAC could theoretically seize control of a space-based capability which it then could use in hostilities against a State (eg by disrupting a key military communication satellite's functionality).
[64] Even if a non-State-organized armed group succeeded in using advanced technology to cause damage to the space-based capabilities of a State and no terrestrial restriction on the formation of a NIAC was observed, the hostilities must nonetheless be of sufficient intensity/duration—and not an isolated incident—to give rise to a NIAC. In other words, although the right of self-defence by a State might be triggered by such an event, the criteria of intensity and organization required to constitute a NIAC would also need to be fulfilled in order to establish a NIAC.

territory of one State, there is wide consensus that a NIAC can extend beyond the territory of just the one State in which the NIAC originated. Common Article 3 has been interpreted as not implying a strict geographical limitation to a single State, at least to the extent that a NIAC spills over into the territory of an adjacent State.[65] Consistent with a broader (and sometimes contested) interpretation, States have engaged in fighting al Qaeda, Daesh, and associated groups around the world[66]—in NIACs that extend to multiple States beyond the territories adjacent to the State in which the conflict originated—and have often done so by means of satellites relaying signals that control drones targeting these non-State organized armed groups. This State practice is consistent with the finding that to the extent a terrestrial NIAC involves military space operations, Common Article 3 to the 1949 Geneva Conventions (which is reflected in customary international law and applied to space by Article III of the OST) and other relevant rules of conventional and customary international law relating to NIACs apply.

---

[65] The lawfulness of an extension or spillover of a NIAC into non-adjacent territories may be unsettled. The ICRC's position is that NIACs 'can spill over into neighbouring countries because of the continuity of hostilities', but 'the IHL criteria of intensity and organization required to constitute a NICA would need to be fulfilled in the territory of each individual third State for the applicability of IHL to be triggered'. ICRC, 'International Humanitarian Law and the Challenges of Contemporary Armed Conflicts' (32nd International Conference of the Red Cross and Red Crescent, Geneva, 2015) (ICRC 2015 IHL Challenges Report) 19. But see also ICRC, 'International Humanitarian Law and the Challenges of Contemporary Armed Conflicts' (31st International Conference of the Red Cross and Red Crescent, Geneva, 2011) 9–10 ('[A] seventh type of NIAC believed by some to currently exist is an armed conflict taking place across multiple states between Al Qaeda and its "affiliates" and "adherents" and the United States ("transnational")'); ICRC 2015 IHL Challenges Report (n 65) 15; and GC I Commentary (n 37) paras 452–482.

[66] As noted by one State at State Consultations, while NIACs may indeed extend beyond the territories adjacent to the State in which the conflict originated (as reflected in the conflict with al Qaeda and Daesh), support for this view does not indicate any endorsement of analysis based on a 'Global War on Terror'.

SECTION 2
CONDUCT IN OR RELATED TO ATTACK

Rule 31
Attack

An 'attack', in the context of a military operation, including a military space operation, in the course of armed conflict, is an act of violence against the adversary whether in offence or in defence.

Overview of Legal Basis of Rule

1. This Rule is based on the definition of 'attack' in Article 49(1) of Additional Protocol I,[67] and reflects the meaning of attack in customary international law applicable in both international and non-international armed conflicts.[68] It is important to understand that the term 'attack', as used throughout the Rules in this *Manual* relating to the law of armed conflict, is to be distinguished from the term 'armed attack', which appears in Article 51 of the UN Charter and is discussed in Rule 23: Armed Attack. The latter applies only in the context of the law governing the resort to force (*jus ad bellum*).[69] By contrast, the following analysis bears on the issue of whether a particular military space operation is an attack under the separate legal regime of the law of armed conflict or the *jus in bello*.

2. An understanding of the term 'attack' is fundamental to compliance with the law of armed conflict in the conduct of military space operations. For example, an attack must be directed at military objectives (see Rule 34: Military Objectives), civilians may never be made the object of an attack (see Rule 32: Distinction), and an attack must conform with other requirements, particularly precautionary measures

---

[67] See Introduction to Part III, paras 9–10 (noting that the text of Additional Protocol I explicitly states in art 49(3) that this Rule is applicable to warfare on land, air, and sea, and this *Manual* interprets Additional Protocol I as also extending to military space operations, that may affect the civilian population, individual civilians, or civilian objects in any domain).

[68] The ICRC takes the position that State practice has established this rule as a norm of customary international law applicable in both international and non-international conflicts. ICRC CIHL Study (n 14) Rule 15 (but see Introduction to Part III, paras 11–13, noting that serious concerns have been expressed by some States about the methodology used in the ICRC CIHL Study). With regard to the application of this Rule in non-international armed conflict, see *Commentary on the Additional Protocols* (n 9) para 4783 (noting that the term 'attack' has the same meaning in Protocol II). See also Michael N Schmitt, Charles HB Garraway, and Yoram Dinstein, *The Manual on the Law of Non-International Armed Conflict with Commentary* (International Institute of Humanitarian Law (IIHL) 2006) (*NIAC Manual*) Rule 1.1.6.

[69] *Commentary on the Additional Protocols* (n 9) para 1882 ('it is appropriate to note that in the sense of the Protocol an attack is unrelated to the concept of aggression or the first use of armed force').

(see Section 3: Precautions in Attack, including Rule 38: Proportionality in Attack). A military space operation that does not qualify as an attack is not subject to the rules that specifically regulate attacks, although it remains subject to other rules of the law of armed conflict applicable to other military space operations (eg see Rule 46: Constant Care).

Attack as an Act of Violence by Means of Traditional Armed Force

3. As reflected in this Rule, the traditional focus of the term 'attack' under the law of armed conflict has been on an act of violence (with requisite intent), as accomplished by the use of armed force and associated weapons.[70] This traditional view reflects a means-based approach. While many actions may have damaging results, the origins of the law of armed conflict, or the *jus in bello*, focused on regulating armed, physical force, and weapons associated with such force. A similar focus can be found in the origins of the prohibition of the use of force in the UN Charter and the *jus ad bellum* (see Rule 21: Use of Force). Armed force has often been characterized by the use of weapons to destroy targets with the force of kinetic energy against targets (bombs, artillery shells, missiles etc). Other armed, physical means and methods of warfare, such as chemical, biological, and nuclear weapons were already part of a wide range of weapons able to achieve acts of violence by the end of the Second World War. These weapons systems were later joined by numerous non-kinetic weapon systems utilizing various parts of the electromagnetic spectrum, including not only electronic measures utilizing radio waves but also directed energy weapons employing high-energy lasers and microwave radiation, which have many possible applications in military space operations. These weapons systems relied on new uses of the electromagnetic spectrum, building on the foundation of electronic warfare that was already present before and during the Second World War. Traditional weapons systems based on kinetic energy have expanded for purposes of military space operations, including new ASAT weapons, robotic mechanisms, and objects that are capable of manoeuvring in space. These modern weapon systems, both kinetic and non-kinetic, are closely associated with weapons systems that formed the traditional basis for both the use of armed force

---

[70] UK LOAC Manual (n 21) para 5.20.2 (Amendment 4, July 2011) ('An "act of violence" involves the use of armed forces including means of warfare (that is, weapons).' The United Kingdom has also recognized that 'a cyber operation is capable of being an "attack" under IHL where it has the same or similar effects to kinetic action that would constitute an attack'. UK Foreign, Commonwealth & Development Office, 'Application of international law in states' conduct in cyberspace: UK statement' (submitted to UN Group of Governmental Experts on Advancing Responsible State Behaviour in Cyberspace in the Context of International Security, 3 June 2021) para 24. One State at State Consultations stressed that a purpose or an intent to cause damage is a fundamental component of an act of violence and thus of an attack—and that State practice clearly supports this requirement (see paras 8 and 12).

and acts of violence under international law. Thus, the use of these weapons would (or could) constitute an attack under the means-based approach for purposes of the law of armed conflict.

Attack by Cyber Means

4. The transmission of data by means of cyber capabilities is different in many respects from traditional weapon systems that rely on armed force. However, cyber actions may nonetheless in some cases cause the same or similar types of damaging effects as these traditional weapon systems. Cyber capabilities have thus highlighted an alternative effects-based approach to defining attacks in armed conflicts. This effects-based approach, which corresponds generally with the position taken by several States,[71] is the position of the ICRC,[72] and enjoys considerable academic support,[73] posits that an 'act of violence' should include an act that created violent consequences, even if the mode of inflicting those consequences was not violent.[74] Under this approach, a military operation qualifies as an act of violence (and thus an attack) if it is 'an act that causes death or injury to a person or that damages or destroys an object').[75] Thus, according to this effects-based approach, any military

---

[71] For the positions of several other States supporting various versions of the effects-based approach, see International Cyber Law in Practice: Interactive Toolkit, 'Attack (international humanitarian law)' (online database, 2021) [https://perma.cc/A7G2-KG2D].

[72] ICRC, 'International Humanitarian Law and Cyber Operations during Armed Conflicts' (2019) 102 International Review of the Red Cross 481, 489–90 [perma.cc/2Z3M-MJNF] (arguing that 'it is widely accepted that cyber operations expected to cause death, injury or physical damage constitute attacks under IHL').

[73] See eg Michael N Schmitt, 'Cyber Operations and the Jus in Bello: Key Issues' (2011) 87 International Law Studies 89, 94: 'it is not the violence of the act that constitutes the condition precedent to limiting the occurrence of an attack, but the violence of the ensuing result'; Yoram Dinstein, *The Conduct of Hostilities under the Law of International Armed Conflict* (3rd edn, CUP 2016) 2: 'The violent essence of an act must be understood in terms of consequences (death/injury to human beings or destruction/damage to property), rather than the immediate cause'; Laurent Gisel, Tilman Rodenhauser, and Knut Dormann, 'Twenty Years On: International Humanitarian Law and the Protection Of Civilians Against the Effects of Cyber Operations During Armed Conflicts' (2020) 102 International Review of the Red Cross 287, 312: 'It is well established that the notion of violence in this definition can refer to either the means of warfare or their effects, meaning that an operation causing violent effects can be an attack even if the means used to cause those effects are not violent as such.'

[74] NATO Cooperative Cyber Defence Centre of Excellence, Tallinn Manual 2.0 on the International Law Applicable to Cyber Operations (Michael N Schmitt ed, 2nd edn, CUP 2017) (Tallinn Manual 2.0) Rule 30, para 3 (observing that acts of violence 'should be considered in the sense of violent consequences and should not be limited to violent acts').

[75] Norwegian Law of Armed Conflict Manual (n 59) para 2.2 ('Examples of non-kinetic acts that may constitute an attack include cyberattacks'); New Zealand Department of the Prime Minister and Cabinet, 'The Application of International Law to State Activity in Cyberspace' (1 December 2020) para 25 ('A cyber activity may constitute an "attack" for the purposes of international humanitarian law where it results in death, injury, or physical damage, including loss of functionality, equivalent to that caused by a kinetic attack.'). UK statement on 'Application of international law in states' conduct in cyberspace' (n 59) para 24 ('A cyber operation is capable of being an "attack" under IHL where it has the same or similar effects to kinetic action that would constitute an attack.'); Italian Ministry for Foreign Affairs and International Cooperation, 'Italian Position Paper on "International Law and Cyberspace"' (2021) 9–10 ('In line with the definition of "attack" under Article 49(1) of [Additional Protocol I], Italy

operation (including a military space operation) that causes damage, destruction, injury, or death qualifies as an attack. However, a necessary addendum to a purely effects-based approach requires that one also consider the *intent* underlying the act of violence, so that unsuccessful attempts are included in the definition of an attack. As noted by one State at State Consultations, the intended or reasonably expected effects of the physical act 'are an inseparable component of the act of violence'. This focus on the act itself and the actor's underlying intentions (and not merely an examination of the damaging effects) may thus be especially important in incidents involving accidents, malfunctions etc. See related discussion in paragraph 8.

5. There are undoubtedly some situations in which cyber capabilities can be employed in military space operations in a manner that constitutes an act of violence, particularly when used to control weapons employing physical, armed force. Consider the case in which a State inserts malware in another State's computer guidance system, effectively hijacking control of a kinetic-kill weapon system (such as an ASAT missile system) to engage in an attack with that weapon system against an adversary's satellite. In such a case, the cyber-enabled control of the missile system engaging a target would constitute an act of violence and an attack.

6. Because of the physical characteristics of the space environment, some uses of armed force that cause even the temporary loss of functionality of a satellite may effectively result in a 'mission kill' by preventing the satellite from accomplishing its military purpose.[76] Such actions may be accomplished using any of the weapon

---

qualifies cyber operations as "attacks" under IHL if they constitute an act of violence resulting in more than minimal physical damage of property or disruption in the functioning of critical infrastructure, or human injury and loss of life.'); Tallinn Manual 2.0 (n 74) Rule 30 ('A cyber attack is a cyber operation, whether offensive or defensive, that is reasonably expected to cause injury or death to persons or damage or destruction to objects.').

[76] With respect to any required seriousness or minimum level of damage of an attack, one State at State Consultations noted that 'depending on the circumstances prevailing at the time of an alleged attack, the nature/importance of the targeted space object, and the context in which the armed forces are deployed, an apparently minor action causing minor or no damage may constitute an attack— particularly during a time of high alert'. Although not explicitly addressing military space operations, other States have taken similar positions regarding a 'loss of functionality' or a 'disruption in the functioning of critical infrastructure' as a form of damage that may constitute the effects of an attack. See New Zealand, 'The Application of International Law to State Activity in Cyberspace' (n 75) para 25; Italian Ministry for Foreign Affairs and International Cooperation (n 75) 9–10. Other States have taken a contrary position. See eg Roy Schöndorf (Israeli Deputy Attorney General (International Law)), 'Israel's Perspective on Key Legal and Practical Issues Concerning the Application of International Law to Cyber Operations' (transcript of the keynote speech delivered at the Stockton Center for International Law, US Naval War College) (2021) 97 International Law Studies 395, 400 ('Only when a cyber operation is expected to cause physical damage, will it satisfy the element of an attack under LOAC. In the same vein, the mere loss or impairment of functionality to infrastructure would be insufficient in this regard, and no other specific rule to the contrary has evolved in the cyber domain.'). A similar view rejecting the inclusion of the loss of functionality as qualifying damage for an attack was expressed by one State at State consultation.

systems discussed above, including cyber capabilities, and may constitute an 'attack'. In this respect, it may not matter whether the space object has been physically damaged or merely temporarily disabled. For example, any action that moves a satellite out of its designated orbit can potentially destroy that satellite or render it temporarily or permanently functionally useless. It should also be noted that in light of the fast-moving and unique environment of a potential armed conflict in space, an action causing even the temporary loss of the functionality of a satellite (without the satellite being physically damaged) may cause irreparable harm to the mission or capabilities of the attacked State and thus such actions must be assessed on a case-by-case basis under the circumstances prevailing at the time. For example, an act that temporarily jams, dazzles, or otherwise temporarily disables a particularly sensitive target during heightened tensions may be more likely to constitute an attack act. Thus, the temporary jamming, blinding, or incapacitation of an early warning satellite during a time of crisis (even if this only results in a temporary loss of functionality) might be regarded as an attack by the attacked State.

7. Cyber capabilities in military space operations[77] may achieve the same results that weapons employing traditional armed force can achieve because the vast majority of space objects are dependent on signals and remote control. This means that actions taken against these space control systems—whether by employing physical force (missiles, robotic mechanisms, kinetic kill vehicles etc), the use of the electromagnetic spectrum (including electronic measures, lasers, high-energy microwave radiation), or the use of cyber capabilities—may cause an adversary's satellite to de-orbit in a manner that it is likely to be physically destroyed or permanently incapacitated, constituting an attack. At the same time, a cyber action taken against a State's missile warning satellite that causes only a temporary disruption in that satellite's functionality—and that does not cause any lasting harm to the satellite itself—could still have a major effect on the targeted State and thus constitute an 'attack'. A more difficult case is presented by the jamming or dazzling of a less critical satellite that causes no physical damage and results in only a temporary disruption of that satellite's functions. Such actions may or may not constitute an attack under the circumstances governing at the time.

8. This *Manual* recognizes both the traditional means-based and the emerging effects-based approach, and regards them as complementary, drawing on both in particular situations. While it may be appropriate in various situations to use an effects-based approach to determine whether a particular cyber-based or other military space operation constitutes an attack, care must be taken to not extend this approach too broadly as the exclusive basis for defining an act of violence in all types of military space operations. There are numerous reasons for this. For

---

[77] It should be noted that cyber actions in military space operations can be directed against the satellite itself, the ground station, or the satellite's up-/down- or cross-links.

example, an ASAT attack employing a missile or other kinetic kill vehicle that misses its target may not cause any damage at all and yet may still constitute an attack.[78] It is also possible that some cyber operations directed at targets on Earth may result in damages, such as purely financial losses or exfiltration of data, that do not represent 'violent consequences', that is, damages that are equivalent to those caused by the use of physical, armed force.[79] Some acts of hostility may also cause damage but do not qualify as an attack. For example, ruses (including actions involving the transmission of misleading information) may result in actions taken by an adversary that result in damage to the adversary's own space assets, but they will not qualify as attacks.[80] Finally, it is also possible that even if damage does occur as a result of a military space operation, the underlying act that caused that damage may lack the requisite intent or purpose for it to constitute an act of violence, as in the case of accidents (see paragraph 12).[81]

---

[78] Thus, a military space operation does not need to be successful to qualify as an attack, as long as an act of violence is involved. As noted, this scenario calls for a modified or amended version of a purely effects-based approach, one that includes an examination of *the intent underlying the attempted act of violence* to determine if damages/violent consequences were 'expected'. See Tallinn Manual 2.0 (n 74) Rule 30 (noting that a cyber attack is a cyber operation 'that is reasonably expected to cause injury or death to persons or damage or destruction to objects'). At the same time, it may be particularly difficult in the cyber context to distinguish an expected attack from other diverse, malicious cyber intrusions (in space or in any other domain), in part because the 'intent' behind such cyber intrusions may be quite difficult to discern. It should also be noted that several States that have adopted an effects-based approach to attacks in the cyber and other domains do not explicitly include 'expected' injuries, death, or damage in their definition of a cyber (or other) attack, although their analysis of the underlying act of violence could include this requirement (see eg examples of State definitions of a cyber attack in n 75 above).

[79] As noted during State Consultations, a cyber action disabling a State's critical infrastructure, including its major financial institutions, seems highly likely to constitute sufficient damage to make such an action an attack. However, the removal of funds from a bank account or other cyber actions causing selected financial losses seems unlikely to qualify as an attack. In addition, the exfiltration or corruption of data would normally be considered an act of espionage, not an attack (even though such an action may cause considerable harm to the victim State). Furthermore, the status of a variety of harmful cyber actions against data is unsettled. See Switzerland Federal Department of Foreign Affairs, 'Switzerland's position paper on the application of international law in cyberspace' (UN GGE 2019/ 2021, May 2021) 10 ('What exactly constitutes a "cyber attack" in an armed conflict has yet to be clarified ... It encompasses at the very least cyber operations that are reasonably expected to cause, directly or indirectly, injury or death to persons, or physical damage or destruction to objects. The question, how exactly data is protected in the absence of such physical damage, remains a challenge.').

[80] However, it could also be it could also be argued that in some cases the damage resulting from ruses, including the transmission of misleading information, may involve an insufficient link between the action and its effects. Nonetheless, in the complex space environment dominated by remotely controlled space objects dependent on reliable information, it is possible that damages could occur as the result of ruses and misinformation affecting an adversary's operators. For example, transmitting misleading information to an adversary's military commander regarding the location of military assets in space that results in the manoeuvre and accidental collision of the adversary's satellites is not an attack.

[81] As noted by one State at State Consultations, 'the definition of an attack, as set forth in Article 49(1) of Additional Protocol I, refers to "acts of violence against the adversary". This phrase, together with the element of "violence" and the term "attack" itself (as well as the contexts in which it is used in Additional Protocol I), reflect the "purpose element" in the definition of attack, which requires that the purpose behind the damaging act would be to harm the adversary, in order for the act to that it qualifies as an attack.' This State further noted that purpose 'is an integral element in the definition of attack'. Attacks thus cannot be defined only by their expected physical damage, since there are other activities that cause such a damage that clearly do not qualify as 'attacks' in the common understanding and practice of States.

Acts of Violence Against the Adversary

9. The definition of an attack, as set forth in this Rule and in Article 49(1) of Additional Protocol I, refers to 'acts of violence *against the adversary*' (emphasis added).[82] This language in Article 49(1), which excludes any reference to attacks against civilians and civilian objects, was adopted by a majority of the State representatives on the relevant drafting committee because they noted that civilians are the subject of numerous express protections in other Articles of the Additional Protocol.[83] It is true that to the extent incidental damage, injury or death is caused to the civilian population as a result of an attack on an adversary's military objectives, the civilian population is further protected by other restrictions on the attacker, such as precautionary measures (see Section 3: Precautions in Attack) and proportionality (see Rule 38: Proportionality in Attack). However, several States at State Consultations commented that the definition of attacks in Article 49(1) of Additional Protocol I should be read as including acts of violence against civilians. Excluding acts of violence that are directed against civilians from the definition of attacks in fact presents something of a logical conundrum because it can be argued that the rule prohibiting attacks against civilians is rendered moot if the definition of attack excludes all actions against civilians.

Scope and Application

10. This Rule covers 'attacks', whether conducted offensively or defensively.[84] For example, if a satellite of State A is engaged in offensive rendezvous operations against a satellite of State B, the firing of an ASAT missile by State B at State A's satellite would be an attack on State A's satellite, even if the reason for the attack was defensive in nature. As noted in the Commentary to Additional Protocol I, 'the definition given by the Protocol has a wider scope since it—justifiably—covers defensive acts

---

[82] Another provision in Additional Protocol I explicitly provides that '[t]he civilian population as such, as well as individual civilians, shall not be the object of attack'. Additional Protocol I (n 4) art 51(2). See also Rule 33: Direct Participation in Hostilities.

[83] See *Commentary on the Additional Protocols* (n 9) para 1877 (some States involved in the drafting of Article 49 of Additional Protocol I sought to remove the phrase 'against the adversary' because they believed that 'the provisions of this Section of the Protocol should apply to the civilian population of all the Parties to the conflict, including the civilian population of the Party concerned'. This proposed deletion was rejected, and the existing language was retained by a vote of 38 votes in favour, 18 votes against, and 10 abstentions on Committee III. In this regard, the Commentary notes that 'this idea was partially retained in paragraph 2 of the article 49'). An alternative view of this Rule, to help ensure protection of the civilian population, would reject this decision by the drafters of the Additional Protocol and interpret the Rule as encompassing the civilian population and not limiting the definition of an attack to just acts of violence (or violent consequences) directed against the adversary.

[84] *Commentary on the Additional Protocols* (n 9) paras 1880 and 4783; UK LOAC Manual (n 21) para 5.20.2.

(particularly "counter-attacks") as well as offensive acts, as both can affect the civilian population. It is for this reason that the final choice was a broad definition'.[85]

11. It is difficult to establish any de minimis standard for an act of violence in space as an attack for purposes of the law of armed conflict. As noted in paragraphs 6 and 9, depending on the circumstances prevailing at the time of an alleged attack, the nature/importance of the targeted space object, and the context in which the armed forces are deployed, an apparently limited action causing minor or no damage may constitute an attack—particularly during a time of high alert. Thus, a laser dazzling operation that momentarily blinds an optical sensor on a surveillance satellite, or the use of electronic measures that disrupt, interfere with, or degrade the Telemetry, Tracking, and Control (TT&C) functions of a satellite, even if that loss is temporary, may constitute an attack for purposes of the law of armed conflict.

12. Accidents do not qualify as acts of violence or attacks, notwithstanding their damaging effects or harmful consequences, and even some actions that cause 'expected' damage may lack the requisite intent for an attack.[86] With respect to accidents, if a State that is a party to the conflict loses control of one of its satellites because it is bumped by a micrometeoroid, thereby knocking it off its intended trajectory, and it accidentally collides with a satellite of State B, another party to the conflict, there is no attack in the absence of intention. This may be a particularly important concept in space, since hazardous conditions, extreme speeds, control of most military space operations from distant locations, disabled or non-functional satellites in decaying and unpredictable orbits, and a host of other challenges confronting space operators, all strongly suggest that allowance must be made for the possibility of accidents. To do otherwise would increase the chances of unnecessarily enlarging armed conflicts in space, to the detriment of all humanity.[87]

---

[85] *Commentary on the Additional Protocols* (n 9) 1880.

[86] As noted by one State at State Consultations, 'many acts of warfare that are technically expected to cause damage (sometimes knowingly or even intentionally) do not amount to "attacks", if the military purpose in those acts is not harming the adversary. For example, this would be the case with disconnecting a space capsule, that might land on property or even persons on Earth, thereby causing physical damage. The purpose element is also grounded in State practice.'

[87] One additional challenging and unsettled issue in this area concerns possible actions by a so-called rogue commander, ie one who acts without or against the orders of State military authorities. Actions by a military commander are attributable to a State under Art 91 of Additional Protocol I, which states that '[a] party to the conflict ... shall be responsible for all acts committed by persons forming part of its armed forces'. In addition, art VI of the OST (n 46) provides that States that are parties to the OST 'shall bear international responsibility for national activities in outer space ... and for assuring that national activities are carried out in conformity with [the OST, including international law]' (see Rule 10: Responsibility of States for National Activities in Outer Space). Although the OST governs the attribution of responsibility for the national activities of States in space, more generally art VII of the Articles on Responsibility of States for Internationally Wrongful Acts provides that 'the conduct of an organ of a State or a person or entity empowered to exercise elements of the governmental authority shall be considered an act of the State under international law if the organ, person or entity acts in that capacity, even if it exceeds its authority or contravenes instructions'. How the military and space law attribution regimes apply with respect to an unauthorized attack in space conducted by a rogue military commander therefore raises untested legal issues.

Rule 32
Distinction

In order to ensure respect for and protection of the civilian population and civilian objects, a party to an armed conflict shall at all times distinguish between the civilian population and combatants and between civilian objects and military objectives and accordingly shall direct its military operations, including military space operations, only against military objectives.

Overview of Legal Basis of Rule

1. This Rule is based on the principle of distinction, as formulated in Article 48 of Additional Protocol I.[88] The principle of distinction is one of the fundamental principles of the law of armed conflict, dating back at least as far as the preamble to the 1868 St Petersburg Declaration, which states that the only legitimate object which States should endeavour to accomplish during war is to weaken the military forces of the enemy. The principle has been described by the International Court of Justice (ICJ) as one of the two cardinal principles of the law of armed conflict[89] and thus forms part of customary international law in both international armed conflicts and non-international armed conflicts.[90] As used in this *Manual*, the term 'military objective' encompasses both objects and persons. Military objectives can include dual-use objects in space, such as some commercial satellites (see Rule 34: Military Objectives).

---

[88] The principle is further reflected in arts 51(2) and 52(2) of Additional Protocol I. Additional Protocol I (n 4).
[89] *Nuclear Weapons* Advisory Opinion (n 3) 226, para 78.
[90] ICRC CIHL Study (n 14) Rule 1 ('Numerous military manuals, including those of States not, or not at the time, party to Additional Protocol I, stipulate that a distinction must be made between civilians and combatants and that it is prohibited to direct attacks against civilians ... In addition, there are numerous examples of national legislation which make it a criminal offence to direct attacks against civilians, including the legislation of States not, or not at the time, party to Additional Protocol I.'). But see Introduction to Part III, paras 11–13, noting that serious concerns have been expressed by some States about the methodology used in the ICRC CIHL Study).

Scope and Application

2. This Rule on Distinction applies to all military space operations. 'Military operations' is a broad term; while it certainly encompasses an 'attack' (see Rule 31: Attack) in the space domain, it should also be understood to mean 'any movements, manoeuvres and other activities whatsoever carried out by the armed forces with a view to combat'.[91]

3. Conversely, the term 'military space operations' does not include many diverse military space activities, such as broadcasting or directing information from outer space towards the civilian population. Instead, the word 'operations' refers to military operations during which violence is used, and not to ideological, political, or religious campaigns.[92] It should also be noted that all Rules in this Part of the *Manual* apply in circumstances during an 'armed conflict'; military space activities outside an 'armed conflict' are not subject to this Rule.

4. This Rule is without prejudice to the application of any special protection enjoyed by persons under the law of armed conflict, such as when a combatant is *hors de combat*. Similarly, medical personnel and religious personnel, both military and civilian, enjoy special protected status during a time of armed conflict.[93] Such medical and religious personnel must be respected and protected in all circumstances, provided that they do not commit, outside their humanitarian function, acts harmful to the enemy.[94]

5. Combatants are any members of the State armed forces, except medical and religious personnel.[95] Relevantly, classification as a member of the armed forces is based on status, not occupation. Therefore, regardless of the role an individual is performing (space-related or otherwise), a member of the armed forces who is not otherwise entitled to special protection is subject to this Rule.

---

[91] *Commentary on the Additional Protocols* (n 9) para 2191; UK LOAC Manual (n 21) para 5.32, fn 187 (noting that the '[c]onduct of military operations has a wider connotation than "attacks" and would include the movement or deployment of armed forces').

[92] *Commentary on the Additional Protocols* (n 9) para 1875 (further noting that the term 'military operations' 'refers to all movements and acts related to hostilities [emphasis added] that are undertaken by armed forces').

[93] Geneva Convention for the Amelioration of the Condition of the Wounded and Sick in Armed Forces in the Field (adopted 12 August 1949, entered into force 21 October 1950) 75 UNTS 31 (GC I) arts 24–26; Geneva Convention for the Amelioration of the Condition of Wounded, Sick and Shipwrecked Members of Armed Forces at Sea (adopted 12 August 1949, entered into force 21 October 1950) 75 UNTS 85 (GC II) art 36; Additional Protocol I (n 4) art 15; see Rule 35: Medical Units and Religious Personnel (regarding protections accorded to medical and religious personnel).

[94] GC I (n 93) art 24; Additional Protocol I (n 4) art 13. See Rule 35: Medical Units and Religious Personnel.

[95] Additional Protocol I (n 4) art 43(2); ICRC CIHL Study (n 14) Rule 8 (notes that '[n]umerous military manuals contain this definition of combatants. It is supported by official statements and reported practice. This practice includes that of States not, or not at the time, party to Additional Protocol I. No official contrary practice was found.').

6. The term 'combatant' is generally reserved for international armed conflicts. Persons who are not members of State armed forces are civilians. This includes private contractors, non-military government employees, and other non-military personnel involved in military space activities. They are protected from attack unless and for such time as they take direct part in hostilities (see Rule 33: Direct Participation in Hostilities). The targeting of organized armed groups in non-international armed conflicts is also addressed in Rule 33: Direct Participation in Hostilities.

Rule 33
Direct Participation in Hostilities

Civilians enjoy protection from attack during an armed conflict, including in a military space operation, unless and for such time as they directly participate in hostilities.

Overview of Legal Basis of Rule

1. This Rule is drawn from Article 51(3) of Additional Protocol I and Article 13(3) of Additional Protocol II.[96] Although the precise definitions or thresholds for some of its terms are subject to debate, it is generally regarded as customary international law in international armed conflicts[97] and may be customary international law in non-international armed conflicts.[98]

Scope and Application

2. This Rule applies only to civilians. It therefore does not apply to members of the regular armed forces, members of organized armed groups (see discussion at paragraphs 10–14), or participants in a *levée en masse*, who are legitimate targets of attack at all times unless *hors de combat*. Civilians who participate directly in

---

[96] See Introduction to Part III, paras 9–10 (noting that the text of Additional Protocol I explicitly states that this Rule is applicable to warfare on land, air and sea, and this *Manual* interprets Additional Protocol I as also extending to military space operations, which may affect the civilian population, individual civilians, or civilian objects in any domain).

[97] See ICRC CIHL Study (n 14) Rule 6 (but see Introduction to Part III, paras 11–13, noting that serious concerns have been expressed by some States about the methodology used in the ICRC CIHL Study). Norwegian LOAC Manual (n 59) paras 1.40 and 3.21; UK LOAC Manual (n 21) paras 15.6 and 15.8; US DoD Law of War Manual (n 5) paras 5.8, 5.8.1.2, and 17.6 (noting, however, that the United States has not necessarily 'adopted the direct participation in hostilities rule that is expressed in Article 51 of AP I', para 5.8.1); see also *The Public Committee Against Torture in Israel v The Government of Israel* (2006) HCJ 769/02 (Targeted Killings Case) 491–94.

[98] The ICRC takes the position that State practice has established the obligations contained in art 13(3) of Additional Protocol II as norms of customary international law applicable in international armed conflicts See CIHL CIL Study (n 14) Rule 6; UK LOAC Manual (n 21) paras 15.6 and 15.8 (see fn 25 and fn 29 which expressly refer to customary international law in a NIAC); US DoD Law of War Manual (n 5) para 17.6 (while fn 228 in the commentary notes that the very similar phrases concerning 'all persons who do not take a direct part or who have ceased to take part in hostilities' are found in both Common Article 3(1) of the four Geneva Conventions and Article 4 of Additional Protocol II, the United States does not accept the precise wording of the obligation in the Additional Protocols.

hostilities are liable to attack during that time by any lawful means, including in, through or from space. Harm to such persons also does not need to be included in assessing the proportionality of an attack (see Rule 38: Proportionality in Attack) or the precautions that must be taken to avoid and minimize harm to civilians during an attack or during military operations generally (see Section 3: Precautions in Attack and Rule 46: Constant Care).

Determining Direct Participation in Hostilities

3. The concept of 'direct participation in hostilities' (DPH) is not explicitly defined in any law of armed conflict instrument.[99] As a result, States have noted the difficulty in determining when an individual's actions meet this legal threshold[100] and there is no universally agreed standard for making such a decision. However, there is a general consensus within the majority of State Military Manuals that DPH must go beyond simply contributing to the war effort in some general way (such as contributing finances, providing food to troops, or participating in scientific development of military capabilities).[101] Those States that do express a formula for assessing DPH generally provide that direct participation requires, *inter alia*, deliberate action in support of one party to an armed conflict, with the intention of causing (or contributing to) harm to the other party's military forces or military operations.[102] Rather than a formulaic approach, some manuals outline a series of cumulative factors that go into the establishment of DPH.[103] Other State manuals do not enumerate specific formulae or identify factors as such, but opt to provide a general narrative and examples of direct participation (ie 'civilians bearing arms and taking part in military operations')[104] and examples of not taking a direct part (ie 'civilians working in military vehicle maintenance depots ... are not [taking a direct part in hostilities]').[105] Some manuals define the requirement of 'direct participation' as requiring 'concrete actions',[106] 'sufficient' involvement,[107] or 'closely linked' actions.[108]

---

[99] ICRC CIHL Study (n 14) Rule 6.
[100] US DoD Law of War Manual (n 5) para 5.8.3; Australian LOAC Manual (n 31) para 5.36; Danish LOAC Manual (n 28) 171; Mando de Adiestramiento y Doctrina, *Orientaciones: El Derecho de los Conflictos Armados, Tomo I, OR7-004* (Ministerio de Defensa 2007) (Spanish Law of Armed Conflict Manual) 1–16 (footnote).
[101] Danish LOAC Manual (n 28) 168; Norwegian LOAC Manual (n 59) para 3.26; US DoD Law of War Manual (n 5) para 5.8.3.2; *Targeted Killings* Case (n 97) 495.
[102] For example, Danish LOAC Manual (n 28) 168–69; Norwegian LOAC Manual (n 59) para 3.24; US DoD Law of War Manual (n 5) para 5.8.3; New Zealand LOAC Manual (n 25) para 6.5.13.
[103] US DoD Law of War Manual (n 5) para 5.8.3.
[104] Australian LOAC Manual (n 31) para 5.36.
[105] UK LOAC Manual (n 21) para 5.3.3.
[106] German LOAC Manual (n 21) para 518.
[107] Israel Defence Force, 'The 2014 Gaza Conflict, 7 July–26 August 2014: Factual and Legal Aspects' (State of Israel, 2015) [perma.cc/587H-ZNTB] (Israeli Gaza Report), para 268; Norwegian LOAC Manual (n 59) para 3.22.
[108] ibid para 3.26.

4. The ICRC has published an 'Interpretative Guidance' on DPH that does enumerate specific requirements as to when an individual can be considered a direct participant in hostilities, offering a series of examples as to what may or may not amount to such participation. This formula of steps includes, *inter alia*, identifiable acts that affect military operations, the establishment of a causal link of a sufficient threshold and that there be a connection between the harm and the armed conflict (belligerent nexus).[109] These elements do find expression in some military manuals and some States have used the Interpretive Guidance as a point of reference in structuring their approach to DPH.[110] However, other States have either not drawn on this structure or have not updated their manuals on the issue of DPH since the Interpretive Guidance was released.[111] The US Department of Defense has expressly stated that it does not accept the Interpretative Guidance, although it acknowledges parts of the guidance 'are consistent with customary international law'.[112] Nevertheless, the Interpretive Guidance remains a useful and influential interrogation of the application of DPH.

5. There is broad agreement in the majority of Manuals that assessment of DPH must be made in each individual case on the basis of all information available.[113] States acknowledge that this is most often performed by forces 'on the ground', frequently in a combat situation where there is little time to fully consider all factors.[114] As a result they generally emphasize a pragmatic view based on the factual situation and the context[115] and provide general guidelines for specific judgment in such situations.[116]

---

[109] Nils Melzer, 'Interpretive Guidance on the Notion of Direct Participation in Hostilities Under International Humanitarian Law (ICRC 2009) 93.

[110] For example, Danish LOAC Manual (n 28) 121; German LOAC Manual (n 21) para 131.

[111] For example, Australian LOAC Manual (n 31); Office of the Judge Advocate General, 'Law of Armed Conflict at the Operational and Tactical Levels' (US Joint Doctrine Manual, Canadian National Defence, 2001); New Zealand LOAC Manual (n 25); Norwegian LOAC Manual (n 59); Spanish Law of Armed Conflict Manual (n 100); Armée Suisse, 'Bases légales du comportement à l'engagement' (Règlement 51.007.04 f, VBS/DDPS 2019) (Swiss LOAC Manual); UK LOAC Manual (n 21).

[112] US DoD Law of Manual (n 6) para 4.26.3 ('[T]he United States has not accepted the ICRC's study on customary international humanitarian law nor its 'interpretive guidance' on direct participation in hostilities.').

[113] Australian LOAC Manual (n 31) para 5.36; New Zealand LOAC Manual (n 25) para 6.5.12; Norwegian LOAC Manual (n 59) para 3.31; UK LOAC Manual (n 21) para 5.3.4; US DoD Law of War Manual (n 5) para 5.8.3; *Targeted Killings* Case (n 97) 495.

[114] New Zealand LOAC Manual (n 25) para 8.5.5; UK LOAC Manual (n 21) para 5.3.4; Israeli Gaza Report (n 107) para 268.

[115] Australian LOAC Manual (n 31) para 5.36; New Zealand LOAC Manual (n 25) para 6.5.13; US DoD Law of War Manual (n 5) para 5.8.3; UK LOAC Manual (n 21) para 5.3.3; Israeli Gaza Report (n 107) para 268.

[116] For example, Danish LOAC Manual (n 28) 169–71; New Zealand LOAC Manual (n 25) 6-15-6-17; Norwegian LOAC Manual (n 59) paras 3.33–3.34; US DoD Law of War Manual (n 5) paras 5.8.3.1–5.8.3.2; UK LOAC Manual (n 21) para 5.3.3; Israeli Gaza Report (n 107) para 268; German LOAC Manual (n 21) paras 518 and 1119.

6. Parties to an armed conflict are obliged to presume civilian status where there is doubt[117] and must exercise caution before concluding that an individual is directly participating in hostilities.[118] This does not require that the matter is beyond all reasonable doubt but instead 'must reflect the level of certainty that can reasonably be achieved in the circumstances'.[119] It is clear as a practical matter that any doubt can be displaced with additional intelligence.[120]

7. A civilian who directly participates in hostilities becomes a legitimate target of attack for such time as that individual is engaged in the act of direct participation.[121] Measures preparatory to the execution of a specific act of direct participation in hostilities as well as the deployment to and the return from the location of its execution constitute an integral part of that act.[122] However, to be considered direct participation in hostilities, an act must be sufficiently proximate to the intended or actual harm. Hence, in the context of space operations, the production of malware designed to target and cause damage to a specific satellite may be considered direct participation in hostilities when it is an integral part of the military operation targeting the satellite,[123] but general development of coding techniques later adapted for this purpose would not be. Similarly, a civilian who is plays an integral role in the direct targeting of an enemy satellite through the use of a kinetic ASAT weapon may come within the terms of DPH.

8. Civilians are extensively involved in all facets of space activity, including some military space activities and operations. The determination of which activities constitute direct participation in hostilities must be undertaken on a case-by-case basis. Despite the different methods of determination discussed above, many States are reasonably agreed on the point that the test for taking a direct part in hostilities 'extends beyond merely engaging in combat and also includes certain acts that are an integral part of combat operations or that effectively and substantially contribute to an adversary's ability to conduct or sustain combat operations'.[124]

---

[117] UK LOAC Manual (n 21) para 5.3.4 states that it must be 'substantial' doubt and Norwegian LOAC Manual (n 59), para 3.23, notes that 'some degree of doubt is acceptable'.

[118] Additional Protocol I (n 4) art 50(1) and reflected in eg Danish LOAC Manual (n 28) 173; New Zealand LOAC Manual (n 25) para 6.5.11; Norwegian LOAC Manual (n 59) para 3.23, although this obligation has been explicitly rejected as customary international law by the United States; see US DoD Law of War Manual (n 5) para 5.4.3.2; regardless, one expressed State view is that the presumption of civilian status may not outweigh the commander's 'duty to protect the safety of troops under his command or to preserve the military situation'; see UK LOAC Manual (n 21) para 5.3.4.

[119] ICRC Interpretive Guidance on Direct Participation in Hostilities (n 109) 76 (but see US DoD Law of War Manual (n 5) para. 4.26.3; ICRC CIHL Study (n 14) Rule 6 ('One cannot automatically attack anyone who might appear dubious').

[120] *Targeted Killings* Case (n 97) 500.

[121] Additional Protocol I (n 4) art 51(3).

[122] Danish LOAC Manual (n 28) 172; US DoD Law of War Manual (n 5) para 5.8.3.1; *Targeted Killings* Case (n 97) 495.

[123] Danish LOAC Manual (n 28) 170.

[124] US DoD Law of War Manual (n 5) 5.8.3. See also Danish LOAC Manual (n 28) 169; New Zealand LOAC Manual (n 25) para 6.5.22; Norwegian LOAC Manual (n 59) paras 3.25–3.26, 3.30. One State at State Consultations noted that space assets are often dual-use in nature and even military space assets

Repeated Acts of Direct Participation

9. Some States take the view that repeated acts of direct participation in hostilities may in special cases result in suspension of civilian protections until such time as there is permanent cessation of involvement, although they express differing opinions as to when this occurs and again, it must generally be assessed on the facts of each individual case.[125] On another view, the period of involvement in each such act must be analysed separately for purposes of identifying direct participation in hostilities and civilian protections are re-engaged between incidents each time.[126] This approach is criticized by at least one State as 'Revolving Door Protection'.[127]

Organized Armed Groups

10. In international armed conflicts, a member of an organized armed group (OAG) that belongs to a State that is a party to the conflict is treated as a combatant and may be targeted in the same manner as a member of the armed forces of that State.[128] The position is more complex in the case of an OAG which does not belong to a State that is a Party to an international armed conflict or a non-State OAG that engages in hostilities in a non-international armed conflict. The ICRC has concluded that for the purposes of the principle of distinction, such organized armed groups consist only of individuals whose continuous function it is to take a direct part in hostilities on behalf of a party to the armed conflict (ie a 'continuous combat function').[129]

11. State military manuals vary as to what level of involvement in a non-State OAG[130] makes a 'member' of that OAG a valid military objective. Some States draw directly from the ICRC Interpretive Guidance and the notion of 'continuous combat function', for example specifying that only those members who directly participate in hostilities on a frequent basis are deemed to become targetable

---

may be operated by private operators/civil companies, which leaves open the question whether current State practice is consistent with the principle of distinction. The representative of this State thus asked what are the criteria for such a consistency and what are the legal consequences of this State practice? To some extent, these issues are addressed in Rule 41: Precautions Against the Effects of Attack.

[125] Norwegian LOAC Manual (n 59) para 3.37; US DoD Law of War Manual (n 5) para 5.8.4.
[126] See eg Danish LOAC Manual (n 28) 172.
[127] US DoD Law of War Manual (n 5) para 5.8.4.2.
[128] Geneva Convention relative to the Treatment of Prisoners of War of August 12, 1949 (opened for signature 12 August 1949, entered into force 21 October 1950) 75 UNTS 135 (GC III) art 4(2).
[129] ICRC Interpretive Guidance on Direct Participation in Hostilities (n 109) 31–35 (but see US DoD Law of War Manual (n 5) para 4.26.3).
[130] This refers to non-State OAGs in both non-international and international armed conflicts.

throughout their involvement with the OAG.¹³¹ Norway's military manual places this threshold slightly lower, indicating that members of an OAG must be conducting some 'activities vital to the group's conduct of attacks' to lose their protection from attack, but do not need to reach the level of involvement that would be considered direct participation in hostilities in the case of an ordinary individual civilian.¹³²

Some States set a considerably lower threshold and deem that any individual who is 'formally or functionally' a member of a non-State armed group is a valid military target at all times—although often specifying that only the armed or military 'wing' of any faction engaging in hostilities can be considered an OAG.¹³³ These States would consider that individual members of such a military 'wing' are targetable based on this status alone, and an additional requirement of a 'continuous combat function' or undertaking 'activities vital to the group's conduct of attacks' would be unnecessary. The United States has taken the position an individual in a specified terrorist OAG in a non-international armed conflict may be targeted if that individual is engaged in hostilities against the US or its allies, has purposefully and materially supported such hostilities, or is a member of a specified terrorist OAG.¹³⁴ **12.**

Regardless of the determination used for when membership of a non-State OAG will render an individual targetable, States have generally specified that once that individual permanently ceases involvement in the OAG, they will regain civilian protection against direct attack.¹³⁵ **13.**

Notwithstanding the continuing use of space assets in non-international armed conflicts (such as the use of satellites to relay signals that control unmanned aerial vehicles/remotely piloted aircraft for targeting), non-international armed conflicts are unlikely to originate in or occur exclusively in space (see Rule **14.**

---

¹³¹ Danish LOAC Manual (n 28) 181–82; New Zealand LOAC Manual (n 25) paras 6.5.24–6.5.26; German LOAC Manual (n 21) para 1308.
¹³² Norwegian LOAC Manual (n 59) para 3.42 and Example 5, at 64.
¹³³ Israeli Gaza Report (n 107) para 264; Australian *Criminal Code Act 1995* (Cth) ss 268.70 and 268.125; Explanatory Memorandum, Criminal Code Amendment (War Crimes) Bill 2016 (Commonwealth of Australia) paras 10–11; US DoD Law of War Manual (n 5) para 5.7.3.
¹³⁴ US DoD Law of War Manual (n 5) para 5.7.3; For example, legislative acts in the United States permit the detention and targeting of individuals as unprivileged belligerents based on their active membership in terrorist armed groups, such as al Qaeda. See US Military Commissions Act of 2009, 10 USC § 948(a)(7) (defining an 'alien unprivileged enemy belligerent' as: an individual (other than a privileged belligerent) who—(A) has engaged in hostilities against the United States or its coalition partners; (B) has purposefully and materially supported hostilities against the United States or its coalition partners; or (C) is a member of al Qaeda.'); US National Defense Authorization Act for Fiscal Year 2012 (reaffirming the authority to detain a 'person who was a part of or substantially supported al-Qaeda, the Taliban, or associated forces that are engaged in hostilities against the United States or its coalition partners, including any person who has committed a belligerent act or has directly supported such hostilities in aid of such enemy forces').
¹³⁵ US DoD Law of War Manual (n 5) para 5.7.3.3; Danish LOAC Manual (n 28) 182.

30: Non-International Armed Conflict, paragraph 4). Although a non-state belligerent is an anomaly in space today, to the extent a terrestrial non-international armed conflict does involves military space operations or the use of military space assets, all relevant rules of the law of armed conflict relating to a non-international armed conflict apply.

Rule 34
Military Objectives

Military objectives are lawful targets in a military operation in a time of armed conflict, including a military space operation. Military objectives are those objects that by their nature, location, purpose, or use make an effective contribution to military action and whose total or partial destruction, capture or neutralisation, in the circumstances ruling at the time, offers a definite military advantage.

Overview of Legal Basis of Rule

1. This Rule is based on Article 52(2) of Additional Protocol I,[136] which is generally accepted as reflecting customary international law in both international and non-international armed conflict.[137]

Requirements

2. In order for an object to constitute a military objective it must satisfy the two related requirements articulated in Article 52(2): it must by its 'nature, location, purpose or use make an effective contribution to military action' and its 'total or partial destruction, capture or neutralisation' must offer 'a definite military advantage' in the circumstances ruling at the time. These two prongs are

---

[136] See Introduction to Part III, paras 9–10 (noting that the text of Additional Protocol I explicitly states in Article 49(3) that this rule is applicable to warfare on land, air, and sea, and this Manual interprets Additional Protocol I as also extending to military space operations, that may affect the civilian population, individual civilians, or civilian objects in any domain).

[137] The ICRC takes the position that State practice has established this rule as a norm of customary international law applicable in both international and non-international armed conflicts. ICRC CIHL Study (n 14) Rule 6 (but see Introduction to Part III, paras 11–13, noting that serious concerns have been expressed by some States about the methodology used in the ICRC CIHL Study). The military manuals of many States contain this rule and even States not party to Additional Protocol I recognize this definition of military objectives. See US DoD Law of War Manual (n 5) para 5.7.3 ('Military objectives, insofar as objects are concerned, include "any object any object which, by its nature, location, purpose or use make an effective contribution to military action and whose total or partial destruction, capture or neutralization, in the circumstances ruling at the time, offers a definite military advantage"'.). See also 'The Operation in Gaza—Factual and Legal Aspects' (Israeli Ministry of Foreign Affairs, July 2009) [https://perma.cc/ZPK2-V85Q] para 238. Additionally, see *Prosecutor v Pavle Strugar* (Trial Judgment) IT-01-42-T (31 January 2005) para 223.

cumulative, and it should not be mistakenly assumed that when one is fulfilled the other is also necessarily fulfilled.[138] The criteria of 'nature, location, purpose or use' take into account an object's current and potential[139] contribution to military action. Objects that facilitate military communications,[140] contribute to command and control of forces,[141] or support intelligence, surveillance, and reconnaissance functions[142] can all be military objectives (subject to meeting the requirements of 'effective contribution to military action' and 'definite military advantage in the circumstances ruling at the time'). Accordingly, satellites and their ground stations that provide service to military forces could—by virtue of their location, nature, purpose, or use—amount to military objectives. Although the focus of most States in ratifying the Additional Protocol was on areas on land, it might also be possible to characterize a specific area in outer space as being a location for purposes of making an object there a military objective.[143] For example, an object located in a Lagrange Point or a particular slot in geostationary orbit might be a 'location' by which it makes an effective contribution to military action, denial of access to which (by capture/control or neutralization of the object) may, depending on the circumstances ruling at the time, offer a definite military advantage.

---

[138] For example, see discussion on this point by International Law Association Study Group, in its final 2017 report, 'The conduct of hostilities and International Humanitarian Law – Challenges of 21st Century Warfare' [2016] Yearbook of International Humanitarian Law (ILA Report on conduct of hostilities) 287, 290 ('These two prongs are cumulative').

[139] See n 144 regarding the current functions of an object vs the intended or possible use of the object in the future.

[140] Australian LOAC Manual (n 31) para 5.31; UK LOAC Manual (n 21) para 5.4.5; US DoD Law of War Manual (n 5) para 5.6.8; Danish LOAC Manual (n 28) 300; Norwegian LOAC Manual (n 59) 7.10; New Zealand LOAC Manual (n 25) para 8.5.8; *Commentary on the Additional Protocols* (n 9) para 2020.

[141] US DoD Law of War Manual (n 5) para 5.6.4.1; Australian LOAC Manual (n 31) para 5.31; Norwegian LOAC Manual (n 59) para 7.3; New Zealand LOAC Manual (n 25) para 8.5.9.

[142] New Zealand LOAC Manual (n 25) para 8.5.9 (It was raised at the State consultation process that in the context of space, this may include space situational awareness assets).

[143] For example, France's declaration at the time of ratification of Additional Protocol I stated that 'une zone spécifique peut être considérée comme un objectif militaire' (a specific area may be considered a military objective) based on the criteria set out in art 52. 'Accession by France to Protocol I of 8 June 1977' (2001) 83 International Review of the Red Cross 549, para 12 [perma.cc/PF2T-SNE6]; Belgium noted a 'specific zone' could be a military objective. Belgium, House of Representatives, Explanatory memorandum on a draft bill for the approval of the Additional Protocols (1984–1985 Session) Doc. 1096-1, 9 January 1985; New Zealand LOAC Manual (n 25) para 8.5.9 includes as a potential military objective 'an area of tactical or strategic importance'; Norwegian LOAC Manual (n 59) para 7.4 similarly includes 'areas of strategic importance'. ILA Report on conduct of hostilities (n 138) 293 (noting that 'in the view of a number of Western States a specific area of land may be a military objective if, because of its location or other reasons specified in Article 52(2) Additional Protocol I, its total or partial destruction, capture or neutralization in the circumstances ruling at the time offers definite military advantage' and citing as examples the declarations made on Article 52 at the time of ratification of Additional Protocol I by Italy, Germany, the United Kingdom, Canada, the Netherlands, New Zealand, and France). However, during State Consultations, some States expressed the view that a location could not be a military objective.

Dual-Use Space Objects

3. Some objects (including many satellites) may be 'dual use'—that is, they serve (or are capable of serving)[144] both civilian and military purposes simultaneously or sequentially. For the purpose of determining whether a dual use object is a military objective, the test stated in the Rule applies: it is a military objective if it meets the definition given, irrespective of whether it might also provide services to civilians. Thus, a satellite that provides both military and civilian communications would be a military objective (and thus targetable) if its military use or purpose meets the test stated in this Rule, despite the civilian functions it may also perform. Even so, the targeting of space systems is always subject to other rules applicable to attacks, such as the prohibition of indiscriminate attacks and compliance with proportionality requirements (Rule 38: Proportionality in Attack) and precautions in attack (Section 3: Precautions in Attack), which regulate the manner of attack, or which may effectively prohibit an attack at all.[145]

4. In the case of a satellite bus that carries distinct military and civilian payloads, as a whole the satellite will qualify as a military objective. However, if the civilian payload is functionally and physically distinguishable as a discrete 'object', the civilian payload itself would not be a military objective, nor a target of attack. When feasible, means and methods of warfare that affect solely the payload used for military purposes and not the rest of the dual-use space object should be chosen, in order to avoid or at least minimize incidental civilian harm. However, if it is not feasible to attack the military payload separately, an attack on the satellite bus as a military objective would be permissible, provided the attacking military force takes the expected incidental damage to the civilian object into account in its proportionality analysis, in addition to complying with all other applicable precautions in attack.

Effective Contribution to Military Action

5. One ongoing debate for those States not party to Additional Protocol I is whether an object making an effective contribution to the enemy's 'war-sustaining' capability can ever be a military objective. While war-fighting and war-supporting

---

[144] See ILA Report on conduct of hostilities (n 138) para 2.4 ('The generally accepted view is that "use" refers to the current function of an object'); but see US DoD Law of War Manual (n 5) para 5.6.6.1 (noting that '"purpose" means *the intended or possible use* in the future. For example, runways at a civilian airport could qualify as military objectives because they may be subject to immediate military use in the event that runways at military bases have been rendered unserviceable or inoperable') (emphasis added).

[145] It should be noted that other rules of the law of armed conflict, such as constant care (see Rule 46: Constant Care), apply generally to military operations, but attacks are governed by a set of rules specifically applicable to attacks (see Rule 31: Attack).

objects are viewed as making an effective contribution to military action and are lawful military objectives under Additional Protocol I, war-sustaining objects are not. This could be important in military space operations. For example:

- 'War-fighting' refers to the conduct of offensive or defensive combat operations (eg an anti-satellite missile);
- 'War-supporting' refers to assisting or contributing to the conduct of offensive or defensive combat operations (eg a reconnaissance or communication satellite, or the launch facility for military satellites); and
- 'War-sustaining' could, in extremis, refer to space objects that indirectly sustain war-fighting capabilities (eg civilian satellites or launch capability not used or intended for use for military purposes, but which nonetheless generate revenue for the State that is used for funding its military operations).

The United States position is that it can. The US Department of Defense Law of War Manual indicates that an 'object's effective contribution to the war-fighting or war-sustaining capability of an opposing force is sufficient' to make it a military objective.[146] This position appears to be at odds with Article 52 of Additional Protocol I (to which the United States is not a party), which requires there to be a 'direct contribution' to military action and a proximate 'definite military advantage'. The generally accepted position is well stated in Norway's Military Manual.[147] An example of the debate surrounding the issue concerns attacks on the oil/petroleum infrastructure based on its status as a source of revenue for an adversary. Although the United States invoked this as a basis for attacking some oil-transport and storage capabilities of the Islamic State group in Iraq and Syria,[148] other States

---

[146] US DoD Law of War Manual (n 5) para 5.6.6.

[147] Norwegian LOAC Manual (n 59) paras 7.13–7.14. ('[A] distinction must be made between objects necessary for the conduct of military actions, ie war-supporting capabilities, and objects that provide only general support to the war effort (war-sustaining capabilities) ... War-supporting capabilities, such as weapons factories, military ports and communications systems used for command and control purposes, will usually be lawful targets because they will qualify as military objectives.... These must be distinguished from objects which support only the general war effort. In most cases, the latter will not qualify as lawful targets, either because their contribution cannot be said to make a direct contribution to military action or because the military advantage of attacking a given object is insufficiently concrete.... An attack with the sole intention of causing the enemy financial losses and thus weakening the enemy's military power in the longer term will be an attack against the general war effort, and therefore not permitted.'); see also ILA Report on conduct of hostilities (n 138) para 2.5 (describing the 'generally accepted view' that 'to qualify as a military objective, there must exist a proximate nexus to military action (or "war fighting")').

[148] US Department of Defense Press Briefing by Col Steve Warren (Baghdad, Iraq 13 November 2015) [https://perma.cc/Y8LB-KFBD] (describing a 'disruption operation' by US forces against a location where 'ISIL's primary oil production capabilities reside', and noting that the operation had inflicted 'a significant damage on ISIL's ability to fund itself'). But see Laurent Gisel, 'The Relevance of Revenue-Generating Objects in Relation to the Notion of Military Objective' (2017 Bruges Colloquium, 19–20 October 2017) 147–48 (examining State practice in this area, including inconsistent US practice, and concluding that 'in most cases, a proximate nexus between oil or oil-related objects and military action is given as the justification for strikes on such objects carried out in armed conflicts of the last decades', that '[r]evenue-generating objects may be seen as the "far end" of the notion of war-sustaining', and that targeting such objects 'risks bringing us back to limitless wars').

involved in military operations against Daesh (ISIS), who are parties to Additional Protocol I, endorsed a different approach: attacking Daesh oil infrastructure only when it involved fuel actually destined for Daesh military action.[149]

---

[149] Marten Zwanenburg and Nelleke Van Amstel, 'Correspondents' Reports' [2016] Yearbook of International Humanitarian Law 1, 3 ('In response to a parliamentary question whether it was possible for Dutch fighter jets operating against ISIS in Iraq and Syria to bomb oil fields/oil depots or money caches, the [Government Ministers] responded that, under IHL, only military objectives may be attacked. Oil refineries and banks will usually not qualify as such, even when they are financially lucrative for ISIS. Only oil refineries that contribute directly to military action—for example because they provide oil to military materiel of ISIS—can form a legitimate target.').

Rule 35
Medical Units and Religious Personnel

In the course of a military operation in an armed conflict, including a military space operation, medical units and religious personnel, wherever located, enjoy special protection in addition to protection from attack afforded to all civilian objects.

Overview of Legal Basis of Rule

1. During military operations, including military space operations, medical units[150] (including personnel,[151] activities,[152] equipment, and transports[153]), whether military or civilian, and which are exclusively assigned to medical purposes[154] must be respected and protected at all times and in all domains. The protections set forth in this Rule are found in their latest and most complete form in Additional

---

[150] Additional Protocol I (n 4) art 12(1) provides that '[m]edical units shall be respected and protected at all times and shall not be the object of attack'. The term 'medical unit' has been defined in art 8(e) as encompassing 'establishments and other units, whether military or civilian, organized for medical purposes and exclusively assigned to those purposes ... The term includes, for example, hospitals and other similar units, blood transfusion centres, preventive medicine centres and institutes, medical depots and the medical pharmaceutical stores of such unit. Medical units may be fixed or mobile, permanent or temporary and include the medical or pharmaceutical stores of these units.'

[151] Additional Protocol I (n 4) art 8 defines 'medical personnel' as 'those persons assigned, by a Party to the conflict, exclusively to the medical purposes enumerated under sub-paragraph e) or to the administration of medical units or to the operation or administration of medical transports. Such assignments may be either permanent or temporary. The term includes: i) medical personnel of a Party to the conflict, whether military or civilian, including those described in the First and Second Conventions, and those assigned to civil defence organizations; ii) medical personnel of national Red Cross (Red Crescent, Red Lion and Sun) Societies and other national voluntary aid societies duly recognized and authorized by a Party to the conflict; iii) medical personnel of medical units or medical transports described in Article 9, paragraph 2.'

[152] ibid art 16(1) states that '[u]nder no circumstances shall any person be punished for carrying out medical activities compatible with medical ethics, regardless of the person benefiting therefrom'.

[153] ibid art 8(f) defines 'medical transports' as 'any means of transportation, whether military or civilian, permanent or temporary, assigned exclusively to medical transportation under the control of a competent authority of a Party to the conflict'. Article 8(g) further defines 'medical transportation' as 'the conveyance by land, water or air of the wounded, sick, shipwrecked, medical personnel, religious personnel, medical equipment or medical supplies protected by the Conventions and by this Protocol'.

[154] In addition to art 8(e) of Additional Protocol I which provides that medical units encompass establishments and other units organized for medical purposes and exclusively assigned to those purposes, art 9(2) provides that relevant provisions of the First Geneva Convention 'shall apply to permanent medical units and transports [other than specified hospital ships covered elsewhere] and their personnel made available to a Party to the conflict for humanitarian purposes: a) by a neutral or other State which is not a Party to that conflict; b) by a recognized and authorized aid society of such a State; c) by an impartial international humanitarian organization'.

Protocol I, but they are founded on historic treaty obligations and reflect customary international law in both international and non-international armed conflicts.[155] Although the foundational legal obligations of this Rule that are found in the Geneva Conventions are in some cases implicitly or explicitly linked to the land, air, and/or sea domains and the relevant articles in Additional Protocols I and II may also be implicitly or explicitly linked to these terrestrial domains, the larger humanitarian objectives underlying those treaties and this Rule transcend these limitations and would generally apply, in principle, in all domains, including space.

Loss of Special Protection

2. Medical units lose their special protection under this Rule if they are being used outside their humanitarian function, to commit acts harmful to the enemy.[156] In such case, a warning has to be issued, whenever appropriate, setting a reasonable time limit, and an attack can only take place after such warning has remained unheeded.[157] It should also be noted that the special protections in this Rule apply to protected persons and objects in all domains, including those on Earth, celestial bodies, and in outer space.

---

[155] The ICRC takes the position that State practice has established that this Rule is a norm of customary international law applicable in both international and non-international armed conflicts. See ICRC CIHL Study (n 14) Rules 25–30 (but see Introduction to Part III, paras 11–13, noting that serious concerns have been expressed by some States about the methodology used in the ICRC CIHL Study). As noted by the ICRC, this long-established obligation to respect and protect medical units in international armed conflicts was first set forth in the 1864 Geneva Convention and was repeated in the subsequent Geneva Conventions of 1906 and 1929. It is now found in the First, Second, and Fourth Geneva Conventions of 1949. Its most recent and comprehensive formulation is found in arts 9–15 of Additional Protocol I. Article 12(2) of the Additional Protocol expands its original scope to cover civilian medical personnel in addition to military medical personnel in all circumstances (see para 4 of the commentary). The ICRC notes that this extension is widely supported in State practice (which generally refers to medical personnel without distinguishing between military or civilian medical personnel). With respect to the application of this Rule to Non-International Armed Conflicts, see ICRC CIHL Study (n 14) Rule 25. The ICRC posits that this protection for medical units is implicit in the requirement in Article 3 common to the four Geneva Conventions to care for the wounded and sick. The ICRC notes that this protection is also explicitly provided for in the Protocol Additional to the Geneva Conventions of 12 August 1949, and Relating to Victims of Non-International Armed Conflicts (Protocol II) (adopted 8 June 1977, entered into force 7 December 1978) 1125 UNTS 609 (Additional Protocol II) art 11(1), for those States that are parties to that Protocol. The ICRC further notes that respect for and protection of medical personnel is included in numerous military manuals which are applicable to or have been applied in non-international armed conflicts. See ICRC CIHL Study (n 14) Rule 25. See also the Rome Statute of the International Criminal Court (n 57), art 8 (e)(ii) (listing as 'Other serious violations of the laws and customs applicable in armed conflicts not of an international character, within the established framework of international . . . any of the following acts: . . . (ii) Intentionally directing attacks against buildings, material, medical units and transport, and personnel using the distinctive emblems of the Geneva Conventions in conformity with international law').

[156] Additional Protocol I (n 4) art 13. GC I (n 93) art 21; GC II (n 93) art 34; Geneva Convention Relative to the Protection of Civilian Persons in Time of War (adopted 12 August 1949, entered into force 21 October 1950) 75 UNTS 287 (GC IV) art 19. Furthermore, Article 15 of Additional Protocol I explicitly provides that 'civilian medical personnel shall be respected'.

[157] Additional Protocol I (n 4) arts 11(2) and 13(1).

Definition of 'Medical Unit'

3. The definition of what constitutes a medical unit under treaty and corresponding customary international law appears to require the exclusive assignment of a building or an area for relevant medical purposes. Hence a multi-function physical area used as a medical facility on an ad hoc basis is not covered by this special protection as it is not used exclusively for medical purposes unless the medical area or facility is a distinct part of the overall multi-function area. This should be distinguished from a physical area designated temporarily, but exclusively, for medical purposes, which would be subject to protection. Likewise, the use of medical equipment to monitor personnel for lawful medical scientific experiments would be protected.

4. For a civilian medical unit to enjoy the additional protection afforded by this Rule, it must belong to a party to the conflict, or be recognized and authorized by one of them.[158] In the case of civilian medical units exclusively designated as such on board a space object or on a celestial body, there is of course no related State practice to review in the absence of an armed conflict in space. To date, there are also very few examples of any medical units on board space objects at all, other than the limited medical equipment and supplies on board the International Space Station (and limited medical supplies and equipment on individual manned space missions). However, to the extent that a civilian medical facility is exclusively designated as such on board a space object that is part of a State's 'national space activities', that State bears international responsibility for the space object, for assuring that the space object's activities are carried out in conformity with the OST, and for its continuing supervision and authorization (see Rule 10: Responsibility of States for National Space Activities in Outer Space). One example raised during the State consultation process was the possible future use of a satellite designated specifically for medical communications and registered accordingly, although the 'marking' of such a satellite in space would present a challenge in the space environment, as discussed shortly.

5. Medical equipment, when forming an integral part of a medical unit—and likely also when such equipment is exclusively assigned to medical purposes[159]—is

---

[158] ibid art 12(2). Civilian medical units also enjoy the additional protection afforded by this Rule if they are authorized in conformity with art 9, para 2 of Additional Protocol I or under art 27 of the First Geneva Convention.

[159] Based on State practice and relevant international agreements, the ICRC supports the interpretation that standalone medical equipment (ie medical equipment that is not an integral part of a medical unit but is exclusively assigned to medical purposes) enjoys specific protection under this Rule. In setting forth a list of persons and objects which are authorized to use 'distinctive emblems' for their protection, art 8(l) of Additional Protocol I lists 'medical units and transports' and separately includes 'medical and religious personnel, equipment or supplies' on the list—suggesting that such protection is available not only to military medical equipment but also to civilian medical equipment. Furthermore, art 39 of Geneva Convention I refers to the possibility of displaying the distinctive emblem on 'all equipment employed'. With respect to medical transports, the term 'medical equipment' is broadly defined

covered by this Rule. For example, it is possible that an ultrasound machine aboard the International Space Station could be subject to special protection (over and above its protection as a civilian object), when used for exclusively medical purposes.[160]

Display of Distinctive Emblems

Medical units, equipment, transports, and personnel are entitled to display distinctive emblems, including the Red Cross and the Red Crescent (and for those party to Additional Protocol III of the Geneva Conventions,[161] the Red 'Crystal') to mark their protected status.[162] The display of a protective emblem only serves as identification of established protected status, it does not confer that protected status.[163] Hence protected status will apply independently of whether medical units, personnel, activities, equipment, and transport display the distinctive emblem, since it is based upon their actual functions. **6.**

Notwithstanding paragraph 6, conventional markings have limited practical applications in the space environment and there is no State practice regarding the display of the protective emblems in military space operations. Moreover, the space law regime does not require the marking of military or civilian space objects, nor does it require that the specific functions of space objects be identified as part of that space object's registration (see Rule 8: Registration of Space Objects and Rule **7.**

under art 8(f) of Additional Protocol I and should include transports that are exclusively dedicated to medical activities. See *Commentary on the Additional Protocols* (n 9) para 382 ('As regards the expression "medical equipment or medical supplies", this should be interpreted broadly. It includes any equipment and supplies necessary for medical care—particularly surgical equipment—but also heavier equipment (for example, the equipment for an operating theatre or even an entire field hospital), or even, quite simply, medicines themselves.'

[160] During State Consultations, a State expressed the view that medical equipment on board the International Space Station is likely to be covered by this Rule.
[161] ICRC Protocol Additional to the Geneva Conventions of 12 August 1949, and Relating to the Adoption of an Additional Distinctive Emblem (Protocol III) (adopted 8 December 2005, entered into force 14 January 2007) 45 ILM 558 (Additional Protocol III).
[162] Under the Statute of the International Criminal Court, 'intentionally directing attacks against buildings, material, medical units and transport, and personnel using the distinctive emblems of the Geneva Conventions in conformity with international law' constitutes a war crime in both international and non-international armed conflicts. Rome Statute of the International Criminal Court (n 57) art 8(2)(b)(xxiv) and (e)(ii). This war crime is relevant to medical units, personnel, equipment, and transport because they are authorized to use and display the distinctive emblems of the Geneva Conventions.
[163] Annex I to Protocol I to the Geneva Conventions of 1949: regulations concerning identification, as amended on 30 November 1993 (adopted 30 November 1993, entered into force 1 March 1994) (1993 Revised Additional Protocol I Annex I) art 1 provides that: '1. These regulations concerning identification in this Annex implement the relevant provisions of the Geneva Conventions and the Protocol; they are intended to facilitate the identification of personnel, material, units, transports and installations protected under the Geneva Conventions and the Protocol; 2. These rules do not in and of themselves establish the right to protection. This right is governed by the relevant articles in the Conventions and the protocol.'

45: Improper Use of Markings). Thus, due to the physical and practical limitations imposed by the space environment and by the framework of the space law regime itself, the conventional application of these rules on protective markings and their relevance to military space operations for the foreseeable future is likely to be very limited. However, medical units and transports can also be identified by signals, at least in the maritime and aeronautical contexts,[164] and Annex I to Additional Protocol I (as amended to 1993) does allow for radio[165] and satellite[166] signals to be used to identify protected status. The future use of digital markings, conveyed by signals, may thus present a possible application of protective markings in space at some time in the future.[167] Currently, States are under no obligation to use such digital signals in space in support of obligations under the law of armed conflict. Although the challenges currently presented by the space environment make the effective identification of medical persons and objects in space extremely difficult, the medical persons and objects afforded protection under this Rule remain specifically protected under the law of armed conflict even without displaying any physical emblem, digital, light, or electronic signals or other marking.

Protection of Religious Personnel

8. The long-established obligation to respect and protect religious personnel was first set forth in the 1864 Geneva Convention and was repeated in the subsequent Geneva Conventions of 1906 and 1929.[168] It is now found in Article 24 of the First Geneva Convention and Article 36 of the Second Geneva Convention and was extended in Article 15 of Additional Protocol I to include civilian religious personnel. These protections reasonably extend to military space operations.

---

[164] See 1993 Revised Additional Protocol I Annex I (n 163) chapter III and IV, concerning light signals, radio signals, and electronic identification. For example, '[p]rotected medical transports may, for their identification and location, use standard aeronautical radar transponders and/or maritime search and rescue radar transponders. It should be possible for protected medical transports to be identified by other vessels or aircraft equipped with secondary surveillance radar by means of a code transmitted by a radar transponder ... The code transmitted by the medical transport transponder should be assigned to that transport by the competent authorities and notified to all the Parties to the conflict.' ibid art 9(2).
[165] ibid art 8.
[166] ibid art 10(2): '2. The medical transports referred to in Articles 40 (Section II, No. 3209) and N 40 (Section III, No. 3214) of the ITU Radio Regulations may also transmit their communications by satellite systems, in accordance with the provisions of Articles 37, N 37 and 59 of the ITU Radio Regulations for the Mobile-Satellite Services.'
[167] It might be noted that art 98 of Annex I of Additional Protocol I provides a review mechanism through which means of identification may be adapted to space operations in the future.
[168] Historical treaties and documents, ICRC International Humanitarian Law Databases, https://ihl-databases.icrc.org/en/ihl-treaties/historical-treaties-and-documents.

SECTION 3
PRECAUTIONS IN ATTACK

Rule 36
Verification

Those who plan or decide upon an attack in an armed conflict, including an attack involving a military space operation, shall do everything feasible to verify that the target is a military objective and is not subject to special protection.

Overview of Legal Basis of Rule

1. This Rule is based on Article 57(2)(a)(i) of Additional Protocol I[169] and is generally accepted as customary international law applicable in international and most likely to non-international armed conflicts.[170] The obligation is continuous and ongoing such that those who plan or decide upon an attack have a legal obligation based upon information reasonably available to them to do everything feasible in order to verify, at all times before the actual execution of the attack, that the military target/objective is indeed a military objective and is not subject to special protections (see Rule 34: Military Objectives).

Application and Scope

2. The obligation applies to 'those who plan or decide upon an attack'. This refers to a wide range of personnel, including commanding officers and subordinate ranks.[171] However, the scope of any particular individual's obligations under this Rule depends upon various factors, such as the means and authority available to such personnel to verify the target.[172] Therefore, depending on the circumstances, the application of the Rule in relation to individuals of various ranks and roles may differ.[173] Implicit in this Rule is an obligation incumbent on those who execute or

---

[169] See Introduction to Part III, paras 9–11 (noting that the text of Additional Protocol I explicitly states in art 49(3) that this Rule is applicable to warfare on land, air, and sea, and this *Manual* interprets Additional Protocol I as also extending to military space operations, that may affect the civilian population, individual civilians, or civilian objects in any domain).

[170] See n 21 (discussing the status of precautionary measures as customary international law in international armed conflict and likely in non-international conflicts).

[171] *Commentary on the Additional Protocols* (n 9) para 2197.

[172] UK LOAC Manual (n 21) 5.32.2; AMW Manual (n 31) 126.

[173] During the negotiations of this provision in Additional Protocol I there was some debate about who is best placed to make these decisions, with some delegations favouring only Commanding Officers and those with relevant seniority. This view was not ultimately accepted, though it is evident that the legal responsibility for such decision making will be greatest for those who have available to

carry out the attack (in addition to those who plan and decide upon an attack) to do everything feasible to verify that the target is a military objective and is not subject to special protection.[174]

3. Consider an attack against a satellite of an adversary that is being used for military operational purposes. The attack is planned by a command centre located on Earth and carried out by a military spacecraft by means of a rendezvous proximity operation (RPO). In this case, both the command centre staff and the military spacecraft operators will bear an obligation to take feasible measures to verify the target; the spacecraft commander may be able to rely on visual identification of the target, and the command centre may use various intelligence resources as well as satellite and telescopic imagery in its verification.[175] In space, intelligence to verify that the target is a military objective may include available sensor information that informs space situational awareness, including infrared, radar, and electronic signatures of space objects. It must be noted, however, that verifying the identity, nature, purpose, and use of space objects may be more difficult in many circumstances than it is for verifying the status of objects located in terrestrial domains. Verification can also be complicated by active measures taken by a belligerent party to deceive or conceal the presence of a space object; there are frequently surprises and persistent unknowns in the space context.

4. As discussed in the Introduction to Part III, paragraphs 19–20, the obligation to take feasible measures is not an absolute requirement to do everything possible but rather an obligation to do what is practicable or practically possible to verify a target, taking into account the circumstances ruling at the time, including humanitarian and military factors.[176] Thus, the scope of what should be considered

them the most information and have the authority and means to delay or cancel an attack depending upon changing circumstances; see *Commentary on the Additional Protocols* (n 9) para 2191.

[174] Regarding continuing verification duties, see New Zealand LOAC Manual (n 25) 8.7.5 ('NZDF commanders are to constantly review target lists and likely military objectives as new information and intelligence becomes available and as circumstances change. All members of the NZDF are to inform their commanders of facts suggesting that earlier information on whether an object is a military objective is wrong, or that new circumstances apply.'); Danish LOAC Manual (n 28) para 2.27 ('If circumstances change during the attack and those conducting the attack become aware of the change, consideration must be given to whether it remains lawful to carry through the attack or whether, for example, there are too many civilians present, as may be the case if civilians or unidentified persons move into the danger zone. If it becomes apparent that the attack would cause disproportionate injury to civilians, it must be cancelled or suspended.'); Norwegian LOAC Manual (n 59) 4.2 ('Even if the required degree of certainty has been attained once, continued verification may still be required, depending on the circumstances, to ensure that the verification basis is sufficiently up-to-date. The verification should be updated in cases in which considerable activity is seen in the objective and/or in cases in which a certain period of time has passed since the last verification.').

[175] See ICRC, *Draft Additional Protocols to the Geneva Conventions of August 12, 1949: Commentary* (ICRC October 1973) 65 [https://perma.cc/H7C9-RJ27] (noting—in relation to draft Article 50(1)(b)—that '[t]o ensure the identification of military objectives, recourse may be had to various methods: land or aerial reconnaissance, by one's own troops or allied troops, by human (scouts or intelligence officers) or technical means (radar, television, satellites, infra-red rays, etc.))'.

[176] Norwegian LOAC Manual (n 59) para 2.5; UK LOAC Manual (n 21) para 5.32.2.

'feasible' may contract due to various military factors, including the operational risks of exposing the forces to casualties or other security risks, available means, and the cost of taking the precaution, in terms of time or other resources.[177] Similarly, the difficulty of gathering information about, and assessing the various functions of space objects should be taken into account when making such an assessment of feasibility. This may depend on the means of an attack. For example, an attack by means of a space vehicle in an RPO mission may be inherently more suited to ongoing verification right up to the last moment prior to contact with the target, using on-board cameras, as opposed to a ground-launched ASAT missile. However, this must be considered in conjunction with other precautions in attack and the feasibility of attack by different means (see Rule 37: Choice of Means and Methods of Attack).

---

[177] Danish LOAC Manual (n 28) 324, 327 (noting that '[o]nly feasible precautions must be taken. This brings an element of pragmatism to the process: parties to a conflict engaging in attacks undertake to do what can reasonably be required within the limits of the time and resources available and without exposing their own forces to unnecessary danger.'); Norwegian LOAC Manual (n 59) para 2.6 (noting that in addition to tactical and operational considerations, available means, and the need to protect one's own forces, '[a]ccount must also be taken of the fact that such decisions are normally made under difficult and confusing circumstances'); New Zealand LOAC Manual (n 25) 8.7.6 (noting that objectives 'will usually be set in accordance with command, strategic and tactical considerations, as well as practical issues such as capability and resources, many of which the commander will be unable to change. Where the opportunity arises to achieve the mission in a number of different ways, the one that causes the least incidental civilian loss and damage is to be selected.').

Rule 37
Choice of Means and Methods of Attack

Those who plan, decide upon or execute an attack during a military operation in an armed conflict, including a military space operation, must:

(a) take all feasible precautions in the choice of means and methods of attack, and
(b) choose among military objectives offering similar military advantage, with a view to avoiding, and in any event to minimizing, incidental loss of civilian life, injury to civilians and damage to civilian objects.

Overview of Legal Basis of Rule

1. This Rule is largely based on Articles 57(2)(a)(ii) and 57(3) of Additional Protocol I.[178] There is general agreement that this Rule reflects customary international law in international armed conflicts and is also likely to reflect customary international law in non-international armed conflicts.[179] The Rule requires specific precautionary measures with a view to avoiding, and in any event minimizing, incidental loss of civilian life, injury to civilians, and damage to civilian objects. Implicit in this Rule is the corresponding obligation incumbent on those who execute or carry out the attack (in addition to those who plan and decide upon an attack) to take all feasible precautions in the choice of means and methods of attack and choose among military objectives offering similar military advantage, with a view to avoiding, and in any event to minimizing, incidental loss of civilian life, injury to civilians, and damage to civilian objects.

Feasible Precautions

2. With respect to the specific obligation to take all feasible precautions in the choice of means and methods of attack, feasibility requires an assessment of which means

---

[178] See Introduction to Part III, paras 9–10 (noting that the text of Additional Protocol I explicitly states in art 49(3) that this Rule is applicable to warfare on land, air, and sea, and this *Manual* interprets Additional Protocol I as also extending to military space operations that may affect the civilian population, individual civilians, or civilian objects in any domain).

[179] See n 21(discussing the status of precautionary measures as customary international law in international armed conflict and also likely in non-international conflicts).

or methods of attack can cause 'the least incidental damage commensurate with military success'.[180] Feasibility should be understood as that which is practicable or practically possible taking into account all circumstances ruling at the time,[181] including humanitarian and military considerations.[182] For further discussion of these considerations see Introduction to Part III, paragraphs 19–20, and Rule 36: Verification, paragraph 4.

3. Subpart (a) of the Rule might require consideration of using a means or method of attack that can selectively target only particular components of a dual-use satellite, as opposed to targeting the entire satellite, if doing so is expected to avoid or minimize damage to civilians or civilian objects. This could be achieved through the employment of effective intelligence, together with available technology that enables more precise methods and means of attack—such as, in some circumstances, cyber operations or targeted RPOs as opposed to ASAT missile attack. However, the use of such alternate means of attack is subject to feasibility, including in this case the availability of effective intelligence and technology—and is also subject to the finding of a 'similar military advantage' under subpart (b).

Similar Military Advantage

4. Subpart (b) of the Rule is based on Article 57(3) of Additional Protocol I and requires an attacker to choose among viable lawful military objectives that offer a 'similar military advantage', and to attack the one likely to cause least incidental civilian injury or damage. The term 'similar military advantage' refers to attacks on either of the two or more target options affording the attacking party comparable operational benefits.[183]

5. For example, a State seeking to disable an adversary's satellite that constitutes a military objective may have available to it several possible options with varying consequences relevant to this determination. Using a kinetic kill anti-satellite weapon could create debris that would create a hazard for satellites that are civilian objects

---

[180] UK LOAC Manual (n 21) para 5.32.4.
[181] *Commentary on the Additional Protocols* (n 9) para 2198
[182] See art 3(10) of Amended Protocol II and art 1(5) of the Convention on Prohibitions or Restrictions on the Use of Certain Conventional Weapons Which May be Deemed to Be Excessively Injurious or to Have Indiscriminate Effects, 10 April 1981, 1342 UNTS 137; US DoD Law of War Manual (n 5) para 5.2.3.2; UK LOAC Manual (n 21) para 5.32, fn 191; German LOAC Manual (n 21) para 412; New Zealand LOAC Manual (n 25) para 2.2.10; Canadian LOAC Manual (n 21) G-L 6.
[183] See eg International Criminal Tribunal for the Former Yugoslavia, 'Final Report to the Prosecutor by the Committee Established to Review the NATO Bombing Campaign Against the Federal Republic of Yugoslavia' (ICTY Final Report to the Prosecutor) 39 ILM 1257, 1263–70 (concluding that since it was safer for a NATO aircraft to operate at a high altitude, there was no legal requirement under the rule of precautions in attack to operate at a lower altitude, even though doing so made it difficult to see the target and therefore could have caused more incidental civilian injury or damage); see also US DoD Law of War Manual (n 5) para 5.11.7.

in nearby orbits and may be particularly hazardous in heavily populated orbits or in orbits that host crewed civilian spacecraft. Alternatively, a directed energy attack could impair the target satellite's sensors, disabling the relevant capability but not creating either debris or collision risk. In choosing the appropriate means or method to achieve the goal of disabling the satellite, the commander must take into account the feasibility of using particular technical capabilities for the attack, with a view to avoiding the particular incidental loss of civilian life, injury to civilians, or damage to civilian property, and the ability of each means or method to achieve a similar military advantage.

6. This Rule applies until (and in some cases, even during) the execution of the attack. Thus, if reliable information becomes reasonably available after approval of an attack, indicating that a different means or method of attack would decrease or eliminate the loss of civilian life, injury to civilians, or damage to civilian objects while achieving a similar military advantage, those who plan, decide upon, or execute the attack shall act, to the extent feasible in the circumstances prevailing at the time, to employ the alternative means or method.

Rule 38
Proportionality in Attack

A Party to an armed conflict may not make an attack, including an attack involving a military space operation, that may be expected to cause incidental loss of civilian life, injury to civilians, damage to civilian objects, or a combination thereof, that would be excessive in relation to the concrete and direct military advantage anticipated.

Overview of Legal Basis of Rule

1. The text of this Rule is based on Article 51(5)(b) of Additional Protocol I.[184] The Rule reflects both customary international law applicable in international and non-international armed conflict.[185]

Application and Scope

2. This Rule reflects the requirement to balance two critical evaluations required by the law of armed conflict: the concrete and direct military advantage anticipated from an attack and the expected incidental loss of civilian life, injury to civilians, damage to civilian objects, or a combination thereof (referred to collectively in this Rule as 'civilian losses').[186] It applies to military space operations to the same

---

[184] See Additional Protocol I (n 4) art 57(2)(a)(iii); see Introduction to Part III, paras 9–10 (noting that the text of Additional Protocol I explicitly states in art 49(3) that this Rule is applicable to warfare on land, air, and sea, and this *Manual* interprets Additional Protocol I as also extending to military space operations, that may affect the civilian population, individual civilians, or civilian objects in any domain).

[185] See n 21 (discussing the status of precautionary measures as customary international law in international armed conflict and likely in non-international conflicts) In addition, see US DoD Law of War Manual (n 5) paras 5.12 and 17.7; New Zealand LOAC Manual (n 25) para 8.6.1; Louise Doswald-Beck (ed), *San Remo Manual on International Law Applicable to Armed Conflicts at Sea* (CUP 1995) (San Remo Manual) Rule 46(d); AMW Manual (n 31) r 14. The ICRC notes that 'while Additional Protocol II does not contain an explicit reference to the principle of proportionality in attack, it has been argued that it is inherent in the principle of humanity which was explicitly made applicable to the Protocol in its preamble and that, as a result, the principle of proportionality cannot be ignored in the application of the Protocol' and that '[m]ilitary manuals which are applicable in or have been applied in non-international armed conflicts specify the principle of proportionality in attack'. ICRC CIHL Study (n 14) Rule 14.

[186] In a larger context, this rule has also been viewed as reflecting the balancing of fundamental principles of the Law of Armed Conflict. See *Commentary on the Additional Protocols* (n 9) para 2208 ('In every attack [military commanders] must carefully weigh up the humanitarian and military interests at

338   RULE 38 PROPORTIONALITY IN ATTACK

degree as any other military operations that may affect the civilian population, individual civilians, or civilian objects in any domain.

3. This Rule applies only in the conduct of attacks (see Rule 31: Attack). It must not be confused with concepts of proportionality set forth in other bodies of law, such as with respect to the *jus ad bellum* notion of self-defence, the concept of proportionality applicable in international human rights law, and the law governing countermeasures.

4. This Rule is closely associated with other precautionary measures in this Section that require those who plan, decide upon, or execute[187] an attack to 'do everything feasible to verify that the objectives to be attacked are neither civilians nor civilian objects';[188] 'take all feasible precautions in the choice of means and methods of attack with a view to avoiding, and in any event to minimizing, incidental loss of civilian life, injury to civilians and damage to civilian objects';[189] and cancel or suspend an attack if it subsequently becomes apparent that the attack may be expected to cause incidental loss of civilian life, injury to civilians, damage to civilian objects, or a combination thereof, that would be excessive in relation to the direct military advantage anticipated.[190] This Rule is also associated with the obligation of States, in the conduct of military operations, to take 'constant care' to spare the civilian population, civilians and civilian objects[191] (see Rule 46: Constant Care). These obligations, together with the Rule of Proportionality, are likely to have great importance in protecting ever-increasing civilian activities and uses of space from the loss of civilian life, injury to civilians, or damage to civilian objects which may be caused by an armed conflict.

Incidental Civilian Losses

5. The incidental civilian losses contemplated in this Rule concern the expected loss of civilian life, injury to civilians, damage to civilian objects, or a combination thereof.

---

stake.'); ibid para 2219 ('this rule, such as it is, is aimed at establishing an equitable balance between humanitarian requirements and the sad necessities of war').

[187] Although the term 'execute' is not included in art 57(2)(a) of the Additional Protocol, it is included here because of the possibility that the original plans for an attack may change. Those responsible for executing the attack may thus be required to modify the plans, and are required to comply with the required precautionary measures—including the obligation under art 57(2)(a)(iii) to refrain from deciding to launch any attack which may be expected to cause incidental loss of civilian life, injury to civilians, damage to civilian objects, or a combination thereof, which would be excessive in relation to the concrete and direct military advantage anticipated.
[188] Additional Protocol I (n 4) art 57(2)(a)(i); see Rule 36: Verification.
[189] ibid art 57(2)(a)(ii); see Rule 37: Choice of Means and Methods of Attack.
[190] ibid art 57(2)(b); see Rule 39: Suspension or Cancellation of Attack.
[191] ibid art 57(1).

These incidental civilian losses thus do not include other possible harm to civilians (such as psychological harm, fear, inconvenience, stress etc) or the loss of life or injury of persons or objects that, at the time of attack, have lost their protection against direct attack, including able-bodied combatants or members of an OAG, civilians for such time as they are directly participating in hostilities,[192] or civilian objects that have become military objectives (see Rule 34: Military Objectives).

6. Relevant incidental civilian losses for the purposes of this Rule are those that may be expected to result from the attack but do not include civilian losses that are speculative, hypothetical or merely risked. In drafting the text of Article 57 of Additional Protocol I, States rejected prohibiting an attack 'which risks causing' civilian losses, instead prohibiting only attacks that 'may be expected to cause' the requisite civilian losses.[193]

7. Relevant incidental civilian losses for purposes of this Rule must also not be too remote, in the sense that these losses must be the proximate result of the attack.[194]

8. The incidental death or injury of civilians and damage to civilian objects considered in this Rule (or, as elsewhere referred to in this Rule, 'civilian losses') 'does not include inconvenience, irritation, stress, fear' or other such intangible effects,[195] including psychological harm or the interruption of non-essential satellite services (particularly on a temporary basis). The proportionality analysis must consider both direct and indirect civilian losses that may be expected (not merely risked) to be caused by the attack.

9. For an attack to be prohibited under this Rule, the expected incidental civilian losses resulting from the attack must be 'excessive' relative to the direct and concrete military advantage anticipated. This Rule offers no fixed standard for how much civilian death or injury or damage to civilian objects is excessive under this Rule—it is a determination made by the commander and those planning, deciding upon, and executing the attack. Even extensive incidental civilian losses would not

---

[192] ICRC Interpretive Guidance on Direct Participation in Hostilities (n 109) 13, n 6 (but see US DoD Law of War Manual (n 5) para 4.26.3.
[193] *Commentary on the Additional Protocols* (n 9) para 2209.
[194] During State Consultations, some States criticized the use of undefined terms and phrases such as 'second or third order effects and beyond' in making proportionality calculations, noting the possibility that such terms and phrases could stray into effects that are quite remote. It was also noted by one State that such terms could be particularly difficult to calculate in the space context. The term 'reverberating effects' may raise similar concerns, particularly in the space context, if it means the effects of an attack pass through layers of different actions, human responsibilities, and diverse complications—which may involve unexpected, contributing, or intervening circumstances—leading to remote losses that are not the proximate result of the attack. Although the term 'reverberating' is found in some popular, academic, and other publications, because of its broad and undefined reach and considerable criticism by States at Sate consultation of similar terms it is not used in this *Manual*.
[195] Norwegian LOAC Manual (n 59) paras 1.27 and 2.21; US DoD Law of War Manual (n 5) paras 5.12.1.2 and 16.5.1.1; Harvard University Program on Humanitarian Policy and Conflict Research, *Commentary on the HPCR Manual on International Law Applicable to Air and Missile Warfare* (CUP 2010) (AMW Manual Commentary) Commentary to r 1(l), para 5.

necessarily be prohibited if the military advantage anticipated from an attack is sufficiently high,[196] unless such losses are specifically prohibited by other rules of law of armed conflict.[197] At the same time, the proportionality rule would prohibit an attack causing even nominal losses to a civilian or a civilian object if excessive in relation to the military advantage anticipated.

Anticipated Military Advantage

10. Military advantage includes 'any consequence of an attack which directly enhances friendly military operations or hinders those of the enemy'.[198] It may also include a combination of benefits derived from the military advantage to friendly forces and military disadvantage to enemy forces. The advantage must be military in nature, and therefore advantages that are solely psychological, social, financial, economic, or moral are not relevant.

11. The military advantage 'anticipated' under this Rule must be 'concrete and direct'.[199] It cannot be merely hypothetical or speculative and must produce a real or clearly identifiable military benefit.[200] The anticipated advantage does not require certainty but rather a 'bona fide expectation that the attack will make a relevant and proportional contribution to the objective of the military attack involved'.[201] In applying the rule of proportionality in Article 51 and the precautionary measures in Article 57 of Additional Protocol I, States have indicated that 'military advantage' is understood to refer to the advantage anticipated from the attack considered as a whole and not only from isolated or particular parts of the attack.[202] Similarly, 'military advantage' is not restricted

---

[196] See eg ibid para 1980.
[197] See UK LOAC Manual (n 21) para 2.6.3; US DoD Law of War Manual (n 5), paras 2.6.3 and 5.12.3; AMW Manual Commentary (n 195) Commentary to r 14, paras 7–8;
[198] ibid Commentary to Rule 1(w), para 3.
[199] See *Commentary on the Additional Protocols* (n 9) para 2209 (noting that the expression 'concrete and direct' was 'intended to show that the advantage concerned should be substantial and relatively close, and that advantages which are hardly perceptible and those which would only appear in the long term should be disregarded'); UK LOAC Manual (n 21) para 5.33.3.; However, as emphasized by one State at State Consultations, 'as a matter of customary obligation there is not any temporal restriction when it comes to military advantage. Situations where the military advantage appears only in the long term frequently happen during hostilities, and it is legitimate to consider them into the proportionality analyses.'
[200] LOAC Manual (n 14) para 5.33.3; Spanish Law of Armed Conflict Manual (n 100) para 4.2.b; ICTY Final Report to the Prosecutor (n 183) para 76 [https://perma.cc/7T9P-PKL4]; see also AMW Manual Commentary (n 195) Commentary to r 14, para 9.
[201] 'Notification by the depositary addressed to the ICRC on 24 June 1991' (Australia—statement made at the time of ratification of Additional Protocol I).
[202] ibid; United Kingdom, Statement on Ratification of Additional Protocol I, 28 January 1998, 2020 UNTS 75, 77; New Zealand LOAC Manual (n 25) para 8.6.4; Norwegian LOAC Manual (n 59) para 2.23; US DoD Law of War Manual (n 5) para 5.12.3; Germany, Statement on Ratification of Additional Protocol I, 14 February 1991, 1607 UNTS 526, 529; Netherlands, Statement on Ratification of Additional

to immediate tactical gains but may be assessed in the full context of the war strategy.²⁰³

12. Thus, the military advantage need not be derived from one attack alone but can be aggregated based on the effects of a series of attacks or a specific operation within a military campaign.²⁰⁴ For example, a military space operation may be directed against a constellation of enemy satellites in order to achieve the anticipated military advantage and a commander must consider the advantage offered by the entirety of these attacks in degrading enemy capabilities, while weighing whether the incidental losses to the civilian population from the aggregate of the attacks is expected to be excessive. In another case, a military space operation may be focused on anticipated advantages that are spread across different domains. Thus, the anticipated advantages of an attack on an adversary's satellite may be assessed in connection with a larger attack that it is part of, including the advantage gained via an attack on a terrestrial target. For example, an attack on a terrestrial target of an adversary may be made in conjunction with an attack on an adversary's satellite if it deprives that terrestrial target of its usual communications and intelligence support.

Judgment of Commander Based Upon Circumstances Prevailing at the Time

13. This Rule relies to some extent on a 'subjective evaluation'²⁰⁵ and 'allows for a fairly broad margin of judgment'.²⁰⁶ Rather than making a retrospective judgment based on the actual results or effects of the attack, any assessment of proportionality must be made on a prospective basis, based on what the military commander (and others responsible for the planning, deciding upon, and execution of the attack) knew or had reason to know, based on all information reasonably available

---

Protocol I, 26 June 1987, 1477 UNTS 300; AMW Manual Commentary (n 195) Commentary to Rule 14, paras 11ff. See also *Commentary on the Additional Protocols* (n 9) para 2208.

²⁰³ US DoD Law of War Manual (n 5) para 5.12.2.1; South Africa, 'Advanced Law of Armed Conflict Teaching Manual' (1 April 2008) (South Africa LOAC) 181; Côte d'Ivoire, 'Law of Armed Conflict Teaching Manual' (2007) Book IV ('The military advantage at the moment of attack is the advantage anticipated from the operation or from the military campaign of which the attack is a part, considered as a whole, and not only from isolated or particular parts of that campaign or that operation.'); US DoD Law of War Manual (n 5) para 5.12.2.1.
²⁰⁴ New Zealand LOAC Manual (n 25) para 8.6.4; Norwegian LOAC Manual (n 59) para 2.23; US DoD Law of War Manual (n 5) para 2.23. See also AMW Manual Commentary (n 195) Commentary to r 14, paras 11ff.
²⁰⁵ *Commentary on the Additional Protocols* (n 9) para 2208 ('Even if this system is based to some extent on a subjective evaluation, the interpretation must above all be a question of common sense and good faith for military commanders. In every attack they must carefully weigh up the humanitarian and military interests at stake.').
²⁰⁶ ibid para 2210.

to them at that time.[207] As stated by the International Criminal Tribunal for the Former Yugoslavia in the *Galić* case, '[i]n determining whether an attack was proportionate it is necessary to examine whether a reasonably well-informed person in the circumstances of the actual perpetrator, making reasonable use of the information available to him or her, could have expected excessive civilian casualties to result from the attack'.[208] The military manuals of numerous States,[209] the decisions of international tribunals,[210] and other State practice[211] provide useful guidance in implementing this test.

Relationship with Principle of Distinction

14. This Rule is not a substitute for, and in no way limits or undermines, the principle of distinction (see Rule 32: Distinction). While it contemplates incidental loss of civilian life and objects, only objects and persons qualifying as military objectives may be targeted (see Rule 34: Military Objectives and Rule 33: Direct Participation in Hostilities). If an attack is intentionally directed against the civilian population as the target itself, then it is a violation of those other rules (including discrimination), and this is not excused by the fact that the civilian losses would be tolerated if they were incidental, as opposed to intentional. Similarly, this Rule does not limit

---

[207] UK Reservation to Additional Protocol I: ('(d) in relation to Articles 51 to 58 inclusive, Military commanders and others responsible for planning, deciding upon, or executing attacks necessarily have to reach decisions on the basis of their assessment of the information from all sources which is reasonably available to them at the relevant time'). Adam Roberts and Richard Guelff (eds), *Documents on the Laws of War* (2nd edn, OUP 1989) 510 Additional similar reservations were made by Austria (p 500), and Canada (p 502).

[208] *Galić* Trial Judgment (n 35) para 58.

[209] For example, the Canadian Law of Armed Conflict Manual (n 25), s 5, para 27, indicates that '[c]onsideration must be paid to the honest judgement of responsible commanders, based on the information reasonably available to them at the relevant time, taking fully into account the urgent and difficult circumstances under which such judgements are usually made' and indicates that the proportionality test must be examined on the basis of 'what a reasonable person would have done' in such circumstances. Similar provisions are contained in the Australian LOAC Manual (n 31) paras 2.8, 2.9, and 5.11; Danish LOAC Manual (n 28) 320; New Zealand LOAC Manual (n 25) paras 8.6.1–8.7.2, fn 43; UK LOAC Manual (n 21) para 5.32.10; and US DoD Law of War Manual (n 5) paras 5.10.2.2, 5.10.2.3, and 5.12.2.

[210] See ICTY Final Report to the Prosecutor (n 183) para 50 ('It is suggested that the determination of relative values must be that of the 'reasonable military commander'.); *Galić* Trial Judgment (n 35) para 58; United Nations War Crimes Commission, 'Law Reports of Trials of War Criminals' (vol VIII, 1949) (The Hostages Trial) 68 (discussing United States Military Tribunal, Nuremberg, 'Trial of Wilhelm List and Others' (8 July 1947)) (noting that although 'an examination of the facts in retrospect can well sustain [the] conclusion' that there was actually 'no military necessity for this destruction and devastation' that the defendant had ordered as the commander of German forces retreating from Soviet troops in Finland, the Tribunal concluded that 'we are obliged to judge the situation as it appeared to the defendant at the time. If the facts were such as would justify the action by the exercise of judgment, after giving consideration to all the factors and existing possibilities, even though the conclusion reached may have been faulty, it cannot be said to be criminal.').

[211] See eg the Interpretive Declaration made by Algeria and the Reservation made by Austria to arts 85 and 86 of Additional Protocol I. Roberts and Guelff (n 207), Algeria (p 499 and Austria (p 500).

or undermine other rules on precautions in attack, which apply concurrently.[212] In particular, an attack expected to cause incidental civilian losses that are not excessive and thus does not violate this Rule, are nevertheless a violation of law of armed conflict if it would have been feasible to take additional precautions to avoid or minimize this incidental losses under other Rules in this Section. In short, satisfying the proportionality test is not sufficient to make an attack lawful.[213]

Special Challenges Related to Military Space Operations

15. The application of the rule of proportionality to military space operations presents some special challenges that are different from those found in other domains. At the outset, since there is no experience with space war, there may be little basis for estimating how much unintentional damage would be caused by an attack, and how much concrete and direct military advantage would be gained by such an attack. This makes it even harder than it usually is in other operational domains to assess the variables that go into the proportionality assessment. Nonetheless, the attacker is obliged to undertake the analysis as fully as possible.

16. One major challenge in applying the rule of proportionality in space concerns destructive attacks on space objects that generate long-lasting space debris. For example, an ASAT system that intercepts and destroys a target in space using a kinetic energy weapon may generate a massive cloud of lethal debris that presents a persistent hazard to the space activities of civilians and all space-faring States.[214] Even small pieces of this 'space junk', travelling at extremely high speed, can destroy or damage any satellite that it encounters in space. Depending on the altitude of the debris, the unpredictable threat posed by this debris may endure for decades or even centuries. This unpredictable threat extends not only to space objects, but also to increasing numbers of persons engaged in diverse space activities.

---

[212] US DoD Law of War Manual (n 5) para 5.10.5.

[213] For example, the law of armed conflict prohibits certain means and methods of warfare (see Rule 42: Means and Methods of Warfare Generally), and the use of prohibited weapon systems (see Rule 5: Weapons of Mass Destruction), even if their use might satisfy the proportionality rule. In this regard, a State that is a Party to Additional Protocol I is prohibited from using means or methods of warfare in military space operations that are intended, or may be expected, to cause widespread, long-term, and severe damage to the natural environment See Additional Protocol I (n 4) art 35(3). Additional, related environmental considerations may apply (see Rule 43: Natural Environment).

[214] For example, a destructive ASAT test by the People's Republic of China in 2007 on one of its own aging weather satellites created a massive cloud of remnants that will last for decades, posing a collision risk to spacecraft in or passing through low Earth orbit. William J Broad and David E Sanger, 'Flexing Muscle, China Destroys Satellite in Test' *NY Times* (New York, 19 January 2007) [https://perma.cc/9TXD-BULX]; Leonard David, 'China's Anti-Satellite Test: Worrisome Debris Cloud Circles Earth' (SPACE.com, 2 February 2007) [https://perma.cc/74VN-GT8P].

17. In the situation above, a commander contemplating an attack on an adversary's military satellite—and planning to employ a destructive ASAT weapon which is likely to generate considerable space debris—is confronted with unique space-related challenges under the rule of proportionality. The commander and those planning and executing this attack must include in their calculation not only the expected short-term effects of the attack but also its expected long-term effects on civilians and civilian objects, including the effects on civilian objects in space, and the consequent risk of additional affects for civilian populations on Earth relying on such space objects, in order to determine whether the expected incidental civilian losses are excessive in relation to the direct and concrete military advantage anticipated. Although the anticipated military advantage may be very significant, the expected civilian losses posed by the attack's generation of lethal space debris, potentially suffered many years after the attack,[215] must also be considered.

18. To date, given the fortuitous absence of any armed conflict in space, there is no State practice to serve as a precedent or a guide for a commander in making the proportionality calculation related to an attack on a space object that is expected to generate space debris. However, it might be argued that several factors relevant to making this calculation might include: where the satellite is operating; how far the debris field might spread (eg Geosynchronous Earth Orbit (GEO) vs Low Earth Orbit (LEO)); how long the debris would remain in orbit; how many and how large the debris pieces would be; and how feasible it would be to track these pieces of debris and manoeuvre to avoid them in the future.[216] This evaluation may be especially important in light of the profound, long-lasting impact that such a debris field could have on all States, not just on the belligerents, who will be engaged in peaceful space operations long after the immediate armed conflict is over.

19. Another major space-related challenge presented by the proportionality rule concerns the diverse and expanding services, functions, and purposes of satellites. Satellites, and constellations of satellites, may support important public and private infrastructure on Earth, as well as special functions such as emergency services, humanitarian relief operations, and medical communications. Essential activities in the commercial, industrial, and financial sectors are also increasingly dependent on satellite services. The civilian life throughout the world has become particularly dependent upon Global Navigation Satellite System (GNSS) signals not only for navigation but also for precision timing synchronization for modern industries, the Internet, environmental and atmospheric monitoring, meteorology,

---

[215] One State at State Consultations observed that '[n]aturally, the more indirect or temporarily distant the effects are, the harder it is to anticipate them, and there would be a lesser tendency to see them as a reasonably expected incidental damage which must be taken into account'.

[216] David Koplow, 'International Legal Standards and the Weaponization of Outer Space' UNIDIR/2008/14 (Security in Space: The Next Generation Conference Report, Geneva, 31 March–1 April 2008) 167.

climate research, security applications, telecommunications, security services, quantum cryptography, cartography, and safety monitoring.[217] As early as 2011, the European Commission estimated that 6–7 percent of gross domestic product in Western countries was dependent on satellite radio navigation.[218]

20. While a targeted satellite may qualify as a military objective based on the facts that it makes an effective contribution to the adversary's military action and that the satellite's total or partial destruction, capture, or neutralization, in the circumstances ruling at the time, offers a definite military advantage, that same satellite may also serve important civilian functions such as those noted above. In some circumstances, an attack on a military satellite might also be expected to damage other satellites that also serve these civilian functions.[219] In either case, a commander will be called upon to make a proportionality calculation to determine whether the expected incidental civilian losses are excessive to the anticipated military advantage of the attack. This proportionality calculation may be complex and hindered by a lack of transparency regarding the functions of a particular satellite. Nonetheless, any attack on a satellite cannot proceed in the absence of a good faith application of the proportionality analysis.

21. In space, both sides of the proportionality calculation are simultaneously large and growing, making the balance dynamic. As technology advances, interconnectivity increases, and the importance of satellites continues to grow, it is likely that the judgments of military authorities with respect to the expected incidental loss of civilian life, injury to civilians, or damage to civilian objects caused by attacks on space objects may be required to adjust accordingly. Yet satellites also increasingly perform many critical, fundamental military functions, and the destruction or incapacitation of satellites may thus present a clear military advantage.[220] Furthermore, the destruction of satellites will not ordinarily be expected to result directly in the loss of human lives, a key factor in the proportionality considerations.[221] This requires a commander, in the circumstances prevailing at the time,

---

[217] 'Global Navigation Space Systems: Reliance and Vulnerabilities' (Royal Academy of Engineering 2011) 3 [https://perma.cc/3LC4-WKT7] (noting that 'the use of GPS signals is now commonplace in data networks, financial systems, shipping and air transport systems, agriculture, railways and emergency services. Safety of life applications are becoming more common.').

[218] ibid.

[219] One State at State Consultations noted that practical considerations may impede the consideration of 'civilian functions' in this proportionality analysis, emphasizing that it may be very hard to identify or quantify such civilian functions, in particular since it may depend on the subjective decisions of civilians regarding how to use the object that is damaged by the attack.

[220] It should be noted that at the current time destruction of a satellite would not ordinarily be expected to result in the loss of human life, a key factor in traditional proportionality calculations; see Additional Protocol I (n 4) art 57(2)(a)(iii), which refers explicitly to only one type of effect to be included in the proportionality calculation: incidental loss of civilian life, injury to civilians, damage to civilian objects, or a combination thereof.

[221] Nevertheless, the attacker must still take into account the possibility of human losses on Earth, assuming they are not too speculative or remote.

to make reasonable use of intelligence resources that are reasonably available to the commander, to determine the incidental loss of civilian life, injury to civilians, or damage to civilian objects that may be expected to result from an attack on a particular satellite or group of satellites. Both the expected incidental direct and indirect civilian losses in space, as well as the civilian losses on Earth caused by impairing the civilian use of the dual-use space object(s), must be included in this calculation.

22. For example, in the case of an attack on a large group of GNSS satellites that serve both military and civilian purposes, the precise losses caused by the disruption of so many different civilian services provided by these satellites may be extremely difficult to calculate. The extent and nature of the expected incidental civilian losses inflicted by such an attack on a modern, inter-connected society (which are likely to include citizens of many States, not just those involved in the conflict) will nonetheless require a legal assessment under the proportionality rule. However, as noted, some effects on the civilian population—such as inconvenience, psychological harm, fear, stress, and the loss of non-essential satellite services (particularly if only a temporary loss)—will not qualify as part of this calculation.[222] Other effects, such as some economic losses, may be difficult to predict or categorize and may not, in themselves, constitute loss of life and/or damage to property which is the focus of the proportionality calculation.[223] It is thus possible that many losses—including long-term second- and third-order effects and other damages that are risked but not 'expected'—may represent difficult *policy* issues for decision-makers that lie outside the scope of *legal* analysis under the rule of proportionality.

---

[222] Fortunately, to date, the precise application of this Rule to incidental civilian losses on earth or in space during an armed conflict in space has not been determined by State practice. However, as the law of armed conflict now provides, it is clear that only those attacks may be expected to cause incidental loss of civilian life, injury to civilians, damage to civilian objects, or a combination thereof, that would be excessive in relation to the concrete and direct military advantage anticipated are to be included in the proportionality calculation.

[223] See Norwegian LOAC Manual (n 59) para 2.21 ('only losses, injuries or damage of a certain impact have to be weighed against the military advantage. These must either entail the loss of life or injury to civilians, or damage to or destruction of civilian objects.'); US DoD Law of War Manual (n 5) para 16.5.1.1. ('In assessing incidental injury or damage during cyber operations, it may be important to consider that remote harms and lesser forms of harm, such as mere inconveniences or temporary disruptions, need not be considered in assessing whether an attack is prohibited by the principle of proportionality.') It must be noted, however, that many essential medical and emergency services are increasingly dependent on satellite communications and that disruption of those services could result in the loss of civilian lives and must, if expected, be included in calculations of incidental civilian losses under this Rule. Similarly, critical national infrastructure and other civilian industries that depend on satellite communications could be damaged by attacks that disrupt those communications and thus potentially qualify as damage to civilian objects that must be included in proportionality calculations.

Rule 39
Suspension or Cancellation of Attack

An attack in an armed conflict, including an attack involving a military space operation, shall be suspended or cancelled if it becomes apparent that:

(a) the object of the attack is not a military objective or is subject to special protection; or

(b) the attack may be expected to cause incidental loss of civilian life, injury to civilians, damage to civilian objects or a combination thereof, which would be excessive in relation to the concrete and direct military advantage anticipated.

Overview of Legal Basis of Rule

1. This Rule is based on Article 57(2)(b) of Additional Protocol I[224] and is generally considered to be customary international law in international armed conflicts and possibly in non-international armed conflict.[225] The essence of this Rule is an obligation that even if an attack, when originally planned, would meet all applicable legal criteria, the attack must not be carried out if subsequent information reveals that the attack would no longer satisfy the applicable tests. This Rule is framed in terms of suspending or modifying the attack; implicit is the additional possibility that the attack could be modified or re-planned so as to bring it into compliance.[226] However, it may not always be possible to alter or delay an attack so as

---

[224] See Introduction to Part III, paras 9–10 (noting that the text of Additional Protocol I explicitly states in Article 49(3) that this Rule is applicable to warfare on land, air, and sea, and this *Manual* interprets Additional Protocol I as also extending to military space operations that may affect the civilian population, individual civilians, or civilian objects in any domain). As noted by one State at State Consultations, this obligation in Additional Protocol I applies to a State that is a party to the conflict, and to those within that State that is a party to the conflict with the authority to take such actions. See eg US DoD Law of War Manual (n 5) para 5.10.2.1 ('As with other aspects of the law of war, the persons within a party to a conflict who are responsible for making the decisions and judgments required by the principle of proportionality are those who have the authority to make these decisions and judgments. The specific responsibilities that individual combatants have to implement the principle of proportionality will depend on their role and assigned military duties in planning or conducting an attack.').

[225] See n 21 (discussing the status of precautionary measures as customary international law in international armed conflict and possibly in non-international armed conflicts).

[226] See UK LOAC Manual (n 21) para 5.32.7 ('[t]here is the duty to cancel or suspend attacks if the incidental damage may be expected to be disproportionate to the military advantage anticipated ... Instead of cancelling or suspending the attack, it can be re-planned so as to bring it within the proportionality principle.').

to bring it into compliance with legal obligations; in that case, it must be cancelled altogether.[227] As noted by one State at State Consultations, it may not always be feasible to suspend or cancel an attack when it becomes apparent that the object of the attack is not a military objective or is specially protected. Conversely, if an intended target is suddenly discovered to be a dual-use object, it may in some cases be feasible to modify the attack to strike only the military component.

When an Attack Will Not Be Against a Military Objective or It is Against a Target that is Subject to Special Protection

2. Subpart (a) applies where it becomes apparent that the object of the attack is not a military objective or is subject to special protection. Thus, for example, an attack must be modified, suspended, or cancelled if the objective was originally classified as a satellite meeting the definition of a military objective, but newly available information makes it apparent that it is actually a satellite that is not a military objective, or if it becomes apparent that the object is (and remains at the time of the attack) subject to special protection warranting additional considerations before the attack (see eg Rule 35: Medical Units and Religious Personnel). There is no requirement to cancel an attack against an object subject to special protection if, for example, this object lost its protection.

3. In many situations, an attack may be able to rely on visual means to find out whether an intended objective is or is not a military objective, but the use of long-range weapons (and the use of weapons in the space environment generally) requires more caution in making this determination because there is often a lack of direct view.[228] In the context of military space operations, this obligation will almost always be fulfilled on the basis of varied intelligence sources that inform targeting decisions. For example, consider a situation in which an attack is approved against what is believed to be a communication satellite used in part by enemy forces in a manner making it fulfil the definition of military objective under the law of armed conflict. The expectation is that the attack will permanently disable its communications transponders. If it later becomes apparent due to new intelligence that the satellite was never, or is no longer, used by the enemy for military purposes, and there is no indication that it is intended to be so used by the enemy in the future, the attack must be suspended or cancelled because the satellite does not qualify as a military objective (see Rule 34: Military Objectives).

---

[227] As noted by one State at State Consultations, it may not always be possible to suspend or cancel an attack when it becomes apparent that the object of the attack is not a military objective or is specially protected.
[228] *Commentary to the Additional Protocols* (n 9) para 2221.

When an Attack Will Not Comply with Proportionality Requirements

Subpart (b) of the Rule provides that an attack shall be suspended or cancelled when it is expected to cause incidental loss of civilian life, injury to civilians, damage to civilian objects, or a combination thereof, which would be excessive in relation to the concrete and direct military advantage anticipated (namely that it does not comply with the Rule 38: Proportionality in Attack). This could be due to new information that has been received or a change in the circumstances prevailing at the time of the attack. In such a case, if the change in assessment would render the expected incidental civilian harm excessive compared to the anticipated military advantage, then the attack must be modified, suspended, or cancelled.   **4.**

Consider an approved attack against a satellite that constitutes a military objective after all feasible precautions have been taken and it has been determined that the attack will comply with the rule of proportionality. However, at the last clear chance to suspend or cancel the attack before it is launched, the operator obtains new information concerning the presence of a satellite that may enter the orbit of the projected debris path that will be caused by the attack. In such a circumstance, a new assessment is needed to reconsider whether the attack may now be expected to cause excessive civilian harm compared to the direct and concrete military advantage that is anticipated and the attack must be suspended or cancelled in the meantime.   **5.**

The obligation to suspend or cancel an attack rests with those to whom it becomes apparent that the objective is no longer a military objective or that civilian harm will be excessive. The issue in practice is whether a subordinate will have enough information (and authority) to make an assessment that it is 'apparent' that the situations in either subparts (a) or (b) of the Rule exist. In the situation relevant to subpart (a), the person executing the attack against the communications satellite may not be privy to the intelligence used to inform the original decision that the target is a military objective. In the situation relevant to subpart (b) of the Rule, the person executing the attack may not fully appreciate the military advantage anticipated from the attack as a whole—and this may be especially true in the case of an attack on a satellite which would almost always be part of a broader campaign.[229] In such a case, when relevant intelligence is received by a person (such as an operator executing the attack) who does not have the power to suspend or cancel the attack, the information must be transmitted, to the extent feasible, to a person who does   **6.**

---

[229] ibid paras 2220–2221; US DoD Law of War Manual (n 5) para 5.12.2.1 ('Lower-level personnel may not be competent to evaluate the broader strategic and operational implications of the entire attack'); UK LOAC Manual (n 21) para 5.32.9; Danish LOAC Manual (n 28) ch 8, s 5; Norwegian LOAC Manual (n 59) para 2.24.

have that authority.[230] However, the obligation is dependent on the information reasonably available from all sources to that person with the requisite authority, under the circumstances ruling at that time,[231] as well as the means at that person's disposal to suspend or cancel the attack.[232]

---

[230] See United Kingdom, 'Instrument of Ratification with Declarations and Reservations to Additional Protocol I' [2001] UNTS 75, 78 para (o) (restricting the obligation to 'those who have the authority and practical possibility to cancel or suspend the attack'); US DoD Law of War Manual (n 5) para 5.11.4 (emphasizing that subordinates generally would not be authorized to cancel or suspend an attack simply because they disagree with the commander's assessment of proportionality, although they may cancel or suspend an attack 'in appropriate circumstances', especially when commanders are not able to maintain situational awareness of the risks of civilian casualties.).

[231] France, for example, has asserted that the obligation to cancel or suspend an attack requires normal due diligence, based on the information available to the one who decides the attack 'calls only for due diligence to cancel or suspend that attack, on the basis of the information available to the person deciding on the attack' [translated from the French]; see Julie Gaudreau, 'The Reservations to the Protocols Additional to the Geneva Conventions for the Protection of War Victims' (2003) March (849) International Review of the Red Cross 143–84. According to Canada's reservation to Additional Protocol I made upon ratification on 20 November 1990, this obligation is dependent on the quality of the information available at the time decisions are made. Commanders must make reasonable, good faith efforts to gather intelligence and to review the intelligence available to them: 'military commanders and others responsible for planning, deciding upon or executing attacks have to reach decisions on the basis of their assessment of the information reasonably available to them at the relevant time ..... such decisions cannot be judged on the basis of information which has subsequently come to light'—see Government of Canada, 'Reservations made at the time of ratification to Protocol relating to the Protection of Victims of International Armed Conflicts' (ICRC 1990) [https://perma.cc/C4ZJ-RZWW].

[232] Koninklijke Landmacht (The Netherlands), 'Humanitair Oorlogsrecht: Handleiding' (Militair Juridische Dienst 2005) para 0544; 'Official Records of the Diplomatic Conference on the Reaffirmation and Development of International Humanitarian Law Applicable in Armed Conflicts—Geneva (1974–1977)—Volume VI' (Federal Political Department 1978) 239 (statement by representative for Cameroon, 27 May 1977) [https://perma.cc/8P6Y-VGL6]; *Commentary on the Additional Protocols* (n 9) para 2221.

Rule 40
Warnings

During military operations in an armed conflict, including a military space operation, effective advance warning shall be given of an attack that may affect the civilian population, unless circumstances do not permit.

Overview of Legal Basis of Rule

1. This Rule is based on Article 57(2)(c) of Additional Protocol I and Article 26 of the 1907 Hague Regulations.[233] It is generally considered to be customary international law applicable to attacks during international armed conflict and possibly during non-international armed conflict.[234]

Whether Circumstances Do Not Permit a Warning

2. The obligation to warn is not absolute. Importantly, a warning shall be given unless 'circumstances do not permit'.[235] Such circumstances could include the need for surprise (or secrecy) as a condition for the success of an attack or when giving such warning would risk the lives of the attacking forces.[236] Thus, if warning the

---

[233] See Introduction to Part III, paras 9–10 (noting that the text of Additional Protocol I explicitly states in art 49(3) that this Rule is applicable to warfare on land, air, and sea, and this *Manual* interprets Additional Protocol I as also extending to military space operations, which may affect the civilian population, individual civilians, or civilian objects in any domain). The origins of this Rule can be traced the 1907 Hague Convention IV (n 6) in relation to warfare on land.

[234] See n 21 (discussing the status of precautionary measures as customary international law in international armed conflict and as likely to be in non-international conflicts). Although the United States is not party to Additional Protocol I, the US DoD Law of War Manual (n 5) para 5.11.5.2 provides that '[u]nless circumstances do not permit, effective advance warning must be given of an attack that may affect the civilian population'. This section of the US DoD Law of War Manual does, however, frame some aspects of this obligation differently than the formulation found in art 57(2)(c).

[235] Additional Protocol I (n 4) art 57(2)(c). See also *Commentary on the Additional Protocols* (n 9) para 2223.

[236] According to the US DoD War Manual, for example, 'legitimate military reasons, such as exploiting the element of surprise in order to provide for mission accomplishment and preserving the security of the attacking force' qualify as circumstances that preclude warning. US DoD War Manual (n 6) 5.11.1.3. See also UK LOAC Manual (n 21) para 5.32.8; *Commentary on the Additional Protocols* (n 9) para 2223; AMW Manual Commentary (n 195) r 37 para 6; Australian LOAC Manual (n 31) para 5.56. However, depending on the circumstances ruling at the time, humanitarian concerns may nonetheless point to the need for consideration of alternatives to a mission that requires no warning be given.

enemy about an imminent attack on one of its satellites (if required because the attack may affect the civilian population by disrupting essential satellite services) would allow the enemy to evade the attack—for instance by manoeuvring its satellite into another orbit or by taking other protective measures, such as shuttering to protect optics—circumstances would not require that a warning be given. Other circumstances that should be considered when assessing the feasibility of issuing a warning include but are not limited to a lack of time to effectively warn, an operational need to carry out the attack immediately, and increased risk to civilians where it is clear that a warning would lead to the use of human shields.[237]

Where an Attack May 'Affect the Civilian Population'

3. The obligation to provide effective advance warnings applies to attacks during military space operations where that attack may 'affect the civilian population'[238] (either on Earth or in space) and is not applied in cases where the attack is not expected to have an effect on the civilian population.[239] Warnings must never be abused as a means of spreading terror among the civilian population, nor should they be used to deceive the civilian population.[240]

4. The term 'affect' is not defined in the law of armed conflict. As a result, uncertainty exists as to the precise threshold at which the obligation manifests. A textual-based view of this term is that the obligation to warn arises only in the context of civilians being injured or killed or civilian objects being damaged or destroyed. This position is derived from the fact that the protections provided by treaty law in the context of attacks attach only to such consequences. In particular, all other requirements under Article 57(2) of Additional Protocol I refer to the loss of civilian lives, injury to civilians, and damage to civilian objects, as is the case with regard to the rule of proportionality (see Rule 38: Proportionality in Attack). Assuming that 'damage to civilian objects' encompasses damage to civilian property (including commercial satellites) and essential services that these satellites provide to the civilian population on Earth, a broad view of the warning obligation in military space would encompass a requirement to consider, where possible, the sustained and widespread loss of essential services (that will result in the loss of civilian lives, injury to civilians, and damage to civilian objects) which are provided to the civilian population by a satellite that is the object of an attack. However, care must be taken in the space context to not extend the phrase 'affect the civilian population' too far and it must be recognized that the ability of an attacker to identify all the services provided by a

---

[237] UK LOAC Manual (n 21) para 5.32.8.
[238] Additional Protocol I (n 4) art 57(2)(c).
[239] UK LOAC Manual (n 21) para 5.32.8; US DoD Law of War Manual (n 5) 5.3.3.2. and 5.11.1.2.
[240] *Commentary on the Additional Protocols* (n 9) para 2225.

particular satellite (and the users of those services) and to provide a warning to the affected civilian population on a timely basis may be quite limited.

5. It is unlikely that effects consisting of mere inconvenience, irritation, stress, fear, or the loss of some non-essential types of satellite services following an attack on a communications satellite would constitute harm to the civilian population that would require an advance warning.[241] However, it is unclear what type and degree of adverse impacts associated with the loss of satellite services require advance warning other than those effects which are likely to be the proximate cause of the loss of civilian lives, injury to civilians and damage to civilian objects. It is clear that the attacking military force must take into account the expected direct incidental damage (and proximate, indirect incidental damage) to civilian objects and the civilian population in its proportionality analysis (see Rule 38: Proportionality in Attack).

Judgment of Commander Regarding Whether Circumstances Permit a Warning and Whether an Attack 'May Affect the Civilian Population' Under this Rule

6. The determination of whether circumstances permit a warning will be based on the information reasonably available to the commander at the time. As stated by the court in the *Galić* case with respect to the application of the proportionality principle, '[i]n determining whether an attack was proportionate it is necessary to examine whether a reasonably well-informed person in the circumstances of the actual perpetrator, making reasonable use of the information available to him or her, could have expected excessive civilian casualties to result from the attack'[242] (see Rule 38: Proportionality in Attack). In evaluating whether an attack 'may affect the civilian population' for purposes of giving warnings under this Rule, the commander is not responsible for knowing every part of the civilian population on Earth or in space that may be affected by a proposed attack and precisely how they will be affected. Rather, a commander must be judged by what could be expected from a reasonable military commander, making use of reasonably available information from all sources, under the circumstances ruling at the time.[243] This may

---

[241] AMW Manual Commentary (n 195) r 37 para 4.
[242] *Galić* Trial Judgment (n 35) para 58.
[243] The military manuals of most States and international court decisions address the requirements for a responsible commander's use of information in making decisions related to an attack in the context of proportionality. For example, the Canadian LOAC Manual indicates that '[c]onsideration must be paid to the honest judgement of responsible commanders, based on the information reasonably available to them at the relevant time, taking fully into account the urgent and difficult circumstances under which such judgements are usually made' and indicates that the proportionality test must be examined on the basis of 'what a reasonable person would have done' in such circumstances. Canadian LOAC Manual (n 21) 4–5; Algeria, 'Interpretive Declarations Made Upon Accession to the 1977 Additional Protocol 1' (16 August 1989) s 2 [https://perma.cc/757S-D38N] ('To judge any decision,

involve a particularly difficult evaluation in military space operations, especially with respect to multi-purpose and dual-use space systems, and comprehensive information may not be reasonably available, but a good faith evaluation is nonetheless required.

Other Requirements for Advance Warnings

7. When an attacking State is required to give advance warning of an attack that is expected to affect the civilian population, the advance warning must be designed to be *effective*. A warning should be designed to facilitate the protection of the civilian population so that civilians and the authorities in control of the civilian population can take measures to reduce the risk that civilians will be harmed by the operation.[244] Consequently, the assessment of the effectiveness of the warning is not measured retrospectively in terms of (for example) the number of citizens who did in fact respond to the warning. However, given the purpose of a warning—namely to enable the local authorities to take steps to enhance the protection of the civilian population, and to allow individual civilians to flee or take other preparatory steps in order to protect themselves from the attack—the warning needs to be given in a manner that will allow it to reach as many as possible of the civilians who are likely to be affected by the attack, and in a way (eg in a language) that is understood by them.[245]

8. The law does not require a set form or method for warnings.[246] The mode of the warning is dependent on the context; it may depend on the available equipment, as well as military and humanitarian considerations. Warnings can include, but are not limited to, broadcasts, leaflets, sound or light signals, text messages, phone calls, and notice to the operators of satellites delivering services to the civilian population that might be affected by the attack. Warnings should be as clear and specific as circumstances permit so as to allow local authorities controlling the civilian population and individual civilians to take relevant protective measures, such as arranging to use other methods of communication or location. The degree of specificity of the warning may depend on the length of time prior to the attack

the circumstances, the means and the information available at the time the decision was made are determinant factors and elements in assessing the nature of the said decision.'); UK Declaration upon ratification of Additional Protocol I, Roberts and Guelff (n 207) 510 ('Military commanders and other responsible for planning, deciding upon, or executing attacks necessarily have to reach decisions on the basis of their assessment of the information from all sources which is reasonably available to them at the relevant time.'); see Rule 38: Proportionality in Attack.

[244] US DoD Law of War Manual (n 5) para 5.11.5.2.
[245] UK LOAC Manual (n 21) para 5.32.8; US DoD War Manual (n 5) 5.11.5.2; AMW Manual Commentary (n 195) r 37 para 8.
[246] US DoD Law of War Manual (n 5) para 5.11.1.1; AMW Manual Commentary (n 195) r 37 para 9.

in relation to which the warning is issued. For example, there are cases in which an imprecise warning issued well in advance of the attack may be more effective than a precise warning immediately preceding it.[247] Whenever different options to warn exist then insofar as the circumstances permit, it could be argued that the most effective warning must be chosen based on the object and purpose of the warning, which is to protect the civilian population from the effects of attacks.[248]

9. During military space operations, an attacking State should give effective advance warning under this Rule of attacks that may affect civilians located in space or that extend to civilians on Earth. For example, if circumstances permit, effective advance warning should be given to civilians on board the International Space Station (ISS) to enable the ISS to manoeuvre or take other precautions to avoid debris that might be created by an attack on a military satellite. In some cases, the advanced warnings under this Rule may need to reach the civilian population on Earth to be effective. For example, an attack against a satellite that is likely to affect aerial navigation or air traffic control in such a way as to threaten civilian lives and property may, if circumstances permit, require a warning to the relevant authorities so as to allow them to take preparatory steps to initiate a transition to relevant backup systems, such as Long-Range Navigation (LORAN), or to temporarily ground flights.[249] The obligation to warn also applies to military space operations that are likely to affect the civilian population on the high seas, international airspace, or neutral territory. Similarly, the warning requirement would attach even where such effects manifest outside the zone of hostilities (such cases are highly likely in the space context because space objects may provide essential services that are regional or even global in nature).

10. Warnings may be conveyed through the enemy forces controlling the local civilian population if it is reasonable to conclude under the circumstances that the enemy will pass on the warning to its civilian population.[250] This option is particularly relevant in the outer space context given that the loss of certain satellite functions is likely to affect a significant proportion of the civilian population, and that often it

---

[247] AMW Manual Commentary (n 195) r 37 para 9.
[248] A State at State Consultations noted that '[w]hile it may be sensible from a policy perspective to choose the most effective warning, it is not clear what the legal basis is for saying that this must be chosen, so long as the warning chosen is an effective one'. There is no form or required 'balancing test' between military requirements and humanitarian concerns applicable to the decision of a commander to determine whether a warning is required or, if it is, how detailed and specific the warning must be. However, where circumstances permit, humanitarian factors should be considered at all stages of the warning process (including selecting the form, timing, and content of the warning).
[249] Another example could be issuing a warning, if circumstances permit, to the civilian corporations that operate satellites that an attack is coming that might jeopardize their satellites, if those satellites provide essential services within the parameters discussed in para 4.
[250] US DoD Law of War Manual (n 5) para 5.11.5.2; AMW Manual Commentary (n 195) r 37 para 15.

will be easier for the enemy to know what effects the loss of satellite functionality is likely to have and on whom,[251] and to reach out to its own population.

11. Civilians who do not heed a warning will usually be subject to a heightened (factual) risk of being affected by the attack than civilians who acted in accordance with the warning. However, such civilians do not lose their protection (unless and for such time as they are directly participating in hostilities (see Rule 33: Direct Participation in Hostilities), and they remain protected from excessive incidental harm in accordance with the obligation of proportionality (see Rule 38: Proportionality in Attack). An effective advance warning therefore does not relieve the attacker from the obligation to take all other feasible precautionary measures to avoid, and in any event to minimize, incidental loss of civilian life, injury to civilians, or damage to civilian property.

---

[251] In this regard, see eg UK LOAC Manual (n 21) para 5.32.8 (foreseeing that warning may *enable the civil defence authorities to take appropriate measures*) (emphasis added).

Rule 41
Precautions Against the Effects of Attack

During and before an armed conflict, a State shall take necessary precautions, to the maximum extent feasible, to protect the civilian population, individual civilians, and civilian objects under its control against the dangers resulting from military space operations.

Overview of Legal Basis of Rule

1. This Rule is based on Article 58 of Additional Protocol I, reflecting Article 58(c) in particular.[252] The phrase 'necessary precautions' should be read as a blanket provision that includes the more specific requirements of Article 58(a) (obligation to remove civilians and civilian objects from the vicinity of military objectives) and Article 58(b) (obligation to avoid locating military objectives within or near densely populated areas), to the degree these provisions are feasible in the particular outer space context in which they are applied. This Rule reflects customary international law applicable in international armed conflicts and also reflects what increasingly appears to be customary international law that is applicable in non-international armed conflicts.[253]

Scope, Requirements, and Obligations

2. This Rule includes measures to protect civilians, the civilian population, and civilian objects (including privately owned satellites) both in the terrestrial domain and in outer space, such as satellites or future populated craft or facilities, under the control of the State.

---

[252] See Introduction to Part III, paras 9–10 (noting that the text of Additional Protocol I explicitly states in art 49(3) that this Rule is applicable to warfare on land, air, and sea, and this *Manual* interprets Additional Protocol I as also extending to military space operations, that may affect the civilian population, individual civilians, or civilian objects in any domain).

[253] See n 21 (discussing the status of precautionary measures as customary international law in international armed conflict and likely in non-international armed conflicts). In addition, with respect to the application of this Rule to non-international armed conflicts, see UNSC Res 2573 (2021) OP 2 ('2. Demands that *all parties* to armed conflicts fully comply with their obligations under international humanitarian law, including … taking all feasible precautions to protect the civilian population and civilian objects within their control against the effects of attacks.') (emphasis added).

3. The term 'to the maximum extent feasible' in this Rule is imprecisely defined in law and practice. It refers to 'those precautions that are practicable or practically possible, taking into account all circumstances ruling at the time, including humanitarian and military considerations'.[254] The particular precautionary measures (passive precautions) that are feasible are always contextually determined.[255] It can be the case that planning and preparation for passive precautions must be taken in peacetime, such as avoiding building a new military space facility in the midst of a concentration of civilian housing.[256]

4. This Rule imposes obligations on both attackers and defenders.[257] Sometimes the primary burden will be on the attacker, who is obliged to shape the attack in order to mitigate consequences; sometimes, the defender will have much more information about the civilian population and objects and more ability to control them and is thus obliged to act to mitigate harm to the civilian population (loss of civilian lives, injury to civilians, and damage to civilian objects).

5. The obligations under this Rule are triggered with respect to the 'dangers' resulting from military operations. It is generally agreed that mere inconvenience or irritation does not rise to the level of 'dangers' triggering this obligation, nor would the temporary loss of non-essential satellite services (particularly if the loss of such services is only temporary). However, the specific meaning of 'dangers' is not clear.

---

[254] See ICRC CIHL Study (n 14) Rule 22, noting that 'State practice indicates that an attacker is not prevented from attacking military objectives if the defender fails to take appropriate precautions or deliberately uses civilians to shield military operations. The attacker remains bound in all circumstances, however, to take appropriate precautions in attack … and must respect the principle of proportionality … even though the defender violates international humanitarian law' (but see Introduction to Part III, paras 11–13, noting that serious concerns have been expressed by some States about the methodology used in the ICRC CIHL Study). Importantly, several States made reservations upon ratifying or acceding to Additional Protocol I with respect to the definition of the term 'feasibility' and several States have addressed the meaning of the term 'feasibility' in their military manuals. See n 265. For further discussion of the term 'feasibility', see Introduction to Part III, paras 19–20, Rule 36: Verification, para 4, and Rule 37: Choice of Means and Methods of Attack, paras 2–3. See also ICRC CIHL Study (n 14) Rule 23 ('Each party to the conflict must, to the extent feasible, avoid locating military objectives within or near densely populated areas.') and Rule 24 ('Each party to the conflict must, to the extent feasible, remove civilian persons and objects under its control from the vicinity of military objectives.').

[255] See US DoD Law of War Manual (n 5) para. 5.3.2. Other States cite this standard for their application of the precautions requirements under art 58 of Additional Protocol I (as well as other feasible precautions language therein). See Australia, Statement on Ratification of Additional Protocol I (21 June 1991) 1642 UNTS 473; Canada, Statement on Ratification of Additional Protocol I (20 November 1990) 1591 UNTS 462, 464; Italy, Statement on Ratification of Additional Protocol I (27 February 1986) 1425 UNTS 438, 439; Netherlands, Statement on Ratification of Additional Protocol I (26 June 1987) 1477 UNTS 300. While arts 57 and 58 of Additional Protocol I generally reflect customary international law and set forth important obligations incumbent on States to limit incidental civilian harm in military operations, the ICTY has noted that 'admittedly, even these two provisions leave a wide margin of discretion to belligerents by using language that might be regarded as leaving the last word to the attacking party'. *Kupreškić* Judgment (n 21) para. 524.

[256] See eg *Commentary on Additional Protocols* (n 9) para 2244 in relation to art 58.

[257] Broadly applied, this Rule requires a belligerent to endeavour to protect, when feasible, the civilian population not only from the applicable adverse consequences of its own military actions, but also from the applicable adverse consequences of the actions of an adversary.

Although no definition of dangers is provided in Article 58 of Additional Protocol I, the loss of civilian life, injury to civilians, and damage to civilian objects is the focus of Chapter IV 'Precautionary Measures' of the Additional Protocol, particularly as reflected in Article 57.[258]

Application of Rule to Ground-Based and Space-Based Segments of Military Space Operations

6. The requirement to take passive precautions applies fully to ground-based segments of military space operations. For example, parties to a conflict must, to the extent feasible in the circumstances, refrain from placing military ground segments (such as control stations, uplink transmitters, or downlink receivers) in densely populated areas.[259] Similarly, a State must, again to the extent feasible, remove civilians from the vicinity of any immobile ground stations that are likely to qualify as military objectives based on their nature, location, purpose, or use in the conflict.[260] In other situations, a feasible precaution under this Rule would be for a State (potentially both the attacking State and the defending State) to warn the population in the vicinity of an immovable ground station of the potential threat of a strike. Note that if the facility is secret and its function is not known to the enemy or surrounding population, issuing such warning may not be feasible under the military considerations prevailing at the time.

7. The requirement to take passive precautions also applies fully to space-based segments of space operations. For example, such precautions could include, to the extent feasible in the circumstances, the physical hardening of civilian satellites or providing them with technological protection against cyber, electromagnetic, or other such dangers. States also could make protections or countermeasures for military space objects available to safeguard civilian space operations. For instance, if a State has a counter-EMP shielding that protects its military-use satellites against certain attacks, it may make such shielding available to manufacturers of civilian satellites under its control in order to protect civilian space infrastructure. Other examples of passive precautions, to the extent they are feasible in the circumstances, could include employing separate satellites to perform civilian and

---

[258] In a resolution adopted in 1970 on basic principles for the protection of civilian populations in armed conflicts, the UN General Assembly required that 'in the conduct of military operations, every effort should be made to spare civilian populations from the ravages of war and *all necessary precautions should be taken to avoid injury, loss or damage to civilian populations*'. UN General Assembly, Res 2675 (XXV) (emphasis added). The resolution was adopted by 109 votes in favour, none against, and 8 abstentions.
[259] See Additional Protocol I (n 4) art 58(b).
[260] ibid art 58(a).

military functions, separating military and civilian payloads, and frequency diversification as between military and civilian communications.[261]

8. Warnings by the States concerned (potentially both the attacking and defending State) of the possibility of an attack may be effective in the space context. A civilian operator, or government operator of a satellite that is not a military objective, may have technological means to protect civilian objects that military operations might endanger, as with the risk that space debris caused by an attack on a military space object could strike a civilian satellite. For example, a warning of potential destructive military operations could allow the operator to shift, where feasible, a civilian space object's orbit. It is important to note that feasibility is always a consideration. Altering the course of a satellite may be impractical when considering the value of the satellite to the civilian population, the likelihood of the threat, the cost of the protective action, or other humanitarian or military factors. Additionally, for a satellite constellation, reconfiguration may negate its functionality, further diminishing the practicality of such precautions.

9. In light of the unique environment of outer space, any civilians in outer space face particular risk from military operations.[262] For example, it is difficult in space to take measures to protect oneself from the effects of military operations, to flee from an area of ongoing military operations, or to evacuate civilians rapidly from the vicinity of military operations. Moreover, there are only limited medical resources in outer space, and the likelihood of death is high in the event a civilian spacecraft is incidentally damaged. Accordingly, it will be particularly important that parties to a conflict carefully consider all feasible passive precautions that may be taken. For example, removing civilians from a space station in anticipation of escalating hostilities that could extend to the space station,[263] or avoiding locating military objectives within the vicinity of these civilians,[264] may be feasible in the circumstances.

---

[261] In this regard, it has also been suggested by the ICRC that States could work towards identifying space systems serving specially protected objects like hospitals and objects indispensable to the survival of the civilian population, such as drinking water installations and supplies and irrigation networks; and although it is not required by the current space law registration regime, when registering space objects, States could also expressly indicate the civilian status of those objects exclusively dedicated to such civilian use.

[262] With respect to densely populated areas, see Additional Protocol I (n 4) art 58(b).

[263] ibid art 58(a).

[264] ibid art 58(c).

Attacking Party's Continuing Obligation to Take Feasible Precautions

10. A defending party's failure to adhere to this Rule, or the fact that certain protections are not feasible, does not absolve an attacking party from its duties to take feasible precautions in conducting attacks or to cancel or suspend attacks that would result in excessive incidental civilian harm (see generally Rules 36–40).[265] Consider an attack by State B on a satellite bus of State A that hosts two payloads. One is a military payload that contains imagery equipment used solely by the military to collect targeting intelligence. The second is a communications link for State A's civilian emergency services network, allowing for search and rescue communication for the benefit of the civilian population. Although State A could have hosted the second, purely civilian, function on a different satellite, its failure to do so does not absolve State B of its duty to take all feasible precautions in attack, or to assess the proportionality of incidental direct and indirect loss of civilian lives, injury of civilians, and damage to civilian objects and the concrete and direct military advantage anticipated. It is important to note that State B may simply not have the capability of detecting and attacking only the military payload of a satellite. A defender should, to the extent feasible, separate civilian and military components and functions on a satellite, and an attacker should, to the extent feasible, attack only the military objectives and in any event minimize the incidental loss of civilian lives, injury to civilians, and damage to civilian objects; however, under current and immediately foreseeable technology, many precautionary measures or actions may not be feasible on either side.[266]

---

[265] See reservations, statements and declarations made by States upon ratification or accession to Additional Protocol I related to the term 'feasibility' in Roberts and Guelff (n 207) (Algeria, 299; Belgium, 501; Canada, 502; Italy 507; United Kingdom, 510); see further discussion of the term 'feasibility' in Introduction to Part III, paras 19–20; Rule 37, paras 19–20; *Galić* Trial Judgment (n 35) para 61; US DoD Law of War Manual (n 5) para 2.5.5; AMW Manual Commentary (n 195) r 46.

[266] One State at State Consultations observed that '[i]n our view this takes a broadly sensible position that acknowledges the importance of feasibility in the context of military space operations'.

SECTION 4
MEANS AND METHODS OF WARFARE

Rule 42
Means and Methods of Warfare Generally

(a) Means and methods of warfare from, to, or within space are prohibited where they:
  i. are specifically prohibited under applicable treaties or customary international law; or
  ii. cannot be directed at a specific military objective as required by the law of armed conflict; or cause the effects which cannot be limited or controlled as required by the law of armed conflict; and consequently, are of a nature to strike military objectives and civilian objects without distinction.
(b) The use of means and methods of warfare, including those employed in a military space operation, which are of a nature to cause unnecessary suffering or superfluous injury is prohibited.
(c) In the study, development, acquisition, or adoption of a new weapon, means or method of warfare in military operations, including military space operations, a State that is a party to Additional Protocol I is under an obligation to determine whether its employment would, in some or all circumstances, be prohibited by Additional Protocol I or by other applicable international law.

Overview of Legal Basis of Rule

1. This Rule encompasses all weapons, weapon systems, and offensive or defensive capabilities which may be employed in military space operations. Methods or means of warfare refer to the way in which such capabilities are to be used. There is no accepted definition of what constitutes a 'space weapon'. Such a definition is particularly elusive since most objects in space possess a potential military capability, particularly any which are capable of being manoeuvred. Accordingly, this Rule applies the general rules of the law of armed conflict governing means and methods of warfare to military space operations, as well as prohibitions or limitations on specific weapon systems under relevant international agreements (such as those related to nuclear weapons and other weapons of mass destruction (WMDs)). The legal basis for subpart (a)(i) of this Rule is examined in paragraphs 3–7 with respect to WMDs and means or methods of warfare which weaponize the environment or are intended to cause widespread, long-term and severe damage to the natural

environment; the legal basis for subpart (a)(ii) of this Rule is examined in paragraph 8 with respect to indiscriminate weapons and indiscriminate attacks and in paragraph 9 with respect to the means or methods of warfare that produce effects that cannot be controlled or limited as required by international law; the legal basis for subpart (b) of this Rule is examined in paragraph 10; and the legal basis for subpart (c) of this Rule is examined in paragraph 12.

Specific Limitations or Prohibitions

2. Subpart (a) of this Rule affirms that prohibitions and limitations on certain weapons under treaty and customary international law apply in outer space, whether such weapons are used from, to, or within space against targets in a terrestrial domain, or in or to outer space against targets in outer space. Although the use in outer space of some weapons that are prohibited or restricted by treaty—for example expanding bullets[267]—is unlikely at present, Article III of the OST makes international law applicable to activities in outer space, including international treaty law governing the use of particular weapons. In general, weapons limitation treaties are not territorial and thus would apply to space.[268] As means and methods of warfare are adapted to outer space and may be employed in a manner similar to their employment in terrestrial domains, States bound by such treaty obligations or equivalent rules under customary international law must adhere to them in military space operations. Furthermore, in any armed conflict—including one in space—the right of the Parties to that conflict to choose methods or means of warfare is not unlimited.[269]

Weapons of Mass Destruction

3. There are very few specific weapons-related prohibitions or limitations that expressly apply to outer space. WMDs are an exception (see Rule 5: Weapons of Mass Destruction). Pursuant to Article IV of the OST, every State is thus prohibited from: (i) placing in orbit around the Earth any objects carrying nuclear weapons or any other kinds of weapons of mass destruction; (ii) installing nuclear

---

[267] Hague Declaration (IV, 3) on the Use of Bullets Which Expand or Flatten Easily in the Human Body (29 July 1899).
[268] For example, at some point in the future, blinding laser weapons could be effectively employed in space and the applicable convention contains no territorial terrain restrictions. 1980 Convention on Prohibitions or Restrictions on the Use of Certain Conventional Weapons which may be deemed to be Excessively Injurious or to have Indiscriminate Effects, Protocol IV on Blinding Laser Weapons, 1342 UNTS 137 (13 October 1995).
[269] Additional Protocol I (n 4) art 35(1); 1907 Hague Convention IV (n 6) art 22; *Nicaragua* case (n 48) para 77.

weapons or any other kinds of weapons of mass destruction on celestial bodies; and (iii) stationing nuclear weapons or any other kinds of weapons of mass destruction in outer space in any other manner. In addition, each party to the Treaty Banning Nuclear Weapon Tests in the Atmosphere, in Outer Space and Under Water (PNTB) is obliged to prohibit, to prevent, and not to carry out any nuclear weapon test explosion, or any other nuclear explosion, at any place under its jurisdiction and control beyond the limits of the atmosphere, including outer space.[270] Additional prohibitions and restrictions related to nuclear weapons with respect to military space activities are discussed in Rule 5: Weapons of Mass Destruction.

Environmental Considerations

Environmental considerations may act as a further limitation to the means and methods of warfare applicable to military space operations. A State that is a party to Additional Protocol I is prohibited from using means or methods of warfare in military space operations that are intended, or may be expected, to cause widespread, long-term, and severe damage to the natural environment.[271] Although there is no consensus among States, there is support for the proposition that States should apply the law of armed conflict in a military operation, including a military space operation, with a view to protect the natural environment (see Rule 43: Natural Environment, including statements by States rejecting this obligation).[272]

4.

There is currently no generally accepted definition under international law of the term 'natural environment'. There is limited support in State practice for a broad interpretation of the meaning of 'natural environment' which suggests it is likely also

5.

---

[270] Treaty Banning Nuclear Weapon Tests in the Atmosphere, in Outer Space and Under Water (entered into force 10 October 1963) 480 UNTS 43, art I(a). See also Agreement governing the Activities of States on the Moon and Other Celestial Bodies (adopted 5 December 1979, entered into force 11 July 1984) 1363 UNTS 3 (which prohibits States that are parties to that agreement from putting objects carrying WMDs into orbit around the Moon or placing or using such weapons on the Moon).

[271] Additional Protocol I (n 4) arts 35(3), 55.

[272] The International Court of Justice refrained from determining if arts 35(3) and 55 of Additional Protocol I should be considered customary international law; *Nuclear Weapons* Advisory Opinion (n 3) para 31 ('The Court notes furthermore that Articles 35, paragraph 3, and 55 of Additional Protocol 1 provide additional protection for the environment. Taken together, these provisions embody a general obligation to protect the natural environment against widespread, long-term, and severe environmental damage; the prohibition of methods and means of warfare which are intended, or may be expected, to cause such damage; and the prohibition of attacks against the natural environment by way of reprisals. These are powerful constraints for all the States having subscribed to these provisions.'). The ICRC takes the position that State practice has established these articles as a norm of customary international law applicable in both international and non-international armed conflicts. ICRC CIHL Study (n 14) Rule 45 (but see Introduction to Part III, paras 11–13, noting that serious concerns have been expressed by some States about the methodology used in the ICRC CIHL Study). It should also be noted that some States have explicitly rejected these Articles in Additional Protocol I as reflecting rules of customary international law. See eg US DoD Law of War Manual (n 5) para 6.10.3.1 ('The United States has not accepted these provisions [Additional Protocol I arts 35.3 and 55)] and has repeatedly expressed the view that these provisions are "overly broad and ambiguous" and "not a part of customary law."').

to encompass the environment of outer space (see Rule 43: Natural Environment). However, Article II of the 1977 Environmental Modification Convention (ENMOD) characterizes the word 'environment' as 'the dynamics, composition or structure of the Earth, including its biota, lithosphere, hydrosphere and atmosphere, or of outer space'.[273] This definition, of course, is limited to the parties to ENMOD and to the specific purposes of ENMOD. Parties to ENMOD are prohibited from deliberately engaging in environmental modification techniques with widespread, long-lasting, or severe effects as the means of causing destruction, damage, or injury to another party.[274] Article II of the ENMOD Convention provides that 'environmental modification techniques' include 'any technique for changing—through the deliberate manipulation of natural processes—the dynamics, composition or structure of the Earth ... *or of outer space*'. The ENMOD Convention therefore prohibits the deliberate manipulation of the environment of outer space as a weapon of war.[275]

6. The ENMOD Convention speaks of the 'environment', absent the adjective 'natural', but its scope of protection is directed at preventing 'manipulation of natural processes'.[276] As stated by the United Nations General Assembly Committee on Disarmament, the ENMOD Convention was not intended as a protection for the natural environment, per se, but rather as a prohibition against the environment itself being weaponized.[277] As such, direct manipulation of human-made objects located in outer space would not be contrary to the ENMOD Convention. Preventing an adversary's ability to utilize the electromagnetic spectrum, for instance by jamming one of its satellites, is not an example of manipulating the environment of space but merely an act preventing an adversary's ability to use natural phenomena found within it.

7. In an Annex to the ENMOD Convention, the Consultative Committee of Experts adopted 'Understandings', which are not incorporated into the Convention but provide guidance with regard to interpretation of key terms.[278] For example, 'widespread' is defined as 'encompassing an area on the scale of several hundred square kilometres'; 'long-lasting' is defined as 'lasting for a period of months, or approximately a season'; and 'severe' damage is said to require 'serious or significant disruption or harm to human life, natural and economic resources or other

---

[273] Convention on the Prohibition of Military or any Hostile Use of Environmental Modification Techniques (adopted 10 December 1976, entered into force 5 October 1978) 1108 UNTS 151 (ENMOD Convention) art II.
[274] ibid art I.
[275] During State Consultation, some States speculated that the deliberate creation of a substantial debris cloud in space that was targeted at an enemy's space object could amount to a violation of the ENMOD Convention (n 273).
[276] ibid art II.
[277] UNGA, 'Report of the Conference on the Committee on Disarmament Volume 1' (1976) UN Doc A/31/27 para 327 [perma.cc/W6AC-PHV4].
[278] ibid 91.

assets'. 'Severe' damage is said to require 'serious or significant disruption or harm to human life, natural and economic resources or other assets'.[279] The threshold of harm envisaged for the ENMOD Convention to apply is manifestly high, using the phrase 'widespread, long-lasting or severe'.[280] Note, however, that the even higher Additional Protocol I threshold of 'widespread, long term *and* severe' damage[281] is replaced with 'widespread, long term *or* severe'.[282]

Indiscriminate Weapons and Indiscriminate Attacks

8. Under subpart (a)(ii) of the Rule, attacks that employ means or methods of warfare in space that cannot be directed at a specific military objective are prohibited. Subpart (a)(ii) is based on Article 51(4)(b) and (c) of Additional Protocol I,[283] reflects customary international law,[284] and is related to the broader prohibition against indiscriminate attacks.[285] Accordingly, the International Court of Justice (ICJ) has observed that 'States must never make civilians the object of attack and must consequently never use weapons that are incapable of distinguishing between civilian and military targets'.[286] For instance, consider the case in which State A has a direct-ascent ASAT. During an armed conflict with State B, the latter party embeds malware in the ASAT control system that makes its target acquisition unreliable. Although State A discovers the malware and is unable to eliminate it or otherwise repair the guidance system, State A decides to employ the system regardless. In these circumstances, the likelihood that the ASAT will strike a military

---

[279] ibid.
[280] ENMOD Convention (n 273) art I.
[281] Additional Protocol I (n 4) arts 35(3), 55.
[282] ENMOD Convention (n 273) art I.
[283] Additional Protocol I (n 4) art 52(4)(b) (prohibiting 'indiscriminate attacks', including 'those which employ a method or means of combat which cannot be directed at a specific military objective').
[284] The ICJ has noted that the principle of distinction, which constitutes the broader obligation underlying this Rule, is one of the two cardinal principles of the law of armed conflict. *Nuclear Weapons Advisory Opinion* (n 3), para 78 (referring to distinction as one of 'the cardinal principles contained in the texts constituting the fabric of humanitarian law'. The military manuals of most States thus restate this obligation and the ICRC takes the position that State practice has established this rule is a norm of customary international law applicable in both international and non-international armed conflicts. ICRC CIHL Study (n 14) Rules 1 and 17 (but see Introduction to Part III, paras 11–13, noting that serious concerns have been expressed by some States about the methodology used in the ICRC CIHL Study).
[285] Article 51 of Additional Protocol I (n 4) prohibits 'indiscriminate attacks' which it defines as those attacks which 'are not directed at a specific military objective', and includes the means and methods prohibited in subpart (a) within this prohibition. It further provides that the following types of attacks, inter alia, are to be considered as indiscriminate: an attack by bombardment by any methods or means which treats as a single military objective a number of clearly separated and distinct military objectives located in a city, town, village or other area containing a similar concentration of civilians or civilian objects; and an attack which may be expected to cause incidental loss of civilian life, injury to civilians, damage to civilian objects, or a combination thereof, which would be excessive in relation to the concrete and direct military advantage anticipated.' See Rule 38: Proportionality in Attack.
[286] ibid.

satellite is accordingly reduced. The use of the system would be indiscriminate and thus prohibited on the basis of subpart (a)(ii).

9. Subpart (b) of the Rule prohibits those means or methods of warfare that produce effects that cannot be controlled or limited as required by international law. This subpart of the Rule is based on Article 52 of Additional Protocol I, which prohibits indiscriminate attacks including 'those which employ a method or means of combat the effects of which cannot be limited as required by this Protocol ... and are of a nature to strike military objectives and civilians or civilian objects without distinction'.[287] It further reflects customary international law.[288] A weapon is indiscriminate when the effects thereof are expected to spread uncontrollably and cause damage to protected space objects, persons in outer space, or persons or objects on Earth.[289] For instance, if the operator of an electromagnetic pulse weapon,[290] deployed in space to attack a specific target, cannot limit or control its widespread and damaging effects so as to avoid or minimize harm to persons or objects protected by the law of armed conflict, it would be considered as indiscriminate.

Unnecessary Suffering of Combatants

10. Subpart (b) of this Rule is based on Article 23(e) of the 1899 Hague Regulations and Article 35(2) of Additional Protocol I stating that '[i]t is prohibited to employ weapons, projectiles and material and methods of warfare of a nature to cause superfluous injury or unnecessary suffering'.[291] This subpart of the Rule reflects customary international law—the ICJ has noted that it is based on one of the 'cardinal principles contained in the texts constituting the fabric of humanitarian law', that it is 'prohibited to cause unnecessary suffering to combatants: it is accordingly

---

[287] Additional Protocol I (n 4) art 52 (4)(b).
[288] ICRC CIHL Study (n 14) Rule 71 ('State practice establishes this rule as a norm of customary international law applicable in both international and non-international armed conflicts. Weapons that are by nature indiscriminate are those that cannot be directed at a military objective or whose effects cannot be limited as required by international humanitarian law.'). The ICRC notes that this Rule is found in the military manuals of numerous States, including Australia, Belgium, Canada, Colombia, Ecuador, France, Germany, Israel, Republic of Korea, New Zealand, Nigeria, Russian Federation, Sweden, Switzerland, United States, and Yugoslavia.
[289] With respect to attacks on military objectives in space that are expected to generate hazardous debris fields, see discussion in Rule 38: Proportionality in Attack.
[290] A High Altitude EMP is 'a near-instantaneous electromagnetic energy field that is produced in the atmosphere by the power and radiation of a nuclear explosion, and that is damaging to electronic equipment over a very wide area, depending on power of the nuclear device and altitude of the burst'. See Clay Wilson, 'High Altitude Electromagnetic Pulse (HEMP) and High Power Microwave (HPM) Devices: Threat Assessments' (Prepared for Members and Committees of US Congress, CRS 2008) [perma.cc/DXU3-ZRLE].
[291] When articulating the prohibition, some States find the term 'calculated', which originates in the English version of the 1907 Hague Convention IV (n 6) as more appropriate than the term 'of a nature'. See eg US DoD Law of War Manual (n 5) para 6.6.1; Australian LOAC Manual (n 31) para 13.29 (prohibiting the use of 'arms, projectiles or material calculated to cause unnecessary suffering').

prohibited to use weapons causing them such harm or uselessly aggravating their suffering'.²⁹² In addition, the Rome Statute of the International Criminal Court lists as a war crime '[e]mploying weapons, projectiles and material and methods of warfare which are of a nature to cause superfluous injury or unnecessary suffering or which are inherently indiscriminate in violation of the international law of armed conflict'.²⁹³

11. The terms 'superfluous injury' and 'unnecessary suffering' are not defined in Additional Protocol I, but the ICJ has referred to it as 'a harm greater than that unavoidable to achieve legitimate military objectives'.²⁹⁴ The military manuals of several States contain similar definitions.²⁹⁵ As such, 'superfluous injury' or 'unnecessary suffering' may be considered those which—in type, intensity, or severity—go beyond what is necessary to render an adversary '*hors de combat*'. The prohibition applies only to injury or suffering caused to combatants.

Legal Review of Weapons and Means and Methods of Warfare

12. In the study, development, acquisition, or adoption of a new weapon, means, or method of warfare, subpart (c) of this Rule reflects the application in the outer space context of the express obligation under Additional Protocol I to determine whether the employment of a new weapon, means, or method of warfare would, in some or all circumstances, be prohibited by Additional Protocol I or by an applicable rule of international law before it is employed.²⁹⁶ Although there is support for the proposition that this subpart of the Rule reflects customary international law, there is a lack of definitive State practice and official expressions of *opinio*

---

[292] *Nuclear Weapons* Advisory Opinion (n 3) para 78. It is not clear whether this Rule applies to non-international armed conflicts, although the ICRC notes that '[p]ractice is in conformity with the rule's applicability in both international and non-international conflicts, as States generally do not have a different set of military weapons for international and non-international armed conflicts'. ICRC IHL Customary International Law Database, Rule 70. The ICTY has also observed that 'elementary considerations of humanity and common sense make it preposterous that the use by States of weapons prohibited in armed conflicts between themselves be allowed when States try to put down rebellion by their own nationals on their own territory. What is inhumane, and consequently proscribed, in international wars, cannot but be inhumane and inadmissible in civil strife.' *Tadić* decision (n 31) para 119.

[293] Rome Statute of the International Criminal Court (n 57) art 8(2)(b)(xx).

[294] *Nuclear Weapons* Advisory Opinion (n 3) para 78.

[295] See eg Australia, which considers avoiding suffering to involve 'averting the infliction of suffering, injury or destruction not actually necessary for the accomplishment of legitimate military objectives'. Australian LOAC Manual (n 31) para 2.7; for Germany suffering is unnecessary when 'the expected impairment does not serve any military purpose or if injuries or suffering are caused by the effects of weapons or projectiles that are not necessary to neutralise the adversary forces'. German LOAC Manual (n 21) para 402. Peru similarly states unnecessary suffering results from any violence not indispensable for gaining an advantage over the enemy. Centro del Derecho Internacional Humanitario y Derechos Humanos de las Fuerzas Armadas, 'Manual para las Fuerzas Armadas: Derechos Humanos, Derecho Internacional Humanitario' (Ministerio de Defensa 2010) para 28(a)(1).

[296] Additional Protocol I (n 4) art 36.

juris.[297] The practice of certain States that are not party to Additional Protocol I, such as the United States and Israel, in regularly conducting weapons reviews prior to fielding any weapons, is also important to note.[298] States are not obliged to reveal the contents of their weapons reviews unless required to do so by an applicable international agreement.

13. The determination of legality required of States under this subpart of the Rule is not binding internationally (in the sense any particular State's internal assessment that a particular weapon is legal is not conclusive for other States or international courts, who would eventually reach their own assessments).[299] A State must determine the legality of the 'normal or expected use' of a weapon, means or method of warfare, though it is not required 'to foresee or analyse all possible misuses of a weapon, for almost any weapon can be misused in ways that would be prohibited'.[300]

14. Based on the language of Article 36 of Additional Protocol I, this subpart of the Rule does not restrict, nor does it exclude, its application to any particular domain, and thus encompasses weapons to be used in military space operations.[301] The practical effect of this subpart of the Rule is that it would encompass all weapons, means, and methods of warfare regardless of the conflict in which they were employed.

---

[297] The military manuals of numerous States contain this Rule. New Zealand LOAC Manual (n 25) para 7.4.1; Danish LOAC Manual (n 28) 379–80; Spanish Law of Armed Conflict Manual (n 100) para 3.2.e.(1). The ICRC also takes the position that this Rule is a norm of customary international law applicable in both international and non-international armed conflicts. ICRC, 'A Guide to the Legal Review of New Weapons, Means and Methods of Warfare—Measures to Implement Article 36 of Additional Protocol I of 1977' (ICRC 2020).

[298] See US DoD Law of War Manual (n 5) para 6.2.3, 'AP I Requirement for Legal Review of a New Weapon, Means, or Method of Warfare' para 19.20.1.2 (noting that 'the DoD policy and practice of conducting weapons reviews preceded this provision of AP I'); Israeli Gaza Report (n 107) para 339.

[299] *Commentary on the Additional Protocols* (n 9) para 1469.

[300] ibid.

[301] The *Commentary on the Additional Protocols* also specifically notes with respect to art 36 that 'space war' is a matter of concern in relation to 'future arms'. ibid para 1476.

Rule 43
Natural Environment

(a) A State that is a party to Additional Protocol I is prohibited from using means or methods of warfare in a military operation, including a military space operation, that are intended, or may be expected, to cause widespread, long-term and severe damage to the natural environment.

(b) Although there is no consensus among States, there is support for the proposition that States should apply the law of armed conflict in a military operation, including a military space operation, with a view to protecting the natural environment.

Overview of Legal Basis of Rule

1. This Rule deals with protection of the natural environment during armed conflict. Subpart (a) of this Rule applies to States that are parties to Additional Protocol I and is based on Article 35(3)[302] and, to a lesser extent, Article 55[303] therein. There are divergent views among States as to whether this Rule reflects customary international law as certain States are on record as expressly denying that these Articles represent customary international law.[304] In light of this divergence of

---

[302] Article 35(3) of Additional Protocol I provides that '[i]t is prohibited to employ methods or means of warfare which are intended, or may be expected, to cause widespread, long-term and severe damage to the natural environment'. See Introduction to Part III, paras 9–10 (noting that the text of Additional Protocol I explicitly states in art 49(3) that, to the extent this Rule is based on art 55, it is applicable to warfare on land, air, and sea, and this *Manual* interprets Additional Protocol I as also extending to military space operations, that may affect the civilian population, individual civilians, or civilian objects in any domain). However, in this regard, the status of the natural environment generally as a 'civilian object' is subject to debate. See following discussion.

[303] Article 55 of Additional Protocol I provides that '[c]are shall be taken in warfare to protect the natural environment against widespread, long-term and severe damage. This protection includes a prohibition of the use of methods and means of warfare which are intended or may be expected to cause such damage to the natural environment and thereby to prejudice the health or survival of the population'.

[304] See ICRC 'Guidelines on the Protection of the Natural Environment in Armed Conflict' (2020) para 48 (regarding the rule that '[t]he use of methods or means of warfare that are intended, or may be expected, to cause widespread, long term and severe damage to the natural environment is prohibited', the ICRC states that '[i]t should be noted that there is a certain amount of practice contrary to this rule and there are diverging views on its customary nature'). This practice includes the United States, France, and the United Kingdom (the latter two States disputing the application of the rule to the use of nuclear weapons). See US DoD Law of War Manual (n 5) para 6.10.3.1 ('The United States has not accepted these provisions and has repeatedly expressed the view that these provisions are "overly broad and ambiguous" and "not a part of customary law."'); United Kingdom, LOAC Manual; United Kingdom, Reservations and declarations made upon ratification of Additional Protocol I (1979) 432,

views, subpart (a) of this Rule is drafted to apply only to States that are parties to Additional Protocol I.[305] However, the ICRC argues that the obligation stated in subpart (a) represents customary international law in both international and non-international armed conflicts[306] and that States like the United States, France, and the United Kingdom that reject this position should be characterized as persistent dissenters.[307]

2. There is currently no generally accepted definition under international law of the term 'natural environment' and there are also questions as to whether this Rule extends to military space operations that affect the environment of outer space[308] or is limited to military space operations that affect the terrestrial environment.

699. ('the UK "understands both of these provisions to cover the employment of methods and means of warfare and that the risk of environmental damage falling within the scope of these provisions arising from the employment of methods and means of warfare is to be assessed objectively on the basis of the information available at the time"'); France, 'Statement on Ratification of AP I', translated in Schindler and Toman(eds) (n 19) 801. The ICRC thus notes that '[s]ome view that, because of the objection of specially affected States, it has not emerged as a rule of customary international law in general and/or with regard to the use of nuclear weapons'). ICRC 'Guidelines on the Protection of the Natural Environment in Armed Conflict' (2020), para 48 (but note that the ICRC further observes that there are ongoing debates regarding 'the notion of "specially affected States"').

[305] States that are not parties to Additional Protocol I remain obliged to respect and protect the natural environment in accordance with applicable international law. In this regard, the ILC has proposed the following principle with respect to the general protection of the natural environment during armed conflict: '1. The natural environment shall be respected and protected in accordance with applicable international law and, in particular, the law of armed conflict. 2. Care shall be taken to protect the natural environment against widespread, long-term and severe damage. 3. No part of the natural environment may be attacked, unless it has become a military objective.' ILC, Draft Principles on the Protection of the Environment in Relation to Armed Conflicts (20 May 2022) UN Doc A/CN.4/L.968, Principle 13. According to the ILC, 'the term "care shall be taken" should be interpreted as indicating that there is a duty on the parties to an armed conflict *to be vigilant of the potential impact* that military activities can have on the natural environment.' ibid Principle 13, Commentary (6) (emphasis added).

[306] See ICRC CIHL Study (n 14) Rule 45 (but see Introduction to *Manual*, paras 11–13, noting that serious concerns have been expressed by some States about the methodology used in the ICRC CIHL Study); see also Principle 13 of the ILC's Draft Principles on the Protection of the Environment in Relation to Armed Conflict (n 305) ('1. The natural environment shall be respected and protected in accordance with applicable international law and, in particular, the law of armed conflict. 2. Care shall be taken to protect the natural environment against widespread, long-term and severe damage. 3. No part of the natural environment may be attacked, unless it has become a military objective.'); but see n 323 regarding concerns expressed by some States regarding the application of ILC Draft Principles to this Rule. Note that the ICJ refrained from determining if arts 35(3) and 55 of Additional Protocol I should be considered customary international law, although it stated that 'Articles 35, paragraph 3, and 55 of Additional Protocol 1 provide additional protection for the environment. Taken together, these provisions embody a general obligation to protect the natural environment against widespread, long-term, and severe environmental damage; the prohibition of methods and means of warfare which are intended, or may be expected, to cause such damage; and the prohibition of attacks against the natural environment by way of reprisals. These are powerful constraints for all the States having subscribed to these provisions.' *Nuclear Weapons* Advisory Opinion (n 3) para 31.

[307] ICRC Guidelines on the Protection of the Natural Environment in Armed Conflict (n 304) para 48 ('It appears that the United States is a "persistent objector" to the customary rule and France, the United Kingdom and the United States are persistent objectors with regard to the application of the customary rule to the use of nuclear weapons.').

[308] Of course, to the extent rules of international law regarding the environment are part of international law, it is applicable to the exploration and use of outer space under Article III of the OST.

There is, however, State practice indicating concern for environmental protection in outer space and describing space activities that lead to negative environmental effects in space or on Earth as actions that should be considered at least 'irresponsible' (but not necessarily unlawful) behaviour.[309]

'Environment' Under the 1977 Environmental Modification Convention

3. Turning to international agreements, Article II of the 1977 Environmental Modification Convention (ENMOD) expressly characterizes the word 'environment' as 'the dynamics, composition or structure of the Earth, including its biota, lithosphere, hydrosphere and atmosphere, *or of outer space*'[310] (see Rule 42: Means and Methods of Warfare Generally, paragraphs 5–7). This definition, of course, is limited to the States Party to ENMOD and to the specific purposes of ENMOD, which is focused on environmental modification as a particular means or method of warfare (discussed more generally in Rule 43: Natural Environment). Another multilateral international agreement that takes a broad view of the environment as extending to space, at least in terms of space containing 'limited natural resources', is the Constitution of the International Telecommunication Union.[311] Based on the above, it is possible to conclude that the law of armed conflict that protects the natural environment applies to the environment of outer space. This Rule proceeds on the basis that, at the least, it applies to military space operations with terrestrial effects on the natural environment, and is likely also to apply to the environment of outer space. The ICRC understands the 'natural environment' to constitute the natural world together with the system of inextricable interrelations between living

---

[309] On 16 December 2020, the UNGA adopted Resolution 75/36 that encourages Members States to submit their views on 'existing and potential threats and security risks to space systems' and on behaviours they would characterize as irresponsible or threatening (but not illegal). UNGA Res 75/36 (2021) UN Doc A/76/77. Written submissions were submitted by several States expressly addressed environmental concerns in outer space, including submissions by Italy, Finland, Germany, and New Zealand. For example, Italy stated that physical damage to a satellite could affect both the space service and the environment and dedicated a paragraph to 'the effects on the environment', which states that 'any space activity that leads to negative environmental effects in space on Earth should be considered at least irresponsible'. 'IT contribution to the report of the UN Secretary-General following Resolution 75/36 on "Reducing space threats through responsible behaviours"' (2021) [perma.cc/6GU9-NZ6P]. In reiterating this point in the latter part of the written submission, Italy mentions 'underestimation of the impacts of new programme launches on the space environment' as a criterion of irresponsible behaviours. ibid.

[310] ENMOD Convention (n 273) art II.

[311] Article 44(2) of the Constitution of the International Telecommunication Union 1992 (to which there are over 190 State Parties) refers to radio frequencies and any associated orbits as 'limited natural resources', which are managed by the processes of the ITU in order that they may be used as economically and efficiently as possible. Constitution and Convention of the International Telecommunication Union (adopted 22 December 1992, entered into force 1 July 1994) 1825 UNTS 3.

organisms and their inanimate environment,[312] in the widest sense possible, and this includes outer space as part of the natural world.

Obligations and Reservations Under Additional Protocol I

4. The Rule prohibits military space activities that are intended or may be expected to cause 'widespread, long-term and severe' damage to the natural environment. Articles 35(3) and 55 of Additional Protocol I do not explain what is meant by 'widespread, long-term and severe'. Hence, there is no quantum of duration, scope, or intensity suggested in the treaty text as an indicator.[313] At a minimum, these provisions were meant to exclude ordinary damage to the environment as a side effect of battle (such as damage to the Earth via the formation of craters as a result of bombing a lawful target).[314] Indeed, the fact that the test in Articles 35(3) and 55 is cumulative ('widespread, long term *and* severe') indicates the threshold for the test to be met is high[315] and some States viewed the phrase 'long-term' as meaning measured in decades.[316] However, the application of the concept of 'normal combat damage' in space has not yet been addressed by States and may call for a closer examination of unique environmental issues in space. For example, cratering on the Moon is likely to constitute 'normal' combat damage in

---

[312] See ICRC Guidelines on the Protection of the Natural Environment in Armed Conflict (n 304) para 16.

[313] The ICRC suggests the term 'widespread' should be understood as referring to damage extending to 'several hundred square kilometres'; 'long-term' should cover damage somewhere between the range of that not considered to be short term or temporary, such as artillery bombardment, and that with impacts in the range of years (possibly a scale of 10–30 years), subject to a variety of factors (including the ability of certain substances to persist in particular natural environments); and the term 'severe' should be understood to cover the disruption or damage to an ecosystem or harm to the health or survival of the population on a large scale, with normal damage caused by troop movements and artillery fire in conventional warfare generally falling outside the scope of this prohibition. See ICRC Guidelines on the Protection of the Natural Environment in Armed Conflict (n 304) paras 35–40 and 50–72. It should be noted, however, that the definition of these terms has been founded to date on experiences in terrestrial environments and has not yet been applied to the complex space environment.

[314] 'Official Records of the Diplomatic Conference on the Reaffirmation and Development of International Law Applicable to Armed Conflicts, vol XV' (Federal Political Department, Bern 1978) 269; German LOAC Manual (n 21) para 435 (referring to art 35: 'Such damage to the natural environment significantly exceeds normal combat damage.').

[315] Danish LOAC Manual (n 28) 424 ('The requirement that all conditions must be met results in the establishment of a very high threshold of violation. Such a threshold does not automatically mean, however, that acts falling below the threshold are permitted. For example, an act may be in violation of the rules on proportionality.').

[316] Official Records of the Diplomatic Conference on the Reaffirmation and Development of International Humanitarian Law Applicable in Armed Conflicts—Geneva (1974–1977)—Volume XV (Federal Political Department 1978) 268–69. It is important to note that the three criteria in the ENMOD Convention are separated by the word 'or' not 'and', and that the criterion 'long-lasting' is defined in the 'Understandings' found in the Annex to the Convention as 'lasting for a period of months, or approximately a season'. UNGA, 'Report of the Conference on the Committee on Disarmament Volume 1' (1976) UN Doc A/31/27, 91 [perma.cc/W6AC-PHV4]; see Rule 42: Means and Methods of Warfare Generally.

most cases. On the other hand, the generation of very large clouds of orbital debris could be 'long term' and potentially 'severe' (although since the threshold is high and cumulative, the damage must also be 'widespread'). An example of a military space operation that could reach the high threshold required by this Rule would be the intentional deorbiting of a nuclear-powered satellite that spreads high levels of radioactive fallout over an area (whether that area is populated or unpopulated).[317]

5. Some States that are parties to Additional Protocol I have submitted reservations, declarations, understandings, or interpretive statements to the effect that Protocol I does not govern or apply to the use of nuclear weapons or nuclear weapons generally.[318] Furthermore, the ICJ determined in the *Nuclear Weapons* Advisory Opinion that it did not consider that environmental treaties cited by States in that case 'could have intended to deprive a State of the exercise of its right of self-defence under international law because of its obligations to protect the environment'.[319] A State that is a party to Additional Protocol I (and has not submitted a relevant reservation) would be in violation of subpart (a) if it used nuclear weapons and inflicted widespread, long-term and severe damage to the natural environment, even if the state had otherwise appropriately complied with the rules regarding proportionality and precautions in attack.

Application of the Law of Armed Conflict with a View to Protect the Natural Environment

6. Outside the prohibitions contained in Additional Protocol I, the specific environmental considerations that must be taken into account by States in an armed conflict are not uniform. This lack of uniformity underlies the wording of subpart (b) of this Rule. The International Court of Justice has noted that 'States must take environmental considerations into account when assessing what is necessary and proportionate in the pursuit of legitimate military objectives'.[320] However, some

---

[317] While 'severe' in the context of art 55(1) is understood to refer primarily to damage prejudicing the health or survival of the population, art 35(2) is understood to address ecological rather than only human concerns. In this regard, the travaux préparatoires of Additional Protocol I gives an example of environmental harm that meets the required threshold of harm that is an unpopulated area. See 'Report to the Third Committee on the Work of the Working Group' (Official Records of the Diplomatic Conference of Geneva of 1974–1977, vol XV, April 1975) CDDH/III/275, 360.

[318] With regard to nuclear weapons, a number of States that are parties to Additional Protocol I made declarations, reservations or statements regarding the non-applicability of Additional Protocol I to nuclear weapons. See Roberts and Guelff (n 207) (Interpretive Declaration by Belgium, p. 501; Statement of Understanding by Canada, p. 502; Declaration by Germany, p. 504; Declaration/Reservation by Ireland, p. 506; Declaration by the Netherlands, p. 508; Interpretive Declaration by Spain, p. 509; Understanding by the United Kingdom, p. 510, and; Understanding by the United States (as non-State Party but Signatory), p. 12. The Rule would not apply to the use of nuclear weapons per se, whether terrestrially or in outer space.

[319] *Nuclear Weapons* Advisory Opinion (n 3) para 30. The ICJ more broadly observed that it could not 'reach a definitive conclusion as to the legality or illegality of the use of nuclear weapons by a State in an extreme circumstance of self-defence, in which its very survival would be at stake') ibid para 96.

[320] ibid para 30.

States have argued that this statement was not intended by the ICJ to apply outside the *jus ad bellum* context.[321] With respect to environmental considerations in the *jus in bello*, the International Law Commission (ILC) has stated that '[t]he natural environment shall be respected and protected in accordance with applicable international law and, in particular, the law of armed conflict', and that 'no part of the natural environment may be attacked, unless it has become a military objective.'[322] The ICRC argues that '[i]t is generally recognized today that, by default, the natural environment is civilian in character'[323] and that this recognition is not only reflected (implicitly) in the ILC's work on the protection of the environment in relation to armed conflicts but also in State practice[324] and other important practice and scholarly work.[325] On the other hand, as noted in paragraph 7, some States are on record as strongly criticizing this approach and this criticism was also reflected in comments by some States at State Consultations.

---

[321] See eg United States of America, 'Comments of the United States on the International Law Commission's draft principles on the protection of the environment in relation to armed conflicts' (submitted to 73rd Session of the International Law Commission, 2021) [https://perma.cc/TYZ4-LJ9D] ('US Comments on ILC Draft Principles') 17 ('As an initial matter, it is unclear from that opinion whether the ICJ intended its statement as one of jus in bello or jus ad bellum ... More broadly, it is clear from the ICJ's opinion that the court was merely making an observation about the ways that existing international law protects the environment.'); Israel, 'Comments from the State of Israel on the International Law Commission's Draft Principles on the Protection of the Environment in Relation to Armed Conflicts as adopted by the Commission in 2019 on first reading' (Submitted to 73rd Session of the International Law Commission, 2021) [https://perma.cc/S8YH-U8DV] ('Israel Comments on ILC Draft Articles') para 90 ('As is apparent from the reference to the relationship between the right of self-defence and environmental obligations, the ICJ's passage is concerned with necessity and proportionality under the jus ad bellum ... the Court's statement in paragraph 30 of the *Nuclear Weapons* advisory opinion, clearly refers to the concepts of necessity and proportionality under the jus ad bellum, and not in the context of LOAC....').

[322] See ILC, Draft principles on protection of the environment in relation to armed conflicts (2022) UN Doc A/77/10, Principle 14.

[323] ICRC Guidelines on the Protection of the Natural Environment in Armed Conflict (n 304) para 18. The ICRC further notes that although Article 55 of Additional Protocol I does not specifically designate all parts of the natural as civilian objects, this provision falls under Part IV, Section I, Chapter III of the Protocol, entitled 'Civilian objects'. ibid para 18. One State at State Consultations strongly contested this view, arguing that States apply the law of armed conflict with respect to each specific element of the environment rather than with respect to the environment in its totality. This State noted that 'overwhelming State practice indicates that in particular cases, a military would not consider a pit of sand, a group of trees, etc. to be "civilian objects" which are relevant to the distinction, precautions, and proportionality analyses. Instead of making an evaluation of an attack on the environment as a whole, a State typically evaluates a particular element of the natural environment to determine whether it is military objective (when it makes an effective contribution to military action) or a civilian object (when it is used or relied upon by civilians for their health or survival).'

[324] See ibid para 18, n 33, noting that numerous states (including Denmark, Finland, Iceland, Norway, Sweden, Italy, Mexico, New Zealand, and Switzerland) expressed support for the ILC's proposed approach according to which 'no part of the [natural] environment may be attacked unless it has become a military objective'. A few States expressed a less expansive view of the protection to be accorded to the environment. For example, the United States stated that 'parts of the natural environment cannot be made the object of attack unless they constitute military objectives'. Only Peru explicitly indicated that the principles of distinction, proportionality, and precautions apply to the natural environment.

[325] ibid para 30, n 35.

While there may be a broadly shared understanding that international law relating to the protection of the environment 'must be taken into account in situations of armed conflict,' the ICRC has also noted that 'determining the extent to which international environmental law applies in parallel to IHL is a more complex question'.[326] This complexity may be particularly apparent with respect to the application of the principle of proportionality in the context of environmental concerns, both on Earth and in space. Although many States agree that the natural environment should not be intentionally targeted and attacked unless it becomes a military objective—and that attacks on the natural environment that are conducted without military necessity and in a wanton[327] or arbitrary[328] are clearly prohibited—this does not directly address the manner in which environmental considerations should be taken into account by a State applying proportionality calculations in attacking military objectives. While the ICRC argues that all parts or elements of the natural environment are civilian objects, unless some become military objectives' and that 'its various parts are, therefore, protected as such by the general rules of IHL protecting civilian objects',[329] State views diverge on precisely how environmental considerations factor into this proportionality analysis and some States reject the formal inclusion of environmental considerations in proportionality calculations.[330]

7.

---

[326] ICRC Guidelines on the Protection of the Natural Environment in Armed Conflict (n 304) para 30.

[327] UK LOAC Manual (n 21) para 12.24 ('Damage to or destruction of the natural environment not justified by military necessity and carried out wantonly is prohibited.'); US Department of the Army and the US Marine Corps Training and Education Command, 'The Commander's Handbook on the Law of Land Warfare' (FM 6-27/MCTP 11-10C, August 2019) para 2-135 ('Wanton destruction of the environment is prohibited.'); San Remo Manual (n 185) Rule 44 ('Methods and means of warfare should be employed with due regard for the natural environment taking into account the relevant rules of international law. Damage to or destruction of the natural environment not justified by military necessity and carried out wantonly is prohibited.').

[328] German Navy, 'Commander's Handbook: Legal Bases for the Operations of Naval Forces' (Wolff Heinstschel von Heinegg tr, German Navy 2002) para 312 ('any damage to or destruction of the natural environment which does not have a military advantage and is carried out arbitrarily is prohibited').

[329] See eg Israel Comments on ILC Draft Articles (n 321) paras 15 and 17, stating that 'Israel's position that the protection of the natural environment under customary LOAC is anthropocentric in nature, in the sense that under customary international law, an element of the natural environment constitutes a civilian object only when it is used or relied upon by civilians for their health or survival ... Importantly, the anthropocentric approach finds ample support in State practice. Thus, States generally do not treat elements of the natural environment that are not used or relied upon by civilians for their health or survival as they would treat civilian objects. For example, Israel is unaware of any State which, upon attacking a military base in a remote area, would consider expected damage to surrounding bushes, rocks or soil as damage to civilian objects that ought to be incorporated in the proportionality assessment relating to the attack.'

[330] See eg US Department of the Navy, *The Commander's Handbook on the Law of Naval Operations* (August 2017 edn, US Office of the Chief of Naval Operations 2007) (US Commander's Handbook of Naval Operations) para 8.4 (stating that 'a commander should consider the environmental damage that will result from an attack on a legitimate military objective as one of the factors during targeting analysis' and thus states a US formulation that does not explicitly invoke the proportionality principle but may implicitly rely upon similar balancing). Some States also explicitly do not support the classification of the natural environment as civilian in nature. See eg statements by El Salvador and Croatia before the Sixth Committee of the UN General Assembly in ICRC guidelines. ICRC Guidelines on the Protection of the Natural Environment in Armed Conflict (n 304) para 18, fn 33.

Rule 44
Prohibition of Perfidy

In the conduct of military operations during an armed conflict, including military space operations, it is prohibited to kill or injure an adversary by resort to perfidy. Acts inviting the confidence of the adversary to believe that they are entitled to, or are obliged to accord, protection under the rules of the law of armed conflict, with the intent to betray that confidence, constitute perfidy. However, ruses of war are not prohibited.

Overview of Legal Basis of Rule

1. The prohibition of perfidy is a long-established rule of customary international law regulating the conduct of hostilities in international armed conflicts and non-international armed conflicts.[331]

2. Perfidy is prohibited under Article 37(1) of Additional Protocol I in the following terms: 'It is prohibited to kill, injure or capture an adversary by resort to perfidy'. There is significant disagreement about whether the prohibition of perfidy under customary international law is limited to acts that result in the killing or injuring of an adversary[332] and thus the Rule does not include capture.

---

[331] The prohibition of perfidy, which is set forth in art 37(1) of Additional Protocol I, is also found in a large number of military manuals and was already widely recognized by States when it was codified in the art 23(b) of the Hague Regulations in 1907. The ICRC thus takes the position that State practice has established this rule as a norm of customary international law applicable in both international and non-international conflicts ICRC CIHL Study (n 14) Rule 65 (but see Introduction to Part III, paras 11–13, noting that serious concerns have been expressed by some States about the methodology used in the ICRC CIHL Study).

[332] For example, the ICRC takes the position that capture is included in the definition of perfidy (see Customary IHL Study (n 14) Rule 65), while neither the Hague Regulations nor the Statute of the ICC mention capture in their definitions of perfidious conduct. Hague Convention IV (n 6) art 23(b); Rome Statute of the International Criminal Court (n 57) arts 8(2)(b)(xi) and 8(2)(e)(ix). US perspectives on this issue have varied—see eg US DoD Law of War Manual (n 5) p 320 para 5.22.2.1, which states that 'resort to perfidy' to capture is not prohibited as a matter of customary international law, cf 2017 US Commander's Handbook of Naval Operations (n 330) which states the opposite view—see p 12-3 para 12.7: 'it is also prohibited to kill, injure or capture an adversary by feigning civilian or noncombatant status'; note also New Zealand regards perfidy as including capture in non-international armed conflict (New Zealand LOAC Manual (n 25) p 8-28, fn 94) and; as noted, Denmark regards perfidy as including capture as part of customary international law in an international armed conflict, but not in non-international armed conflicts (Danish LOAC Manual (n 28) 395–96).

Perfidy Distinguished from Ruses

Perfidy must be distinguished from ruses, which are lawful under the law of armed conflict.[333] Ruses, like perfidy, are also intended to mislead an adversary or to induce them to act recklessly. However, ruses do not invite the confidence of an adversary with respect to protection under the law of armed conflict with an intent to betray that confidence and therefore are not prohibited so long as they infringe no other rule under the law of armed conflict. Article 37(2) of Additional Protocol I provides examples of legitimate ruses which include the use of camouflage, decoys, mock operations, and misinformation.

In the context of military space operations, permissible ruses may include using satellites made of radar-absorbent material in order to make them harder to detect and track by the enemy; launching dummy satellites and pretending these have an active military function; transmitting deceptive satellite signals with a view to those signals being intercepted by the enemy; or pretending to communicate with space objects which do not exist in reality. The central requirement is that the conduct in question does not rely upon a protected legal status with an intent to betray such confidence relied upon or to a violation of any other rule of the law of armed conflict.

Summary: Four Elements or Requirements of Perfidy

Perfidy has four elements or requirements. The first is that the conduct in question must relate to a protection enjoyed by a particular person, object, or activity that is specifically provided for in the law of armed conflict. Relevant examples include the protection available to civilians, medical personnel, UN personnel, and those who have surrendered or who are otherwise *hors de combat*. The Rule also covers protections accorded to objects, including medical facilities, and, to some extent, civilian objects.[334] Protection owed on the basis of a norm of a different body of

---

[333] 2017 US Commander's Handbook of Naval Operations (n 330) s 12.1.1; UK LOAC Manual (n 21) paras 5.17 and 15.12; German LOAC Manual (n 21) para 471; AMW Manual Commentary (n 195) r 113; *NIAC Manual* (n 68) para 2.3.6; ICRC CIHL Study (n 14) Rule 57.

[334] It should be noted that there is considerable ambiguity associated with perfidy when military forces make use of civilian objects. On the one hand, the misuse of medical facilities and related infrastructure can clearly constitute perfidy. On the other hand, the lawfulness of ruses, ambushes, camouflage, and decoys may in some battlefield settings (especially urban ones) involve the legitimate use by military forces of civilian objects such as buildings and other structures. For example, there is a long history of states camouflaging military bases and other military facilities (including production centres and aircraft assembly plants) as farms or even small towns with houses, streets, and trees. See Kevin Jon Heller, 'Disguising a Military Object as a Civilian Object: Prohibited Perfidy or Permissible Ruse of War?' (2015) 91 International Law Studies 517, 522–25 (further observing that 'although soldiers can ambush the adversary by hiding inside a burned-out school bus or behind a hedgerow, they cannot ambush the adversary by dressing as civilians and hiding within a civilian population ... States simply refuse to equate feigning civilian status with feigning civilian-object status.').

law (including domestic law) or a moral obligation does not suffice to meet this requirement.[335]

6. Second, perfidy requires that there be an act inviting the confidence of the adversary to lead them to believe that they are entitled to, or are obliged to accord, protection under the law of armed conflict. A simple failure to distinguish oneself as a combatant is not perfidy, although it may carry certain negative consequences, including the loss of entitlement to prisoner of war (POW) status and the possibility of criminal prosecution for participation in hostilities under domestic law. Moreover, there is no general obligation under the law of armed conflict to prospectively mark military assets as such and there are significant practical and legal obstacles to the conventional use of markings in space (see Rule 45: Improper Use of Markings). Thus, in the space context, the failure to specify a military function of a space object in spite of its intended military use does not satisfy this criterion. Indeed, many military space objects are not explicitly registered as military and there are many ambiguous statements regarding the purpose and function of satellites in the UN Register of Objects Launched into Space (see Rule 8: Registration of Space Objects). However, it is possible that explicitly indicating an exclusively civilian function or a protected status when registering a military satellite could meet this criterion.

7. Third, to come within the scope of the prohibition, the perpetrator of the perfidious act must intentionally betray the confidence of the adversary.

8. Fourth, in order for acts of deception to constitute acts of perfidy under this Rule, they must carry particular consequences. Thus, an *illegal* perfidious act must result in the death or injury (or, for some States, also capture) of an adversary. This requirement excludes from the application of the Rule conduct resulting in the destruction of property through the use of perfidious deception. Moreover, the act of perfidy must be the proximate cause of the death or injury. This means that a remote causal relation characterized by other intervening causes in addition to the perfidious act would not amount to a violation of this Rule. A deceptive action feigning a protected status that is intended to enable an actor to escape (but not to harm) the enemy may violate other rules of the law of armed conflict, but it does not constitute perfidy.

---

[335] Waldemar A Solf, 'Article 37: Prohibition of Perfidy' in Michael Bothe and others (eds), *New Rules for Victims of Armed Conflicts* (Martinus Nijhoff Publishers 2013).

Unsuccessful Perfidious Acts

9. There are two views regarding the issue of whether an unsuccessful perfidious attack violates this Rule. One view is that the intended harm must occur before the Rule is violated; the plain text of Article 23(b) of the Hague Regulations and Article 37 of Additional Protocol I underpins this proposition. The other view is that the Rule will be violated whenever a perfidious act (including an attack) is launched or undertaken; thus, under this view, attempted or unsuccessful acts of perfidy also fall within the scope of this prohibition.[336]

---

[336] *Commentary on the Additional Protocols* (n 9) paras 1493 and 1524; San Remo Manual (n 185) Rule 111; see also Rome Statute of the International Criminal Court (n 57) art 25(3)(f) (which provides as follows: 'In accordance with this Statute, a person shall be criminally responsible and liable for punishment for a crime within the jurisdiction of the Court if that person: ... (f) Attempts to commit such a crime by taking action that commences its execution by means of a substantial step, but the crime does not occur because of circumstances independent of the person's intentions ....') See also the Rome Statute of the International Criminal Court (n 57), which includes the crime of perfidy in art 8(2)(b)(xi): 'killing or wounding treacherously [note the US view at n 241 that treacherously and perfidy are interchangeable] in an international armed conflict' and art 8(2)(e)(ix) '[k]illing or wounding treacherously a combatant adversary' in a NIAC. This was certainly the view of the delegations involved in the Diplomatic Conferences drafting Additional Protocol I. See 'Official Records of the Diplomatic Conference on the Reaffirmation and Development of International Law Applicable to Armed Conflicts, vol XIV' 255. See also 259, statement by delegate of Ireland, and 268, statement by delegate of India; UK LOAC Manual (n 21) 59–60, paras 5.9.2–5.9.3; Canadian LOAC Manual (n 21) 6-2, para 603; Norwegian LOAC Manual (n 59) p 201, para 9.24—these manuals make it clear that it is the intent of the perfidious actor that makes their actions unlawful, not the outcome.

Rule 45
Improper Use of Markings

(a) Subject to the development of suitable technology and its adoption for military space operations, during an international armed conflict in space, a State shall not use:
  i. enemy national or military markings improperly during a time of combat; or
  ii. national or military markings of a State not party to the conflict.

(b) Subject to the development of suitable technology and its adoption for military space operations, during both international armed conflict in space and in non-international armed conflict in space, a State shall not use:
  i. internationally recognized protective markings, signs or signals for other than their intended purposes; and
  ii. the distinctive emblem of the United Nations, except as authorised by that Organisation.

Overview of Legal Basis of Rule

1. Due to the physical and practical limitations imposed by the space environment and by the framework of both the space law regime itself and the law of armed conflict, the conventional application of these rules and their relevance to military space operations for the foreseeable future is likely to be very limited.[337] Improper use of the national and/or military markings of an adversary to the conflict (subpart (a)(i) of this Rule), or the national and/or military markings of a State not a party to the conflict (subpart (a)(ii) of this Rule), is prohibited in an international armed conflict under treaty and customary international law.[338] There is

---

[337] Note generally that art 39(1) and (2) of Additional Protocol I provide that '[i]t is prohibited to make use in an armed conflict of the flags or military emblems, insignia or uniforms of neutral or other States not Parties to the conflict' and that '[i]t is prohibited to make use of the flags or military emblems, insignia or uniforms of adverse Parties while engaging in attacks or in order to shield, favour, protect or impede military operations'. As discussed below, arts 6–9 of Annex I of Additional Protocol I (addressing distinctive signals used by medical units or transports, including light, radio and electronic identification) explicitly refer to transports on land, aircraft, and naval vessels.

[338] Hague Convention (IV) (n 7) art 23(f); US DoD Law of War Manual (n 5) para 5.24.1. Note, however, that this prohibition appears to be viewed by some States as relating only to concrete visual objects. See eg US DoD Law of War Manual (n 5) para 5.23.1.5 ('The prohibition on misuse of enemy flags, insignia, and military uniforms refers only to concrete visual objects, rather than enemy codes, passwords, and countersigns.'). The ICRC takes the position that State practice establishes this rule as

no agreement whether these prohibitions also apply in a non-international armed conflict, and if so, to what extent.[339] This Rule does not extend to prohibiting the non-perfidious use of false national or military signals, which is permitted as a ruse (see Rule 44: Prohibition of Perfidy). The legal basis for subparts (b)(i) and (b)(2) of this Rule are set forth in paragraphs 5 and 8, respectively.

Markings and Their Very Limited Current Application to Space

2. These prohibitions apply only to national and military *markings*, noting that current use of such markings on space objects is very limited. Under the space law regime, objects in space do not have nationality and thus are not 'flagged' the way naval vessels or aircraft are, nor are they subject to any of the other widely recognized rules or conventions applicable to maritime and air operations (see Rule 7: Jurisdiction and Rule 8: Registration of Space Objects). Space objects with military functions may have no markings indicating such functions or status. Furthermore, the information about space objects provided by States in registering them often does not indicate that any military operations are involved, nor is there a requirement to do so (see Rule 8: Registration of Space Objects). In addition, the practical utility of 'markings' in space, in any conventional sense, is extremely limited due to the absence of visual observation. For these reasons, and in the absence of any related State practice to date, it cannot be definitively stated how much application the general legal regime governing national markings in the terrestrial environments of land, sea, and air warfare has to a State's military objects in space. This said, if States were to develop, or render public existing, national or military markings for space objects, it is possible that the relevant provisions on improper use could be applied to such markings.

Improper Use of National or Enemy Markings

3. While there is no settled legal position on the outer limits of what amounts to improper use of national or enemy markings in a general sense, at a minimum it is clear that their use during combat is improper. If these rules of the law of armed conflict could be applied in space during an international armed conflict, it would

---

a norm of customary international law applicable in both international and non-international armed conflicts. ICRC CIHL Study (n 14) Rule 63 (but see Introduction to *Manual*, noting that serious State concerns have been expressed about the methodology used in the ICRC CIHL Study).

[339] See ICRC CIHL Study (n 14) Rule 62; *NIAC Manual* (n 68) rule 2.3.5; AMW Manual Commentary (n 195) r 112(c) para 7.

be prohibited for a State to launch an attack from a space object displaying the military markings of its adversary.[340]

4. As indicated in subpart (b)(i) of the Rule, the improper use of national and military markings of a State that is not a party to the conflict is prohibited.[341] The exception in naval warfare for flying a false flag is a distinct feature of naval warfare and, in the absence of State practice in space (where space objects do not have 'flags' of nationality), this exception is restricted solely to the law of naval warfare context.[342]

Improper Use of Protective Markings

5. Improper use of protective markings in subpart (b)(1) of the Rule is prohibited in international and non-international armed conflicts, including those involving military space operations.[343] With respect to military space operations and non-international armed conflicts, space assets have played an important role in some non-international armed conflicts on Earth, for example in targeting terrorist groups in the terrestrial domain by using surveillance satellites and by operating drones via communications satellites. However, due to a lack of State practice with respect to rules of the law of armed conflict in space, practical and technological considerations created by the space environment, and the space law regime itself, for the foreseeable future it is difficult to hypothesize a non-international armed conflict originating in or occurring in space itself (see Rule 30: Non-International Armed Conflict).

6. The law of armed conflict framework provides for the use of several protective markings, including for military medical units, transports, and personnel; civilian medical units, transports, and personnel; cultural property; and civil defence buildings and materiel. In light of the practical limitations of space affecting the visibility and conventional use of markings, the current relevance of these

---

[340] Additional Protocol I (n 4) art 39(1) ('It is prohibited to make use in an armed conflict of the flags or military emblems, insignia or uniforms of neutral or other States not Parties to the conflict.'); *Commentary on the Additional Protocols* (n 9) para 1574; see also ICRC CIHL Study (n 14) Rule 62; US DoD Law of War Manual (n 5) para 5.23.1; UK LOAC Manual (n 21) para 5.11.1; New Zealand LOAC Manual (n 25) para 8.9.13; Danish LOAC Manual (n 28) ch 10 ss 2.3, 2.4, 2.5; German LOAC Manual (n 21) para 480.

[341] *Commentary on the Additional Protocols* (n 9) para 1565. The ICRC takes the position that State practice establishes this rule as a norm of customary international law applicable in both international and non-international armed conflicts. ICRC CIHL Study (n 14) Rule 63; see also *NIAC Manual* (n 68) rule 2.3.4.

[342] Commentary to HPCR Manual (n 174) commentary accompanying rule 112(c) para 3.

[343] Hague Convention (IV) (n 7) art 23(f); GC I (n 93) art 44; GC II (n 93) art 44; Hague Convention for the Protection of Cultural Property in the Event of Armed Conflict (adopted 14 May 1954, entered into force 7 August 1956) 249 UNTS, 240, art 17(3); Additional Protocol I (n 4) art 66(8); Additional Protocol II (n 60) art 12; Danish LOAC Manual (n 28) 404. The ICRC takes the position that State practice establishes this rule as a norm of customary international law applicable in both international and non-international armed conflicts. ICRC CIHL Study (n 14) Rule 61.

protective markings in the context of military space operations is very limited. However, it may be worth noting that medical units and transports can also be identified by signals and if a State were to develop dedicated medical spacecrafts, it is possible that such spacecraft could use a specific signal that was adopted for the space environment in the future.[344] Annex I of Additional Protocol I also specifically identifies the use of satellites as being the means through which medical transports may transmit their distinct and urgent communications.[345] The use of digital markings, conveyed by signals, may thus present a possible application of some of these protective markings in space at some time in the future. Currently of course, States are under no obligation to use such digital signals in space in support of the requirements of the law of armed conflict.

7. For protective markings, 'improper use' has a different meaning from when that term is used in relation to the national and military markings. In this context, 'improper use' is any use not consistent with the proper purpose of the protective markings under the law of armed conflict.[346] Accordingly, to the extent these rules are able to be applied in space, it would be prohibited to conduct a military space operation while displaying protective markings inconsistent with the type of space operation being conducted (or engaging in conduct inconsistent with the proper use of protected signs or signals).[347] Although it is possible to imagine a space vehicle in the future that indicates it is exclusively dedicated to medical purposes (like an ambulance) that could misuse its designated status and protective electronic signals/markings by actually carrying only weapons and armaments, such a scenario is beyond this *Manual*'s time frame.

---

[344] See 1993 Revised Additional Protocol I Annex I (n 163) chs III and IV (concerning light signals, radio signals, and electronic identification). For example, '[p]rotected medical transports may, for their identification and location, use standard aeronautical radar transponders and/or maritime search and rescue radar transponders. It should be possible for protected medical transports to be identified by other vessels or aircraft equipped with secondary surveillance radar by means of a code transmitted by a radar transponder ... The code transmitted by the medical transport transponder should be assigned to that transport by the competent authorities and notified to all the Parties to the conflict.' 1993 Revised Additional Protocol I Annex I (n 163) art 9.2. It must be noted, however, that arts 6–9 of Annex I to Additional Protocol I (addressing distinctive signals used by medical units or transports, including light, radio, and electronic identification) refer to signals for medical vehicles on land, aircraft, and naval vessels. Once technology becomes available for this purpose, it may be adopted for use in space.
[345] 1993 Revised Additional Protocol I Annex I (n 163) art 10. Articles 6–9 of Annex I of Additional Protocol I applies to transports on land, aircraft, and naval vessels.
[346] ICRC CIHL Study (n 14) Rules 59–61.
[347] 2017 US Commander's Handbook of Naval Operations (n 330) § 12.2; AMW Manual (n 197) Rule 112(a).

Improper Use of the Distinctive Emblem of the United Nations

8. Subpart (b)(ii) of the Rule concerns the use of the distinctive emblem of the United Nations,[348] which is prohibited, except as authorized by the organization,[349] in both an international and non-international armed conflict.[350] As with improper use of national and military markings of States not a party to the armed conflict, the prohibition in this Rule is absolute.

---

[348] The distinctive emblem of the United Nations was approved by the General Assembly on 7 December 1946. UNGA, 'Official Seal and Emblem of the United Nations' (7 December 1946) UN Doc A/RES/92(I) [https://perma.cc/JE3Z-YPFH]. See generally Dag Hammarsköld Library, 'Maps, Flags, Boundaries' (UN, 14 April 2021) [https://perma.cc/Y8BM-YTJZ].

[349] For example, for operations authorized by the UN Security Council under Chaps VI or VII of the UN Charter. See *Commentary on the Additional Protocols* (n 9) para 1560. The first dedicated UN space mission was scheduled for launch in 2021, but the Sierra Nevada Corporation has since stated that the mission is expected to occur around 2024. 'UNOOSA and Sierra Nevada Corporation announce Call for Interest to provide landing site for Dream Chaser® spacecraft mission carrying experiments from UN Member States' [https://perma.cc/72KZ-2GTZ].

[350] Additional Protocol I (n 4) art 38(2). The ICRC takes the position that State practice establishes this rule as a norm in both international and non-international armed conflicts. ICRC CIHL Study (n 14) Rule 60. See also *NIAC Manual* (n 68) rule 2.3.4; San Remo Manual (n 185) 1 rule 110(e); HPCR Manual commentary accompanying rule 112(e) para 5.

SECTION 5
OTHER OBLIGATIONS

Rule 46
Constant Care

In the conduct of military operations, including military space operations, a Party to Additional Protocol I shall take constant care to spare the civilian population, individual civilians, and civilian objects.

Overview of Legal Basis of Rule

1. This Rule is based on Article 57(1) of Additional Protocol I which provides that '[i]n the conduct of military operations, constant care shall be taken to spare the civilian population, civilians and civilian objects'.[351] While this Rule is binding on States that are parties to Additional Protocol I, there is debate whether the requirement of constant care has customary international law status and what its precise contours would be.[352]

Application to Military Operations Not Governed By More Specific Rules Regarding Attacks

2. The term 'military operations' should be understood to mean 'any movements, manoeuvres and other activities whatsoever carried out by the armed forces with a view to combat'[353] and includes 'all movements and acts related to hostilities that

---

[351] See Introduction to Part III, paras 9–10 (noting that the text of Additional Protocol I explicitly states in Article 49(3) that this Rule is applicable to warfare on land, air, and sea, and this Manual interprets Additional Protocol I as also extending to military space operations, that may affect the civilian population, individual civilians, or civilian objects in any domain).

[352] The ICRC takes the position that this rule is a norm of customary international law applicable in both international and non-international armed conflicts. ICRC CIHL Study (n 14) Rule 15 (but see Introduction to *Manual*, paras 11–13, noting that serious concerns have been expressed by some States about the methodology used in the ICRC CIHL Study); the US DoD Law of War Manual acknowledges that constant care is an obligation binding on Additional Protocol I Parties under Article 57(1), but notes 'this obligation is susceptible to a range of interpretations' and that Parties to Additional Protocol I 'may also interpret it in a manner that is consistent with the discussion in this section [setting forth rules governing the conduct of hostilities, including feasible precautions]'. US DoD Law of War Manual (n 5) para 5.3.3.4. The failure of the military regulations of most States to precisely define what the term 'constant care' means, together with the term's frequent conflation with feasible precautions, further complicates its independent customary international law status. In this regard, during the lengthy discussions and difficult negotiations at the diplomatic conference that resulted in the text of art 57(1), several delegations considered that 'the article was dangerously imprecise.' *Commentary on the Additional Protocols* (n 9) para 2187.

[353] ibid para 2191.

are undertaken by armed forces'.[354] Accordingly, military space operations comprise those military space activities that have a nexus to such conduct by a party engaged in a conflict, including communications, reconnaissance, and surveillance by means of space-based assets as part of those activities.

3. The term 'constant care' is not specifically defined in Additional Protocol I. However, it has been described as an obligation upon those charged with approving and executing a military operation to always bear in mind that civilians and civilian objects might be harmed as a result of the operation, and therefore to take into account the likely effects of their space operations on the civilian population, civilians, and civilian objects.[355]

4. The ICRC describes the obligations contained in Article 57(1) and 57(2) of Additional Protocol I to be 'inter-related'.[356] In this regard, it might be noted that during the negotiation of Additional Protocol I, a clear distinction was not made between what became Article 57(1) and the more specific obligations to take precautions when undertaking attacks under Article 57(2). Despite this, as discussed above, it is clear that Article 57(1) by its very wording ('military operations') does apply outside of the context of 'attacks' and hence has a broader scope of application in terms of military functions and activities.[357] However, the obligations are expressed in general terms and are thus subject to the more specific duties and obligations contained within Article 57(2). Indeed, the practical application of this obligation has been described as being fulfilled by the 'other paragraphs' of Article 57 which relate to precautions in attack.[358] This point is expressed most clearly in the UK Joint Service Manual, which provides that 'the commander will have to bear in mind the effect on the civilian population of what [he/she] is planning to do and take steps to reduce that effect as much as possible. In planning or deciding on or carrying out attacks, however, those responsible have more specific duties.'[359] Those specific duties relate to obligations under both 'precautions in attack' requirements, including the principle of proportionality, and will, when applied according to their own context, extend beyond and *supersede the more general obligations of constant care* (see Section 3: Precautions in Attack, including Rule 38: Proportionality in Attack).

---

[354] ibid para 1875.
[355] UK LOAC Manual (n 21) para 5.32.1.
[356] ICRC CIHL Study (n 14) Rule 15 (the ICRC notes the constant care obligation and the obligation to take precautions are 'interrelated').
[357] UK LOAC Manual (n 21) footnote 187 to para. 5.32.1 (distinguishing between art 57(1) and 57(2), pointing out that the phrase military operations 'has a wider connotation than 'attacks' and would include the movement or deployment of armed forces').
[358] *Commentary on the Additional Protocols* (n 9) para 2191.
[359] UK LOAC Manual (n 21) para 5.32.1.

Application to Military Space Operations in Particular

5. Exercising constant care is of particular importance in the planning and execution of military space operations due to the complex—including dual-use—nature of many space objects; the effects, both direct and indirect, of such operations; the potentially long-lasting nature of the effects; and the high likelihood that civilian systems will be affected. For instance, in considering an operation other than an attack such as one designed to temporarily disrupt enemy use of a communications satellite, the commander approving the operation must consider the impact that doing so will have on civilian communications. If an attack is contemplated, this general obligation transitions into the specific requirements of feasible precautions in attack (Section 3: Precautions in Attack), including the specific requirements of proportionality (Rule 38: Proportionality in Attack).

Rule 47
Belligerent Reprisals

Military acts during international armed conflicts, including acts during military space operations, which constitute belligerent reprisals are prohibited against protected objects and persons, with limited possible exceptions under stringent conditions.

Overview of Legal Basis of Rule

1. Belligerent reprisals are acts in international armed conflicts, including those involving military space operations, that would violate the law of armed conflict but for the fact that they are in response to violations of the law of armed conflict by the adversary party and meet certain stringent conditions set forth in the following paragraphs. The status of armed reprisals in non-international armed conflicts is debated.[360] Reprisals must be distinguished from countermeasures (see Rule 25: Countermeasures).

---

[360] This Rule and commentary cover only the law applicable to international armed conflict. To date, there is some ambiguity as to whether the concept of belligerent reprisal applies to a non-international armed conflict. There is no express prohibition or recognition of belligerent reprisals found in Common Article 3 of the 1949 Geneva Conventions nor in Additional Protocol II. Military manuals appear to accept the permissibility of reprisals and their limits regardless of, or without addressing, conflict classification. These include the United States (US DoD Law of War Manual (n 5) para 18.18)); United Kingdom (UK LOAC Manual (n 21) paras 5.18 and 16.16)); Canada (Canadian LOAC Manual (n 21) para 1507)); Denmark (Danish LOAC Manual (n 28) para 2.16); and New Zealand (New Zealand LOAC Manual (n 25) paras 17.10.1–17.10.5)). The United Kingdom notes that to the extent the ICTY concluded in *Prosecutor v Kupreškić* Judgment (n 21) 533–36 that 'attacks on civilians [in any type of conflict] by way of reprisal can never be justified ... the court's reasoning is unconvincing and the assertion that there is a prohibition in customary law flies in the face of most of the state practice that exists. The UK does not accept the position as stated in this judgment.' UK LOAC Manual (n 21) para 16.19.1, fn 63. Another State at State Consultations emphasized that the prohibitions on belligerent reprisals do not reflect customary international law and viewed the Court's decision in *Kupreškić* (n 21) as assuming that the doctrine of reprisals applied in NIACs. This State also referred to another ICTY case as another example of where the Court did not question the use of reprisals, per se, in NIACs. *Prosecutor v Milan Martić* (Appeals Judgment) IT-95-11-A (8 October 2008) paras 263 and 267 (noting the Trial Court's statement that 'a reprisal is subject to strict conditions and is only to be used as an exceptional measure' and finding that Martić 'failed to show that the Trial Chamber erred in concluding that two conditions justifying reprisals had not been met'). The ICRC, however, viewed these cases differently as implying that such a general prohibition in all conflicts is already in existence, based largely on the imperatives of humanity or public conscience, and that there appears to exist a trend in favour of prohibiting such reprisals. More broadly, the ICRC takes the position that parties to a non-international armed conflict do not have the right to resort to belligerent reprisals and, in addition, are prohibited from taking other countermeasures against protected persons. See ICRC CIHL Study (n 14) Rule 148 (but see

Under the 1949 Geneva Conventions, reprisals are prohibited against the wounded, sick, and shipwrecked; personnel, buildings, vessels, and equipment protected by the Convention;[361] POWs;[362] civilians who are interned, are in occupied territory, or are otherwise in the hands of an adverse party to the conflict, and their property;[363] medical and religious personnel, vehicles, equipment, and facilities;[364] and cultural property as defined under the 1954 Hague Convention on Cultural Property.[365] In addition, the scope of this prohibition is dependent on whether the State is a party to Additional Protocol I.[366] If a State is a party to Additional Protocol I (and has not made any reservations related to reprisals), the prohibition extends to actions against the civilian population,[367] individual civilians,[368] civilian objects,[369] places of worship,[370] objects indispensable to the survival of the civilian population,[371] the natural environment,[372] historic monuments, works of art or places of worship which constitute the cultural or spiritual heritage of peoples,[373] and works or installations containing dangerous forces.[374] Notably, although Additional Protocol I provides that attacks against the civilian population or civilians by way of reprisals are prohibited, some States made statements upon ratification of Additional Protocol I reserving the right to undertake reprisal action if the adverse party makes 'serious and deliberate attacks' upon the civilian population or civilian objects of these States.[375]

2.

Introduction to Part III, paras 11–13, noting that serious concerns have been expressed by some States about the methodology used in the ICRC CIHL Study).

[361] GC I (n 93) art 47.
[362] GC III (n 128) art 13.
[363] Geneva Convention relative to the Protection of Civilian Persons in Time of War (adopted 12 August 1949, entered into force 21 October 1950) 75 UNTS 287, art 33.
[364] GC I (n 93) art 46; US DoD Law of War Manual (n 5) 18.18.3.2.
[365] Hague Convention for the Protection of Cultural Property in the Event of Armed Conflict (n 343) art 4(4).
[366] As emphasized by several States at State Consultations, it is important to note that some States have made reservations to Additional Protocol I regarding reprisals, and that the reprisals prohibited by that Protocol are not prohibited as a matter of customary international law. See n 375 regarding States making such reservations. See Introduction to Part III, paras 9–10 (noting that the text of Additional Protocol I explicitly states in art 49(3) that this Rule is applicable to warfare on land, air, and sea, and this *Manual* interprets Additional Protocol I as also extending to military space operations, that may affect the civilian population, individual civilians, or civilian objects in any domain).
[367] Additional Protocol I (n 4) art 51(6).
[368] ibid art 51(6).
[369] ibid art 52(1).
[370] ibid art 53(c).
[371] ibid art 54(4).
[372] ibid art 55(2).
[373] ibid art 53(a) and (c).
[374] ibid art 56(4).
[375] See statement made by Egypt (Statement on Ratification of Additional Protocol I [adopted 9 October 1992, entered into force 9 April 1993] 1712 UNTS 435, 439); Germany (Statement on Ratification of Additional Protocol I [14 February 1991] 1607 UNTS 526, 529); Italy (Statement on Ratification of Additional Protocol I [27 February 1986] 1425 UNTS 438, 440); and France, Schindler and Toman (n 19) 800, 801, which also clarified that France reserved the right to react to serious violations of Additional Protocol I with any means permitted by international law to prevent further

Application of Rule in Space

3. The specific persons and property protected by this Rule are unlikely to be located in outer space in any appreciable numbers for the foreseeable future, however a wide range of military operations from space could be directed against these protected groups or property in the terrestrial domain. In addition, belligerent reprisals in military space operations may be used to respond to violations of the law of armed conflict undertaken in the terrestrial domain; there is no requirement that reprisals be in kind or limited to the same domain, provided such acts remain within the law's parameters (see paragraph 5).

Requirements for States that are Parties to Additional Protocol I

4. For States that are parties to Additional Protocol I, the range of options available to undertake belligerent reprisals in space would appear to be very limited. For those State parties of Additional Protocol I that have made statements concerning reciprocity regarding responses to specified unlawful attacks, and for those States that are not parties to Additional Protocol I, the range of options is wider, but still may be limited by other international law. For these States, civilian nationals of the belligerent State and civilian property in space (that have no function in relation to protected categories under the 1949 Geneva Conventions) would, *prima facie*, be susceptible to attack as a measure of belligerent reprisal (subject to any applicable restrictions).[376]

Restrictions on Reprisals Under Customary International Law

5. Where specific actions in reprisals are not prohibited outright by other applicable international legal obligations (eg using prohibited weapons), including those conducted from, to, or within space.[377] These are as follows:

violations, that all seem to suggest that the categories listed in Additional Protocol I may lose their protection in the case of the exercise of the right of belligerent reprisal).

---

[376] In the view of the ICRC, customary international humanitarian law significantly limits the range of reprisal options, regardless of treaty language and related declarations. See ICRC CIHL Study (n 14) Rule 145—Reprisals, Rule 146—Reprisals against Protected Persons, Rule 147—Reprisals against Protected Objects, and Rule 148—Reprisals in Non-International Armed Conflict. The ICRC notes, however, that because of existing contrary practice (albeit very limited in its view), it is difficult to conclude that there has yet crystallized a customary rule specifically prohibiting reprisals against civilians during the conduct of hostilities.

[377] See ICRC CIHL Study (n 14) Rule 148 ('Where not prohibited by international law, belligerent reprisals are subject to stringent conditions'). Examples of military manuals of States setting forth such

A. Reprisals—including in military space operations—may be taken only as a response to a prior serious violation of the law of armed conflict[378] and only for the purpose of inducing the adversary to comply with the law; they cannot be taken in retaliation, revenge, or for the purpose of punishment;[379]
B. Reprisals may only be used as a measure of last resort when there are no other lawful means available to induce the adversary to respect the law;[380]
C. Reprisals must be proportionate to the original violation of the law;[381]
D. Reprisals must be approved at the highest level of command/government;[382]
E. Reprisals must cease as soon as the adversary complies with the law;[383] and
F. Reprisals must be made public, announced as such,[384] and given with reasonable notice under the circumstances prevailing at the time.[385] This communication requirement ensures the purpose of reprisals (to induce a change in an adversary's illegal behaviour) is respected by clearly linking the timely action taken in reprisal to an adversary's wrongful acts.

---

stringent conditions on reprisals include the US DoD Law of War Manual (n 5) para 18.18.2. and the UK LOAC Manual (n 21) para 16.19.1.

[378] See New Zealand LOAC Manual (n 25) para 17.10.1 ('A reprisal is an action taken by a party to conflict which would otherwise be unlawful, for the purpose of forcing an opposing party to comply with LOAC. To be justified, a reprisal must be preceded by a breach of LOAC by the opposing party.').

[379] The Hostages Trial (n 210) 34.

[380] *In re Hass and Priebke* (Judgment) ILDC 1599-322 (22 July 1997); United Nations War Crimes Commission *Hans Albin Rauter v Netherlands* (1949) 14 WCR 120. See also US DoD Law of War Manual (n 5) para 18.18.2.2 (listing acts such as 'protests and demands, retorsion, or reasonable notice of the threat to use reprisals' as necessary and appropriate steps before resorting to reprisals).

[381] See The Hostages Trial (n 210) 85; US Law of War DoD Manual (n 5) para 18.18.2.4; UK LOAC Manual (n 21) para 16.17 ('A reprisal must be in proportion to the original violation. Whilst a reprisal need not conform in kind to the act complained of, it may not significantly exceed the adverse party's violation either in degree or effect. Effective but disproportionate acts cannot be justified as reprisals on the basis that only an excessive response will forestall further violations.').

[382] UK LOAC Manual (n 21) para 5.18; US DoD Law of War Manual (n 5) para 18.18.2.4; Australian LOAC Manual (n 31) para 13.18; Danish LOAC Manual (n 28) para 3.16; Norwegian LOAC Manual (n 59) para 14.72.

[383] Australian LOAC Manual (n 31) para 13.18; Canadian LOAC Manual (n 21) para 1507.2, 1507.6h; UK LOAC Manual (n 21) para 16.17.

[384] United Nations War Crimes Commission *Richard Wilhelm Hermann Bruns and Two Others v Norwegian State* (1948) 3 WCR 21-22; see also UK LOAC Manual (n 21) para 16.17(g); Canadian LOAC Manual (n 21) para 1507.6g; German LOAC Manual (n 21) para 489; US DoD Law of War Manual (n 5) para 18.18.2.5.

[385] Canadian LOAC Manual (n 21) para 1507.6c ('There must be reasonable notice that reprisals will be taken. What degree of notice is required will depend on the particular circumstances of each case. Notice is normally given after the violation but may, in appropriate circumstances, predate the violation. An example of notice is an appeal to the transgressor to cease its offending conduct and punish those responsible. Thus, such an appeal may serve both as a plea for compliance and a notice to the adversary that reprisals will be undertaken.'); US DoD Law of War Manual (n 5) 18.18.2.2 ('[C]onsideration should be given to using protests and demands, retorsion, or reasonable notice of the threat to use reprisals before resorting to reprisals.'); UK LOAC Manual (n 21) 16.16.c ('Reasonable notice must be given that reprisals will be taken. What degree of notice is required will depend upon the particular circumstances of the case.').

Special Considerations Regarding Reprisals in Space

6. With respect to military space operations in particular, great care must be taken in the conduct of any belligerent reprisal to not infringe upon the rights that other, non-belligerent States enjoy under the OST or under any other agreements making up the space law regime. For example, in undertaking a belligerent reprisal, a State must show due regard for the interests of these other States (see Rule 17: Due Regard) and undertake appropriate international consultations before proceeding with any activity would cause potentially harmful interference with the activities of these other States (see Rule 18: Harmful Interference). There is no right to resort to belligerent reprisals against non-belligerents, including military and civilian astronauts of non-belligerents.

7. With respect to military astronauts of the adversary who would qualify as lawful targets, reprisals against them would be prohibited only when they fall into one of the listed categories of persons protected in paragraph 2 (see Rule 13: Astronauts and Personnel of a Spacecraft). For example, reprisals against wounded astronauts are prohibited.

8. With respect to civilian populations of the belligerent State in the terrestrial environment, some States that are not parties to Additional Protocol I have asserted the right to undertake reprisals against such civilians or against civilian property in particular limited circumstances.[386] In principle, civilians and civilian-owned property of the belligerent State in space would be included in this reservation. In addition, as noted, some States that are parties to Additional Protocol I have made reservations to similar effect.

---

[386] US DoD Law of War Manual (n 5) para 18.18.3.4 fn 225. 'The Position of the United States on Current Law of War Agreements: Remarks of Judge Abraham D. Sofaer' (Legal Adviser, United States Department of State, 22 January 1987) 2 American University Journal of International Law and Policy 460, 469 ('To take another example, article 51 of Protocol I prohibits any reprisal attacks against the civilian population, that is, attacks that would otherwise be forbidden but that are in response to the enemy's own violations of the law and are intended to deter future violations. Historically, reciprocity has been the major sanction underlying the laws of war. If article 51 were to come into force for the United States, an enemy could deliberately carry out attacks against friendly civilian populations, and the United States would be legally forbidden to reply in kind. As a practical matter, the United States might, for political or humanitarian reasons, decide in a particular case not to carry out retaliatory or reprisal attacks involving unfriendly civilian populations. To formally renounce even the option of such attacks, however, removes a significant deterrent that presently protects civilians and other war victims on all sides of a conflict.').

Rule 48
Neutrality in Space

The fundamental principles of the law of neutrality apply to military space operations during international armed conflict, although the precise application of these principles from, to, or within space is yet to be determined.

Overview of Legal Basis of Rule

1. The law of neutrality applies in space during international armed conflict and regulates the relationships between parties to that armed conflict and neutral States (ie States that are not a party to the conflict).[387] Its key purposes are to: protect neutral States from effects of the conflict; safeguard neutral rights; and protect parties to the conflict against action or inaction on the part of neutral States that benefit their enemies.[388] These purposes also help prevent neutral States from being unwittingly drawn into an armed conflict, a risk that is particularly acute for military space operations as States regularly use satellites registered or operated by other States or private actors for military purposes[389] and space objects may have legal connections with multiple States (see Note on Legal Connections Between States and a Space Object).

---

[387] See eg German LOAC Manual (n 21) para 1201 (defining neutrality as 'the status of a State that is not participating in an armed conflict between other States'); UK LOAC Manual (n 21) para 1.42 ('[t]he traditional law of neutrality defines the relationship under international law between states engaged in an armed conflict and those that are not participating in that conflict'). The ICRC further notes that the concept of a 'neutral person' has a distinct meaning under international humanitarian law, namely that of a national of a non-belligerent state. In this regard, the ICRC emphasized that such nationals enjoy specific protections for as long as their country of nationality does not become a party to the armed conflict, even if the State violates (some of) its obligations under the law of neutrality. However, it should be noted that individual persons also lose any protections afforded by neutrality through their own actions, even if their state of nationality remains neutral (just as civilians can lose their protected civilian status by directly participating in hostilities).

[388] US DoD Law of War Manual (n 5) para 15.1.3.

[389] Office of the Chairman of the Joint Chiefs of Staff, 'Joint Publication 3-14—Space Operations' (rev edn, US Department of Defense 26 October 2020) I-6 [https://perma.cc/66EN-A7QB].

Limitations of Some Rules of Neutrality to Terrestrial Domains

2. Many of the rights and obligations of the law of neutrality have been codified in treaty law with a particular territorial domain in mind, the most significant of which are the Hague Conventions V and XIII from 1907, which relate to the land and sea domains, respectively.[390] These rules will nonetheless apply to space activities, space infrastructure (such as launch facilities or mission control facilities), or space objects located in those territorial domains (although no space-related objects or facilities existed when these conventions were concluded, as no outer space activities yet existed).

Underlying Principles

3. Despite the conventional focus on the terrestrial domains, some underlying principles of the law of neutrality are general in essence and based primarily on behaviour or conduct. That is, there is arguably an underlying general principle of law of neutrality that is conduct based, rather than domain based, and those general principles apply to military space operations, including those that occur in space.[391] In this context, it is relevant to note several attempts to define what such general principles of neutrality might be.[392] While these efforts are interesting or even persuasive, they have not yet been accepted through State practice and *opinio juris* as reflecting international law that would apply to the space domain. To the extent that neutrality law would apply in space,[393] its general principles would require belligerents to refrain from attacking neutral states, persons, and property in space, to respect the rights of neutrals in areas outside the jurisdiction of any State (including

---

[390] See Hague Convention (V) respecting the Rights and Duties of Neutral Powers and Persons in Case of War on Land (adopted 18 October 1907, entered into force 26 January 1910) 205 CTS 299; Hague Convention (XIII) concerning the Rights and Duties of Neutral Powers in Naval War (adopted 18 October 1907, entered into force 26 January 1910) 205 CTS 395. As reflected in the titles of these conventions, the Hague V Convention applies 'in case of war on land' and the Hague XIII Convention applies 'in naval war'. Moreover, Article 20 of the 1907 Hague V Convention provides that '[t]he provisions of the present Convention do not apply except to the Contracting Powers, and then only if all the belligerents are parties to the Convention.' 36 Statutes at Large 2433.

[391] *Nuclear Weapons* Advisory Opinion (n 3) 226 paras 88–89 ('international law leaves no doubt that the principle of neutrality, whatever its content ... is applicable ... to all international armed conflict, whatever type of weapons might be used').

[392] For example, Lassa Oppenheim suggested in early twentieth century that such basic duties include impartiality in actions related to the belligerents, respect of the neutral status and of free commerce and acquiescence in the exercise of either belligerent's right to punish neutral merchantmen for rendering unneutral service to the enemy. Lassa Oppenheim, *International Law: A Treatise—Volume 2, War and Neutrality* (2nd edn, Longmans, Green and Co 1912) 379 [https://perma.cc/QD3H-3GPD]; see also US DoD Law of War Manual (n 5) para 15.3; German LOAC Manual (n 21) paras 1207–1209.

[393] It should be noted that to the extent that any general international law exists on neutrality, it is applicable to space, via art III of the OST.

rights under the OST), and to spare them the consequences of hostilities, to the extent feasible. The law of neutrality would, to the extent applicable, provide that in the space environment any State not party to an international armed conflict and seeking to maintain neutral status, must remain impartial, abstain from space activities deemed non-neutral, and take certain actions to end or prevent belligerent military activities that would violate its neutrality. Failure to fulfil such neutral obligations could therefore lead to loss of neutral status of an object, person, or State, depending on the circumstances.

Lack of State Practice

4. There is very little academic commentary on the subject of neutrality in space and no State practice authoritatively confirming that conventional or customary obligations concerning neutrality apply in space. In fact, only one State's military manual has been identified that explicitly addresses attacks or any other type of military operation against a neutral State's assets in space.[394] Hence, whether and how conventional or customary international legal obligations apply to particular military activities or operations in space must be assessed by States on a case-by-case basis. The lack of State practice and *opinio juris* related to military space operations during armed conflict makes specific determinations as to how the general law of neutrality applies difficult to determine at the present time. This lack of State practice (let alone consensus) must also be noted with respect to the actions of a non-governmental entity (NGE), such as a corporation, that engages in actions in space that appear to be inconsistent with the neutrality of that NGE's State of nationality (usually also the State that is responsible for that NGE that is part of its national space activities). There is no State practice regarding what actions in space by an NGE might constitute actions inconsistent with the responsible neutral State's obligations, in part because many of the rules found in international law in this area are domain-specific (notably often developed for the maritime domain). However, it does not seem consistent with the object and purpose of the OST to enlarge conflicts in space by forcing a State to automatically forfeit its neutral status on the basis of the actions of an NGE over which that State does not have effective control (see Rule 10: Responsibility of States for National Activities in Outer Space, paragraph 14(c)).

---

[394] Danish LOAC Manual (n 28) para 3.5.1 ('Nor is it permissible to attack, State-owned infrastructure of neutral States, even if the infrastructure is located in outer space.'); ICRC, 'Working paper submitted by the International Committee of the Red Cross to the open-ended working group on reducing space threats through norms, rules and principles of responsible behaviours, as convened under United Nations General Assembly Resolution 76/231' [https://perma.cc/DQH7-VE6Y] ('Military operations in, or in relation to, outer space do not occur in a legal vacuum but are constrained by existing international law, notably ... the law of neutrality.').

Questions Regarding Non-Governmental Entities Providing Space-Based Services Used By a Belligerent State

5. A State representative at State Consultations asked, in light of the ongoing conflict in Ukraine, how a State's neutrality (State A) is affected by one of its NGEs providing space-based (commercial) internet or space-based imagery that is used by the armed forces of a belligerent State B in an armed conflict. In this regard, the State representative asked what the threshold is for a neutral State A becoming a party to the conflict. Assuming that the fundamental principles of neutrality do apply to space—but given the undeveloped application of neutrality law to space—this question can be answered only by posing the questions needed to establish the correct legal framework for analysis. These unsettled questions are:

    A. Which specific neutrality rules are part of customary international law that extend to space and which rules are specific or limited to domains other than space?
    B. In particular, what actions taken by a space object or services provided by a space object to one of the belligerents would violate a neutral's obligation of impartial conduct?
    C. What legal relationship must a space object have with a State in order for the space object's actions to be attributed to that State? Only the responsible State under Article VI of the OST? Or also a State with a different legal connection, such as the State of Registry?
    D. If a space object's actions are inconsistent with the attributed State's neutral obligations, under what circumstances does that State lose its neutral status?[395]

6. Regardless of a State's neutrality during an armed conflict, if one of its space objects makes an effective contribution to the military actions of belligerent State A, that object may become a legitimate military objective (and be targeted) if its total or partial destruction or neutralization, in the circumstances ruling at the time, offers a definite military advantage to belligerent State B (see Rule 34: Military Objectives).

---

[395] See para 5 and Rule 10: Responsibility of States for National Activities in Outer Space, para 14(c), regarding the difficulties in finding that a State automatically forfeits its neutral status based on the actions of an NGE in space (for which that State is responsible), even if that State has no effective control over that NGE's actions.

Index

For the benefit of digital users, indexed terms that span two pages (e.g., 52–53) may, on occasion, appear on only one of those pages.

access *see* freedom of use, access, exploration, and scientific investigation and principles of cooperation (Rule 1)
accidents, mistakes, and other non-intentional acts
   armed attack (Rule 23) 203–4, 229–30, 236–37, 293
   attack, definition of (Rule 31) 303–4, 305–6
   mechanical errors 236–37
   missing intended targets 206–7, 213–14
   negligence 236–37
   radio interference (Rule 19) 186
   State practice 236–37
Additional Protocol I to Geneva Conventions,
   application of 277–78, 279–80
   adversary, definition of acts of violence against the 307
   attack, definition of (Rule 31) 301, 307–8
   belligerent reprisals (Rule 47) 395, 396, 398
   choice of means and methods of attack (Rule 37) 274–75, 334, 335
   civilian populations and objects, protection of 277–78, 279–80
   constant care (Rule 46) 391, 392
   customary international law 301, 319
   declarations, understandings, or interpretive statements 377
   direct participation in hostilities (DPH) (Rule 33) 312
   distinction (Rule 32) 309
   improper use of markings (Rule 45) 386–87
   international armed conflicts (IACs) (Rule 29) 290–91
   means and methods of warfare (Rule 42) 367, 368–69, 370–72
   medical units and religious personnel (Rule 35) 324–25, 328
   military objectives (Rule 34) 319–20, 321–23
   natural environment (Rule 43) 14–15, 368–69, 373–74, 376–79
   perfidy, prohibition of (Rule 44) 380–81
   precautions against the effects of attack (Rule 41) 357, 358–59
   precautions in attacks 278, 280–82
   proportionality in attack (Rule 38) 337, 339
   reservations 377
   suspension or cancellation of attack (Rule 39) 347–48
   verification (Rule 36) 331
   warnings (Rule 40) 351, 352–53
Additional Protocol II to the Geneva Conventions of 1949 295, 312, 324–25
Additional Protocol III to Geneva Conventions 327
aggression
   collective security measures (Rule 28) 265–66, 267–69
   definition 204–5, 265
   peaceful purposes in outer space (Rule 3) 49–50
   threat of force (Rule 22) 225
Agreement on Rescue and Return of Astronauts (ARRA) 19–20
   astronauts, use of term 129–31
   capacity to assist 19–20
   interpretation 19–20
   number of parties 19
   Outer Space Treaty (OST) 19–20, 129, 134–35
   parties 19–20
   persistent objectors, lack of 20
   personnel of a spacecraft, use of term 129–30
   Preamble 129–30
   ratification 19–20
   rescue elsewhere on Earth 133
   return of personnel 134–35
   signatories 19
   space objects, capacity to handle 19–20
   space tourism 130, 131
   State practice 19–20
   withdraw, no expressions of intent to 19
air and sea domains, comparison with 159–60
Air Defence Identification Zones (ADIZ) 162–63

404   INDEX

airspace 162–63, 166–67, 355 *see also* **airspace and outer space (delimitation of outer space)**
airspace and outer space (delimitation of outer space) 26–29
  atmosphere, concept of 27–28
  boundary, fixing a 28
  combination of spatial approaches and other proposals 28
  conflicting approaches 27–29
  functionalist approach 27, 28–29
  gravitational effects, demarcation based on Earth's 28
  navigable air space, theory of 28
  satellites, lowest perigee of 28
  spatialist approach 27–29
  State sovereignty 26–27, 28–29
  von Karman line (aerodynamic characteristics) 28–29
  zones (Rule 16) 28
analogies 15, 172–73
Antarctic Treaty 1961
  demilitarization 64, 66
  negotiating history 65–66
  visits 147–48, 150–51
anticipatory self-defence 254–56
Apollo 11 Mission
  flag, planting of the 41–42
  landing sites 168–69
  Lunar Module of (the Eagle) 167–68
Apollo 17 landing sites 168–69
appropriation *see* **non-appropriation of outer space and celestial bodies (Rule 2)**
armed attack (Rule 23) 154, 226–37
  accidents, mistakes, and other non-intentional acts 154, 203–4, 229–30, 236–37
  accumulating incidents 236
  attack, definition of (Rule 31) 301
  attribution 259
  collective self-defence (Rule 27) 235
  counterspace weapons systems 154–55
  customary international law 226
  cyber capabilities 228–29, 231
  definition 226–27
  degrading of the functions of space objects 231–33
  effects-based approach 203–5, 229–30, 231–32
  gravity threshold 226–28, 229–32, 236
  harmful actions 228–29
  imminence
    in anticipatory self-defense 250, 254–56
    in warning zones 163–64
  interference with space objects 231–33
  international armed conflicts (IACs) (Rule 29) 291
  International Court of Justice (ICJ) 229–30, 233, 236
  jamming 228–29
  legal basis 226, 235–36
  military objectives (Rule 34) 235
  nationality 233
  non-intervention principle (Rule 20) 195
  Outer Space Treaty (OST) 226, 234
  registration of space objects (Rule 8) 234, 235
  satellites 230–31, 235–36
  scale and effects test 205, 229–32
  self-defence (Rule 26) 226–27, 233, 235–36, 250, 252–56, 259
  space objects 230–37
  State practice 231–32, 233, 234, 235–37
  temporary or partial disruption of space objects 231, 232–33
  territory and border incursions 236–37
  UN Charter 226, 227, 231, 301
  unfriendly acts amounting to attacks 154, 228–29
  use of force (Rule 21) 226–29
armed conflicts *see* **international armed conflicts (IACs) (Rule 29)**; **non-international armed conflicts (NIACs) (Rule 30)**
armed groups *see* **organized armed groups (OAGs)**
ARRA *see* **Agreement on Rescue and Return of Astronauts (ARRA)**
Artemis Accords 47–48, 100–1, 165–66, 169, 174
ASATs (anti-satellite weapons)
  armed attack (Rule 23) 229–30
  attack, definition of (Rule 31) 302–3, 304, 305–6, 307–8
  choice of means and methods of attack (Rule 37) 335–36
  co-orbital ASAT weapons 206–7, 227–28
  destructive tests 174–76, 180–82
  direct-ascent 206–7, 227–28, 255, 369–70
  direct participation in hostilities (DPH) (Rule 33) 315
  due regard (Rule 17) 174–76
  electronic, cyber, and high energy laser capabilities against satellites 183
  harmful contamination, avoidance of (Rule 14) 140
  harmful interference (Rule 18) 180–82
  kinetic energy 315, 335–36, 343
  kinetic kill weapons 180–82, 335–36
  malware 369–70

INDEX 405

means and methods of warfare (Rule 42) 369–70
non-international armed conflicts (NIACs) (Rule 30) 296
proportionality in attack (Rule 38) 343–44
space debris 140, 180–82
Tenets of Responsible Behaviour in Space (US DoD) 174–76
testing 174–76
threat of force (Rule 22) 223–24
use of force (Rule 21) 206–7, 227–28

asteroids
collective security measures (Rule 28) 270–71
resources, recovery of 42–43, 46–48, 101, 169
threats 75, 80, 270–71
3D printing 100–1

astronauts and personnel of a spacecraft (Rule 13) 129–38 *see also* Agreement on Rescue and Return of Astronauts (ARRA)
all possible assistance duty 132–33
astronauts, use of term 129–31
belligerent reprisals (Rule 47) 398
belligerent rights 137
capacity to assist 133, 136
compensation for damage 135
customary international law 54–55
distinction (Rule 32) 129–30
distress at sea, duty to rescue persons in 54–55
emergency landings 133, 135
envoys of mankind, astronauts as 130, 131
hostilities, effect of 136–38
internment of civilians and abled-bodied combatants 137
jurisdiction (Rule 7) 135–36
launching authorities 55–56, 132–33, 134–35
law of armed conflict 137–38
lawful targets, military astronauts as 398
legal basis 129
life or health of astronauts, reports on any phenomena which could constitute a danger to 136
mandatory reporting 39–40
medical and religious personnel under law of armed conflict, special protections for 137
military personnel 135
Moon and other celestial bodies 55–56, 135, 136
neutral States 137
Outer Space Treaty (OST) 40, 129–33, 134–35, 136
personal scope of application 129–31
personnel of a spacecraft, use of term 129–30
prisoners of war (POWs) 137–38

privileges and immunities of diplomatic envoys 131
professional astronauts and spaceflight participants, difference between 130–31
protected persons, as 398
purposive interpretation 130
registration of space objects (Rule 8) 135–36
rescue
armed conflicts, during 136
Earth, on 133
outer space, in 55–56
sovereign territory, on 132–33
return of personnel 134–35, 137
scientific activities, military astronauts engaged purely in 137
space tourism 130–31
State practice 130–31, 137
atmosphere, concept of 27–28 *see also* **airspace**
attack, definition of (Rule 31) 301–8
accidents and mistakes 303–4, 305–6
Additional Protocol I to Geneva Conventions 301, 307–8
adversary, definition of acts of violence against the 307
armed attack (Rule 31), distinguished 301
ASAT weapons 302–3, 304, 305–6, 307–8
civilians 307
constant care (Rule 46) 301–2
customary international law 301
cyber means, attack by 303–6
de minimis standards, difficulty in establishing 308
defensive acts 307–8
distinction (Rule 32) 301–2, 310
effects-based approach 303–4, 305–6
electromagnetic spectrum, weapons systems using 302–3
intent 303–4, 305–6, 308
international armed conflicts (IACs) (Rule 29) 301
jamming 305
law of armed conflict 301–3, 308
legal basis 301–2
manoeuvred in space, objects capable of being 302–3
means and methods of warfare (Rule 42) 301–3, 305–6
military objectives (Rule 34) 301–2, 307
non-international armed conflicts (NIACs) (Rule 30) 301
precautions in attack 301–2, 307
proportionality in attack (Rule 38) 301–2, 307, 338
robotic mechanisms 302–3

406 INDEX

attack, definition of (Rule 31) (*cont.*)
   ruses 305–6
   satellites 304–5, 307–8
   scope and application 307–8
   traditional armed force, acts of violence by 302–3, 305
   use of force (Rule 21) 301–2
attacks *see* attack, definition of (Rule 31); choice of means and methods of attack (Rule 37); conduct in or related to attack; precautions against the effects of attack (Rule 41); precautions in attack; proportionality in attack (Rule 38); suspension or cancellation of attack (Rule 39)
attribution of State responsibility in space 290–92
   instructions, State agents acting on 290–91
   international agreements, violation of 155
   international armed conflicts (IACs) (Rule 29) 290–93
   legal connections with space objects 291–92
   neutrality in space (Rule 42) 110, 113–14
   non-government entities (NGEs) 105, 110–14, 291, 292
   official capacity, State agents acting in an 290–91
   paramilitary groups 290–91
   responsibility of States for national activities in outer space (Rule 10) 105, 106, 110–14, 155, 291
   self-defence (Rule 26) 259
   special attribution regime 105, 110–11, 112–13, 115, 155, 290–91
Australia
   cyber operations, damage caused by 216–17
   Moon Agreement 24, 65
   Woomera Village/Town 9

ballistic missile technology, use of 265–66
belligerent occupation, terrestrial domain limitations in situations of 293
belligerent reprisals (Rule 47) 394–98
   application of rule in space 396
   astronauts 398
   cease as soon as adversary complies with the law, reprisals must 397
   civilian population or civilians 395, 396, 398
   customary international law 396–97
   due regard (Rule 17) 398
   Geneva Conventions 1949 395, 396, 398
   harmful interference (Rule 18) 398
   highest level of command/government, approval at the 397
   international armed conflicts (IACs) (Rule 29) 394
   last resort, as measures of 397
   law of armed conflict 395–97
   legal basis 394–95
   non-belligerents 398
   non-international armed conflicts (NIACs) (Rule 30) 394
   proportionality in attack (Rule 38) 396–97
   protected persons 396, 398
   public, as 397
   reasonable notice 397
   restrictions 396–97
   special considerations 398
benefit and interests of all countries 36, 38
benefit-sharing regime, requirement for a 44
Benefits Declaration (UN General Assembly Resolution) 38
biological weapons 73, 74, 75, 265–66, 302–3
Brazil
   peaceful purposes in outer space (Rule 3) 51–52
breach of the peace, threats to 265–66, 267–69

camouflage 381
cancellation of attacks *see* suspension or cancellation of attack (Rule 39)
capacities/capabilities *see also* cyber capabilities
   all possible assistance duty 133, 136
   Astronauts, Agreement on Rescue and Return of (ARRA) 19–20
   astronauts and personnel of a spacecraft (Rule 13) 133, 136
   environmental monitoring 1–2
   intelligence, surveillance, and reconnaissance (ISR) 1–2
   international organizations, responsibility of (Rule 11) 119–20
   means and methods of warfare (Rule 42) 365–66
   Outer Space Treaty (OST) 119–20
   position, navigation, and timing (PNT) functionality 1–2
   Registration Convention 22
   rescue 136
   self-defence (Rule 26) 256
   space objects, handling 19–20
   technological capabilities 133
   threat of force (Rule 22) 225
causation 203–4, 314, 339, 382
celestial bodies *see* non-appropriation of outer space and celestial bodies (Rule 2); Moon

INDEX 407

and other celestial bodies; specified military establishments and activities on celestial bodies, restrictions on (Rule 4); visit to facilities on the Moon and other celestial bodies (Rule 15)
change of circumstances 12–13
Chapter VII of UN Charter *see* enforcement measures (Chapter VII)
characterization of conflicts
   international armed conflicts (Rule 29) 287–93
   non-international armed conflicts (Rule 30) 294–97
chemical weapons 73, 74, 75
China
   alleged close encounter of Starlink satellite with Chinese space station (2021) 136n. 483
   ASAT weapons 58–59, 140, 180–82
   national security in space 58–59
   satellites, destruction of 180–82
   space debris 180–82
choice of means and methods of attack (Rule 37) 281–82, 334–36
   Additional Protocol I to Geneva Conventions 274–75, 334, 335
   ASAT weapons 335–36
   civilian life, injury and damage to civilian objects, avoiding/minimizing loss of incidental 334–36
   customary international law 274–75, 334
   cyber capabilities 335
   dual-use satellites 335
   feasible precautions 334–35
   intelligence collection (Rule 6) 335
   international armed conflicts (Rule 29) 334
   legal basis 334
   military advantage 334, 335–36
   military objectives (Rule 34) 334, 335–36
   non-international armed conflicts (Rule 30) 334
   practicable or practically possible, what is 334–35
   precautions against the effects of attack (Rule 41) 361
   rendezvous and proximity operations (RPOs) 335
   satellites 335–36
   space debris 335–36
   verification (Rule 36) 332–33, 334–35
civilian populations, civilians, and civilian objects *see also* **distinction (Rule 32)**
   Additional Protocol I to Geneva Conventions 277–78, 279–80
   adversary, definition of acts of violence against the 307
   attack, definition of (Rule 31) 307
   belligerent reprisals (Rule 47) 395, 396, 398
   choice of means and methods of attack (Rule 37) 334–36
   civilians, definition of 311
   constant care (Rule 46) 391–93
   dangerous forces, space objects containing 279–80
   direct losses 339, 345–46, 361
   direct participation in hostilities (DPH) (Rule 33) 312–18, 356
   due regard (Rule 17) 174
   essential services, loss of 352–53
   excessive incidental civilian harm 361
   excessive losses harm 339–40, 341, 349, 356
   harmful contamination, avoidance of (Rule 14) 139, 145
   incidental civilian losses 337–46
   inconvenience, stress, fear or loss of non-essential services 353
   indirect losses 339, 345–46, 361
   internment 137
   law of armed conflict 276
   Liability Convention 124
   military objectives (Rule 34) 357, 359
   natural environment (Rule 43) 379
   organs of the State 289–90
   perfidy, prohibition of (Rule 44) 381–82
   precautions against the effects of attack (Rule 41) 357–61
   precautions in attack 278
   presumption of civilian status 315
   proportionality in attack (Rule 38) 337–46
   return 137
   return of personnel 137
   space objects exclusively for civilian use 94–95
   speculative, hypothetical or merely risked losses 339
   suspension of civilian protections 316
   suspension or cancellation of attack (Rule 39) 349
   warnings (Rule 40) 352–56
claims commissions, establishment of 21, 122–23
coercion *see also* **use of force (Rule 21)**
   armed intervention 195–96
   definition 194–95
   diplomatic actions 196–97
   economic disruptions 197–98
   electoral processes, interference with 198–200

collective security measures (Rule 28) (*cont.*)
    non-intervention principle (Rule 20) 191–92, 194–200
    State practice 194–95
    threat of force (Rule 22) 223–24
collective security measures (Rule 28) 263–71
    see also **collective self-defence (Rule 27)**
    aggression 265–66, 267–69
    authorization by UN Security Council 263–64, 266–71
    breach of the peace, threats to 265–66, 267–69
    cessation of hostilities 264
    collective self-defence (Rule 27) 266–67
    conflicting international agreements, primacy of enforcement measures over 270–71
    countermeasures (Rule 25) 243
    enforcement measures (Chapter VII) 263–71
    exceptional powers under Article 41 and 42 263–64, 265, 266–68
    international organizations, responsibility of (Rule 11) 120
    legal basis 263–64
    maintenance or restoration of international peace and security 263–64, 265, 266, 268–71
    mutual assistance 266
    non-forcible measures 263–64, 267–69
    non-intervention principle (Rule 20) 200
    peacekeeping operations 269–70
    provisional measures 263–65
    regional arrangements, agencies, or organizations 266–67, 269–70
    satellites 265–66, 267–68, 269–70
    State practice 268
    threats to peace 265–66, 267–69, 270–71
    UN Charter 263–71
    UN Security Council 263–71
    use of force (Rule 21) 202, 265–66, 268–69
    WMDs (Rule 5) 265–66, 270–71
collective self-defence (Rule 27) 260–62
    armed attack (Rule 23) 235
    assistance, right to seek 260–62
    collective security measures (Rule 28) 266–67
    customary international law 260–61
    legal basis 260
    requirements and application 260–62
    right to assist 260
    use of force (Rule 21) 202
    WMDs (Rule 5) 76–78
combatants *see also* **distinction (Rule 32)**
    definition 310–11
    failure to distinguish oneself as a combatant 382
    hors de combat persons 310, 312–13
    internment 137

superfluous injury, definition of 371
unnecessary suffering of combatants 370–71
commercial sector *see* private sector
Committee on Space Research *see* COSPAR (Committee on Space Research)
Common Article 2 of the Geneva Conventions 276, 287–88, 293
Common Article 3 of the Geneva Conventions 276, 294–97
common heritage of mankind 24, 44
communications *see also* ITU harmful radio interference (Rule 19); jamming electronic communications
    command and communication systems 220–21
    constant care (Rule 46) 391–92
    dual-use objects 321
    GNSS 185–86, 211–12, 219, 344–45
    medical communications 326
    military objectives (Rule 34) 319–20, 321
    proportionality in attack (Rule 38) 341
    satellites 1–2, 220–21, 321, 332
    telegraphic, radio, and other means of communication, complete or partial interruption of 202–3
    zones (Rule 16) 162, 163–64
compensation for damage
    aircraft flights 122–23
    astronauts and personnel of a spacecraft (Rule 13) 135
    courts, tribunals, or agencies, through 122–23
    damages 25, 91–92, 123, 125
    diplomatic channels, seeking compensation through 122–23
    liability for damage to space objects (Rule 12) 122–24, 125, 236–37
    procedures and requirements 122–23
    reparations 116
    return of personnel 135
    surface of the Earth 122–23
Comprehensive Nuclear Test Ban Treaty (CTBT) 80
concealment of space objects 332
conduct in or related to attack
    attack, definition of (Rule 31) 301–8
    direct participation in hostilities (Rule 33) 312–18
    distinction (Rule 32) 301–11
    medical units and religious personnel (Rule 35) 324–28
    military objectives (Rule 34) 319–23
confidence, betrayals of 381, 382
conflict of laws 10–11
constant care (Rule 46) 391–93

INDEX

Additional Protocol I to Geneva Conventions 391, 392
- application to military space operations 393
- civilian population, civilians and civilian objects 391–93
- communications 391–92
- dangerous forces, space objects containing 279–80
- definition, lack of agreed 392
- direct participation in hostilities (DPH) (Rule 33) 312–13
- dual-use objects 393
- legal basis 391
- military operations, definition of 391–92
- precautions in attack 281, 392, 393
- proportionality in attack (Rule 38) 338, 392, 393
- reconnaissance 391–92
- specific rules regarding attacks, military operations not governed by 391–92
- surveillance 391–92

contamination *see* harmful contamination, avoidance of (Rule 14)
continuing obligation of attackers 281–82, 331, 361
continuous combat function 316–17
cooperation *see* international cooperation
corporations *see* private sector
COSPAR (Committee on Space Research)
- biological and organic contamination, guidelines on 141, 144–45
- Planetary Protection Policy 143–44

Cosmos 954 Incident (1978) 123, 142
countermeasures (Rule 25) 243–49
- active countermeasures 244
- cessation 246
- collective countermeasures 246
- conditions 244–45
- customary international law 243
- definition 244
- due regard (Rule 17) 249
- free use principle (Rule 1) 246–47
- in-kind, countermeasures 244–45
- injury, notion of 247–48
- International Court of Justice (ICJ) 246
- jamming 248
- land-based assets 244–45
- legal basis 243
- non-government entities (NGEs) 245–46
- radio interference (Rule 19) 247–48
- reciprocity 244–45
- reparations 116–17, 247
- requirements and application 244–49
- responsibility of States for national activities in outer space (Rule 10) 245–46
- retorsion, distinguished 241, 244, 246, 249
- satellites 359–60
- space objects 245–46
- temporary, as 248
- termination 248
- third States 245–46
- use of force prohibited 245
- zones (Rule 16) 160–61

counterspace weapons systems and capabilities 154–55, 206–9, 213–14, 227–28, 231
crisis, times of *see* tension and crisis, military activities during times of
cultural property 167–68, 395
customary international law *see also opinio juris*
- Additional Protocol I to Geneva Conventions 301, 319
- airspace and outer space (delimitation of outer space) 26–27
- analogy, mechanism of 15
- armed attack (Rule 23) 226
- Astronauts, Agreement on Rescue and Return of (ARRA) 20
- astronauts and personnel of a spacecraft (Rule 13) 133
- attack, definition of (Rule 31) 301
- belligerent reprisals (Rule 47) 396–97
- choice of means and methods of attack (Rule 37) 274–75, 334
- collective self-defence (Rule 27) 260–61
- constant care (Rule 46) 391
- countermeasures (Rule 25) 243
- Declaration of Legal Principles 1963 (UNGA) 18–19
- direct participation in hostilities (DPH) (Rule 33) 312
- distinction (Rule 32) 309
- distress at sea, duty to rescue persons in 54–55
- *erga omnes* obligations 246–47
- general practice of States, evidence of 18–19
- harmful contamination, avoidance of (Rule 14) 142–43
- improper use of markings (Rule 45) 384–85
- international armed conflicts (IACs) (Rule 29) 319
- International Committee of the Red Cross (ICRC) study on customary humanitarian international law 278–79
- interpretation 10, 11–12
- jurisdiction (Rule 7) 85–86
- *jus cogens* 10, 111–12
- law of armed conflict 11–13, 14–15

410 INDEX

customary international law (*cont.*)
  lex specialis 10, 11–12
  Liability Convention 21–22
  means and methods of warfare (Rule 42) 366, 370, 371–72
  medical units and religious personnel (Rule 35) 324–25, 326
  military objectives (Rule 34) 319
  Moon Agreement 24, 44, 65, 134
  natural environment (Rule 43) 373–74
  neutrality in space (Rule 48) 401, 402
  non-international armed conflicts (NIACs) (Rule 30) 294, 296–97, 319
  non-intervention principle (Rule 20) 191–92, 197–98, 199–200
  nuclear weapons 207–8
  Outer Space Treaty (OST) 4, 17–19, 24
  perfidy, prohibition of (Rule 44) 380
  precautions against the effects of attack (Rule 41) 357
  precautions in attack 280–81
  proportionality in attack (Rule 38) 337
  Registration Convention 23–24
  retorsion (Rule 24) 241–42
  self-defence (Rule 26) 250, 251, 252–53, 254–55
  silence or inaction of States 1–2
  suspension or cancellation of attack (Rule 39) 347–48
  treaty law, no hierarchy with 10
  UN Charter, hierarchy with 10
  use of force (Rule 21) 201, 207–8, 216–17
  verification (Rule 36) 331
  warnings (Rule 40) 351
  WMDs (Rule 5) 78–79, 207–8, 227–28
  zones (Rule 16) 166–67
cyber capabilities
  armed attack (Rule 23) 228–29, 231
  ASAT weapons 183
  attack, definition of (Rule 31) 303–6
  choice of means and methods of attack (Rule 37) 335
  customary international law 216–17
  defence 216–17
  democratic processes 192–94
  denial-of-service attacks 214–15
  early warning satellites 305
  economic stability 192–94, 197–98
  effects-based approach 303–4
  electoral processes 198–200
  energy security 192–94
  essential medical care 192–94
  hijacking of weapons 215
  intent 303–4
  malicious cyber actions 213–14
  malware 304, 315, 369–70
  manipulation or destruction of data 216–17
  non-international armed conflicts (NIACs) (Rule 30) 296
  non-intervention principle (Rule 20) 192–94, 197–98, 214–15
  remote controlled systems 215
  responsibility of States for national activities in outer space (Rule 10) 112
  ruses 305–6
  satellite 'mission kills' 304–5
  self-defence (Rule 26) 217–18
  State practice 214–15, 217–18
  UN Charter 213–15, 216–19
  use of force (Rule 21) 203–4, 213–19, 228–29

dangerous forces, space objects containing 279–80
dazzling 212–14, 305, 308
debris *see* space debris
deception 332, 382
  Declaration of Legal Principles Governing the Activities of States in the Exploration and Use of Outer Space (1963) 18, 37, 41, 108, 135
  Astronauts, Agreement on Rescue and Return of (ARRA) 135
  harmful interference (Rule 18) 177
  non-appropriation of outer space and celestial bodies (Rule 2) 41
  Outer Space Treaty (OST) 18–19, 36–37
decoys 381
defensive measures 216–17, 259, 307–8
delimitation of outer space *see* airspace and outer space (delimitation of outer space)
demilitarization 49–50, 53–54, 55–56, 59, 66
densely populated areas, obligation to avoid location of military objectives in 357, 358, 359, 360
destruction of property
  data, manipulation or destruction of 216–17
  destructive ASAT weapons 174–76, 180–82
  perfidy, prohibition of (Rule 44) 382
  satellites 180–82, 230–31, 343–44, 345–46
  space debris, by 343–44
deterrence 222–23
direct participation in hostilities (DPH) (Rule 33) 312–18
  belligerent nexus 314
  civilians, application to 312–18
  constant care (Rule 46) 312–13
  continuous combat function 316–17
  customary international law 312

determination of direct participation 313–15
direct participation, definition of 313
distinction (Rule 32) 311, 316
guidelines 314
hors de combat persons 312–13
international armed conflicts (IACs) (Rule 29) 312
law of armed conflict 313
legal basis 312
levée en masse, participants in 312–13
malware 315
military manuals 313, 314, 316–17
military objectives (Rule 34) 316
non-international armed conflicts (NIACs) (Rule 30) 312, 316–18
non-State armed groups 316–17
organized armed groups (OAGs) 316–18
precautions in attack 312–13
preparatory acts 315
presumption of civilian status 315
proportionality in attack (Rule 38) 312–13, 342–43
repeated acts of direct participation 316
satellites 315, 317–18
scope and application 312–13
suspension of civilian protections 316
targeting of organized armed groups 311
terrorists 317
threshold 316–17
warnings (Rule 40) 356
directed energy weapons 208–9, 227–28, 335–36
distinction (Rule 32) 301–11
Additional Protocol I to Geneva Conventions 309
armed forces, classification as a member of 310
attack, definition of (Rule 31) 301–2, 310
civilians, definition of 311
combatants, definition of 310–11
customary international law 309
direct participation in hostilities (DPH) (Rule 33) 315, 316
dual-use objects 309
harmful contamination, avoidance of (Rule 14) 139, 145
hors de combat combatants 310
international armed conflicts (IACs) (Rule 29) 309, 311
International Court of Justice (ICJ) 309
law of armed conflict 309–11
legal basis 309
medical units and religious personnel (Rule 35) 310
military objectives (Rule 34) 309

military operations, definition of 310
military space operations, definition of 310
non-international armed conflicts (NIACs) (Rule 30) 309, 311
operations, definition of 310
organized armed groups (OAGs) 315, 316
proportionality in attack (Rule 38) 342–43
St Petersburg Declaration 1868 309
satellites 309
scope and application 310–11
special protections enjoyed by persons under the law of armed conflict 310
distress at sea, duty to rescue persons in 54–55
distress, alarm, urgency or safety communications 187–88, 189
DPH *see* **direct participation in hostilities (DPH) (Rule 33)**
dual-use objects
choice of means and methods of attack (Rule 37) 335
constant care (Rule 46) 393
distinction (Rule 32) 309
military objectives (Rule 34) 309, 321
proportionality in attack (Rule 38) 346
satellites 321, 335, 346
suspension or cancellation of attack (Rule 39) 347–48
warnings (Rule 40) 353–54
due regard (Rule 17) 170–76
ASAT tests 174–76
balancing rights and interests 170, 172–73
belligerent reprisals (Rule 47) 398
benefit of mankind 170–72
civilians and civilian property, treatment of 174
common law 154
countermeasures (Rule 25) 249
due diligence obligation 173
free use principle (Rule 1) 38
harmful contamination, avoidance of (Rule 14) 139, 173
harmful interference 173
international cooperation 170–72, 173, 174
interpretation 170–74
legal basis 170
liability for damage caused by space objects (Rule 12) 174
mutual assistance 173
origins 170–72
Outer Space Treaty (OST) 40, 170–72, 173–76
stand-alone obligation, as 173
State practice 170–72
veto on activities, imposition of a 170–72
zones (Rule 16) 159–60, 162, 166–67

Early Warning Satellites/Systems
as consistent with the use of space for peaceful purposes 64
electronic measures against as possible use of force 210
fundamental stabilization role 220–21
inferred actions and intent of the space object may viewed as possible use of force or armed attack 290
interference with as possible use of force 204
jamming against as potential use of force 242
placement of objects in close proximity as possible use of force 224
Russian view 221
strategic nuclear stability and international peace and security dependent 210
temporary blinding, jamming, or incapacitation 305
temporary or partial disruption as possible armed 232
economic disruptions 192–94, 197–98, 202–3
effects-based approach 203–5, 229–30, 231–32, 303–4, 305–6
electoral processes, interference with 198–200
electromagnetic pulse (EMP) weapons 208–9, 227–28
electromagnetic spectrum 141, 178–79, 186, 189, 209–12, 228–29, 302–3, 368
emblems, display of distinctive 327–28
emergencies 56, 133, 135, 187–88, 189, 282–83
electoral processes, interference with 198–200
enforcement measures (Chapter VII) 263–71
all necessary measures 268–69
armed attack (Rule 23) 226
collective security measures (Rule 28) 263–71
conflicting international agreements, primacy of 270–71
exclusion zones 224
forcible measures 263–64, 268–69
limits 268–69
mandatory measures 266
non-forcible measures 263–64, 267–69
non-intervention principle (Rule 20) 200
provisional measures 263–65
regional arrangements, agencies, or organizations 266–67
sanctions 265–66
satellites 267–68
self-defence (Rule 26) 125, 259
use of force (Rule 21) 265–66, 268–69
zones (Rule 16) 163–64, 166–67
ENMOD Convention 1977 (Convention on the Prohibition of Military or Any Other Hostile Use of Environmental Modification Techniques) 367–69, 375–76
environment *see* natural environment (Rule 43)
envoys of mankind, astronauts as 130, 131
equality and non-discrimination 36–37, 39, 43
erga omnes obligations 246–47
essential services, loss of 352–53, 355
Ethiopia
harmful radio interference 187–88
peaceful purposes in outer space (Rule 3) 60
European Code of Conduct for Space Debris Mitigation (ISO Standard) 144–45
European Space Agency (ESA) 56, 144–45
EUTELSAT, interference with 211–12
exclusion zones, enforcement of 224
exploration *see* freedom of use, access, exploration, and scientific investigation and principles of cooperation (Rule 1)
extraterrestrial matter on Earth, introduction of 141–43, 145

feasibility
choice of means and methods of attack (Rule 37) 334–35
continuing obligation of attackers 361
free use principle (Rule 1) 39–40
maximum extent feasible, definition of 358
neutrality in space (Rule 48) 400–1
precautions against the effects of attack (Rule 41) 349, 357, 358, 359–60, 361
precautions in attack 282–83, 334–35, 349
proportionality in attack (Rule 38) 338
suspension or cancellation of attack (Rule 39) 347–48, 349
verification (Rule 36) 332–33
warnings (Rule 40) 351–52
force majeure 116–17
foreseeable future, rules with limited relevance to 276
France
close approach of Luch- Olymp satellite, protest of 180
ICRC study on customary humanitarian international law 279
natural environment 373–74
peaceful purposes in outer space (Rule 3) 56
satellite jamming, protest of 187–88
free navigation, right of 163–64, 241–42
freedom of use, access, exploration, and scientific investigation and principles of cooperation (Rule 1) 35–40
benefit and interests of all countries, requirement for any use be carried out for the 36, 38

INDEX 413

Benefits Declaration 38
countermeasures (Rule 25) 246–47
due regard (Rule 17) 38, 40
erga omnes obligations 246–47
feasible and practicable, compliance
 when 39–40
legal basis 35–36
limitations and obligations 35–36, 40
mankind, recognition that space is province of
 all 36, 38
non-discrimination and equality, principle
 of 36–37, 39
Outer Space Treaty (OST), free use principle
 in 35–40, 246–47
retorsion (Rule 24) 241
threat of force (Rule 22) 224
UN Charter 35–36, 40
voluntary reporting 39–40
zones (Rule 16) 159–60, 163–64, 168–69
Friendly Relations Declaration 192–94,
 195, 204–5

Geneva Conventions of 1949 *see also* **Additional
 Protocol I to Geneva Conventions;
 Additional Protocol II to Geneva
 Conventions; Additional Protocol III to
 Geneva Conventions**
application 273–74
belligerent reprisals (Rule 47) 395, 396
Common Article 2 of the Geneva
 Conventions 276, 287–88, 293
Common Article 3 of the Geneva
 Conventions 276, 294–97
First GC, 2016 Commentary to 290–91
non-international armed conflicts (NIACs)
 (Rule 30) 295–96
Second GC, protection of religious
 personnel in 328
Third GC, release and return of POWs
 under 138
genocide 189, 245
geographical limitations 287–88, 293, 296–97
**global navigation satellite systems
 (GNSS)** 185–86, 211–12, 219, 344–45
good faith 256, 282–83, 345
**gravitational effects, demarcation of airspace
 based on Earth's** 28
**ground-based segments of military space
 operations** 359–60

**Hague Convention on Cultural Property
 1954** 395
Hague Regulations 1899 and 1907
application 274–75

Hague Conventions V and XIII 1907 400
perfidy, prohibition of (Rule 44) 383
warnings (Rule 40) 351
harm *see* **harmful contamination, avoidance of
 (Rule 14); harmful interference (Rule 18)**
**harmful contamination, avoidance of (Rule
 14)** 139–45
appropriate measures to avoid harmful
 contamination 142–44
ASAT tests 140
avoid harmful contamination, obligation
 to 141, 142–43, 145
backward contamination of the Earth,
 avoidance of 139, 141–43, 145
biological and organic contamination,
 guidelines on 141, 144–45
civilian and military activities as encompassed
 by the Rule 139, 145
customary international law 142–43
due regard (Rule 17) 139, 174
Earth, adverse changes in the environment on
 the 139, 141–43, 145
electromagnetic spectrum 141
exploration of outer space 139–40
extraterrestrial matter on Earth, introduction
 of 141–43, 145
forward contamination of outer space,
 avoidance of 139–41, 142–43, 145
harmful contamination, definition of 140
hostilities 145
interpretation 141
ITU recommendation on environmental
 protection of the geostationary-satellite
 orbit 144–45
legal basis 139
licensing 142–43, 144–45
military and civilian activities, lack of
 distinction between 139, 145
Moon and other celestial bodies 139–40
nuclear power sources 140
outer space, contamination of 139–41, 142–
 43, 145
Outer Space Treaty (OST) 40, 139–41, 142–44
space debris, creation of 140, 144–45
State practice 140, 142–43
voluntary, non-binding
 guidelines 141, 143–45
harmful interference (Rule 18) 177–84 *see also*
 ITU harmful radio interference (Rule 19)
application of Rule 177–78
appropriate consultations 179–83
armed conflict, during 184
ASAT weapons 180–82
belligerent reprisals (Rule 47) 398

harmful interference (Rule 18) (*cont.*)
  broad meaning 178–79
  collisions 178–79, 180
  common law 154
  consultations 177–78, 179–84
  due regard (Rule 17) 173, 177
  electronic, cyber, and high energy laser capabilities against satellites 183
  harmful, definition of 180
  jamming electronic communications 183
  legal basis 177
  mandatory reporting 39–40
  nationals, activities of 177–78
  non-intervention principle (Rule 20) 200
  Outer Space Treaty (OST) 40, 178–83
  physical means, through 178–79
  private companies, satellites launched by 178
  rendezvous and proximity operations (RPOs) 180
  responsibility of States for national activities in outer space (Rule 10) 178
  satellites 178, 180–83
  space debris, creation of 180–82
  State practice 179–83
  States, activities of 177–78
  zones (Rule 16) 159–60, 162, 165–66
heritage sites
  in armed conflict, protection of 395
  high-energy lasers 209
  Artemis Accords voluntary zones for protection of 167–69
hijacking, of satellites by cyber means 215, 296
hors de combat persons 310, 312–13
hostilities *see also* **direct participation in hostilities (DPH) (Rule 33); international armed conflicts (Rule 29); non-international armed conflicts (Rule 30)**
  astronauts and personnel of a spacecraft (Rule 13) 136–38
  harmful contamination, avoidance of (Rule 14) 145
  Moon Agreement 24
human rights 245, 338
human shields, use of 351–52

imminent armed attacks 163–64, 250, 254–56
impossibility of performance due to supervening events 12–13
improper use of markings (Rule 45) 384–88
  Additional Protocol I to Geneva Conventions 386–87
  combat, use during 385–86
  customary international law 384–85
  enemy markings 385–86
  international armed conflicts (IACs) (Rule 29) 384–86, 388
  jurisdiction (Rule 7) 385
  law of armed conflict 385–87
  legal basis 384–85
  means and methods of warfare (Rule 42) 384–88
  medical units and religious personnel (Rule 35) 327–28, 386–87
  military markings 384–86
  national markings 384–86
  naval warfare 386
  non-international armed conflicts (NIACs) (Rule 30) 384–85, 386, 388
  perfidy, prohibition of (Rule 44) 382, 384–85
  protective markings 386–87
  registration of space objects (Rule 8) 385
  satellites 386–87
  State practice 385, 386
  UN, improper use of the distinctive emblem of the 388
  visual observation in space, absence of 385
India
  ASAT weapons 59, 140, 180–82
  peaceful purposes in outer space (Rule 3) 51–52
  visits to facilities on the Moon and other celestial bodies (Rule 15) 149–50
  weapons in outer space, no general ban of 61
indispensable objects 94, 360, 395
indiscriminate weapons and indiscriminate attacks 369–71
inspections 148, 150–51
instructions, State agents acting on 290–91
intelligence collection (Rule 6) 82–84
  choice of means and methods of attack (Rule 37) 335
  intelligence, definition of 83
  legal basis 82–83
  national technical means of verification (NTMs) 82–83
  non-military and commercial entities 84
  precautions against the effects of attack (Rule 41) 361
  proportionality in attack (Rule 38) 341
  reconnaissance satellites 82–83
  silence or inaction of States 1–2
  space situational awareness (SSA) systems 83
  State practice 83–84
  suspension or cancellation of attack (Rule 39) 348, 349–50
  verification (Rule 36) 332
Inter-Agency Space Debris Coordination Committee (IADC) 141

INDEX 415

interference *see* harmful interference (Rule 18)
international armed conflicts (IACs),
    characterization of (**Rule 29**) 287–93
  accidents and mistakes 293
  armed attack (Rule 23) 291
  armed conflict, definition of 288
  attack, definition of (Rule 31) 301
  attribution 290–92
  belligerent reprisals (Rule 47) 394
  choice of means and methods of attack (Rule 37) 334
  civilian organs of the State 289–90
  combatants, definition of 311
  customary international law 287–88, 319
  direct participation in hostilities (DPH) (Rule 33) 312
  distinction (Rule 32) 309, 311
  existence of armed conflict, determination of 288–90
  fact, as a question of 289
  improper use of markings (Rule 45) 384–86, 388
  instructions, State agents acting on 290–91
  intensity of fighting 288–89
  law of armed conflict 287–88
  legal basis 287–88
  legal connections with space objects 291–92
  medical units and religious personnel (Rule 35) 324–25
  natural environment (Rule 43) 373–74
  neutrality in space (Rule 48) 399, 400–1
  non-international armed conflicts (NIACs) (Rule 30) 276
  official capacity, State agents acting in an 290–91
  organized armed groups (OAGs) 316
  Outer Space Treaty (OST) 290–92, 293
  parties to armed conflicts, determination of 291
  perfidy, prohibition of (Rule 44) 380
  precautions against the effects of attack (Rule 41) 357
  proportionality in attack (Rule 38) 337
  registration of space objects (Rule 8) 292
  responsibility of States for national activities in outer space (Rule 10) 291–92
  satellites 292
  space debris, accidents causing 293
  State practice 288–89, 292
  threshold requirement 288–90
  UN, improper use of the distinctive emblem of the 388
  warnings (Rule 40) 351
International Civil Aviation Convention 26–27

International Committee of the Red Cross (ICRC)
  attack, definition of (Rule 31) 303–4
  constant care (Rule 46) 392
  direct participation in hostilities (DPH) (Rule 33), guidance on 314, 316–17
  effects-based approach 303–4
  emblems, display of distinctive 327
  international armed conflicts (IACs) (Rule 29) 288–89
  law of armed conflict 273, 274–75
  medical units and religious personnel (Rule 35) 327
  military operations, definition of 3
  natural environment (Rule 43) 373–74, 375–76, 379
  non-State armed groups 316–17
international cooperation *see also* **freedom of use, access, exploration, and scientific investigation and principles of cooperation (Rule 1)**
  due regard (Rule 17) 170–72, 173, 174
  non-appropriation of outer space and celestial bodies (Rule 2) 43, 47–48
  ownership of space objects (Rule 9) 101
  zones (Rule 16) 165–66
International Criminal Court (ICC), Rome Statute of the 189, 370–71
International Criminal Tribunal for the former Yugoslavia (ICTY) 341–42
international humanitarian law (IHL) *see* law of armed conflict
International Law Association (ILA) Use of Force Committee 288–89
International Law Commission (ILC)
  Articles on State Responsibility 243, 246
  draft articles on armed conflict 12–13, 68–70, 76, 78–79
  draft principles on protection of the environment in relation to armed conflicts 278–79
  interpretation of treaties and conventions, study on 7–8
  law of armed conflict, priority of 13
  lex specialis 13
  natural environment (Rule 43) 377–78
  reparations 116
  return of personnel 137
  self-defence (Rule 26) 12
  WMDs (Rule 5) 76–79
international liability for damage caused by space objects (Rule 12) 121–25 *see also* **Liability Convention**
  civilian use of space objects 124

international liability for damage caused by space objects (Rule 12) (*cont.*)
  claims commissions, establishment of 122–23
  compensation 122–24, 125, 135, 236–37
  contractual relationships 121
  damages 91–92, 123, 125
  diplomatic channels, seeking compensation through 122–23
  Earth, damage to the 123
  fault 174
  launching States 26, 121, 122–24
  law of armed conflict 124–25
  legal basis 121
  national activities, international responsibility for 125
  non-government entities (NGEs) 125, 295–96
  Outer Space Treaty (OST) 121, 122, 123–25
  ownership of space objects (Rule 9) 98–99
  Registration Convention 22
  registration of space objects (Rule 8) 95–96
  self-defence (Rule 26) 258–59
  State practice 123
  suspension of rules 125
  zones (Rule 16) 162
international organizations, responsibility of (Rule 11) 118–20
  capacity to comply 119–20
  intergovernmental organizations 119–20
  international tribunals 288
  law of armed conflict 118
  legal basis 118
  legal issues 118–20
  lex specialis 118, 119
  non-intervention principle (Rule 20) 192–94, 197–98, 200
  Outer Space Treaty (OST) 118–20
  reparations 120
  responsibility of States for national activities in outer space (Rule 10) 118–20
    Rule 10 120
  satellites, armed force against 292
  self-defence (Rule 26) 120
  UN Charter 118, 119–20
  use of force (Rule 21) 120
International Space Station (ISS)
  Approach Ellipsoid 161–62
  docking 161–62
  intellectual property created on board, ownership of 100
  jurisdiction (Rule 7) 85–86
  medical units and religious personnel (Rule 35) 326–27
  Multilateral Control Board. International Rendezvous System Interoperability Standards 161–62
  professional astronauts and spaceflight participants, difference between 130–31
  registration of space objects (Rule 8) 95–96
  warnings (Rule 40) 355
  zones (Rule 16) 161–62
International Telecommunication Union (ITU) *see also* **ITU harmful radio interference (Rule 19)**
  Constitution and Regulations 185–86, 187–89, 375–76
  environmental protection of the geostationary-satellite orbit, recommendation in 144–45
international tribunals 288, 341–42
Internet 185–86, 344–45
internment 137
intervention *see* **non-intervention principle (Rule 20)**
investigations *see* **freedom of use, access, exploration, and scientific investigation and principles of cooperation (Rule 1)**
Iran
  military reconnaissance satellite 60
  satellite jamming 187–88, 212
Israel
  on ICRC study on customary humanitarian international law 278–79
  means and methods of warfare (Rule 42) 371–72
  peaceful purposes in outer space (Rule 3) 60
ITU harmful radio interference (Rule 19) 185–90
  application of rule 186–88
  armed conflicts, during 190
  command and control 185–86
  countermeasures (Rule 25) 247–48
  distress, alarm, urgency or safety communications 187–88, 189
  electromagnetic spectrum 178–79, 186, 189
  exemption for military radio installations 188–89
  Genocide Convention, incitement to genocide contrary to the 189
  global navigation satellite systems 185–86
  harmful interference, definition of 187–88
  intentional, accidental or incidental interference 186
  international legal obligations, application of other 189
  jamming 183, 187–88, 189
  legal basis 185–86

military radio installations, exemption for 188–89
non-intervention principle (Rule 20) 200
optical sensors in satellites, interference with 186
Outer Space Treaty (OST) 186, 189
private sector 186
Radio Regulations, services operating in accordance with 187–88
reciprocity 189
rendezvous and proximity operations (RPOs) 186
satellites
 Internet services 185–86
 jamming 183, 187–88
 national technical means (NTM) of verification 177–78
 optical sensors, interference with 186
 private sector 186
 satisfactory service, signals as strong enough only to ensure a 186
satisfactory service, signals as strong enough only to ensure a 186
space station, definition of 185–86
spoofing 189
telemetry 185–86
zones (Rule 16) 159–60

jamming electronic communications
armed attack (Rule 23) 228–29
attack, definition of (Rule 31) 305
countermeasures (Rule 25) 248
counterspace weapons systems and capabilities 209
GNSS (global navigation satellite systems) 211–12
harmful interference (Rule 18) 183
radio frequency part of the electromagnetic spectrum, using the 209–12, 228–29
radio interference (Rule 19) 183, 187–88, 189
retorsion (Rule 24) 241–42
satellites 183, 187–88, 209–12, 228–29, 305
signals, concept of 210–11
UN Charter 209–11
use of force (Rule 21) 183, 209–14, 220–21
Japan
ASAT weapon test, criticism of 180
harmful contamination, avoidance of (Rule 14) 143–44
peaceful purposes in outer space (Rule 3) 57
resources, exploitation of space 46–47
judgment of commanders based upon circumstances prevailing at the time 341–42

jurisdiction (Rule 7) 85–89
Apollo 11, Lunar Module of (the Eagle) 167–68
astronauts and personnel of a spacecraft (Rule 13) 135–36
customary international law 85–86
enforcement 86–87
exclusive jurisdiction 86–87
improper use of markings (Rule 45) 385
international agreements 85–86
International Space Station (ISS) 85–86
legal basis 85–86
Moon and other celestial bodies 86–87
nationality 85–86, 87–88, 234
non-appropriation of outer space and celestial bodies (Rule 2) 42
non-intervention principle (Rule 20) 200
Outer Space Treaty (OST) 85–89, 135–36
ownership of space objects (Rule 9) 98–99, 100
passive nationality principle 85–86
prescriptive jurisdiction 85–86
protective principle 85–86
registration of space objects (Rule 8) 92, 135–36
self-defence (Rule 26) 258–59
sovereign immunity 88–89
space objects 88–89, 98–99, 100, 234
State sovereignty 85–87
States in space, jurisdiction of 86–89
States of Registry 86–87, 88–89
territorial jurisdiction 85–86
universality 85–86
use of force (Rule 21) 201–2
visit to facilities on the Moon and other celestial bodies (Rule 15) 147, 149–50
zones (Rule 16) 167–68
jus ad bellum 12–15
armed attack, definition of (Rule 23) 226
cyber capabilities 216–17
natural environment (Rule 43) 377–78
responsibility of States for national activities in outer space (Rule 10) 110–12
self-defence (Rule 26) 226, 338
threat of force (Rule 22) 110
UN Charter 12
use of force (Rule 21) 110
jus cogens 10, 111–12
jus in bello *see* **law of armed conflict**

Kazakhstan
Moon Agreement 24, 65
keep out zones,
 declarations of 163–64, 166

418   INDEX

kinetic energy, weapons based on 302–3, 304, 315, 343
kinetic-kill weapon systems or vehicles 180–82, 206–7, 304, 335–36
  use of force (Rule 21) 206–8, 227–28

lasers
  dazzling 212–14, 305, 308
  high-energy lasers 209
  satellites, high energy capabilities against 183
launching authorities/States
  Astronauts, Agreement on Rescue and Return of (ARRA) 132–33
  astronauts and personnel of a spacecraft (Rule 13) 132–35
  joint and several liability 122
  legal connections with States 291–92
  liability for damage to space objects (Rule 12) 26, 121, 122–24
  ownership of space objects (Rule 9) 98–99
  registration of space objects (Rule 8) 90, 91–92, 95–97, 292, 295–96
  rescue
    inform launching authorities and Secretary-General of UN, duty to 56
    outer space, in 55–56
    sovereign territory, on 132–33
  return of personnel 134–35
  space objects and States, legal connections between 26
  States of Registry 26
  visit to facilities on the Moon and other celestial bodies (Rule 15) 147
law of armed conflict 12–15, 273–76 *see also* Additional Protocol I to Geneva Conventions; Additional Protocol II to Geneva Conventions; Geneva Conventions of 1949
  astronauts and personnel of a spacecraft (Rule 13) 137–38
  attack, definition of (Rule 31) 301–3, 308
  attribution 112–13
  choice of means and methods of warfare (Rule 37) 274–75
  conflict of laws 11–12
  customary international law 11–13, 14–15, 278–79
  direct participation in hostilities (DPH) (Rule 33) 313
  distinction (Rule 32) 309–11
  domain-specific, rules as 14–15
  facilities in space, existence of 276
  foreseeable future, rules with limited relevance to 276
  fundamental change of circumstances 12–13
  Hague Regulations 1899 and 1907 274–64, 383, 400
  humanity, preservation of a measure of 273
  impossibility of performance due to supervening events 12–13
  improper use of markings (Rule 45) 385–87
  international armed conflicts (IACs) (Rule 29) 287–88
  International Court of Justice (ICJ) 273–74
  international organizations, responsibility of (Rule 11) 118
  lex specialis 13, 70, 137
  liability for damage to space objects (Rule 12) 124–25
  means and methods of warfare (Rule 42) 365–66, 367
  militarization of outer space 273
  military astronauts, return of 137
  natural environment (Rule 43) 14–15, 375–76, 377–78
  non-government entities (NGEs) 110
  non-international armed conflicts (NIACs) (Rule 30) 294–97
  Outer Space Treaty (OST) 13, 273–75
  perfidy, prohibition of (Rule 44) 381–82
  priority 13
  prisoners of war (POWs) 137–38
  proportionality in attack (Rule 38) 337–38, 339–40, 342–43
  responsibility of States for national activities in outer space (Rule 10) 110, 112–14
  space domain, rules relevant to 275
  special protections 310
  State practice 276
Law of the Sea Convention 1982 (UNCLOS) 44, 70, 172–73
lex specialis
  conflict of laws 10–11
  customary international law 10, 11–12
  hierarchy of laws 10, 11–12
  international organizations, responsibility of (Rule 11) 118, 119
  interpretation 10–12
  law of armed conflict 13, 70, 137
  multiple legal regimes, existence of 10–11
  nuclear weapons, prohibitions of placement in orbit and installation of 12
  Outer Space Treaty (OST) 11–12
  reparations 115
  responsibility of States for national activities in outer space (Rule 10) 115
  self-defence (Rule 26) 70
  space law 115, 118, 119, 124–25

UN Charter 10, 11–12
WMDs (Rule 5) 12
liability *see* **international liability for damage caused by space objects (Rule 12)**
Liability Convention 20–22, 121, 122–25, 155
　aircraft flights, compensation for 122–23
　civilian use of space objects 124
　Claims Commission, establishment of a 21
　claims procedures 21
　customary international law 21–22
　interpretation 20–21
　jus standi 21
　non-government entities (NGEs) 125
　number of parties 20
　Outer Space Treaty (OST) 20–22
　parties 20–22
　persistent objectors, lack of 21
　ratifications 20–21
　Registration Convention 22
　specially affected States 20–21
　State practice, dissenting 21
　subsequent agreements 20–21
　subsequent practice 20–21
　surface of the Earth, compensation for damage caused on 122–23
　Vienna Convention on the Law of Treaties (VCLT), interpretation under 20–21
　withdraw, no expressions of intent to 20
Libya
　use of force, enforcement measures involving the 268–69
Limited Test Ban Treaty *see* **Partial Nuclear Test Ban Treaty (PNTB)**Luch/Olymp Satellite incident (2016) 56, 160–61
Luxembourg
　resources, exploitation of space 46, 101

maintenance or restoration of international peace and security 52, 263–64, 265, 266, 268–71
malware 304, 315, 369–70
mankind, recognition that space is province of all 36, 38
manuals *see* **military manuals**
maritime analogies 172–73
markings *see* **improper use of markings (Rule 45)**
means and methods of warfare (Rule 42) 365–72 *see also* **choice of means and methods of attack (Rule 37)**
　Additional Protocol I to Geneva Conventions 367, 368–69, 370–72
　attack, definition of (Rule 31) 301–3, 305–6
　customary international law 366, 370, 371–72
　definition 365–66
　environmental considerations 365–66, 367–69, 373–79
　improper use of markings (Rule 45) 384–88
　indiscriminate weapons and indiscriminate attacks 369–71
　International Court of Justice (ICJ) 369–70, 371
　law of armed conflict 365–66, 367
　legal basis 365–66
　legal reviews, obligation to carry out 371–72
　limitations or prohibitions 365–67
　military objectives (Rule 34) 369–70
　natural environment (Rule 43) 367, 373, 375
　nuclear weapons 365–67
　perfidy, prohibition of (Rule 44) 380–83
　potential military capability 365–66
　space weapons, definition of 365–66
　State practice 367–68, 371–72
　superfluous injury, definition of 371
　unnecessary suffering of combatants 370–71
　weapons
　　indiscriminate 365–66, 369–71
　　international agreements 366
　　legal review, obligation to carry out 371–72
　　limitations or prohibitions 365–66
　　unnecessary suffering of combatants 370–71
　　WMDs (Rule 5) 365–67
medical units and religious personnel (Rule 35) 324–28
　astronauts and personnel of a spacecraft (Rule 13) 133–34
　customary international law 324–25, 326
　distinction (Rule 32) 310
　emblems, display of distinctive 327–28
　equipment 326–27
　Geneva Convention II, protection of religious personnel in 328
　improper use of markings (Rule 45) 327–28, 386–87
　international armed conflicts (IACs) (Rule 29) 324–25
　ISS 326–27
　legal basis 324–25
　loss of special protection 325, 348
　markings 327–28, 386–87
　medical experiments 326
　medical unit, definition of 326–27
　multi-function areas 326
　non-international armed conflicts (NIACs) (Rule 30) 324–25
　Outer Space Treaty (OST) 326
　perfidy, prohibition of (Rule 44) 381–82
　Red Cross and Red Crescent, emblems of 327

420 INDEX

medical units and religious personnel (Rule 35) (*cont.*)
    registration of space objects (Rule 8) 327–28
    satellites used for medical communications 326
    signals, identification of medical units by digital 327–28, 386–87
    space objects 326, 327–28
    State practice 326, 327–28
    suspension or cancellation of attack (Rule 39) 348
    warnings (Rule 40) 325

meteorology 1–2

methodology of the Woomera Manual 7–15
    interpretive issues 7–8, 10–12
    jus ad bellum 12
    law of armed conflict and space 12–15
    lex specialis 10–12
    State silence or inaction, significance of 9–10
    State practice 7–9

methods of warfare *see* **choice of means and methods of attack (Rule 37); means and methods of warfare (Rule 42)**

microwave weapons 209, 212–13, 227–28

militarization of outer space 273

military activities, definition of 3

military advantage
    aggregation 341
    anticipated advantage 340–41
    choice of means and methods of attack (Rule 37) 334, 335–36
    concrete and direct, as 337–38, 340–41, 343, 344
    direct advantage 338, 349
    excessive losses in relation to military advantage 339–40, 341, 349
    military objectives (Rule 34) 319–20, 322–23
    precautions against the effects of attack (Rule 41) 361
    proportionality in attack (Rule 38) 337–38, 339–41, 343, 344, 345–46
    satellites 345–46
    similar military advantage 335–36
    suspension or cancellation of attack (Rule 39) 349–50

military establishments *see* **specified military establishments and activities on celestial bodies, restrictions on (Rule 4)**

military objectives (Rule 34) 319–23
    Additional Protocol I to Geneva Conventions 319–20, 321–23
    armed attack (Rule 23) 235
    attack, definition of (Rule 31) 301–2, 307
    choice of means and methods of attack (Rule 37) 334, 335–36
    civilians, obligation to move 357, 359
    communications, objects facilitating military 319–20, 321
    cumulative criteria 319–20
    current and potential contribution to military action 319–20
    customary international law 319
    definition 309
    densely populated areas, obligation to avoid location of military objectives in 357, 358, 359, 360
    direct participation in hostilities (DPH) (Rule 33) 316
    distinction (Rule 32) 309
    dual-use objects 309, 321
    effective contribution to military action 321–23
    indiscriminate weapons and indiscriminate attacks 369–70
    international armed conflicts (IACs) (Rule 29) 319
    legal basis 319
    military advantage 319–20, 322–23
    natural environment (Rule 43) 377–78, 379
    nature, location, purpose or use criteria 319–20
    neutrality in space (Rule 48) 402
    non-international armed conflicts (NIACs) (Rule 30) 319
    organized armed groups (OAGs) 316
    precautions against the effects of attack (Rule 41) 357, 358, 359, 360
    precautions in attack 281, 321
    proportionality in attack (Rule 38) 321, 338–39, 342–43, 345
    requirements 319–20
    satellites 235, 309, 321, 345, 349
    secret facilities 359
    suspension or cancellation of attack (Rule 39) 347–48, 349–50
    verification (Rule 36) 331–33
    war-fighting and war-supporting objects 321–23
    war-sustaining objects 321–23

military operations, definition of 3, 310, 391–92

military space operations during armed conflict 273–83 *see also* **conduct in or related to attack; means and methods of warfare; precautions in attack**
    Additional Protocol I to Geneva Conventions, application of 277–78, 279–80
    astronauts and personnel of a spacecraft (Rule 13) 133–34
    belligerent reprisals (Rule 47) 394–98
    constant care (Rule 46) 391–93

customary humanitarian international law, status of ICRC study on 278–79
dangerous forces, space objects containing 279–80
humanity, preservation of a measure of 273
international armed conflicts (IACs) (Rule 29) 287–93
law of armed conflict, application of 273–76
neutrality in space (Rule 48) 399–402
non-international armed conflicts (NIACs) (Rule 30) 276–77, 294–97
misinformation/disinformation 199–200, 381
mock operations 381
Moon Agreement 24
astronauts and personnel of a spacecraft (Rule 13) 134
common heritage of mankind 24
customary international law 24, 44, 65, 134
harmful contamination, avoidance of (Rule 14) 140
hostile acts or threats or hostile acts, prohibition of 24
inapplicability to non-State parties 65
number of parties 65
opposition of States 24
Outer Space Treaty (OST) 24, 134
ratifications 24
restrictions on military activities 24
specified military establishments and activities on celestial bodies, restrictions on (Rule 4) 65, 66
Moon and other celestial bodies *see also* **Moon Agreement; visit to facilities on the Moon and other celestial bodies (Rule 15)**
Apollo 11 Mission
 flag, planting of the 41–42
 landing sites 168–69
 Lunar Module of (the Eagle) 167–68
Apollo 17 landing sites 168–69
armed conflict, establishment of zones during 166–67
Artemis Accords 165–66
demilitarization regime 64, 66
emergencies 56
exclusion zones 168–69
harmful contamination, avoidance of (Rule 14) 139–40
international cooperation 165–66
jurisdiction (Rule 7) 86–87, 167–68
military equipment 67–68
military personnel 63–64
NASA's Lunar Surface Innovation Initiative 47–48, 100–1
Outer Space Treaty (OST) 67–68
ownership of space objects (Rule 9) 100–1

peaceful purposes in outer space (Rule 3) 62
rescue 55–56
responsibility of States for national activities in outer space (Rule 10) 109–10
specified military establishments and activities on celestial bodies, restrictions on (Rule 4) 63–64, 66–68
tardigrades to surface of the Moon, introduction of 140
weapons 62, 67–68
WMDs (Rule 5) 67–68, 73
zones (Rule 16) 164–69

national activities in outer space *see* **responsibility of States for national activities in outer space (Rule 10)**
national security
ASAT tests 58–59
peaceful purposes in outer space (Rule 3) 56–60
State practice 7
zones (Rule 16) 162–64
national space defence policy, existence of 222–23
nationality
aircraft 87
armed attack (Rule 23) 233
corporations 87
jurisdiction (Rule 7) 85–86, 87–88, 234
passive nationality principle 85–86
registration of space objects (Rule 8) 92, 292
space objects 25, 233–34
vessels 87
natural environment (Rule 43) 367, 373, 375 *see also* **harmful contamination, avoidance of (Rule 14)**
Additional Protocol I to Geneva Conventions 14–15, 368–69, 373–74, 376–79
civilian objects, natural environment as 379
customary international law 373–74
definition 367–68, 374–75
electromagnetic spectrum, use of the 368
environment, definition of 375–76
Environmental Modification Convention (ENMOD) 1977 14–15, 367–69, 375–76
guidance 368–69
international armed conflicts (IACs) (Rule 29) 373–74
International Court of Justice (ICJ) 377–78
irresponsible behaviour 374–75
law of armed conflict 14–15, 375–76, 377
legal basis 373–74
long-lasting, definition of 368–69, 376–77
manipulation of outer space 367–68

natural environment (Rule 43) *(cont.)*
    means and methods of warfare (Rule 42) 365–66, 367–69, 373, 375
    military objectives (Rule 34) 377–78, 379
    non-international armed conflicts (NIACs) (Rule 30) 373–74
    nuclear weapons 377
    precautions in attack 377
    proportionality in attack (Rule 38) 377–78, 379
    satellites, nuclear-powered 376–77
    self-defence (Rule 26) 377
    severe damage, definition of 368–69, 376–77
    space debris 376–77
    space environment 374–75
    State practice 374–75, 377–78
    uniformity, lack of 377–78
    widespread, definition of 368–69, 376–77
navigable air space, theory of 28
necessity 116–17, 167, 250, 251–52
Netherlands
    cyber operations, damage caused by 216–17
neutrality in space (Rule 48) 399–402
    astronauts and personnel of a spacecraft (Rule 13) 137
    attribution 110
    behaviour or conduct 400–1
    civilian personnel, return of 137
    corporations 401
    customary international law 401, 402
    domain-specific, rules as 14–15
    feasibility 400–1
    general principles 400–1
    Hague Conventions V and XIII 1907 400
    international armed conflicts (IACs) (Rule 29) 399, 400–1
    internment of able-bodied combatants 137
    legal basis 399
    limitations of some rules to terrestrial domains 400
    military manuals 401
    military objectives (Rule 34) 402
    non-government entities (NGEs) 113–14, 401, 402
    non-international armed conflicts (NIACs) (Rule 30) 399
    opinio juris 400–1
    Outer Space Treaty (OST) 400–1, 402
    responsibility of States for national activities in outer space (Rule 10) 110, 113–14, 401
    risk of being drawn into armed conflict 399
    satellites 399
    space infrastructure 400
    space objects 400, 402
    State practice 400–1
    threshold 402
    treaty law 400
Nigeria
    peaceful purposes in outer space (Rule 3) 60
non-appropriation of outer space and celestial bodies (Rule 2) 41–48
    Artemis Accords 47–48
    asteroid resources, recovery of 46
    authorization and continuing supervision of non-government entities (NGEs), responsibility of States for 45–47
    benefit-sharing regime, requirement for 44
    common heritage of mankind 44
    flag, planting of the US 41–42
    international cooperation 43, 47–48
    jurisdiction (Rule 7) 42
    legal basis 41–42
    non-governmental entities 42–43, 45–47
    non-international armed conflicts (NIACs) (Rule 30) 295
    Outer Space Treaty (OST) 40, 42–48, 293, 295
    private entities 46–47
    registration of space objects (Rule 8) 42
    removal of resources from their place 44–46
    resources, unsettled status of 42–48
    responsibility of States for national activities in outer space (Rule 10) 45–47
    State practice 43
    State sovereignty 41–42, 45–46
    threat of force (Rule 22) 224
    zones (Rule 16) 159–60, 167
non-discrimination and equality 36–37, 39, 43
non-forcible security measures 263–64, 267–69
non-government entities (NGEs)
    attribution 105, 110–14, 115, 290–91
    authorization and continuing supervision 45–47, 105, 106–7, 114–15
    categories 109
    countermeasures (Rule 25) 245–46
    effective control 112–13
    liability for damage to space objects (Rule 12) 125, 295–96
    neutrality in space (Rule 48) 113–14, 401, 402
    non-appropriation of outer space and celestial bodies (Rule 2) 42–43, 45–47
    Outer Space Treaty (OST) 186
    radio interference (Rule 19) 186
    responsibility of States for national activities in outer space (Rule 10) 105, 106–9, 110–14, 115, 291
    self-defence (Rule 26) 110–11, 258–59
    threat or use of armed force 105, 108

INDEX   423

non-international armed conflicts (NIACs), characterization of (Rule 30) 294–97
  attack, definition of (Rule 31) 301
  belligerent reprisals (Rule 47) 394
  capabilities of non-State armed groups 295–96
  choice of means and methods of attack (Rule 37) 334
  customary international law 294, 296–97, 319
  cyber capabilities 296
  definition 276, 294
  direct participation in hostilities (DPH) (Rule 33) 312, 315, 316–18
  distinction (Rule 32) 309, 311
  Geneva Conventions 1949 276, 294–97
  geographic limitations 296–97
  improper use of markings (Rule 45) 384–85, 386, 388
  intensity of conflicts 294
  internal disturbances and tensions, such as riots, isolated or sporadic violence or other acts of a similar nature 294
  international armed conflicts (IACs) (Rule 29) 276
  law of armed conflict 294–97
  legal basis 294
  limitations imposed by space and the space law regime 295–96
  medical units and religious personnel (Rule 35) 324–25
  military objectives (Rule 34) 319
  neutrality in space (Rule 48) 399
  non-State actors 276–77, 295–97, 316–17
  organized armed groups 316–18
  Outer Space Treaty (OST) 295, 296–97
  perfidy, prohibition of (Rule 44) 380
  precautions against the effects of attack (Rule 41) 357
  precautions in attack 280–81
  proportionality in attack (Rule 38) 337
  registration of space objects (Rule 8) 295–96
  responsibility of States for national activities in outer space (Rule 10) 276–77, 295–96
  satellites 296–97
  self-defence (Rule 26) 259
  spillovers 296–97
  suspension or cancellation of attack (Rule 39) 347–48
  technological challenges 276–77
  territorial limitations 295–96
  terrorists 317
  UN, improper use of the distinctive emblem of the 388
  verification (Rule 36) 331
  warnings (Rule 40) 351
non-intervention principle (Rule 20) 154, 191–200
  armed attack (Rule 23) 195
  armed intervention 195–96
  coercion 191–92, 194–200
  collective security measures (Rule 28) 200
  customary international law 191–92, 197–98, 199–200
  cyber capabilities 192–94, 198–200, 214–15
  declarations 191–92
  democratic processes as vulnerable to cyber conduct 192–94
  diplomatic actions 196–97
  economic disruptions 192–94, 197–98
  electoral processes, interference with 198–200
  energy security as vulnerable to cyber conduct 192–94
  enforcement 200
  essential energy security 192–94
  freely, matters which state is permitted to decide 192–94
  harmful interference (Rule 18) 200
  indirect use of force 195–96
  interference 191–92
  International Court of Justice (ICJ) 191–94, 195, 197–98
  international organizations 192–94, 197–98, 200
  jurisdiction (Rule 7) 200
  legal basis 191–92
  non-forcible prohibited intervention 197–200
  Outer Space Treaty (OST) 191, 200
  radio interference (Rule 19) 200
  reserved domain/exclusive competence 192–94, 198–99
  satellites 196–97, 198, 200
  sovereign equality of States 191
  State practice 200
  State sovereignty 192–94
  UN Charter 192–94, 200
  unwanted interference or non-forcible prohibited interference 196–97
  use of force (Rule 21) 191–92, 194–96, 198–99, 200
  use of space assets against another State 191
non-kinetic weapon systems 302–3
non-repetition, guarantees of 116–17
non-State actors *see also* organized armed groups (OAGs)
  non-international armed conflicts (NIACs) (Rule 30) 276–77, 295–97
  self-defence (Rule 26) 256–59

424   INDEX

North Atlantic Treaty Organization (NATO) 1–2, 214–15, 216–17, 261–62, 266–67
North Korea (DPRK)
  enforcement action, UN Security Council 265–66
  satellite jamming 211
Norway
  military action, effective contribution to 322
  organized armed groups 316–17
nuclear power 140, 376–77 *see also* nuclear weapons
nuclear weapons 73–75
  Additional Protocol I to Geneva Conventions 377
  asteroids, deflecting 75
  collective security measures (Rule 28) 265–66
  Comprehensive Nuclear Test Ban Treaty (CTBT) 80
  customary international law 78, 216–17
  definition 74
  International Court of Justice (ICJ) *Nuclear Weapons Advisory Opinion* 74, 77–79
  limitations or prohibitions 365–67
  means and methods of warfare (Rule 42) 75, 365–67
  natural environment (Rule 43) 377
  nuclear power sources, use of 74–75
  orbit, prohibition of installation and placement in 12
  Partial Nuclear Test Ban Treaty (PNTB) 79–80, 366–67
  place in orbit, definition of 72
  planetary defence, issue of 75
  satellites 256
  self-defence (Rule 26) 77–79, 256
  stationing 72, 73
  testing 79–80
  Treaty on the Prohibition of Nuclear Weapons 81
  use of force (Rule 21) 207–8, 227–28

occupation, terrestrial domain limitations in situations of belligerent 293
official capacity, State agents acting in an 290–91
oil/petroleum infrastructure 322–23
opinio juris
  airspace and outer space (delimitation of outer space) 26–27
  means and methods of warfare (Rule 42) 365–66, 371–72
  neutrality in space (Rule 48) 400–1
  Outer Space Treaty (OST) 17–19
  Red Cross study on customary humanitarian international law 278
  State practice 4–5

WMDs (Rule 5) 71–72
organized armed groups (OAGs)
  continuous combat function 316–17
  direct participation in hostilities (DPH) (Rule 33) 316–18
  distinction (Rule 32) 311, 316
  international armed conflicts (IACs) (Rule 29) 316
  military objective, as (Rule 34) 316
  non-international armed conflicts (NIACs) (Rule 30) 311, 316–18
  non-State armed groups 259, 316–18
  paramilitaries 290–91
  targeting 311, 316–17
  terrorists 317
OST *see* Outer Space Treaty (OST)
outer space, definition of 4
Outer Space Treaty (OST) 16–17 *see also* Outer Space Treaty (OST), *travaux préparatoires* of
  all possible assistance duty 132–33, 136
  appropriation 293
  armed attack (Rule 23) 226, 234
  ASAT tests, space debris caused by 140
  Astronauts, Agreement on Rescue and Return of (ARRA) 19–20, 129, 133–35
  astronauts and personnel of a spacecraft (Rule 13) 129–33, 136
  attribution 290–91
  background 18
  belligerent occupation 293
  belligerent rights 70
  Benefits Declaration (UN General Assembly Resolution) 38
  capacity to comply 119–20
  civilian use of space objects 124
  countermeasures (Rule 25) 243, 245–46
  Declaration of Legal Principles 1963 18–19, 36–37
  collective security measures (Rule 28) 270–71
  collective self-defence (Rule 27) 76–78
  customary international law 4, 17–19, 24
  distinction (Rule 32) 139
  due regard (Rule 17) 40, 170–72, 173–76
  elaboration by other treaties 15–16, 19–22
  entry into force 16
  free use principle (Rule 1) 35–40, 246–47
    astronauts and personnel of a spacecraft (Rule 13) 40
    due regard (Rule 17) 40
    harmful contamination, avoidance of (Rule 14) 40
    non-appropriation of outer space and celestial bodies (Rule 2) 40

INDEX 425

ownership of space objects (Rule 9) 100–1
visits (Rule 15) 40
harmful contamination, avoidance of (Rule 14) 40, 139–41, 142–44
harmful interference (Rule 18) 40, 178–83
intelligence collection (Rule 6) 82–83
international armed conflicts (IACs) (Rule 29) 291–92, 293
international organizations, responsibility of (Rule 11) 118–20
interpretation 4–5, 7, 11–12, 19–20, 50–51
jurisdiction (Rule 7) 85–89, 135–36
jus ad bellum 12
law of armed conflict 11–12, 70, 273–75
lex specialis 11–12
liability for damage to space objects (Rule 12) 121, 122, 123–25
limitations and obligations 35–36, 40
means and methods of warfare (Rule 42) 366–67
medical units and religious personnel (Rule 35) 326
Moon and other celestial bodies 24, 67–68, 134
negotiations 52–54
neutrality in space (Rule 48) 113–14, 400–1, 402
non-appropriation of outer space and celestial bodies (Rule 2) 42–48, 100–1
non-government entities (NGEs) 125, 186
non-international armed conflicts (NIACs) (Rule 30) 295, 296–97
non-intervention principle (Rule 20) 191, 200
nuclear weapons 12, 79–80
number of parties and signatories 16–17
object and purpose 16, 50–51, 113–14, 401
ownership of space objects (Rule 9) 98–101
parties 4, 16–17, 18–19
peaceful purposes in outer space (Rule 3) 49–56, 61–62, 110
Preamble 50–52, 53–54
priority 12
radio interference (Rule 19) 186, 189
ratifications 4, 16–17, 18–19
registration of space objects (Rule 8) 25–26, 90, 92, 94–95, 96–97
reparations 115
resources, unsettled status of 42–43, 44–46
responsibility of States for national activities in outer space (Rule 10) 45–47, 105–10, 111–14, 291, 292
return of personnel 134–35
self-defence (Rule 26) 68–69, 70, 250–51, 258–59

signatories 16–17
silence or inaction of States 1–2
space objects
  legal connections with States 25–26
  ownership (Rule 9) 98–101
  responsibility (Rule 10) 45–47, 105–10, 111–14, 291, 292
specified military establishments and activities on celestial bodies, restrictions on (Rule 4) 63–64, 65–70
State practice 18–19
surface of the Earth, compensation for damage caused on 122–23
suspension of parts of Treaty 70
terrestrial domain limitations 293
third party rights 13
UN Charter 12, 251
use of force (Rule 21) 11–12, 201
Vienna Convention on the Law of Treaties (VCLT), interpretation under 4–5, 20–21
visit to facilities on the Moon and other celestial bodies (Rule 15) 40, 146–50, 164–65
weapons, no general ban on 61–62, 63–64, 67–68
withdraw, no expressions of intent to 16
WMDs (Rule 5) 67–68, 71–81
zones (Rule 16) 154, 159–61, 162–63, 164–65, 166, 167–69

ownership of space objects (Rule 9) 98–101
abandonment 99
armed conflict, capture in 99
Artemis Accords 100–1
changes in ownership 92–93, 96–97
construction of objects on spacecrafts or other objects 100–1
international cooperation, principle of 101
ISS, creation of intellectual property on the 100
juridical persons 99
jurisdiction (Rule 7) 98–99, 100
landed on celestial bodies, objects 99–100
launching States 98–99
legal basis 98
legal connections with States 26, 98–99, 291
legal issues 98–101
liability 98–99
mined resources 101
Moon and other celestial bodies 100–1
national laws 99, 100
natural persons 99
Outer Space Treaty (OST) 98–101
registration of space objects (Rule 8) 98–100

ownership of space objects (Rule 9) (*cont.*)
   responsibility of States for national activities in outer space (Rule 10) 98–99
   return of objects 99
   satellites 235
   State practice 53–54
   States of Registry 98–99, 100
   transfer of ownership 99

Partial Nuclear Test Ban Treaty (PNTB) 79–80, 366–67
participation *see* direct participation in hostilities (DPH) (Rule 33)
peacekeeping operations 269–70
peaceful means, settlement of disputes by 153
peaceful purposes in outer space (Rule 3) 49–62
   astronauts and personnel of a spacecraft (Rule 13) 135
   demilitarization 49–50, 53–54, 55–56, 59
   diverse and growing military space activities 58–60
   exclusively peaceful purposes, definition of 49–50
   interpretation 50–51, 54, 55–56
   legal basis 49–50
   Moon and other celestial bodies, no prohibition on weapons on the 62
   national security 56–60
   non-aggressive uses 52–57, 63–64, 110
   non-military, as meaning 49–57, 58–59
   object and purpose of treaties 50–51
   Outer Space Treaty (OST) 49–56, 61–62
   peaceful purposes, definition of 63–64
   responsibility of States for national activities in outer space (Rule 10) 110
   satellites 53–55, 56–58, 60
   self-defence (Rule 26) 49–50, 54, 251, 253–54
   specified military establishments and activities on celestial bodies, restrictions on (Rule 4) 63–64, 65–66
   State practice 49–50, 54–60
   UN Charter 49–50, 52, 55–56, 61
   Vienna Convention on the Law of Treaties (VCLT), interpretation of 50–51
   weapons, no general ban on 61–62
peacetime, routine military activities in 3–4, 31
   astronauts and personnel of a spacecraft (Rule 13) 36, 129–38
   belligerent rights by States, exercise of 31
   civilian population from hostilities, protection of 31
   freedom of use, access, exploration, and scientific investigation and principles of cooperation (Rule 1) 35–40
   harmful contamination, avoidance of (Rule 14) 40, 139–45
   intelligence collection (Rule 6) 82–84
   international liability for damage caused by space objects (Rule 12) 40, 121–25
   international organizations, responsibility of (Rule 11) 118–20
   jurisdiction (Rule 7) 85–89
   non-appropriation of outer space and celestial bodies (Rule 2) 40, 41–48
   ownership of space objects (Rule 9) 98–101
   peaceful purposes in outer space (Rule 3) 49–62
   registration of space objects (Rule 8) 90–97
   responsibility of States for national activities in outer space (Rule 10) 37, 40
   self-defence (Rule 26) 35–36
   space law regime 3–4, 35–36
   specified military establishments and activities on celestial bodies, restrictions on (Rule 4) 40, 63–70
   visit to facilities on the Moon and other celestial bodies (Rule 15) 40, 146–51
   WMDs (Rule 5) 40, 71–81
peremptory norms 10, 111–12, 245
perfidy, prohibition of (Rule 44) 380–83
   Additional Protocol I to Geneva Conventions 380–81
   camouflage 381
   capture 380
   civilian objects 381–82
   combatant, failure to distinguish oneself as a 382
   confidence, betrayals of 381, 382
   customary international law 380
   death or injury of adversaries 382
   deception 382
   decoys 381
   destruction of property 382
   four elements or requirements 381–82
   Hague Regulations 1899 and 1907 383
   improper use of markings (Rule 45) 382, 384–85
   international armed conflicts (IACs) (Rule 29) 380
   law of armed conflict 381–82
   legal basis 380
   means and methods of warfare (Rule 42) 380–83
   medical facilities 381–82
   misinformation 381
   mock operations 381
   non-international armed conflicts (NIACs) (Rule 30) 380
   proximate cause 382
   registration of space objects (Rule 8) 382
   ruses 305–6, 381, 384–85

INDEX 427

space objects, failure to specify the military functions of 382
special protections 381–82
unsuccessful perfidious acts 383
personnel of a spacecraft, use of term *see* **astronauts and personnel of a spacecraft (Rule 13)**
place in orbit, definition of 72–73
planetary defence 75, 80, 270–71
Planetary Protection Policy (COSPAR) 143–44
platforms in space 149–50
position, navigation, and timing (PNT) functionality 1–2
precautions against the effects of attack (Rule 41) 281, 357–61
Additional Protocol I to Geneva Conventions 357, 358–59
attackers, obligations on 358
choice of means and methods of attack (Rule 37) 361
civilian losses 357–61
continuing obligation of attackers 361
countermeasures (Rule 25) 359–60
customary international law 357
dangers, definition of 358–59
defenders, obligations on 358
densely populated areas, obligation to avoid location of military objectives in 357, 358, 359, 360
excessive incidental civilian harm 361
feasibility 349, 357, 358, 359–60, 361
ground-based segments of military space operations 359–60
inconvenience or irritation 358–59
intelligence collection (Rule 6) 361
international armed conflicts (IACs) (Rule 29) 357
legal basis 357
military advantage 361
military objectives (Rule 34) 357, 358, 359, 360
necessary precautions, definition of 357
non-international armed conflicts (NIACs) (Rule 30) 357
passive precautions 358, 359–60
planning and preparation 358
practicable or practically possible, precautions which are 358, 360
proportionality in attack (Rule 38) 361
satellites 359–60, 361
scope, requirements and obligations 357–59
secret facilities 359
space-based segments of military space operations 359–60
space debris, warnings on 360

suspension or cancellation of attack (Rule 39) 349
verification (Rule 36) 361
warnings (Rule 40) 360, 361
precautions in attack 280–83 *see also* **verification as precaution in attack (Rule 36)**
Additional Protocol I to Geneva Conventions 278, 280–82
attack, definition of (Rule 31) 301–2, 307
choice of means and methods of attack (Rule 37) 281–82, 334–36
civilian populations and objects 278
constant care (Rule 46) 281, 392, 393
context 282
continuous obligation, as an 281–82
costs and resources 282–83
customary international law 280–81
dangerous forces, space objects containing 279–80
direct participation in hostilities (DPH) (Rule 33) 312–13
duration of obligation 281–82
feasibility 282–83, 334–35
good faith 282–83
humanitarian benefits 282–83
military objectives (Rule 34) 281, 321
military personnel, application to all 281–82
natural environment (Rule 43) 377
non-international armed conflicts (NIACs) (Rule 30) 280–81
operational risks 282–83
planning of attacks 281–82
precautions against the effects of attack (Rule 41) 281, 357–61
proportionality in attack (Rule 38) 337–46
success of military missions, effect on the 282–83
suspension or cancellation of attack (Rule 39) 281, 347–50
urgency 282–83
verification (Rule 36) 281, 331–33
visit to facilities on the Moon and other celestial bodies (Rule 15) 147–48, 150, 164–65
warnings (Rule 40) 351–56
preparatory acts 315
prisoners of war (POWs) 137–38
private sector
harmful interference (Rule 18) 178
nationality of corporations 87
neutrality in space (Rule 48) 401
non-appropriation of outer space and celestial bodies (Rule 2) 46–47
radio interference (Rule 19) 186
satellites 178, 186, 309, 352–53
privileges and immunities 88–89, 131

428 INDEX

proportionality in attack (Rule 38) 337–46
  Additional Protocol I to Geneva Conventions 337, 339
  application and scope 337–38
  ASAT systems 343–44
  attack, definition of (Rule 31) 301–2, 307, 338
  belligerent reprisals (Rule 47) 396–97
  causation 339
  civilian losses 337–46
  communications support, attacks on 341
  constant care (Rule 46) 338, 392, 393
  countermeasures (Rule 25) 247–49, 338
  customary international law 337
  dangerous forces, space objects containing 279–80
  direct participation in hostilities (Rule 33) 312, 342–43
  distinction (Rule 32) 342–43
  dual-purpose satellites 346
  feasible precautions 338
  good faith 345
  human rights 338
  incidental civilian losses 337–46
  intelligence support 341
  intention 342–43
  international armed conflicts (IACs) (Rule 29) 337
  International Criminal Tribunal for the former Yugoslavia (ICTY) 341–42
  international tribunals, decisions of 341–42
  judgment of commanders based upon circumstances prevailing at the time 341–42
  jus ad bellum 338
  law of armed conflict 337–38, 339–40, 342–43
  legal basis 337
  military advantage 337–38, 339–41, 343, 344, 345–46
  military manuals 341–42
  military objectives (Rule 34) 321, 338–39, 342–43, 345
  military space operations, special challenges related to 343–46
  natural environment (Rule 43) 377–78, 379
  non-international armed conflicts (NIACs) (Rule 30) 337
  precautions against the effects of attack (Rule 41) 361
  precautions in attack 337–46
  psychological harm 339
  satellites 343–46
  self-defence (Rule 26) 247, 250, 251, 252–54, 338
  space debris 343–44
  space objects, attacks on 343–44
  State practice 341–42, 344
  subjective evaluation 341–42
  suspension or cancellation of attack (Rule 39) 349–36
  warnings (Rule 40) 352–54, 356
protected persons *see also* civilian populations, civilians, and civilian objects; medical units and religious personnel (Rule 35)
  astronauts and personnel of a spacecraft (Rule 13) 398
  belligerent reprisals 396, 398
  distinction (Rule 32) 310
  perfidy, prohibition of 381–82
  special protections 310, 325, 348, 381–82
  suspension or cancellation of attack (Rule 39) 348
provisional measures 263–65
proximity to space objects of other States, intentional placement of hostile objects in 224
psychological harm 338–39, 346
psychological operations 203–4, 216, 228–29

radio communications *see* ITU harmful radio interference (Rule 19)
radio frequency part of the electromagnetic spectrum, using the 209–12, 228–29
reciprocity 147–51, 244–45
reconnaissance 1–2, 82–83, 391–92
Red Crescent, International Federation of the 327
regional arrangements, agencies, or organizations 120, 266–67, 269–70
Registration Convention 22–24
  belligerent reprisals (Rule 47) 398
  capacity of States 22
  customary international law 23–24
  diminishing compliance, trend of 23
  general principle of registration 23–24
  interpretation 23–24
  Liability Convention 22
  loopholes or escape clauses 23
  number of parties 22
  Outer Space Treaty (OST) 23–24
  parties 22, 23
  ratifications 22
  signatories 22
  subsequent agreement 23
  subsequent practice 23
  transparency 23
  withdraw, no expressions of intent to 22
registration of space objects (Rule 8) 90–97 *see also* Registration Convention

INDEX   429

armed attack (Rule 23) 235–36
challenges 92–93
change in status of objects 92–93
changes in ownership 92–93, 96–97
civilian use, identification as exclusively
    dedicated to 94–95
connecting States to objects 91–92
de-orbiting or decaying objects 92–93
failure to register 91–92
foreign objects 92–93
functional objects 92–93
hijacking or control 296
improper use of markings (Rule 45) 382
information provided by States 92–95
international armed conflicts (IACs) (Rule
    29) 292
jurisdiction (Rule 7) 92, 135–36
launching States 90, 91–92, 95–97,
    292, 295–96
legal basis 90
legal connections with States 25–26, 291–92
liability 95–96
medical units, marking of 327–28
missiles 90
nationality 92, 292
non-appropriation of outer space and celestial
    bodies (Rule 2) 42
non-functional objects 92–93
non-international armed conflicts (NIACs)
    (Rule 30) 296–97
non-State armed groups, use to target 296–97
orbital parameters 93
Outer Space Treaty (OST) 25–26, 90, 92,
    94–95, 96–97
ownership of space objects (Rule 9) 98–100
perfidy, prohibition of (Rule 44) 382
Registration Convention 90–91, 93–
    97, 98–100
responsibility of States for national activities in
    outer space (Rule 10) 91–92, 96, 295–96
satellites 93–94, 95–96, 292, 296–97
self-defence (Rule 26) 247
space debris 91
States of Registry 25–26, 91–92, 95–97
sub-orbital flights 90
transparency, lack of 93–95
visit to facilities on the Moon and other
    celestial bodies (Rule 15) 147
religious personnel *see* **medical units and
    religious personnel (Rule 35)**
remote controlled systems 215, 305
**rendezvous and proximity operations
    (RPOs)** 180, 186, 332–33, 335
reparations 105, 106, 115–17, 120, 247

reprisals *see* **belligerent reprisals (Rule 47);
    countermeasures (Rule 25)**
rescue of astronauts *see also* **Agreement on Rescue
    and Return of Astronauts (ARRA)**
armed conflicts, during 136
capacity to assist 136
Earth, elsewhere on 133
joint rescue operations 132
outer space, in 133–34
refusal of access by territorial State 132–33
Secretary-General of UN, duty to
    inform 132–33
sovereign territory, on 132–33
suspension of duty 136
resources 42–48, 100–1, 169, 282–83
response actions 154–55
collective security measures (Rule
    28) 263–71
collective self-defence (Rule 27) 260–62
countermeasures (Rule 25) 243–49
harmful interference (Rule 18) 155
Liability Convention 155
Outer Space Treaty (OST) 155
retorsion (Rule 24) 241–42
self-defence (Rule 26) 250–59
UN Charter 155
responsibility *see* **international organizations,
    responsibility of (Rule 11);
    responsibility of States for national
    activities in outer space (Rule 10)**
**responsibility of States for national activities in
    outer space (Rule 10)** 105–17
attribution of international responsibility 105,
    106, 110–14, 291
authorization and continuing supervision of
    non-government entities, requirement
    of 105, 106–7, 114–15
countermeasures (Rule 25) 245–46
cyber capabilities 112
effective control 111–12, 113–14
government entities 108–9, 291
harmful interference (Rule 18) 178
International Court of Justice (ICJ) 111–12
international organizations, responsibility of
    (Rule 11) 118–20
interpretation 106–7, 108–9, 115
jus ad bellum 110–12
law of armed conflict 110, 112–14
legal basis 105
lex specialis 115
liability for damage to space objects (Rule
    12) 121
military space activities, concept of 109–14
Moon and other celestial bodies 109–10

430   INDEX

responsibility of States for national activities in outer space (Rule 10) (cont.)
  national activities, concept of 105, 106–10, 234
  neutrality 110, 113–14, 401
  non-appropriation of outer space and celestial bodies (Rule 2) 45–47
  non-government entities (NGEs), activities of 105, 106, 108–9, 295–96
    attribution of responsibility 105, 110–14, 291
    authorization and continuing supervision, requirement of 105, 106–7, 114–15
    special attribution rule 105, 110–11, 112–13, 115
    threat or use of armed force 105, 108
  non-international armed conflicts (NIACs) (Rule 30) 276–77, 295–96
  Outer Space Treaty (OST) 40, 105–10, 111–14, 291
  ownership of space objects (Rule 9) 98–99
  peaceful purposes, concept of 110
  registration of space objects (Rule 8) 91–92, 96, 295–96
  reparations for internationally wrongful acts 105, 106, 115–17
  sale or transfer of space objects 99
  self-defence (Rule 26) 110–12, 116–17
  State practice 106–7, 112–13
  UN Charter 110–12, 113–14
  use of force (Rule 21) 111–12
  WMDs (Rule 5) 109–10
retaliation 247
retorsion (Rule 24) 241–42
  application of rule 241–42
  belligerent reprisals (Rule 47) 241
  countermeasures (Rule 25) 241, 243, 247
  customary international law 241–42
  definition 241
  free use principle (Rule 1) 241
  jamming 241–42
  legal basis 241
  unlawful but friendly acts 241–42
return of astronauts/personnel see also Agreement on Rescue and Return of Astronauts (ARRA)
  armed conflicts, during 137
  civilian personnel 137
  compensation for damage 135
  International Law Commission (ILC) 137
  internment of civilians 137
  military personnel 135
  prisoners of war (POWs) 137
  representatives of launching States, to 134–35
  scientific activities, military astronauts engaged purely in 137
  States of Registry, to 134–35
reviews of weapons, obligation to carry out legal 371–72
robotic mechanisms 302–3
Rome Statute of the International Criminal Court 189, 370–71
Roscosmos 46–47
ruses 305–6, 381, 384–85
Russia see also Soviet Union
  arms control 220–21
  ASAT weapons 180–82
  Luch/Olymp Satellite incident (2016) 56, 160–61
  peaceful purposes in outer space (Rule 3) 54
  space debris 180–82

safety
  heritage sites, protection of space 168–69
  personnel, of 149–51
  rendezvous proximity operations (RPOs) 186
  safety-based manoeuvre zones 160–62
  satellites 165–66
  visit to facilities on the Moon and other celestial bodies (Rule 15) 149–51
  zones (Rule 16) 165–66
St Petersburg Declaration 1868 309
sale or transfer of space objects 99
sanctions 265–66
satellites see also ASATs (anti-satellite weapons)
  airspace and outer space (delimitation of outer space) 26–27
  armed attack (Rule 23) 235–36
  arms control 220–21
  attack, definition of (Rule 31) 304–5, 307–8
  ballistic missile technology, use of 265–66
  choice of means and methods of attack (Rule 37) 335–36
  collective security measures (Rule 28) 265–66, 267–68, 269–70
  collision, risk of 224
  commercial/private satellites
    armed attack (Rule 23) 235
    distinction (Rule 32) 309
    harmful interference (Rule 18) 178
    military objectives (Rule 34) 321
    precautions against the effects of attack (Rule 41) 357, 359–60
    radio interference (Rule 19) 186
  communications 1–2, 220–21, 321, 332
  countermeasures (Rule 25) 359–60
  cyber capabilities 304–5
  defensive acts 307–8

INDEX

de-orbiting 162
destruction 180–82, 230–31, 343–44, 345–46
direct participation in hostilities (DPH) (Rule 33) 315, 317–18
directed energy attacks 335–36
diverse and expanding services, functions and purposes 344–45
dual-use satellites
　choice of means and methods of attack (Rule 37) 335
　distinction (Rule 32) 309
　military objectives (Rule 34) 321
　proportionality in attack (Rule 38) 346
early warning satellites 220–21
economic disruptions 198
electronic, cyber, and high energy laser capabilities 183
enforcement measures (Chapter VII) 267–68
Global Navigation Satellite Systems (GNSS) 185–86, 211–12, 219, 344–45
harmful interference (Rule 18) 178, 180–83
hijacking 215
improper use of markings (Rule 45) 386–87
inciting violence or civil unrest via satellite transmissions 196–97
international armed conflicts (IACs) (Rule 29) 292
international organizations, responsibility of (Rule 11) 292
Internet services 185–86, 344–45
jamming 183, 187–88, 209–12, 219, 228–29, 305
legal connections with States 25, 26, 292
malware 315
medical communications 326
military advantage 345–46
military functions 235
military objectives (Rule 34) 235, 309, 321, 345, 349
national technical means of verification (NTMs) 177–78
neutrality in space (Rule 48) 399
non-essential services, loss of 358–59
non-intervention principle (Rule 20) 196–97, 198, 200
nuclear-powered satellites 376–77
nuclear weapons 256
offensive rendezvous operations 307–8
optical sensors in satellites, interference with 186
ownership of space objects (Rule 9) 235
peaceful purposes in outer space (Rule 3) 53–55, 56–58, 60
peacekeeping operations 269–70

precautions against the effects of attack (Rule 41) 358–60, 361
proportionality in attack (Rule 38) 343, 344–46
proximity to space objects of other States, intentional placement of hostile objects in 224
radio interference (Rule 19) 186
radio navigation 344–45
reconnaissance 82–83
registration of space objects (Rule 8) 93–94, 95–96, 292, 399
ruses 381
satisfactory service, signals as strong enough only to ensure a 186
self-defence (Rule 26) 235–36, 256
space debris 335–36, 343–44, 360
spoofing 219
State practice 200
suspension or cancellation of attack (Rule 39) 348, 349–50
temporary or partial disruption 154, 212–13, 228–29, 304–5
use of force (Rule 21) 154, 209–13, 215, 219–21, 227–29, 265–66
verification (Rule 36) 332
warnings (Rule 40) 220–21, 305, 351–53, 354–55, 360
zones (Rule 16) 160–61, 162, 163–64, 167
scale and effects test 205, 229–32
scientific investigations *see* freedom of use, access, exploration, and scientific investigation and principles of cooperation (Rule 1)
secret facilities 359
security *see* national security
security measures *see* collective security measures (Rule 28)
self-defence (Rule 26) 250–59, 260 *see also* collective self-defence (Rule 27)
　anticipatory self-defence 254–56
　application to space 251
　armed attack (Rule 23) 226, 233, 250, 252–56, 259
　attribution 259
　capabilities 256
　civilian protection and civilian objects, protection of 70
　countermeasures (Rule 25) 252–53
　customary international law 78, 250, 251, 252–53, 254–55
　cyber capabilities 217–18
　defensive measures, reporting and termination of 259

self-defence (Rule 26) (*cont.*)
   direct-ascent ASAT 255
   extraterritorial military operations 256–57
   imminent armed attacks 226, 250, 254–56
   incursions 163–64
   International Court of Justice (ICJ) 252–53
   international organizations, responsibility of (Rule 11) 120
   jurisdiction (Rule 7) 258–59
   jus ad bellum 226, 338
   law of armed conflict 70
   legal basis 250
   legitimate aims 252
   lex specialis 70
   liability (Rule 12) 258–59
   military manuals 251
   natural environment (Rule 43) 377
   necessity 250, 251–52
   non-government entities (NGEs) 110–11, 258–59
   non-international armed conflicts (NIACs) (Rule 30) 259
   non-State actors 256–59
   nuclear weapons 77–79, 256
   Outer Space Treaty (OST) 68–69, 70, 76–78, 250–51, 258–59
   peaceful purposes in outer space (Rule 3) 49–50, 54, 251, 253–54
   proportionality in attack (Rule 38) 247, 250, 251, 252–54, 338
   regional organizations 120
   registration of space objects (Rule 8) 258–59
   reparations 116–17
   responsibility of States for national activities in outer space (Rule 10) 106–7, 112–13
   satellites 235–36, 256
   space objects 163–64, 235–36
   specified military establishments and activities on celestial bodies, restrictions on (Rule 4) 68–70
   State practice 76, 256–57
   State sovereignty 256–57
   terrestrial domains to space, extension from 253–54
   threat of force (Rule 22) 110, 222
   UN Charter 68–69, 163–64, 250–52, 253–55, 256–57, 259
   use of force (Rule 21) 110, 201–2, 217–18, 250
   weapons testing 68–69
   WMDs (Rule 5) 76–79
   zones (Rule 16) 160–61, 163–64
signals 210–11, 305, 327–28
silence or inaction of States 9–10
sovereign immunity 88–89

sovereignty *see* **State sovereignty**
Soviet Union (USSR) *see also* **Russia**
   arms control 220–21
   ASAT weapons 140, 180–82
   Astronauts, Agreement on Rescue and Return of (ARRA) 134–35
   due regard (Rule 17) 170–72
   international organizations, responsibility of (Rule 11) 118–19
   military equipment 67–68
   Outer Space Treaty (OST) 51–54
   peaceful purposes in outer space (Rule 3) 51–54
   visit to facilities on the Moon and other celestial bodies (Rule 15) 147–48, 150–51
space capabilities *see* **capacities/capabilities; cyber capabilities**
space debris
   accidents and mistakes 293
   ASAT tests 140, 180–82
   choice of means and methods of attack (Rule 37) 335–36
   European Code of Conduct for Space Debris Mitigation (ISO Standard) 144–45
   harmful contamination, avoidance of (Rule 14) 140
   harmful interference (Rule 18) 180–82
   IADC guidelines 141, 144–45
   international armed conflicts (IACs) (Rule 29) 293
   licensing 144–45
   long-lasting 343, 344
   natural environment (Rule 43) 376–77
   precautions against the effects of attack (Rule 41) 360
   proportionality in attack (Rule 38) 343–44
   registration of space objects (Rule 8) 91
   satellites 335–36, 343–44, 360
   UNCOPUOS Space Debris Mitigation Guidelines 144–45
   warnings (Rule 40) 360
Space Defence Identification Zones (SpaDIZ) 162–63
space, definition of 4
space objects *see also* **international liability for damage caused by space objects (Rule 12); registration of space objects (Rule 8); satellites; space debris**
   armed attack (Rule 23) 201–2, 230–37
   concealment 332
   countermeasures (Rule 25) 245–46
   dangerous forces, space objects containing 279–80

INDEX 433

deception 332
degree of damage, evaluation of 231–32
facilities versus space objects 146–47, 149–50
international armed conflicts (IACs) (Rule 29) 291–92
jurisdiction (Rule 7) 88–89, 234
legal connection between a State and a space object 25–26, 233–36, 291–92
medical units and religious personnel (Rule 35) 326, 327–28
military functions, failure to specify 382
nationality 25, 233–34
neutrality in space (Rule 48) 400, 402
non-international armed conflicts (NIACs) (Rule 30) 296
Outer Space Treaty (OST) 25–26
ownership of space objects (Rule 9) 26, 98–101
perfidy, prohibition of (Rule 44) 382
proportionality in attack (Rule 38) 343–44
proximity to space objects of other States, intentional placement of hostile objects in 224
registration of space objects (Rule 8) 25–26, 147, 234, 296
remote control 305
responsibility, determination of 25–26
self-defence (Rule 26) 201–2, 235–36
signals 305
temporary or partial disruption, interference with, or degrading of functions 201–2, 231–33
use of force (Rule 21) 201–2
verification (Rule 36) 332
visit to facilities on the Moon and other celestial bodies (Rule 15) 147, 149–50
war-fighting and war-supporting objects 321–23
war-sustaining objects 321–23
space situational awareness (SSA) systems 83
space station, definition of 185–86
space tourism 130–31
special protections 310, 325, 348, 381–82
specified military establishments and activities on celestial bodies, restrictions on (Rule 4) 63–70
demilitarization 64, 66
list of prohibited military activities, nature of 65–66
Moon and other celestial bodies 63–64, 66–68
non-aggressive uses 63–64
Outer Space Treaty (OST) 63–64, 65–70
peaceful purposes (Rule 3) 63–64, 65–66
self-defence (Rule 26) 68–70

weapons 63–64, 67–69
spoofing 189, 219, 220–21
State consultations 5–6
State responsibility *see* **responsibility of States for national activities in outer space (Rule 10)**
State security *see* **national security**
State sovereignty
airspace and outer space (delimitation of outer space) 26–27, 28–29
freely, matters which State is permitted to decide 192–94
jurisdiction (Rule 7) 85–87
non-appropriation of outer space and celestial bodies (Rule 2) 41–42, 45–46
non-intervention principle (Rule 20) 192–94
self-defence (Rule 26) 248
sovereign immunity 88–89
use of force (Rule 21) 201–2
States of Registry *see also* **Registration Convention; registration of space objects (Rule 8)**
definition 90
jurisdiction (Rule 7) 86–87, 88–89, 92
launching States 26, 98–99
legal connections with States 292
ownership of space objects (Rule 9) 98–99, 100
registration of space objects (Rule 8) 90, 91–92, 93–94, 95–97
return of personnel 134–35
return of space objects 99
Secretary-General, provision of information to 93–94
two or more States 96
which State is the State of Registry 95–97
superfluous injury, definition of 371
surveillance 1–2, 391–92
suspension or cancellation of attack (Rule 39) 281, 347–50
Additional Protocol I to Geneva Conventions 347–48
authority 349–50
civilian losses 349
collective security measures 263–64
communication satellites 332, 349–50
customary international law 347–48
dual-use objects 347–48
feasibility 347–48, 349
intelligence collection (Rule 6) 332, 349–50
international armed conflicts (IACs) (Rule 29) 347–48
legal basis 347–48
long-range weapons 332
medical units and religious personnel (Rule 35) 348

suspension or cancellation of attack (Rule 39) (*cont.*)
  military advantage 349–50
  military objectives (Rule 34) 347–48, 349–50
  non-international armed conflicts (NIACs) (Rule 30) 347–48
  precautions against the effects of attack (Rule 41) 349, 361
  proportionality in attack (Rule 38) 349–50
  satellites 332, 349–50
  special protection, targets subject to 348
  visit to facilities on the Moon and other celestial bodies (Rule 15) 151

telegraphic, radio, and other means of communication, complete or partial interruption of 202–3 *see also* ITU harmful radio interference (Rule 19)
telemetry 185–86
tension and crisis, military activities during times of 153–55 *see also* **response actions**
  armed attack (Rule 23) 154, 203–4, 226–37
  attribution of internationally wrongful acts 155
  due regard (Rule 17) 154, 170–76
  harmful interference (Rule 18) 154, 177–84
  legal obligations and prohibitions of particular relevance 154
  legal framework 153
  non-intervention principle (Rule 20) 154, 191–200
  peaceful means, settlement of disputes by 153
  radio interference (Rule 19) 154, 177–79, 183, 185–90
  threat of force (Rule 22) 154, 222–25
  times of tension and crisis, meaning of 154
  UN Charter 3–4, 153
  unfriendly acts and responses to unfriendly acts 3–4
  use of force (Rule 21) 154, 183, 201–21
  zones (Rule 16) 154, 159–69
terminology 4
terrorism 317, 352
threat of force (Rule 22) 154, 222–25
  aggression, threats of 225
  application of Rule 222–25
  ASAT capabilities 223–24
  capability to use force 225
  coercive intent or purpose 223–24
  credible intention to use force 222–24, 225
  deterrence 222–23
  exclusion zones, enforcement of (Rule 16) 224
  free use principle (Rule 1) 224
  grey areas 224

International Court of Justice (ICJ) 222–23
jus ad bellum 110
legal basis 222
national space defence policy, existence of 222–23
non-appropriation of outer space and celestial bodies (Rule 2) 224
non-government entities (NGEs) 105, 108
proximity to space objects of other States, intentional placement of hostile objects in 224
satellites, risk of collision with 224
self-defence (Rule 26) 222–23
UN Charter 222–23
threats to peace 265–66, 267–69, 270–71
three-dimensional (3D) printing 100–1
Tlatelolco Treaty (Treaty for the Prohibition of Nuclear Weapons in Latin America) 74
transparency 93–95
travaux préparatoires 4–5, 8–9, 129–30
treaty law 4–5, 10, 11–12, 400–1 *see also travaux préparatoires*; **Vienna Convention on the Law of Treaties (VCLT), interpretation under**
Treaty on the Elimination of their Intermediate-range and Shorter-range Missiles 83, 220
Treaty on the Limitation of Anti-Ballistic Missile Systems 83, 220
Treaty on the Prohibition of Nuclear Weapons 81

Ukraine
  satellite jamming 211–12
  neutrality in space (Rule 48) 402
UN Charter 3–4, 153
  armed attack (Rule 23) 226, 231, 301
  attack, definition of (Rule 31) 301–2
  Chapter VI 269–70
  collective security measures (Rule 28) 266–70
  collective self-defence (Rule 27) 260
  countermeasures (Rule 25) 243
  counterspace weapons systems and capabilities 207–8, 213–14
  customary international law 10
  cyber capabilities 213–15, 216–19
  defensive measures, reporting and termination of 259
  distinction (Rule 32) 61
  economic measures 202–3
  enforcement measures (Chapter VII) 263–71
  exceptional powers under Article 41 and 42 263–64, 265, 266–68
  free use principle (Rule 1) 35–36, 40
  geographical scope 201–2

international organizations, responsibility of (Rule 11) 118, 119–20
jamming 209–11
law of armed conflict 274–75
maintenance of peace and security 52, 155
means and methods of warfare (Rule 42) 61
non-intervention principle (Rule 20) 192–94, 200
non-State actors 256–57
object and purpose 268
Outer Space Treaty (OST) 35–36, 40, 251
peaceful purposes in outer space (Rule 3) 49–50, 52, 55–56, 61
peaceful settlement of disputes 155
political independence 201–2
responsibility of States for national activities in outer space (Rule 10) 110–12, 113–14
self-defence (Rule 26) 12, 120, 250–52, 253–55, 256–57, 259
State practice 202–3, 212–13
territorial integrity 201–2
threat of force (Rule 22) 49–50, 110, 222–23
use of force (Rule 21) 35–36, 40, 49–50, 110, 201–3, 206–14, 216–18
weapons, restrictions on 61
zones (Rule 16) 163–64
UNCOPUOS *see* United Nations Committee on the Peaceful Uses of Outer Space
United Arab Emirates (UAE)
peaceful purposes in outer space (Rule 3) 60
resources, exploitation of space 46
United Kingdom
due regard (Rule 17) 170–72
harmful contamination, avoidance of (Rule 14) 142–43
ICRC study on customary humanitarian international law 278–79
peaceful purposes in outer space (Rule 3) 58
visits to facilities on the Moon and other celestial bodies (Rule 15) 148
United Nations (UN) *see also*; UN Charter; United Nations Security Council (UNSC)
Declaration of Legal Principles 1963 (UNGA) 18–19, 36–37, 41, 135, 177
distinctive emblem, improper use of the 388
Online Index of Objects Launched into Outer Space 96
rescue, duty to inform Secretary-General of 56
UN Office for Outer Space Affairs (UNOOSA) 91, 93–94, 96–97
United Nations Committee on the Peaceful Uses of Outer Space (UNCOPUOS)

airspace and outer space (delimitation of outer space) 27–29
due regard (Rule 17) 170–72
harmful interference (Rule 18) 178
Moon Agreement 24
peaceful purposes in outer space (Rule 3) 51–52, 53–54
Space Debris Mitigation Guidelines 144–45
specified military establishments and activities on celestial bodies, restrictions on (Rule 4) 67–68
visit to facilities on the Moon and other celestial bodies (Rule 15) 148
United Nations Security Council (UNSC)
collective security measures (Rule 28) 263–71
  authorization 263–64, 266–71
  discretion 265–66, 268
  enforcement measures (Chapter VII) 263–71
  exceptional powers under Article 41 and 42 263–64, 265, 266–68
discretion 265–66, 268
enforcement measures (Chapter VII) 263–71
exceptional powers under Article 41 and 42 263–64, 265, 266–68
legally binding decisions 263–64
peacekeeping operations 269–70
provisional measures 263–65
use of force (Rule 21) 265–66, 268–69
United States
Apollo 11 Mission
  flag, planting of the 41–42
  landing sites 168–69
  Lunar Module of (the Eagle) 167–68
Apollo 17 landing sites 168–69
armed attack (Rule 23) 227, 255
arms control 220–21
ASAT weapons 140, 174–76
asteroid resources, recovery of 46
cyber capabilities 216–17
due regard (Rule 17) 174–76
ICRC 278–79, 314
imminent armed attack 255
means and methods of warfare (Rule 42) 371–72
military equipment 67–68
military objectives (Rule 34) 322–23
non-appropriation of outer space and celestial bodies (Rule 2) 41–42, 44–46
oil/petroleum infrastructure 322–23
Outer Space Treaty (OST) 51–54
peaceful purposes in outer space (Rule 3) 51–54
private entities 46

436 INDEX

United States (*cont.*)
  resources, exploitation of space 46
  satellites, destruction of 180–82
  space debris 180–82
  Tenets of Responsible Behaviour in Space 174–76
  terrorists 317
  visit to facilities on the Moon and other celestial bodies (Rule 15) 147–49, 150–51
  Webster formula 255
  zones (Rule 16) 167–69
universality 85–86
unnecessary suffering of combatants 370–71
use of force, prohibition of (Rule 21) 154, 201–21 *see also* **coercion; threat of force (Rule 22)**
  aggression 204–5
  armed attack (Rule 23) 201–2, 226–29
  arms control 220–21
  ASAT weapons 206–7, 227–28
  attack, definition of (Rule 31) 301–2
  attribution 111–12
  causation 203–4
  collective security measures (Rule 28) 202, 265–66, 268–69
  collective self-defence (Rule 27) 202
  command and communication systems 220–21
  countermeasures (Rule 25) 245
  counterspace weapons systems and capabilities 154, 206–9, 213–14, 227–28, 231
  customary international law 201, 207–8, 216–17
  cyber capabilities 203–4, 213–19, 228–29
  direct-ascent ASAT weapons 206–7, 227–28
  directed energy weapons 208–9, 227–28
  early warning satellites 220–21
  economic relations 202–3
  effects-based approach 203–5
  electoral processes 198–99
  electromagnetic pulse (EMP) weapons 208–9, 227–28
  enforcement measures 265–66, 268–69
  free use principle (Rule 1) 35–36, 40
  Friendly Relations Declaration 204–5
  high-energy lasers 209
  high-powered microwave weapons 209
  hijacking satellites 215
  indirect force 195–96, 204–5
  international organizations, responsibility of (Rule 11) 120
  jamming 183, 209–14, 220–21

  jurisdiction (Rule 7) 201–2
  jus cogens 111–12
  legal basis 201
  non-government entities (NGEs) 105, 108
  non-intervention principle (Rule 20) 191–92, 194–96, 198–99, 200
  physical damage or injury 202–7, 216–18, 227–28
  radio frequency part of the electromagnetic spectrum, using the 209–12, 228–29
  remote controlled systems 215
  responsibility of States for national activities in outer space (Rule 10) 111–12
  satellites 154, 209–13, 219–21, 227–29, 265–66
  scale and effects 205
  self-defence (Rule 26) 201–2, 217–18, 250
  space objects 154, 201–2
  spoofing 219, 220–21
  State practice 210–12, 214–15, 217–18, 268
  State sovereignty 201–2
  telegraphic, radio, and other means of communication, complete or partial interruption of 202–3
  temporarily disrupt, interfere with, or degrade space systems, capabilities across the electromagnetic spectrum that 212–13, 220–21, 228–29
  terrestrial application of use of force 207–8
  traditional approach to use of armed force 203–5, 216–18
  UN Charter 201–3, 206–8, 217–18
    cyber conduct 213–15, 216–19
    free use principle (Rule 1) 35–36, 40
    jamming 209–11
    State practice 202–3, 212–13
    traditional approach 204–5, 216–17
    use of force, definition of 202–3
  UN Security Council 265–66, 268–69
  unfriendly acts amounting to 154
  use of force, definition of 202–4
  WMDs (Rule 5) 207–8, 227–28
  weapons systems and capabilities 154, 206–9, 227–28

VCLT *see* **Vienna Convention on the Law of Treaties (VCLT), interpretation under**
verification as precaution in attack (Rule 36) 281, 331–33
  Additional Protocol I to Geneva Conventions 331
  application and scope 331–32
  choice of means and methods of attack (Rule 37) 332–33, 334–35

command centre personnel 332
concealment 332
continuous obligation, as 331
customary international law 331
deception 332
feasibility 332–33
intelligence collection (Rule 6) 332
legal basis 331
military objectives (Rule 34) 331–33
national technical means of verification (NTMs) 82–83, 177–78
non-international armed conflicts (NIACs) (Rule 30) 331
personnel, application to various 331–32
practically possible, obligation to do what is 332–33
precautions against the effects of attack (Rule 41) 361
precautions in attack 281, 331–33
rendezvous proximity operations (RPOs) 332–33
satellites 332
space objects 332
Vienna Convention on the Law of Treaties (VCLT), interpretation under
Astronauts, Agreement on Rescue and Return of (ARRA) 19–20
impossibility of performance due to supervening events 12–13
Liability Convention 20–21
non-application to armed conflict 12–13
Outer Space Treaty (OST) 4–5, 20–21
peaceful purposes in outer space (Rule 3) 50–51
State practice 7
WMDs (Rule 5) 76–77
visits to facilities on the Moon and other celestial bodies (Rule 15) 146–51
advance notice 147–49, 150, 164–65
armed conflicts, suspension during 151
conditions 148–49, 150–51
consultation 150
facilities, definition of 146
facilities versus space objects 146–47, 149–50
inspections 148, 150–51
interference with normal operations 147–48, 149–51, 164–65
jurisdiction (Rule 7) 147, 149–50
launching States 147
legal basis 146
military personnel, presence of 149
military use of facilities 149
normal operations, impeding 147–48, 149–51, 164–65

number of facilities 148
open access 147–49, 150–51
Outer Space Treaty (OST) 40, 146–50, 164–65
permanence and ongoing operational capacity, element of 149–50
platforms in space 149–50
precautions 147–48, 150, 164–65
prior agreements 147–49
procedural requirements 149–51
reasonable advance notice 150
reciprocity 147–51
registered space objects 147
safety of personnel 149–51
Soviet Union 147–48, 150–51
space objects 147, 149–50
State practice 151, 164–65
substantive requirements 149–50
timing, agreements on 147–48
visit, definition of 150–51
zones (Rule 16) 164–65
von Karman line (aerodynamic characteristics) 28–29

war, law of *see* law of armed conflict
warnings (Rule 40) 351–56
airspace 355
circumstances not permitting a warning 351–52
civilian population, where attacks affect the 352–56
customary international law 351
direct damage 353
direct participation in hostilities (DPH) (Rule 33) 356
dual-use and multi-purpose systems 353–54
effective warnings 354–55
enemy forces, warnings through 355–56
essential services, loss of 352–53, 355
excessive harm, protection from 356
feasibility 351–52
fixed-distance warning zones 164
form or method 354–56
free navigation 163–64
human shields, leading to use of 351–52
identification zones 162–63
inconvenience, stress, fear or loss of non-essential services 353
indirect damage 353
information, making use of reasonably available 353–54
international armed conflicts (IACs) (Rule 29) 351
judgment of commanders whether circumstances permit warnings 353–54

438 INDEX

warnings (Rule 40) (*cont.*)
  languages 354
  legal basis 351
  lives of attacking forces, risk to 351–52
  medical units and religious personnel (Rule 35) 325
  method 354–56
  national security 162–64
  non-international armed conflicts (NIACs) (Rule 30) 351
  precautions against the effects of attack (Rule 41) 360, 361
  precautions in attack 351–56
  proportionality in attack (Rule 38) 352–54, 356
  protective measures 354–55
  satellites 220–21, 305, 351–53, 354–55, 360
  self-defence (Rule 26) 163–64
  space debris 360
  space objects and systems 163–64
  specificity and clarity 354–55
  State practice 162–64
  surprise, need for 351–52
  terror, as means of spreading 352
  time, lack of 351–52
  time limits 325
  zones (Rule 16) 162–64
weapons *see also* **ASATs (anti-satellite weapons); cyber capabilities; nuclear weapons; weapons of mass destruction (WMDs) (Rule 5)**
  arms control treaties 79–80, 82–83, 177–78, 366–67
  ballistic missile technology, use of 265–66
  biological weapons 73, 74, 75, 265–66, 302–3
  counterspace weapons systems and capabilities 154–55, 206–9, 213–14, 227–28, 231
  customary international law 67–68
  directed energy weapons 208–9, 227–28, 335–36
  electromagnetic pulse (EMP) weapons 208–9, 227–28
  high-energy lasers 209
  indiscriminate weapons and indiscriminate attacks 369–71
  kinetic energy, weapons based on 302–3, 304, 315, 343
    kinetic-kill weapon systems or vehicles 180–82, 206–7, 304, 335–36
    use of force (Rule 21) 206–8, 227–28
  law of armed conflict 273
  long-range 332

  means and methods of warfare (Rule 42) 365–66, 369–72
  microwave weapons 209, 227–28
  Moon and other celestial bodies 62, 67–68
  Outer Space Treaty (OST) 61–62, 63–64, 67–68
  peaceful purposes in outer space (Rule 3) 61–62
  remote controlled systems 215
  reviews of weapons, obligation to carry out legal 371–72
  self-defence (Rule 26) 68–69
  space weapon, definition of 365–66
  specified military establishments and activities on celestial bodies, restrictions on (Rule 4) 63–64, 67–69
  superfluous injury, definition of 371
  testing 67–69, 162
  treaty law 67–68
  UN Charter 61
  unnecessary suffering of combatants 370–71
  use of force (Rule 21) 154, 206–9, 227–28
weapons of mass destruction (WMDs) (Rule 5) 71–81 *see also* **nuclear weapons**
  armed conflicts, applicability in 78–79, 80
  asteroid threats 270–71
  biological weapons 75, 265–66
  chemical weapons 73, 74, 75, 265–66
  collective security measures (Rule 28) 265–66, 270–71
  customary international law 78–79
  definition 73–74
  installation
    definition of 72–73
    self-defence (Rule 26) 76–78
  legal basis 71–72
  limitations or prohibitions 365–67
  means and methods of warfare (Rule 42) 365–67
  Moon and other celestial bodies 67–68, 73
  Outer Space Treaty (OST) 67–68, 71–81
  Partial Nuclear Test Ban Treaty (PNTB) 79–80
  peaceful purposes in outer space (Rule 3) 61
  place in orbit, definition of 72–73
  responsibility of States for national activities in outer space (Rule 10) 109–10
  self-defence (Rule 26) 76–79
  specified military establishments and activities on celestial bodies, restrictions on (Rule 4) 67–69
  State practice 71–72, 76
  stationing 72–73, 76

testing 73, 79–80
toxic chemicals 75
use of force (Rule 21) 207–8, 227–28
WMDs *see* weapons of mass destruction (WMDs) (Rule 5)

zones (Rule 16) 28, 154, 159–69
   air and sea domains, comparison with 159–60
   Air Defence Identification Zones (ADIZ) 162–63
   airspace 162–63, 166–67
   Apollo 11
      landing sites 168–69
      Lunar Module of (the Eagle) 167–68
   Apollo 17 landing sites 168–69
   armed conflict, establishment of zones during 166–67
      belligerent rights 166–67
      immediate area of operations, definition of 166–67
      military necessity 167
      State practice 166–67
   communication tools, as 162, 163–64
   countermeasures (Rule 25) 160–61
   customary international law 166–67
   declarations 154, 159–61, 162, 163–64, 166–67
   due regard (Rule 17) 159–60, 162, 166–67
   enforcement 163–64, 166–67
   exclusion zones, enforcement of 224
   fixed-distance warning zones 164
   free navigation, right of 163–64, 241–42
   free use principle (Rule 1) 159–60, 163–64, 168–69
   harmful interference 159–60, 162, 165–66
   heritage, zones on celestial bodies for the protection of space 167–69
   identification zones 162–63
   immediate area of operations, definition of 166–67
   imminent armed attacks 163–64
   incursions 163–64
   international cooperation 165–66
   jurisdiction (Rule 7) 167–68
   keep out zones, declarations of 163–64, 166
   legal basis 159–60
   liability for harm caused by space objects (Rule 12) 162
   maintenance 154
   mechanics of zones in space 160
   military bases, installations, or fortifications 159–60
   military necessity 167
   Moon and other celestial bodies, establishment of zones on the 164–69
   national security 162–64
   non-appropriation of space and celestial bodies (Rule 2) 159–60, 167
   Outer Space Treaty (OST) 154, 159–61, 162–63, 164–65, 166, 167–69
   radio interference (Rule 19) 159–60
   safety zones 160–62, 168–69
   satellites 160–61, 162, 163–64, 167
   self-defence (Rule 26) 160–61, 163–64
   Space Defence Identification Zones (SpaDIZ) 162–63
   State practice 162–65, 166–67
   territorial-based zones, extension into outer space of 162–63
   territorial sovereignty 162–63
   UN Charter 163–64
   visit to facilities on the Moon and other celestial bodies (Rule 15) 164–65
   warning zones 162–64
   weapons testing 162